Bank Management

[*Ensuring Growth Enhancing Value*]

Vasant Desai

Himalaya Publishing House
ISO 9001 : 2015 CERTIFIED

First Edition : 2009
Reprint : 2010
Reprint : 2023
Reprint : 2024

Published by : Mrs. Meena Pandey
for **HIMALAYA PUBLISHING HOUSE PVT. LTD.,**
"Ramdoot", Dr. Bhalerao Marg, Girgaon, Mumbai - 400 004.
Phone: 022-23860170, 23863863; **Fax:** 022-23877178
E-mail: himpub@bharatmail.co.in; **Website:** www.himpub.com

Branch Offices :

New Delhi : "Pooja Apartments", 4-B, Murari Lal Street, Ansari Road, Darya Ganj, New Delhi - 110 002. Phone: 011-23270392, 23278631; Fax: 011-23256286

Nagpur : Kundanlal Chandak Industrial Estate, Ghat Road, Nagpur - 440 018. Phone: 0712-2721215, 2721216

Bengaluru : Plot No. 91-33, 2nd Main Road, Seshadripuram, Behind Nataraja Theatre, Bengaluru - 560 020. Phone: 080-41138821; Mobile: 09379847017, 09379847005

Hyderabad : No. 3-4-184, Lingampally, Besides Raghavendra Swamy Matham, Kachiguda, Hyderabad - 500 027. Phone: 040-27560041, 27550139

Chennai : No. 34/44, Motilal Street, T. Nagar, Chennai - 600 017. Mobile: 09380460419

Pune : "Laksha" Apartment, First Floor, No. 527, Mehunpura, Shaniwarpeth (Near Prabhat Theatre), Pune - 411 030. Phone: 020-24496323, 24496333; Mobile: 09370579333

Cuttack : Plot No. 5F-755/4, Sector-9, CDA Markat Nagar, Cuttack - 753 014, Odisha. Mobile: 09338746007

Kolkata : 3, S.M. Bose Road, Near Gate No. 5, Agarpara Railway Station, North 24 Parganas, West Bengal - 700 109. Mobile: 09674536325

DTP by : **Sri Siddhi Softtek,** Bangalore.

Printed at : Geetanjali Press Pvt. Ltd., Nagpur. On behalf of HPH.

PREFACE

Banks are in the forefront of economic development. They are the heart of Indian financial system. Banks in India have been playing a unique role in mobilising saving credit disbursement, investment and providing other services. According to the latest figures released by the Reserve Bank of India (RBI), commercial banks' deposits touched Rs.30,75,224.33 crore, outstanding bank credit amounted to Rs.22,72,602.73 crore,investments touched Rs.9,86,052.21 crore and Rs.9,66,516.17 crore on March 14, 2008. The ability of the banking system to perform its tasks efficiently and in harmony with our needs and economic goals depends in a large measure on its efficient management. In fact, bank management by itself is a multidisciplinary subject, cutting across many recognised disciplines. In India, however, the subject has yet to get recognition as a discipline in its own right. The subject, therefore, merits recognition and study, so as to run the financial system in consonance with our objectives as well as to accelerate economic growth. The banking system must be managed prudently, safely and profitably if we are to have a strong, growing and adaptable banking system capable of meeting the demands of society.

Globalisation, financial deregulation, accelerating economic growth and improvement have had a profound effect on the bank management in recent years. The main challenge for the banking sector would be to expand while maintaining sound financial health. Banks, therefore, would need to focus on sound management.

Issues in Bank Management

This has propelled the banks to become conscious of their performance on a continuous basis and shift the focus from expansion (volume) to efficiency (margin).

1. Technology: The banks have a challenging task ahead to remain competitive in an environment of ever advancing technology levels in banking. They will need new Banking Solutions to replace their existing Legacy Systems and to network their branches. Government and the Reserve Bank will need to facilitate this transition by determined actions within the next five years. In this connection, there is need to create an Apex Body with statutory powers to develop, disseminate and regulate technology for interbank networks, and payment systems so as to enable the banks to reach the global standards.

2. Human Resource Management: At present the human resource policies in banks are mainly guided by the concept of permanent employment and its necessary concomitants of creating career paths, terminal benefits, etc. for the employees. In this fast-changing world of worker mobility—both horizontally and vertically—and value systems, the public sector banks will need the freedom not only to hire the right talent at market related compensation but also to shed surplus manpower. Bank-centric wage negotiations should be allowed. All this calls for a close relook into the Statute Books as well as Management Practice of the banks.

3. Risk Management and Regulatory Implications: To reach the international standards of capital adequacy, risk management and accounting practices, the right talent at appropriate levels of management needs to be inducted laterally and the banks should have the necessary freedom to do so.

4. Structural Issues: Structure of a bank is generally business and technology driven. Therefore, whether or not the Government reduces its holdings to 1/3 levels, the initiative to decide on the best structure should be left to the individual banks themselves. Also, issues internal to the organizational structure should be left to the individual banks, while the Government and the Regulator could confine their role to providing a stable macro-environment and supervision to protect the interests of the stakeholders and the shareholders.

5. Corporate Governance: Irrespective of the nature of the organization, corporate governance has to ensure transparency and efficiency in the running of the organization. Accordingly, the Government's decision to reduce its equity holdings to 1/3 levels should get reflected in corporate governance also. Therefore, all structural strengthening to exercise flexibility and autonomy should be ensured.

6. Rural Banking: Having committed 75 per cent of their branch network to serving rural and semi-urban population, public sector banks have to adopt a financial engineering approach to rural banking. The delivery systems have to be made cost effective. Therefore, there is a need for redesigning the rural banking system to deliver new products and services and to make the priority sector more receptive and productive. In this connections, the regulatory constraint on banks' allocation of credit flows also needs a relook. Commercialized agriculture should be considered as a potential avenue for new business. There is need for a paradigm shift in rural finance and in both mobilization and allocation of resources through other intermediaries including NBFCs.

7. Management of NPAs: There are several impediments including statutory, legal and political in the recovery of bank loans and advances. Therefore, restructuring of borrowal accounts should be left to individual bank decision subject to full transparency. Then only the public sector banks can better function as business organizations in pursuit of excellence and sound financial performance.

The Process

The study of organization and management of banks has encountered many innovations in its evolutionary stages. Significant contributions have been made by the various schools of management thought such as scientific management, administrative or process school, behavioural sciences, quantitative (operations research) school, systems approach and contingency or environmental school of management thought. Recent awareness and emphasis of management's social responsibilities has introduced rethinking and reassessment of the traditional principles of management. Based on these directions and other new trends, this book attempts to bring together and integrate the past and present developments within a systematic and rational framework for studying the management fundamentals. In fact, a sound banking system is premised on the principles of sound corporate governance. Corporate governance lays down the fundamental rules by which banks are managed. The quality of corporate management has become important in the banking system in view of growing competition and consolidation.

Management of Operations

The leading banks now are increasingly focussing on differentiating their product offering by allowing customers to build products and creating 'brands.' Preferred customers of the bank have the ability to create product variants to suit their individual needs, often requiring banks to collaborate with other players. Most of the banks have invested in sophisticated touch points (both self-serviced and human interaction) that are either owned, shared or source through a third party service provider. All these touch points have the ability to capture and use customer intelligence for marketing efforts and for adhering to service stands to ensure customer stickiness.

The customer strategies adopted by the successful players are focussed on retaining profitable customers, while also developing specific marketing initiatives to attract customers from other banks with incentive schemes, packaged service and competitive service standards. In addition, the search for profitable customers by the banks has taken them beyond the traditional metro and urban areas, with the rural sector being viewed as a serious market, and not just a priority sector commitment.

Organisation of the Bank

The Prime objective of the book is to provide a comprehensive and up-to-date information about Bank Management. The teachers and students will get an insight into the Principles, operational priorities and practices of the key players in the field.

The whole text has been discussed in TWENTY-FIVE chapters grouped in sections. Chapter one introduces the subject and provides an insight into the varied facets of Bank Management unfolding in the course of next TWENTY-FOUR chapters.

The study discusses and analysis the new challenges and new initiatives of Banks and their unique role in the economy. In short, the study acts as a motivator to pursue a career in the growing and innovative core banking, portfolio management, investment banking, Micro Financing, insurance and allied areas.

Wealth Management, Credit Management

I shall feel duly rewarded, in meeting the needs of students and teachers squarely as well as in arousing adequate interest in the minds of readers and students on the important multi-dimensional facets of the Indian banking system and assess its contribution to economic development and growth.

The author welcomes any comments and suggestions for making the book more effective, informative, innovative and knowledgeable.

Acknowledgements

My debt to those who have helped me in one way or the other is worth appreciating. While I take this opportunity to thank all of them—they are too numerous to mention individually in a brief preface—I would like to acknowledge my deep sense of gratitude to Mr. K. N. Pandey,

Mr. Anuj Pandey, Mr. Neeraj Pandey, Nimisha Kadam and Mr. S. K. Patil for their cooperation and encouragement.

I take this opportunity to express my sincere appreciation and gratitude to Ms. Pratibha Chaudhari for reading the book carefully and suggesting changes to make it more crisp, lucid and informative.

No words can adequately express my debt of gratitude to my late father, Shri. Ranganath Balawant Mutalik Desai (1909-1996) and my late mother Smt. Laxmidevi (1914-2000), for generating in me a perennial interest in higher studies.

I am particularly indebted to my wife, Mandaramala, whose patience, support, encouragement, understanding, and love helped this effort to fruition.

I acknowledge the secretarial assistance rendered by varied people at varied stages.

The Himalaya Publishing House, which is in the forefront of publications, enthusiastically came forward to undertake the publication of this unique study. I wholeheartedly thank them.

Finally, I thank all those who directly or indirectly helped me in bringing out this unique study.

Mumbai
April 19, 2008

Vasant Desai

CONTENTS

Evolution of Commercial Banking in India

The East India Company set up Bank of Bombay in 1720 with the objective of increasing trade and thereby the revenue of the Company. In 1773, Warren Hastings floated the General Bank of Bengal and Bihar, which was a private establishment but under the patronage of East India Company's government. The General Bank was closed in 1775 due to opposition in the Governor-General's Council. In 1786, the General Bank of India was floated, which claimed limited liability on the shareholders. But neither British nor the Indian law existed at that time to confer the right of limited liability on the shareholders except by the Royal Charter. Subsequently, other banks, viz., the Carnatic Bank (1788), the Madras Bank (1795), the British Bank (1795) and the Asiatic Bank (1804) were established as private institutions.

On February 1, 1806, the Government Bank started functioning in Madras by the passing of the resolution by Bentinck in his Council. The Government Bank was empowered to issue notes subject to some conditions. Apart from Bank of Hindustan, two other European banks operated for various periods in eighteenth century Bengal. The Commercial Bank (1819) and the Bank of Calcutta (1824) were floated mainly by the agency houses. The Union Bank was born by the merger of the Calcutta Bank and the Commercial Bank. These private banks were owned by few individuals and managed by a few men and were legally termed as partnership firms with limited liability.

The Bank of Calcutta was established in 1806 as a joint stock bank with limited liability, which was brought under the Royal Charter in 1809 and renamed as Bank of Bengal. Subsequently, the Bank of Bombay (1840) and the Bank of Madras (1843) were established by Act III of 1840 and Act IX of 1843 by the East India Company. The Government Bank founded by Bentinck was replaced and closed simultaneously with the opening of the Bank of Madras in June 1843. The business of these Presidency banks were initially confined to discounting of bills or other negotiable private securities, keeping cash accounts, receiving deposits and issuing and circulating cash notes. The major innovations in banking method and organisation came with the establishment of Bank of Bengal, which included (a) use of joint stock system for raising capital; (b) conferring of limited liability on shareholders by means of a charter; (c) provision for the note issue which could be accepted for public revenue payments; (d) general provision for acceptance of deposits from the general public; (e) imposition of explicit limit on credit and the kind of securities it could accept; and (f) provision for regulatory changes in the board of directors. The Royal Charter governed the three Presidency banks, which was revised from time to time. There were no legally recognised commercial banks with special right within India other than the Presidency banks. The East India Company's government reserved the right to regulate the monetary and credit system to itself.

With the passing of the Paper Currency Act, 1861, the right to issue currency notes by the Presidency banks was abolished and the same function was entrusted to the Government. With the collapse of the Bank of Bombay, the New Bank of Bombay was established in January 1868. In 1876, the Presidency Bank Act came into existence, which brought the three Presidency banks under the common statute and restriction on business. In terms of Act XI of 1876, the Government of India decided on strict enforcement of the charter and the periodic inspection of the books of these banks. In 1921, the three Presidency banks and their branches were merged to form the Imperial Bank of India, which acquired the triple role of a commercial bank, a banker's bank and a banker to the government. In 1951, when the first Five Year Plan was launched, the development of rural India was accorded the highest priority. The All India Rural Credit Survey Committee recommended the creation of a State-partnered and State-sponsored bank by taking over the Imperial Bank of India and integrating with it, the former State-owned or State-associated banks. Accordingly, an Act was passed in the Parliament in May 1955 and the State Bank of India was constituted on July 1, 1955. Later, the State Bank of India (Subsidiary Banks) Act was passed in 1959 enabling the State Bank of India to take over eight former State-associated banks as its subsidiaries.

Source: Evolution of the State Bank of India (Part I and II).

Falling Interest

Commercial Banks' Business

(Rs.crore)

	Feb.29, 2008	*Mar.14, 2008*	*Change*
Aggregate deposits	30,80,859.14	30,75,224.33	-5,634.81
Demand deposits	4,59,128.27	4,42,720.44	-16,407.83
Time deposits	26,21,730.83	26,32,503.89	10,773.06
Investments	9,86,851.30	9,86,052.21	-799.09
Government bonds	9,67,011.46	9,66,516.17	-495.29
Other approved securities	19,839.84	19,536.04	-303.80
Bank credit	22,51,212.98	22,72,602.73	21,389.75
Food credit	44,311.27	43,505.17	-806.10
Non-food credit	22,06,901.71	22,29,097.56	22,195.85

Bank Group-wise Averages for 2005-06 and 2006-07

(Amount in rupees crore)

Items	SBI & its Associates		Nationalised Banks		Other SCBs		Foreign Banks		All Banks	
	2005-06	*2006-07*	*2005-06*	*2006-07*	*2005-06*	*2006-07*	*2005-06*	*2006-07*	*2005-06*	*2006-07*
Total number of banks	8	8	20	20	27	24	29	29	84	81
No.of offices	1774	1807	1780	1845	251	296	9	9	676	725
No.of employees	33826	32028	23686	23647	4093	5756	763	960	10440	11051
Business per employee (in Rs.lakh)	337.79	435.52	383.07	490.21	670.67	697.75	955.41	995.08	419.77	522.29
Profit per employee (in Rs.lakh)	2.20	2.56	2.23	2.87	4.51	4.69	13.89	16.46	2.81	3.49
Capital and reserves & surplus	4708	5368	3869	4634	1623	2095	838	1141	2181	2704
Deposits	67801	79184	54004	68036	15861	22921	3922	5200	25768	33273
Investments	28095	26458	20440	22649	6685	8914	1806	2464	10315	11729
Advances	46460	60303	36730	47885	11588	17239	3364	4357	18056	24447
Interest income	6163	7042	4429	5588	1304	2123	424	621	2207	2927
Other income	1191	975	619	654	300	463	185	239	421	480
Interest expended	3505	4232	2623	3480	796	1365	178	263	1276	1776
Operating expenses	1970	1998	1277	1363	446	636	202	267	705	818
Cost of Funds (CoF)	4.84	4.92	4.27	4.81	4.32	5.16	3.63	4.03	4.38	4.85
Return on advances adjusted to CoF	2.93	3.55	3.86	3.99	4.39	4.37	4.90	5.74	3.80	4.08
Wages as % to total expenses	24.35	21.01	21.42	17.89	12.15	10.93	18.22	20.06	20.11	17.20
Return on Assets	0.87	0.86	0.89	0.94	1.07	1.03	2.08	2.27	1.01	1.05
CRAR	11.95	12.30	12.27	12.50	12.42	12.10	13.02	12.00	12.32	12.30
Net NPA ratio	1.75	1.10	1.27	1.00	1.05	1.00	0.82	0.80	1.31	1.00

Explanatory Notes

Bank Group Level Averages

(a) Business per employee (or profit per employee) is computed by dividing the total business (or profit) for the group (as available in annual accounts) by the number of employees in the group (as obtained from IBA).

(b) CoF is computed as the ratio of interest paid on deposits and borrowings to average of deposits and borrowings of the group for the years 2005-06 and 2006-07.

(c) Return on advances adjusted to CoF is computed by subtracting CoF for the group from return on advances for the group; the latter is computed as the ratio of interest earned on advances by the group to average of total advances of the group for the years 2005-06 and 2006-07.

(d) Return on assets for a group is obtained as weighted average of return on assets of individual banks in the group, weights being the proportion of total assets of the bank as percentage to total assets of the group.

(e) Capital adequacy ratio and net NPA ratio for the four bank groups and also for all banks have been obtained from OSMOS, Department of Banking Supervision, RBI.

(f) For rest of the items, simple averages are used at the group level.

(g) Similar definitions are used at all banks' level.

(h) All banks' averages are computed based on state bank group (8 banks), nationalised banks (20), foreign banks (29) and other scheduled commercial banks (24 banks, excluding erstwhile Lord Krishna Bank).

(i) IDBI Limited is considered as a nationalised bank.

Source: RBI

The Best and the Biggest

The Top 10 Big Banks by Some Key Parameters

Figures in R. scrore

By Balance Sheet Size	
State Bank of India	**5,66,565.24**
ICICI Bank	3,44,658.11
Canara Bank	1,65,961.05
Punjab National Bank	1,62,422.50
Bank of Baroda	1,43,146.17
Bank of India	1,41,636.99
IDBI Bank	1,03,839.33
Union Bank of India	1,02,677.88
Central Bank of India	93,008.08
HDFC Bank	91,235.61

Figures in Rs.crore

By Operating Profit	
State Bank of India	**9,999.94**
ICICI Bank	5,874.41
Punjab National Bank	3,230.65
Canara Bank	2,912.47
HDFC Bank	2,805.00
Bank of Baroda	2,415.01
Bank of India	2,394.99
Standard Chartered	2,337.95
Citibank N.A.	2,180.45
Union Bank of India	2,000.83

Figures in per cent

By Growth in Operating Profit	
ABN AMRO	**75.05**
Bank of Maharashtra	67.06
Indian Bank	52.03
ICICI Bank	51.07
HSBC	50.53
HDFC Bank	41.76

State Bank of Bikaner and Jaipur	41.20
Bank of India	40.78
Citibank N.A.	38.26
Syndicate Bank	37.16

Figures in basis points

By Change in Mkt Share of CASA

ICICI Bank	**0.5971**
Axis Bank	0.4551
HDFC Bank	0.2869
IDBI Bank	0.1985
Corporation Bank	0.1105
Union Bank of India	0.1058
Bank of Maharashtra	0.1031
State Bank of Mysore	0.0168
Federal Bank	0.0161
Dena Bank	0.0137

Figures in Rs. crore

By Operating Profit/Employee

Citibank N.A.	**0.42**
Standard Chartered	0.32
HSBC	0.29
ABN AMRO	0.29
ICICI Bank	0.18
Axis Bank	0.14
HDFC Bank	0.13
IDBI Bank	0.12
Corporation Bank	0.10
Federal Bank	0.09

FASTEST GROWING BIG BANK

AXIS BANK

What would you call a Bank that has grown its profits at 30 per cent or more in 28 of the last 30 quarters? At the least, a consistent performer. But what has earned P. J. Nayak-led Axis Bank (formerly UTI Bank) its distinction as the fastest growing big bank is its equally impressive growth in other areas such as deposits, and loans and advances. Overall ranked $5, Axis has grown at a five-year CAGR of 38 per cent. "We want to be known as an Asian Bank," says Nayak, Chairman and Managing Director. "In the last year and a half, our overseas operations have accounted for 7-8 per cent of our business, which will account for 15-20 per cent in the next couple of years." Currently the bank is present in Singapore, Dubai and Hong Kong, with a representative office in Shanghai. In the domestic market, the growth strategy is to diversify capital market operations and grow inorganically as and when opportunities arise. "Apart from normal banking operation (including core banking and non-interest income), we would like to take advantage of the strong capital market by venturing into private equity, broking, asset management and insurance businesses," says Nayak. The only hitch: Nayak is due to retire mid-2009.

Axis Bank's Nayak: Surging ahead

FASTEST GROWING SMALL BANK

YES BANK

Among the small banks (Balance Sheet size less than Rs.24,000 crore), YES Bank comes in at $ 2 right behind Punjab & Sind Bank. That means it has beaten other relatively young banks such as Rana Talwar's Centurion Bank of Punjab, Uday Kotak's Kotak Mahindra Bank, and the Hindujas' IndusInd Bank to emerge as the fastest growing bank. Of course, the fact that YES Bank has a smaller balance sheet (Rs.11,103 crore) than either Centurion (Rs.18,483 crore) or Kotak (Rs.19,915 crore) helps, but there's no denying that Rana Kapoor-founded YES Bank is not just clipping, but also well differentiated in the industry. "We have clearly positioned ourselves differently from the rest. We have adopted a knowledge-driven approach that goes beyond the traditional realm of banking," says Managing Director & CEO Kapoor, referring to the bank's diversified portfolio, which has specific focus on sunrise sectors such as food and agriculture, biotechnology, life sciences, and infrastructure. YES Bank is also moving deeper into financial services in areas such as investment banking, asset reconstruction, asset management (read: mutual funds) and also private equity. "We are looking at organic opportunity in all our businesses," says Kapoor, former head of Rabo India Finance.

THE MOST EFFICIENT SMALL BANK

KARUR VYSYA BANK

Karur Vysya is one of the older private sector players but a relatively new convert to technology (it introduced core banking solutions in 2005). Just the same, the Tamil Nadu-based bank has lost no time in leveraging technology to expand and become efficient. Currently, the bank has 281 branches (and will expand to 300 in next two months), 279 ATMs of its own including 18 in rural areas and 108 in semi urban areas, and piggybacks on 10,000 other ATMs. Still, the bank is keen to build its physical presence. It plans to increase the number of branches to 300 shortly and create a pan-India presence. "We find value in increasing branches and this is reflected in our results," says Chairman P.T. Kuppuswamy, adding that such a strategy also helps Karur reach out to customers who are not computer savvy. Karur also runs a tight ship. Its NPA as a percentage of net advances in 2006-07 was a minuscule 0.23, although the more recent figure puts it at 0.05 per cent. "We are in no hurry really, but in the next quarter we can bring it down to zero," says Kuppuswamy, whose bank also had one of the lowest cost-to-income ratios of 41 per cent.

Chapter 1

Introduction

In Perspective

Banking is the epicentre of economic development. And, sound management is the basic need to create confidence and accelerate the process of economic growth.

The banking system in India is undergoing structural transformation under the influence of globalisation, deregulation, technological advances, and institutional and legal reforms. While the liberalised environment has opened new avenues of business for banks, it has led to competitive environment. To survive and excel in a competitive environment, banks have been innovating, diversifying and sharpening their banking skills. Banking regulation and supervision has been progressively aligned with international best practices with suitable adaptations. The management practices are reoriented and reinvented to excel. The corporate governance framework in banks has also been strengthened.

Since a safe and sound banking system is a prerequisite for sustained growth of the Indian economy, emphasise has been led on a sound bank management.

Economic development is a complex process in which both the private and public sectors have important roles to play. Their roles are best played if they can be cast as partners in helping to achieve growth in a given country's economic development. The optimum scenario calls for a mutually reinforcing partnership among all the elements of the international development community: multilateral, bilateral, the private sector, specialized groups, concerned individuals — everyone is involved — all playing their roles against a background of appropriate economic and social policies. The word "development" involves not merely economic changes but also social and institutional changes in many underdeveloped countries. It calls for new sets of values and new concepts of society and government. No path to development is likely to be smooth. Banking is the base for economic development.

Economic Growth

Economic growth has been widely accepted by economists as a major goal of national policy, both in the industrialised countries and in countries that are developing. The concept of economic growth has almost become a commonplace in economic studies, particularly those of underdeveloped countries. In fact, economic growth is a complex process which, despite intensive study, is still not understood in its true perspective. It was only in the period since World War II that the concept received wide publicity and recognition. In his commentaries on the Social Framework — An Introduction to Economics (1960), Prof. J. R. Hicks, observes: "There is indeed no single index which is a perfect measure of economic growth; in order to see whether an economy is growing properly, we need to look at far more things than can possibly be expressed in a single figure." He preferred national income to consumption as a better measure. In a conventional sense, economic growth has been defined as progress in per capita income measured in the currency units of constant purchasing power. Strictly speaking, the growth which results from a more complete utilisation of capacity is easier to achieve and less fundamental than growth, which involves the actual expansion of an economy's capacity. Some economists have defined economic growth as a relation between the rates of increase in capital and the working force, on the one hand, and in population, on the other, such as higher per capita output (not necessarily consumption). Under this contention, the composition of investment would steadily change. Prof. Rostow is of the opinion that the process of economic growth should be regarded as continuity of a brief time interval of two or three decades when the economy progresses automatically. But Prof. Ragnar Nurkse states: "The technical physical productivity of capital can be realised in economic terms only through balanced growth, enlarging the aggregate size of the market and increasing individual investment incentives all round."

In the post-nationalisation period, significant changes have been seen in banking in consonance with the sea changes in the social, economic and political spheres. Though the average population serviced per bank office improved from 65,000 to 12,000 and a large segment of the incremental credit was channelled into exports, agriculture, small industries and small businesses, it bred inefficiency, corruption, lower productivity, poor customer services, chaotic work ethics and poor management. The 1992 banking scam indicts the banking system's working environment. This is the result of not having commercial adaptations in time. The problems of prudence and professional management techniques, communication and co-ordination, decentralization, delegation, monitoring of management information and control are associated with branch banking.

New Factors

It is difficult to identify any single factor as being the most important. Nevertheless, it would appear that changing technology may have had that role. In previous years we had seen the intensification of the use of technology in foreign exchange dealing rooms and in the treasury function. This created a large corps of people with experience in handling this kind of financial transaction, together with the technology to effect the calculations quickly, accurately, and on a massive scale. This technology could be used at extremely low marginal cost to support new markets. In some fields the concepts of the markets were previously well-known, such as options or forward rate agreements but it was simply impractical to run a market on a significant and controlled scale before the computer hardware to support it was available.

A second pressure was the marketing and competitive structure of the banking industry. With the globalisation of finance, many banks and innovative investment houses moved into other markets, taking their ideas with them. The nature of marketing in banking is in some fields through innovation. Those finance houses attempted to think of new products which they could take to their customers and use them in justification for being given their business.

The traditional relationship between a bank and its customer had been a one-to-one link, with the bank and the customer meeting across a table to negotiate a loan or other deal. But in the new structure the innovative finance house puts itself between the bank and its customer, suggesting ideas to the customer, and expecting the banks to compete in price and quality to provide whatever financial instruments the customer wished. This new marketing structure thus accelerated the introduction of innovations and at the same time, forced more competitive pricing.

TABLE 1.1

Impact and Status on M. Narasimhan Committee Recommendations on Banking

Recommendations	*Impact*	*Status*
• Stringent capital adequacy norms.	• Banks become financially stronger.	• RBI directives out, with deadlines.
• Treat private banks at par with public ones.	• More, and new competition.	• No guidelines, but many plans.
• Abolish licences for branch expansion, free entry of foreign banks.	• Those already here expand, others set up shop.	• Not done. Clearances still subjective.
• Bring down SLR and CRR.	• Funds released.	• Partially done.
• Curtail 'priority' lending.	• Profitability up.	• Work started.
• Change to a four-tier banking structure.	• Better focus, stability. Costs cut.	• No policy. Dicey proposition.
• Formation of a body for tackling bad debts — mainly affects public sector banks.	• Reduce debt on paper, speed up slow-moving assets.	• Nothing as yet. May not happen. It's impractical.
• De-regulation of interest rates.	• Fund costs go up. More bank profits.	• Lending, not floor, rates freed.
• Create a quasi-autonomous body, RBI-plus.	• More freedom, less administration.	• Nothing as yet, a slow go.
• Depoliticise banking, and key appointments.	• Public sector bank efficiency up.	• Years away, if it happens at all.
• Redefine the role of institutions in takeovers and mergers.	• Will make low-equity managements feel very shaky.	• Nothing as yet. Possible opposition from industry.

During the mid-1980s, the margins on wholesale business were reduced significantly. This stemmed from many factors. There was excess of capital in banking, in particular as the Japanese banks benefited from the enormous commercial success of Japan, and began to take their due place on the world banking scene. Corporate treasurers became increasingly concerned about price, and at being seen to obtain the best deal in the market place.

From the economic point of view, the major task of banks and other financial institutions is to act as intermediaries, channeling savings into investment and consumption: through them, the investment requirements of savers are reconciled with the credit needs of investors and consumers.

If this process of transference is to be carried out efficiently, it is absolutely essential that the banks are involved. Indeed, in performing their tasks they realise important economies of scale: the savings placed at their disposal are employed in numerous and large transactions adapted to the specific needs of borrowers. In this way they are able to make substantial cost savings for both savers and borrowers, who would otherwise have to make individual transactions with each other. However, there is more to these economies of scale than just the cost aspect. Indeed, for the saver/investor, the bank's mediation leads principally to a very important reduction in risk, which is not only a result of risk-spreading that the bank accomplishes in reinvesting savings (diversification in banking) in productive avenues.

Banks and Development

The following critical path of development shows how banks and other catalysts are interlinked with development:

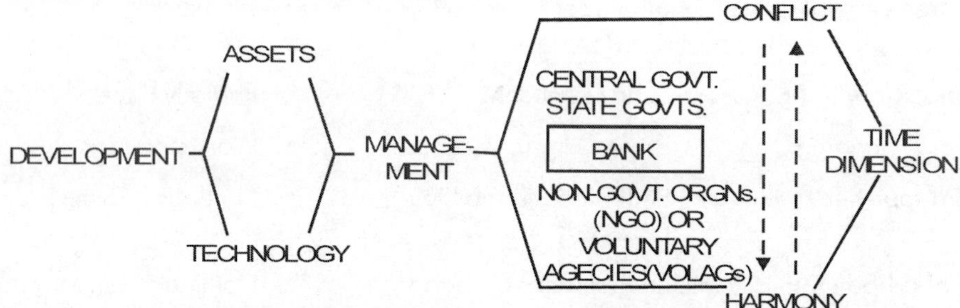

Fig.1.1 Critical Path of Development.

Nowadays, banking has gone far beyond the conventional confines of traditional banking and assumed the epithet and role of development banking. The role of a banker has become a multi-faceted one. He has to be a pen pusher and a go-getter. His role is of being a catalyst, a nucleus, a pacesetter, an experimenter and even a practical theorist. He can be an ideal conduit for realizing the 'Lab to Land' programmes. A development banker is looked upon as one who can bridge the gap between professor and practitioner, between research labs (like R&D labs or RRLs) and end-use beneficiaries on the farm, between specialised national institutions and voluntary agencies (VOLAGs), between visionary and visualiser. He has been, and continues to be, a platform where educative and awareness programmes are organized and knowledge disseminated. In a nutshell, he is a developmental crusader himself with an infinite number of possibilities.

Retail Banking

The banks have taken up "retail" banking in a big way and have made significant inroads into new markets; their aggregate lendings to agriculture, small industry, small business, and other indigent borrowers belonging to the weaker sections of the community, covering nearly 358.40 lakh accounts, amounted to Rs. 4,09,748 crores in March 2006 and formed over 40.2 per cent of their total credit portfolio.

The banks have been making every endeavour, both on their own and in partnership with Government-sponsored development organisations and associations of private trade and industry, to promote the growth of entrepreneurship and self-employment ventures in the country by granting credit on easy terms.

In the context of the continuing paucity of entrepreneurial talent and scarcity of investible resources, commercial banks in India have increasingly been called upon to play a more positive and dynamic role in igniting the forces of innovation and investment, and helping to foster and broad base new entrepreneurship in the country. The development of entrepreneurship — one of the social responsibilities enjoined on the banks — is a complex process. The functions of this development-banking include, in addition to the traditional functions of providing term loans and working capital, the formulation of project ideas, identification of specific projects suitable to local conditions, location of, and inducing, new entrepreneurs to take up these well-formulated projects, and provision of a package of counselling services, including technical and managerial guidance.

Over the past decade or so, public sector banks have been experimenting with a wide range of special schemes designed to "tailor" credit to the specific requirements of individual enterprisers. These include schemes for financing engineers, doctors, craftsmen and other technically qualified entrepreneurs, apart from several other schemes for the promotion of self-employment among the weaker sections of the community, such as newspaper vendors, cobblers, hawkers, handloom weavers as well as disabled defence personnel. For schemes for entrepreneurial development, all that the banks require is a worthwhile project, technically feasible and economically viable, coupled with technical competence and ability to manage the enterprise, apart from the character and integrity of the entrepreneur. Credit from banks is no problem even where the entrepreneur is not in a position to bring in the normal owner's equity. There are quite a few projects of new entrepreneurs where the banks have, in fact, granted 100% finance.

Promoting Entrepreneurship

The banks' experience in promoting entrepreneurship has been that if all the multi-dimensional aspects of this process are to be handled by them alone, the progress would be tardy, with the added disadvantage of duplication of their organisational and technical machinery and higher cost implications. Accordingly, they have been endeavouring, wherever possible, to operate a research clinic in collaboration with the State development agencies and the various organisations representing industry, commerce and trade. Various schemes have been designed by them to help entrepreneurs exploit opportunities in the ancillary industrial sector. The bank has already compiled an exhaustive dossier from which a prospective entrepreneur can get information on the various components of the schemes. Once the prospective entrepreneur has chosen his line of manufacture, the schemes put him in touch with the large industrial unit which is in need of that particular item. The large industrial unit will help and guide the entrepreneur in:

(i) The preparation of project report;

(ii) Arranging for in-plant training, if necessary;

(iii) Commissioning the project;

(iv) Solving technical problems in the process of manufacture; and

(v) Standardising the quality of the product and assuring a minimum purchase order for a specific period of time.

The entrepreneurial clinic also helps the entrepreneur in securing registration, selecting plant and machinery, locating sources of supply of raw materials and advice and guidance in technical matters, besides arranging for full financial assistance on attractive terms. A distinguishing feature of these schemes is the linking of the prospective entrepreneur with an operating industrialist who will act as his foster-father for all his needs.

The banks have been making vigorous and sustained efforts in discharging their social responsibilities in other sectors as well. The banking philosophy is to provide credit and technical and financial guidance to suit the specific requirements of each case. Banks also believe in the philosophy of creative banking with emphasis on dynamic lending, i.e., lending which will facilitate the expansion of production and result in increase in incomes and employment.

The banks have simultaneously been aggressive in promoting exports through a package of wide-ranging services. The small industrial sector has responded to the banks' efforts and has made a contribution, though small, to the export effort.

The main thrust of banks' promotional work has been to support activities that help step up the pace of viable industrializations and ensure balanced regional growth. These activities are designed to promote the healthy growth of small enterprises, widening of the entrepreneurial base and spread industrial culture among weaker and under-privileged sections of the community. IDBI sponsors and supports research activities related to industry, economy and technology. IDBI has also been making concerted efforts to strengthen and enlarge the institutional base that supports all these activities.

Marketing

After the nationalisation of 14 major commercial banks in 1969, banks woke up from their isolation and found themselves in a highly competitive and rapidly changing environment. As a result, their approach to customers and market underwent a change and their focus was gradually shifted to the marketing of products. So also development banks became product-oriented organisations, placing before the prospective customer a wide range of services, expecting him to choose, presuming that the customer had the knowledge, time, interest and skills to pick out the service that would suit him best. At the same time, they became conscious of their corporate image and its projection; and this introduced the public relations philosophy in banks.

The first major step in the direction of marketing was initiated by the State Bank of India when, in 1972, it reorganized itself on the basis of major market segments, dividing the customers on the basis of their activities, and carved out four major market segments, viz., the commercial and institutional segment, the small industries and small business segment, the agriculture segment, and the personal and services banking segment. The new organisational framework embodies the principle that the existence of an organisation was primarily dependent upon the satisfaction of customer needs. The objectives of the scheme, among others, were:

(i) Deeper penetration and coverage of markets by looking outwards;

(ii) Adequate flexibility of organisation to accommodate growth and rapid change; and

(iii) Delegation of work with a view to releasing senior management for more futuristic tasks.

The hallmark of the reorganized set-up was customer orientation. It aimed at:

(i) A total view of a customer's needs;

(ii) Meeting the identified needs in the best possible manner by developing appropriate and suitable services;

(iii) The identification of potential customers; and

(iv) Conducting the activities at the branches on the basis of a carved out market instead of job-wise segments.

Planning was separated from operations, and the posts of Development Managers for each segment were created to provide the necessary expertise to the operating functionaries in their respective market segments for better market penetration and development strategies. Yet another major leap forward in the marketing direction was taken when the bank took upon itself the responsibility of involving itself in the neighbourhood affairs and winning the co-operation of the community in its developmental efforts. The then Chairman of the State Bank of India observed: "I cannot seriously attempt to provide a set of specific guidelines to follow for initiating innovations, for, in each place, in every situation, at any given point of time, we will have to try out new approaches to resolve the increasingly intricate growth problems faced by individuals and the community — we must develop alertness to opportunities and should be able to tell our story effectively to the people we serve."

Research and Development

But banks have not been content with pioneering new schemes of financing and providing adequate credit to the priority sectors. Realising the importance of research and development in enriching the life of the common man, the major banks have established a Research and Development Fund. The Fund promotes research which aims at raising the productivity of agricultural and allied activities and small-scale and cottage industries to improve the living conditions of the rural population and to identify and train new entrepreneurs. The scope of the scheme is quite wide and includes agriculture and allied activities, village reconstruction, improvements in the economic and social well-being of the rural community, development of entrepreneurship, assistance to the handicapped; and it provides for the institution of chairs in universities for the conduct of research in such fields as agriculture, rural development, entrepreneurship and others, which are relevant to the policy of the banks. Innovative banking is an eternal quest for new avenues for serving the common man, and the response of the bank's staff to this quest has been encouraging. A new culture is slowly developing in this institution, as a result of which the barriers between the banks and the society are being demolished and the hopes and aspirations of the common man find an immediate echo in the policies and practices of the banks. This, it may be said without hesitation, is one of the ideals of public sector banking. Innovative banking has made a significant contribution to the realisation of this deal.

Catalyst in Social Change

The development banks, as financial institutions, are only a catalyst in social change. With training programmes, they try to impress upon their staff that banks are for the people and that in a country in which the people are poor, the major objective of the bank is to associate itself with all the programmes for the amelioration of the conditions of life of the weaker sections. Training has been redesigned to meet the ever-growing and changing growth needs of bank personnel and to prepare them to meet the emerging challenges of the future. New methods of assessing training needs, new processes of involving the critical functionaries in the training areas, systems to evaluate the effectiveness of training and systems to take training to the branches — these are some of the new developments in the bank's training system.

The viability and excellence of an organisation depend upon the competence of its people. Having regard to this, the banks have introduced a Human Resources Development system. The HRD is a continuous process, which enables every individual, as a member of a team, to realise and activate his potential so as to effectively contribute to the achievement of the organisational goals. Banks also believe in building a culture of collaboration and team work at all levels. To achieve these objectives, appropriate systems have been designed by the banks. A comprehensive and scientific manpower plan has been evolved with the help of which it is now possible to assess not only the present manpower needs but also forecast future requirements. To enable our managers to perform optimally, a new performance appraisal system has been designed and introduced. This system, in addition to bringing about clarity in respect of roles, provides timely feedback and promotes a healthier superior-subordinate relationship in the bank. A career plan model which helps in systematically building up skills and capabilities through a proper placement policy has also been evolved.

The Indian banking scene, particularly that of development banking, has thus undergone a profound transformation during the last two decades! Banks are now expected to play a leading role in bringing about economic and social change. With a wide expansion of branches, banking is now closer to the masses; and the policies of the banks are increasingly oriented towards helping the weakest of the weak sections of society. The evolution of the banks' policies in the field of rural credit, financing of small-scale industries and other weaker sections, the initiative taken under the lead bank scheme in accepting the challenge of banking development in the most difficult areas of the country, in preparing comprehensive development-oriented district credit plans for sustained development, and the numerous other innovative banking schemes introduced by their offices are noteworthy features of the operations of the banks.

The New World of Banking

The new world of banking is undergoing a sea change. Four trends are fundamentally altering the financial world: consolidation of institutions, globalization of operations, development of new technologies, and universalization of banking. Each of these poses challenges for the effective supervision and regulation of the financial sector.

Financial institutions around the world are consolidating at a rapid pace. The number of institutions is declining, their average size is increasing. The consolidation drive has created powerful banking institution.

Globalisation has facilitated risk diversification by banks and improved the overall performance.

Developments in technology, and especially the impressive growth of Internet banking and brokerage services, have allowed globalization to go beyond the ownership structure of financial conglomerates and to reach the retail markets. In fact, many banks are using their online operations to expand into foreign markets, avoiding the costly process of building retail brick-and-mortar networks of branches. Moreover, the emergence of alliances between major banks and telecommunications conglomerates suggests that, in the future, competition in the electronic marketplace will be fierce. In addition, the appearance of virtual banks and the development of electronic money for the global Internet market have created the possibility for the growth of nonbank (and, possibly, largely unregulated) institutions that provide credit to, and collect funds from, the public. Faster communications require faster reactions from both markets and policymakers but also quickly make information obsolete.

The final vehicle for this transformation of the financial sector is the universalization of banking, which is increasingly blurring the boundary between bank and nonbank financial services.

In short, the banking sector is entering a new world in which national and institutional boundaries are becoming less important. Inevitably, supervisory and regulatory systems will have to adapt their work methods in order to remain effective. The growing emphasis on risk management, exchange of information, and coordination at the international level is evidence of efforts to adapt.

In a rapidly changing world of banking, one has to understand how one has gained from multiple intelligence to meet with the multiple challenges as well as opportunities. There are five kinds of minds — disciplinary, synthesising, creating, respectful and ethical. In the process, these minds work and put into place a personal strategy to develop these minds in the self. And, this will help the new world of banking to extend services promptly across the borders and board. This will help in ushering a new concept of banking practices for the benefit of all stake-holders.

Tasks Ahead

Banking is a very sensitive industry which is constantly under the public gaze. Better customer service, whether in the urban or rural area, whether to the depositor or to the borrower, and the productivity of banks are the most vital factors to which this industry has to pay closer attention if it is to discharge its responsibilities in a satisfactory manner. However, the tasks before the banks are still unfinished and gigantic. With a greater emphasis on agriculture, the development of backward areas, on integrated rural development and the development of small and tiny industries in the Tenth Five-Year Plan, the banking system is expected to play a crucial role by the deployment of its funds in rural areas, particularly in assisting agriculture, rural industries, and the small-scale sector on a preferential basis. Moreover, in view of the Government's aim of full employment to all able-bodied persons, the banks will be required to improve the flow of credit under self-employment schemes. The Working Groups set up by the Government have made several recommendations to improve the flow of bank credit to the weaker sections under the programmes envisaged under the Seventh Plan; and commercial banks will no doubt put forth their very best efforts to achieve these socially-desirable goals. They have all along been in the vanguard of all the programmes which help the common man and have actively associated themselves with the financing of schemes under the Antyodaya programme. Block level plans have been drawn up under the Integrated Rural Development Programme with a view to assisting in the fulfilment of the objective of providing full employment to the rural poor. The widening network of the banks' branches has taken them nearer and nearer to the masses, and given them increasing opportunities of ameliorating their living conditions. Simultaneously, banks play a catalytic role in increasing industrial production and exports and accelerate the process of economic development, without compromising on productivity and profitability.

In recent years, banks in India have been functioning more as leaders in development and instruments of national policy than as dealers in money. The concept of banking as mere depositories of the community's savings and lenders to creditworthy parties having substantial worth has given way to the concept of purposeful banking sub serving the growing and diversified financial needs of planned economic development. The emphasis has now shifted to lending according to national priorities and helping the hitherto neglected and weaker sections of the community in their productive activities. The direction in favour of mass and rural banking in a big way is unmistakably clear.

As the economy becomes more diversified, as the money and capital markets grow more vibrant, as the financial sector gets liberalised, there will be a greater need for professionalism in financial services and integrity and autonomy in the operations of financial institutions within a broad regulatory framework. That would lend credibility and respect to the exercise of judgement in individual cases and build up investor confidence which is the only sure foundation for a healthy development of a capital market. But this can only happen in an environment of greater competition and a more liberal framework. If every aspect of balance sheet operations and every aspect of management is subject to controls and approvals, it tends to do damage to the essential qualities bankers and financial managers are associated with, viz., innovation and risk-taking. Bankers tend to become financial bureaucrats bound by rules and regulations and subject to direction.

The issue of providing commercial banks with greater autonomy in their operations is closely related to the larger issue of greater autonomy for all public financial institutions such as the term-lending institutions and most importantly, of the Reserve Bank of India. In the Reserve Bank we have an institution which should command respect, credibility and authority. In recent years, there has been some erosion of that authority and it is necessary to restore to that institution the authority and autonomy in its discharge of the functions entrusted to it by law and expected of it by the public. It is a legitimate function of the Reserve Bank to operate monetary policy in respect of the quantum, direction and cost of credit and regulated the banking system, and I would add, the term-lending institutions catering both to industry and agriculture, to safeguard the solvency, viability; and profitability of the financial system and ensure that its operations are in conformity with our development objectives. Detailed regulation by government in the area of credit development and branch expansion has led to needless and avoidable duplication of authority. There is indeed no need for government separately and in parallel involving itself in matters of credit allocation and direction. The banking and credit system should not look to two masters. The roles of the government and the Reserve Bank ought to remain distinct and distinguish between the proprietary and the supervisory.

The argument for a measure of deregulation or liberalisation rests not on ideology but on the practical case that it would help to foster efficiency, taking into account the stage of development our banking and credit system and the capital markets have reached. We have a strong enough geographical base and functional spread and we have a cadre of professional managers who if left free to take credit and investment decisions, could do so without interference but in pursuit of broader policy objectives set by the Reserve Bank.

The Indian banking system currently is set for changes. Sufficient ground has been created for Narasimham Committee norms to take off. Banking in India has to swim in tempestuous waters and competitive environment and can no longer be protected. Its important observations are:

— The emphasis on reform policies is to inject productivity, efficiency, upgradation of technology, reduction of cost and improvement in customer service.

— Good banking is to combine social banking with commercial bar king.

— Most central banks in the world do not intervene or direct the business of banking. But in India, pressures on balance of payments have been building up since the mid- 1980s, accentuated by more imports. We averaged GNP at 5% in the 1980s and 5, 6% between 1985-90. The oil crisis and Gulf War forced drawing down our reserves, and commercial borrowings and NRI sources started drying up, creating pressure on current account deficit, though the level of this has been of 1984-85 level only. How to finance this?

Higher interest rates will result in better management of resources, productivity, inventory holding by producers at economic order levels etc. A higher interest rate acts as an antiinflation many mechanism, will bring about an effect through a decline in the aggregate demand. There is a slow down in industrial production too. Devaluation has resulted in less absorption in the economy.

A hike in interest rates does not affect government expenditure/borrowing as their borrowing rates are not changed. The expected reduction in government expenditure did not take place resulting in increasing money supply. The policy of RBI should not, of course, be a "continued hike in interest rate" and government expenditures have to come down.

While monetary authority (RBI) decides the level of interest rates, administered rates may be necessary to take care of certain segments of society but rates charged on different monetary instruments should be linked to the level of interest rates. Determine lending rate and then determine deposit rates.

— To induce deposits, despite keeping them low like in Japan (to affect lending rates also), give fiscal concessions.

— Fundamental reform in the financial system is a fundamental reform in the interest rate structure.

— Government is the most favoured sector, pre-empting credit through cutback of SLR at 38.5%, CRR at 15% together with 10% of this as incremental.

— If Government reduces its fiscal deficit from 8.5% to 6.5% and then to 5% of GDP, then it is possible and can be expected from GOI/RBI to reduce CRR and slowly SLR also by 1993-94. Some other tangible measures are: rise in bond rates and better rates on small savings..

— Availability of timely credit is more important than the cost of credit.

— As recommended by the Chakravarty Committee Report, have two rates — one minimum lending rate (MLR) and another below this MLR.

— Fix the minimum deposit rate at 2% above the inflation rate.

— Fix MLR at 3% above the maximum deposit rate and leave all other rates to be fixed by the different banks.

— As competition gets intense, liability management and funds management become more important. Banks have to shift from protected waters of structured rates to the tempestuous waters of flexible interest rates.

Conclusion

India is a vast country with rural and urban areas in different stages of financial development. The disintermediation process requires that the final saver must be directly accessible to the corporate borrower. This is feasible in urban centres but presents difficulties in the widely-dispersed rural areas where the intermediation role of banks is necessary. Banks, therefore, have important developmental responsibilities in the semi-urban and rural areas which constitute a major part of the Indian economy.

Further, banks in India are basically retail banking organisations. Profits from wholesale banking business used to cross-subsidise the high costs of retail banking. In recent years, however, the wholesale banking business is gradually going out of the folds of the banks to other units, which can quote much more attractive rates than banks, on account of their low costs. Increasing proportion of retail banking business, coupled with high reserve costs, is threatening to make Indian banks uneconomic.

For the success of the overall macro-economic objectives, monetary controls are, no doubt, necessary but the reserve costs are pushing up the overall costs of commercial banks and affecting their competitive efficiency in the financial services industry. If this situation continues, the banking industry will be rendered uncompetitive. Effective cost of funds to the banking system being high, banks will be constrained to raise their charges and, in an intensely competitive industry, it could be priced out in the long run. Besides the higher operational costs, the other burden which the banks alone have to carry is in the form of high reserve costs. Low-yield assets, in which the banks are obliged to invest a substantial part of their funds, raise the costs for the banks.

While breaking new ground in the socio-economic field, where the cost factor is relatively higher, banks have not ignored their overall business, domestic as well as overseas. Their overseas offices and subsidiaries have recorded significant improvement in the magnitude of business operations. The banks are also gradually changing the character of their overseas operations — from multinational to international banking.

Domestically, banks have made good progress in mobilising higher deposits and simultaneously, their lending and investment portfolio has increased, for they now cater to the needs of millions of new entrepreneurs and assist them in their ancillary business activity, with the result that they have managed to improve steadily their operating results. All in all, the banks are today in a much stronger position in terms of financial and organisational strength to enable them to meet the emerging challenges that lie ahead than they were in the past. Already the 1980s have witnessed a phenomenal growth of the banking industry, both in size and in the variety of operations. The banks' involvement in the rural areas has also undergone multi-dimensional changes. The development banks' penetration in project financing and schematic financing will accelerate the process of economic growth in the 90s. A planned approach to operations — prudent and professional management, efficient administration and participative management — would help increase their activities in a multi-directional as well as well-diversified way for the benefit of mankind and, at the same time, sustain economic growth and development.

Chapter 2

The Banking System in India

Banking system plays a vital role in the economic development of a country. The structure of the banking system in India consists of two parts: (i) unorganized sector; and (ii) organized sector. The organized sector comprises moneylenders and indigenous bankers. The organized sector consists of commercial banks, co-operative banks and regional rural banks. Besides the above institutions which provide mainly short-term credit to business there are a number of specialized term lending institutions which provide long-term requirements of industry, agriculture and foreign trade. Post office savings bank which is 115 years old is another segment of the banking system. The Reserve Bank of India, the Central Bank of the country is at the apex of the banking structure in India.

Indigenous Bankers

The indigenous bankers occupy an important place in the Indian financial system. From ancient times, indigenous bankers lend money, act as money changers and finance internal trade by means of internal bill of exchange. The business of indigenous bankers is generally a family concern. With their own capital they grant loans against securities such as gold, jewellery, land, promissory notes, etc. They also buy and sell remittances and discount hundies.

The indigenous bankers do not have contact with other sections of the banking world. They combine banking with trading commission business. They generally deal with agriculturist and small traders. The interest rate charged by them is higher than the interest charged by other banking institutions. In spite of all these defects, the indigenous bankers occupy a prominent position in the money market. According to the Reserve Bank of India, about 50 per cent of internal trade is financed by these indigenous bankers. The Banking Commission (1972) has pointed out that, "they are much sought after because of their flexibility, absence of formalities and promptness." The commission has noted that, "if they are linked with the Reserve Bank, the entire financial system in the country will get strengthened."

BOX 2.1

LOOKING BACK

Private bankers have existed in India since antiquity. At the time the British took over the subcontinent, an extensive network of Indian banking houses already existed.

Francis Buchanan Hamilton, writing around 1811-12, refers to "24 proper bankers (kothiwals) at Patna and to the house of Jagat Seth. Later, Colonel Wade described the banking and mercantile network of Bogotee Ram, treasurer of the Nawab of Fatehpur.

Modern banking in India emerged between the 18th and the beginning of the 19th centuries when a structure of European controlled banks was erected primarily by European agency houses. Joint stock banking emerged after Act III of 1860 conferred limited liability on joint stock banking companies in India.

In 1683, the first bank was set up in Madras by the officers of the East India Company. Between 1788 and 1804 three more banks appeared. In 18th century Bombay, private merchants and bankers practically directed the activities of the city's government. The government's involvement in expensive wars made it dependent on private merchants for loans. Till 1806, agency houses such as Forbes and Co., Bruce Fawcett and Co., Shotton and Co., Jamshetjee Jeejeebhoy, and others retained their control over the credit markets of Bombay.

In Calcutta, an agency house, Alexander and Co., established the Bank of Hindostan in the 1770s. In 1819 the Commercial Bank, and in 1824 the Calcutta Bank, were floated by agency houses Mackintosh and Co., and Palmer and Co., respectively. Later, the two banks merged to form the Union Bank.

The end of the East India Company's monopoly over trade in 1833 led to the entry of new European firms and new business for second class agency houses. The Bank of Calcutta and the Bank of Bombay were the next banks to emerge.

The most permanent institutional gain of this period was the emergence of the three Presidency Banks between 1809 and 1843, all destined to play a pivotal role in Indian banking. In 1921, these banks were amalgamated into the Imperial Bank of India, and eventually became the State Bank of India.

While the progress of banking was slow till 1900, one constituent of the banking system developed remarkably during the last decade of the 19th century. These were the Indian joint stock banks which benefited from the sudden boom of investment in this country at the time.

Leading Indian joint stock banks that emerged were:

- The Bank of India, 1906
- The Central Bank of India, 1911; in 1923 the Tata Industrial Bank was merged with this bank
- The Punjab National Bank, 1895
- The Bank of Baroda, 1909
- The Indian Bank, 1907
- The Union Bank of India, 1919

It was only in the 1850s that British banking actually reached India, when four banks began functioning as chartered institutions. These were:

- The Chartered Bank of India, Australia and China, 1853
- The Chartered Bank of Asia, 1853

- The Chartered Mercantile Bank of India, London and China, 1857; acquired by the Hongkong and Shanghai Bank in 1959
- The Agra and United Services Bank, 1857

Started by Captain Robert Melville Grindlay of the East India Company, Grindlay's Bank opened branches in Calcutta in 1854 and Bombay in 1865.

Founded by James Wilson, who also founded the *Economist* magazine, the Standard Chartered Bank began operations in India as the Chartered Bank in 1858. In the same year, a bank was started in Africa, called the Standard Bank. The two were merged in 1969 to form the Standard Chartered Bank.

Commercial Banks

Commercial banks are the oldest banking institutions in the organized sector. They constitute the predominant segment of the banking system in India. They cater to the needs of trade, commerce, industries, agriculture, small business, transport and other activities with a wide network of branches throughout the country. Commercial banks command a major share in the total banking operations. The commercial banking system consists of scheduled banks and non-scheduled banks.

Scheduled Bank

Scheduled bank is one, which is registered in the Second Schedule of the Reserve Bank of India. The following conditions should be fulfilled by a bank for inclusion in the Schedule:

(1) The bank concerned must be carrying on a business of banking in India.

(2) The bank must have paid-up capital and reserve of an aggregate value of not less than Rs. 5 lakhs.

(3) It must satisfy Reserve Bank of India that its affairs are not being conducted in a manner detrimental to the interest of the depositor.

The scheduled banks come within the direct purview of the credit control measures of the Reserve Bank. They are entitled to borrowings and rediscounting facilities from the Reserve Bank of India. (Non-scheduled banks are not entitled to such facilities).

Non-Scheduled Bank

Bank which is not included in Second Schedule of the Reserve Bank of India is known as non-scheduled bank. As at end March, 2005 there were 4 Non-Scheduled Banks.

All banks which are included in the Second Schedule to the Reserve Bank of India Act, 1934 are Scheduled Banks. These banks comprise Scheduled Commercial Banks and Scheduled Co-operative Banks. As of March 2006, 354 banks were included in the Second Schedule.

Scheduled Commercial Banks in India are categorised into five different groups according to their ownership and/or nature of operation. These bank groups are (i) State Bank of India and its

Associates, (ii) Nationalised Banks, (iii) Regional Rural Banks, (iv) Foreign Banks and (v) Other Indian Scheduled Commercial Banks (in the private sector).

Scheduled Co-operative Banks consist of Scheduled State Co-operative Banks and Scheduled Urban Co-operative Banks.

At the end of March 2006, there were 283 Scheduled Commercial Banks. It comprised State Bank of India, 7 SBI Associates, 19 Nationalised banks, IDBI Ltd., 196 Regional rural Banks, 31 Foreign Banks and 28 Private Sector banks (8 new and 20 old private sector).

There were 71 Scheduled Cooperative Banks consisting of 16 Scheduled State Co-operative Banks and 55 Scheduled Urban Co-operative Banks.

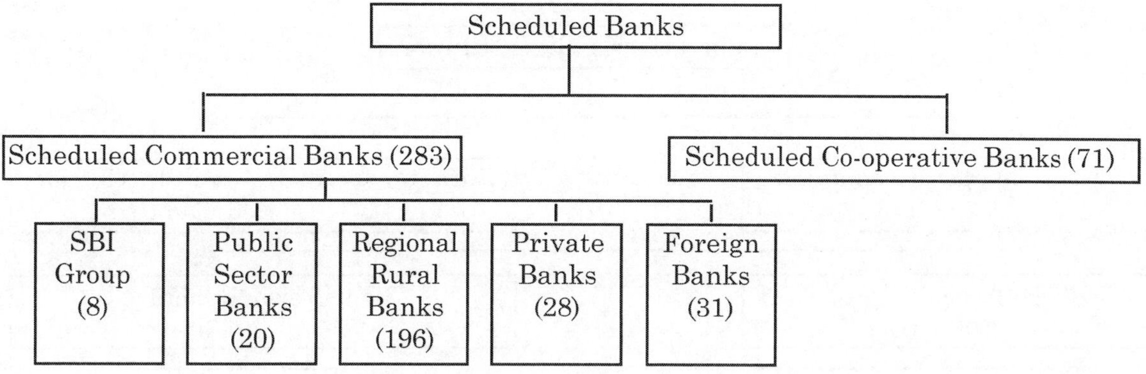

Chart 1 Structure of Scheduled Banks

Co-operative Banks

Co-operative banks, another component of the Indian banking system, originated with the enactment of the Co-operative Credit Societies Act of 1904. The Act provided for the establishment of credit societies for financing agriculturists. Under the Act number of co-operative credit societies were started. The Co-operative Credit Societies Act, 1912 provided for the establishment of co-operative central banks by a union of primary credit societies. The Maclagan Committee appointed in 1914, recommended the establishment of a State Co-operative Apex Bank. Following this, Central Co-operative Banks were started in many provinces. However, the co-operative movement to cater to the needs of agriculturist received momentum only during post independence era.

Co-operative banks in India have come a long way since the enactment of the Agricultural Credit Co-operative Societies Act in 1904. The century old co-operative banking structure is viewed as an important instrument of banking access to the rural masses and thus a vehicle for democratisation of the Indian financial system. Co-operative banks mobilise deposits and purvey agricultural and rural credit with a wider outreach. They have also been an important instrument for various development schemes, particularly subsidy-based programmes for the poor.

The co-operative banking structure in India comprises urban co-operative banks and rural co-operative credit institutions. Urban co-operative banks consist of a single tier, *viz.*, primary co-operative banks, commonly referred to as urban co-operative banks (UCBs). The rural co-operative credit structure has traditionally been bifurcated into two parallel wings, *viz.*, short-term and long-term. Short-term co-operative credit institutions have a federal three-tier structure consisting of a large number of primary agricultural credit societies (PACS) at the grass-root level, central co-operative banks (CCBs) at the district level and State co-operative banks (StCBs) at the State/apex level. The smaller States and Union Territories (UTs) have a two-tier structure with StCBs directly meeting the credit requirements of PACS. The long-term rural co-operative structure has two tiers, *viz.*, State co-operative agriculture and rural development banks (SCARDBs) at the State level and primary co-operative agriculture and rural development banks (PCARDBs) at the *taluka/tehsil* level. However, some States have a unitary structure with the Sate level banks operating through their own branches; three States have a mixed structure incorporating both unitary and federal systems.

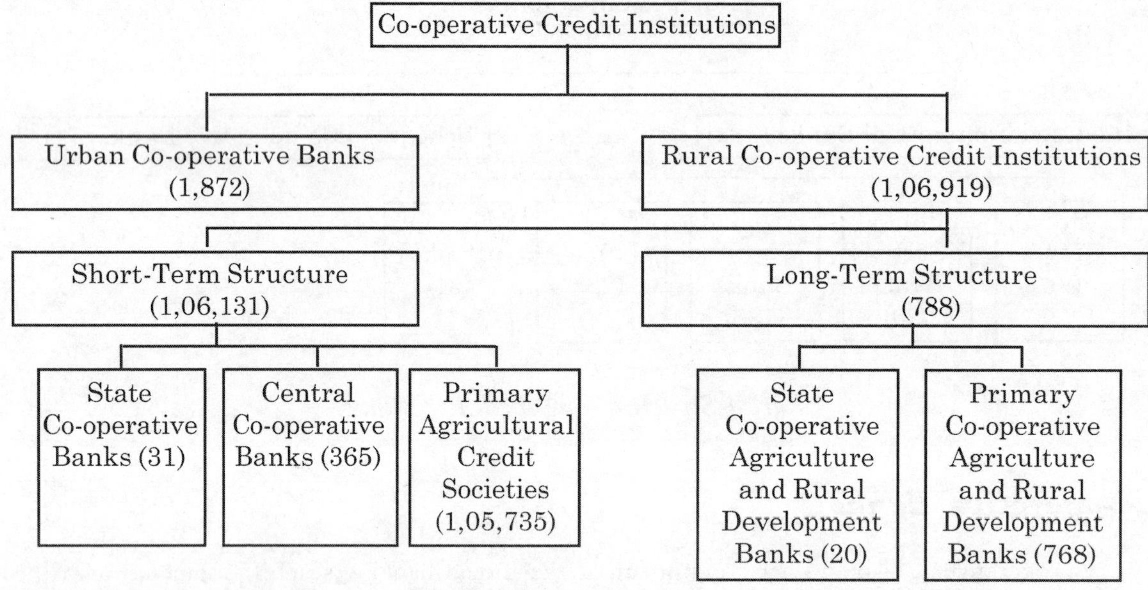

Chart 2 Structure of Co-operative Credit Institutions

Note: Figures in parentheses indicate the number of institutions at end-March 2005 for urban co-operative banks and at end-March 2004 for rural co-operative credit institutions.

The co-operative banking structure in India is a pyramid type of a three tier structure comprising: *(i)* Primary Agricultural Co-operative Credit Society at the village level, *(ii)* District Central Co-operative Banks at the district level, and *(iii)* State Co-operative Bank at the state level.

Primary Co-operative Credit Societies

The primary co-operative societies function at the base of the co-operative credit system. It may be organized by ten or more persons normally belonging to a village or a cluster of villages. The societies raise funds by way of share capital, deposits from members and non-members and loans from District Central Co-operative Banks. The borrowing powers of members as well as society is limited.

Central Co-operative Banks

A Central Co-operative Bank is a federation of primary credit societies in a specified area normally extending to the whole district. The central banks raise funds by way of share capital from member societies, deposits from public and loans from the State Co-operative Bank. The main task of these banks is to finance member societies. In addition to this, they carry on commercial banking activities. They also act as 'balancing centres' making available temporary excess funds of one primary society to another which is in need of them.

State Co-operative Banks

The State Co-operative Bank is a federation of Central Co-operative Banks. It acts as a watch dog of the co-operative banking structure in the state. It receives deposits from the public and from local boards, municipalities, etc. Further they receive loans at call and short notice from the Commercial Banks and from the Reserve Bank of India. The state governments contribute a certain portion of their working capital. The state co-operative banks lend money to central co-operative banks which in turn lend to primary societies. The central banks act as intermediaries between the state co-operative bank and primary credit societies.

Urban Co-operative Banks

Primary (urban) co-operative banks play an important role in meeting the growing credit needs of urban and semi-urban areas. UCBs mobilise savings from the middle and lower income groups and purvey credit to small borrowers, including weaker sections of the society. The number of UCBs stood at 1,872 at end-March 2005, including 79 salary earners' banks and 119 *Mahila* banks. Total number of scheduled UCBs were 55 at end-March 2005. Scheduled UCBs are under closer regulatory and supervisory framework of the Reserve Bank.

BOX 2.2

MEDIUM-TERM FRAMEWORK FOR URBAN CO-OPERATIVE BANKS

The Medium-Term Framework (MTF), which is being finalised based on responses to the draft Vision Document, seeks to achieve the following objectives:

- To rationalise the existing regulatory and supervisory approach keeping in view the heterogeneous character of the entities in the sector.
- To facilitate a focused and continuous system of supervision through enhancement of technology.
- To enhance professionalism and improve the quality of governance in UCBs by providing training for skill upgradation and also by including large depositors in the decision making process/management of banks.
- To put in place a mechanism that addresses the problems of dual control, given the present legal framework and the time-consuming process in bringing requisite legislative changes.
- To put in place a consultative arrangement for identifying weak but potentially viable entities in the sector and provide a framework for nursing them back to health including, if necessary, through a process of consolidation.

- To identify the unviable entities in the sector and provide an exit route for such entities.

The above framework is proposed to be implemented through:

- A differentiated regulatory regime as opposed to a "one-size-fits-all" approach.
- A two-tier regulatory regime: (a) simplified regulatory regime for unit banks and single district banks with deposits less than Rs.100 crore; and (b) regulation for all other banks on the lines of commercial banks.
- As the strategy to deal with UCBs may need to be State-specific, a State Level Task Force for Urban Co-operative Banks (TAFCUB) is to be constituted comprising senior officials from the Reserve Bank, State Governments and local/central co-operative Federations.
- The TAFCUB would be responsible for (i) identifying weak but viable UCBs and devise a time-bound programme for revival; and (ii) recommending (a) the nature and extent of financial support, (b) future set up of unlicensed banks, and (c) the manner and timeframe for exit of unviable banks.
- To address issues/difficulties relating to dual control within the existing legal framework, it has been proposed to evolve a working arrangement in the form of Memorandum of Understanding (MoU) between the Reserve Bank and the State Government.

Various entities in the urban co-operative banking sector display a high degree of heterogeneity in terms of deposits/asset base, areas of operation and nature of business. In view of its importance, it is imperative that the sector emerges as a sound and healthy network of jointly owned, democratically controlled and professionally managed institutions. In order to achieve these objectives, the Reserve Bank took a series of policy initiatives in 2004-05. The most significant initiative in this regard was the Vision Document and Medium-Term Framework (MTF) for UCBs. With a view to protecting depositors' interests and avoid contagion on the one hand, and enabling UCBs to provide useful service to local communities and public at large on the other, a draft Vision Document was prepared and placed in public domain for eliciting comments. Based on the feedback received from different quarters, the necessary modifications were carried out in the vision document to evolve as the medium-term framework for the sector.

Land Development Banks

Besides short-term and medium-term advances, agriculturists require long-term loans for effecting permanent improvement in land, for purchase of pumpsets, tractors, digging up of wells, etc. Land Development Banks meet the long-term credit requirements of the agriculturists. It is two tier structure with central land development banks at the state level and primary land development banks at taluka or district level. The banks of Tamil Nadu, Mumbai, Andhra Pradesh and Karnataka are of this type. In states like Gujarat, Uttar Pradesh and Jammu and Kashmir there is unitary structure, i.e., the Apex Land Development Banks operate directly through their own branches at the district or taluka level.

The land development banks obtain funds mainly by the issue of long-term debentures. Such debentures carry the guarantee of the state government and are subscribed by the central and state governments, commercial banks, Life Insurance Corporation and Reserve Bank of India. Special debentures are floated for which resources are provided by state government and NABARD.

Regional Rural Banks

Regional Rural Banks (RRBs) form an integral part of the banking system with focus on serving the rural sector. RRBs combine the local feel and familiarity with rural problems, which the co-operatives possess, and the degree of business organisation as well as the ability to mobilise deposits, which the commercial banks possess. RRBs are specialised rural financial institutions for catering to the credit requirements of the rural sector.

In the early 1970s there was a growing realization that the benefits of the co-operative system has not reached all strata of farmers. The public sector banks, due to constraint of manpower resources and high cost of operation were not able to satisfy the credit needs of rural population, especially those of weaker sections. Therefore, in 1975, the Central Government appointed a working group under the chairmanship of M. Narasimhan to review the flow of institutional credit to weaker section of the rural community and to devise alternative agencies to provide institutional credit to people in rural areas. The working group felt that the co-operative institutions and commercial banks would not be able to fill the credit gap within a reasonable time. Therefore, it recommended a new type of institutions which could combine the local knowledge and familiarity with the rural problems which the co-operatives possess and the degree of organizational ability to mobilize deposits, access to money market and modernized outlook which the commercial banks have.

Following the recommendations, the Central Government promulgated an ordinance in September 1975 for the establishment of Regional Rural Banks (RRBs). The first five Regional Rural Banks were established on October 2, 1975. The ordinance was later replaced by the Regional Rural Banks Act, 1976.

Objectives: The main objective of the RRBs was to provide credit and other facilities mainly to the small and marginal farmers, agricultural labourers and artisans who had, by and large, not been adequately served by the existing credit institutions.

Organization: The RRBs are established by 'sponsor bank', usually a public sector bank. The steering committee on RRBs identifies the districts requiring RRBs. Later, the Central Government, with the consultation of the state government and the sponsor bank setup RRBs. Each RRB is separate body corporate with perpetual succession and common seal. But it is closely linked with the sponsor bank. Each RRB operates within local limits with such name as may be specified by the Central Government. The head office of the RRB will be within the local limit as specified by the Central Government. The rural bank may establish its braches or agencies at any place within the notified area.

Capital: The authorized capital of each RRB is Rs. 1 crore and the paid up capital is Rs. 25 lakhs. Of this 50 per cent is subscribed by the Central Government, 15 per cent by the state government and 35 per cent by the sponsor bank. At present the formula for subscription to RRBs has been fixed at 60:20:20 between central government, state government and the sponsor bank. The Central Government contribution is made through NABARD.

Management: The general superintendence, direction and management of the affairs and business of RRBs vests with the nine member Board of Directors. The Central Government nominates 3 directors, the state government has 2 directors and the sponsor bank nominates 3 directors. The chairman is usually an officer of the sponsor bank but appointed by the Central Government. The Board of Directors is required to act on business principles and in accordance with the directives and guidelines issued by the Reserve Bank. At the state level, State Level Co-ordination Committee have also been formed to have uniformity of approach of different RRBs.

Resources of RRBs: The resources of RRBs consist of:

(i) Share capital,

(ii) Deposits from public,

(iii) Borrowing from sponsor banks,

(iv) Refinance from NABARD.

The Reserve Bank of India has put RRBs on par with co-operative banks for refinance facilities, i.e., 2% below the bank rate. Like commercial banks, the RRBs have been made eligible for accommodation against a mere declaration of eligible loans and advances by them.

The RRBs are allowed to offer 1 ½ per cent additional rate of interest on their deposits over the rate offered by commercial banks. The facilities provided by the Deposit Insurance and Credit Guarantee Corporation of India have been extended to the RRBs to protect the interest of depositors.

Operations: The RRBs are required to undertake the following business:

(i) Granting of loans and advances to small and marginal farmers and agricultural labourers, whether individually or in groups or to cooperative societies including agricultural marketing societies, agricultural processing societies, co-operative farming societies, primary agricultural societies for agricultural purposes or for other related purposes.

(ii) Granting of loans and advances to artisans, small entrepreneurs and persons of small means engaged in trade, commerce or industry or other productive activities within its area of operation.

The RRBs now meet the consumption needs of small and marginal farmers and other borrowers of small means for certain specific purposes such as education, medical expenses, etc.

In the case of regional rural banks (RRBs) sponsor banks are being encouraged to amalgamate the RRBs sponsored by them at the State level. The Government of India (Ministry of Finance), after consultation with NABARD, the concerned State Governments and the Sponsor banks, issued nine notifications on September 12, 2005 under Section 23-A of the Regional Rural Banks Act, 1976 providing for amalgamation of 28 RRBs into nine new RRBs sponsored by nine banks in six States, *viz.*, Bihar, Gujarat, Karnataka, Maharashtra, Punjab and Uttar Pradesh. These amalgamations have become effective from September 12, 2005.

In order to reposition RRBs as an effective instrument of credit delivery in the Indian financial system, an Internal Working Group on RRBs was set up by the Reserve Bank in February 2005 (Chairman: Shri A.V. Sardesai) to examine various alternatives available within the existing legal framework for strengthening the RRBs and making them viable rural financial institutions. The Group, in its final report submitted in June 2005, made several recommendations for restructuring the RRBs (Box 2.3). The main recommendations of the Working Group relating to restructuring options, change of sponsor banks, minimum capital requirements, governance and management, regulation and supervision have been sent to the Government of India for consideration.

BOX 2.3

INTERNAL GROUP ON REGIONAL RURAL BANKS (RRBS)

The major recommendations of the Group are set out below:

- To improve the operational viability of RRBs, the route of merger/amalgamation of RRBs may be considered along two lines: (i) merger between RRBs of the same sponsor bank in the same State; and (ii) merger of RRBs sponsored by different banks in the same State.
- A change in sponsor banks may, in some cases, help improve competitiveness, work culture and efficiency of concerned RRBs for which new banks, both public and private sector, could be considered.
- The merged entities and existing RRBs that have accumulated losses can be capitalised to wipe out the losses and satisfy minimum capital requirement. The CRAR may initially be kept at 5 per cent.
- For those RRBs which may not turn around within a specified time limit, say 3 to 5 years, an exit route may be considered subject to extent legal provisions.
- The process of appointment of Chairmen of RRBs may be re-examined to explore the possibility of appointing them from the open market through a transparent process.
- The Boards of RRBs may be strengthened by making them broad-based through inclusion of professionals such as agricultural experts, bankers, etc.
- An appropriate recruitment policy, providing for greater flexibility and freedom, may be required for RRBs.
- An appropriate incentive structure, career planning, relevant training, especially in skill upgradation and information technology, be evolved for employees of RRBs.
- It would be appropriate if both the regulatory and supervisory functions relating to RRBs are exercised by the Reserve Bank.
- RRBs may be encouraged to actively consider distribution of products of mutual fund/insurance companies, rationalisation of branch network, participate in consortium lending within their areas of operations.
- RRBs may be considered for currency chest facility and empowered to collect taxes by the State Governments.

The RRBs have played an important role in mobilizing the savings of the small farmers, artisans and agricultural labourers. The presence of the banks has helped to develop banking habits among rural masses. In spite of the progress made the following are some of the drawbacks:

(i) The ratio of advances to deposits was supposed to be 10:15 but the RRBs are able to manage at 1:1 ratio.

(ii) The RRBs have made losses continuously. Some banks have eroded their share capital. The losses exceeded the share capital in some other banks.

(iii) The overdues and the number of defaulters is on the increase. The recovery rate has been deteriorating despite continuous effort and increase in the number of field staff.

The RRBs have become an integral part of the Indian rural banking system. The Kelkar Working Group in its report in 1986 has pointed out that RRBs are eminently suited for the jobs envisaged for them. Hence there is an urgent need to revitalise the RRBs by augmenting their resources, rationalising the lending procedure, imparting training to the staff and getting co-operation of the state governments.

Regional Rural Banks form an integral part of the Indian Banking System with focus on serving the rural sector. The state-wide amalgamation of RRBs over the year has reduced the number from 196 to 90 by the end of December, 2006. The logic of this process is to enable the RRBs to function in a competitive environment by taking advantage of economies of scale and reducing transaction costs.

Local Area Banks

Four local area banks (LABs) were functional at end-March 2005. These banks have a very small base of assets, deposits and advances. Cumulatively, they made the operating profit of Rs.3.4 crores in 2004-05.

Foreign Banks

In addition to domestic banks, 31 foreign banks with 245 branches were operating in India at the end of September 2005. These banks originated from 19 countries. While four banks have 10 or more branches [Standard Chartered Bank (83), HSBC Ltd. (39), Citibank N.A.(35) and ABN AMRO Bank N.V.(19), 12 banks were operating only one branch each. The branches of foreign banks are spread over 35 centres in 17 States/Union Territories. In addition, 27 foreign banks from 13 countries have also set up representative offices in India. At present, 58 banks have presence in India either through branches or representative office. The Banks have also been suitably reorienting the regulatory and supervisory framework so as to meet the challenges of a new environment. It has been the endeavour of the Reserve Bank to develop a competitive, strong and dynamic banking system so that it plays an effective role in supporting the growth process of the economy. The emphasis has been on safeguarding the financial stability of the overall system through increased emphasis on prudential guidelines and effective monitoring, improving institutional soundness, strengthening the regulatory and supervisory processes by aligning with international best practices and by developing the necessary technological and legal infrastructure. While the approach towards the reforms has essentially been gradual and relevant to the context, consultative processes and appropriate timing and sequencing of measures have succeeded in aiding growth, enhancing efficiency, avoiding crises and imparting resilience to the financial system. The foreign banks hold about 8 per cent of the total commercial banks' assets in India. Almost all the foreign banks operating in India are multinationals. These banks operate mainly in big trading centers and cater to the needs of big customers who can provide them with the entire spectrum of business. The profitability of these banks is higher than Indian banks.

Development Banks

A development bank is a multipurpose institution which provides medium and long-term credit to industrial undertakings, discover investment projects, undertake the preparation of project reports, provide technical advice and managerial services and assist the management of industrial units. Thus rendering Financial assistance and promotional services are the main functions of development banks.

There is a network of development banks in India at the all-India and state levels. Besides development banks for Financing industrial undertakings, development banks for providing finance for agriculture, export and housing have been established in India. A brief description of the bank is given in the succeeding pages.

Conclusion

The banking system in India is quite unique and widely diversified. It plays a distinct role in the development and growth of the economy. The banking sector has played a critical role in fulfilling the needs of the growing and increasingly diverse economy, offering high-quality services to businesses and individuals alike. The availability of efficient banking and financial services has been a key driver of business growth and profitability, and the ability of people to meet their needs for housing, education, health and other lifestyle aspirations. Banks have successfully created world-class financial products and services catering to the entire gamut of needs of households and businesses. Change and growth are throwing up new opportunities and challenges for the Indian banking and financial services sector in the 21st century.

Chapter 3

Commercial Banking: Structure and Evolution

Introduction

Banking is the lifeline of an economy. They are the catalytic agent and in the driver's seat of the financial system. The importance of commercial banks in the process of economic development has been stressed from time to time by the economic thinkers and progressive bankers in the country. Commercial banks play a very important role in our economy; in fact, it is difficult to imagine how our economic system could function efficiently without many of their services. They are the heart of our financial structure, since they have the ability, in cooperation with the Reserve Bank of India, to add to the money supply of the nation and thus create additional purchasing power. Banks' lending, investing and related activities facilitate the economic processes of production, distribution and consumption.

What is A Bank?

Time was when it was a reasonably simple exercise to identify a bank. Essentially, it was an institution which took deposits from the public and lent money. Of course, there have always been institutions of rather different character which fell within the definition — the UK merchant banks, for example, or (a special and unique case) the discount house. There have also been banks which have developed extensively into other areas of financial activity such as the West German universal banks with their substantial securities interests. And it is universally acknowledged that because of the special nature of banking, the institutions involved needed special supervisory treatment for the protection both of the public and of the financial system as a whole.

A whole range of changes are taking place which together are blurring the accepted definitions. Over a long period, there has been the growth of the inter bank and wholesale money markets, reducing dependence on retail deposits and making possible the emergence of banks operating virtually exclusively with wholesale money. In the US there has been the creation of that contradictory beast, the 'non-bank Bank', which gets round the rules by operating on only one side of the balance sheet.

Then there has been the steady breakdown of accepted barriers between different types of bank. Historically, for example, savings banks in most countries had different origins from the commercial banks and a different mission in life. In recent years, though they moved over in most countries into straight coercible and, more and more, international banking. So have many of the more specialised financial institutions such as the French 'green bank', Credit Agricole. Barriers are also coming down between banks and other types of financial institutions — in the UK, for example, building societies are gearing up to put their toes into banking waters; do we eventually take some of them into the list?

Then there is the 'securitisation' of banking, effectively by passing the accepted banking practice in a way which leads to marketable instruments superseding traditional borrowing and lending. At the same time, the banks themselves are moving out into activities which in many countries have been fenced off; in particular, securities trading, common on the continent of Europe but hitherto not in the United Kingdom and still not permitted in the United States of America. The potential impact of securities holdings is dramatically illustrated in the year 1986 by the Danish banks, with huge 'Profit' increases as a result of revaluation of their portfolios.

Commercial and Development Banks

The importance of commercial and development banks in the process of economic development has been stressed from time to time by economic thinkers and progressive bankers in the country. Commercial development banks play a very important role in our economy; in fact, it is difficult to imagine how our economic system could function efficiently without many of their services. They are the heart of our financial structure since they have the ability, in co-operation with the Reserve Bank of India, to add to the money supply of the nation and create additional purchasing power. Banks' lending, investments and related activities facilitate the economic processes of production, distribution and consumption. Economic development is a continuous process. Broadly, there are two schools of thought on the concept of economic development. According to some, economic development is both the widening flow of production and the deepening flow of income. Others are of the opinion that it is the presence of various facilities that induce further development. In fact, economic development is a socio-economic political puzzle, for it exists within the limits set by the economic environment. Economic development is deliberately organised or left to the action of private enterprise. As such economic development is quite a weighty issue. Ragnar Nurkse advocates

the idea of balanced growth as against the concept of rapid growth achieved through the actions of individual entrepreneurs, producing recurrent waves of industrial progress.

The success of economic development depends essentially on the extent of mobilization of resources (both internal and external) and investment, and on the operational efficiency and economic discipline displayed foreign aid and assistance are dim, one has to rely upon internal resources for economic development.

Economic development is a continuous process. Broadly, there are two schools of thought on the concept of economic development. According to some, economic development is both the widening flow of production and the deepening flow of income. While others consider that it is the presence of various facilities that induce further development. In fact, economic development is a socio-economic political puzzle as it exists within the limits set by the economic development which are deliberately organised or left to the action of private enterprise, economic development is quite a weighty issue. Ragnar Nurkse advocated the idea of balanced growth as against the concept of rapid growth, achieved through the action of individual entrepreneurs, producing recurrent waves of industrial progress.

The success of economic development depends essentially on the extent of mobilisation of resources (both internal and external) and investment and on the operational efficiency and economic discipline displayed by the various segments of the economy. At a time when the prospects of foreign aid and assistance are dim, one has to rely upon the internal resources for economic development. It is, therefore rightly emphasised that the rate of investment to a large extent depends upon the mobilisation of internal savings. The mobilised savings are put in the productive manner, so that the economy is on the move. Since Independence and more particularly since the commencement of the planned development, the economy has moved rapidly forward in several directions.

Role of Banks

Banks play a positive role in economic development of a country as repositories of community's savings and as purveyors of credit. Indian banking has aided the economic development during the last fifty years (1949-1999) in an effective way. The Banking sector has shown remarkable responsiveness to the needs of planned economy. It has brought about a considerable progress in its efforts at deposit mobilisation and has taken a number of measures in the recent past for accelerating the rate of growth of deposits. As a recourse to this, the commercial banks opened a number of branches in urban, semi-urban and rural areas and have introduced a number of attractive schemes to foster economic development.

The activities of commercial banking have grown in multi-directional ways as well as multi-dimensional manner. Banks have been playing a catalytic role in area development, backward area development, extended assistance to rural development all along helping agriculture, industry, international trade in a significant manner. In a way, commercial banks have emerged as the key financial agencies for rapid economic development.

PROCESS OF COMMERCIAL BANKING DEVELOPMENT IN INDIA

1949	REGULATION	BANKING COMPANIES ACT 1949
1955	NATIONALISATION PHASE-I	STATE BANK OF INDIA (SBI)
1959	NATIONALISATION PHASE-II	SBI SUBSIDIARIES
1961	INSURANCE COVER TO DEPOSITS	DEPOSIT INSURANCE CORPORATION
1968	SOCIAL CONTROL	NATIONAL CREDIT COUNCIL
1969	NATIONALISATION PHASE-III	14 MAJOR COMMERCIAL BANKS
1971	CREDIT GUARANTEE	CREDIT GUARANTEE CORPORATION
1975	NEW RURAL BANKS	REGIONAL RURAL BANKS
1980	NATIONALISATION PHASE-IV	SIX COMMERCIAL BANKS WITH DEPOSITS OF OVER Rs. 200 CRORES
1985	REORGANISATION OF BANKING	
1996	NEW BANKS	PRIVATE BANKS
1998	REVIEW	RE-EXAMINATION

Fig. 3.1

Banks in India were started on the British pattern in the beginning of the 19th century. In those days, all banks were joint stock banks and were governed by the companies law. Banks are broadly classified into those that are statutory as those that are based on the area of their operations.

The scheduled commercial banks in the country comprise the State Bank of India and its associate banks (8), the nationalised banks (19), private sector banks (29), regional rural banks (196) and foreign banks (44).

By pooling the savings together, banks can make available funds to specialised institutions which finance different sectors of the economy, needing capital for various purposes, risks and durations. By contributing to government securities, bonds and debentures of term-lending institutions in the fields of agriculture, industries and now housing, banks are also providing these institutions with an access to the common pool of savings mobilised by them, to that extent relieving them of

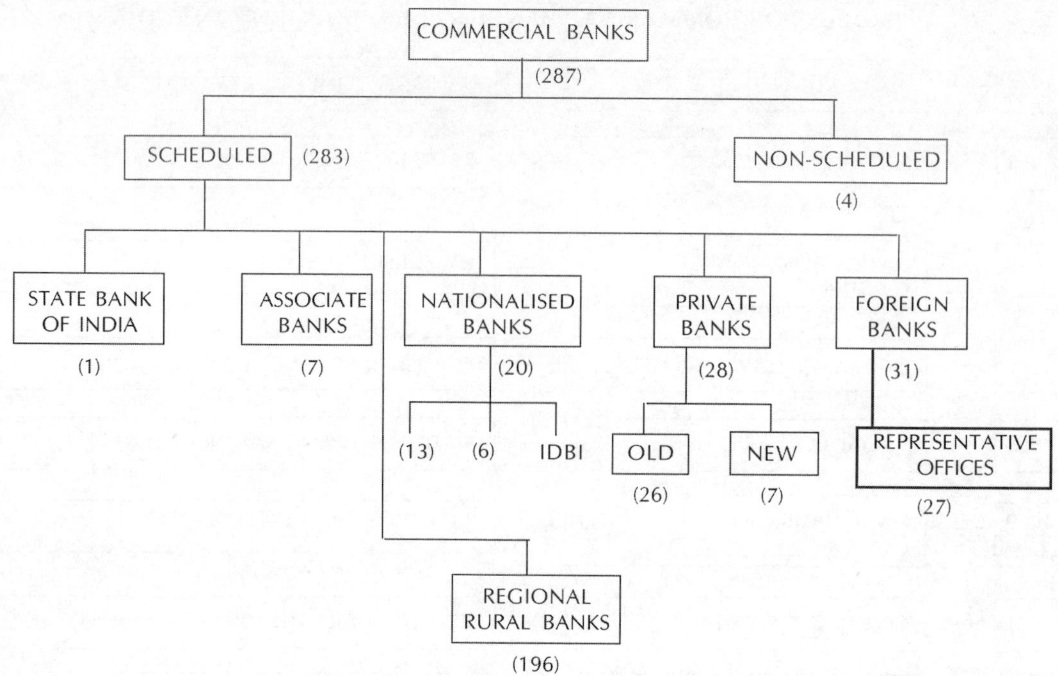

Fig. 3.2 Structure of Commercial Banks in India

the responsibility of directly approaching the saver. This intermediation role of banks is particularly important in the early stages of economic development and financial specialisation. A country like India, with different regions at different stages of development, presents an interesting spectrum of the evolving role of banks, in the matter of intermediation and beyond.

Mobilisation of resources forms an integral part of the development process in India. In this process of mobilisation, banks are at a great advantage, chiefly because of their network of branches in the country. And banks have to place considerable reliance on the mobilisation of deposits from the public to finance development programmes. Further, deposit mobilisation by banks in India acquired greater significance in their new role in economic development.

Commercial banks provide short-term and medium-term financial assistance. The short-term credit facilities are granted for working capital requirements. The medium-term loans are for the acquisition of land, construction of factory premises and purchase of machiney and equipment. These loans are generally granted for periods ranging from five to seven years. They also establish letters of credit on behalf of their clients favouring suppliers of raw materials/machinery (both Indian and foreign) which extend the banker's assurance for payment and thus help their delivery. Certain transactions, particularly those in contracts of sale to Government Departments, may require guarantees being issued in lieu of security/earnest money deposits for release of advance money, supply of raw materials for processing, full payment of bills on the assurance of the performance etc. Commercial banks issue such guarantees also.

Risk Management

The banks are committed to a healthy credit culture that recognizes the need to ensure high asset quality. In this endeavour, improvement in the existing measures in the risk management process is receiving special attention. A major step in this direction is the introduction of the revised in-house Credit Risk Assessment (CRA) system, which captures financial risks as also other types of risks, such as industry risk in a borrowal account. The system has well stabilized, and covers a major part of the bank's large commercial and industrial loan portfolio. In order to bring about uniformity in the risk assessment methodology, the CRA system has also been extended to high value accounts in the SSI and agricultural segments as well.

The bank's credit portfolios are well diversified cutting across various industries with exposures in each category restricted to reasonable levels. Exposures to different industries are within limits set on the consideration of management of different risks and are kept under close monitoring.

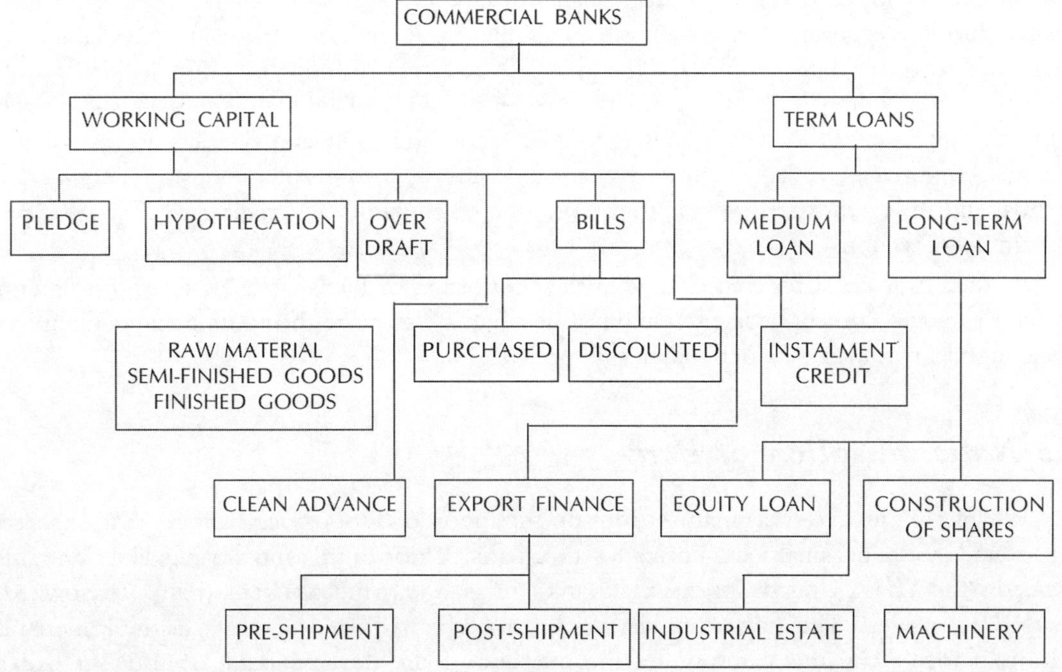

Fig. 3.3 Types of Financial Assistance Provided by Commercial Banks

Even as the Reserve Bank of India took several steps to widen the financial infrastructure by taking the initiative to establish several new institutions such as those for providing long-term finance to industries, an important banking development in the Fifties was the conversion of the Imperial Bank of India into State Bank of India. This was done on the recommendations of the Rural Credit Survey Committee. The majority of the shares of Imperial Bank of India was acquired by the Reserve Bank of India and this was the first step towards widening the scope of the banking system in this country.

By early Sixties, it came to be realised, that, apart from ignoring the growing needs of sectors such as agriculture, the credit flow from banks was highly concentrated, catering only to a limited segment of the society, the need to give the banking system a new sense of direction, in order to make it an instrument of economic growth was keenly felt. It was, therefore, decided to extend what came to be known as 'Social Control' over the banking industry by issuing guidelines regarding the deployment of credit. The National Credit Council was set up by the Government in February 1969, as a follow-up measure to the introduction of the scheme of 'Social Control.' The Council's main functions were envisaged as (*i*) to assess the demand for bank credit from various sectors of the economy, (*ii*) to determine priorities for grant of loans and advances, having regard to the availability of resources and requirements of priority sectors, particularly agriculture, small-scale industry and exports; and (*iii*) to co-ordinate the lending and investment policies between commercial banks and co-operative banks and the specialised agencies, to ensure optimum and efficient utilisation of resources.

A Study Group of the National Credit Council was set up under the chairmanship of Prof. D.R. Gadgil to suggest an organisational framework for implementation of social objectives. The Study Group identified that uneven distribution of credit existed not only between states but also between different economic sectors and observed that bank credit was virtually unavailable to small borrowers and weaker sections. The Group recommended the adoption of an 'area approach' towards branch expansion for the proper growth of banking system. This approach led to the formulation of the Lead Bank Scheme. Under this scheme, districts were assigned to individual commercial banks, which were entrusted with the responsibility of estimating the deposit potential and the credit gaps, so that steps could be taken to fill the credit gaps through a phased programme of action.

As there was no significant change in the proportion of loans available to priority sectors, it was felt that social control by itself would not be adequate to make the commercial banking system a meaningful instrument of socio-economic policies.

The Nationalisation of Banks

1969 wasn't just the year man set foot on the moon or Woodstock happened; it was also the year Indira Gandhi nationalised 14 private sector banks. Prior to that most banks like Central Bank (owned by the Tatas), United Commercial Bank (Birlas) and Syndicate Bank (Pais) were owned and managed by business. The only exception was the State Bank of India. Known as the Imperial Bank of India before 1955, this came under the purview of the Reserve Bank of India; it had been nationalised in July 1955 under the SBI Act of 1955. The businessmen who owned these banks channelised most deposits into their own companies, often ignoring the government's focus areas, agriculture and small-scale industries.

That neglect was one reason for the nationalisation of banks. Another was Gandhi's desire to spread the banking habit in rural and semi-urban areas, freeing farmers from the clutches of usurious moneylenders. And still another was the odd name like Nath Bank that went bust.

Nationalisation: A Chronology

Fig. 3.4

1949:	Enactment of Banking Regulation Act
1955: (PHASE I):	Nationalisation of State Bank of India
1959: (PHASE II):	Nationalisation of SBI subsidiaries
1961:	Insurance cover extended to deposits
1969: (PHASE III):	Nationalisation of 14 major banks
1971:	Creation of Credit Guarantee Corporation
1975:	Creation of regional rural banks
1980: (PHASE IV):	Nationalisation of six banks with deposits over Rs. 200 crore.

Accordingly, on 19th July 1969, fourteen large commercial banks having deposits of Rs. 50 crores and above were nationalised.

Twenty eight key banks were nationalised in four stages. State Bank of India in 01-07-1955, 7 associate banks in 1959-60, 14 banks on 19-07-1969 and 6 banks on 15-04-1980. With the merger of one bank there are at present 27 banks in the public sector.

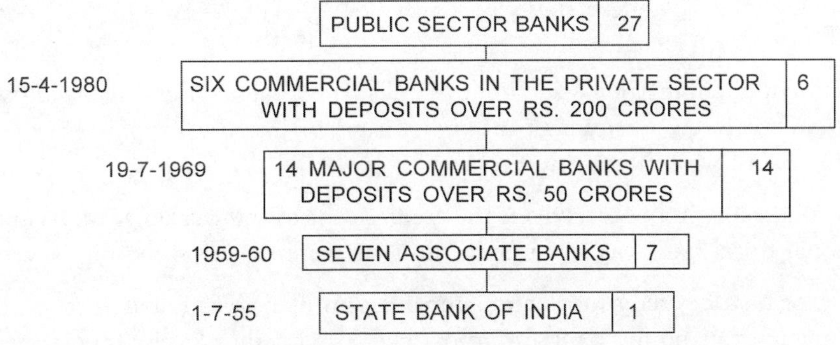

Fig. 3.5 Evolution of Public Sector Banking

The Role of the Public Sector in Banking

A major role now tends to be given to the public sector banks. This change is brought about by the social responsibilities and the need to accelerate the process of economic development in hitherto neglected areas and spheres. As at the end of March 1998, 224 of the 299 banking institutions were in the public sector. The share in branch network, deposits and advances accounted for 92.7, 90.7 and 88.9 per cent respectively. The effort of merging weak private sector units with public sector banks will enhance the role of the public sector banks. Care must be taken to improve the efficiency of banks and inculcate a competitive spirit in them.

The major objectives of nationalisation were:

(*a*) widening the branch network of banks particularly in the rural and semi-urban areas;

(*b*) greater mobilisation of savings through bank deposits; and

(*c*) re-orientation of credit flows so as to benefit the hitherto neglected sectors such as agriculture, small-scale industries and small borrowers.

With a view to achieving these objectives, several steps have been taken since 1969. Some of the important measures are —

1. Under successive branch licensing policies, banks were required to open offices in rural and semi-urban areas with a view to increasing the coverage of branch network outside metropolitan and urban areas.
2. Banks were required to lend a certain proportion of the net bank credit for priority sectors which included agriculture, small-scale industries and small business. This proportion was initially fixed at 33 per cent and was later raised to 40 per cent. Under the overall target, sub-targets were also laid down for credit to specific sectors such as agriculture and for weaker sections of the society.
3. With a view to ensuring that deposits mobilised in rural and semi-urban areas were deployed in those areas, banks were required to maintain a credit-deposit ratio of 60 per cent in rural and semi-urban areas.
4. Specific targets were also laid down for bank participation in poverty alleviation programmes such as IRDP.
5. In determining the lending rate structure of banks, an element of cross subsidisation was built into it. While large borrowers paid higher rates of interest, certain other sectors of the economy paid lower rates of interest.
6. With a view to meeting more effectively the credit needs of the weaker sections in the rural areas, Regional Rural Banks as separate institutions were set up in the mid-seventies.
7. Formulation of district credit plans and annual action plans was initiated so as to ensure that credit made available by banks were dovetailed with the developmental plans.
8. To prevent large borrowers from pre-empting credit from the banking system, the Credit Authorisation Scheme was introduced.
9. Every bank was asked to formulate a credit plan for the bank as a whole each year so that the objectives of overall monetary and credit policy could be achieved.

By and large, the major objectives of nationalisation have been fulfilled. There has been a dramatic change in the profile of Indian banking. A structural transformation of far reaching significance has occurred in the deployment of commercial bank credit. Banking has thus emerged as an effective catalytic agent of socio-economic change in the country.

BOX 3.1

ATTACKING RURAL POVERTY AND USHERING IN RURAL PROSPERITY

Financial assistance to farmers has shot up from Rs. 5970 crores in 1984 to nearly Rs. 65,741 crores in 2002. Under IRDP scheme, over 42.5 lakh families have been assisted to the extent of Rs. 1200 crores. Under DRI scheme Rs. 690 crores have been lent just at 4% interest. Village adoption schemes, development schemes, special programmes of upliftment, financing, alternate sources of energy, deep sea fishing, trawlers, mechanised fishing boats etc. and now the 'Service Area Approach' — all towards rural prosperity.

All out Assistance to Scheduled Castes and Scheduled Tribes

Be they Adivasis, or Santals or Todas — every small tribe constitutes a large segment of rural India. Banks have provided greater thrust to the socio-economic schemes aimed at development of scheduled castes and scheduled tribes. Credit assistance to the tune of Rs. 1957 crores has benefited 73 lakh families of which Rs. 1,100 crores have been specifically channelised to their agriculture and allied activities.

Big Scale Help to the Small Scale Industry

All small business units, artisans and craftsmen have been given priority in receiving assistance to boost their progress. Financial assistance has jumped from Rs. 655 crores in 1984 to Rs. 57,060 crores in 2002.

Helping Entrepreneurs to set up New Industries

By providing much needed finance, Public Sector Banks help entrepreneurs to set up new industries. Feasibility studies and entrepreneurial development programmes are conducted to guide and assist them.

From Unemployment to Self-employment

Under SEPUP and SEEUY, in the last two years alone, 668 lakh people have been gainfully self-employed. Banks have provided greater support to identify and free bonded labour to undertake self-employment ventures.

Equal Opportunities for Women

Banks are constantly encouraging more and more women in their entrepreneurial efforts. Banks are participating in a national programme of training and employment for women by providing credit to their self-employment ventures.

Homes for the Roofless

Under the Bank's housing schemes, financial assistance has been provided to various sections especially to the rural poor for the construction of houses to the tune of Rs. 29,148 crore.

Assistance to Students

Educational loans are provided to students for higher studies. Vocational guidance is also provided for helping the younger generation to face the future with confidence.

'Roads' to Progress

The Banks play a major role in providing loans to the road transport operators — helping link the country's transport network to the remotest corners.

A Thrust to the Economy

Financial assistance to medium and large industries has increased from Rs. 13,400 crore in 1984 to Rs. 57,872 crore in 1994 and further to Rs. 1,88,829 crore in 2003.

Generating Greater Savings Through Deposits

Total deposits have registered a tremendous growth (26 fold) from Rs. 64,000 crores in 1985 to Rs. 16,65,457 crores as at end December 2004.

Helping People Advance with 'Advances'

The funds mobilised have been channelised for productive purposes and enterprises. Advance have risen from Rs. 44,500 crores in 1985 to Rs. 10,41,631 crores in December 2004 and investments in government and other securities stood at Rs. 6,74,595 crores and Rs. 25,946 crores respectively as at end December, 2004.

Commitment towards Customer Service

Several concrete steps have been taken to provide a high degree of courteous and efficient customer service to our 26 crore account holders. It is their earnest endeavour to come up to customers' expectations.

Serving People Everywhere

The banks reach the masses wherever they may be with over 62056 branches all over the country. A majority of these are in rural and semi-urban areas.

A GUIDE TO HELP YOU INVEST WISELY

Take the Cure from Nature

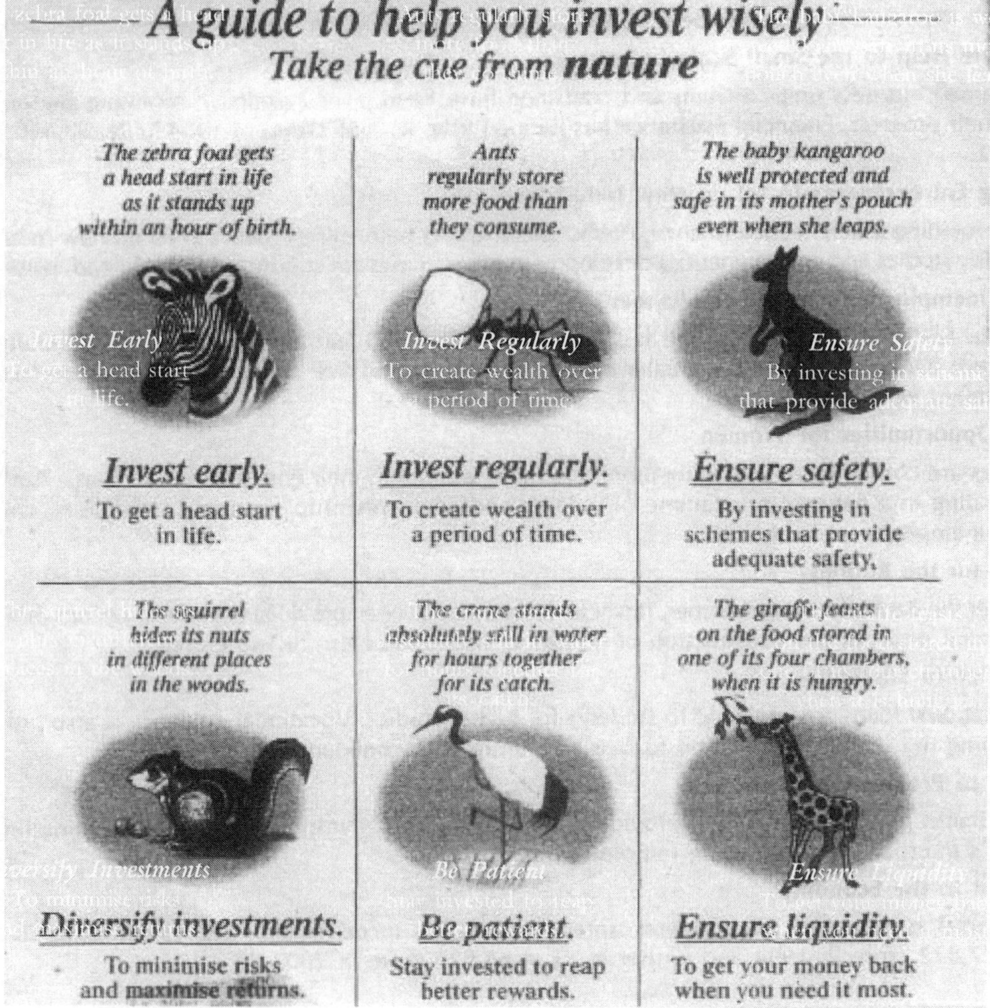

A critical factor in the long-term sustainability of social development and economic prosperity in India is engaging rural India in the process of economic growth. The agriculture sector continues to be plagued by dependence on the vagaries of climatic conditions and inefficiencies in the agricultural value chain. It is, in a way, 'the weak link' in India's growth equation and impacts not only those directly dependent on agriculture for livelihood but the entire economy.

Enhancing access to financial services is a major element of the approach towards realising the potential of rural India. The rural economy represents a large latent demand for credit, savings and risk mitigation products like insurance. It is only by delivering financial services to people in the rural areas and lower income categories that they can be brought within the ambit of economic activity and the full potential of the country's physical and human resources can be realised. The rural markets are, therefore, the next horizon of growth and banks will have to create holistic propositions to address this opportunity. This will call for a deeper and more comprehensive understanding of rural needs. Banks have to invent a new business model where they can create a distribution base effectively in 600,000 villages in India and learn to do that at one-tenth the cost of urban India.

Banks are working with key stakeholders (agri-based industries, government authorities and existing rural financial intermediaries) towards this end. We seek to use technology as a tool to accelerate the penetration of financial services, by using smart cards with biometric authentication and hand-held devices for banking transactions, not yet available to our urban customers. This radical approach of channels and products based on a technology reinvention and delivery architecture will bring financial services to the rural poor in a sustainable manner.

In summary, the financial services sector in India is poised for a period of sustained growth. This will be driven by continued urban consumer demand, expansion into rural markets, corporate investment in India and overseas, and leveraging of core competencies in international markets.

New Banking Order

Banking in India is getting more complex and sophisticated and passing through a period of transformation. Never before has the banking terrain been changing so fast nor have the banking and non-banking boundaries been so malleable. Banking system has transited from overly regulated atmosphere to a relatively more relaxed but competitive open environment. Competition is increasing as never before with banks being exposed to challenges of fluctuating interest rates, exchange rates, asset liability mismatches and increasing margin strains not to speak about growing disintermediation. Used as they were for a long time to well regulated and orchestrated financial system, banks in India had to graduate themselves to the new market induced regime and it is to their credit that they have taken such financial transitions in their stride. Transparency, standardisation in disclosure of financial and prudential information and consistency and compliance with recognised banking norms are the beneficial results of the reform process. In the evolving regulatory environment with freedom of operation, one has to be careful against control weaknesses and control failures too. No doubt banks in India have come of age and they are well poised to tread on the emerging volatile environment with caution, restraint and optimism. New banking order may appear to be threatening and unstable but that is the price of progress worth paying too.

In a competitive economy as only to be expected, the final say is with the customer. Most profound changes touching the industry is from customers. We are very conscious that giving customers much more service than they expect is the surest way to build and retain their loyalty and in the process, aiming long-term profitability by creating customer value and trust.

In a market led economy, success would depend on how quickly and meaningfully we respond to changes and seize the available opportunities which are only for the prepared. Human resources development takes centre stage in fast changing business environs. To take on the competition and to ensure customer creation and his retention, highly motivated and knowledgeable people have to be in place. People only develop an institution and knowledge is a means to it. Luckily, your Bank has such invaluable human resources, development of which has been our responsibility. We have therefore created more opportunities for our people for continued learning to update their banking and personnel skills just to make them feel at home with "high-tech" and "high-touch" services. We have made them to be conscious that in a knowledge based industry like banking, there is nothing like self-development. We have created hospitable and challenging atmosphere for them and also ample scope for their career advancement which compares well with the ideal in the system.

BOX 3.2

MANAGEMENT OF OPERATIONS

The leading banks now are increasingly focussing on differentiating their product offering by allowing customers to build products and creating 'brands.' Preferred customers of the bank have the ability to create product variants to suit their individual needs, often requiring banks to collaborate with other players. Most of the banks have invested in sophisticated touch points (both self-serviced and human interaction) that are either owned, shared or source through a third party service provider. All these touch points have the ability to capture and use customer intelligence for marketing efforts and for adhering to service stands to ensure customer stickiness.

The customer strategies adopted by the successful players are focused on retaining profitable customers, while also developing specific marketing initiatives to attract customers from other banks with incentive schemes, packaged service and competitive service standards. In addition, the search for profitable customers by the banks has taken them beyond the traditional metro and urban areas, with the rural sector being viewed as a serious market, and not just a priority sector commitment.

THE OUTSOURCING MODEL

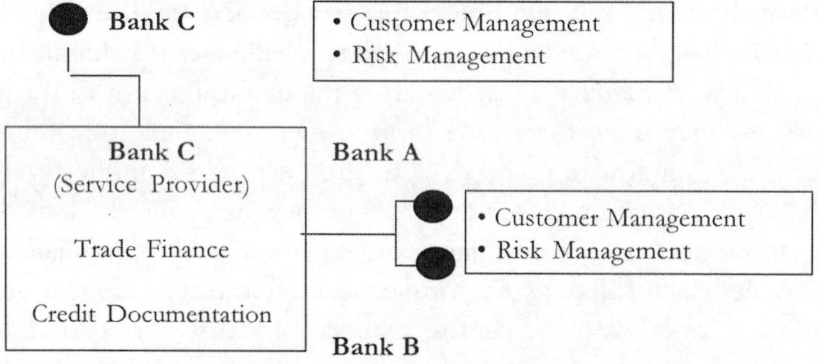

Banking in the New Millennium

Banks are changing; their business is changing, their ownership pattern is changing and the way they are managed is changing. Loan-loss provisioning norms have become mandatory. Compliance with capital adequacy ratios will drive them deeper into the equity and debt markets and non-compliance for any reason, will severely threaten their ability to take on new business. Shareholders will constantly clamour for higher dividend payouts and issue of bonus shares.

In short, a new banking environment has emerged, compelling banks to stay lean, mean and hungry. In this new environment, technology, data bases and provision of value added services and

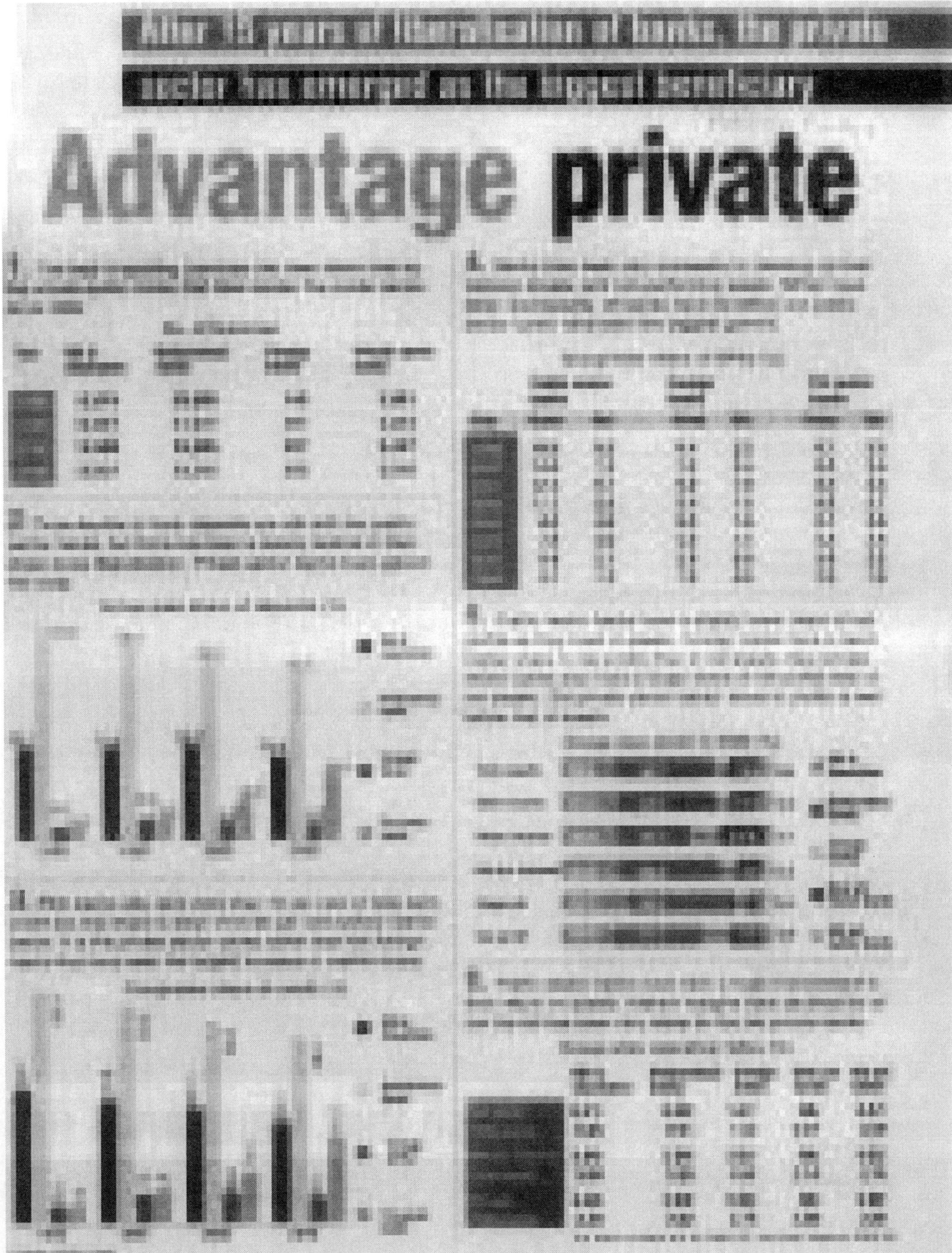

Advantage private

not in cement and concrete branches, following a mindless 10 a.m. to 2 p.m. routine. On-line banking thus represents the new paradigm in banking and by embracing it willingly and confidently, public sector banks have increased their efficiency, upgraded quality of service and improved productivity. This paradigm should strategically develop over the years.

The Future

Adjust, adapt, and change. That's the message that technology has sent across to modern day banking. As technology ingrains itself in all aspects of a bank's functioning, the challenge lies in exploiting the potential for profiting from investments made in technology.

Is the business of banking financially viable? It certainly is not, the way it is conducted in India. There are several challenges confronting the sector. These could be broadly classified into the development of funds in quality assets and the management of revenues and cost.

It is generally observed that public sector banking is not very competent to plan and manage revenues. There are several practices that need a close look. We need stable and long-term leadership in these banks to ensure sustained performance. There is also a need for these banks to examine its resource utilisation. These banks possess substantial branch network and manpower. Are these utilised effectively? Why do these banks underutilise technology? Why are they slow to identify opportunities that arise from the substantial resources base? Their fee income, compared to total income, can be improved if they can be efficient in their transaction conduct, and they can cross-sell third party products.

The foreign and new private sector banks are very mindful of the inefficiencies in the public sector banking. They manage their fee based income far more aggressively. We see them participating in the distribution of insurance and mutual funds products effectively. Some of the progressive players have identified process outsourcing and shared services as a sunrise opportunity. The banking sector has an uphill task considering the challenges it is facing. The gap between thinking and debating the solutions and the implementation of these is widening. This will erode the viability and the economic value of the business.

Despite the radical new trends emerging, banks will continue to play their role as trust-enablers in all commercial activities. Their role as financial intermediaries and payment enablers will also continue, but they will be outsourcing all non-core activities to specialised service providers and insource opportunities where they have a saleable value proposition. The transfer of money will not generate profits — it will, however, be the basis of other services that banks will provide. The level of integration that banks achieve with their customers supply chain will determine profitability.

Financial Services: Then & Now

Old World	*New World*
Confined market place	Unlimited market space
Competition between banks	Competition from brands
Limited product line	Extensive product breadth
One-size-fits-all product	Customisation and innovation
Branch-focussed	e-Enabled, multi-channel players
Focus on business growth	Focus on revenue growth as well as cost-reduction
Revenues through margin	Revenues generated through fees and value-added services.

The Impact of IT

Technology Trends	*Product/*	*Outsourcing Service Mgmt.*	*Insourcing*	*Analytics*	*Payment Systems*
Increase in processing power	●	N/A	N/A	●	N/A
Increase in networking	○	●	●	N/A	○
Development of modular software components	○	●	●	N/A	○
Development of messaging standards	○	●	●	○	●

○ Minor Impact ● Major Impact

Globalisation

Implementation of the WTO accord and the subsequent liberalisation of rules for foreign banks have had a significant impact on the banking sector. Although not too many new banks entered the market, the existing foreign banks grew bigger by purchasing market share wherever they perceived value. The new banks were mostly specialists, which licenses as their entry vehicles. Some foreign banks exited India as part of their global rationalisation and decision to concentrate on.

Analysis of data in any major Indian bank shows that 15-20% of the branches contribute to 70-80% of business. If banks are computerised and Net-enabled, data from the remaining 80-85% branches can be captured on the server of a branch LAN or a PC and then communicated to a central host via a regional data processing centre.

Bank managements should not look at IT upgrades in isolation. By issuing unique customer IDs, it is possible to access detailed customer information, making it possible to differentiate between profitable and non-profitable customers. A similar approach can be adopted in the case of products and services. Plans need to be put in place to utilise this information.

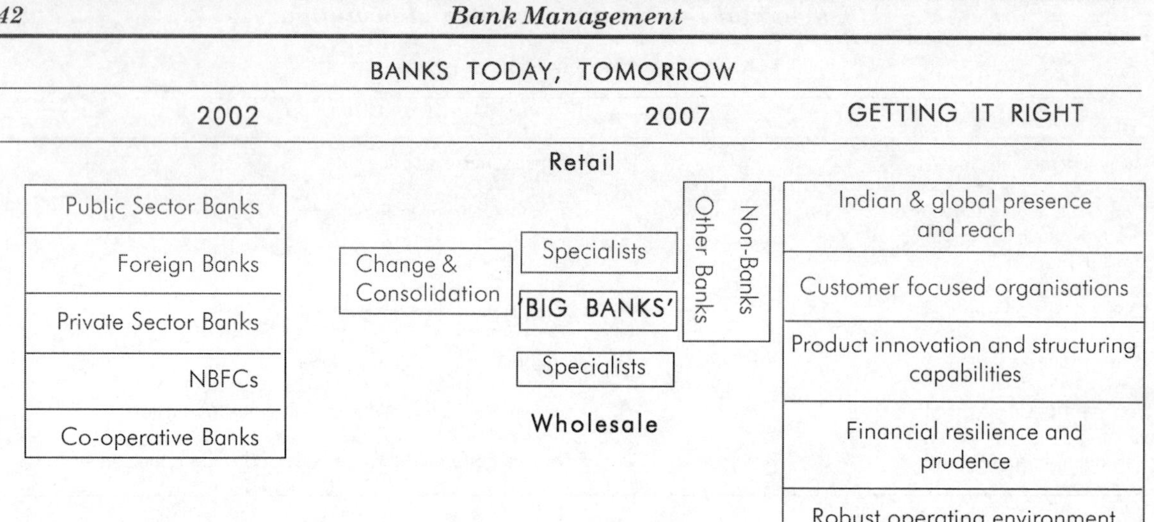

The indicators of this transformation have been visible for the past few years.

The increase in the number of foreign transactions and the growth in banks' investment portfolios requires an efficient, computerised treasury management system. This becomes all the more important because they add immediately to a bank's bottomline.

BOX 3.3

BANK SOLVENCY AND LIQUIDITY

A bank is solvent if the value of its assets is greater than the value of its liabilities to depositors and other creditors; "net worth" is the amount by which assets exceed liabilities. The larger a bank's net worth, the larger its cushion against insolvency — that is, the larger the fall in asset values that the bank can sustain and still be solvent. Bank supervisors try to ensure that banks have adequate capital, which is often defined as some minimum fraction of total or risk assets. If the required capital-to-assets ratio is 5 per cent, for example, a bank with $100 million in assets and $98 million in liabilities (hence a networth of $2 million) would be instructed to find $3 million of additional capital to bring networth up to $5 million. Many banks in developing countries are insolvent and unable to earn the large sums needed to regain solvency; the negative net worth of some of these banks is many times their capital.

A bank is liquid as long as it can meet day-to-day operating expenses and withdrawals. Because it is highly leveraged, a bank can remain liquid long after becoming insolvent. That some countries have not experienced runs does not signify that their banks are sounder than banks in countries where runs did occur but merely that they are more liquid. Public ownership of banks, implicit or explicit deposit guarantees, periodic provision of liquidity to weak banks, and macroeconomic stability make depositors less likely to withdraw funds from insolvent banks and thereby help those banks to remain liquid.

Conclusion

Commercial banks are likely to remain the dominant institutions for some time. Banks have to gradually rise to provide services in response to market requirements. This, in turn, calls for more competition and better management. Banks can be made more efficient by improving their management systems. Better management requires new lending policies, better loan recovery procedures, more sophisticated information systems, better-trained and highly motivated staff and less government interference. The entry of new private banks, domestic or foreign, can stimulate competition. In spite of competition, commercial banks are to spearhead the financial system in India and continue to foster accelerated economic development and growth with merit.

Like in any developing country, in India too, commercial banking has the hub of the financial system and has played a pivotal role in economic development. Apart from performing the key functions of providing liquidity and payment services to the real sector and managing bulk of the financial intermediation process, the banking sector has contributed to the process of economic development by serving as a major source of credit to all sections of the economy, be it the household, industry, Government or the weaker sections of society. It would be, therefore, in fitness of things to state that, like anywhere else in the world, in India too, the banks have played their role as growth facilitators and the evolution of banking is closely intertwined with the growth and evolution of the real sector.

Beyond the millennium, the Indian commercial banks will emerge larger in size, technologically better equipped and stronger in capital base. The regulatory mechanism will ensure that the health of the Indian commercial banks is preserved and improved and that they continue to play an important role in the Indian economy.

ANNEXURE 1

BANKING CHALLENGES IN THE NEW MILLENNIUM

The changes affecting the banking sector in the wake of globalization and opening up of the economy in the early nineties has provoked much reflection on ways to strengthen the banking system. A conference of the Chief Executives of banks has identified a number of priorities to make the banking sector sound and vibrant to play a crucial role in the accelerated development of the economy. The banking sector reforms, implemented since 1991, have brought in a near-total metamorphosis of the sector and made the PSBs serious about the risk-return trade-off on one hand and maximization of the shareholders' value, on the other. Maximizing the shareholders' value has, in fact, assumed paramount importance, particularly for the banks, which have gone public, because these banks are now accountable to millions of their shareholders rather than the Union Government as their single shareholder. This has propelled the PSBs to become conscious of their performance on a continuous basis and shift the focus from expansion (volume) to efficiency (margin).

1. Technology: The public sector banks have a challenging task ahead to remain competitive in an environment of ever advancing technology levels in banking. They will need new Banking Solutions to replace their existing Legacy Systems and to network their branches. Government and the Reserve Bank will need to facilitate this transition by determined actions within the next five years. In this connection, there is need to create an Apex Body with statutory powers to develop, disseminate and regulate technology for interbank networks, and payment systems so as to enable the banks to reach the global standards.

2. Human Resource Management: At present the human resource policies in banks are mainly guided by the concept of permanent employment and its necessary concomitants of creating career paths, terminal benefits, etc. for the employees. In this fast-changing world of worker mobility — both horizontally and vertically — and value systems, the public sector banks will need the freedom not only to hire the right talent at market related compensation but also to shed surplus manpower. Bank-centric wage negotiations should be allowed. All this calls for a close relook into the Statute Books as well as Management Practice of the banks.

3. Risk Management and Regulatory Implications: To reach the international standards of capital adequacy, risk management and accounting practices, the right talent at appropriate levels of management needs to be inducted laterally and the banks should have the necessary freedom to do so.

4. Structural Issues: Structure of a bank is generally business and technology driven. Therefore, whether or not the Government reduces its holdings to 1/3 levels, the initiative to decide on the best structure should be left to the individual banks themselves. Also, issues internal to the organizational structure should be left to the individual banks, while the Government and the Regulator could confine their role to providing a stable macro-environment and supervision to protect the interests of the stakeholders and the shareholders.

5. Corporate Governance: Irrespective of the nature of the organization, corporate governance has to ensure transparency and efficiency in the running of the organization. Accordingly, the Government's decision to reduce its equity holdings to 1/3 levels should get reflected in corporate governance also. Therefore, all structural strengthening to exercise flexibility and autonomy should be ensured.

6. Rural Banking: Having committed 75 per cent of their branch network to serving rural and semi-urban population, public sector banks have to adopt a financial engineering approach to rural banking. The delivery systems have to be made cost effective. Therefore, there is a need for redesigning the rural banking system to deliver new products and services and to make the priority sector more receptive and productive. In this connections, the regulatory constraint on banks' allocation of credit flows also needs a relook. Commercialized agriculture should be considered as a potential avenue for new business. There is need for a paradigm shift in rural finance and in both mobilization and allocation of resources through other intermediaries including NBFCs.

7. Management of NPAs: There are several impediments including statutory, legal and political in the recovery of bank loans and advances. Therefore, restructuring of borrowal accounts should be left to individual bank decision subject to full transparency. Then only the public sector banks can better function as business organizations in pursuit of excellence and sound financial performance.

✲ ✲ ✲

LEADERS OF THE PACK

CAPITAL ADEQUACY

BANK	CAR	Debt Equity	Adv/Total Assets	% Sec/Total Investments	% Sec/Assets
YES BANK	16.40	5.90	57.80	60.10	19.30
IDBI	14.80	11.20	60.00	55.10	18.40
CORPORATION BANK	13.90	10.20	59.00	83.50	20.00
FEDERAL BANK	13.73	14.78	36.86	90.51	27.51
BANK OF BARODA	13.65	12.60	53.00	71.20	22.00
ICICI BANK	13.48	9.20	38.10	71.40	30.30
INDIAN BANK	13.20	17.09	47.06	84.23	33.66
PUNJAB & SIND	12.83	13.85	47.83	82.83	39.23
CENTURION BANK OF PUNJAB	12.52	10.30	57.66	81.87	21.12
ORIENTAL BANK OF COMMERCE	12.50	9.90	37.00	80.90	23.10
PNB	12.00	13.00	50.84	82.21	25.76
STATE BANK OF INDIA	11.88	15.62	53.72	85.55	22.97
HDFC BANK	11.40	11.40	47.60	69.10	26.70
CITIBANK	11.33	8.30	53.82	90.08	20.93
KOTAK BANK	11.27	5.06	57.99	35.13	15.49
CANARA BANK	11.22	13.40	39.82	82.74	22.89
UCO BANK	11.12	22.70	60.44	83.51	26.52
UTI BANK	13.30	15.10	44.90	54.80	23.79
CENTRAL BANK	11.02	19.47	50.34	81.44	31.13
BANK OF INDIA	10.75	19.46	57.97	68.65	18.51
ING VYSYA BANK	10.70	14.14	61.00	86.00	22.00
HSBC	10.61	6.74	44.86	73.86	22.98
INDUSIND BANK	10.54	17.94	52.83	84.72	26.01
STANDARD CHARTERED	9.93	5.74	49.97	81.35	20.87

RESOURCES DEPLOYED

BANK	Total Assets (Rs cr)	Liquidity/Total Assets	Investments/Total Assets	Fixed Assets*	Other Assets*
STATE BANK OF INDIA	496,832	6.23	32.71	4.75	4.78
ICICI BANK	251,389	6.80	21.90	1.60	3.20
PNB	148,325	16.94	28.89	2.58	2.58
CANARA BANK	133,779	9.57	27.87	0.53	2.41
BANK OF BARODA	113,393	12.00	30.90	1.00	3.50
BANK OF INDIA	112,421	10.18	26.40	0.72	2.73
IDBI	90,302	6.00	28.20	1.00	4.80
CENTRAL BANK	74,863	8.40	38.22	0.97	4.06
HDFC BANK	73,506	9.40	38.60	1.10	3.00
UCO BANK	61,839	5.41	31.25	0.98	1.41
ORIENTAL BANK OF COMMERCE	58,937	9.40	26.50	0.70	4.00
UTI BANK	49,731	7.30	43.30	1.10	3.40
STANDARD CHARTERED	48,182	9.86	24.51	1.85	13.80
INDIAN BANK	47,825	10.09	39.96	1.11	3.77
CITIBANK	45,457	5.56	23.23	1.22	7.79
CORPORATION BANK	40,507	10.00	26.00	1.00	4.00
HSBC	37,473	7.67	32.40	1.12	13.94
FEDERAL BANK	20,642	9.07	30.38	0.64	2.83
PUNJAB & SIND	19,043	11.27	36.53	1.49	2.85
KOTAK BANK	17,367	5.55	28.10	6.97	6.97
INDUSIND BANK	17,023	8.60	30.70	1.93	6.14
ING VYSYA BANK	16,787	6.70	26.00	2.40	3.80
CENTURION BANK OF PUNJAB	11,330	9.37	25.80	2.75	4.56
YES BANK	4,165	5.20	32.40	0.80	2.70

ASSET QUALITY

BANK	Net NPAs/Total Advances	Advances/Total Assets	Investments/Total Assets	Yield on Advances	Yield on Investments
YES BANK	0.00	57.80	32.40	8.60	5.40
KOTAK BANK	0.24	57.99	28.10	8.71	4.33
PNB	0.30	50.84	28.89	7.19	9.04
ORIENTAL BANK OF COMMERCE	0.50	57.00	28.50	8.00	9.20
HDFC BANK	0.50	47.60	38.60	7.50	6.80
HSBC	0.58	44.86	32.40	7.94	5.85
CORPORATION BANK	0.60	59.00	26.00	7.80	8.30
ICICI BANK	0.70	58.70	28.50	8.15	6.05
INDIAN BANK	0.79	47.66	39.96	7.94	8.02
BANK OF BARODA	0.85	53.00	30.90	7.10	8.20
FEDERAL BANK	0.95	56.86	30.38	7.80	7.31
CITIBANK	0.95	53.82	23.23	8.33	8.37
IDBI	1.00	60.00	28.20	9.00	3.30
UTI BANK	1.00	44.90	43.30	8.10	7.20
CENTURION BANK OF PUNJAB	1.10	57.66	25.80	8.87	6.15
CANARA BANK	1.12	59.82	27.87	6.87	7.23
BANK OF INDIA	1.30	57.97	28.40	7.02	6.77
STANDARD CHARTERED	1.57	49.97	24.51	8.37	7.37
ING VYSYA BANK	1.80	61.00	26.00	8.50	7.20
STATE BANK OF INDIA	1.87	53.72	32.71	8.92	8.47
INDUSIND BANK	2.09	52.83	30.70	9.19	5.75
UCO BANK	2.10	60.44	31.75	7.04	7.93
PUNJAB & SIND	2.43	47.83	36.53	7.28	8.44
CENTRAL BANK	2.59	50.34	38.22	6.94	7.95

MANAGEMENT QUALITY

BANK	Credit/Deposit	Profit/Emp (Rs '000)	Business/Emp (Rs '000)	RONW
IDBI	209.00	1,200	118,630	8.40
KOTAK BANK	185.52	1,089	73,935	12.48
ICICI BANK	88.50	1,000	122,600	14.60
CITIBANK	87.63	2,170	160,792	16.23
STANDARD CHARTERED	84.40	1,450	83,729	19.84
YES BANK	82.70	180	38,400	8.70
ING VYSYA BANK	77.04	20	20,500	0.90
CORPORATION BANK	72.90	400	52,800	13.70
CENTURION BANK OF PUNJAB	69.51	190	35,437	9.37
BANK OF INDIA	69.39	172	37,696	14.12
STATE BANK OF INDIA	68.81	278	46,200	14.96
CANARA BANK	68.53	294	41,968	18.21
UCO BANK	68.53	80	37,333	7.99
HSBC	67.37	1,207	91,565	17.56
ORIENTAL BANK OF COMMERCE	66.90	400	56,800	10.80
FEDERAL BANK	65.65	356	46,319	16.08
BANK OF BARODA	64.00	200	39,600	12.30
PNB	62.97	264	35,627	15.47
HDFC BANK	62.85	600	61,100	17.70
INDUSIND BANK	62.04	252	108,325	4.25
CENTRAL BANK	56.65	67	27,980	7.36
UTI BANK	55.60	700	85,300	18.80
INDIAN BANK	54.99	222	27,200	20.66
PUNJAB & SIND	53.81	114	27,292	8.88

EARNINGS QUALITY

Bank	Net Profit (Rs cr)	Net Profit Growth (%)	Spread (%)	Other Inc to [illegible]	Net Profit/Total Assets
STATE BANK OF INDIA	5,550	-1.20	3.46	50.96	0.79
ICICI BANK	2,540	26.70	4.90	119.07	1.00
PNB	1,532	9.49	4.36	25.41	1.03
CANARA BANK	1,379	1.54	3.07	41.03	1.03
STANDARD CHARTERED	905	38.41	5.35	44.03	0.19
HDFC BANK	872	30.80	3.70	44.15	1.10
BANK OF BARODA	827	22.20	2.90	36.95	0.70
KOTAK BANK	730	326.99	3.11	278.27	4.06
BANK OF INDIA	723	130.99	2.83	45.26	0.84
CITIBANK	706	17.57	5.97	50.67	0.16
ORIENTAL BANK OF COMMERCE	537	-23.30	2.70	34.44	0.90
IDBI	544	70.70	3.40	298.57	0.60
INDIAN BANK	515	22.47	3.78	15.58	1.08
HSBC	515	32.84	4.50	87.36	0.14
UTI BANK	485	45.00	3.10	67.67	1.00
CORPORATION BANK	345	10.50	3.00	44.58	1.00
CENTRAL BANK	250	-30.51	3.63	22.34	0.33
FEDERAL BANK	225	139.79	3.35	36.17	1.08
UCO BANK	197	-43.11	2.68	29.62	0.32
PUNJAB & SIND	108	[illegible]	4.13	23.95	0.57
CENTURION BANK OF PUNJAB	68	249.66	4.21	62.43	0.72
YES BANK	55	[illegible]	2.50	116.63	1.30
INDUSIND BANK	37	-82.09	2.45	71.76	0.21
ING VYSYA BANK	[illegible]	[illegible]	2.80	19.53	0.19

LIQUIDITY

Bank	Liquidity/Total Assets	G. Sec/Investments	A. Sec/Assets
CANARA BANK	9.57	82.74	0.30
CENTURION BANK OF PUNJAB	9.23	91.87	0.00
UCO BANK	5.41	83.51	0.67
PUNJAB & SIND	11.27	92.81	2.62
INDIAN BANK	10.09	84.23	1.15
FEDERAL BANK	9.07	90.54	0.04
INDUSIND BANK	8.40	84.72	0.01
BANK OF INDIA	10.28	69.69	0.07
CENTRAL BANK	8.40	83.44	1.14
PNB	16.84	92.23	0.32
KOTAK BANK	5.94	55.13	0.00
STATE BANK OF INDIA	8.23	85.51	0.65
ORIENTAL BANK OF COMMERCE	9.40	80.90	0.60
CORPORATION BANK	10.00	83.50	0.30
BANK OF BARODA	12.00	71.20	1.14
IDBI	6.00	65.30	0.00
HDFC BANK	9.40	69.30	0.01
ICICI BANK	6.80	71.40	0.01
UTI BANK	7.30	54.80	0.00
ING VYSYA BANK	6.70	56.90	0.00
YES BANK	5.20	60.10	0.00
CITIBANK	5.56	90.08	0.00
HSBC	7.62	78.88	0.15
STANDARD CHARTERED	9.86	81.85	0.00

Methodology

For the purposes of the panel discussion, *Business India* looked closely at the numbers of 24 banks. While other banks were still eligible to be selected Best Bank by the panel (a couple of names were indeed discussed in passing as future candidates), this 24-bank universe was essentially the *BI* shortlist. The selection was based on considerations such as size and visibility. The basic numbers for the entire universe of 88 banks are in the tables that follow (*see Key Financial Figures: All Banks*).

CAPITAL ADEQUACY

Simply stated, this is each bank's leverage calculated after assigning different risks announced by the Reserve Bank of India (RBI) to assets. Other ratios which have a bearing on the capital adequacy ratio have been calculated to include debt-equity ratio, which is the proportion of total outside liability to networth.

RESOURCES DEPLOYED

In banking, the size of the balance sheet is very significant. The ranking on this parameter is based on total assets. There are other factors that have a bearing on resources and, in turn, on efficient deployment. Like liquid assets. This is defined as the total proportion of resources deployed in liquid assets, which generate relatively low yields.

ASSET QUALITY

Asset quality is another important aspect in the evaluation of banks. Net NPAs to Net Advances is the best indicator of the quality of a bank's assets. The other parameters include advances-to-assets, which is used to gauge the credit disintermediation of a bank.

EFFICIENCY, MANAGEMENT

Although any evaluation of management is subjective, we have tried to segregate the parameters that best reflect the management quality based on the data available in the balance sheets. Like the credit-deposit ratio (total advances as proportion of total deposits), which indicates a management's aggressiveness to improve income.

EARNINGS QUALITY

Banks are ranked on profit after tax and provisions. The other parameters are Net Profit growth: to factor in growth in profits. Other related ratios are the spread which is, in fact, the operating margin of a bank. Spread is net interest income/total average assets expressed as a percentage.

LIQUIDITY

As banks are in the business of borrowing and lending, an asset-liability mismatch can wreak havoc on a bank's operation. The more liquid the assets the better, while, on the liability (deposits) side, the longer the maturity period, the better. Here the banks are ranked on proportion of liquid assets to total assets.

CAR - CAPITAL ADEQUACY RATIO; RONW-RETURN ON NET WORTH; OTHER NII - OTHER NET INTEREST INCOME; G.SEC - GOVERNMENT SECURITIES; A. SEC - APPROVED SECURITIES; * PROPORTION OF RESOURCES DEPLOYED IN FIXED ASSETS; **PROPORTION OF RESOURCES DEPLOYED IN OTHER ASSETS

Chapter 4

Functions of Commercial Banks

Introduction

Commercial banks play a very important role in our economy, in fact, it is difficult to imagine how our economic system could function efficiently without many of their services. They are the heart of our financial structure. In addition to mobilising deposits by inculcating banking habit and spreading the message of thrift, by lending and investing these resources productively, as by transferring funds throughout the nation and even internationally, the banks make possible a more complete utilisation of the resources of the nation. Thus by their lending, investing as related activities banks facilitate the economic process of production, distribution and consumption. By their mopping up savings, they maintain a balance between present consumption and future and thus act as a lever regulating the prices.

Commercial banks have been referred to as "department stores of finance", a term that has been forwarded by commercial banks since it implies that they provide a wide variety of financial services and, consequently, places them in a stronger competitive position.

The Role of Banks

From the economic point of view, the major task of banks and other financial institutions is to act as intermediaries channelling savings to investment and consumption; through them, the investment requirements of savers are reconciled with the credit needs of investors and consumers.

If this process of transference is to be carried out efficiently, it is absolutely essential that the banks are involved. Indeed, in performing their tasks they realize important economies of scale; the savings placed at their disposal are employed in numerous and large transactions, adapted to the specific needs of borrowers. In this way they are able to make substantial cost savings for both savers and borrowers, who would otherwise have to make individual transactions with each others. However, there is more to these economies of scale than just the cost aspect. Indeed, for the saver/investor, the bank's mediation leads principally to a very important reduction in risk, which is not only a result of risk-spreading that the bank accomplishes in reinvesting savings (diversification in both investment and its concentration), but also as a financial intermediary taking over from the saver the greater share of the risks entailed.

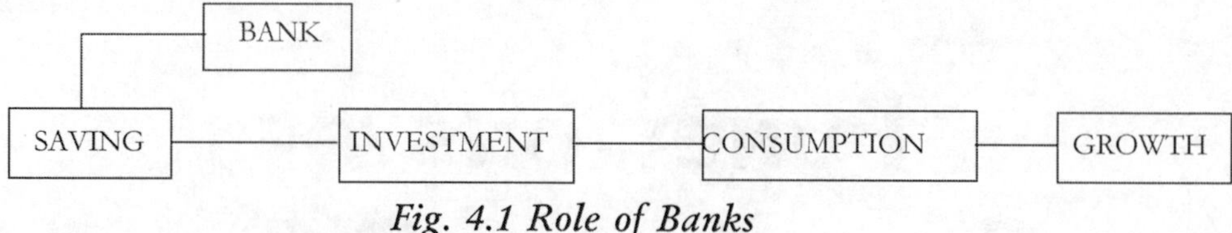

Fig. 4.1 Role of Banks

One major risk has directly to do with the transformation deposits into loans. Not only does the difference between the two have to be bridged, but also interest rate differential consequent on the differing terms. In the last decade, this latter aspect has weighed very heavily with the banks, due to the rising trend of interest rates and particularly their increased volatility.

Obvious risks are naturally those connected with lending. Recession has landed many borrowers in difficulties. Often, they have not been able to repay their loans. On the other hand, the growing internationalization of banking has brought new risks to the fore, such as the exchange risks.

Besides this, transactions themselves and the general management of the banking institution entail risks. Technological advance, the internationalization of business and banking and the increasingly sophisticated demands for financial services make banking ever more difficult, so that expertise is more than ever essential in the provision of financial services.

Indian banking has aided the economic development in an effective way in the post independence period. The banking sector has shown remarkable responsiveness to the needs of the planned economy. It has brought about a considerable progress in its efforts at deposit mobilisation and has taken a number of measures in the recent past to accelerate the rate of growth of deposits. To achieve this end commercial banks opened a number of branches in urban, semi-urban and rural areas and introduced a number of attractive schemes and free services to customers to attract more deposits. As at end March, 1995, aggregate deposits of commercial bank and amounted to Rs. 3,92,759 crores, outstanding credit and investments stood at Rs. 2,07,543 crores and Rs. 1,67,231 crores respectively. The Credit-Deposit ratio was lower at 52.8 per cent.

Permitted Banking Activities

First, the legal position as to the services permissible for commercial banks in India may be stated. The traditional functions covered by the term 'banking' are defined in Section 5(b) of the Banking Regulation Act, 1949 as follows:

"Banking means the accepting for the purpose of lending or investment, of deposits of money from the public repayable on demand or otherwise, and withdrawable by cheque, draft, order or otherwise."

Section 6(1) of the Banking Regulation Act, 1949 elaborates on this and gives a list of permissible activities for banks which include, in addition to raising deposits and the grant of secured and unsecured advances, various ancillary services. This list is as follows:

(1) the borrowing, raising or taking up of money, the lending or advancing of money either upon or without security;

(2) the drawing, making, accepting, discounting, buying, selling, collecting and dealing in bills of exchange, 'hundis', promissory notes, coupons, drafts, bills of lading, railway receipts, warrants, debentures, certificates, scrips and other instruments and securities whether transferable or negotiable or not;

(3) the granting and issuing of letters of credit, travellers' cheques and circular notes;

(4) the buying, selling and dealing in bullion and species;

(5) the buying and selling of foreign exchange including foreign bank notes;

(6) the acquiring, holding, issuing on commission, underwriting and dealing in stocks, funds, shares, debentures, debentures stock, bonds, obligations, securities and investments of all kinds;

(7) the purchasing and selling of bonds, scrips or other forms of securities on behalf of constitutes or others, the negotiating of loans and advances;

(8) the receiving of all kinds of bonds or valuables, on deposit or for safe custody or otherwise;

(9) the providing of safe deposit vaults;

(10) the collecting and transmitting of money and securities;

(11) acting as agents for any government local authority or any person or persons;

(12) the carrying on of agency business of any description including the clearing and forwarding of goods, giving of receipts and discharges and otherwise acting as an attorney on behalf of customers, but excluding the business of a managing agent or secretary and treasurer of a company;

(13) contracting for public and private loans and negotiating and issuing the same;

(14) the effecting, insuring, guaranteeing, underwriting, participating in managing, and carrying out of any issue, public or private, of State, municipal or other loans or of shares, stocks, debentures, or debenture stock of any company, corporation or association and the lending of money for the purpose of any such issues;

(15) carrying on and transacting every kind of guarantee and indemnity business;

(16) managing, selling and realising any property which may come into the possession of the company in satisfaction or part satisfaction of any of its claims;

(17) acquiring and holding and generally dealing with any property or any right, title or interest in any such property which may from the security or part of the security for any loans or advances or which may be connected with any such security;

(18) undertaking and executing trusts;

(19) undertaking the administration of estates as executor, trustee or otherwise.

Activities which are not Allowed

Commercial banks are not allowed to undertake activities other than those covered by these two sections of the Banking Regulation Act, 1949. While such restriction of activities of commercial banks is necessary for discouraging them from indulging in non-banking activities like trading, it has hindered the introduction of a new type of service by commercial banks, namely, equipment leasing, which is in vogue in foreign countries. Under 'equipment leasing', the bank purchases an equipment, say a tractor, and leases it to its actual users. Another type of services which is not provided by commercial banks in India owing to legal difficulties is the issue of negotiable certificates of deposits. These are not covered by the Negotiable Instruments Act, 1881 and as such protection available to bankers for other negotiable instruments like cheques is not available in respect of these certificates.

Services Provided by Commercial Banks in India

Commercial banks in India, like their counterparts all the world over, have been performing for their customers — and in some instances also for the public at large — most of these activities. The range of services offered differs from bank to bank, depending mainly on the size and type of banks; but the acceptance of deposits from the public and provision of credit form the mainstay of the banking business in India. The services offered by commercial banks can be classified into (i) services to depositors, (ii) services to borrowers for providing credit to them, and (iii) ancillary services. A list of various bank services usually provided by banks in India is given in Annexure-I.

The traditional services mainly relate to (i) maintenance of different types of deposit accounts; (ii) grant of advances through cash credit, overdraft and loan accounts and through purchasing/discounting demand and usance bills; (iii) collection of cheques, bills and other instruments (inland and foreign); (iv) issue of performance and financial guarantees; (v) provision of remittance facilities by issue of drafts, mail transfers and telegraphic transfers; (vi) provision of facilities of safe deposit and safe custody; and (vii) purchase and sale of securities.

With the accent on deposit mobilisation and grant of credit to weaker sectors of society during recent years, banks have introduced a number of new schemes. Besides these, banks have also introduced certain services such as credit cards, gift cheques, emergency vouchers, participation certificates, for the convenience of customers. Of these various new services, the schemes relating to deposit mobilisation have been described in Chapter 8 'Deposit Mobilisation by Banks.' A brief account of the other new services is given in the succeeding paragraphs.

Personal Loan Scheme

In the last decade, a few major banks in India have introduced a new facility, namely, the personal loan scheme, or the instalment loan scheme, the purpose of which is to offer to individuals, either employed or in business and having a steady income, a convenient way to borrow money from banks to purchase durable goods, such as radios, refrigerators and sewing machines which they may not be in a position to purchase outright. The personal loan system is specially designed to meet the needs of the salary and wage earners group in receipt of modest but regular income.

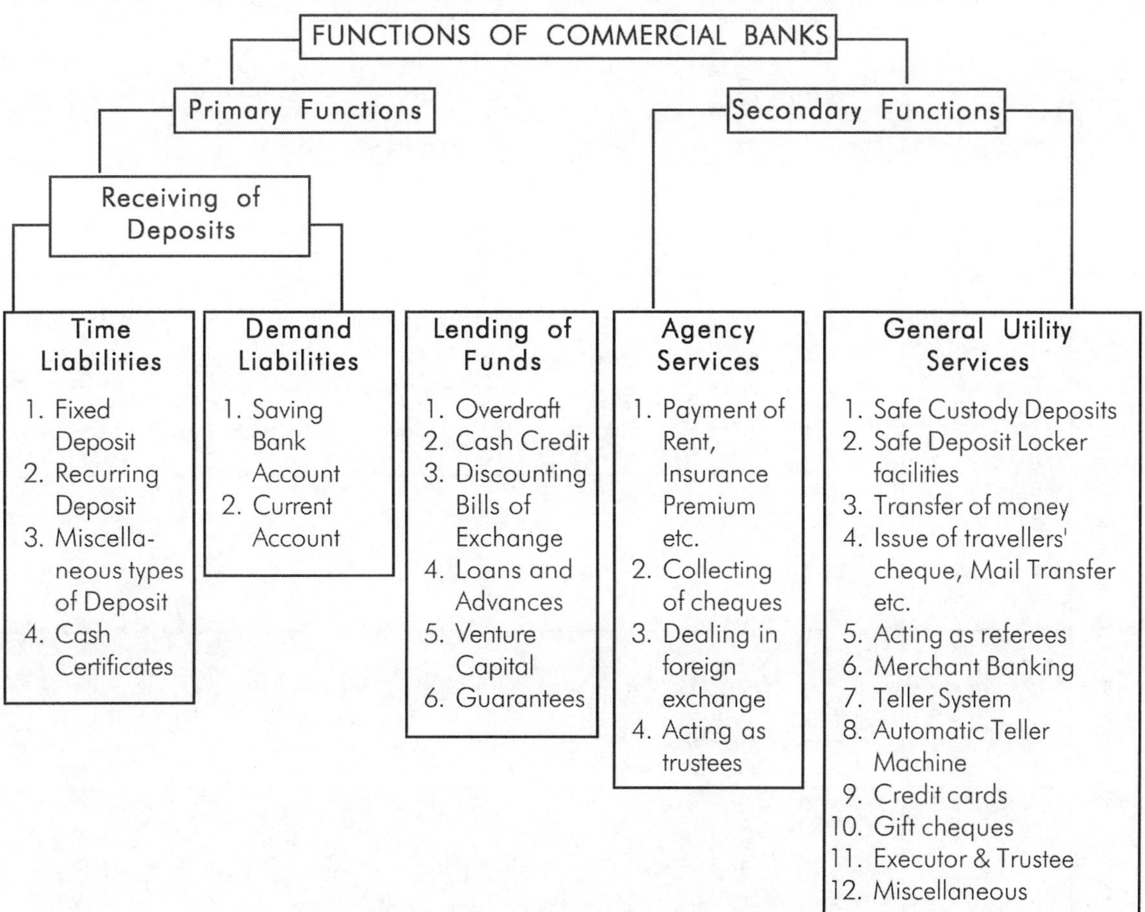

Fig. 4.2 Functions of Commercial Banks

These are clean loans and banks keep a lien on the goods and reserve the right to seize them if the borrower fails to fulfil his part of the contract. Default in payment is not a criminal offence in India; it is only a cause for civil action and though banks charge a penalty on overdue instalments, the possibility of a number of defaults in repayment of instalments cannot be ruled out. The scheme has not been introduced on an extensive scale in India for the above reason and also as the scope for this service is relatively limited because of the low level of income and the limited demand for durable consumer goods. However, in the years to come as the general standard of living improves, at least the major banks may be in a position to popularise this service.

Loan Participation

Some of the larger borrowers are financed by more than one institution on a participation basis, either because the amount involved is very large and beyond the resources of a single institution or because the amount is beyond what an institution would like to risk on a single borrower. In July 1970, one of the foreign banks introduced Participation Certificates (PC) — a new credit instrument — by which it sells to a third party a loan it has already made to one of its customers. PC is a deed

CHART 4.1
SUBSIDIARY/ACTIVITIES TAKEN UP BY PUBLIC SECTOR BANKS

Merchant banking/ equipment leasing		*Housing finance*		*Factoring*		*Venture fund*		*Mutual funds*	
Subsidiary	*Equity participation*	*Subsidiary*	*Equity participation*	*Subsidiary*	*Equity participation*	*Subsidiary*	*Equity participation*	*Domestic*	*Off-shore*
1. State Bank of India	1. Indian Overseas Bank	1. Andhra Bank	1. State Bank of India	1. State Bank of India	1. State Bank of Indore	1. Canara Bank	1. Bank of India	1. State Bank of India	1. State Bank of India
2. Canara Bank	2. Union Bank of India	2. Punjab National Bank	2. Canara Bank	2. Canara Bank	2. Union Bank of India		2. Union Bank of India	2. Canara Bank	2. Canara Bank
3. Punjab National Bank	3. UCO Bank of India	3. Bank of Baroda	3. Union Bank of India		3. SB of Saurashtra		3. Bank of Baroda	3. Punjab National Bank	
4. Central Bank of India	4. State Bank of India	4. Central Bank of India	4. Syndi-cate Bank		4. Andhra Bank			4. Bank of India	
5. Bank of India	5. Punjab National Bank	5. Indian Bank						5. Indian Bank	
6. Indian Bank	6. Central Bank of India	6. State Bank of India						6. Bank of Baroda	
7. Andhra Bank	7. Bank of India	7. Bank of India							
8. Allaha-bad Bank									

of transfer legally transferring title of the customers' hypothecated current and moveable assets. It indicates that the bank undertakes to repay the loan directly on maturity; the participator need not, therefore, look to the customer. The minimum amount of a PC was fixed at Rs. I lakh; it has three tenures — 30 days, 60 days and 90 days also introduced similar participation schemes. Participation Certificates introduced by some commercial banks in India are unrelated to particular maturities of term loans and are of relatively short maturities.

Schemes for Financing Small Industrial Units

Banks grant term loans to small industrial units for expansion, modernisation, renovation and also provide them with working capital finance. Besides industrial units, loans are also granted to technocrats, technologists, technicians and entrepreneurs to set up small scale industrial units. Banks also give finance for promotion of industrial estates — for purchase of land and construction of sheds.

Schemes for Financing of Agriculture

Banks have introduced a number of schemes to help agriculturists. They provide short-term loans for financing seasonal agricultural operations including purchase of inputs; medium-term loans for purchase of equipment such as tractors, agricultural machinery and long-term loans for the purchase of land and other assets of long durability. Under the 'area approach' some banks have adopted certain villages for providing credit facilities for all productive purposes in the villages adopted. A few banks have also introduced Farm Graduate Schemes, under which financial assistance is provided to agricultural graduates, to enable them to acquire land and become progressive agriculturists. Many of the banks have also launched schemes for financing farm-based activities such as poultry, dairy-farming, pisciculture, etc. Loans are also provided to fishermen for purchase, construction and mechanisation of boats.

Under the various schemes owner-cultivators possessing generally 4 acres of land and above are eligible for short-term and medium-term loans. Tractor loans are, however, sanctioned to those possessing a minimum holding of 25 acres each. Joint loans are sanctioned where a borrower's holding is less than 25 acres. For term-loans, a period of 12 months is allowed subject to repayment being made when the crop is sold, while for medium-term loans the period is generally 2 to 5 years.

One of the schemes, which has been launched in co-ordination with a fertiliser manufacturer, provides short-term loans to meet input requirement and labour costs of agriculturists. The fertiliser manufacturer helps in soil testing, provides technical assistance for selection of suitable seeds and recommends a combination of fertilisers and its proper application, use of plant protection materials etc. The manufacturer has set up an appropriate number of fertiliser distributors and dealers in the areas concerned who are assisted by agricultural development assistants. Under another scheme, 'Credit Cards' are issued to the participant farmers. They cover all their credit requirements for seed, fertiliser and cultivation expenses for the full year. Schemes have also been evolved for providing financial assistance for establishment of custom service units, such as tractor and trailer units, sprayer and dusting units, bull-dozers, cold storage units, etc. and for construction of godowns.

By and large, banks advance loans against collateral of assets created out of the loan such as tractors, pump-sets, etc. supported by mortgage of land, and, where necessary, personal guarantee acceptable to the bank. Short-term advances are granted against hypothecation of standing crop supported by land by collateral security and, where necessary guarantee of two persons. Further, some banks give loans against gold ornaments for agricultural purposes. In deserving cases, unsecured loans against personal guarantee of two persons are also made.

The object of one of the liberalised schemes for agricultural finance launched by a major bank on a pilot basis on some districts assist those farmers, who are potentially viable, or groups of such farmers to undertake diversified farming activities. In respect of group borrowing — the size of group ranging from two to ten — in addition to group guarantee, short-term loans were also secured by hypothecation of crops. In cases where group loans were not possible, individual loans were advanced against hypothecation of crops. Loans for purchase of implements were secured by hypothecation of implements with or without collateral security. Medium-term loans were, however, secured registered or equitable mortgage.

Financing of Road Transport Operators, Other Small Borrowers, Self Employed Persons, etc.

Loans to road transport operators are granted for purchase of vehicles, i.e., scooters, taxis, trucks, auto-rickshaws, cycle-rickshaws on hypothecation of the vehicle concerned. Loans are also granted, to self-employed persons, i.e., professionals like doctors, lawyers, architects, etc. to start or expand trade or vocation, to develop business and for buying equipment, tools, furniture, etc. Banks also grant loans to retail traders to acquire and hold stocks or for repairing/furnishing renovating shops or for purchase of ancillary equipment. Schemes have also been introduced by banks for providing finance to unemployed graduates for purposes such as running business as retail dealers of manufacturers (e.g., Indian Oil Company), for undertaking building or electrical installation contracts, etc. One bank has opened a branch to serve as a multi-service agency for financing tailors initially. A scheme to finance vegetable, fruit and flower stall holders was also introduced by another bank. A number of banks have introduced housing deposit schemes for financing acquisition/construction of houses. Some banks have also introduced schemes for granting educational institutions for buying laboratory and workshop equipment and scientific and technical books. Another new scheme is the 'Salary Reserve Scheme', under which savings bank account holders, who credit their net salary to their savings bank accounts, can get an advance of a month's salary subject to a maximum of Rs. 2,000.

Credit Transfer System

The increased network of branches has expanded the scope of remittance facilities. As a result of increased customers expectations, a number of banks have introduced schemes for free remittance of funds by their customers, subject to certain conditions. One of such schemes is the 'Special Credit Transfer System', under which any person can remit free of charge amount up to Rs. 2,500 at a time from one branch of the bank for credit to any personal account with any of its branches. Under another scheme known as the 'Special Cheque Transfer Scheme', cheque upto Rs.

25,000 drawn on any personal accounts with any of the branches of the bank can be collected or negotiated at par for the payee or last endorsee.

Collection/Payment of Certain Periodical Receipts/Payments on Behalf of Customers

A few banks provide collection/payment facilities on behalf of joint stock companies, public utility concerns or Government. For example, some banks collect subscription to share capital on behalf of joint stock-companies at the time of a new share issue and refund share application money on behalf of these companies when the share issues are over-subscribed and/or share applications are not accepted. Certain banks arrange for payment of salaries of staff members of companies on behalf of such companies. A few banks arrange payment of dividend warrants on behalf of joint stock companies and a few others collect electricity bills for electricity boards. There are some banks which collect school fees on behalf of schools at certain centres. Many banks collect for the personnel of the Indian Armed Forces, cheques and salary/pension bills drawn on the Accountant General's office. Collection of National Defence Fund contributions and occasional donations towards noble cause is also undertaken by banks. A few banks also undertake to distribute State lottery tickets and payment of prize money as permitted by the State Governments.

Credit Cards

A few banks in India have introduced credit cards on an experimental basis. Credit cards or 'courtesy' cards as these are sometimes called, are issued to valued constituents as identification cards. On presentation of the credit card, the constituent can encash his cheques drawn on his account at any of the offices of the bank upto a specified amount on any particular day, at any one office. Under another scheme, special cheques of specified amounts signed by the customer holding the credit card can be encashed by authorised establishment such as departmental stores which are reimbursed by the bank in respect of the cheques.

Travellers Cheques

Travel within as well as outside India has increased considerably of late and a few banks in India have seized this opportunity and started providing customers with the facility of travellers cheques so as to avoid the risk of loss or inconvenience in having to carry large amount of cash while travelling. These cheques are issued in suitable denominations and are encashable at any office of the bank.

Travel Agency Work

Another facility closely associated with the travel habit is the travel work, i.e., securing of passage, accommodation in hotels, obtaining details of passenger sailings and general travel information from travel agents for their customers as also the furnishing of introduction to them entitling them to the courtesies of their correspondents abroad. Only a few commercial banks in India provide this service. Certain banks undertake to inform Railway/State Transport timings to their depositors. They also arrange reservation of tickets for a small charge, for their customers only.

Gift Cheques

One of the new devices adopted by new banks to attract customers is the issue of gift cheques, artistically designed in attractive folders and covers. The purchaser of a gift cheque need not be an account holder with that bank or with any other bank to avail of this service. The cheque is collectable at par at all the offices of the issuing bank in India.

Lock-Box and Night Safe Services

A few banks have been also experimenting with the 'Lock-Box Service' at selected centres, to lodge the cheques and other remittances in a box kept at the branch of a bank during office hours, to be collected by the bank the next day and the necessary entries passed. It obviates the need for the customers to go to the bank during customers' own office hours and thus saves time for them. Some attempts are also made at selected branches to offer night service facilities whereby, the customers, particularly the traders, can lodge cash overnight.

Service after the Usual Banking Hours

In order to provide facilities to customers to encash their cheques for small specified amounts after usual office hours, some banks have introduced various schemes. One such scheme is known as 'Emergency Vouchers Scheme.' The vouchers which are sold free of charges are encashable at the banks' branches during office hours and at selected Burmah Shell Stations after office hours. A few banks have also started evening centres where cheques can be encashed after usual office hours. A number of banks provide morning and/or evening banking facilities in residential areas.

Other Services

Only a few banks in India provide tax assistance service to their customers. The major difficulty in extending this service appears to be its highly technical nature which involves employment of experts by banks. With a larger number of persons being covered by taxation, the demand for this service is likely to increase. Similarly, only a few banks provide executor and "trustee service." Some of the banks had formed subsidiaries to undertake this business which is of a highly specialised nature. As regards standing instructions, most of the banks undertake on behalf of customers to pay insurance premia, collect interest on Government securities, pensions; pay bills, etc., but the services have not been extended to payment of rent, hotel bills, electricity bills, etc.

Conclusion

In the liberalised environment of today the dynamics of a market driven economy has multiplied manifold the choices available to an individual, both as a consumer and producer. At the core of this change has been the need for each banks to examine itself from the point of customers — depositors, entrepreneurs and self-employed persons — needs productivity, quality, and costs. Cutting costs, improving productivity and offering better customer service. At the same time banks should also offer varied and dovetailed services to their ever growing clientele.

One of the welcome features of competition is that the customer is again back on the centre stage. With technology providing new alternatives, the race is now on winning over the customers with improved products and services. True to our image as a customer-friendly bank, we are constantly on the lookout for upgrading our services and, at the same time, strengthening our R & D efforts. But people in the operations have a vital role to play in providing valuable feedback about the customers' needs and expectations which are of immense value in designing new products and services. I would also like to emphasise the fact that a careful analysis of the customer complaints can also provide us new insights into their feelings and expectations and help up in evolving innovative services to meet their felt needs.

Exhibit 4.1 Instruments of Collection in India

Instruments	*Advantages*	*Disadvantages*
Cheques	• No charge • Payable through clearing • Can be discounted after receipt • Low discounting charge • Requires customer limits which are interchangeable with overdraft limits	• Can bounce • Collection time can be long • Collection charge
Drafts	• Payable in local clearing • Chances of bouncing are remote	• Cost of collection • Buyers account debited on day one
Documentary bills	• Low discounting charge • Theoretically, goods are not released till payments are made or the bill is accepted • No charge except stamp duty • Can be discounted • Discipline of payment on due date	• Not payable through clearing • High collection cost • Long delays
Trade bills	• No charge except stamp duty • Can be discounted • Discipline of payment on due date	• Procedure is relatively cumbersome • Buyers are reluctant to accept the due date discipline
Letter of credit	• Good credit control as goods are released on payment or acceptance of bill • Seller forced to meet delivery schedule because of expiry date	• Opening charges • Transit period interest • Negotiation charges • Need bank lines to open LC • Stamp duty on usance bills

Source: Based on handout prepared by Mr. Sanjeev Sirpal, IIM, Ahmedabad. See page 647 of *Financial Management* by Professor I.M. Pandey.

Exhibit 4.2 Principal Short-term Investment Opportunities in Indian Money and Capital Markets

Instrument/ Investment	*Borrower*	*Maturity When issued*	*Marketability*	*Basis for Calculating Interest/Discount*	*Comments*
Treasury Bills(T-Bills)	Reserve Bank of India issues on behalf of the Government of India	Issued at discount, redeemed at par after 91 days. Issued for periods ranging from 14 days to 364 days through regular auction	Excellent secondary market	Discount weekly	Auctioned Highly liquid
Central Government Securities (Gillt-edged) Securities	Government of India	1 year to 10 years	Riskless. Less liquid than treasury bills	Fixed rate of interest or through auction	They are demanded by banks
Commercial Paper (CP)	Industrial firms, companies, banks, private sector companies and public sector companies	30 days or more	Redeemed on maturity	Interest or discount RBI	Negotiable guidelines CPs are sold directly or through dealers
Inter-corporate deposits	Companies	One month time required to convert into cash	Rate of interest is at 12-15% per annum	Short-term deposits High degree of risk	Reputed companies' deposits have the opportunity to use this source
Certificate of Deposit (CDs)	Banks	Payable on fixed date without grace period. 3 months period to one year	Secondary market exists	Interest Discounted like treasury bills and commercial papers	Short-term issuance promissory notes. Lock-in period is 45 days
Repurchases Agreement (Repos). One party sells a security to another with an agreement to buy it back at a specified time and price	Between Commercial banks Banks avail itself of funds against pledge of securities. It is a pledge transaction	1-14 days	RBI permits repos between banks, cooperative and eligible institutions, i.e., Discount and Finance House of India (DFHI), and Securities Trading Corporation of India (STCI)	Sale and buy-back price banks is the interest cost lender	RBI guidelines Collateral security is offered to the banks

ANNEXURE

BANK SERVICES

Deposits Schemes Tailored for Various Types of Depositors

1. Current Account
2. Savings Account
3. Fixed or Term Deposits
4. Monthly Interest Income Deposit Schemes
5. Cash Certificates
6. Annuity or Retirement Schemes
7. Farmers' Deposit Schemes
8. Daily Savings Schemes
9. Minor's Savings Schemes
10. Marriage/Educational Savings Plan

Deposits Linked with Other Benefits

1. Insurance Linked Savings Bank Accounts
2. Housing Deposit
3. Salary Reserve Scheme

Services Provided for Depositors

1. Collection of cheques, demand drafts, bills of exchange, promissory notes, hundis, inland and foreign documentary and clean bills.
2. Purchase of local and foreign currency documentary/clean bills, negotiation of bills under inland and foreign letters of credit, advising of inland and foreign letters of credit established by branches and correspondents.
3. Carrying outstanding instructions of deposits for (a) payment of insurance premia, (b) payment of subscription, (c) payment of certain taxes, (d) gift remittances etc.

Loan Schemes Tailored for Various Types of Borrowers

1. Call Loans
2. Term Loans
3. Cash Credit
4. Overdrafts
5. Letters of Credit
6. Personal Loans for (a) durable consumer goods (b) construction of residential houses (c) electrification, gas connection
7. Loan Participation
8. Loans to farmers —
   (*a*) Short-term
   (*b*) Medium-term
9. Loans to Small Scale Industry
   (*a*) Medium-term
   (*b*) Working capital
10. Loans to Road Transport Operators
11. Loans to Self-employed Persons
12. Loans to Technocrats, Technologists, Technicians and Entrepreneurs
13. Loans to Retail Trade
14. Educational Loans
    (*a*) Graduates and Post-graduate Courses in India
    (*b*) Higher Studies Abroad
15. Assistance for Industrial Estates

16. Leasing
17. Factoring

Ancillary Services

1. Gurantees
   (*a*) Performance Guarantee
   (*b*) Financial Guarantee
2. Safe Custody of Deeds, Securities
3. Safe Deposit Vault
4. Purchase and Sale of Securities
5. Collection of Interest on Securities/Debentures and Dividend on Shares, Collection of Pension Bills
6. Remittance of Funds — Bank Drafts, Mail Transfers, Telegraphic Transfers to other parts of the country and to foreign countries
7. Executor and Trustees — (a) Executor and Trustee Under a Will, (b) Trustee under a Trust Deed Security Mortgage Debentures, (c) Trustee under a Deed of Settlement, (d) Trustee for Life Insurance Policies under Married Women's Property Act, 1874.
8. Personal Tax Assistance, Preparing Income Tax/Sales Tax/Wealth Tax Returns
9. Investment Facilities — Underwriting, Banker to New Issues, Guidance to Investment, Stock Exchange Assistance
10. Credit Transfers
11. Credit Cards
12. Travellers Cheques
13. Gift Cheques
14. Emergency Vouchers
15. Sale of units of the Unit Trust, National Savings Certificates, etc.

Chapter 5

Liabilities and Assets of Banks

Introduction

Annual report and balance sheet of a bank can be fascinating for anyone with a special interest, because between the covers of this one publication can be found a great deal of information about the bank. One can learn from the report the major events as business results of the bank during the year. The balance sheet is a statement of banks' liabilities and assets at a particular time. Banks in India have to prepare their balance sheet and profit and loss account in forms set out in the III Schedule of the Banking Regulation Act, 1949. The balance sheet of a bank is of greater importance, because it deals in other 'money.'

The difference between the two is this: The balance sheet shows the financial position of a bank on a particular day as compared to the corresponding period in the previous year. The profit and loss statement shows the operating record of a bank income, expenditure and profit/loss of the bank over a period of time, i.e., one year.

The balance sheet has been defined as a "list of the balance in the assets, liability or network accounts." This definition may be accurate but it is sketchy. It would perhaps, be more meaningful to say that a balance sheet shows the sources from which funds currently used to operate business have been obtained the liabilities and owners' equity and the types of property and the property rights in which these funds are currently locked up, i.e., assets. Thus a balance sheet is a statement of assets and liabilities at a given moment of time.

The Banking Regulation Act and the Companies Act requires that the balance sheet of a bank should give a true and fair view of its state of affairs and should be drawn within the prescribed form.

The following table is an active balance sheet of a public sector commercial bank in India. It serves as a model to understand the intricacies of liabilities and assets of a commercial bank.

In India, it is customary to list the assets on the right hand side and the liabilities on the left hand side. While in some countries like the U.S.A., the practice adopted is in the reverse of this practice.

Liabilities of a Commercial Bank

Of the total liabilities, 3-7 per cent are internal to the system, i.e., liabilities to the banking system and borrowings from the Reserve Bank. The rest of total liabilities, i.e., 93-97% constitute the net or external liabilities to others.

Liabilities to the banking system consist mainly of demand and time deposits from banks — 60-80%. Borrowings from banks — 20-40%. There is a residual term generally below 4% but in the interval 1992-96, it was high at 12.4-18.5%.

Deposits

In the Liabilities to Others component, aggregate deposits constitute 92-94%, borrowings are negligible being less than half a per cent, and the remainder is a residual term. Within aggregate deposits, 80-82% are time deposits and 18-20% are demand deposits. Since aggregate deposits account for close to 90% of the total liabilities of the banking system, and this 90% is uniformly following the 80:20 rule, it appears that 70% of the liabilities of the banking system are contracted with time covenants and only 20% without time covenants. The implications of this behaviour on banking profits are obvious — much of bank liabilities are contracted at a cost and are not free which would have been the case if demand deposits predominated. On the positive side, asset-liability management becomes easier when the deposits involve time covenants. In line with the theory of banking, aggregate liabilities of the banking system is a linear function of the aggregate deposits.

The liabilities of a bank are grouped under the following heads:

1. Capital.
2. Reserve fund and other reserves.
3. Deposits.
   (*i*) from the public.
   (*ii*) from other banks.
4. Borrowings from other Banking Companies, Agents etc.
5. Bills payable.
6. Other liabilities.
7. Profit & Loss.
8. Contingent liabilities.

Bills for collection being bills receivable and acceptances, endorsements and other obligations are shown on both sides. Hence, they are not generally considered as liabilities.

Capital: In banking, no less than in other business enterprises survival and growth depend on capital resources and their efficient use. All banks need capital to cover and extend fixed assets and business investments, to enable trading to continue and increase, to maintain the confidence of depositors and to ensure viability in the face of loss arising from inevitable business and political fluctuation and uncertainty, particularly in an inflationary climate.

For banks, the concept of capital adequacy must relate to the totality of capital resources employed in the business. What is adequate in this respect may be judged from a different viewpoint which must in practice be reconciled, namely: first, the bank itself has an obvious responsibility to its depositors and its shareholders to be capitalised in a prudent manner.

Second, the central bank has responsibilities for the stability of the banking sector as a whole. In discharging this task, its contact with individual banks enables it to form a unique view of quality of their management and balance sheet structure.

Third, what the well-informed outside observer expects to see in the balance sheet may not be an irrelevant consideration. It is of unquestionable importance that a paucity of capital should not, at some future time, become a major constraint on the growth of the banks and hence on their ability to compete in the world.

BALANCE SHEET AS AT 31ST MARCH, 2003

	As at 31.03.2003 (Rs. '000)	*As at 31.03.2002 (Rs. '000)*
CAPITAL AND LIABILITIES		
Capital	410,00,00	577,86,81
Reserves and Surplus	3738,82,83	2893,62,69
Deposits	72094,82,25	64030,00,94
Borrowings	93,82,23	267,39,84
Other Liabilities and Provisions	5717,45,75	4366,24,29
Total	82054,93,06	72135,14,57
ASSETS		
Cash & Balances with Reserve Bank of India	5607,51,12	7859,85,52
Balances with banks and money at call and short notice	2089,63,92	4637,84,15
Investments	30458,24,40	23220,10,56
Advances	40471,59,83	33126,70,52
Fixed Assets	659,61,63	659,01,25
Other Assets	2768,32,16	2631,62,57
Total	82054,93,06	72135,14,57
Contingent Liabilities	51176,14,39	36024,25,93
Bills for Collection	3316,93,15	3920,21,33
Notes on Accounts		

PROFIT AND LOSS ACCOUNT FOR THE YEAR ENDED 31ST MARCH, 2003

	For the year ended 31.03.2003 (Rs. '000)	*For the year ended 31.03.2002 (Rs. '000)*
I. INCOME		
Interest earned	6657,72,29	6370,56,11
Other income	1512,13,13	1428,53,43
Total	8169,85,42	7799,09,54

II. EXPENDITURE		
Interest expended	4424,77,28	4550,24,84
Operating expenses	1747,70,57	1592,60,69
Provisions and contingencies	978,48,38	914,84,01
Total	7150,96,23	7057,69,54
III. NET PROFIT FOR THE YEAR	1018,89,19	741,40,00
IV. Appropriations transfers to		
Statutory reserve	255,00,00	186,00,00
Capital reserve	25,03	98,43
Investment fluctuation reserve	299,00,00	164,00,00
Revenue Reserves	303,20,41	310,41,57
Proposed dividend	143,50,00	80,00,00
Dividend tax	17,93,75	
Total	1018,89,19	741,40,00
Notes on accounts		
Earnings per share	20.56	12.83

SCHEDULES FORMING PART OF THE PROFIT & LOSS ACCOUNT FOR THE YEAR ENDED 31ST MARCH, 2003

	For the year ended 31.03.2003 (Rs. '000)	*For the year ended 31.03.2002 (Rs. '000)*
SCHEDULE 13 — INTEREST EARNED		
I. Interest/Discount on advances/Bills	3590,97,21	3130,48,05
II. Income on Investments	2652,32,71	2496,70,92
III. Interest on balances with RBI and other inter-bank funds	414,04,61	707,56,71
IV. Others	37.76	35,80,43
Total	6657,72,29	6370,56,11
SCHEDULE 14 — OTHER INCOME		
I. Commission, exchange and brokerage	359,47,60	322,16,91
II. Profit on sale of investments — Net	674,26,02	662,81,20
III. Profit on sale of land/buildings and other assets	1,38,09	73,66
IV. Profit on exchange transactions — Net	132,97.02	129,44,16
V. Income earned by way of dividend etc. from subsidiaries/companies and/or joint ventures abroad/in India	53,19,47	53,77,97
VI. Miscellensous income	290,84,93	259,59,53
Total	1512,13,13	1428,53,43
SCHEDULE 15 — INTEREST EXPENDED		
I. Interest on deposits	4224,94,39	4350,48,70
II. Interest on reserve abank of India/Inter-bank borrowings	9,01,56	21,71,07
III. Others	190,81,33	178,05,07
Total	4424,77,28	4550,24,84
SCHEDULE 16 — OPERATING EXPENSES		
I. Payments to and provisions for employees	1162,19,90	1122,52,01
II. Rent, taxes, lighting	162,88,83	144,31,82
III. Printing and stationery	19,05,72	16,42,10
IV. Advertising and publicity	9,66,67	5,97,77

V. Depreciation on bank's property (Net of transferred from revaluation reserve)	108,65,39	92,67,75
VI. Directors' fees, allowances and expenses	35.70	23.31
VII. Auditors' fees and expenses (includes for branch auditors)	10,40,77	9,92,32
VIII. Law charges	1,84,35	85,32
IX. Postage, Telegrams, Telephones etc.	17,91,43	18,09,30
X. Repairs and maintenance	32,07,61	25,42,91
XI. Insurance	33,76,07	30,86,54
XII. Other expenditure	188,88,13	125,29,44
Total	1747,70,57	1592,60,69

CASH FLOW STATEMENT FOR THE YEAR ENDED 31ST MARCH, 2003

(Rs. '000)

	31.03.2003	*31.03.2002*
I. OPERATING ACTIVITIES		
Interest & Commission received	6310,24,07	6079,88,54
Interest & Commission paid	(4423,18,55)	(4491,49,68)
Other Revenues	423,81,95	389,03,69
General & Administrative expenses	(1621,41,91)	(1604,78,76)
NET CASH FLOW FROM OPERATING ASSETS PRIOR TO THE EFFECT OF CHANGES IN ASSETS AND LIABILITIES	689,45,56	373,63,79
II. NET (INCREASE)/DECREASE IN OPERATING ASSETS		
Government and approved securities	(6353,66,15)	(1820,11,46)
Funds advanced to customers	(7821,04,31)	(5680,62,01)
Other operating assets	25,19,30	658,31,14
III. NET INCREASE/(DECREASE) IN OPERATING LIABILITIES		
Deposits from customers	8059,81,31	4952,48,10
Borrowings from banks & financial institutions	(173,57,61)	45,78,62
Other operating liabilities	307,95,31	(136,14,59)
CASH FLOW FROM OPERATING ACTIVITIES BEFORE TAXATION	((5,265,86,59)	(1607,66,41)
Taxes paid	(316,77,53)	(176,37,44)
CASH FLOW FROM OPERATING ACTIVITIES	(5582,64,12)	(1784,03,85)
IV. INVESTING ACTIVITIES		
(Purchase of fixed assets	(112,01,40)	(105,66,06)
(Purchase)/sale of Investments	(884,47,69)	32,95,24
Dividend received	53,19,47	53,77,97
Investment income	1261,75,92	1209,42,93
CASH FLOW FROM INVESTING ACTIVITIES	318,46,30	1190,50,08
V. FINANCING ACTIVITIES		
Return of capital to government	(167,86,81)	—
Share premium received	275,00,00)	—
Dividend paid	(143,50,00)	(80,00,00)
Subordinated debts	500,00,00	—
CASH FLOW FROM FINANCING ACTIVITIES	(4800,54,63)	(673,53,77)
CASH & CASH EQUIVALENTS AT THE BEGINNING OF THE YEAR	12497,69,67	13171,23,44
CASH & CASH EQUIVALENTS AT THE END OF THE YEAR	7697,15,04	12497,69,67

Reserves: Reserves of a bank also indicate the health of the institution. It is obligatory on the part of banks to transfer 20 per cent of profit to reserves to strengthen the capital base of the bank. Capital and reserves together constitute the network of a bank.

The reserve fund is built to meet unforeseen and unexpected contingencies. It is a source of strength for the bank as it can withstand heavy losses. The reserve fund is invested in first class securities. This apart, banks are also permitted to build secret reserves too.

Deposits from Banks

Deposits from banks and from the public are the life blood of commercial banks. They are the chief sources of bank and account for approximately 83 per cent of bank liabilities. Banks deposits are classified into (*a*) Fixed deposits (*b*) Savings bank deposits and (*c*) Current deposits, contingency accounts etc. Contingency accounts include head office funds and other inter-bank and inter-branch adjustments classified as deposits.

Borrowings from other Banking Companies, Agents

With a view to replenish their funds, banks borrow from the Reserve Bank of India (presently refinance is given for food credit and export credit), bills rediscounted with the Reserve Bank. In addition, banks borrow from other refinance bodies like IDBI, SIDBI, NABARD, EXIM BANK, IFC, IRBI and other financial institutions.

Bills Payable: Outstanding bills constitute the liability of a bank.

Other Liabilities: Generally include provision of dividend, unclaimed dividends, interest provision accounts and inter-office adjustments.

Profit and Loss Account represents the balance of profits after making all appropriations. Since Profit is payable to the shareholders, it represents the liability of the bank.

Contingent Liabilities invariably include: (1) claims against the bank not acknowledged as debts (2) bills of exchange rediscounted (3) outstanding forward exchange controverts (4) partly paid shares (5) guarantees given on behalf of others and other moneys for which the bank is contingently liable.

Assets of a Commercial Bank: The assets of the commercial bank are given on the right hand side of the balance sheet. These are grouped under following heads:

1. Cash — in hand and with Reserve Bank of India (including foreign currency notes.)
2. Balances with other banks — on current account and on deposit accounts.
3. Money at call and short notice.
4. Investments — (*a*) Central and State Government securities and Treasury Bills (*b*) Other Trustee securities (including shares which are Trustee securities).
5. Advances
   (*i*) Loans, cash credits, overdrafts etc.
   (*ii*) Bills discounted and purchased.
6. Premises less depreciation.
7. Furniture & Fixtures less depreciation.
8. Other assets

BOX 5.1

GROWING SIGNIFICANCE OF NON-DEPOSIT RESOURCES

Banks have traditionally funded their lending operations mainly with deposits. However, in recent years, some changes have taken place on the liability side of the banks' balance sheet. While deposits continue to be the main source of funding, the relative significance of non-deposit resources has increased. Within non-deposit resources, the shares of borrowings and reserves in total liabilities have increased gradually (Chart 1). Although the share of capital has declined over the years, the share of net-owned funds has gone up marginally. In order to meet the capital adequacy requirements, banks have relied mainly on retained earnings. Banks' profitability in recent years has improved significantly as a result of which they are able to plough back their profits.

Two significant sources of borrowings in recent years have been subordinated debt, issued to augment their Tier II capital in the domestic capital market and increase in foreign currency borrowings. The sharp expansion in foreign currency borrowing has been on account of various liberalisation measures relating to the capital account for facilitating residents' foreign currency requirement for productive purposes. Flexibility given to banks to tap the source of foreign borrowings, especially for granting pre-shipment credit in foreign currency (PCFC)/export bills rediscounting (EBR) to exporters has been another factor contributing to higher foreign currency borrowings. Banks have also been allowed to use funds generated through buy-sell swaps in domestic forex markets for granting such loans subject to Aggregate Gap Limit approved by the Reserve Bank.

To the extent banks rely on borrowings to fund their lending operations, they are exposed to uncertainties as players in the securities market are more sensitive to interest rates and market conditions. Borrowings from the market generally also tend to be expensive than deposits and large reliance on market borrowings could erode the interest margin. However, long-term nature of such borrowings reduces liquidity risk and enables banks to finance long-term projects.

A sharp growth of non-deposit resources has also monetary implications as conventional broad monetary aggregate does not adequately reflect the growth of assets in the balance sheet. This is evident from the ratio of net non-monetary liabilities (NNML), which after declining steadily between 1990-91 and 1998-99, rose sharply in 2004-05 (Chart 2).

Cash and Balances

Among assets, the cash and balances with Reserve Bank component is theoretically a function of the Cash Reserve Ratio (CRR) prescribed by the Reserve Bank in line with monetary and credit policy. It has moved in a band of 9-14.4% of total assets, sticking somewhat to the higher side in 1987-89, 1991-92, and 1993-95. In the three post-reform years when cash and balances went upto 14%, the credit fell below 50% of total assets. In the 1987-89 period, it was marginally above 50%. Within the component, there is a significant trend which is seen in the first 5 years of our analysis, i.e., cash has come down from 13.2% in 1984-85 to 6.3% in 1988-89 and thereafter remained in the 4.5-6.5% range barring a couple of years. Conversely, balances with the RBI have climbed from 86.8% to 93.7%, staying between 93.5% and 95.5%. This is apparently due to the practice of charging notional interest (opportunity cost) on cash held by branch, but not on balances held with the Reserve Bank. The interest is transferred to the head office, but reduces branch profit.

Investments

Investments by banks comprise of two broad categories, *viz.*, Government and other approved securities (SLR Investments), and commercial paper, shares, bonds and debentures issued by the corporate sector and public sector undertakings (non-SLR investments).

The Investments component is ostensibly a function of the Statutory Liquidity Ratio prescribed by the RBI in line with monetary and credit policy. The proportion of investments to total assets was always below 33% upto 1989-90 but never went below 33.7% after that year. In 1993-94, it was 37% when credit fell below 46%. The mean for the six years is 38.4%. Within investments, an interesting phenomenon is observed. The mix of government securities and other approved securities, which was 2:1, prior to 1991-92 has over just 6 years become 5:1. In 1996-97, there was redistribution in rupee terms from approved securities to government securities. In the light of the Rakesh Mohan Committee Report 1997, this is clearly an adverse development.

Credit

Credit is the broadest and most important component of the assets of the banking system. It is also the most complex because in developing economies, it is not merely an outcome of credit policy but also a tool of agricultural and industrial policy. Nationalisation was part of a broad developmental plan to increase the flow of scarce resources to productive purposes, which had otherwise been monopolised by a few deeply entrenched vested interests. From a level of 54-55% in the 1984-86 period, credit fell below 52% in 10 out of the remaining 11 years, and below 49% in 3 out of 6 post-reform years. The mean for these 11 years is 50.2% implying that just about half of banking assets have supported mainstream production for the last decade. Notably, whereas other assets in the portfolio have grown at compounded annual growth rates of 17%+, in keeping with 17%+ growth rate in deposits, bank credit has grown at 15.6% only. Within Bank credit, loans, cash credits and overdrafts constitute 90% and the rest are inland and foreign bills. Interestingly, the ratio of inland to foreign bills has changed from 3:1 to 1:1 which is probably due to the liberalisation of foreign trade as well as export finance coming under the scheme of priority-sector advances.

Assets with the Banking system consttitute between 2.5-4.7% of total assets of the banking system and is a contra variable to liabilities with the banking system. About 80% is represented by Balances with other banks (in current or other accounts) plus Money at call and short notice. The rest is composed of advances to banks and other assets with the banking system.

Considering cash in hand and balances witth Reserve Bank, as a percentage of both incremental assets and incremental liabilities, the ratio was quite high in the years 1991-92, 1993-94 and 1994-95, being 28%+, 32%+ and 15%+ respectively. There have been counterbalancing decrements in 1992-93 and 1995-97. These cyclical movements are not exhibited upto 1990-91; the incremental cash function till that date is monotone decreasing. The identical feature is also obtained from the incremental cash-deposit ratio. The system seems to move from situations of normal liquidity to excess liquidity and back with amazing speed and the magnitude of adjustment can exceed 40% of incremental assets or liabilities. Were the participants in the Indian financial markets to be capable enough to interpret such volatility coupled with a managed yield-to-maturity curve, the expectations arising out of such volatility would be unhealthy because markets tend to overreact. However, given an immature market, with low integration and low capability of participants to assimilate information, the impact of liquidity volatility becomes somewhat indeterminate.

Given that investments as a per cent of total assets have been rising and credit as a percentage of total assets falling, if we analyse the behaviour of these two variables simultaneously, we see the clearly inverse and counter cyclical nature of these two variables, whether taken as a percentage of total assets or total liabilities or total deposits. Interestingly, post reform, the frequency of cyclical variation has increased (with consequential reduction of the time period between crest and trough), but more disturbingly, the magnitude of the fluctuation has increased. This can be due to either or both of two reasons first, our banking system is very fragile and prone to overreact to exogenous shocks in the form of fiscal imbalances, capital market fluctuations, etc.; second, we have been taking excessive recourse to monetary action for whatsoever causes. In the context of a developing economy, such continuous adjustments cannot by any length of economic logic be deemed healthy.

Composition of Funds

The sources and uses of funds in terms of the new balance sheet format by the RBI with effect from March 1992, as categorised by banks is given above. The cost and return structure of these sources and uses and the availability constraints and risk element, is also given against each item.

Sources	*Cost Structure/Availability*
(1) Share capital	Free of cost except for payment of dividend. It needs generation of profits to service the capital in the absence of which shareholders would hardly be encouraged to contribute more in future.
(2) Reserves — Statutory reserve — Capital reserve — Revaluation reserve — Revenue and other reserves	Available free of cost. Additions would generally be made out of surplus from year to year, except for revaluation reserve.
(3) Deposits — Demand deposits — From banks — From others	No or negligible financial cost but operational cost is very high. A high degree of customer orientation and right kind of staff attitude is the pre-requirement to bring sizeable funds. Volumes matter, to keep the cost low.
— Savings	Reasonable financial cost and high operational cost. The largest segment in commercial banks in terms of member of customers.
— Term deposits — From banks — From others	Highest financial cost but the operational cost is low. The banks have to maintain a balance between the level of funds in this category and other two categories. Otherwise the position may turn out to be unaffordable especially if proper deployment becomes difficult.
(4) Borrowings and refinance — RBI — Other banks — Other institutions and agencies	Financial cost reasonable and operational cost low, but the constraints are many on availability and firm repayment commitments.
(5) Liabilities and provisions — Bills payable — Interest accrued — Others	Servicing cost high.

There are off-balance sheet liabilities also, known as contingent liabilities like claims against the bank, guarantees and letters of credit issued on behalf of the customers, liabilities on account of outstanding forward exchange contracts, etc.

The mix of sources and uses in percentage terms is given above in the illustration. It would be observed that the above sources and uses have their own cost and income structure and risk elements. One cannot choose between funds mobilisation and deployment as both these have to be carried simultaneously. The objective of mobilisation as well as of deployment is to earn to sustain and meet other requirements such as provisioning, cost of non-performance or maintenance of capital adequacy. Failure to mobilise or deploy effectively would lead to the one and the same thing, i.e., losses.

Uses	*Return Structure/Risk Element*
(1) Cash in hand Balance with RBI — In current account — In other accounts	No return on funds for cash in hand and return on balance with RBI is just enough to cover Saving Bank cost. The deployment is risk free.
(2) Balance with banks/money at call and short notice — Balance with banks — In current accounts — In other deposit a/cs — Money at call and short notice with banks	Rate of return is highly fluctuating and uncertain and is hovering around the saving bank deposit rate but the deployed funds do not carry any risk.
(3) Investment — Government securities — Other approved securities — Shares — Debentures and bonds — Subsidiaries and/or joint ventures — Others	Return is adequate to cover the financial cost and part of the operational cost which is low and the investments are risk free except the risk of depreciation in value due to ever changing coupon rates and capital market fluctuations.
(4) Advances (including bills) — Bills purchased — Cash credit and overdrafts and loans payable on demand — Term loans	A major portion carries interest around 18 per cent. The operational cost is very high and the funds deployed carry very high degree of risk. Prudential guidelines on income recognition and provisioning can reduce the average yield substantially, if record of recovery turns out or continues to be poor.
(5) Fixed assets — Premises — Other fixed assets (including fixture & furniture)	No return from the funds deployed and there is recurring cost of depreciation and maintenance.
(6) Other assets — Inter-office adjustments — Interest on investments not collected — Tax paid in advance — Stationery and stamps — Non-banking assets acquired — Others	Operational cost is generally high and these assets generally do not yield any income.

Consolidated Balance Sheet of Scheduled Commercial Banks

(Amount in Rs.crore)

	As at end-March					
	2004		2005		2006#	
	Amount	Per cent to total	Amount	Per cent to total	Amount	Per cent to total
1	2	3	4	5	6	7
Liabilities						
1. Capital	22,348	1.1	25,183	1.1	25,905	1.1
2. Reserves and Surplus	94,254	4.8	1,18,326	5.2	1,23,530	5.2
3. Deposits	15,78,450	80.0	18,21,884	80.1	18,36,987	78.0
3.1 Demand Deposits	2,03,237	10.3	2,30,709	10.1	2,34,595	10.0
3.2 Savings Bank Deposits	3,73,677	18.9	4,43,052	19.5	4,44,944	18.9
3.3 Term Deposits	10,01,536	50.7	11,48,123	50.5	11,57,447	49.1
4. Borrowings	95,562	4.8	1,18,311	5.2	1,68,316	7.1
5. Other Liabilities and Provisions	1,83,402	9.3	1,90,918	8.4	2,01,244	8.5
Total Liabilities/Assets	**19,74,017**	**100.0**	**22,74,622**	**100.0**	**23,55,983**	**100.0**
Assets						
1. Cash and Balances with RBI	1,13,246	5.7	1,15,711	5.1	1,18,087	5.0
2. Balances with Banks and Money at Call and Short Notice	82,033	4.2	92,927	4.1	96,204	4.1
3. Investments	8,04,199	40.7	8,43,081	37.1	8,68,135	36.8
3.1 In Government Securities (a+b)	6,39,143	32.4	6,84,005	30.1	6,98,903	29.7
(a) In India	6,36,266	32.2	6,80,641	29.9	6,95,540	29.5
(b) Outside India	2,877	0.1	3,363	0.1	3,363	0.1
3.2 In Other Approved Securities	18,100	0.9	16,291	0.7	16,291	0.7
3.3 In Non-approved Securities	1,46,956	7.4	1,42,785	6.3	1,52,941	6.5
4. Loans and Advances	8,64,271	43.8	11,05,725	48.6	11,51,138	48.9
4.1 Bills Purchased & Discounted	66,968	3.4	87,188	3.8	89,544	3.8
4.2 Cash Credit, Overdrafts, etc.	3,72,207	18.9	4,35,777	19.2	4,37,060	18.6
4.3 Term Loans	4,25,096	21.5	5,82,760	25.6	6,24,534	26.5
5. Fixed Assets	21,409	1.1	22,161	1.0	23,051	1.0
6. Other Assets	88,860	4.5	95,018	4.2	99,367	4.2

Including the impact of conversion of a non-banking entity into a banking entity.

Source: Balance sheets of respective banks.

The illustration also provides an insight into the fact as to how the cost aspects of various liabilities affect the total expenditure and resultantly the spread and profit earning capacity and similarly the income yielding aspect of various assets adversely or positively disturbs or supports, the profit position of the banks.

In any economy, the central government will *ipso facto* be a better risk than a state government because of its recourse to monetisation — however, in our credit planning, we adopted adhocism by asking banks to buy approved securities without first seeing whether state governments had the institutional expertise to raise debt competitively in the investor's risk-return framework, given the poor state of their public finances. Even now, if reforms are not holistically envisaged, credit will flow in the Pareto-skewed style to a few market-savvy states like Gujarat, Maharashtra, Karnataka, Andhra Pradesh, Tamil Nadu, etc.

In order to free resources for infrastructure and agrarian development, it is imperative to redirect flow of credit to the private economy. This should not be done exclusively by reducing coupon rates on gilts because that would have two adverse fall-outs-first, banks' profitability would decline in the absence of concurrent SLR deduction. Second, the reduction of interest expenditure in the government's revenue account would be used to reduce revenue and fiscal deficits in the short-run but would encourage profligate borrowing in the medium-to-long-run, given our political economy.

Conclusion

The liabilities and assets of a commercial bank reflect the health of the bank and inherent risk. A healthy picture reassures depositors. The commercial banks should present still more transparent accounts, so that a proper analysis and rating is made from time to time. With the implementation of the Asset Liability Management (ALM) System by banks from April, 1999, risk management covering credit risk and market risk, the interest rate risk will be minimised. Further, it will improve the quality of assets portfolio and enhance financial soundness of the banks. Asset Liability management is a continuous process of planning, organising and controlling asset liability volumes, maturities, yields and rates.

Annexure - I

Table – 1: Scheduled Commercial Banks – Business in India (Rs. in crore)

(Amount in Rs.crore)

	Outstanding as on 2007 Jan. 19#	Variation over Financial Year so far	
		2005-06	2006-07
Liabilities to the Banking System			
Demand and Time Deposits from Banks	34,703	–10,232	–2,375
Borrowings from Banks	30,964	–5,696	1,750
Other Demand and Time Liabilities	9,017	2,634	127
Liabilities to Others			
Aggregate Deposits	23,89,110	1,60,417	2,80,061
		(9.0)	(13.3)
Demand	3,56,701	16,366	–7,939
Time	20,32,408	1,44,051	2,88,000
Borrowings	83,772	6,513	629
Other Demand and Time Liabilities	2,14,840	–8,877	26,060
Borrowings from Reserve Bank	**3,706**	**1,740**	**2,218**
Cash in hand & Balanaces with RBI	**1,52,109**	**13,287**	**12,003**
Cash in hand	13,314	537	268
Balances with Reserve Bank	1,38,795	12,750	11,735
Assets with the Banking System			
Balanace with other Banks	25,100	–50	–1,363
Money at call and short notice	13,951	–13,369	331
Advances to Banks	5,569	–5,305	1,378
Other Assets	19,249	490	9,129
Investments	**7,59,291**	**–24,882**	**41,836**
		(–3.4)	(5.8)
Government Securities	7,37,496	–22,885	36,754
Other Approved Securities	21,795	–1,997	5,082
Bank Credit	**17,66,491**	**2,09,964**	**2,59,414**
		(18.2)	(17.2)
Food Credit	41,210	–1,673	520
Non-food Credit	17,25,281	2,11,637	2,58,895
Loans, Cash-Credit and Overdrafts	16,86,567	–2,07,831	2,56,112
Inland Bills - Purchased	11,159	–748	–1,755
Discounted	31,650	2,292	834
Foreign Bills - Purchased	14,142	–1,035	1,067
Discounted	22,973	1,624	3,156
Cash-Deposit Ratio	**6.37**		
Investment-Deposit Ratio	**31.78**		
Credit-Deposit	**73.94**		

Source: Reserve Bank of India

Table – 2: Kisan Credit Cards-State-wise Progress as on March 31, 2006

(Amount in Rs.Lakh)

Sl. No.	Name of State	Commercial Banks		Regional Rural Banks	
		Card Issued (in numbers)	Amount Sanctioned	Card Issued	Amount Sanctioned
1	Andhra Pradesh	10,63,529	3,49,595	1,61,069	59,632
2	Assam	47,782	6,759	15,080	2,193
3	Arunachal Pradesh	1,615	133	351	7
4	Bihar	1,46,268	43,415	62,981	20,878
5	Chhattisgarh	41,919	14,972	48,399	9,567
6	Gujrat	1,11,400	62,863	43,248	63,612
7	Goa	2,519	3,708	–	–
8	Haryana	93,751	1,10,335	88,259	63,372
9	Himachal Pradesh	19,415	10,271	5,835	8,136
10	Jammu & Kashmir	1,048	442	1,741	11,145
11	Jharkhand	48,917	9,623	59,491	17,752
12	Karnataka	2,75,305	1,55,918	1,09,199	2,83,737
13	Kerala	97,189	43,101	25,988	9,939
14	Madhya Pradesh	1,91,504	1,36,436	86,179	44,786
15	Maharashtra	2,70,492	1,34,654	29,484	8,226
16	Manipur	5,885	744	96	19
17	Meghalaya	7,680	1,317	1,455	188
18	Mizoram	3,690	580	52	12
19	Nagaland	4,278	797	43	5
20	Orissa	1,27,076	24,561	81,856	25,345
21	Punjab	97,371	1,37,102	14,584	19,023
22	Rajasthan	1,76,588	1,25,687	97,268	59,354
23	Sikkim	959	240	–	–
24	Tamilnadu	4,30,953	1,26,966	32,144	7,441
25	Tripura	6,066	1,200	4,921	844
26	Uttaranchal	36,296	19,847	4,558	1,535
27	Uttar Pradesh	6,77,700	3,17,394	2,73,897	1,41,441
28	West Bengal	1,72,413	37,391	1,296	64
	Union Teritories	4,943	1,896	–	–

Source: NABARD

Chapter 6

MERCHANT BANKING

Introduction

During the seventies, Indian banking witnessed metamorphic changes. From the basic function of mobilising deposits and money lending, the banking industry has grown into a catalytic agency for the promotion of economic development. With the ever-increasing responsibilities cast on it, its concepts and attitudes have also changed considerably to meet the challenges of the Indian economy. Rapid innovations in the field of banking have resulted in many activities which were hitherto unknown to Indian banking. Along with innovations, banks have tended to lay emphasis on the increased specialisation of various activities. One such innovation is the merchant banking facilities.

Banking is essentially a service industry. Commercial banks are normally engaged in two major types of services, *viz.*, mobilisation of deposits and ancillary services, the one relating to lending is more prestigious because clients more often seek the banker for funds. Merchant banking is, however, exclusively a service function. The merchant banker has to seek a client, establish good relations with him, offer him the kind of services he needs and maintain a continuing relationship with him. Informed and efficient service is the *sine qua non* of merchant banking. A client will come for advice only if he is convinced that the merchant banker knows more than he does, and is capable of doing the work better than his own organisation. In addition, he would expect that he receives proper attention, and that his interests would be adequately served within the prescribed time schedule. The merchant banker should, therefore not only be knowledgeable and efficient, but imbued with the spirit of service so that the client may feel that his interests are safe in his hands.

Merchant Banking — Meaning

Dictionary meaning of "merchant bank" refers to an organisation that underwrites corporate securities and advises such clients on issues like corporate mergers, etc. involved in the ownership of commercial ventures. This organisation may be a bank, corporate body, firm or proprietary concern.

In Indian context this definition suits well. Merchant banking in India started with management of public issues and loan syndication and has been slowly and gradually covering activities like project counselling, portfolio management, investment counselling and mergers and amalgamation of the corporate firms. Although, merchant banking organisations present a long list of services they contemplate to render to their clients but the main services so far being rendered by them are those as authorised by the Securities and Exchange Board of India.

Role of Merchant Banks

To promote the new issue market there is need for a qualitative improvement in the offer of new issues both in terms of time taken and the cost of floatation. At present the time taken for organising a new issue is between 12 to 18 months and the cost of raising new capital varies from 3% to 8% and sometimes even 20%. This can be brought down relatively by specialized merchant banking institutions by catering to the requirements of both large and small industrial units. Cost of floatation of equity and preference capital is higher for new companies than for existing companies, indicating thereby the difficulties experienced by new companies in making a new issue. Merchant banks can help saving in the cost of new companies.

The new issue market has not succeeded fully in mobilising savings partly due to the preference of the public to company deposits and partly due to low yield on equities as compared to those on fixed interest securities. There has been a decline in the proportion of share capital in the total capital employed due to the steep rise in the cost of new issues. There are certain minimum costs to be incurred in respect of fees to brokers, promoters' expenses, underwriting commission etc., irrespective of the size of the project. While bigger companies are able to manage this, small industrialists find it extremely difficult to meet this minimum cost with uncertain prospects of public response. The existing big companies have been relying more on their own internal resource in order to avoid the high cost of making public issues.

Merchant Banking Services

Let us first see how merchant banking services are understood and what is the nature of the services that are offered at present in India. Merchant banking services are activities, i.e., counselling corporate clients, who are in need of capital, on capital structure, form of capital to be raised, the terms and conditions of issue, underwriting of the issue, timing of the issue and preparation of the prospectus and publicity for grooming the issue for the market. They may also relate to the private placement of capital and the raising of long-term loans, either in foreign exchange or in rupee currency, from the national/state financial institutions, and short-term working capital from commercial banks. These activities are mainly stock-exchange-oriented, relating as they do to the issue of fresh capital for a new company setting up an enterprise, or for the existing ones which want to finance the expansion and diversification of other businesses. A few proposals of mergers and amalgamations have also been handled. In essence, therefore, in India, merchant banking services have been looked upon mainly as those consisting of issue house functions connected with the raising of capital from financial institutions and the market and sometimes shaping the proposals for mergers and amalgamations of existing companies into integrated corporate enterprises. It may be recalled that, in the old days, many of these functions were discharged by prominent firms of brokers and that some of them have recently set up consultancy organisations which function as managers to the issue of capital in the market. In addition, proposals for the dilution of equity capital of foreign majority companies and the issue of capital by branches of foreign companies are now sponsored by merchant banks.

While there is no doubt that one of the important functions of merchant banking relates to issue house activities, there are others which are equally important. It would, therefore, be most useful to study first the functions which the merchant banks in the United Kingdom and investment banks in the United States generally perform, and then attempt to analyse which of them are essentially relevant in Indian conditions. It would then be possible to find out in what way these functions may be adapted to our requirements within the framework of the government's industrial policy and the programme of industrial development under the Five-Year-Plans.

Merchant Banking in Britain

Merchant banking services in Britain developed partly as a result of the operation of historical factors and partly in response to the requirements of trade and industry for their short and long-term needs. Though merchant banks themselves collect deposits and grant credit to a limited extent, they act mainly as intermediaries —

(*a*) in channelling short-term credit from commercial banks through discount house to merchants engaged in the import and export trade or in the marketing of goods in the domestic market;

(*b*) in channelising medium and long-term capital from those who wish to lend to those who are in need of funds.

In addition, they render a variety of advisory services to individuals and corporate bodies, including such financial institutions as investment trusts and unit trusts, of which they are the promoters and managers. Merchant banks, therefore, form an integral part of the complex of financial institutions like commercial banks, discount houses, long-term financial institutions and capital markets and have, therefore, established intimate business relationships with them through daily contacts and advisory services.

The prominent merchant banks do acceptance business; many of them act as issuing houses; some are financial bankers; some do foreign exchange business; some are engaged in the bullion business; a few undertake merchanting. All of them do banking in some form by keeping money in current or other accounts for their customers at home or abroad. This type of banking activity is ancillary to other services; but the keeping of current accounts on which their customers draw by cheque is a substantial business for many of them. Allied with this is the keeping of securities in safe custody including the accounts of customers, and making and realising investments on their behalf. This has led in many cases to giving advice to customers on their investments as well as on the management of pension funds, college endowments and other funds of a similar nature. Some of them have an active trustee business which either a department or a separate subsidiary company handles. They also act as registrars and transfer agents for industrial companies. Many merchant banking houses have promoted and are managers of Investment Trusts and Unit Trusts. By developing unit-linked insurance business, they have set up their own life insurance companies, or have established business connections with the existing life insurance offices.

As a group, the merchant banks are active in the following four special areas:

(*i*) They manage individual funds — of individuals, firms or charitable trusts — on a large scale, which now aggregate to many million pounds;

(*ii*) They finance foreign trade, both in acceptance business and in the post-war practice of arranging medium-term export credits;

(*iii*) They advise a growing number of industrial companies not only on how and when to raise capital but also on their financial affairs generally;

(*iv*) To an increasing extent, they are now engaged in foreign security business, placing American shares in Europe and vice versa; running European and off-shore trusts; thus concerning themselves with foreign loan business.

Merchant Banking in USA

In the USA, investment bankers are now mainly engaged in marketing corporate and other obligations. In this function, they have developed great expertise. The investment banking firm forms and manages any syndicate to market public offerings of the issue made by a client corporation. The investment banker is a good judge of the timing of the issue; secondly, he is adept in formulating the terms and conditions which are acceptable to investors in the prevailing conditions. The investment banking firms are, therefore, mainly engaged in investment advisory services bearing on domestic issues of capital as well as in arranging consortia for the issue of capital on behalf of foreign governments and foreign corporate enterprises.

It is important to bear in mind that these institutions have grown and functioned over the years in the environment of freedom wherein they have diversified their activities in tune with the changing circumstances. They have developed qualities of integrity, financial expertise, high management stability, loyalty and close relationship with clients. Many of them have substantial resources of their own and command additional resources through access to commercial banks, financial institutions and the stock market, with which they have established intimate relations and enjoy a high creditworthy status.

In the post-war period, new trends have emerged in the work frame of commercial banks in the West European countries which indicate that banks are now prepared to offer multiple services, including merchant banking services, to their individual and corporate clients. Taking advantage of this, several British banks have set up either subsidiary companies or separate divisions in their own organisations to offer these services. Commercial banks have thus been competing with the old established merchant banks in Britain. In India, the Grindlays Bank opened its merchant banking division in 1967; this was followed by New York based Citibank in 1970. The State Bank of India started its Merchant Banking Division in 1972. The Industrial Credit & Investment Corporation of India Ltd. (ICICI) set up its own division to offer merchant banking services, which relate mainly to the management of the issues floated on the stock exchange. Other commercial banks are reported to have set up their own merchant banking services.

For a systematic organisation of these services, it is necessary:

(*a*) To recognise the importance of these services in the context of the programme of industrial development in India;

(*b*) To state clearly the functions which these organisations would perform so that clients would know the services to expect from them;

(*c*) To spell out the principles which would guide these services; and

(*d*) To set up a competent and efficient organisation to meet the requirements of both individual and corporate clients.

Since 1951, a wide-based and highly diversified industrial structure has been built up which is capable of producing a variety of consumer goods, basic raw materials, intermediate goods and capital goods. Owing to import control regulations, the domestic market is sheltered against foreign competition. Since the demand for all types of goods remained firm, except during the period of recession in 1966-68, and prices in the domestic market were high, the profitability of most of the undertakings was very good. The investment markets were somewhat uncertain, and though the new issues of share of companies with growth prospects were received well by the investing public, a number of issues fared rather badly. Since November 1973, there has been a firm trend in cost escalation, which has eroded the profit margins of various industries. The prospects for the development of various categories of industries became somewhat uncertain. But the industrial sector is bound to grow because increased industrial production is imperative to meet the growing requirements of the people and contain the inflationary pressures in the economy. It is all the more essential in the present situation, therefore, to assess the demand conditions, the supply position of raw materials and other inputs, and estimate the viability of any projected enterprise. This situation demands the services of well-informed and competent financial intermediaries, who would assist the new class of small and medium entrepreneurs.

Importance and need of merchant banking in India: Important reason for the growth of merchant banking has been the developmental activity throughout the country, exerting excess demand on the sources of funds for ever expanding industry and trade, thus, leaving a widening gap unbridged between the supply and demand of investible funds. All India financial institutions had experienced resource constraint to meet the ever increasing demand for funds from the corporate sector enterprises. In the circumstances corporate sector had the only alternative to avail of the capital market services for meeting their long-term financial requirements through capital issues of equity and debentures. With the growing demand for funds there was pressure on capital market that enthused the commercial banks, share brokers and financial consultancy firms to enter into the field of merchant banking and share the growing capital market. With the result, all the commercial banks in nationalised and public sector as well as in private sector including the foreign banks in India have opened their merchant banking windows and are competing in this field. There has been a mushroom growth of financial consultancy firms and broker firms doing advisory functions as merchant bankers as well as managing public issues in syndication with other merchant bankers.

Notwithstanding the above facts, the need of merchant banking institutions is felt in the wake of huge public savings lying still untapped. Merchant banks can play highly significant role in mobilising funds of savers to investible channels assuring promising return on investments and thus can help in meeting the widening demand for investible funds for economic activity. With the growth of merchant banking profession corporate enterprises in both public and private sectors would be able to raise required amount of funds annually from the capital market to meet the growing requirements for funds for establishing new enterprises. This reinforces the need for a vigorous role to be played by merchant banks.

Merchant banks have been procuring impressive support from capital market for the corporate sector for financing their projects. This is evidenced from the increasing amount raised from the capital market by the corporate enterprises year after year.

Increased Responsibilities

The financial community in this country consists of commercial banks, long-term lending institutions and industrial investment and development institutions set up by various state governments. Commercial banks are engaged primarily in the supply of short-term capital for trade and industry. Since 1969, they have been increasingly required to step up their services to the priority sectors. During the last decade, commercial banks have extended medium-term credit and have been engaged in term-lending. Some of them have developed the expertise to apply sophisticated criteria for project appraisal. The specialised financial institutions, led by the Industrial Development Bank of India, are mainly concerned with financing new projects and the expansion of the existing ones; investment institutions like the Life Insurance Corporation of India and the Unit Trust of India are chiefly disposed to make investments on their own account. The State-sponsored institutions, in relatively advanced States, have been functioning efficiently and have contributed to a remarkable extent to the development of backward areas; in other states, some of the institutions, having been set up only recently, have contributed to a remarkable extent to the development of backward areas; in other States, some of the institutions have to acquire experience and develop the requisite expertise for project analysis and evaluation. While the All-India financial institutions have acquired considerable experience and developed expertise of appraisal of the most sophisticated types of industries, they have hardly any personnel or time to spare for assisting or guiding entrepreneurs in preparing their proposals. It would not be out of place here to cite the findings of industries of medium and large size that were incorporated in the Second and Third Plan periods in the private sector: "*Inadequate preparations of projects, defective technical planning, insufficient care in selecting machinery suppliers or foreign collaborators, and, in certain cases, indifferent and inefficient management have all contributed to prolonging unduly the completion of projects.*" Companies which went to financial institutions for assistance, frequently made their approach at a premature stage, and consequently, in a number of projects, changes and modifications, both in technical and financial aspects, were introduced later. These delays in their turn caused overruns in the capital costs of the projects and imposed a heavy burden on financial overheads and pre-production costs.

In this context, there are three or four important points which should be noted. In the Fifth Five-year Plan, in the sphere of large industries, emphasis was laid on the development of such industries as fertilisers, petrochemicals and electronics and others which were highly sophisticated and complex in character. Both the scale of operations and the investment outlay on some of them were much bigger than before. At the same time, there was a distinct stress on decentralisation and the encouragement of small and medium entrepreneurs. In a statement on its industrial policy, the Government announced that it would prefer medium entrepreneurs to large business houses. This implies not only emergence of a new class of entrepreneurs having technical or managerial qualifications but deliberate assistance to successful small industrialists evolving into medium ones. Both classes of entrepreneurs need expert advice and assistance in the preparation and implementation of their projects. Secondly, the concept of security in respect of short-term and long-term lending has undergone a significant change. Instead of the commercial credit of the borrower, it is the creditworthiness and viability of the project that are assessed and taken as the basis for long-term loans, medium-term credit or working capital. In the context of the new bank-client relationship which was spelt out by Shri R. K. Talwar in his A.D. Shroff Memorial Lecture, *Banker and Corporate Customer,* the corporate enterprises would need the services and expert advice of a financial intermediary on the financial management of their short and long-term credit requirements. The banks' "*objective is to identify the precise purpose for which* funds *are sought and to quantify the need; also to ensure that there is proper planning and that, for a specified need, an appropriate type of finance will be raised.*"

Expert Know-how Essential

Thirdly, in many business enterprises, the managing agents offered their services to companies under their management for securing adequate financial resources from commercial banks and other financial institutions. With the termination of the managing agency system, the professional management was in need of services of objective and impartial agencies, having the necessary experience and expert knowledge of financial management. The financial institutions and commercial banks are interested "*in the borrowing customer's quality of management, financial planning and viability of operations.*" Fourthly, there was a need for industrial rationalisation. This could be achieved by mergers and integration between the existing public or privately-owned companies or by the private companies going public. There was also a distinct possibility of Indian enterprises investing in joint ventures abroad with a view to getting a foothold in the overseas markets. In all these respects, there was a need for sophisticated financial planning and management standards. The expanding scope for financial services called for the services of specialised institutions which had a flexible approach and were equipped to deal with corporate problems.

Having regard to the requirements of business and industry in India, it would seem that the functions of merchant banking type of service institutions should, in the initial stages, be in the areas of:

(*i*) Promotion, financing and syndication of Indian projects;

(*ii*) Investment advisory services;

(*iii*) Investment management;

(*iv*) Acceptance credit.

There are several agencies in the country, mainly at the state level which encourage new entrepreneurs to set up industries in the backward areas. Efforts are also made by various state level investment or development institutions to set up industries in the joint sector. The established small and medium entrepreneurs are engaged in either expanding or diversifying their manufacturing activities. It is common knowledge that industrial development is regulated by the Industrial Development & Regulation Act and by the priorities laid down within the framework of the Five-Year Plans. The entrepreneur, especially a new or small-scale one, would require comprehensive services on how to start an enterprise in India. He may or may not need a letter of intent; after he gets one, he has to take a series of steps to implement the project so as to qualify for the actual licence.

Then there are various sanctions and approvals of Government authorities before he can proceed further. If the project involves sophisticated technology not available within the country, the entrepreneur may require foreign technical collaboration, the terms and conditions of which require government approval. In addition to these formalities, steps would have to be taken to have a feasibility study or a market survey, if required, and a project report would be prepared in due course. The merchant banking institutions can assist the entrepreneurs in all these areas; and, after the project appraisal, formulate a plan for financing it. They can assist the clients in raising the funds they require. They ensure that the amount sought is reasonable. They do not themselves provide large resources for their function is mainly to act as sponsors and underwriters rather than a source of finance. They, however, lend their reputation to the issue which would make it easier to raise the money in the market. They act as intermediaries between the borrowers and lenders, and offer their services to both. They cultivate every class of client, particularly the medium and small business enterprises which are today greatly in need of these services. Maintaining a close and constant contact with clients, they acquire familiarity with their problems relating to, or arising from, the activities in which they are engaged. They advise the clients on the best method of raising capital and the best time in which to float their issues. Their advice, therefore, is not merely confined to actual issues but covers all the areas to ensure that their clients receive the necessary assistance in the financial management of their respective enterprises.

The sponsorship of the issue house helps in enlisting the confidence of the investor who would have to have the assurance that the issue was scrutinised by financial experts and was made on reasonable terms and under reputable clients who want to raise the money. They then consult the underwriters and brokers to the issue and recommend its floatation at the appropriate time so as to ensure its success in the market. This includes not only the issue of capital by a new enterprise but also assistance to a private company to go public, in reorganisation, acquisition or mergers and in generally negotiating the terms for them. The institution may take a minority position in financing an equity issue, but this is generally on a temporary basis. Its main role is that of an issue house and sometimes of the manager of a financial syndicate for specific issues. The institution, on the basis of its scrutiny of each project, designs and negotiates a financing package which meets the specific types and terms of financing required by it. It is not always possible for medium-sized businesses to float an issue in the market; but the issue houses can assist them privately with financial institutions on reasonable terms. The activities of the issue houses can be extended to sponsor offers for sale by foreign subsidiaries or branches which are not advised by the Government to bring down their holding to 40 per cent of the total equity capital.

The advisory service is in the nature of corporate counselling including matters regarding financial conditions, performance, and the prospects and needs of a corporate enterprise. In respect of mergers, acquisitions and reorganisations, the merchant bank helps in handling the actual operations. These services also include the provision of information to its clients on the developments affecting their business in India and abroad and the establishment of foreign contacts, whenever required. It may assist in the information and preparation of investment studies and proposals, tender advice on financial planning and control on management changes and needs. The projects to be sponsored and financed may include new projects of new companies; new projects of existing companies; and expansions and modernisation of existing companies. There is also the problem of financially weak or sick units. They require a thorough analysis of the causes of their sickness and recommendations on the remedial measures to be taken to restore them to normal health and viability. All these categories offer a promising market for the merchant bank's services.

With the exception of the firms of brokers registered with the stock exchanges, there is practically no investment advisory service in this country. The merchant banks in the United Kingdom maintain accounts of individual clients, which now run into several hundred millions and act as investment advisers to their clients. Some of the accounts are small or purely discretionary in the sense that the merchant bank is given the discretion to invest the money according to the instructions received from its clients. In India, there are thousands of persons in small and medium income groups who are unable to manage their funds and who sometimes fall victims to unscrupulous manipulators. It would be an excellent idea if a merchant banking institution agrees to maintain accounts from Rs. 25,000 and above and invest funds on behalf of their individual clients. This is not a highly remunerative operation, but would be of great benefit to small savers in the country. It should be remembered that, in the olden days, some of the commercial banks used to maintain accounts on behalf of their large clients — ruling princes, zamindars and wealthy merchants — and made investments in securities and shares on their behalf. Investment management would also include the management of provident funds, pension funds and trusts of various types. In due course, merchant banking divisions should set up genuine investment trusts having independent and flexible investment policies.

During the late seventies, it was evident that a number of industrial concerns were, during the period of recession, forced to work far below their installed capacity. As a consequence, many found it difficult to break-even; and some of them operated at a considerable loss. With the revival of demand for their products, some of these companies had their order books full, but were short of working capital. Many of them were soundly managed and financially viable concerns; but owing to the shortage of current finance, their operations were considerably hampered. In such a case, what was needed was a quick assessment of their financial requirements to help them tide over a temporary period of embarrassment so that they may execute the orders on hand and achieve a profitable working of their enterprises. In such cases, the merchant banking institution came forward to help them to obtain medium-term credit for three to five years from commercial banks or from financial institutions. Again, there are a number of cases in which manufacturing concerns require a medium-term loan for renovation and modernisation as well as for minor plant or balancing equipment which would enable them to increase production by 10 % to 25 per cent — an increase which is permissible without an industrial licence. At present, commercial banks advance a medium-term loan with refinance facilities from the Industrial Development Bank of India (IDBI). A new dimension has been added to the Government's export policy, under which construction and consultancy contracts, including turn-key jobs, by Indian firms in other countries, either on their own or in association with their counterparts in developed countries, are actively encouraged. This required short-term and medium-term finance for the supply of materials and for the purchase of equipment, if required. In addition, these firms would require support in terms of performance guarantees. The banks may consider giving these guarantees after assessing the risk in each case in association with the Industrial Development of India.

Merchant Banking in India

Till early 1960s, there was no merchant banking in the Indian Banking System. It was the Grindlays Bank which started merchant banking services as far back as 1967. After Grindlays Bank, other foreign banks like Citibank and Chartered Bank, started these services in India. Till 1970s, the main services rendered were management of share issues and sub-aspects of financial consultancies. In mid 1970s, there was a boom in the capital market with the introduction of "Foreign Exchange Regulation Act (FERA) (1973)." This created an awareness in the investing public about the capital market. This also encouraged a few commercial banks and financial institutions to set up merchant banking divisions. In addition, private financial brokers also started private merchant banking organisations. Today, the Merchant Banking set up in the country is broadly divided into the following groups:

1. *Foreign Banks*: Along with Grindlays Bank, Citibank, Chartered Bank and Hong Kong Bank are also active in merchant banking.
2. *Indian Banks*: State Bank of India took the lead among Indian banks and is at present well established in the merchant banking field. The other banks that followed suit are Bank of India, Central Bank of India, Bank of Baroda, Punjab National Bank, UCO Bank and Canara Bank which have established similar divisions at their respective head offices and other important centres.
3. *Private Merchant Bankers:* Leading private broker firms were already doing consultancy for Portfolio Investment. They took advantage of the situation and started 'Merchant Banking and Consultancy' services in a big way. Today, firms like J. M. Financial Consultants, Champaklal Investments and Financial Consultancy, V. B. Desai Consultants etc. are some of the leading private merchant bankers in our country.

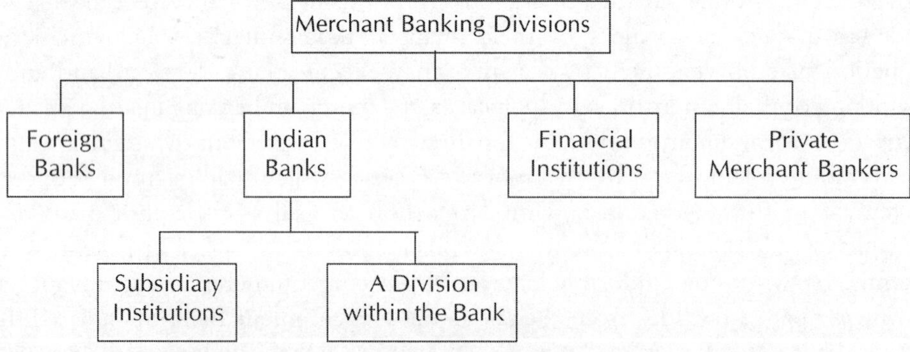

Fig. 6.1 Set-up of Merchant Banking in India

Financial Institutions: Industrial Credit and Investment Corporation of India (ICICI) has a well established merchant banking office. Recently, Industrial Reconstruction Corporation of India

(IRCI) has also started its merchant banking operations though its main concentration and attention is on mergers, amalgamations and takeovers.

In the early stages, the role of merchant banking in India was largely confined to the management of public issues of equity capital. This was due to the fact that several public issues (which came to be popularly known as FERA issues) came to the market at that time and there was, at that stage, an almost total absence of competent issue management services in the country. Today, the scope of merchant banking has gone much beyond just issue management. Banks' merchant banking divisions are now engaged in providing a wide spectrum of financial and related services to their customers.

Merchant banking activities: Merchant banking services in India cover a wide range of activities which are fund-based, non-fund based financial and investment services encompassing both capital as well as money market activities in domestic as well as in international financial markets.

The non-fund based activities include: Capital issues management and private placement of securities, loan/credit/fund syndication, corporate counselling, project counselling, NRI counselling, trusteeship management, portfolio management, management of mergers and amalgamations, management of Buy-ins and Buy-outs, financial engineering or capital restructuring, reorganisation, inter-corporate investment of funds, lease-broking, equipment procurement finance liaison, etc.

The fund-based activities include underwriting of equity/preference shares, bonds and debentures in new capital issues, dealing in money market instruments, like placement of commercial papers, certificates of deposits, treasure bills, transactions, etc. Undertaking equipment leasing, venture capital/fund activities, dealing in secondary market operations with or without stock exchange membership, inter-corporate placement of funds, etc.

All the above services do not fall within the regulatory framework of SEBI. According to the definition of the merchant banker given in clause (e) of rule 2 of Securities and Exchange Board of India (Merchant Bankers) Rules, 1992, the activities a merchant banker is expected to do include, 'the business of issue management either by making arrangements regarding selling, buying or subscribing to securities as manager, consultant, adviser or rendering corporate advisory service in relation to such issue management.'

The healthy growth of the capital market has necessitated the diversification and deepening of merchant banking activities. The sharpening of practices and professionalisation of management has widened the scope of merchant banking activities include:

Role of merchant bankers: The role of merchant banker is dynamic in the wake of diverse nature of merchant banking services. Merchant banker's dynamism lies in promptly attending to the corporate problems and suggest ways and means to solve it. The nature of merchant banking services is development oriented and promotional to help the industry and trade to grow and survive. Merchant banker is, therefore, dedicated to achieve this objective through his dynamism. He is always awake to renew his skills, develop expertise in new areas so as to equip himself with the knowledge and techniques to deal with emerging new problems of corporate business world. He has to keep pace with the changing environment where Government rules, regulations and policies affecting business conditions frequently change; where science and technology create new innovations in production processes of industries envisaging immediate renovations, diversifications, modernisations or replacements of existing plant and machinery or other equipments putting new demands for finances and necessitating overhauling of the capital structure of the firms. Merchant banker has to think and devise new instruments of financing industrial projects. He has to assume wider responsibilities of saving industrial units from going sick and guiding industries to be set up in industrially backward areas to eliminate regional imbalances in industrial development of the country. He has to guide the wider section of the community possessing surplus money to invest in corporate securities and other productive investment channels. He has to help the industry in different forms to ensure that it runs risk free and devoid of uncertainty by assisting the promoters with his knowledge and skills to resolve the problems being faced by them. He has to watch the interest and win over the confidence of the Government, its agencies, along with the entrepreneurs, the investors and the whole community. He must bridge the communication gap between different sections and resolve the problem being faced in different areas concerned with the business world. To discharge the above role, a merchant banker has to be dynamic. For this reason, a merchant banker is sometimes, called M.B., i.e., Moving Bottom, i.e., one who never sits at one place, always moving — attending meetings and meeting clients and constituents, doing business and getting business by attending meetings and conferences, imparting knowledge to others and acquiring new knowledge to maintain his supremacy in possession of latest information. His role depicts a personality cult which is unique and envious to be followed by others.

In the days ahead, merchant bankers have very significant role to play tuning their activities to the requirements of the growth pattern of corporate sector, the industry and the economy as a whole which is, in itself, a challenging task and to meet these challenges merchant bankers will have to be more vigorous and strategic in playing their role. They will have also to adopt new ways and means in discharging their role.

Challenges ahead: Merchant bankers have to tap the opportunities lying ahead with the developing pace of the economy. These opportunities arise in the form of challenges before the merchant bankers to test their skills, expertise and efforts to attune their activities with the programme of economic development of the country, adopt new instruments and innovative means of financing to meet the growing financial requirements of the corporate clients.

Project Finance

Once a client has decided upon the specific project he wishes to set up, the Merchant Banking Division provides a comprehensive package of services for financial structuring and funding. The Division works in close collaboration with the customer and the technical consultants for the preparation of a complete financial dossier; negotiates on behalf of the client with financial institutions and banks for the term finance, and assists him in the preparation of the complex loan documentation.

A project finance assignment fully tests the creativity of the merchant banker; and, quite often, the entire gamut of merchant banking services, including loan syndication, issue management, euro-currency financing and supplier or buyer credits are brought to bear on a single large assignment.

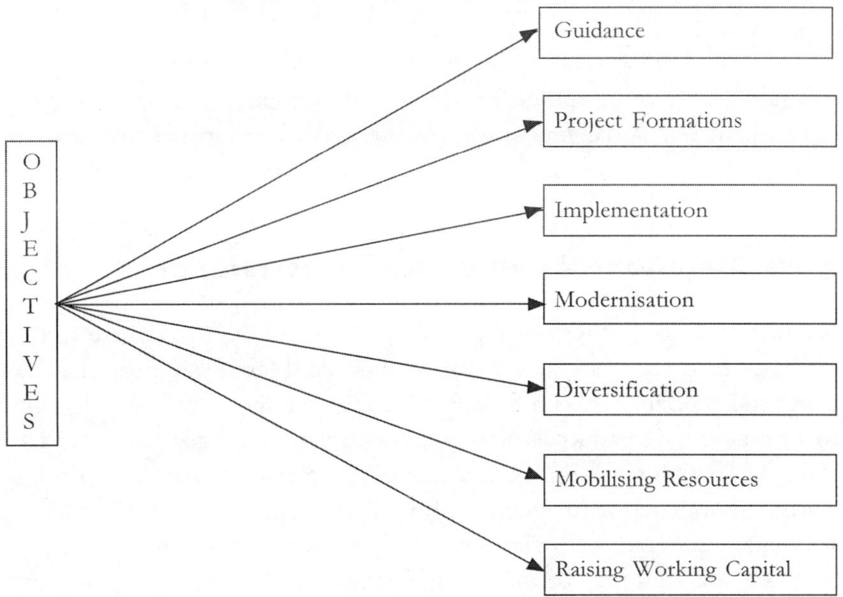

Fig. 6.2 Objectives of Merchant Banking

Corporate Finance

The pioneering role and expertise of the Merchant Division in the sphere of public issue management is well-known. This product has been important in the banks' portfolio of services; and its continuing importance seems assured in the foreseeable future in the context of the recent and welcome growth witnessed in the capital markets in India.

The involvement of the Merchant Banking Division with a public issue, be it of equity, convertible debentures or non-convertible debentures, includes the structuring of the issue, obtanining all approvals (including the consent of the Controller of Capital Issues), appointment of underwriters, brokers and bankers to the issue, preparation of the prospectus, and coordination of all the agencies concerned with clock-work precision.

The merchant banker's presence in all the major financial centres as well his long established relationships with the underwriter and broker fraternities, makes possible the high degree of synchronisation required to ensure the success of an issue.

Entrepreneur Starting a New Project

An entrepreneur who is the promoter of a new project first obtains a Letter of Indent (LoI) from the Government of India and then gets it converted into an Industrial Licence for setting up the proposed project. Generally speaking, the project report is ready and the company is incorporated, by the time the promoter approaches the merchant banker. Though, technically speaking, the promoter can take the help of the merchant banker for projects of any size, it is generally the projects costing over Rs.1 crore which are taken by the promoters to the merchant bankers.

Existing Units

Companies planning modernisation, expansion or diversification for their existing units need the help of merchant bankers. Amalgamation, absorption and reconstruction are some of the additional activities for which merchant banking assistance is availed of.

What Comprises Merchant Banking (MB) Assistance

For small size projects, a promoter can raise the required funds by recourse to the traditional source of finance, *viz.,* bank finance. However, for medium and large size projects, the promoters cannot exclusively depend on banks who normally do not give large term loans. In such cases, the promoters have to find alternative sources of finance which are all-India and state level financial institutions, international markets and the capital market. A merchant banker, who is in constant touch with these different sources of finance, can help these promoters effectively in funding the project. There is a wide range of activities which may be grouped under merchant banking assistance. Broadly, these activities may be divided under two heads, *viz.,* counselling and procuring finance. The main activities which are undertaken by a bank as merchant banking services are mentioned below:

1. *Project counselling or reinvestment studies for investors*: Under this head, a merchant banker is expected to:
   (*a*) identify promising projects,
   (*b*) prepare feasibility studies (economic and financial),
   (*c*) prepare indepth project reports,
   (*d*) assist investors in obtaining licences,
   (*e*) do precise capital structuring,
   (*f*) arrange and negotiate foreign collaborations and
   (*g*) give guidance on amalgamations, mergers and takeovers.
2. *Syndication of loans and project finance:* Once the project is identified and clearance is obtained from the Government departments, the undermentioned steps are to be taken:
   (*a*) Aid in applying to financial institutions, banks and other sources of finance.
   (*b*) Expert advice on government policies, demand-supply gaps, raw material availability, product-mix, plan capacity utilisation, requirements of plant and machinery and the like.
   (*c*) Consultation about alternative sources of finance, debt-equity ratios, 'over-run' finance.
   (*d*) Liaison with government departments, financial institutions, banks etc.
   (*e*) Advice and assistance for modernisation, expansion and diversification.
3. *Issue Management (including equity dilution):* Management of the public issue of shares/ debentures (or even an offer for sales) has been the traditional service rendered by

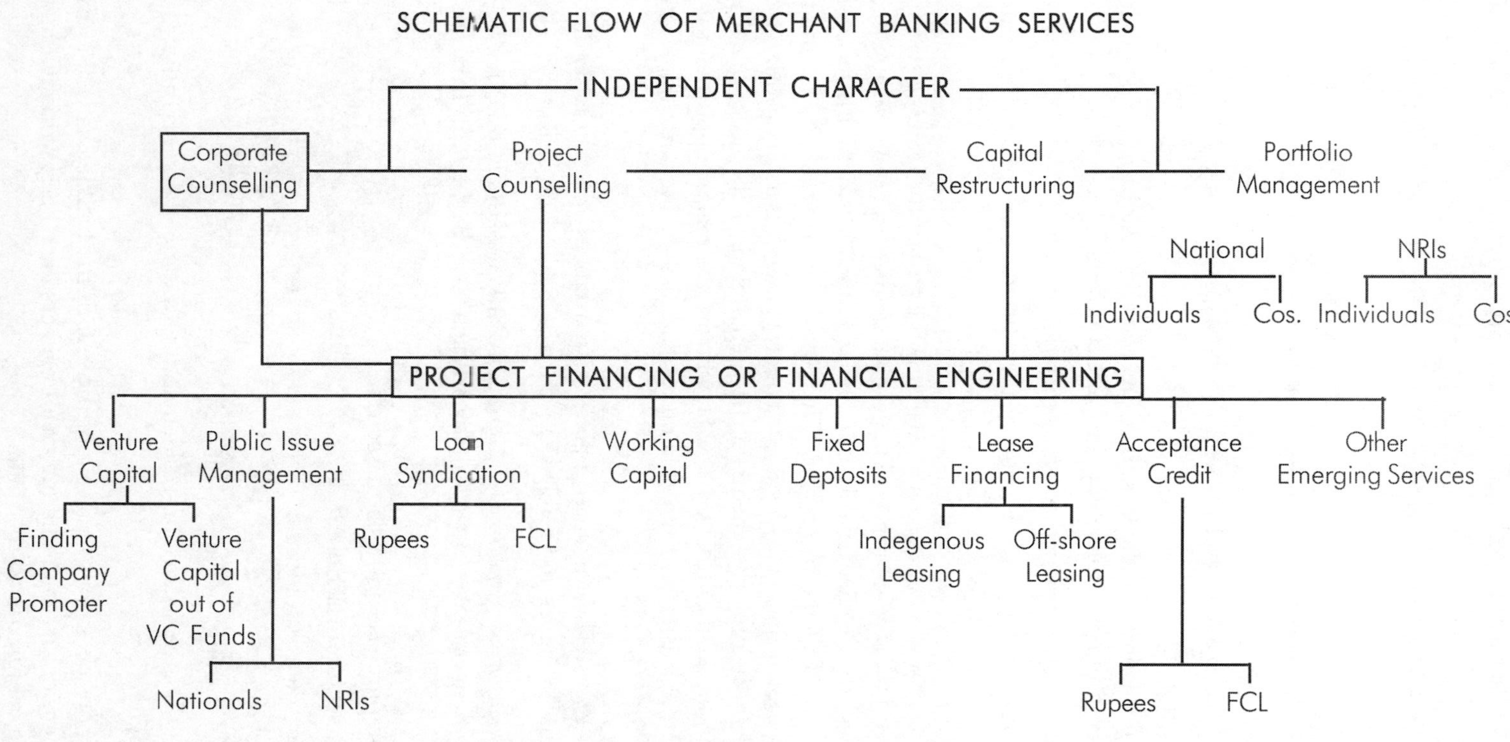

COs = Companies; NRIs = Non-Resident Indians; VC = Venture Capital; FCL = Foreign Currency Loans

Fig. 6.3

Merchant Bankers in India. Actually, with this service, the Merchant Banker was introduced in the Indian financial world. Following are the services rendered by the Merchant Banker under this head:

(*a*) deciding on the size and timing of a public issue in the light of the market condition,

(*b*) preparing the base of successful issue marketing from the initial documentation, liaison with the SEBI, stock exchange, Registrar of companies for clearances etc., to the preparation of the actual launch of the proposed issue,

(*c*) optimum underwriting support,

(*d*) appointment of bankers and brokers as well as issue houses,

(*e*) issue management,

(*f*) professional liaison with share market functionaries like brokers, portfolio managers and financial press for pre-selling and media coverage,

(*g*) preparation of draft prospectus and other documents,

(*h*) wide coverage throughout the country for collection of applications and

(*i*) preparation of advertising and promotional material.

4. *Provision of working capital*: Since Merchant Banking is a part of the banking system, the client has to be assisted in arranging for working capital finance especially for the new ventures. If the requirement of the client is substantially large, then it is desirable to arrange for the syndication on behalf of the promoters. There has been a recent change in arrangement for the working capital finance by issue of debentures on 'Rights' basis. Merchant Bankers play a great role in helping the clients in the preparation of the necessary forms for the financial institutions such as LIC, GIC, UTI, who are the major supporters for such issue. He arranges for the trustees for the debentures and also ensures that the balance portion is tied up with the other bankers.

5. *Foreign Currency Loans*: The merchant banker also arranges for export credit for various countries. He also arranges for foreign currency loan like Eurodollar, IFCI loans etc.

6. *Portfolio management for non-residents*: The Merchant Banker assists in this area by identifying suitable arrangements of investment suitable to each Non-Resident Indian. In short, these include:

(*a*) guidance on purchase and sale of securities

(*b*) handling of such transactions

(*c*) advice on market conditions

(*d*) safe custody of documents

(*e*) collection of earnings (dividend, interest etc.)

(*f*) service as a link between non-residents and Reserve Bank of India for obtaining necessary permission.

Besides this, leasing business is also being talked about in the banking as well as the financial sector. This is a new dimension in which the merchant bankers have been working on, and in fact, a few banks have already ventured into this field.

Moreover, marketing is also a very important function which the merchant banker has to take into account since he has to create the business for himself. He also has to have a close association with his own clients, understand their future expansion/modernisation programmes and advise them the way in which these programmes are to be carried out. His imagination and expertise plays a great role in this area.

He is also expected to be very active in finding out the new ventures opening up in the country. This information can be gathered from the Controller of Capital Issues, Registrar of Companies and State and Central financial institutions.

Project Counselling

If it consists of mere technical appraisal, the department makes use of the services of the Technical and Industrial Consultancy Division. Once convinced of the technical feasibility and commercial viability of the project, the merchant banker's next job is to prepare a *structure of finance.* To determine the structure of finance on the basis of different available sources, the department keeps in view:

(*i*) The norms laid down by term-lending institutions regarding the debt-equity ratio and the promoter's minimum contribution to the total cost of the project;

(*ii*) The availability of various backward area subsidies; and

(*iii*) In case of equity issue, the norms laid down by the stock exchanges for the listing of shares.

The structuring of finance also covers advice on setting up units in the 'joint sector', where state level financial institutions contribute 26% of the equity share capital, while the private promoter contributes 25% and the balance of 49% of the shares are made available to the public. On the other hand, in a 'state assisted unit', state financial institutions contribute 11%, the promoters 40% and the public 49% of the equity share capital. For listing purposes, stock exchanges require that the minimum 60% of the equity share capital should be offered to the public in case of units promoted by private promoters and 49% in the case of a joint sector or state assisted project.

Syndication of Term Loans

This involves the preparation and submission of applications to All-India financial institutions, such as:

IDBI — Industrial Development Bank of India

ICICI — Industrial Credit & Investment Corporation of India Limited

IFCI — Industrial Finance Corporation of India or to state level institutions, such as mentioned below:

SIICOM — State Industrial Investment Corporation of Maharashtra

GIIC — Gujarat Industrial Investment Corporation

MPAVN — Madhya Pradesh Audyogik Vikas Nigam Ltd.

PICUP — Pradeshiya Industrial Investment Corporation of Uttar Pradesh.

In case the above insitutions do not tie up the entire term loan requirement and leave some gap in the term loan, to fill such a gap the merchant banker turns to commercial banks. To finalise the cost of the project, he scrutinises the various items under capital cost and requires the following:

(*i*) Estimates of the cost of land and building;

(*ii*) The latest quotations for plant and machinery;

(*iii*) The estimates of preliminary and pre-operative expense;

(*iv*) The rate of interest on term loans during the construction period;

(*v*) Public issue expense;

(*vi*) Margin money for working capital, etc.

Once the total cost of the project is determined, a finance model is worked out, keeping in mind the norms of financial institutions regarding the debt-equity ratio (generally 2:1), the promoters' contribution (generally 17.5% to 20% of the project cost), etc. The syndication of the term loans not only covers rupee term loans but takes into account foreign currency loans for the import of capital goods, if any, under the line of credit available with the term-lending institutions. The assistance for raising foreign currency loans in the Euro dollar market is also given when the licence granted specifically permits the raising of such finances.

Management of Public Issue

This comprises assistance in:

(*i*) Obtaining the acknowledgement or consent of Controller of Capital Issues (CCI);

(*ii*) The tying up of underwriting of the issue as per requirement;

(*iii*) The preparation of the prospectus;

(*iv*) Grooming the issue to ensure full subscription;

(*v*) Obtaining compliance of the listing requirements of stock exchanges;

(*vi*) Appointing registrars to the issue, advertisers and printers, etc.

A strong liaison with stock broking firms is absolutely necessary for the successful management of public issues.

Underwriting of Public Issues

Generally speaking, a condition is stipulated by the CCI that all public issues should be underwritten. This being so, the merchant banker managing the public issues to the bank benefits as follows:

(*i*) The bank earns a commission on the commitment given;

(*ii*) Since these commitments are sub-underwritten by the bank with brokers, the bank's liaison with them improves; and

(*iii*) As a matter of right, the bank is appointed as the *banker to the issue concerned.*

Since banks are not interested in holding equity shares, it is necessary not only to choose underwriting very carefully but to sub-underwrite every underwriting commmitment of the bank to ensure that they do not devolve on it.

Bankers to the Issue

The bank can automatically get the assignment of bankers to the issues in the following cases:

(*i*) The bank is a banker to the company;

(*ii*) It has given the underwriting commitment;

(*iv*) It is acting as *managers to the issue.*

However, it may also, through the good offices of the promoter or the merchant bankers, get appointed as bankers to the issue, even in the absence of the above circumstances. As bankers to the issue, the work involved is to accept the applications for the shares and debentures and the amount thereof. The amount and the applications are transferred to the consent-giving branch which is also known as the *controlling branch.* Most banks have a branch which is the controlling branch. Other branches, too may have been given consent to act as bankers to the issue. Huge amounts are collected and retained by the bank, pending the allotment of shares, for two to three months at a nominal rate of interest in each issue. The bank can make a mark in this aspect of merchant banking; and this fact is acknowledged by almost all merchant bankers.

Who Can Secure Merchant Banking (MB) Assignments

In many banks, there is full-fledged Merchant Banking Department at the Head Office, which is often headed by an Assistant General Manager(AGM). In addition, there is a merchant banking cell, looked after by an officer of the metropolitan branch at Delhi, Kolkata, Chennai and Ahmedabad. Vigorous and aggressive efforts are made by the department and these cells to secure potential MB assignments. However, it is of utmost importance that these assignments are secured at the very initial stage of the project. Being in constant touch with corporate borrowers, the chief managers of industrial finance branches as well as exceptionally large branches and sometimes managers of large branches obtain early information on possible assignments for the proposed projects of their corporate borrowers or even non-borrowers. This information is conveyed immediately to either the cells or the merchant banking department. In fact, it is very essential to realise that securing assignments are the responsiblility of not only of the department or cells but of every officer of the bank.

How to Tap Merchant Banking Assignments

There are many sources which yield information on new ventures or expansion, diversification, modernisation programmes of existing units. Interviews with customers, new items, review of proposals — these are some ways in which information on possible MB assignments can be obtained. This information can also be obtained from the directors' reports which are published in the newspapers or in the annual reports of companies. The directors' reports invariably contain information on plans for expansion and on foreign collaboration, if any. Contact with customers at this initial stage can help in securing these assignments. As regards procuring underwriting business and assignments of bankers to the issue, it is helpful to contact other merchant banking agencies as well as brokers.

Scale of Fees

The scale of fees depends on the nature of services expected and the time schedule thereof. Apart from the likely man-hours spent on the assignment, the responsibility to be undertaken by the department in completing it is a vital determinant. In addition to the above, the department gives due weightage to the bank's past connections in case of existing customers and the future business potential in the case of new customers.

Advantages to the Bank

Securing merchant banking assignments has the following advantages:

(*i*) Contacts with new customers increase the advances portfolio with the possibility that ancillary business would accrue;

(*ii*) Earning by way of fees for technical appraisals, loan syndication, public issue managements as well as commission on bankers to the issue and underwriting assignments;

(*iii*) Collection of substantial funds by way of monies collected for the public issue held either in current account or in short-term deposits for 46 days.

Who Will Handle the Assignment

Merchant Banking assignments are normally handled by the department at the Head Office. The cells at Delhi, Kolkata, Chennai and Ahmedabad can also render possible assistance required by the customers. These cells may, in due course, be converted into full-fledged divisions in the zonal offices so that they may handle the assignments independently.

Sanctions Required

Though the preliminary discussions for possible MB assignments may be initiated without taking any sanctions, it is necessary to take the sanction of the head office. Committee for assignments of project counselling, loan syndication and management of public issues look into the applications before they are sent out to the various agencies. Normally, for a promoter who is creditworthy, and where the project is viable, there is no difficulty in obtaining the sanction of the Committee. All underwriting proposals upto Rs.10 lakh are taken to the Comittee for sanction, and for higher amounts, to the Board. For consent to act as bankers to the issue, the decision is taken by the Chief Manager in charge of ELB, regional manager or zonal manager. The decision is based on two factors, *viz.,*

(*i*) The branch should be authorised to collect application money, and

(*ii*) It should have the necessary infrastructure to take up the work.

Merchant banking has now secured a place in corporate plans and has received careful attention of the top management. Realising its importance, many nationalised banks have opened merchant banking departments. Even foreign banks and many brokers' firms are now operating in this field.

Specialised Banking

Besides ordinary banking, for which they compete with the commercial banks, the merchant banks operate in specialised fields to earn a substantial income by way of fees, dividend, commission, discount and brokerages on operations.

(*a*) *Syndication of loan:* A large, experienced and specialised staff is able to put through a package for the client's entire requirement of funds by syndicating the loan among various institutions.

(*b*) *Managing public issues:* In doing this, a whole range of legal and financial help is offered in putting through a prospectus, in underwriting arrangements for the public issue and stock exchange listing procedures.

(*c*) *Management of porfolio and institutional funds:* Most merchant bankers possess tremendous economic power by virtue not merely of the total assets that they have in their balance sheets but also because of the large institutional or private funds that they control or manage for a fee. They manage unit trusts, provident pension funds, and insurance company investments, and advise overseas governments and central banks. These fees fetch income for a merchant bank without any commitment of funds on its part.

(*d*) *Acquisition, mergers, takeovers:* With the frequent takeover bids and company raids, and the requirement to comply with statutory and other codes, the investor inevitably turns to the merchant banker for advice. Merchant bankers can give expert advice either for defence against takeover bids or for making takeover bids, acquisitions and mergers.

(*e*) *Project finance and export credits:* The merchant bank, with its overseas contacts and knowledge of different financial markets the world over, is able to put together very intricate packages whereby it brings together suppliers of machinery in the overseas country, prepares project and feasibility reports, offers pre-shipment credits for the suppliers and arranges term-loans for the buyers. It is able to co-ordinate the entire range of activities from the location of suppliers to the procurement of soft loans from government institutions to completion of all the necessary legal and financial arrangements.

(*f*) *Venture capital and bond dealings:* Many merchant bankers also provide venture capital by backing viable projects, and deal in the secondary market for government securities and Eurobonds.

Leasing: For a merchant banker, the search for new financing techniques is an unending one. The Merchant Banking Division of Grindlays Bank has played an important role in introducing leasing as a financially viable alternative source for capital acquisitions. The services offered by this division include arrangement for lease finance facilities for leasing companies, advice on the optimal structuring of the transaction, legal documentation and tax counselling. The bank's vast experience in this line ensures for its clients, both lessors and lessees, leasing transactions on the most favourable terms. There is, at present, a widespread public debate on whether commercial banks in India should be permitted to undertake leasing transactions as a part of their banking activity. Should the necessary policy changes be introduced, the entry of banks into the leasing business will give companies attractive alternative sources of financing and boost the leasing industry in India.

Supplier/Buyer Credits: For clients wishing to import capital goods from the UK, merchant banking divisions can arrange for supplier/buyer credits under the ECGD plan for export finance. Offers on the most favourable terms can be negotiated with the ECGD and the UK suppliers through Grindlays Brandts Ltd. in London. The ECGD credits are available for varying periods at fixed and concessional rates of interest. Similar government backed export credits can also be arranged from other countries such as France and Italy.

The Future

For the merchant banking division, the development of new services to meet the changing market conditions is an ongoing process. Today, the entire merchant banking industry in India is faced with the challenge of attracting Non-Resident Indian (NRI) investment into India, particularly under the scheme for portfolio investments through stock exchanges. Despite the several policy liberalisations which have been announced by the Government in the past year, the response from NRIs, to date, is far below expectations. One important reason for the poor response to the portfolio investment scheme is quite clearly the lack of information with the non-resident investor perturbed regarding the changing conditions in the Indian stock markets. The Merchant Banking Division is now in the process of introducing a comprehensive portfolio advisory service which will try to fill up this information gap, offer expert counselling on investment opportunities, undertake to buy/sell orders, periodically evaluate the portfolio, and look after all the administrative formalities, such as attending to tax returns, collections and remittances of dividend, etc., in compliance with the Reserve Bank of India's and Securities and Exchange Board of India (SEBI) guidelines.

Conclusion

Merchant banking essentially involves selling an issue for a company and handling related work. In the wake of liberalisation of the financial sector, we are seeing certain merchant banking prospects emerging — be it an Indian company or foreign or a multinational, playing in the primary and secondary markets competitively. They are the *prima donnas* of the primary stage. There are about 1200 merchant bankers in the country of which, the SEBI has granted registration to 790 merchant bankers in four different categories. SEBI also granted registration to 36 underwriters and 8 portfolio managers on the basis of its rules and regulations, 1993, upto the end of March, 1995. They compete on an average for about 1000 issues for about Rs. 15,000 crore every year. They act as lead managers, co-managers, issue managers, financial advisers, etc. The domination of the public sector continues, with seven of the top ten managers coming from its ranks. The mushroom growth of merchant banks has given rise to unethical means to sell shares. For a healthy growth of the market operation, the SEBI should enforce strict control on merchant banks and remove the weeds of manipulation and corruption in the market. Stipulation of proper checks and regulation will raise the confidence of investing public in the dynamic and vibrant market mechanism which will be in the larger interests of the society as well as of the economy.

The growth of the capital market in India in the 90s is mainly due to the key role played by the merchant banking divisions of leading development banks as well as commercial banks. In a way, the merchant banks have come to occupy an important place in the Indian financial scene with seven of the top ten merchant bankers coming from the development banks and other financial institutions. They dominate the market in providing professional service to the corporate sector. The future growth of the capital market depends, to a large extent, on the financial services made available by them.

In fact, merchant banks should replace brokers in trading, in course of time, so that the market operations will be beneficial both to the industrial sector and investors as well as other operators in the primary and secondary markets. And the merchants bankers should also pass on the profits to investors, depositors and shareholders equitably.

ANNEXURE - 1

SEBI GUIDELINES FOR MERCHANT BANKERS

1. Authorisation

Any person or body proposing to engage in the business of merchant banking would need authorisation by the Securities and Exchange Board of India (SEBI) in their prescribed format. This will also apply to those presently engaged in merchant banking activity, including as Managers, Consultants or Advisers to issues.

2. Authorised Activities

(*a*) Issue Management, which will inter alia consist of preparation of prospectus and other information relating to the issues, determining financing structure, tie-up of financiers and final allotment services relating to the issue.

(*b*) Corporate advisory services relating to the issue.

(*c*) Underwriting.

(*d*) Portfolio management services.

(*e*) Managers, consultants or advisers in the issue.

3. Authorisation Criteria

All merchant bankers are expected to perform with high standards of integrity and fairness in all their dealings. A code of conduct for merchant bankers will be prescribed by SEBI. Within this context, SEBI's authorisation criteria would take into account mainly the following:

(*a*) Professional competence.

(*b*) Personnel, their adequacy and quality, and other infrastructure.

(*c*) Capital adequacy.

(*d*) Past track record, experience, general reputation and fairness in all their transactions.

4. Terms of Authorisation

(*a*) All merchant bankers, including the existing ones, must obtain the authorisation from SEBI within three months from the issue of these guidelines. SEBI may extent this period at its discretion by a maximum of three more months.

(*b*) All merchant bankers must have a minimum net worth of Rs. one crore.

(*c*) The authorisation will be for an initial period of three years.

(*d*) SEBI may collect from the merchant bankers an initial authorisation fee, an annual fee and a renewal fee.

(*e*) All issues should be managed by at least one authorised merchant banker, functioning as the sole manager or the lead manager. Ordinarily, not more than two merchant bankers should be associated as lead managers, advisers and consultants to a public issue. In issues of over Rs. 100 crores, the number could go up to a maximum of four.

(*f*) The specific responsibilities of each lead manager must be submitted to SEBI prior to the issue.

(*g*) While directors, promoters and every person who authorises the issue of prospectus, shall bear full responsibility for the contents of the prospectus, merchant bankers shall exercise due diligence independently verifying the contents of the prospectus and reasonableness of the views expressed therein. The merchant bankers of the issue shall certify to this effect to SEBI.

(*h*) To ensure a direct stake of merchant banker(s) in the issue managed by them, lead managers would be required to accept a minimum 5%, underwriting obligation in the issue, subject to a ceiling. Details in this regard are prescribed by SEBI.

(*i*) Lead managers/merchant bankers would be responsible for ensuring timely refunds and allotment of securities to the investors.

(*j*) The involvement of merchant bankers in an issue should continue at least till the completion of essential follow-up steps, which must include the listing of the instrument, and despatch of certificates/refunds.

Even if many of these activities are handled by other intermediaries, merchant bankers shall be responsible for ensuring that these agencies fulfill their functions, and must enable themselves to discharge this responsibility through suitable agreements with the issuer company.

(*k*) The merchant banker shall make available to SEBI such information, documents, returns and reports as maybe prescribed, and called for.

(*l*) SEBI shall prepare and prescribe a Code of Conduct for merchant bankers which they should adhere to.

(*m*) SEBI may suspend/cancel the authorisation of merchant bankers for a suitable duration in case of violations of the Guidelines.

(*n*) Nothing in these Guidelines shall exempt the company, its functionaries, or others from any responsibility placed on them by any existing law, regulation, guidelines or conditions imposed with any sanction.

ANNEXURE - 2

FINANCIAL SERVICES BY MERCHANT BANKS

Merchant banking institutions have brought together a multitude financial services with the singular objective of proving tailor-made services to suit the clients' needs. The varied financial services offered by the merchant bankers are as follows:

A. Advance against Shares
Advisors to Euro Issues
Arranging Mergers and Acquisitions
Arranging Syndication
Assets Syndication
Auto Finance

B. Bills Discounting
Bought-out Deals
Bridge Loan/Finance
Business Law Consulting

C. Capital Structuring/Restructuring
Corporate Finance
Corporate Advisory Services
Corporate and Personal Taxation
Corporate Planning
Consumer Financing
Corporate Financial Restructuring

D. Direct Investment
Discounting of Commercial Papers

E. Equipment Leasing
Equity Brokerage
Equity Derivatives
Equity Participation
Equity Research
Euro-issue Advisory Services

F. Fairness Opinion Reports
Financial Consultation
Fixed Deposits

Foreign Exchange
Foreign Exchange Advisory Services
Foreign Investment Consulting
Fund Mobilisation

H. Hire-Purchase
Human Resource Planning

I. Inter-Corporate Deposits
International Financial Advisory Services
International Taxation
Integrated Financial Services
Issue Management
Issue Marketing & Private Placement
Investment Banking
Investment Management
Investment Service

L. Leasing
Leasing Syndication
Loans against Shares and Securities
Loan Syndication

M. Management of Public Rights Issues
Marketing of Primary Market Issues
Merchant Banking Services
Mergers and Acquisitions
Mergers and Amalgamation
Money Changers
Money Market Operations

N. NCD Placement
NSE Operations

O. Organising Foreign Currency Loans and Equity
Organising Funding
OTCEI Finance
OTC Operations

P. Personal Finance
Portfolio Management
Project Advisory Services
Project Appraisals
Project Counselling
Placement of Equity & Debt
Placement with Mutual Funds
Project Finance
Private Placement of Securities
Public Deposits
Privatisation

R. Registrars and Share Transfer Agents

S. Securities and Stocks Trading
Share Shops
Stocks and Securities Broking
Stock Market Operations

Structuring of Means of Finance

Syndication

T. Term Loans

U. Underwriting.

ANNEXURE – 3

MERCHANT BANKING SERVICES

The banks offer package financial arrangement and assitance to small-scale industries in their promotional and expansion activities and act as banker to capital issues. The banks —

- study the economic viability and technical feasibility of the proposals and help in preparation of market survey reports with the assistance of technical consultants;
- provide assistance to entrepreneurs in obtaining various government consents required for industrial projects right from the time the application for letter of intent is made;
- assist the entrepreneur in raising rupee resources in the form of debentures, term loans, deferred payment guarantees from financial institutions;
- assist in raising foreign exchange resources required for import of plant and machinery, components, raw materials, etc., by arranging through the Bank's foreign correspondents, suppliers' credit, buyers' credit and foreign currency loans;
- determine capital structure, assist obtention of consent of Controller of Capital Issues, finalisation of syndication of underwriting arrangements, handling of share applications and relative allotment in consultation with stock exchange;
- finance export of capital equipment on deferred payment terms;
- manages public issues for raising capital, helps establish liaison with government lending bodies for raising long-term development finance, assesses the strengths and weaknesses of the company through management audits and suggests tailor-made solutions to eliminate the weaknesses;
- provides practical training in the line, if necessary;
- provides assistance in obtaining government clearance, procurement of machinery and equipment and marketing of products;
- extends assistance and guidance in implementation of the project.

A novel feature of the scheme is that the bank will provide from a panel of industrialists a 'foster father' to guide and assist the budding entrepreneurs.

Entrepreneurial Assistance by Banks

Many of the scheduled commercial banks provide counselling to industry, mostly in the small-scale and a few of them provide merchant banking services to the corporate sector. Besides, providing working capital, banks play a key role in entrepreneurial assistance and development.

New Entrepreneur Development Agency

1. *Scope.* New Entrepreneur Development Agency is established to assist educated unemployed graduates to set up Small-Scale Industrial Units in urban and metropolitan areas.

2. *Identification and selection of entrepreneurs.* Sponsorship of Government Institutions and Agencies like Small Industries Service Institute (SISI), University Employment Guidance Bureau, Directorate of Industries and Commerce (DICs) and such other agencies is essential. The candidates, thus identified, will be interviewed by a panel of experts for final selection.

3. *Selection of projects.* The selected candidates will be provided with identified project profiles and will be assisted in selecting the projects suitable to their aptitude and backgrounds.

4. *Training.* The candidates on identifying the projects will undergo training under the Entrepreneur Development Programme to be conducted by Agencies like SISI, ITCOT etc. Practical training will also be arranged in industries, wherever possible.

5. *Marketing tie-up.* The candidates will be assisted in getting marketing tie-up with user industries, wherever possible.

6. *Size of the project.* Projects with credit requirements upto Rs. 5.00 lakhs are only eligible for finance under this scheme. 100% finance will be provided in the beginning and the margin will be built up to 20% over a period of time, depending on the profitability envisaged.

7. *Security.* Assets created with bank finance and personal guarantee of the parents wherever necessary.

8. *Repayment.* Repayment of term loans will be based on the profitability projection and within 7 years.

9. *Registration.* The units will have to be registered as Small Scale Industries with the DICs or the District Industries Centers as the case may be.

ANNEXURE – 4

THE THEORETICAL PARADIGM OF THE ROE MODEL

The risk-return model splits the overall bank performance into two components: (i) return on equity (RoE) and (ii) risk. The second component, i.e., risk explains the variability in RoE. The RoE model can be divided into three stages as under:

Stage I

The RoE measures bank accounting profits per rupee of book equity capital, and is defined as 'net income' divided by 'average equity.' Thus,

RoE = Net Income/Average Equity* ... (1)

Dividing both the numerator and the denominator by 'average assets', equation 1 can be re-written as:

RoE = (Net Income/Average Assets) × (Average Assets/Average Equity) or, RoE = Return on Assets (RoA) × Equity Multiplier (EM) ... (2)

where, the RoA is defined as 'net income' divided by 'average total assets' and measures bank profits per rupee of assets, and the EM is defined as 'average assets' divided by 'average equity', and measures a bank's leverage or the rupee amount of assets pyramided on the bank's base of equity capital. The EM is nothing but the reciprocal of the capital/asset ratio.

A bank's EM compares assets with equity and large values indicate a large amount of debt financing related to equity. EM thus measures financial leverage and represents both a profit and a risk measurement. EM affects bank's profits because it has a multiplier impact on RoA to determine bank's RoE. It is also a risk measure because it reflects how many assets can go into default before a bank becomes insolvent.

Stage II

Stage II of the RoE decomposition analysis splits the RoA further into two components. From above,

RoA = Net Income/Average Assets ... (3)

Dividing both the numerator and the denominator by 'Total Income', equation 3 can be re-written as:

RoA = (Net Income/Total Income) × (Total Income/Average Assets)

= Profit Margin (PM) × Asset Utilization (AU) ... (4)

Where, the PM is defined as 'net income' divided by 'total income' (both interest and non-interest income), and measures profits per rupee of total income, and the AU is defined as 'total income' divided by 'average total assets', and measures total income per rupee of assets. Thus, equation 2 can be re-written as under:

RoE = PM × AU × EM ... (5)

The advantage of this method is that one can pinpoint the basic variables that determine the RoE performance. The RoE model contains three alternative measures of profitability, i.e., RoE, RoA and PM, which have the same numerator, i.e., net income, but different denominators, i.e., average equity, average assets and total income, respectively, and thus provides different perspectives on profitability analysis.

Stage III

Stage III further decomposes both the PM and AU. Each component of Stage III is analyzed with respect to a bank's 'total income' or 'total assets.' For example, it is possible to look at wages and salaries per rupee of income or assets. The objective of Stage III analysis is to identify symptoms of good or bad performance by focussing on trends and significant peer-group differences. This facilitates identification of the proximate causes for poor performance as also formulation of appropriate remedial measures.

* Since net income, reported on annual basis, is a "flow" variable, and assets and equities, reported as at the financial year-end, are "stock" variables, to ensure stock-flow compatibility, the "stock" variables have been averaged out. A two-year moving average has been taken for the purpose.

Sources: Sinkey, Joseph F. (Jr.) (1999), 'Commercial Bank Management, 4th edition. pp. 269-278. Taxmann (1999), 'Practical Guide to Instructions of the Reserve Bank of India for Banks and Banking Operations', Volume 1, p. 99.

Efficiency Indicators of Top 25 Global Banks

Efficiency Indicator	*Average (Median)*	*Range*
Capital/Assets Ratio	4.98	2.06-7.56
Real Profit Growth	25.7	(–) 217.1-2070.8
Profit on Average Capital	13.45	(–) 1.0-35.6
Return on Assets	0.52	(–) 0.05-2.22
Cost/Income Ratio	68.33	54.04-98.03
BIS Capital Ratio	11.46	8.9-19.10
Non-Performing Loans to Total Loans	2.4	0.3-14.86

Source: The Banker, July 2000, p. 178.

Note: (1) For some of the banks, data relate to 31.12.1999 and for others data relate to 31.3.2000. (2) There are conceptual differences between the indicators as exist in the case of global banks in India. Therefore, the above-mentioned data can at best be treated as approximations.

Chapter 7

BANKING INNOVATIONS

Introduction

The current phase of the banking cycle appears to be driven by the downturn in economic activity rather than financial distress. Significantly, the largest financial institutions are among those affected by credit concerns. The slowdown in the demand for financing has been aggravated by deterioration in the quality of portfolios on the assets side and the consequent tightening of lending norms. All this has rendered the short-term outlook uncertain. The silver lining in the otherwise somber global macroeconomic and financial situation has been Asia which has been experiencing a stronger than expected recovery. Although equity markets have exhibited a decline, most countries of the region have retained access to international capital markets and international bank lending.

Worldwide financial systems have undergone structural changes. The global factors driving these changes have been advancements in technology and computing, external financial liberalisation and organisational changes in corporate world. Banking and finance in emerging economies has been no exception. But the structural shifts in these economies have been motivated by their country's specific factors also including macro economic pressures, disintermediation pressures and banking crisis of 1990s. These developments have been instrumental in formation of a 'Global Village' making the dividing line between financial products, types of financial institutions and their geographical locations as irrelevant. Globalisation of banking operations and expansion of financial activities as a result of technology advancements, in an increasingly market-driven environment have redefined the business models and changed the way the banks used to do the banking business. The banking industry has virtually seen a shift from brick and mortar banking to banking virtually across time zones, geographical reach and alternative delivery channels.

Indian banking has also come a long way in absorption of technology. Beginning from the installation of ALPMs, banks have moved fast to optimize IT resources. IT is no longer limited to new generation private sector banks, even PSU banks have adopted it in a big way. Technology has become an "enabler" and is moving on to become a "driver" of business.

The Indian economy has recently been exhibiting signs of staying ahead of global activity. Some signs of cyclical recovery are currently evident, although border tensions, a relatively weak and uneven monsoon and concerns relating to the fiscal position are downside risks restraining a fuller surge of growth.

Further, rapid globalisation and increased competitiveness has forced banking innovations in a diversified ways.

Innovation Concept

Innovation means the introduction or application of something new — either new goods and services or new ways of producing them. Innovation differs from invention in one essential respect. An invention is the discovery of something new, whereas an innovation is the actual introduction or application of something new. Entrepreneurs and producers must innovate and adopt new methods and ideas to increase their productive capacity and improve working conditions, thereby raising production and consequently the national income. Innovation is, therefore, an important factor responsible for a country's economic development.

Innovation in Banking

Innovations in banking have become the order of the day and the concept of a bank as a mere manager of liquidity belongs to the past. New services, both credit and non-credit ones, have been introduced and existing services developed by banks throughout the world as they meet increasing competition for business from within the banking industry and from without, fill gap in their range of services or try to steal a march over their competitors by endeavouring to satisfy the needs of their present and potential customers demanding more flexible, advantageously priced and comprehensive facilities. Apart from selective introduction of modern technology to speed up banking operations requiring an increasing degree of sophistication, there will be changes in the composition of banking business reflecting the changes is occurring in trade and industry. The banks, the world over, are becoming financial supermarkets in which a wide variety of services can be purchased and often conduct business that do not always resemble banking.

Many significant changes are taking place in our country in response to changes in national and international economic environment. These changes have also affected the financial sector and are forcing it to move towards a deregulated and more competitive environment. A marked feature of the financial system in the decade of 1980s has been changes which have occurred in the institutional framework and financial instruments. When viewed in historical context, such has been the pace of change which has occurred in the financial systems of developed countries and more particularly in the U.K. and U.S.A. in the last two decades and particularly in the recent years that it is frequently referred to as constituting a "revolution of financial services." Whether this description is an appropriate one is a matter on which opinions differ but nevertheless, observers of the financial system have identified a number of major interlocking trends which have changed and are changing the institutional characteristics of the financial system.

Simultaneously, the trends towards diversification by banks abroad, particularly by those banks which have branches in India and are trying to introduce innovations in their business activities in India so as to enable them to have a higher market share, inevitably had its impact on Indian banks. The demand for diversified financial services was also created by the structural changes that have taken place in the Indian economy over the last decade, as shown below:

(*i*) the share of primary and secondary vectors in national income declined and the share of service sector increased;

(*ii*) the salaried middle class has risen fast and they are in need of financial assets with higher income growth potential than usual commercial bank deposits;

(*iii*) the strategy of accelerating the pace of development has been undertaken by giving an impetus to increased consumption of industrial products through tax concessions and other means; and

(*iv*) the industrial growth appears to be largely anchored to the consumption needs of urban middle class which has emerged with much potential demand for variety of financial services.

The process of disintermediation is part of the process of meeting the financial asset needs of the customers coming from the urban middle class. Many of the financial services offered by banks are oriented towards this class of customers. Diversification in this direction will be largely successful because here commercial banks with their urban orientation are in their home ground. Moreover, following the example of international banks, many Indian banks have tried to shift from traditional business to fee producing business as a step towards their efforts to innovate, adopt new market strategies and diversify.

Innovative Financial Services

The eighties have been years of exciting and progressive change in the banking business emerging from disintermediation process that has set in and consequential diversification being resorted to by banks in India in a big way. Pursuant to this, certain new non-conventional and sophisticated services, based on customer conveniences and preferences, have been added to the banking arena. Significant among those are housing finance, hire-purchase, leasing, factoring, merchant banking, mutual funds, consumer loans and venture capital finance, being provided by banks on their own or through subsidiaries set up exclusively to look after and manage these new areas of business. Some of these activities were there earlier too, but they have got a major fillip with more entrants into the business due to increased opportunities perceived or with certain liberalisation measures in these lines of activities.

Apart from the above, we are experiencing computer revolution and many other important innovations such as introduction of new financial instruments like certificates of deposits, commercial paper, participation certificates and cheques and credit cards, to cope with the emergent competitive environment. Besides, investment management including investment counselling and tax services are also evolving innovative packages to meet consumer demands.

Further, in view of the growing equity culture in the economy, banks may have to become active in distributing stock and shares, debentures and bonds even their own depositors. We also find corporate sector companies branching out as finance companies, undertaking a vast array of financial services.

Several banks have expanded their overseas operations and have undertaken financing the import-export business of their clients in a professional manner, many times competing with large international banks. The international banking scene has undergone drastic changes, with the introduction of computer and telecommunication technology, which have led to geographical and financial integration of international financial market in recent years. International banks have diversified their business into capital market operations since new profit opportunities have been noticed in this field. Responding to these changes in the international environment commercial banks in India have also been trying to diversify in such areas as consumer credit, credit cards, travellers' cheques, etc. It is, however felt that we should not aim at something which is not in our competence and that overseas bank offices should be used more as centres for information for exports.

Retail Loans

Retail loans are comparatively high-yielding and safer, as risk is diversified among a large number of separate individuals, located across the geographic dimensions, as wide as the network of bank branches. Besides this, retail loan offer handsome miscellaneous income by way of upfront fees as against corporate loans with no or negligible upfront fees. Retailing also offers further opportunities to cross-sell various other retail products like credit cards, insurance products, mutual funds and demat facilities to the depositors.

In the recent past, banks, irrespective of their size, have been increasingly focusing on retail segment for both, resource mobilization and lending. The retail market/banking, which was the stronghold of non-banking financial institutions has now attracted the attention of banks, including nationalized banks. Now, realizing the importance and also the necessity, banks in India are busy evolving strategies to tap this emerging retail banking market.

The Concept of Retail Banking

Retail banking is about providing banking services to individuals and joint individuals as opposed to wholesale banking, which focuses on industry and institutional clients. The concept of retail banking is not new to the banks. Retail banking is now being viewed as an attractive market segment, which offers opportunities for growth with profits. It is only in the recent times, that it has attracted special attention of the banks as a solution to some of their immediate concerns. The essence of retail banking lies in individual customers. While retail banking and retail lending are often used synonymously, but as a matter of fact, latter is just one side of the retail banking. In retail banking, all the banking needs of the individual customers are taken care of in an integrated manner. Though retail banking encompasses all types of individual customers, often banks tend to focus on high networth individuals. Retail banking portfolio encompasses deposit and asset-linked products as well as other financial services offered to individuals for personal consumption.

Retail Banking Products and Services

Though a wide-range of retail banking products and services are being offered by banks, which cover both the deposits and the advances, major products offered under retail lending to suit various segments of customers like salaried persons, businessmen, traders, professionals, technocrats, pensioners, labourers, etc., are: housing loans, personal loans, educational loans, vehicle loans, loan for consumer goods, credit and debit cards, global and international cards, loans for holidays, insurance products, gold loans, event loans, etc.

Thus, the banks are offering all the life-cycle products under their 'cradle to grave' strategy to take care of all the credit needs of individuals.

Retail banking products for depositors in various segments, like children, housewives, salaried class, professionals, technologists, pensioners, etc., include: Flexi Deposit Accounts, Savings Banks Accounts, Recurring Deposit Accounts, Other Short Term Deposits.

Banks are coming out with more and more features to add value to retail banking products and services. Few value-added services being offered by banks are:

- Free collection of specified member of outstation instruments per month.
- Instant credit of outstation cheques.
- Concession in commission/exchange for issuance of pay orders of demand drafts.
- Issuance of free cheque books.
- Concession in commission/exchange for issuance of pay orders or demand drafts.
- Issuance of free ATM cards.
- Waiver of credit card issuance fees.
- Issuance of free Add-on cards to members of the cardholder's family.
- Execution of standing instructions of customer.
- Free investment advisory services.

Other retail banking services offered by banks include:

- Payment of utility bills like electricity, telephone and water bills on due dates.
- Payment of monthly/quarterly education fees of children.
- Payment of insurance premium on due dates.
- Demating of shares, debentures and bonds.
- Selling of insurance products.
- Housing Finance.

Micro-Financing

Micro-financing is being practiced world over to combat the menace of poverty. In India it has become well accepted. There are numerous variants of micro finance as prevalent in the country today. These may differ in modalities but the basic premise on which they work is to offer financial services to the poor who have been unorganized and neglected by the financial sector thus far since they are perceived as un-bankable. One of the systems of that has been widely adopted is the linkage through SHGs. In fact, a large number of developing nations has tried this approach for poverty amelioration. Micro financing is a tool to empower the poorest, particularly village women, by improving their lot through micro finance. Its design is quite inspiring and recovery rate is almost cent-percent. Emboldened by the success of NABARD's experiment of linking SHGs and also that of various financial institutions in other developing countries, the banking sector in India adopted SHG concept.

BOX 7.1

RETAIL BANKING

"The only reason a great many American families don't own an elephant is that they have never been offered an elephant for a dollar down and easy weekly payments."

Mad Magazine

Personal Loans Dominate

Personal loans other than home loans have been outperforming even housing loans of late. Data released by the Reserve Bank of India shows that personal loans (other than housing) topped the various categories of loans advanced by banks during 2003-04. Bankers say that the trend is likely to be the same in 2004-05 as well. The latest Basic Statistical Returns of Scheduled Commercial Banks in India reveals that loans worth Rs.8,80,312 crore were disbursed by commercial banks during 2003-04. On top of the list were other personal loans, which amounted to Rs.89,537 crore. Home loans came in a close second at Rs.85,346 crore.

Shopping Patterns

The shopping patterns are changing rapidly across India. In 1999, for instance, Indian consumers spent a full 44 per cent of their income on grocery, followed by 9 per cent on books, music, movies and entertainment and 8 per cent on eating out. Savings took away another 14 per cent, and clothing and consumer durables, 11 per cent. Five years later in 2003, Indians have clearly emerged as big-ticket spenders, with savings and investments as proportion of incomes down to a mere 5 per cent. And where are they spending their bucks? More than 14 per cent on books, music, movies and entertainment, 13.5 per cent on clothing and consumer durables, and almost 11 per cent on eating out.

Meanwhile, according to retail researchers, over half of the shopping in India takes place between five and eight in the evenings, whereas shopping for heavy-ticket item is done generally on weekends.

Source: Times News Network

That's where one has to take a comprehensive approach. There is no single instrument. Different instruments have different lags. That's where one aspect is the self-help and the microcredit scheme. One could think of those as instruments that can increase well-being of the rural sector very rapidly, if programmed well. It may not be the basis of the long-term solution to the development problem, but it could be an important stage in the process. In other words, the woman who is able to supplement her income by raising chickens or vegetable gardens can have her income increase two-three fold very quickly, say from $300 to $800. It's very little, but it's a massive change in quality of life. They'll harness the human capital and her children would then be able to make the transition into the full-fledged market economy. Raising chickens in villages isn't the basis for long-term strategy for development, but it's a step in the transition. One has to see them not as the end point but a stage. You can't ignore the other stages — with all this focus on microcredit, you have to also focus on the small and medium enterprises.

Plastic Smiles: Credit-Debit Cards

The payment industry is undergoing a mixed transformation. At end-March 2004, the number of credit cards stood at 10 million, up by 37 per cent over the previous year. By the end of 2006, this will be somewhere close to 20 million. India has emerged among the fastest growing markets in the world. The credit card market is not confined to the bigger cities any more.

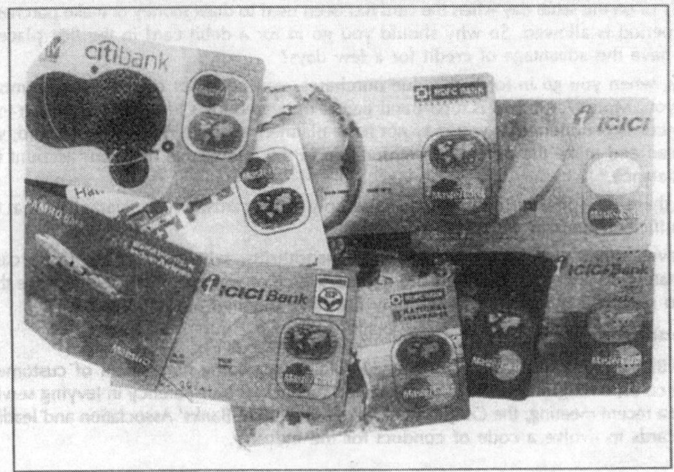

Fig. 7.1

In the cards business, ICICI Bank is in 67 cities, SBI in 41 cities followed by HDFC Bank in 23 cities and Stanchart in 18 cities.

Fig. 7.2

Debit cards, on the other hand do not allow credit. Your account is usually debited immediately or on the same day when the card has been used to draw money or make purchases. No credit period is allowed. So why should you go in for a debit card in the first place, if you don't have the advantage of credit for a few days?

Firstly, when you go in for high-value purchases, you need not carry huge amounts of cash with you. Moreover, travel is a part and parcel of everybody's life today. During a tour, you may incur expenditure that you may not have planned earlier. With the credit card, you can go ahead and make the purchase, comfortable in the knowledge that your account has sufficient balance.

BOX 7.2

CREDIT CARDS

• The Jet Airways Citibank Gold Credit Card is a complete travel card. The annual membership fee for the primary card is Rs. 2,500. One can also get add-on cards for five members of one's family absolutely free. Cardholders are automatically enrolled in the Jet Privilege (JP) programme and will be able to combine the JPMiles you earn on your card with your JP membership account. This is how it works: you earn four JPMiles for every Rs.100 charged to the Gold card. And like any credit card, it can be used to pay for hotel tariffs, car rentals, meals at restaurants or when you shop. In other words, you will keep earning JPMiles even when you are not flying.

• StanChart offers 5 per cent and 6.5 per cent off on the basic fares for domestic and international air travel, respectively. One can book air and rail tickets over the phone and charge them to the credit card. Although this is only in select cities, there is free home delivery of tickets and attractive car hire rates as well as foreign exchange and documentation services that have also been thrown in.

• The State Bank of India and the Tata group have introduced the Tata credit card. Under the Tata Privilege Programme, credit card holders can avail of benefits from the Tata group companies like Tata Motors, Titan, Tanishq, Voltas, Tata AIG.

• The 'StanChart's Cricket Card' enables you to book tickets for cricket matches. There are also double reward points on any transactions made on the card on the day after India wins any one-day international match. The annual fee is Rs.1,500 for four years. The annual fee for each supplementary card is Rs. 350 and add-on card is Rs.400.

• Thomas Cook has introduced a 'GlobalMoney Card.' The card allows one to withdraw cash in the local currency from global VISA ATMs and to pay for goods and services across the world. It is issued by State Bank of India (SBI) and backed by VISA. All you need to do is load your funds into the card before you travel. You can choose to load funds in US dollars, euro or pounds.

• The Yes Bank International Gold Card is the first debit card in India to offer zero per cent surcharge on petrol bills across any petrol pump resulting in a saving up to 2.5 per cent of the transaction value. Yes Bank customers will also benefit from 10 per cent off on domestic holidays through SOTC, easy bookings to over 600 hotels and 3 per cent off on air tickets booked through Sita travels amongst others.

• ICICI Bank and Big Bazaar-promoted by Pantaloon-have launched ICICI Bank-Big Bazaar Gold credit card. Customers will earn six reward points instead of one, for every Rs.100 spent through the card to make a purchase at any of the Big Bazaar outlets. A welcome Gift Voucher of Rs. 250 will be redeemable at Big Bazaar on one-time spends on the card of Rs.500. Moreover, on purchase of Rs.1,500 and above, the co-branded card customer will have an option to pay back the amount in three equal monthly installments, without incurring any financing charges. The bank has also launched "Free for Life" credit cards. The annual fee on all ICICI Bank cards has been waived. The bank has said that this facility will be applicable retrospectively to all its existing credit cards customers.

Also, there are some institutions that issue only debit cards, which guarantees that the user has sufficient funds in his account.

However, credit cards are hazardous for spendthrifts, who tend to use these cards indiscriminately. In a way, credit cards are a great source of wastage of money because they tempt us to go in for purchases that we may not have planned or do not need.

A Big Headache

The RBI has been receiving scores of complaints regarding harassment of customers, unsolicited cards, wrongful activation of cards, and the lack of transparency in levying service charges. The

BOX 7.3

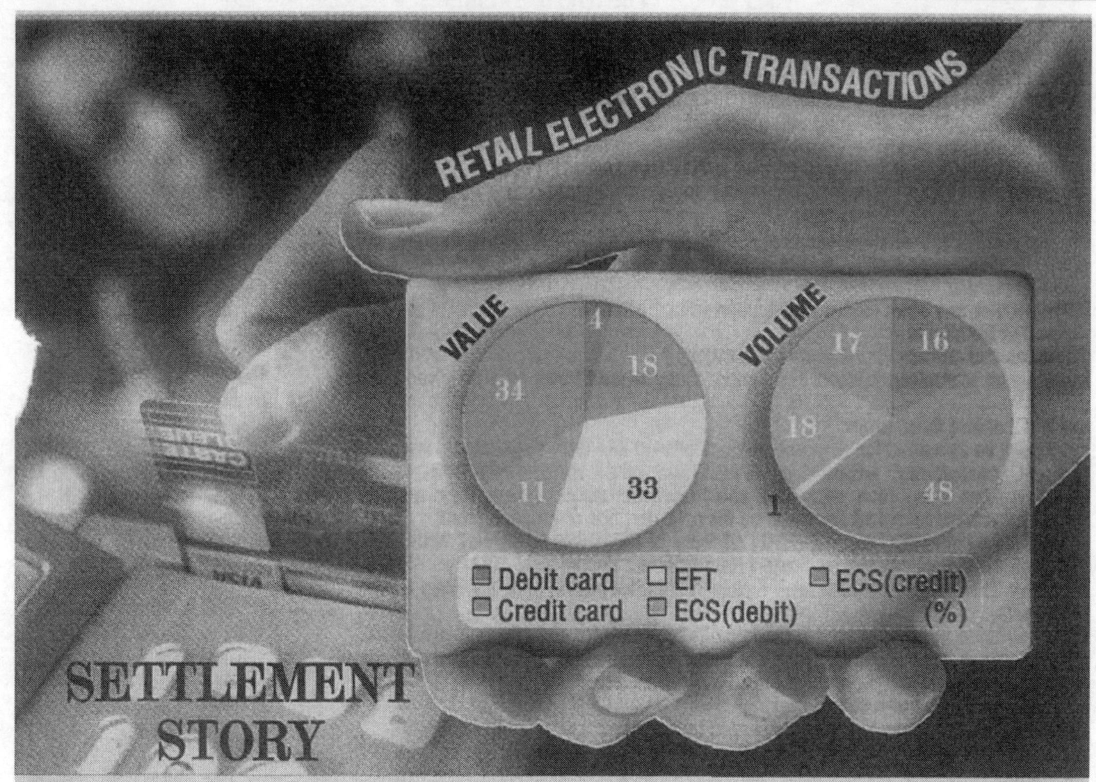

Central Bank asked the Indian Banks' Association and leading issuers of cards to evolve a code of conduct for the industry.

One big headache is that there is no control over direct sales agents (DSA) and also collection teams. Customer databases also float around. On their part, banks have pointed out that while they had systems in place to check the level of service rendered by DSAs and mechanisms for redressal of customer grievances, it was difficult to prevent sale of databases in the absence of any strict privacy laws in the country which in turn made it difficult to control unsolicited calls. For sometime now, there has been a clamour that DSAs must be subject to controls. With the RBI getting into the act, banks will now have to issue appropriate code of conduct to the DSA marketing their credit card products.

Technological Development

Technology has transformed the global world of Banking and Financial Services beyond recognition.

No other industry offers more complex challenges or more exciting opportunities.

Technological initiative spans Retail and Wholesale Banking, Lending Solutions, Payment Systems, Mortgages, Securities, Fund Management, Straight-through-Processing, Risk Management, Compliance, as well as Messaging Systems, Lending Banking and Financial Services Firms. Design and build new age, web based solutions. Expand your domain knowledge while maintaining and enhancing mission-critical production systems. Fine-tune your design skills while working on n-tiered architectures supporting high transaction loads. Work on sophisticated work flow and rule engines. Build real-time, high throughput trading and settlement systems. Design sophisticated Risk and Compliance frameworks. Master best-of-breed processes.

This would benefit the customer in the banking sector. Computerisation of the business of banks has been receiving high importance. The public sector banks have already crossed the 70 per cent level of computerisation of their business. The directive from the Central Vigilance Commission (CVC) to achieve 100 per cent computerisation has resulted in renewed vigour towards computerisation of branches.

Networking has been receiving focused attention by banks. This activity is also being monitored by the Reserve Bank. Most banks have their own corporate networks to facilitate interbranch and branch-controlling office communication in an electronic mode. Inter-bank and inter-city communication takes place through the Indian Financial Network (INFINET). As part of the INFINET, the terrestrial lines have been augmented to provide for increased data transfer capabilities. All these have resulted in the dependence of banks on network-based computing which has benefited the customer. INFINET also provides for safe and secure transmission of electronic messages with the use of Public Key Infrastructure (PKI) which has the legal backing of Information Technology Act, 2000. It also provides for messages to flow in a structured environment, using the SFMS, which provides for inter-operability of messages so that straight through processing (STP) is achieved.

BOX 7.4

FINANCIAL SECTOR TECHNOLOGY VISION DOCUMENT

vDevelopment and Research in Banking Technology (IDRBT). IT for the Financial Sector and IT for Government related functions.

The Vision Document envisages emerging challenges in the form of implementation of standardisation across a variety of hybrid systems at different financial entities, need for decision support systems and the technology to facilitate risk based off-site supervision. If envisions common inter-operatable web-based structures for transmission of data relating to regulatory functions and the use of a single centralised database for all information, apart from hiving off the operation of non-critical functions by the Reserve Bank.

The Vision Document visualises the IDRBT to be a premier research institute, concentrating on research and development for the banking and financial sector, providing educational/training facilities and hiving off business related activities.

Recognising the requirements of IT for the financial sector, the Vision Document elucidates the thrust areas of the Reserve Bank by providing generic information on various standards and approaches. IS Audit and requisite focus on business continuity plans. The Vision Document proposes that specific attention would be devoted to percolation of technology efforts to all types of banks and all sections of the customers in the banks with specific reference to the rural areas and the use of affordable technology products which can be easily used by the target clientele with inter-shareable resources.

The document also details the use of IT in the Government sector transactions (which has the largest potential to grow significantly in the years to come), with specific attention on the need for business process re-engineering, changes in rules and procedures for aligning them with e-governance in a manner so as to achieve implementable objectives.

BOX 7.5

BS7799 STANDARDS

BS7799 is comprehensive in its coverage of security issues, containing a significant number of control requirements. Compliance with it is, thus, a major task for most organisations. By following this standard, financial institutions including banks can ensure compliance to most of the information security requirements. The objectives of these standards are:

- To provide management direction and support for information security, which is a base prerequisite for BS7799.
- To manage information security within the organisation, maintain the security of organisational information processing facilities and information assets accessed by third parties, and to maintain the security of information when the responsibility for information processing has been outsourced to another organisation.
- To maintain appropriate protection of corporate assets and ensure that information assets receive an appropriate level of protection.
- To reduce risks of human error, theft, fraud or misuse of facilities and minimise the damage from security incidents and malfunctions and learn from such incidents.
- To ensure the correct and secure operation of information processing facilities, minimise the risk of systems failures, to protect the integrity of software and information and maintain the integrity and availability of information processing and communication.
- To control access to information, prevent unauthorised access, detect unauthorised activities and ensure information security when using mobile computing and tele-networking facilities.
- To ensure security is built into operational systems, to prevent loss, modification or misuse of user data in application systems.
- To counteract interruptions to business activities and critical business processes from the effects of major failures or disasters.
- To prevent breaches of any criminal or civil law, statutory, regulatory or contractual obligations and of any security requirements, ensure compliance of systems with organisational security policies and standards and minimise interference to/from the system audit process.

ATMs Galore

Automated Teller Machines have been springing up all over the place. There were about 16,000 ATMs in the country in 2004.

ATMs are increasingly providing functionalities that take away the routine teller functions and are an effective personalised and secure customer information and cross-sell channel. With the Reserve Bank of India working towards the implementation of the cheque truncation initiative, this deposit module will facilitate faster cheque processing as the scanned image of the cheque can directly be sent for clearing with the ATM being the point of deposit and truncation. This will facilitate faster access to funds for consumers as well as cost and operational efficiencies for the banks.

Mobility in Banking

Mobile phone banking takes you one step ahead of Internet and tele-banking. You can do your banking, without even making a phone call.

- The most obvious advantage of mobile phone banking over tele-banking and Internet banking is that it is truly "anytime-anywhere banking."
- There are broadly two types of services that you could avail of through your mobile phone — alert services and requests.
- Alert services help you keep a track of the activity in your accounts.
- Requests allow you to call for information pertaining to your bank accounts and conduct transactions.
- Mobile banking works through a set of text messages.

The use of mobile phones in the country has become revolutionary, it is no surprise, therefore, that banks are offering services over mobile phones, as part of their tech banking initiatives.

Services Available

There are broadly two types of services that you could avail of through your mobile phone. One is called alert services and the other is requests. Alert services are a convenient way of keeping a track of the activity in your accounts. If you give your bank standing instructions to alert you, you will be intimated by a text message on your mobile phone via Short Messaging Service (SMS) about a number of developments in your account. These developments include, for example, an increase or decrease in your bank balance above or below a particular level, conclusion of transactions that are greater than a specified amount, accrual of interest, etc. StanChart popularly calls these the "push facilities" as you are informed when the events you have subscribed for get triggered.

Requests, as the name suggests, allows you to request the bank for information pertaining to your bank accounts. In addition, it also allows you to conduct transactions. You could request the bank to let you know your account balance, call for the last few transactions, order a new cheque book, inquire about the status of cheques which are issued or deposited, issue a stop cheque order, etc. Some banks, like HDFC Bank and ICICI Bank, allow you to issue instructions to pay your utility bills under this facility.

Bank on the Net

Internet banking has become a necessity in today's busy lifestyles. Using this mode to transact, saves precious time and effort.

From across the seven seas, as long as you have access to the Internet, you have access to your bank.

Internet banking allows you to conduct a plethora of banking activities using the net.

The best part about Internet banking is the convenience offered along with total confidentiality and safety.

The virtual ease with which you can bank today is reassuring. From across the seven seas, as long as you have access to the Internet, you have access to your bank — and the bank is open 24-7-365.

Fund Transfers

Internet banking or online banking allows you to transfer funds from one of your accounts to another, across branches and cities. Some banks go a step ahead by offering you the facility to transfer money from your account to that of any person with an account at the same bank, any time and from anywhere. All you have to do is submit a signed declaration form stating that you want access to this facility.

Fixed Deposits and Demand Drafts

As part of Internet banking activities, a majority of banks allow you to create a new fixed deposit. To do this you are simply required to fill in the details of the bank account from which you wish to transfer funds, the amount and duration of the deposit, etc. The bank will do the rest and transfer the interest and maturity amount back to the account from which you have created the deposit. A number of banks are willing to issue demand drafts from your account, once you provide them with details of the amount, location and beneficiary, over the net.

Pay Utility Bills

You could now even pay your telephone, mobile and electricity bills over the net. However, some banks limit facilities like these and creation of new fixed deposits and demand draft requests to regular banking hours. In case you put in your request after banking hours, the bank promptly executes it on the next working day. Even that is definitely better than standing in queues at utility offices or a bank premises on a working day.

Other Banking Activities

Naturally, you can carry out other mundane banking activities too, such as checking your account balance and downloading a statement, changing your customer profile, i.e., update your mailing address, etc.

The best part about all these transactions is that they remain totally confidential and safe. What's more, most banks do not charge you any additional fee for this service. So don't let a visit to the bank or a utility office fill up your leisure hours on a weekend or be the reason for your absence at work. Conveniently sit down at your computer, visit your bank's website and transact.

Banks are also innovating on the company and treasury operations fronts. In corporate loans, plain loans are passe. Mumbai inter-bank offered rate (MIBOR)-linked and commercial paper-linked interest rates on loans are common. MIBOR is a reference rate arrived at every day at 4 p.m. by Reuters. It is the weighted average rate of call money business transacted by 22 institutions, including banks, primary dealers and financial institutions.

The State Bank of India was the first to usher in MIBOR-linked loans for top companies. Soon enough, other banks followed.

ICICI Bank carried out the world's first ever securitisation of a micro finance portfolio last year. The bank securitised Rs. 4.2 crore for Bharatiya Samruddhi Finance Ltd. for crop production.

Wealth Management

Banks have begun to recognise the potential of wealth management as a very profitable business. Banks aim to help individuals to preserve and systematically grow their wealth.

Most private banks offer basic investment advisory services under the umbrella of their private or priority banking services. Banks may offer complimentary financial planning services to help one to know exactly what to do with one's money so that one realises their financial objectives. Banks may organise investor meets, circulate market information reports and more under their private banking investment advisory services.

The salient features are:

- Banks offer niche wealth management programmes under their private banking services to customers with predefined limits of portfolio sizes.
- Wealth management services include risk assessment and asset allocation advice tailor-made to individual needs.
- Long-term goals and objectives are discussed and a careful provision is made to help you preserve and grow your wealth.
- Banks either have in-house expertise to guide customers or they have tie-ups with specialised organisations for investment advice.

The wealth management process includes the development of a financial plan (based on your needs and preferences and your risk appetite) and an asset allocation plan. Long-term goals and objectives are discussed and a careful provision is made to help you preserve and grow your wealth. Wealth management services may also include estate planning, tax and legal consultancy, custodial services and more.

INDIAN WEALTH PYRAMID

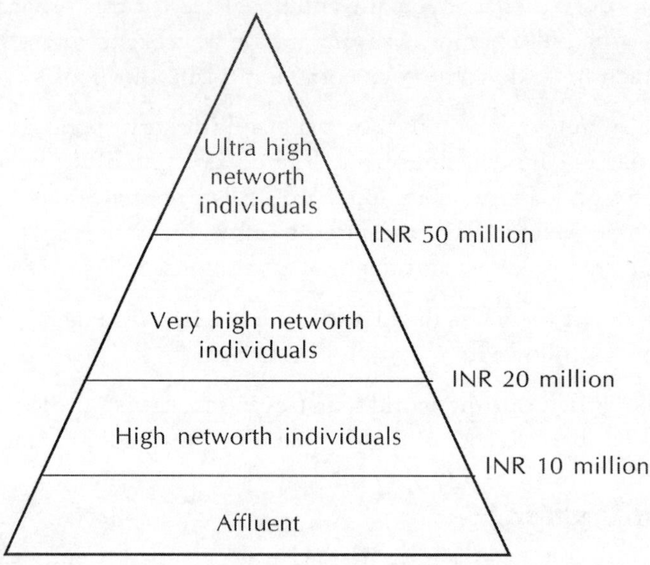

Source: IBM Business Consulting Services.

Fig. 7.3

CHANGING WEALTH PROFILES

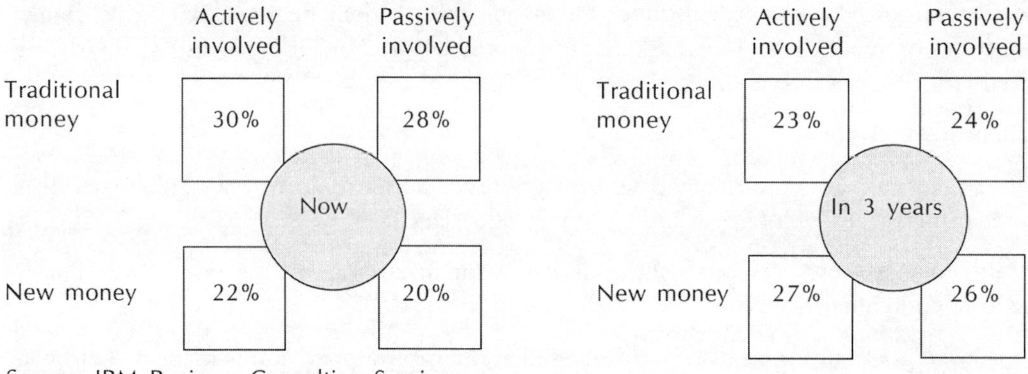

Source: IBM Business Consulting Services.

Fig. 7.4

Harnessing Technology

Banking at your doorstep is no more a distant reality.

Welcome to the world of instant Banking.

Where customers want more, and they want it now! As the Retail Banking Industry in India gears up for the battle royale, retaining and growing a loyal customer base will be the only competitive advantage by your side.

Thus, more and more Banking and Financial Institutions across the country are actively seeking technological partners with the desired domain expertise, who understand legacy banking systems, and can create made-to-order technology modules that plug into the existing systems without disrupting the ongoing processes.

The Indian banking sector is on the threshold of a major technological leap with the advent of the national switch at the Institute for Development and Research in Banking Technology (IDRBT), an institute of the Reserve Bank of India at Hyderabad.

As the national switch takes shape at the premises of the IDRBT, Indian banking will never be the same again.

The other banking innovations that are currently gaining significance in the banking industry are:

Customer Relationship Management (CRM) Solution

CRM is the industry term for the set of methodologies and tools that help an enterprise manage customer relationships in an organized way. It is a process or methodology used to learn more about customers' needs and behaviours in order to develop stronger relationships with them. There are many technological components to CRM. It is a process that will help bring together lots of pieces of information about customers, sales, marketing effectiveness, responsiveness and market trends. CRM helps businesses use technology and human resources to gain insight into the behaviour of customers and the value of those customers.

Fig. 7.5

In simpler terms, Customer Relationship Management (CRM) is defined as finding, getting, and retaining customers. CRM is the core of any customer-focused business strategy and includes the people, processes, and technology associated with sales, marketing, and service. For a successful CRM, technology provides the base on which processes are built by the people for tracking customer behaviour in order to develop marketing and relationship building programs that bond consumers to a brand.

Using CRM, a business can:

- ❑ Provide better customer service
- ❑ Discover new customers
- ❑ Help sales staff close deals faster
- ❑ Increase customer revenues
- ❑ Cross Sell/Up Sell products more effectively
- ❑ Make call centres more efficient

Risk Management, MIS and Data Warehouse

Risk Management is a fairly new concept to the Indian banking industry. Presently most of the banks are on the learning curve and the information systems used by the banks for addressing the risks are scattered in separate applications. Good risk management practices require robust, account level and enterprise wide database. Banks should have access to various kinds of data, which will have to be captured by the bank over a period of time. It was with this background that RBI's committee on Technology Upgradation in the Banking Sector had advised the Indian banks to put in place their strategy for setting up an enterprise wide data warehouse.

According to Dr. Gulati, Director of IDRBT, changes have been drastic, and growth is going to happen exponentially. These days, Indian public sector banks are in the midst of a whirlpool of activity, trying to implement the concept of core banking. About half of them are in the process for working on it, and the other half is on the lockout for the right kind of solution.

The expectation is that by 2008-09, every bank in the country will have a centralised core banking solution. The scenario will be such that, every bit of data about the customer will be in one location — a data centre. With the enormous amount of data at their command, banks can offer products and services, based on the analysis done from a centralised database. Data warehousing and data mining will become a part of the banking lexicon. In the future, bank branches will become delivery channels and offer banking solutions to their customers.

The second aspect is that in this kind of situation, the entire banking scenario will undergo a comprehensive change. For one, the concept of back office and administration will be reduced substantially. Indian public sector banks have a large number of award staff, clerks and officers on their rolls. Today, about 15 % of the workforce is involved in back office operations and that will come down to 5 to 6% in the future. In times ahead, about 85% of the workforce will be in the officer category, and 15% of the staff will be in other areas. There will be a need for a change in attitude and banks will need to look at customer orientation as its frontline activity.

The use of technology is coming up in very big way and changing the entire banking scenario. In a way, the banking industry is no different from others when it comes to the technology adaptation. As the situation evolves, delivery channels will undergo a sea change and banks will seek to provide remote banking services like ATMs, Internet and Mobile Banking. By 2008-09, remote services are likely to contribute about 55 to 60% of the total business volumes of banks in our country.

Technology is also changing the economy of the country and everything is going the electronic way — from e-governance to e-commerce. Given such a scenario, the banking sector cannot remain an island in the midst of the electronic revolution. No deal done electronically is valid unless the financial transaction is completed and banks need to be a part of it. This way, banks will get involved in activities like e-banking, internet banking and e-commerce, e-governance can go around that.

For the Indian consumer, nothing has been more visible than the number of ATMs that dot the urban landscape. With a 24 x 7 concept, these ATMs are mirror services to those provided by the banks. Banks in our country have taken up initiatives on their own by setting up ATMs on an individual basis. Presently, there are about 16,000 ATMs across the country and it is likely to double in the next one and half years. But the catch is that in many cases, the customer of a particular bank can only access the services of the ATM belonging to his bank. Avers Dr. Gulati, "We asked ourselves why should be this so, and got to work out a solution." The concept at work is to optimise resources by getting the ATMs to talk to each other through a national financial switch. This mother switch which is being set up at IDRBT has two components. One, where the customer can access ATM services of all banks from anywhere in the country. The second advantage is that the switch could also act as an inter-bank payment gateway. Thirdly, when one connects everything with everything else, security becomes an important issue. Banks, traditionally have been places where a lot of trust is reposed and it will be no different when it came to electronic transactions.

The popularity of ATMs is another talking point in the banking industry. Industry sources expect that in the next five years, the number of ATMs should touch the one lakh mark. ATMs are going to become a place which will have most of the features of the branch. The payment scenario will also see a major change and one reason for that is the growing popularity of debit cards. There are some 25 million ATM cum debit cards compared to 11 million credit cards. More and more transactions will be through debt cards and people will dispense the practice of carrying cash.

A number of moves are being initiated by banks on the technology front and expenditure on IT and Cyber security related issues are increasing. Public sector banks in India are expected to spend close to Rs. 5,000 crores every year, for the next three to four years. 15% of this amount will be spent on security related issues and Reserve Bank of India is insisting on Basel 2 compliance. This means that more and more technology will have to come into the banking sector.

Autobank E — An Example

An example of 'Autobank E' developed by Standard Bank of South Africa can be quoted which offers a simplified package of services to the mass market. It has been a massive success.

- One of the major strengths of the banks is their "franchise" and technology can undermine such value. Further, the geographic segmentation (rural, semi-urban, urban and metro) of business will call for separate technology responses which need to be integrated in a seamless way to contribute to overall improvement in performance. Achieving such integration will be crucial.

- Opening of new channels of delivery like ATMs need to be followed up by channel migration of the targeted clientele. If this does not happen, the costs of setting up such channels would only add to costs. Banks will have to manage effective the likely "channel conflicts." Transaction costs are saved only if customers use the new channel instead of, rather than in addition to, existing ones.
- The perceived cost reduction through internet-banking needs to be carefully evaluated. According to estimates, in USA Internet-based transactions cost a bank only one cent — a fraction of the cost of other channels. But this figure seems either far too high or far too low. The incremental cost of an online transaction is negligible. But if all costs are fully allocated — incremental IT expenditure, regulatory compliance, credit control and accounting, let alone "customer acquisition" — one cent is hardly likely to cover the bill. Lehman Brothers, an investment bank, cites one estimate that it costs just 14% less to service on online account than an off-line one.
- As new channels of delivery develop with in-built cost and service efficiencies, customer behaviour also changes. The customer may be prepared to pay more if he gets better and quicker service. In other words, the cost barrier breaks down and customer loyalty ceases to be. Customer will exercise his choice and will migrate to the service provider who gives the best service and at the most competitive price. This also calls for products innovation, expanding the range of their products and service offerings because today's value-added products could easily be tomorrow's commodity. Many Internet banks like Egg have taken the lead in offering innovative products like Egg Card — a credit card that features an introductory zero per cent interest rate.

IDRBT IMPACT

The Indian Financial Network is launched by Shri S.P. Talwar, Dy. Governor, Reserve Bank of India	June 1999
IDRBT launches its Research Fellow (Ph.D) Programme in collaboration with the University of Hyderabad	Aug. 1999
The Institute offers Mail Messaging Services to the Indian Banking and Financial Sector	Jan. 2000
IDRBT is bestowed with the Golden Peacock National Training Award 2001	Aug. 2001
Dr. Y.V. Reddy, Dy. Governor, Reserve Bank of India, inaugurates IDRBT's collaborative M.Tech. Programme with the University of Hyderabad	Sep. 2001
The First IDRBT Awards for Excellence in Banking Technology is given away by Shri Vepa Kamesam, Chairman, IDRBT Governing Council and Dy. Governor, Reserve Bank of India	Nov. 2001
IDRBT launches EnDeSign — an indigenously developed Encryption, Decryption, Signature Software	Nov. 2001
IDRBT becomes Certifying Authority for the Indian Banking & Financial Sector	Aug. 2002
IDRBT wins the Computer-world Honors Laureates' Medal for Innovativeness in Development and Management of Indian Financial NETwork	Apr. 2003
The Institute's flagship programme, the Post Graduate Programme in Banking Technology Management, is launched	Sept. 2003
IDRBT launches Mirror-NET — an indigenously developed Corporate Intranet Framework	May 2004

- Concerns about the security of Internet transactions are paramount, particularly in case of financial dealings.
- Another important aspect is integrating customer service interfaces and channels so that the customer deals with a single channel that caters to diverse needs such as kiosks. ATMs, mobile phones, pagers, branch counters, etc. The banks need to be 'one-stop shops' for an entire range of personal finance products, from loans to insurance to mutual funds and even tax saving instruments. This is being done by 'account aggregators' such as Yodlee, Corillian, e-Balance and Vertical One. One can log into one Web site, enter his/her user name and password. This tracks information as diverse as bank and credit card balances, value of investments and frequent flier miles from several sites, each of which has its own user name and password.
- Most of the Indian banks have gone for computerisation without any clear IT strategy and therefore the basic questions remain unattended. What do they want to achieve through computerisation? A low-cost leadership? Better customer service? Higher market share? These questions will be answered only if they have a clear IT strategy, which in turn should be closely aligned to business strategy. In contrast, it appears that IT strategy is driving business strategy in Indian banks and there is no clear linkage between HR strategy. Banks need to overcome this dichotomy.

Conclusion

It is clear that banks in India will now need to operate in an increasingly competitive environment. Not only will the banking market see a large number of players competing with one another but also the new entrants will have the advantage of starting with strong capitalisation, modern technology, lean network and, more importantly, without any accumulated problem of the past. It is also fair to expect that the initial target of the new competitors will be the most profitable segment of the banking business, i.e., high value corporate customers, business relating to high net worth individuals, foreign trade related business, and so on. Customers will now have a real choice. Banks will have to be more customer responsive. The future of Indian banking, therefore, holds greater promise for those who are willing to accept the challenge.

Since the future will be dominated by the technology, investments in newer technology have to be made to modernize existing oerations, to face competitive challenges and to meet customer expectations. But costs of technology emerge much before the generation of expected revenues. Operational risk also may increase or decrease as a result of major technological investments. Thus, a careful monitoring of the progress of technological projects is essential. Also, the management have to make sure that the IT strategy remains aligned with their business strategy so as to avoid being saddled with dead investment.

As the Indian banking industry moves into the neither world, consumers wait with bated breath to soak up the impact once it all starts working. One thing is for sure, the situation in the banking sector will be a lot better. Technology for one, will make sure that consumers will dance all the way to the bank.

Chapter 8

Non-Banking Finance Institutions

Introduction

In recent times, the non-banking finance companies (NBFCs) have emerged as substantial contributors to the Indian economic growth by supplementing the efforts of banks and other development financial institutions. They play a key role in the direction of savings and investments. They offer a wide variety of financial services and play an important role in providing credit to the unorganised sector and small borrowers.

Core financial services provided by financial intermediaries include payments and liquidity, maturity transformation, store of value, information processing and pooling of risks. Banks have traditionally provided most of these services and are increasingly diversifying into other areas. However, banks typically have an edge in providing payment and liquidity related services and they usually select a portfolio mix with an overriding objective of providing a certain return. Non-banking financial institutions (NBFIs), on the other hand, tend to offer enhanced equity and risk-based products. NBFIs play a crucial role in broadening access to financial services, enhancing competition and diversification of the financial sector. They are increasingly being recognised as complementary to the banking system capable of absorbing shocks and spreading risks at times of financial distress.

Mobilisation of financial resources outside the traditional banking system has witnessed tremendous growth all over the world in recent years. The boundaries separating commercial banks and NBFIs are also getting increasingly blurred. Rapid financial diversification has thus posed new challenges for regulators, especially in the area of devising appropriate regulatory safeguards for the highly complex NBFI sector. Owing to their diversified nature, NBFIs may require specific regulatory prescriptions particular to their nature of business, in addition to the general guidelines applicable for the financial sector.

In the wake of rapid industrial development and liberalisation of the financial sector, the entrepreneurs, corporate sector as well as the key financial institutions have diversified their activities to cater to the specific needs of the economy. In this context, the key financial institutions and professionals have promoted financial institutions to create a diversified and competitive financial system.

Growth of Non-Bank Financial Services

The role of banks in non-bank financial services began to grow from the time of the amendment to the Banking Regulation Act in 1983. Many merchant banking divisions and mutual funds were set up by the public sector banks since then. Banks began to increase their non-bank and non-funded business which are called financial services. More recently some more development took place to expand the scope for such services: (1) Keeping open Indian capital market to foreign financial institutions and oversea corporate bodies to invest in India. (2) FERA dilution to encourage both the inflow and outflow of funds and foreign investment in India, some of which might flow into the stock and capital markets. (3) Opening up mutual fund business and even banking to the private sector. Already a number of private sector companies/ firms are engaged in financial services, such as investment financing, hire-purchase, mortgage financing and housing finance etc. Private sector was permitted to set up mutual funds, banks and financial institutions. Financial deregulation, freeing of interest rates on debentures, banks' lending rates and their practices, etc., has helped the growth of the financial sector. Today the emerging trends in this sector are as follows:

1. Faster rate of growth made it a sunrise industry.
2. Deregulation and liberalisation of procedures, reduction in government redtape and discretionary controls and revolution in information technology and in communication led to globalisation of financial markets.
3. Interlinkages between all segments of financial sector began to grow faster and deeper.

Non-Banking Finance Companies

The Non-Banking Finance Companies (NBFCs) when compared to commercial and co-operative banks are a heterogenous group of finance companies. These companies also intermediate between the savers and the investors. The NBFCs, in advanced countries have grown phenomenally and are now coming up in a massive way in the developing countries like Brazil, India, Jordan, Korea and Malaysia. The different categories, of the NBFCs include loan companies, investment companies, hire-purchase finance companies, equipment leasing companies, mutual benefit finance companies, miscellaneous finance companies, miscellaneous non-banking companies, residuary non-banking companies and housing finance companies. A wide variety of companies and markets are operating in an environment of macro-economic stability.

Types of Non-Bank Financial Services

1. Merchant Banking and New Issue Marketing.
2. Underwriting and Loan Syndication.

3. Bill Discounting and Money Market Operations.
4. Housing Finance.
5. Lease and Hire-Purchase Financing.
6. Venture Capital Funds.
7. Investment Financing.
8. Investment Consultancy and Advise.
9. Mergers, Acquisitions, Amalgamations.
10. Capital Restructuring, Revaluations and Designing Capital Structure.
11. Portfolio Management Services.
12. Corporate Asset Management Services.
13. Technical Consultancy and Project Preparation.
14. Mutual Funds.
15. New Issue House Services.
16. Depositories.

Role of NBFCs

Non-Banking Finance Companies (NBFCs) are an integral part of India's financial system. They play an important role in financial intermediation by acting as a link between savers and investors, and have been able to mobilise deposits on a substantial scale in recent years. As estimated by the RBI, regulated deposits of NBFCs at the end of March 1997 formed 12.5 per cent of the aggregate deposits of scheduled commercial banks. Besides, during 1981-1996 non-banking deposits with households increased from 0.5% of GDP to 1.3%, while bank deposits held by households increased from 3.6% of GDP to 4.4% of GDP in the same period.

There are various categories of NBFCs including loan companies, investment companies, hire-purchase finance companies, equipment leasing companies, mutual benefit finance companies, chit funds and housing finance companies. Historically, NBFCs were no regulated till the mid-sixties, but after several unhealthy practices came to light, the RBI Act was amended and regulation extended to the non-banks.

While housing finance companies are regulated by the National Housing Bank, other NBFCs are regulated by the Reserve Bank of India, under the provisions of Chapter IIIB of the RBI Act and the respective directions issued to the different categories of NBFCs. Regulation covers their deposit-taking activity including period of acceptance of deposits, quantum, interest rate, etc. Ceilings stipulated on acceptance of deposits are related to net owned funds (NOF)[1+] and are different for different types of companies.

Competitive Edge of NBFCs

NBFCs supplement the activities of banks in deposit taking and lending and play a dynamic role in the economy. By providing more options to savers and investors; they have helped broaden the market. Because they accept a large volume of small deposits, they reach depositors in all segments, particularly the small savers. Another advantage enjoyed by NBFCs lies in their reach to cater to the specialised credit requirements of certain categories of borrowers not served by the organised banking system. The growth of NBFCs and their edge over banks in certain resects are explained by the fact that there was greater regulation over banks, while NBFCs were relatively free and would offer marginally higher rates of interest on deposits. Their simple procedures and greater customer orientation, and ability to offer higher returns on investment and extend credit to those who are not eligible to receive loans from commercial banks also helped the sector grow.

In particular, as the government pre-empted banks' resources in the form of high reserve requirements, banks had to ration credit. This gap in supply of credit was sought to be met by NBFCs who mobilised deposits from households not covered by banks and made credit available for investment in real assets, consumption and other purposes of which bank credit was not available. In comparison, NBFCs faced lower reserves than commercial banks and therefore had more loanable funds. Further, NBFCs were not constrained by government controls and could adopt modern technology and communications quickly to add value to their products and improve customer service and profits.

Growth of Non-Banking Financial Services

As the demand for financial services grows, countries will need to encourage the development of non-banking financial intermediaries and securities markets in order to broaden the range of services and to stimulate competition and efficiency. India has made considerable progress towards more diversified financial systems.

The role of banks in non-banking financial services began to grow from the time of the amendment to the Banking Regulation Act in 1983. Many merchant banking divisions and mutual funds were set up by the public sector banks since then. Banks began to increase their non-banking and non-funded business which are called *financial* services. More recently, some more developments took place to expand the scope for such services: (1) Keeping open Indian capital market to foreign financial institutions and overseas corporate bodies to invest in India. (2) FERA dilution to encourage both the inflow and outflow of funds and foreign investment in India, some of which might flow into the stock and capital markets. (3) Opening up mutual fund business and even banking to the private sector. Already a number of private sector companies/firms are engaged in financial services, such as investment financing, hire-purchase, mortgage financing and housing finance etc. Private sector was permitted to set up mutual funds, banks and financial institutions. Financial deregulation, freeing of interest rates on debentures, banks' lending rates and their practices, etc., have helped the growth of the financial sector. Today, the emerging trends in this sector are as follows:

1. Faster rate of growth made it a sunrise industry.
2. Deregulation and liberalisation of procedures, reduction in government redtape and discretionary controls and revolution in information technology and in communication led to the globalisation of financial markets.
3. Interlinkages between all segments of financial sector began to grow faster and deeper.

CHART 1

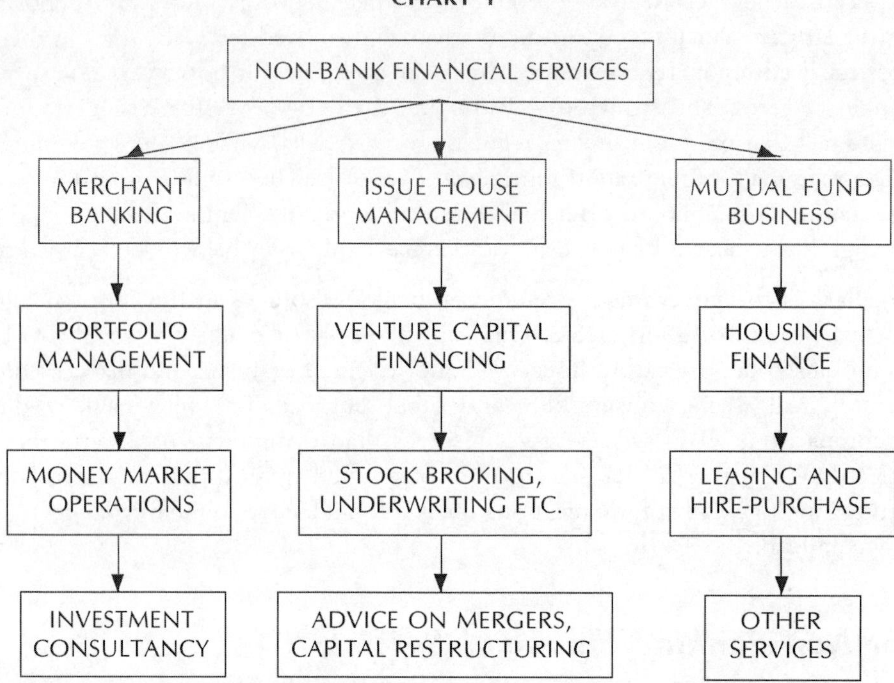

As at end June 2006, the total number of NBFCs registered with RBI stood at 13,014, of which 428 companies were authorised to accept deposits from the public. Total assets/liabilities of NBFCs were Rs. 35,561 crore at end March 2006.

In other developed and some developing countries too, such non-banking financial companies are subject to certain restrictions so as to provide a level playing field for all participants in the financial sector. In some countries, the regulations are same as for banking companies. In some others, separate regulations are there for NBFCs. Self-regulating organisations are also a part of the regulatory system. Broadly, the prudential norms applicable to such organisations include capital adequacy, credit concentration ratio, liquidity ratio and creation of reserves. Punitive action in case of non-compliance is strict. Finance Corporation and State Finance Corporations are also guided by the general economic policy. The data for financial and investment companies relate to about 175 sample companies. The paid-up capital of these companies amount to about 85 per cent of the total paid-up capital of all non-government financial and investment companies, excluding banks and insurance companies. Their total assets form a very small proportion of the total assets of all banks and NBFCs and hence they are not likely to prove dangerous for the effectiveness of monetary controls. This only confirms the predominant position of commercial banks in our financial structure and since none of the other important financial intermediaries is free from controls, the threat from the growth of NBFCs for monetary policy in this country appears to be based on illusionary grounds.

NBFCs and the Reserve Bank of India

The focus of regulatory initiatives in respect of financial institutions (FIs) during 2004-05 was to strengthen the prudential guidelines relating to asset classification, provisioning, exposure to a single/group borrower and governance norms. Business operations of FIs expanded during 2004-05. Their financial performance also improved, resulting from an increase in net interest income. Significant improvement was also observed in the asset quality of FIs, in general. The capital adequacy ratio of FIs continued to remain at a high level, notwithstanding some decline during the year.

The Reserve Bank of India has a separate Department to deal with the NBFCs. It was originally called the Department of non-banking companies. Now, it is referred to as Department of Financial Companies. The main objective of this Department is to exercise some control over the NBFIs by collecting data, issuing directions and inspecting them wherever necessary. Its central office is situated at Kolkata and it has four regional offices.

Functions of the Department

The main functions of the Department of Financial Companies are the following:

(*i*) To identify financial companies and classify them.

(*ii*) To review the classification of such companies then and there.

(*iii*) To attend to legislative matters and issue directions to NBFCs on various matters.

(*iv*) To advise the Central Government and State Governments on matters pertaining to NBFCs.

(*v*) To receive and scrutinise the balance sheets, returns, accounts and statements of NBFCs.

(*vi*) To inspect them and take follow-up action.

(*vii*) To deal sternly with those companies which contravene any of the directions of the RBI.

(*viii*) To consider requests for grants of exemptions.

(*ix*) To carry out studies on the working of these companies.

(*x*) To deal with the complaints received from the public and to do any other work which are incidental to the above functions.

RBI's Control over NBFCs

In the interest of the economy as a whole and in order to pursue an effective monetary policy, it is desirable that the NBFCs should be brought under the control of the Reserve Bank (RBI) in the same way as the commercial banks are controlled. It is so because, whenever the RBI increases its bank rate or changes the lending rates or deposit rates, they will have no impact on the rates charged by these non-banking financial intermediaries. Again, when the RBI follows a policy of 'credit squeeze', the industrial houses can escape from this policy by resorting to the system of financing through 'public deposits.' Besides, any person with any type of security can approach NBFCs at any time and obtain a loan. The RBI has no say over it. Yet another drawback of these companies has been the conspicuous lack of transparency of operations and proper financial disclosure. Again, several residuary non-banking companies are found to be operating with meagre capital and some of them even with negative capital. Moreover, some of the NBFCs have been found to be issuing misleading advertisements for attracting deposits. In these circumstances, the RBI cannot function effectively and implement its fiscal and monetary policies unless the NBFCs are brought under its control. Hence, the RBI has been taking several steps in this direction. Some of them are as follows:

Issue of Directions

The Reserve Bank has issued various directives from time to time to control the deposit acceptance activities of these companies. For instance, the non-banking financial companies are regulated by the RBI under the Non-banking Financial Companies (Reserve Bank) Directions, 1977. The Miscellaneous companies are governed by the Miscellaneous Non-banking Companies (Reserve Bank) Directions 1977. The residuary Non-banking Companies are regulated under the Residuary Non-Banking Companies (Reserve Bank) Directions, 1987. The Housing Finance Companies come under the Housing Finance Companies (National Housing Bank) Directions, 1989. The RBI regulates the activities of non-banking and non-financial companies under the Companies (Acceptance of Deposits) Rules 1975. The RBI exercises control over NBFCs by the issue of various directions as stated above.

Restriction on Deposits

The Reserve Bank has also prescribed certain ceiling limits for the acceptance of deposits by these non-banking financial intermediaries. In the absence of these restrictions, they would go for hunting deposits enormously without any regard to their net equity. Ultimately, the innocent depositors would be affected. Generally, these companies can accept deposits to the tune of 10 times of their net owned funds. A mutual benefit company can accept deposits only from its shareholders. Hence, there is no ceiling limit. Housing finance companies with 20 crores of net owned funds can go up to 15 times of their net owned funds. Similarly, in the case of loan companies and investment companies, there is some relaxation in the ceiling limit.

The RBI has started regulating the period as well as the rates of interest of the deposits of these companies. For instance, recently the RBI issued a circular notifying that these companies should accept deposits for a minimum period of one year and the maximum being 10 years. Further, all these deposits are subject to a ceiling limit of 14 per cent per annum. It is necessary that the NBFCs are subject to the same administered interest rate regime as that of commercial banks.

Regulation of Brokerage

It has been the practice of the NBFCs to attract more and more deposits by paying attractive rates of brokerage or commission or incentives or by whatever name it may be called to the middlemen. Now, the RBI has prescribed certain limits on the payment of brokerage also. For instance, for deposits not exceeding one year, the rate of brokerage shall be 1 per cent of such deposit per annum, for a period 1 year to 2 years, it shall not exceed 1.5 per cent of such deposit and for a period of above 2 years, it shall not exceed 2 per cent of such deposits.

Regulation of Liquidity

Realising the importance of maintaining liquidity, particularly for certain companies like equipment leasing companies and hire-purchase financing companies, the RBI has issued directions insisting these companies to maintain 10% of their deposits in liquid assets.

Compulsory Registration

Now, the RBI requires all non-banking financial intermediaries with net owned funds of Rs. 50 lakh and above to register compulsorily with the former by the end of July 1993. This registration would be a prerequisite for a company to expand its business further.

Submission of Returns

All the NBFCs are required to submit periodical returns to the RBI on various matters pertaining to their operations. Though it is a statutory requirement, most of the companies do not file the returns in time. Some do not file at all. It is found that less than one-third of NBFCs are regular in the submission of periodical returns.

Designation of Banks

The RBI has stipulated that these companies must designate a commercial bank of their own. Yet, most of them have not designated their bank.

Growth of Trade Credits and Other Non-bank Sources

It is argued that in times of credit stringency, trade credits tend to take the place of bank credit and thus defeat the objectives of monetary policy. Since they are little affected by changes in interest rates, they introduce considerable elasticity into the response of business to efforts by the monetary authority to compress liquidity. It is, therefore, important to verify the significance of trade credits in the financing of Indian companies.

A New Approach

The working group of financial companies under the chairmanship of Dr. A. C. Shah, was of the view that a thriving, healthy and growing non-banking financial sector is necessary for promoting the growth of an efficient and competitive financial system.

The approach of the committee towards NBFCs has been for ensuring their healthy growth, for improving the efficacy of the monetary and credit policy as also for inculcating financial discipline among the users and providers of funds.

BOX 8.1

GUIDELINES TO NON-BANKING FINANCIAL COMPANIES ON PRUDENTIAL NORMS FOR INCOME RECOGNITION, ACCOUNTING STANDARDS, ASSET CLASSIFICATION, PROVISIONING FOR BAD AND DOUBTFUL DEBTS, CAPITAL ADEQUACY AND CONCENTRATION OF CREDIT/INVESTMENTS

A. Income Recognition

Income past due but not received within a period of six months is not to be booked till such time income it is actually received. Assets are to be classified as non-performing, based on recovery record. Interest on non-performing assets should not be booked as income if such interest has remained outstanding for more than six months on and from March 31, 1995.

B. Calculation of Provisioning Requirements against Non-Performing Assets* as at the end of March 31, 1995

	Status as		*Provision required*	
(i)	*Sub-standard Asset (Classified as NPA for a period not exceeding two years)*		*A general provision of 10 per cent of total outstanding amount*	
(ii)	*Doubtful Asset (Classified as NPA for a period exceeding 2 years)*	*Period for which asset has been considered as doubtful*	*Provision required on secured portion (as % of secured portion)*	*Provision on unsecured portion (as % of unsecured portions)*
		(a) Upto 1 year	20	100
		(b) 1 to 3 years	30	100
		(c) More than 3 years	50	100
(iii)	Loss Asset, i.e., an asset considered un-collectable (Identified so by the NBFC or external auditors or the RBI inspection)		Entire asset should be written off. If the asset is permitted to remain in the books, 100 per cent of the total outstanding amount should be provided for.	

C. Capital Adequacy

Ratio of capital to risk weighted assets and off balance sheet items should be a minimum of 6 per cent by March 31, 1995 and 8 per cent by March 31, 1996.

D. Credit Rating

NBFC and residuary non-banking companies are required to get themselves rated at least once every year for fixed deposits by one of the following three credit rating agencies and secure minimum rating as indicated below:

Name of the Credit Rating Agency	*Minimum Rating*
CRISIL	FA
ICRA	MA
CARE	CARE BBB(FD)

While companies with net owned funds of Rs. two crore and above had to the rating by March 31, 1995, those having net owned funds below Rs. two crore were given the option to get the rating by March 31, 1996.

* A "non-performing asset" is defined as a credit-facility in respect of which interest remained "past due" in the year ended March 31, 1995 for a period of more than 6 months.

***Source*:** Currency and Finance, 1993-94.

Recommendations

The following recommendations have been made by the working group for the NBFCs:

(*i*) All the existing deposit-taking companies with net owned funds of Rs. 50 lakhs and over should compulsorily register with the regulatory authority. This cut-off point may be reviewed subsequently. Companies with net owned funds below this cut-off point may, if they so prefer, opt for registration. Registered companies will be allowed to accept public deposits up to a multiple of their net owned funds. Unregistered companies with net owned funds of less than Rs. 50 lakhs will be allowed to accept public deposits at a lower level, i.e., in accordance with provisions of Section 58A of the Companies Act, 1956.

(*ii*) Entry norms should be prescribed for all new NBFCs such as: (*a*) minimum net owned funds of Rs. 50 lakhs at the time of commencement; (*b*) registration with the regulatory authority; (*c*) restriction on deposit-acceptance activity at the level permitted to unregistered companies in first two full financial years of operation; and (*d*) permission for deposit acceptance at par with the existing registered companies after completion of this period, on the basis of track record, quality of management, methods of operation, etc.

(*iii*) The function of registration and regulation should be undertaken by the proposed High Powered Supervisory Board.

(*iv*) The focus of NBFC — regulation should be shifted from liability side to asset side of NBFC balance sheet. Capital adequacy standard based on risk-weighted assets as recommended for commercial banks should be prescribed. The regulatory authority, in co-ordination with the representatives of NBFCs, Self-Regulating Organisations and the Institute of Chartered Accountants, may complete the exercise of computing risk weights and credit conversion factors by March 31, 1994 and that capital adequacy ratio at the rate of 8 per cent of the risk weighed assets and off-balance sheet items be introduced by March 31, 1995.

(*v*) Until the time, capital adequacy framework is introduced, the existing limits on deposit acceptance may be continued subject, however, to an overall debts equity ratio in 15:1.

(*vi*) Restrictions should be placed on the portfolio management activities of these companies.

(*vii*) In addition, NBFCs should be required to: (*a*) maintain liquidity ratio of 10 per cent of their total deposit liabilities, (*b*) limit their risk exposure to single and group borrowers to 15 and 25 per cent of their net owned funds respectively, (*c*) transfer at least 20 per cent of their net profit to reserves every year until reserves equal the company's share capital, and (*d*) refrain from investing in certain undesirable activities as defined by the regulatory authority.

(*viii*) Until the time commercial bank deposit interest rates are regulated, NBFC interest rates should also continue to be regulated and that the latter be pegged two to three percentage points above the former. NBFCs should be allowed to accept deposits for periods ranging between 12-84 months as against the existing range of 24-120 months.

(*ix*) The existing distinction between the terms 'exempted' and 'regulated' deposits for purposes of calculating the gearing ratio should be abolished and instead a distinction be made between 'borrowings' and 'deposits.' The regulatory authority may, if it deems fit, create a distinction between 'exempted' and 'regulated' deposits for the purpose of tenor of deposit rate of interest, etc. Deposit insurance is not recommended at this stage.

(*x*) Credit rating should be compulsory for all registered companies not in the immediate future but after a period of five years. Relaxation in the Advertisement Rules has also been recommended.

(*xi*) Norms regarding income recognition, disclosure or transparency of accounts, provision for bad and doubtful debts, etc., should be prescribed. A committee may be constituted for formulating these norms. Suitable reporting formats may also be devised so that effective supervision may be undertaken by the regulatory authority.

(*xii*) Auditors, in the supervisory process, may be assigned a greater role. Periodical statements to be submitted by NBFCs to regulatory authorities will need certification by the auditors. Based on the rule of exception, NBFCs may be inspected by the regulatory authority.

(*xiii*) The regulatory authority should be empowered to suspend/cancel registration of these companies and even move for winding up where it so deems necessary.

(*xiv*) As regards unincorporated entities, apart from the existing restriction on the number of depositors, a ceiling on the quantum of deposits they can accept should be prescribed. A Standing Advisory Committee may be constituted for reviewing regulatory requirements for these bodies.

(*xv*) The regulatory authority should publish the list of all NBFCs periodically.

(*xvi*) The regulatory authority and the self-regulating organisations may initiate a public awareness programme for educating the depositors about the risks associated in placing deposits with various kinds of NBFCs.

Overall, it would appear that the recommendations of the working group have been pragmatic and keeping in line with the changes being contemplated in the financial sector at large. The positive approach of the recommendations is highlighted by the consideration that the role of NBFCs is complementary to the economic growth. The committee has shown not only great promptitude in addressing the problems of the NBFCs but also shown a great deal of selectivity in classifying the NBFCs and meeting their demands. Some of the suggestions, particularly the one relating to public awareness programme sound innovative. If the recommendations of the working group are accepted, they will launch the NBFCs in a healthy trajectory of growth path. If non-banking finance companies are to be efficient and robust, they must be set within a suitable legal and regulatory frame work. A vital test in deciding on the extent of regulation is the number and type of creditors. Last but not the least, the NBFCs will have to cooperate in various ways with the regulatory agencies to keep themselves and the economy healthy.

The RBI has accepted most of the above recommendations. If the above recommendations are implemented, it would go a long way in encouraging the healthy and orderly growth of non-banking financial companies and also in ensuring the solvency and safety of the financial system.

Thus NBFCs are wrestling with a multitude of problems threatening their very survival. Their sources of funds are drying up, they have a poor public image, lending has become riskier, rising menace of non-performing assets and increased competition in retail finance from banks and financial institutions is reducing the spreads. The NBFCs need steady deposit renewals and inflow of fresh deposits to take care of their assets portfolio which are hard to come by on account of their tarnished image except by offer of high interest rates, resulting in inflating their cost of funds. It is like a vicious circle.

There is no denying the fact that NBFC sector is headed for a major shakeout. A major reason is that medium and small NBFCs are not able to mobilise public deposits. Only NBFCs which are financially sound and have access to low-cost funds would be able to survive, which is also in the interest of the depositors. Thus, while the smaller ones could merge to attain greater size, some of the well established players may like to convert themselves into banks. Another lucrative area that has been opened is the insurance sector and RBI has also allowed NBFCs with Rs. 500 crore net worth to float insurance ventures. Further, any NBFC registered with RBI having net-owned funds of Rs. 5 crore will be permitted to undertake insurance business as an agent of insurance companies on fee basis, without any risk participation. RBI has also decided to allow 100% foreign direct investment in the NBFC segment to invite better and larger players in the financial services sector and to enable further development of the market. This in turn can bring in international players as in the case of mutual funds industry, paving the way for increased competition in the financial sector.

Regulation for NBFCs

In view of the important role played by NBFCs, and the need to integrate their activities into the financial system, the scope of regulations to control the activities of NBFCs was expanded from time to time in the recent past and several policy measures initiated to monitor their activities.

1. **Entry Norms:** Prior to the amendment of the RBI Act in 1997, there were practically no entry norms for NBFCs. Now, however, (a) it has been made mandatory for NBFCs to register with RBI and comply with minimum capital requirements; (b) a minimum NOF of Rs. 2.5 million has been stipulated for a company operating as NBFCs, and a minimum NOF of Rs. 20 million in respect of NBFCs which are incorporated on to after April 20, 1999.

2. **Capital Adequacy Requirements:** Overall borrowings of NBFCs had been regulated by linking their fund-raising ability to the NOF, but RBI has now shifted the focus of regulation from the liability side to the asset side by prescribing the capital adequacy requirements apart from stipulating other prudential norms. Accordingly, the capital to risk assets ratio has been raised from 6% in March 1995, to 8% by March 1996, 10% by March 1998, and 12% from March 31, 1999.

3. **Maintenance of Liquid Assets:** As a measure of depositor protection, all NBFCs irrespective of their classification are required to maintain liquid assets at 12.5% and 15% of public deposits with effect from April 1, 1998 and April 1, 1999 respectively. Liquid assets are to be maintained in Government securities and Government-guaranteed securities only and kept free from all encumbrances, for making payment to depositors. It has been suggested that the liquid assets should be increased in a phased manner to 25% of the outstanding public deposits.

4. **Prudential Norms:** In order to regulate the assets of companies, in June 1994, RBI prescribed prudential norms on income recognition, accounting standards, asset classification, provisioning for bad and doubtful debts, credit/investment concentration norms, as in the case of

banks. RBI has also prescribed half-yearly returns to be submitted by NBFCs or ensure compliance with the norms.

Norms relating to NPAs that are prescribed for NBFCs are similar to those applicable to commercial banks for loans. However, for the leasing and hire-purchase assets, the NPA norms are less stringent because the ownership of the underlying assets is vested in the NBFC itself and such assets being marketable, can be realised to refuse the loan losses.

5. Exposure Norm: Recently, NBFCs accessed substantial public deposits at high rates of interest, but the funds were not always invested prudently. To prevent deployment of public deposits in high risk and speculative ventures, the Vasudev Committee (1998) has recommended that in respect of NBFCs taking public deposits, RBI should prescribe ceilings for exposure to real estate, investment in capital markets, especially unquoted shares, and exposure to connected companies in which directors are interested.

6. Acceptance of Deposits: The prescriptions relating to ceiling for public deposits have been, at different times, related to different indicators of the underlying strength of the NBFC. The general approach has been to allow a higher ceiling for equipment leasing and hire-purchase companies whose assets are secure, while prescribing a lower ceiling for loan and investment companies.

(i) Credit Rating Requirement: In June 1994, RBI made it mandatory of NBFCs accepting deposits from the public to get themselves rated by any of the four credit rating agencies in India, and the extent of public deposits that can be accessed by them was corrected to the rating obtained by them, i.e., higher the rating, the higher is the limit up to which the public deposits may be accepted. The objective was to raise the ceiling for acceptance of deposits by registered rated companies, while restricting unrated companies from accepting deposits from the public.

Recently, there have been some reactions with respect to credit rating. While NBFCs with NOF of less than Rs. 2.5 million are not allowed to accept public deposits at all, equipment leasing and hire-purchase companies can accept deposits without any credit rating upto 1.5 times NOF or Rs. 100 million whichever is lower, provided they have a CRAR of 15% or above.

Equipment leasing and hire-purchase companies with NOF above Rs. 2.5 million and minimum investment grade credit rating can accept deposits four times their NOF provided they have a capital adequacy of 10% as on March 31, 1998 and 12% by March 31,1999. Loan and investment companies with investment grade credit rating can raise deposits up to 1.5 times their NOF provided they have a capital adequacy of 15%.

(ii) Interest Rate Ceiling: In 1996, companies having minimum investment grade credit rating, registered with the RBI and complying with prudential norms, were exempted from the ceiling on interest rate, permitted to access borrowings/deposits with any limit or up to a higher ceiling, and required to maintain reduced liquid assets. However, this at times led to intense competition and unethical practice including excessive deposits mobilised at unreasonable high interest rates, and creation of illiquid or non-performing assets. Consequently, the interest rate ceiling was reintroduced in January 1998, and RBI has stipulated interest rate ceiling of 16% on deposits accepted by NBFCs.

Perspective

For the development of a healthy, integrated financial system, there is a need to exploit the synergies between commercial banks and NBFCs and complement their efforts. In particular, NBFCs, which are smaller and more flexible intermediaries, can be more efficient in retailing banks' activities in consumer finance, hire-purchase and equipment leasing. Besides development of linkages, a sound regulatory framework for NBFCs will prevent widespread financial distress and facilitate the emergence of a strong and mature financial sector in the country.

Conclusion

The NBFCs are playing a unique role in mobilising funds, directing investments, providing a push to development, especially in the industrial sector, catering to the varied financial needs of the medium and the rural sector. All in all, a thriving, healthy and growing non-banking financial sector is necessary for promoting the growth of an efficient and competitive economy. Thus, NBFCs have emerged as a unique institution in the Indian financial system, bridging the credit gaps in several sectors.

As NBFCs Provide important services in certain niche areas of the financial sector, improvement in the efficiency of these entities is of crucial importance. Protection of deposits, improvement in corporate governance practices and financial disclosures by NBFCs needs to be focused in future. At the same time NBFCs need to make concerted efforts to reduce their high operating expenses and simultaneously rise the level of the operating efficiency. They should inculcate professionalism in managing the NBFCs.

ANNEXURE

REPORT OF THE TASK FORCE ON NBFCS (CHAIRMAN MR. C. M. VASUDEV): OCTOBER 1998: MAIN HIGHLIGHTS

- Higher CRAR of say 15% for NBFCs accepting public deposits without credit rating; continue 12% CRAR of all rated NBFCs.
- Need for upward revisions of present minimum capital requirement of Rs. 2.5 million.
- RBI to review prudential norms applicable to NBFCs. To prevent deployment of public deposits in high-risk avenues, RBI to lay down ceilings for exposure to real estate and capital markets and tighten exposures to connected companies.
- Quantum of deposits may not be linked to the rating per se provided the rating is above the minimum investment grade. Proposed ceilings could be as under:

Type of Company	*Limit of Public Deposits*
NBFCs with NoF less than Rs. 2.5 million	No access to public deposits
EL/HP company without credit rating	1.5 times NoF or Rs. 100 million whichever is lower (higher CRAR of 15%)
EL/HP company with investment grade credit rating or above	4 times NoF
Loan/investment companies with investment grade credit rating or above	1.5 times NoF (higher CRAR of 15%)

- RBI to consider measures for easing the flow of credit from banks to NBFCs and also prescribe a suitable ratio between secured and unsecured deposits for NBFCs.
- Liquid asset ratio to be increased gradually to 25% of public deposits.
- RBI to be statutorily empowered to appoint depositors' grievance redress authorities with specified territorial jurisdiction. In the meantime, tighten procedures for dealing with complaints of depositors by putting in place a mechanism for speedy disposal of complaints.
- Intensive publicity campaigns through print and electronic media for increasing depositors' awareness. No deposit insurance for depositors in NBFCs.
- Setting up of a separate mechanism for regulation and supervision of NBFCs under RBI, with representation of experts and other professionals. Strengthening offsite surveillance of NBFCs and ensuring sensitive market intelligence.

Chapter 9

Major Issues of Banking

Introduction

The Indian financial system has been broad based as well as expanded and gained a solid foundation during the last two decades. It is characterised by the predominance of public sector institutions and a high degree of regulation, motivated mainly by socio-economic considerations. In the process, certain rigidities and weaknesses have developed in the system. In this chapter, major issues in the Indian financial system are examined to enable the financial system to play its role in ushering in a more efficient and competitive economy.

Progress in Some Spheres

The Indian banking and financial system has made commendable progress in extending its geographical spread and functional reach. The spread of the banking system has been a major factor in promoting financial intermediation in the economy and in the growth of financial savings. The credit reach also has been extensive and the banking system now caters to several million borrowers especially in agriculture and small industry. The Development Financial Institution (DFIs) have established themselves as a major institutional support for investment in the private sector. The last decade has witnessed considerable diversification of the money and capital markets. New financial services and instruments have appeared on the scene.

Despite this commendable progress, serious problems have emerged, reflected in a decline in productivity and efficiency, and erosion of the profitability of the banking sector. The major factors responsible for these are: (a) directed investments; and (b) directed credit programmes. In both these cases, rates of interest that were available to banks were less than the market related rates or what they could have secured from alternate deployment of funds. There has been a deterioration in the quality of the loan portfolio which in turn has come in the way of banks' income generation and enhancement of their capital funds. Inadequacy of capital has been accompanied by inadequacy of loan loss provisions. The accounting and disclosure practices also do not always reflect the true state of affairs of banks and financial institutions. The erosion of profitability of banks has also emanated from the side of expenditure as a result of fast and massive expansion of branches, many of which are unremunerative especially in the rural areas, a considerable degree of over-manning especially in the urban and metropolitan centres and inadequate progress in updating work technology. Both management weaknesses and trade union pressures have contributed to this. There has also been weaknesses in the internal organisational structure of the banks, lack of sufficient delegation of authority and inadequate internal controls and deterioration in what is termed '*house-keeping*' such as balancing of books and reconciliation of inter-branch and inter-bank entries. The DFIs also suffer from a degree of portfolio contamination. This is more pronounced in the case of the State Financial Corporation (SFCs). Being smaller institutions, the internal organisational problems of the DFIs have been less acute than those of the banks. However, both banks and the DFIs have suffered from excessive administrative and political interference in individual credit decision making and internal management. The deterioration in the financial health of the system has reached a point where unless remedial measures are taken soon, it could further erode the real value of and return on the savings entrusted to them and even have an adverse impact on depositor and investor confidence.

BOX 9.1

A PRACTICAL APPROACH TO FINANCIAL STABILITY

Policy makers and academics have proposed several definitions of financial stability. Some define it in terms of what it is not: a situation in which financial instability impairs the real economy. Others take a macro-prudential viewpoint and specify financial stability in terms of limiting risks of significant real output losses associated with episodes of system-wide financial distress. Several complexities arise when financial stability policy is put in practice. First, developments in financial stability cannot be summarised into a single quantifiable measure. In contrast to many other economic policy objectives price stability, budgetary equilibrium, etc., there is no unequivocal unit of measurement for financial stability. This reflects its multi-faceted nature. Second, developments in financial stability are inherently difficult to forecast. Assessing the state of financial stability not only seeks to take stock of disturbances as they emerge, but also identify the build-up of vulnerabilities that could lead to future disturbances. The difficulty here is that financial crises are hard to predict because of contagion effects and that they often reflect the far-reaching consequences of unlikely ('tail') events. Third, policies aimed at financial stability typically involve a trade-off between resilience and efficiency. Often, the pursuit of an efficient allocation of financial resources needs to be weighed against the ability to exclude or absorb shock to the financial system. Finally, policy requirements for financial stability might be time inconsistent. In particular, a short-term stability gain may come at the cost of a longer-term stability loss. For example, the provision of lender-of-last-resort finance or deposit guarantee may undermine market discipline and create a problem of moral hazard or adverse selection.

The challenge, therefore, is to develop a practical policy framework (Chart).

This comprises several stages. The first stage is to know what is happening in the financial system. Monitoring and analysis involves comprehensive and ongoing examination of relevant factors, aimed at early identification of vulnerabilities. Subsequently, an assessment is made to identify whether these vulnerabilities pose a threat to financial stability and what policy responses may be appropriate.

Accordingly, in the first case, appropriate policies are mainly preventive, aimed at maintaining stability. In the second case, when imbalances are developing, safeguarding the stability of the system will call for remedial action. Obviously, owing to its multi-faceted nature, the distinction between the policy categories is seldom clear-cut. Many instruments can be employed to maintain financial stability (Table). In the prevention mode, existing policies are maintained and updated for structural changes in order to prevent future imbalances. Surveillance of financial markets, institutions and infrastructure constitutes an important element of preventive policy. The situation changes if the financial system is close to, or at the boundary of the range of stability.

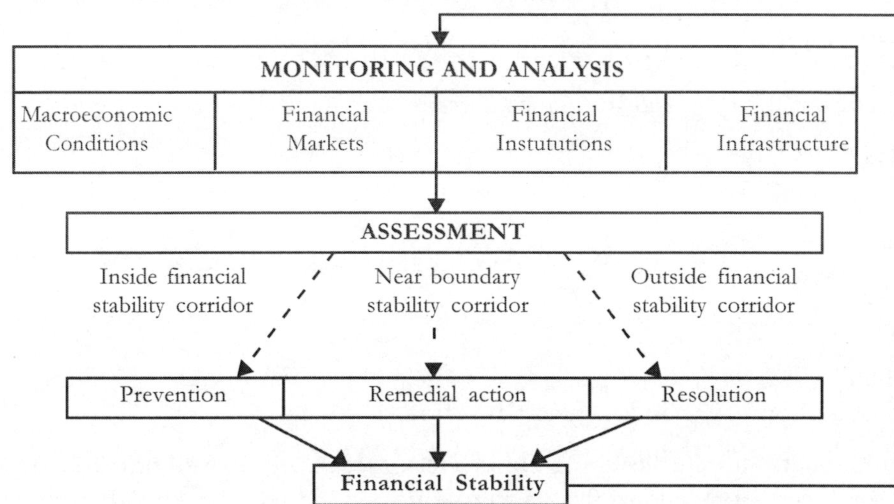

Chart: A Framework for Maintaining Financial System Stability

Table: Policy Instruments for Financial Stability

	Prevention	*Remedial Action*	*Resolution*
	Implementing existing policies to safeguard financial stability	Implementing pre-emptive measures to reduce emerging risks to financial stability	Reactive policy interventions aimed at restoring financial stability
Market disciplining mechanisms	Maintain, Update	Strengthen	Discretionary measures
Self-regulation	Maintain, Update	Strengthen	Discretionary measures
Financial safety nets	Maintain, Update	Strengthen	LOLR, deposit insurance
Surveillance	Maintain, Update	Intensify	Further intensify
Supervision/regulation	Maintain, Update	Intensify	Discretionary measures
Official communication	Existing policies	Moral suasion	Restore confidence
Macroeconomic policies	Maintain, Update	Reduce imbalances	Discretionary measures
Legal system	Maintain, Update	Strengthen	Discretionary measures

LOLR-Lender of last resort.

Looking forward, the shift to a larger, more integrated, leveraged, complex and market-based financial system will continue to change the nature of financial risks. In this respect, the financial stability framework needs to be viewed as a flexible tool that can be used to interpret changes and translate these into policy implications. A major challenge, therefore, remains in developing a deeper understanding of how the different dimensions of financial stability interact with each other and with the real economy, and how these interactions are influenced by policy actions.

References

Houben, A., G.Schinasi and J.Kakes (2004). 'Towards a Framework for Safeguarding Financial Stability', *IMF Working Paper* No.101, Washington DC.

Maintaining Financial Stability in a Global Economy (1997), Symposium sponsored by Federal Reserve Bank of Kansas City, Jackson Hole, Wyoming.

Major Issues

The major issues of the Indian financial system are:

1. Bank capital adequacy,
2. Income recognition,
3. Profitability,
4. Capital market,
5. Banking reforms,
6. Supervision and
7. Consolidation of the Indian financial sector.

Indicators of the current health of the financial system are derived primarily by aggregating data on the soundness of individual financial institutions. One such framework is macroprudential indicators.

Macroprudential Indicators

Aggregated Microprudential Indicators		*Macroeconomic Indicators*
Capital adequacy	**Liquidity**	**Economic growth**
Aggregate capital ratios	Central bank credit to financial institutions	Aggregate growth rates
Frequency distribution of capital ratios	Deposits in relation to monetary aggregates	Sectoral slumps
Asset quality	Segmentation of inter-bank rates	**Balance of payments**
Lending institution	Loan-to-deposit ratios	Current account deficit
Sectoral credit concentration	Maturity structure of assets and liabilities	Foreign exchange reserve adequacy
Foreign currency denominated lending	Measures of secondary market liquidity	External debt (including maturity structure)
Nonperforming loans and provisions	**Sensitivity to market risk**	Terms of trade
Loans to public sector entities	Foreign exchange risk	Composition and maturity of capital flows
Risk profile of assets	Interest rate risk	**Inflation**
Connected lending	Equity price risk	Volatility in inflation
Leverage ratios	Commodity price risk	**Interest and exchange rates**
Borrowing entity	**Market-based indicators**	Volatility in interest and exchange rates
Debt-equity ratios	Market prices of financial instruments	Level of domestic real interest rates
Corporate profitability	Indicators of excess yields	Exchange rate sustainability
Other indicators of corporate conditions	Credit ratings	Exchange rate guarantees
Household indebtedness	Sovereign yield spreads	**Lending and asset price booms**
Management soundness		Lending booms
Expense ratios		Asset price booms
Earnings per employee		**Contagion effects**
Growth in number of financial institutions		Financial market correlation
Earnings and profitability		Trade spillovers
Return on assets		**Other factors**
Return on equity		Directed lending and investment
Income and expense ratios		Government recourse to banking system
Structural profitability indicators		Arrears in the economy

Segments of Indian Financial Sector

1. Banking system
   - (i) commercial banks
   - (ii) cooperative banks
   - (iii) regional rural banks
   - (iv) private banks (new)
2. Development Finance Institutions
3. Stock Exchanges
4. Merchant bankers
5. Non-banking financial companies
6. Other financial companies/institutions

Apex Body	*Institutions*		*Operating Markets*	
IDBI	IFCI ICICI Banks SFCs Development Agencies PFs	LIC UTI GIC Finance Companies Investment Companies Brokers	New Issue Market Securities Market Direct Borrowing From Banks From Public Deposits Others	Initial Issues Further Trading

Fig. 9.1 Segments of Capital Market

Bank Capital Adequacy

Banks need capital to absorb unusual losses. The need to maintain an adequate capital-to-assets ratio exerts discipline on lending. Regulations should set minimum guidelines for capital adequacy that cover both assets and items not listed on the balance sheet (such as guarantees and lines of credit). Standards of capital adequacy can take account of different degrees of risk by requiring, for example, 100 per cent capital for high-risk items such as industrial shares, 10 per cent for unsecured loans, 5 per cent for secured loans, and so on.

In the past, Indian banks were subjected to varying capital requirements stipulated under the statutes. On the pattern of BASLE Committee recommendations, RBI has stipulated that commercial banks should attain capital adequacy in a phased manner. For the purpose, guidelines have been issued on risk weights to be assigned to assets (both funded and off-balance sheet) and banks are required to maintain minimum unimpaired capital funds to conform to the norm. For Indian banks which have branches abroad, the norm of 8 per cent was set to be met by March 31, 1994, foreign banks operating in India were to meet this norm by March 31, 1993. Other Indian banks were told to attain the adequacy norm of 4 per cent by the same month.

BOX 9.2

WHAT ARE CAPITAL ADEQUACY NORMS

In July 1988, the Committee of Banking Regulations and Supervisory Practices (BASLE Committee) released an agreed framework on international convergence of capital measures and capital standard for commercial banks. As a method of measuring capital adequacy, the committee had adopted a risk weighted assets approach which assigned weights to both on and off balance sheet exposures of banks according to their perceived risk and set a minimum standard at 8 per cent to be achieved by commercial banks, particularly for banks conducting significant international business.

The framework suggested by the BASLE Committee was to be applied by the Banking Supervisory Authorities of the various countries. The Reserve Bank of India (RBI), being the central bank of our country, had issued guidelines to all the scheduled commercial banks in the country to implement capital adequacy measures and strengthen their respective capital bases in a phased manner.

As a part of the financial sector reform process, the RBI has asked domestic banks to achieve 4 per cent capital to risk assets ratio by March 1993 and 8 per cent by March 1996. Accordingly, banks are required to adopt a weighed risk assets approach for their on and off balance sheet exposure for measuring capital adequacy.

The capital is divided into two parts — Tier I and Tier II.

Tier I capital consists of the bank's paid up capital, statutory reserves and other disclosed free reserves after deducting equity investments in subsidiaries, intangible assets and losses.

Tier II capital consists of undisclosed reserves and cumulative perpetual preference shares, the discounted value of revaluation reserves, general provision and loss reserves (upto a maximum of 1.25 per cent of the weighted risk assets), hybrid debt capital instruments and subordinated debt instruments (upto a maximum of 50 per cent of Tier I capital). The total Tier II capital should not exceed the Tier capital.

A Guide to Capital Adequacy

International banking supervisors laid out capital adequacy standards in 1988 as a measure of the safety or solvency of a bank in what came to be called the Basle Capital accord. According to this, a bank was required to maintain capital equivalent to 8% of its risk weighted assets.

Capital is divided into Tier I and Tier II capital. Tier I is the core capital and provides the most permanent and readily available support to a bank against unexpected losses. Tier II capital or supplementary capital contains elements that are less permanent or less readily available.

In India, capital adequacy was introduced on April 22, 1992 in a phased manner by the Reserve Bank of India.

Tier I capital comprises paid up capital, statutory reserves and other disclosed free reserves. Capital reserves representing surplus arising out of sale proceeds of assets is also included.

Tier II capital includes undisclosed reserves, cumulative perpetual preference shares, revaluation reserves arising from revaluation of assets that are undervalued on the bank's books (typically bank premises and marketable securities), general provisions and loss reserves, hybrid debt capital instruments and subordinated debt. To qualify as Tier II capital, subordinated debt must have a maturity of not less than five years. Such instruments may be treated as capital upto a limit of 50 per cent of Tier I capital.

The capital gap is the shortfall between the banks required capital and the banks' actual capital after transferring the retained profits to its reserves.

$$\frac{\text{Present capital (Tier I \& II)}}{\text{Aggregate risk weighted assets}} = \text{Required capital of 8\%}$$

The New Basle Accord specifies a continuum of approaches for banks to traverse the path from basic capabilities towards sophisticated risk management. The two sets of approaches specified by Basle Committee for credit risk measurement include the Standardised Approach and the Internal Ratings Based (IRB) Approaches.

Standardised Approach

Under this approach, banks are required to categorise their exposures into supervisory categories, *viz.*, Sovereigns, Non-central government public sector entities, Banks, Corporate, Regulatory retail portfolio, Claim secured by residential property, Past due loans, Higher risk categories, Off balance sheet items etc. Fixed risk weights are assigned corresponding to each supervisory category based on ratings assigned by external rating agencies approved by supervisor. The standardised approach also provides for reduction in credit exposure to a counter party based on the eligible collateral available.

Under the Standardised Approach, the calculation of the capital ratio is expressed as follows which should be a minimum of 8%:

$$\frac{\text{Capital}}{\text{Credit Risk Weighted Assets} + (\text{Operational Risk Charge} \times 12.5) + (\text{Market Risk Charge} \times 12.5)}$$

The IRB Approach

In contrast to the Standardised approach, which is a relatively modest refinement of the Basle I, the IRB approaches represent fundamental shift to a Capital Adequacy system based on the bank's own internal assessments of its risks. The IRB framework is calibrated to cover the bank's potential economic losses, namely:

- **Expected Loss** (EL), i.e., the mean or average loss a bank can reasonably expect to incur on the assets it holds. These are to be covered by a bank's Loan Loss Reserves (LLR).
- **Unexpected Loss** (UL), i.e., losses that exceed the bank's expectation for which the banks are required to maintain the capital. The capital requirement for the UL is arrived at through the Risk weight functions.

The key inputs used in the Risk weight function to estimate capital are:

- Probability of Default (PD), or the likelihood that the borrower defaults over a specified time horizon.

- Loss Given Default (LGD), or the amount a bank would expect to lose in the event of a default (the inverse of the recovery rate).
- Exposure at Default (EAD), which for example reflects the forecast amount that a borrower will draw on a commitment or other type of credit facility.
- Maturity (M) for large exposures.

Under the IRB, the calculation of the capital ratio differs from the Standardised Approach as under:

$$\frac{\text{Capital} + (\text{LLR} - \text{Credit Risk EL})}{(\text{Credit Risk UL} \times 12.5) + (\text{Operational Risk Charge} \times 12.5) + (\text{Market Risk Charge} \times 12.5)}$$

In effect the capital that a bank holds must fully cover its Unexpected Losses, with capital being adjusted for any surplus/shortfall in the amount of Loan Loss Reserves (LLR) required to cover Expected loss. Therefore, if the bank's EL exceeds its reserves, then it must deduct this shortfall from its capital. The ratio above is expressed at the prescribed Basle II minimum of 8%, but national supervisors may decide to set the minimum at a higher level if they deem fit, as has been the practice for a number of countries in their implementation of Basle I. In India, RBI has already prescribed a minimum of 9% Capital adequacy for the Banks.

The IRB approach provides two variants, *viz.*, Foundation IRB and Advanced IRB approach.

Bank Supervisors Add Teeth to Basle Accord

International banking supervisors have updated Basle Capital Accord by setting standards for how banks can test the accuracy of their own risk management models.

The final version of the amended capital accord, approved recently by the central bank governors of the group of 10 nations (G10) and now published, broke new ground by allowing banks to use their own internal models to measure market risks. But supervisors also want to be sure these models can predict possible losses on trading positions and the final version of the accord contains a framework for how to perform and interpret these tests.

Tests are critical to banks because the more accurate the model is, the less capital the bank has to set aside as a cushion against a possible collapse in market prices.

Supervisors, however, will penalise banks with inaccurate models by levying a higher capital charge to reflect the model's inability to accurately gauge risks.

Banks with models that show a high number of lapses will have to multiply their capital charges by four times, while banks with accurate models will only multiply it by three.

The latest version of the accord updates and extends the 1988 Basle Accord, which established minimum capital standards to protect banks against credit risks, such as countries or other lenders defaulting on loans. But banks are facing growing risks from their exposure to volatile financial markets and last year, the Basle Committee issued a proposal with guidelines for how much capital banks should set aside as a cushion against market risks.

Another important aspect of prudential regulations relates to adequate provisioning for bad and doubtful debts. If the profits of banks and other financial institutions are to be a true reflection of their functioning, loan losses must be adequately provided for. Both in relation to banks and the term lending institutions, prescription of uniform accounting practices relating to income recognition and provisioning against doubtful debts has become imperative.

It is in this context that the Reserve Bank introduced in April 1992 a capital risk-weighted asset ratio system for banks (including foreign banks) in India as a capital adequacy measure. Indian banks which have branches abroad were asked to achieve the norm of 8 per cent as early as possible and in any case by March 31, 1994. Foreign banks operating in India were asked to achieve this norm by March 31, 1993. Other banks had to achieve a capital adequacy norm of 4 per cent by March 31, 1993 (Tier I or core capital having been set at not less than 50 per cent of total capital) and the 8 per cent norm by March 31, 1996. The total of Tier II elements will be limited to a maximum of 100 per cent of total of Tier I elements for the purpose of compliance with the norms. Banks have been advised to review the existing level of capital funds vis-a-vis the prescribed level and plan to increase funds in a phased manner to achieve the prescribed ratio by the end of the period stipulated.

What has been said about banks holds good in relation to term lending institutions as well as other financial institutions. Whether they be leasing companies or hire-purchase companies or investment companies, prescription of appropriate capital requirements is must since capital is the last line of protection for all depositors.

Under Basle II, increased capital should not be viewed as the only option for addressing increased risks confronting the bank. Other means of addressing risk must also be considered such as strengthening risk management, applying internal limits, strengthening level of provisions and reserves and improving internal controls. The Second Pillar of the Revised Framework on Supervisory Review Process is intended not only to ensure that banks have adequate capital to support all their risks, but also to encourage banks to develop and use better risk management techniques in monitoring and managing the risks.

BOX 9.3

BASLE II AND RISK MANAGEMENT WITH SPECIAL EMPHASIS ON PILLAR II

The Pillar II of Basle II, i.e., Supervisory Review Process recognises the responsibility of bank management in developing an internal capital adequacy assessment process and setting capital targets that are commensurate with bank's risk profile and control environment. Supervisors are expected to evaluate how well banks are assessing their capital needs relative to risk and to intervene where appropriate.

There are three main areas that are relevant under Pillar II. First, risks considered under Pillar I that are not fully captured by the Pillar I process such as credit concentration risk. Second, certain risks that have not been taken into account by Pillar I process such as interest rate risk in the banking book, business and strategic risk. Third, factors external to the bank, such as business risk cycle effects. An important aspect of Pillar II is the assessment of compliance by banks, on an on-going basis, with the minimum standards and disclosure requirements prescribed for the advanced approaches under Pillar I, particularly the Internal Rating Based framework for credit risk and Advanced Measurement Approaches for operational risk.

The Basle Committee on Banking Supervision has identified four key principles of supervisory review. These are:

- Banks should have a process for assessing their overall capital adequacy in relation to their risk profile and a strategy for maintaining their capital levels. The fundamental elements of this assessment include policies and procedures designed to ensure that the bank identifies, measures, and reports all material risks – a process that relates capital to the level of risk.
- Supervisors should review and evaluate banks' internal capital adequacy assessments and strategies, as well as their ability to monitor and ensure their compliance with regulatory capital ratios. Supervisors should take appropriate supervisory action if they are not satisfied with the result of this process. The supervisors should assess the degree to which internal targets and processes incorporate the full range of material risks faced by the bank.
- Supervisors should expect banks to operate above the minimum regulatory capital ratios and should have the ability to require banks to hold capital in excess of the minimum. Pillar I capital requirements will include a buffer for uncertainties surrounding the Pillar I regime that affect banks. Bank-specific uncertainties will be treated under Pillar II.
- Supervisors should seek to intervene at an early stage to prevent capital from falling below the minimum levels required to support the risk characteristics of a particular bank and should require rapid remedial action if capital is not maintained or restored.

Several measures have been undertaken by the Reserve Bank to prepare the banking system to make a smooth migration to Basle II. Following the amendment to the Banking Companies (Acquisition and Transfer of Undertakings) Act in 1994, several public sector banks (PSBs) have raised capital both in India and abroad through Global Depository Receipts (GDRs). Several PSBs have also raised subordinated debt through the private placement route for inclusion under Tier II capital. There is a proposal to allow banks to raise subordinated debt from the capital market to augment their capital base by making suitable amendment to the Banking Regulation Act, 1949.

Banks can be divided into four categories: Basle skeptics, who are adopting a wait-and-watch approach and want further delay; cautious lobbyists, who have some level of awareness, but expect significant changes in the accord; early adopters, who have high-level understanding of the impacts and are considering budgetary implications; and advanced leaders, where awareness of impact is throughout the organisation, gap analysis has been performed and a programme structure is in place.

Basle II encourages accurate collection, analysis, management and digitisation of data. Thus, banks are looking for solutions to data capture and warehousing from software providers. Data pools creation, data standardisation and data analysis conducting systems are also on their lists. The challenge facing them now is to analyse their existing systems, their current limitations, and the areas needing improvement.

Income Recognition, Asset Classification and Provisioning for Bad Assets

The implementation of stricter asset classification and income recognition guidelines will have an effect on both the profit and loss statements and the balance sheets of commercial banks. In fact, a more transparent recognition of non-performing loans has three separate effects on the financial position of a bank. There is *first* a liquidity effect. If the bank was not in fact receiving cash payments of interest but merely capitalising these in the borrower's loan account, the bank loses flexibility and in particular loses the opportunity to redeploy this income stream to better purpose. *Second*, the non-performing portfolio has a profitability effect. Interest which is not received should not be booked as income as it often is when the true position is not acknowledged. This may seem to be harmless window-dressing but, in fact it has important real implications. Quite apart from eroding the credibility of bank financial statements, unrealistic profit declarations can accelerate the erosion of the capital of bank through unjustified tax and dividend payments. *Third*, there is the balance sheet effect, as loans that are not performing need to be provisioned against and ultimately written off against capital and reserves. If adequate provisions have not been made for loans that are not likely to be recovered, this will impair the bank's capital base, reducing the protection available to depositors and other creditors of the bank, including other banks.

With a view to bringing consistency and uniformity in the accounting policies of all the banks, so as to reflect the real position of banks' financial performance and strength, guidelines have been issued for compliance by banks in a phased manner.

Interest income on loan assets has to be reckoned on realisation basis and not on accrual basis, as per standard international accounting practice. Some banks (e.g., State Bank of India) have already been following the 'realisation' practice for quite some time. Income from advances in respect of codes five to eight is not recognised until it is realised. The new guidelines clearly define the procedure for classifying advances into 'past due' and 'non-performing' for income recognition.

Similarly, for provisioning for loan losses, detailed guidelines have been issued to banks. Assets are to be classified into four categories, *viz.*, standard, sub-standard, doubtful and loss, assets. Instructions for provening in respect of assets falling under the categories substandard, doubtful and loss assets have been issued. Separate instructions have also been issued for provisioning for losses on investment and other assets.

Profitability

The growth of the financial system and its ability to handle the challenges of the future depends, in the ultimate analysis, on its financial strength and profitability.

The erosion of profitability is in a sense the critical issue and epitomises the constraints under which the system has been operating. The problems faced by the banking and financial system which have affected its productivity, efficiency and profitability are thus the combination of factors, both internal to themselves, arising out of organisational and managerial weaknesses and external in the form of policy directions and political and administrative interferences.

Causes of Erosion of Profitability and Efficiency of the System are:

1. Absence of operational flexibility;
2. Excessive degree of regulation;
3. Unplanned growth of business;
4. Wrong priorities;
5. Preemptive diversion of resources;
6. Directed credit programmes;
7. Misplaced emphasis on concessional credit;
8. Subsidisation of credit;

9. Immobilisation of credit, depriving of its revolving character;
10. Lack of direction;
11. Political population and Government interference; and
12. Poor management and inefficiency.

The object of improving banks' profitability and consequently their ability pertains to adding to their reserves and capital funds and to be able to withstand adverse turns in the economic conjuncture. As the economy is deregulated and liberalised and the shelter of protection against internal and external competition reduced, one is likely to expect an element of industrial Darwinism where only the strong and the viable will succeed. In such a situation, the banking and financial system should be prepared to meet any eventualities arising out of a failure of some of the weaker elements in the economic system. The need for a strong and viable financial sector is, therefore, even greater in a period of economic liberalism than in a period of a protected economic environment. From this point of view, therefore, it is imperative that banks' operations be viable and profitable.

The recommendations, therefore, seek to address the issues of declining profitability and efficiency and seek to restore autonomy and flexibility of operations within an overall framework of reasonable monetary stability. They cover policy aspects, organisational issues, accounting practices and operational procedures but underlying them all is the central point of qualitative improvement of the portfolio and attention to enhancing the inherent strength of the institutions. It is in this sense that they have to be seen as an integrated set of recommendations rather than be viewed as piecemeal.

Competitive Efficiency

The measures adopted pertaining to financial systems aim at introducing an element of competitive efficiency in the Indian banking system. It would improve their operational efficiency and strengthen the financial position of banks, which is a pre-requisite of their exposure to the globalised banking environment. Banking, nine-tenth of which is in the public sector, has been subjected to administrative controls in respect of interest rates, directed lending, personnel policies, expansion of offices, etc., over the years. These controls are now sought to be eased in a gradual manner.

Both the deposit rates structure and the lending rates structure were determined by the regulatory authority in the past. In addition, banks used to be subjected to various guidelines on priority sector lending investment in Government securities, etc., which were a part of the policy to ensure that a certain percentage of credit went to specified subsectors. Till recently, banks were required to keep investment in Government and other approved securities at 38.5% of their net demand and time liabilities by way of Statutory Liquidity Ratio (SLR), of which investments in effect were banks' funds lent to the Government at concessional rates. In the 'private' sector category also, banks were required to dispense 40% of credit to 'pre-defined' priority sectors, again most of it at concessional rates. The concessionality in interest charged and a high level of pre-empted funds, affected bank profitability adversely despite a measure of cross-subsidisation. Under the new policy regime, the SLR has been reduced in stages. As to the interest structure, fixed rates have been done away with. Banks have been given freedom to offer deposit rates subject to a maximum and charge lending rates subject to minimum on their non-priority advances. Significantly, the banks can now charge interest at commercial rates on priority advances, if the amount advanced exceeds Rs. 200,000. These steps should help banks shore up profitability to an extent. In respect of larger industrial advances the erstwhile Credit Authorisation Scheme has been replaced by a relaxed Credit Monitoring Arrangement, which permits individual banks the opportunity to tone up their credit appraisal skills.

To rationalise banking presence on efficient lines, banks have been given permission to open, close or relocate branches in non-rural areas without prior approval of the Reserve Bank of India subject to their fulfilling certain norms, thus virtually doing away with the branch licensing policy. A proposal is also said to be under active consideration to segregate the regional rural bank subsidiaries of the commercial banks and reorganise them into separate units with different norms to judge their viability.

– Product Diversification

- Consumer credit cards
- Farm credit cards
- Travellers cheques
- Investors club
- Home loan accounts
- Industrial finance branch
- Automated teller machines
- Overseas branches
- Stock invest

– Business Diversification

- Merchant banking
- Leasing
- Factoring
- Mutual funds
- Portfolio management
- Venture capital
- Housing finance
- Share deals
- Securitisation of debts

Financial Products

Fund Based

- Cash credit
- Overdraft
- Demand loans
- Term finance
- Import credit
- Export credit
- Bill financing

Fee Based

- Letter of credit
- Guarantees
- Bid bonds/Financial performance
- Loan syndication
- Project management
- Counselling
- Investment management
- Portfolio management
- Treasury products Options/Future/Swamps/ Currency switch
- Credit cards

To restore financial health of banks, prudential norms have been set, adherence to which will reflect, in the first phase, the true picture of their financial condition. Guidelines have also been issued on the transparency of their financial statements, on income recognition, asset classification as well as on provisioning for bad and doubtful assets. Simultaneously, capital adequacy norms have been prescribed for various banks (please see box).

These guidelines are to be implemented over a period of time. One other important aspect of banks' health which will need to be dealt with is the present accumulation of their Non-Performing Assets (NPAs) and their present comparatively weak capital base. It is essential that the accumulated NPAs are removed from the banks' balance sheets by means of a mechanism like the Asset Reconstruction Fund, recommended by the Narasimham Committee. This undoubtedly involves substantial separate funding. But, without it, touching capital adequacy norms will pose a very difficult problem for banks.

Regulation of Banking

One of the major issues is that of the regulation of the domestic banking system. At an early stage of development, it is necessary and appropriate that the extent of regulation should be somewhat strict, the main reason being to infuse depositors' confidence and that the depositors should know that the banks are being run as per RBI and Banking Regulation Act. Further, a bank's affairs are being conducted in a manner not detrimental to the depositors' interest. There is, however, a danger that regulation becomes over regulation. If every aspect of balance sheet operations, every aspect of management is a subject of control and approvals, then it is going to damage one quality with which banks are associated their innovative character. Bankers ought not to become government officials following only rules and regulations. The eminent authority on banking, Professor Sayers says that the art of banking lies in making a clean loan. Indian bankers were looking at what they are lending against rather than what they are lending for. In the present context, purpose oriented rather than security oriented banking is important. Excessive regulation tends to make people more security conscious. Of course, while regulation is good, the danger of excessive regulation is that banks can become subject to behest lending whether through loan melas or otherwise. I think it is this that we need to guard against. Regulation should not become excessive. In keeping with the modern trend towards liberalisation of the economy whether be in a import trade or in industrial policy, what we need is to take another look and see whether even in areas of banking and credit, we should not move towards a measure of liberalisation of policies.

The evolving regulatory regime as reflected in the Basle II Accord is aimed at ensuring financial stability and building a robust financial system. There will be more and more reliance on the individual bank's own assessment of risks and the way they go about managing them. This will also be supplemented by the market scrutiny for better financial discipline. This approach to capital regulation, with its market discipline component, signals that sound accounting, auditing and transparency and disclosure will continue to be important parts of 'regulatory and supervisory' approach.

The Basle Committee's paper on "Enhancing bank transparency" emphasis the need of 'transparency' to hold the board of directors and senior management properly accountable for their actions and performance. In order to monitor directors, shareholders and various stakeholders need 'optimal and well designed' timely information. The external audit process provides an independent check on the quality of these reports, limiting the effects of the moral hazard problem to which directors might be susceptible.

The OECD and the World Bank have now combined their efforts to create and support round tables on corporate governance, where national policy makers, regulators and market participants can share experiences and debate corporate governance policies and reforms. The OECD's recent 'white paper on Corporate Governance in South East European Countries' emphasis the need of disclosing "all relevant information material to an informed understanding and assessment of the company's business, activities and situation; ongoing disclosure of significant events should be considerably improved; the respective responsibilities of the different company organs and the external auditors regarding disclosure should be clarified; shareholders' access to information needs to be enhanced through the use of efficient and modern communication by companies as well as authorities; the role of media in the dissemination of company information and in promoting global transparency in business practices needs to be strengthened and supported and shareholders should have access to effective redressal mechanism, including professional arbitration and low cost collective efforts."

Corporate Governance Benchmarking 'Transparency and Disclosures'

Effective corporate governance may be described as a reconciliation between the power and obligations of the Board of Directors to ensure good performance, awareness of the rights and duties of stakeholders and the expectation of the society.

The management consulting firm McKinsey's world wide surveys show "corporate governance remains a great concern for institutional investors", with an overwhelming majority of them being willing to pay a premium for companies demonstrating consistent adherence to high governance standards. In USA, California Public Employees Retirement System (CalPERS) has a three pronged strategy to invest in a company (i) promoting effective shareholder participation in selection of management-nominated directors; (ii) proxy reform, especially for confidentiality in collection, independence in tabulation and uniformity in the treatment of abstention and non-votes; and (iii) setting meaningful criteria for director qualifications, to be adopted publicly by the board of each company.

While in India, the principal characteristics of good corporate governance, as identified by respondents to the ICRA survey (October-December 2003) are: high level of transparency and disclosures; integrity of accounts; appropriate governance structure; strong and independent Board of Directors; care for minority shareholders and active Board Committees.

The key requirements for a high level of transparency and disclosure as identified by the respondents to the survey are speedy dissemination of price sensitive information; presentation of all relevant details in annual accounts and high quality of 'Management Discussion and Analysis.'

Capital Market

With activity on the capital market increasing, consistent with Government's liberalisation policy in other spheres, liberalised operations were permitted on the capital market and the market was opened to global investment. Over the past 3-4 years, major liberalisation measures were taken in this regard.

(a) The office of the controller of capital issues was disbanded. Corporates are now allowed to enter the market directly, without prior approval. For the purpose of control and regulation in the process, the Securities and Exchange Board of India (SEBI) has laid down certain guidelines for disclosures, etc.

(b) A new company set up by an existing company with a five-year track record of consistent profitability, is now free to price its issue (in the past, such issues used to be at par). Similarly, private or closely held companies, with a 3-year track record of consistent profitability, can now price their issue freely.

(c) Stringent disclosure norms have prescribed for compliance by corporates by SEBI.

(d) For debentures, companies are now allowed to determine interest rates, the premium amount on fully convertible debentures, etc. Credit rating has been made mandatory for issue of debentures or any debt instrument by a company.

(e) The capital market has now been opened to foreign institutional investors (An earlier issue of this publication carried a feature on the scheme, which are registered with SEBI, and have been listed in the box).

(f) New institutions, *viz.*, Stock Holding Corporation of India Ltd., Over the Counter Exchange of India (OTCEI) have been set up to cater to investor requirements and improve the working of stock exchanges in the country.

With growing equity cult and investment awareness among savers, the capital market is poised to play a much enlarged role in the financial sector.

In the short-term money market, many new instruments have been introduced such as certificates of deposit, commercial paper, upto 364 days treasury bills, etc. To regulate activities in the money market, which is not as developed as the capital market, Discount and Finance House of India was (DHFI) set up. Commercial banks and financial institutions have been permitted to set up Money Market Mutual Funds. Steps have also been taken to regulate the activities of Mutual Funds set up by banks and financial institutions. They have been brought under the purview of SEBI.

Supervision

An adequate system of supervision follows prudential guidelines. A strong system of supervision becomes necessary in order to ensure that prudential regulations are followed faithfully by financial institutions.

In the last decade, several new institutions have appeared on the financial scene. Merchant banks, mutual funds, leasing companies, venture capital companies and factoring companies have now joined hire-purchase companies in expanding the range of financial services available. However, the regulatory framework for these new set of institutions has still to be developed.

The supervision of these institutions which form an integral part of the financial system, should come within the purview of the new agency to be set up for this purpose under the aegis of the RBI. The control of these institutions should be principally confined to off-site supervision with the on-site supervision being resorted to cases which call for active intervention. The SEBI, which is changed with the responsibility of ensuring orderly functioning of the market should have jurisdiction over these institutions to the extent that their activities impinge on market operations. In regard to mutual funds, there is a good case for enacting new legislation on the lines obtaining in several countries with a view to providing an appropriate legal framework for their constitution and functioning. the present guidelines with regard to venture capital companies are unduly restrictive, and affecting the growth of this business and they need to be reviewed and amended from time to time.

The process of liberalisation has brought in systemic changes in the operations of Development Financial Institutions (DFIs). In tandem with the emerging needs of industry in the new competitive and deregulated financial environment, these institutions have re-oriented their policies and portfolio structure with much sharper customer focus, by developing and introducing a variety of products and services, improving cost efficiency and diversifying into newer areas which in some cases were the exclusive business domain of commercial banks. In the changed milieu, the harmonisation of a modicum of co-ordination between the role and operations of banks and DFIs has become an important issue.

BOX 9.4

ELEMENTS OF A BANK SUPERVISION SYSTEM

An adequate system of bank supervision should allow for both off-site supervision and on-site inspection. The task of the off-site supervisors is to analyse reports of the banks, identify possible problems and propose remedies. Banks in most countries have to submit monthly balance sheet information for purposes of monetary control. It would make sense to combine the two reporting requirements.

After receiving the reports, the *off-site* supervisors should:

- Check their completeness, accuracy and consistency of facts.
- Check their compliance with prudential ratios and regulations.
- Analyse the financial situation of the bank and identify the main changes in financial ratios.
- Identify other risks such as foreign exchange risks, interest rate risks, and concentration risks.
- Prepare a summary for the management of the supervisory agency and recommend its plan of action.

The *on-site* inspectors should check the accuracy of the periodic reports to the supervisor and analyse those aspects of a bank that cannot be adequately monitored by off-site supervision. Inspections, however, should not become audits. they should focus on the bank's main activities and on the potential problems that were identified by off-site supervision. Inspections should assess the quality of assets, management and control procedures and accounting systems. The inspectors should:

- Study the main credit files (and a sample of smaller files) to assess the lending procedures and the quality of the loans.
- Evaluate lending procedures and review minutes of meetings of the credit committee and the board of directors.
- Check management information system and internal controls, especially with regard to the activities of branches and subsidiaries.
- Evaluate accounting procedures, especially those for provisioning and interest accrual.

As in the case of banks and financial institutions, there is need to lay down prudential norms and guidelines governing the functioning of these institutions. These prudential guidelines should relate, among other things, to capital adequacy, debt equity ratio, income recognition provisioning against doubtful debts, adherence to sound accounting and financial policies, disclosure requirements and valuations of assets. The eligibility criteria for entry, growth and exit should also be clearly stipulated so that the growth of these institutions take place on proper lines.

Banks, the world over, are increasingly outsourcing a significant part of their regulated and unregulated activities from specialist providers which they would have traditionally conducted in-house. The opportunities for such outsourcing of activities have increased significantly in recent years with the evolving and improving communication systems and information technology. Although outsourcing can have a positive impact on a bank's cost efficiency and allow it to access specialist expertise that would ordinarily not be available to it internally, it may also expose the bank to certain risks, which if not managed adequately, could be a matter of regulatory and supervisory concern.

BOX 9.5

OUTSOURCING BY BANKS

'Outsourcing' may be defined as use of a third party (either an affiliated entity within a corporate group or an entity that is external to the corporate group) to perform activities on a continuing basis that would normally be undertaken by the bank itself. Third party or service provider refers to the entity that is undertaking the outsourced activity on behalf of the bank. There are some key risks in outsourcing such as strategic risk, reputation risk, compliance risk, operational risk, exit strategy risk, counterparty risk, country risk, contractual risk, access risk, concentration risk and systemic risk. It would be imperative for the bank outsourcing its activities to ensure effective management of these risks.

The failure of a service provider in providing a specified service, a breach in security/confidentiality, or non-compliance with legal and regulatory requirements by either the service provider or the outsourcing bank can lead to financial losses for the bank and could also lead to systemic risks within the entire banking system in the country. Hence, its board of directors and management of bank need to provide direction and guidance to banks to adopt sound and responsive risk management practices for effective oversight, due diligence and management of risks arising out of such outsourcing activities.

Some outsourcing arrangements, if disrupted, have the potential to significantly impact bank's business operations, reputation of profitability. Such arrangements are considered 'material outsourcing.' Banks should use qualitative judgement to assess whether or not an outsourcing arrangement that is in existence or being planned, is to be considered 'material outsourcing' or not.

Before entering into, or significantly changing, an outsourcing arrangement, a bank should: (i) analyse how the arrangement will fit into its organisation and reporting structure; (ii) consider whether the agreement establishing the outsourcing arrangement will allow it to monitor and control its operational risk exposure relating to the service provider; (iii) conduct appropriate due diligence of the service provider's financial position and expertise; (iv) consider how it will ensure a smooth transition of its operations from its current arrangements to a new or changed outsourcing arrangement (including what will happen on the termination of the contract); and (v) consider any concentration risk implications such as the business continuity implications that may arise if a single service provider is used by several banks.

The bank should require its service providers to develop and establish a robust framework for documenting, maintaining and testing business continuity and recovery procedures. Outsourcing often leads to the sharing of facilities operated by the service provider. The bank should ensure that service providers are able to isolate the bank's information, documents and records, and other assets. This is to ensure that in adverse conditions, all documents, records of transactions and information given to the service provider, and assets of the bank can be removed from the possession of the service provider in order to continue its business operations, or deleted, destroyed or rendered unusable.

The bank should have in place a management structure to monitor and control its outsourcing activities. A bank that has entered into or is planning material outsourcing, or is planning to vary any such outsourcing arrangements, should adhere to the regulatory and supervisory requirements. It is imperative for the bank, when performing its due diligence in relation to outsourcing, to consider all relevant laws, regulations, guidelines and conditions of approval, licensing or registration. The engagement of service providers in a foreign country exposes a bank to country risk – economic, social and political conditions and events in a foreign country that may adversely affect the bank. Such conditions and events could prevent the service provider from carrying out the terms of its agreement with the bank. To manage the country risk involved in such outsourcing activities, the bank should take into account and closely monitor government policies and political, social, economic and legal conditions in countries where the service provider is based.

Reference

Bank for International Settlements (2005), 'Outsourcing in Financial Services', Basle Committee of Banking Supervision, February, 2005.

E-Finance

In India, which depends heavily on cash transactions, the use of e-money can be beneficial in terms of reduced miscellaneous costs such as cost of printing and minting of smaller denomination notes and coins and transportation and storage costs. However, the setting up of network infrastructure to operate nationwide electronic payment systems entails heavy cost. On the flip side, the use of e-finance also poses several challenges from the financial stability point of view.

Consolidation

The solutions to the major issues of the Indian banking system aim at consolidating the gains made in the Indian financial sector while improving the quality of the portfolio, providing greater operational flexibility and most importantly, greater autonomy in the internal operations of the banks and financial institutions so as to nurture a healthy, competitive and vibrant financial sector. This will, above all else, require depoliticisation of appointments, implying at the same time a self-denial by the Government and the perception that it has to distance itself from the internal decision-making of the banks and the financial institutions. The proposed deregulation of the financial sector and the measures aimed at improving its health and competitive vitality would, in the Committee's view, be consistent with the steps being taken to open up the Indian economy, enable the Indian financial sector to forge closer ties with the global financial markets and enhance India's ability to take competitive advantage.

Way to Grow

In an industry where size is equated with financial soundness, the small size of Indian banks is reason for much heart-burn. This is all the more so because foreign banks are widely expected

BOX 9.6

E-FINANCE: CHALLENGES

Rapid advances in communication technology in recent years have led to several innovations in the delivery of financial services through the internet and other electronic media (collectively known as e-finance).

In developing economies, the use of e-finance is low in comparison with the advanced industrial economies (Table). However, in some respects, developing countries have an advantage. They can learn from the experience of advanced economies. It may even be possible for them to 'leapfrog' straight to the most advanced technologies.

The growth of e-finance raises several important challenges. First, security concerns are important factors which often discourage many internet users from using e-banking. Supervisors will need to be assured that banks have conducted adequate assessments of the vulnerability of their operating systems, back-up facilities, firewalls and emergency procedures. The complexity of internet-related activity encourages outsourcing, which often raises the problem of concentration risk when several banks depend on the same service provider. Another challenge for both providers of financial services and those who supervise them is the sheer uncertainty. It is difficult to predict which technologies will work best and what would be the response of customers and competitors. In an attempt to maintain profitability, banks might adapt poorly to e-banking (which could involve either under or over-spending on new technology), prompting them to move into riskier business to maintain returns.

Table E-Finance: Select Indicators

Country	*Internet users as percentage of inhabitants*	*Mobile phones per 1000 inhabitants*	*Per cent bank customers using on-line banking*
	2000	*2000*	*1999*
1	*2*	*3*	*4*
Developed Countries			
Australia	34	45	4
Germany	29	59	12
Italy	23	74	n.a.
UK	30	73	6
US	35	40	6
Emerging Markets			
Brazil	3	14	4
Malaysia	16	21	Less than 1
South Africa	5	19	n.a.
South Korea	40	57	n.a.
Indonesia	1	2	n.a.
India	Less than 1	Less than 1	n.a.
Thailand	4	5	n.a.

n.a=not available.

References

Turner, P. (2001), 'E-finance and Financial Stability', in R. Litan, P. Masson and M. Pomerleano (eds.), *Open Doors:Foreign Participation in Financial Systems in Developing Countries*, Brookings.

Claessens, S., T. Glaessner and D. Klingebiel (2001), 'E-finance in Emerging Markets: Is Leapfrogging Possible', World Bank Discussion Paper No.4, June.

to be given more operational freedom from 2009 and there's a question mark whether some of the smaller Indian banks will be able to compete. It is worth noting that the top 25 banks in India account for 85 per cent of total assets, which means that the other banks are very small indeed. How would they be able to compete with the massive economies of scale generated by the big foreign banks?

These concerns have led to a call for consolidation in Indian banking. That is nothing new. In 1991, the first Narasimham Committee recommended that three large banks had become big enough to go international and that this was best done through a process of mergers and acquisitions based on market considerations. The process has now acquired greater urgency, perhaps because of the 2009 deadline. Nevertheless, although in the last two years the finance minister has been talking of the need for consolidation to create world-class banks, nothing much has happened. Since the PSU banks dominate the Indian banking system, M&As among them hold the key for change in the dynamics of the banking sector.

India has been no stranger to M&As in banking. In fact, the Imperial Bank of India, SBI's predecessor, was born from the consolidation of three Presidency Banks in 1920. However, forced M&A as a tool for rescuing ailing banks, besides protecting public and depositor confidence in the banking system, began in 1960. In recent times, private banks have seen voluntary M&A activity based on market considerations. The merger of Times Bank with HDFC Bank was the first of such marriages after liberalisation. Others have followed: the merger of Bank of Madura with ICICI Bank, reverse merger of ICICI with ICICI Bank, the coming together of Centurion Bank and Bank of Punjab and the recent decision of Lord Krishna Bank to amalgamate with Centurion Bank of Punjab. Sometimes, mergers have been forced, usually to rescue weak banks. Take the amalgamation of New Bank of India with Punjab National Bank, the takeover of Global Trust Bank by Oriental Bank or, most recently, the takeover of Sangli Bank by ICICI Bank and United Western Bank by IDBI Bank. Most of these mergers are not market-driven, and it is doubtful whether they create value. Also, the size of these mergers has been small. The big question remains: When will we see mergers in the public sector?

BOX 9.7

THE ASIAN EXPERIENCE

Banking consolidation came to the fore after the 1997 economic meltdown. Japan, which had seen a virtual collapse of its system, made consolidation its forte. This resulted in the emergence of three large banks — Mitsubishi UFJ, Mizuho and Sumitomo Mitsui. Today non-performing asset levels have come down to 2 per cent from a peak of 8.4 per cent in 2002. The crisis exposed the vulnerability of a weak banking system to economic shocks. Hong Kong allowed complete FDI in banking and this facilitated the takeover of several banks by Singaporean and Taiwanese banks. In Indonesia, banks that had capital adequacy ratios below 25 per cent were marked for immediate closure. Consolidation among banks was encouraged and, as a result, the number of banks in Indonesia, which stood at 239 in 1996, came down to 138 by 2003. Post-restructuring, the banks' branch network and coverage has increased significantly. In Malaysia, the regulator Bank Negara has created 10 anchor banks through the consolidation of 22 banks and 39 finance companies. This is a precursor to a second phase of reforms scheduled to commence in 2007. Consolidation has led to the strengthening of the banking systems of these countries and customers are serviced better as a result.

The banking sector plays an important role as fulcrum for the activities in the real sector of the economy. It has to perform its functions most efficiently. Alive to this need, many structural and operational reforms have been and are being implemented and the financial system is being liberalised to let market forces determine its efficiency. In the words of the then Union Finance Minister Dr. Manmohan Singh, *'Both in banking and stock market reforms, we have taken important initial steps. But we have an ambitious agenda ahead of us. Our objective is a vibrant, internationally competitive financial system which is adequately responsive to the needs of India's economic and social development.'*

Conclusion

While restoring the health of the banking system is quite independent of macro structural adjustment, financial sector reforms would have a surer foundation for success if macro-economic balance in the system were restored. No programme of liberalisation can succeed in the absence of such macro-economic stability. The progress of liberalisation also requires movement in phased sequence rather than a sudden splurge of deregulation and, also if we are to avoid the dislocation and adverse consequences that marked such experience in some countries abroad, as for example in the Southern Cone of Latin America. Indeed as Diaz Alejandro pointed out, in this context, financial liberalisation in the absence of fiscal and monetary discipline could lead to financial chaos, which in our country calls for non-inflationary or low-inflationary financing of the Government budget. Even for interest rates to be aligned to productivity in the real sector, a measure of price stability is called for. There is indeed no effective substitute for fiscal and monetary discipline to achieve macro-economic stability.

The Indian banking system has served the country's economy reasonably well so far. It is capable of doing better. The Concise Oxford Dictionary defines reform as making or becoming "*better by removal or abandonment of imperfections, faults or errors.*" The issue is of correcting the imperfections, faults and errors of the past in the hope that the financial sector will enhance the progress of the economy and that *credit would be in Schumpeter's* memorable phrase, "*a phenomenon of development.*"

ANNEXURE I

DEFINITION OF CAPITAL FUNDS

Tier 1 Capital (Core Capital)

- Paid up capital
- Disclosed free reserves (statutory reserves, share premium, other revenue reserves)
- Capital reserve (surplus from sale of capital assets)
- Unallocated surplus (P&L balance carried over)

Tier 2 Capital

- Undisclosed reserves and cumulative perpetual preference shares
- Revaluation reserves (at discount of 55%)
- Investment fluctuation reserve
- General provisions and loss reserves (upto a maximum of 1.25% risk weighted assets)
- Hybrid debt (maturity of above 5 years, fully paid up, unsecured, subordinate to claims of other creditors, not redeemable at the initiative of the holder or without RBI consent).
- Tier 1 Capital should be not less than 50% of total Capital. Tier 2 Capital cannot exceed 100% of Tier 1 Capital. Investment by banks in the subordinated debt of other banks should not exceed 10% of a bank's capital funds and will carry 100% risk weight.
- Some of the options for raising subordinated debt in the domestic market as Tier 2 Capital include Regular Income Bonds with an interest reset clause, Cumulative Interest Bonds, Tax Benefit Bonds (benefit under section 54EA & 54EB), Double Benefit Bonds (bonds with detachable, tradable warrants), Tax Free Bonds, etc.
- With effect from October 2001, RBI has withdrawn the exemption from CRR and SLR requirements on subordinated debt. Consequently, the cost of raising Tier 2 capital has gone up. At present banks already hold Government securities in excess of SLR requirements but will have to find additional resources to meet CRR requirements. However, it would be a very unfair burden on banks if they have to provide for CRR on funds raised in the past, particularly in the case of RBI/IMF as these were raised to shore up the country's foreign exchange resources at a critical time. Also, the exemption has been factored into the cost of funds and these have also been deployed accordingly. Therefore, RBI could consider favourably banks' request for exemption from reserve requirements on Tier 2 capital raised in the past as also resources raised under RBI/IMD.

Tier 3 Capital

Introduced in 1996 by BIS as part of its proposals for market risk. However, the same has not yet been introduced by RBI for India.

- Same characteristics of subordinated debt as in Tier 2 Capital except for original maturity of at least 2 years
- Lock in clause, i.e., no repayment if bank's minimum capital requirement fails
- Tier 3 capital is limited to 250% of Tier 1 capital
- Unused Tier 1 capital may be substituted for Tier 3 upto the 250% limit.

ANNEXURE II

ALLOCATION OF TIER 3 CAPITAL

- As a first step, total risk assets need to be segregated into credit risk and market risk (calculations are as per current regulations and do not include operational risk as it has not yet been introduced).
- Tier 3 capital cannot exceed 250% of Tier 1 capital for market risk. For instance, if Tier 1 capital for market risk is Rs.100, then Tier 3 capital cannot exceed Rs. 250.

- Assume a bank needs to set aside:

  Minimum capital for credit risk: Rs. 600

  Minimum capital for market risk: Rs. 350

- Bank actually has:

  Tier 1 capital: Rs.700

  Tier 2 capital: Rs.100

  Tier 3 capital: Rs.600

- What bank actually does:

  Covers Credit risk by : Rs.500 Tier 1 capital

  and : Rs.250 Tier 2 capital

  Total capital for market risk : Rs.350

- So to cover further asset expansion, bank has balance of Rs.100 Tier capital plus balance of Rs.350 Tier capital (i.e., 600-250).
- But since Tier 3 capital cannot exceed 250% of Tier 1 capital, unused but eligible Tier 3 capital is only Rs. 250 and remaining Rs.100 is not eligible for being counted as Tier 3 capital. So bank does not gain by raising additional Tier 3 capital. Thus, bank will have to carefully plan not only the quantum of capital required, but also its composition.

Chapter 10

Management in Banks

Introduction

Just as any other organisation, banks too must be managed efficiently. For there is too much money at stake. Banks facilitate both the production of goods and services as well as the flow of these goods and services from producers to consumers. Precisely because of these reasons, banks are the heart of our financial system and play a very important role in our economy. Although banks create no new wealth, their lending, investing and related activities facilitate the economic processes of production, distribution and consumption. Banks are, therefore, rightly referred to as a "department store of finance." The banks must be managed prudently, safely and profitably if we are to have a strong, growing and adaptable banking system capable of meeting the demands of society.

The Indian banking system has made commendable progress in extending its geographical spread and functional reach. The spread of the banking system has been a major factor in promoting financial intermediation in the economy and in the growth of financial savings. The credit reach also has been extensive and the banking system now caters to several million borrowers, especially in agriculture and small industry.

Banks today have come of age. They are, and have been acknowledged to be, the prime movers of change. They have been, and remain, in the vanguard of professionalised management as well as of a better system of management. They are promoters and vehicles of more rapid and broad-based economic growth through wide-ranging stimulus to entrepreneurship development in their respective economies. Banking has, indeed, travelled a long way. One of its durable concerns, indeed, is to assist in setting up viable productive projects with the supplementation of capital. Time was when the assistance given by a development bank was related primarily to the security that a borrower could offer. In this respect, the shift to the wider considerations of profitability and productivity of a venture and its contribution to the economic strategies of the country, as well as furtherance of the objectives of its social policy, is now an accomplished fact.

The banking sector is the most dynamic force of the economy. With a view to keeping this sector vibrant, healthy, strong and dynamic, it is of utmost importance that it should be managed well. The key to success is good management.

Good Management

Management is that process by which managers create, direct, maintain and operate purposive organisations through systematic, co-ordinated, and co-operative human effort. Bank management is a multi-disciplinary subject. The scope of good management widens with the scale and scope of diversity of banking activities in consonance with the rapid changes in the political, social and economic environment.

Fig. 10.1 (Courtesy: Times of India, Mumbai, 15.5.92)

Objectives of Bank Nationalisation

The important objectives of bank takeover were:

(i) To mobilise deposits on a massive scale throughout the country and not only in cities and large towns;

(ii) To accelerate lending for productive purposes of diverse kinds, irrespective of the size and social status of the borrower, particularly in the hitherto neglected sectors such as agriculture, small industry and exports, and promote the rapid growth thereof;

(*iii*) To sustain and generate gainful employment in a direct and indirect manner on a much larger scale than before;

(*iv*) To secure a more equitable distribution of credit throughout the country by having a balanced programme of branch expansion, particularly in the states and areas which had lagged behind or were unbanked or underbanked;

(*v*) To encourage new entrepreneurs and contribute to the development and growth of all backward areas;

(*vi*) To serve as active catalysts in viable development programmes in as many sectors of the economy as possible;

(*vii*) To provide improved and extended service to the general public;

(*viii*) To achieve the organisational and functional reorientation of the banking system to facilitate growth;

(*ix*) To ensure the professionalisation of banks.

There have been many changes in the functional, institutional and structural aspects of banking during the post-nationalisation period. The coverage of the country with bank offices has been growing, and there has been a rapid expansion in banking business, in terms of both deposits and advances. Banks made a beginning in increasing their involvement in the financing of agriculture, small-scale industries, small borrowers, retail trade and the self-employed. They have acted as effective intermediaries for accelerated economic growth. Keeping in view the fundamental objective that the banking system must play the fullest possible role in achieving the desired level and rate of economic growth in the country, the Banking Commission observed:

(*i*) With the growth of economy, the commercial banks should expand at a rapid rate, which should be accompanied by a continuous increase in the share of bank money in the total money supply.

(*ii*) There is need for a clear formulation of policy, a policy of action. The banking policy has to be based on the economic goals set by the country.

(*iii*) It is the responsibility of the banks to provide working funds for production.

(*iv*) In providing working funds for production and distribution, the banks have to follow the priorities laid down in the economic plans.

(*v*) Banking is a service industry, and therefore, increased productivity of manpower is an essential component of banking development, a necessary precondition for increased prosperity of all the sections of the community.

Objectives of Bank Management

The banking industry has been passing through a phase of transition which was initiated with the liberalisation of financial policies that led to disintermediation, diversification and deregulation of the financial system. But the increased competition coupled with interventionist policies has jeopardised the cost-benefit of funds. This has given way to non-conventional banking in place of traditional banking so as to capture the increased interest sensitivity of depositors. "Manage the Change' has become the stepping stone for the success of the banks.

The important management objectives of banks are:

1. To organise the structure to meet the challenges of changing environment;
2. To improve customer services;
3. To introduce new schemes;
4. To improve housekeeping;
5. To improve technology in banks;
6. To modernise office equipment;
7. To train employees on an ongoing basis;
8. To improve work ethics;
9. To improve the quality of banking service;
10. To improve the health of the organisation;
11. To imbibe value system;
12. To improve productivity through participative management.
13. To improve inspection and social audit;
14. To follow instructions and stick to rules and guidelines;
15. To rise above and serve the community;
16. To utilise human resources for improving quality of life;
17. To develop leadership and entrepreneurial spirit among the cadre;
18. To motivate employees to work efficiently, productively and profitably;
19. To evolve a unique monitoring and controlling system; and
20. To improve the image and strengthen the confidence of the people in the system.

Evolution of Management Process in Banks

The evolution of management process in banks has been keeping pace with the sea changes that are taking place in the social, economic and political environment. Political will has also had a greater influence on this process.

The threshold years of the nineties witnessed emphasis on consolidation, deregulation, diversification, innovation and induction of new technology. The evolution of the Indian banking scenario has been on the lines of development on the international scene. Far-reaching changes surfaced in the management process in banks in the eighties which are continuing. The transition is from control management in a hierarchical organisation through management by objectives in a flat type or matrix organisation to differential management in a network organisation.

To a large degree, the above changes in the management process have been taking place in Indian banks also. The training system has to take cognisance of this change and prepare its managers for a more participative role in strategy and policy formulation. The change in the management process has been the result of the change in the management environment. The change in the management environment in banks internationally has been one of progress from managing stability through coping with change, managing change to managing diversity.

Evolution of Management Environment in Banks

Pre-1979 Managing stability	*1979-84 Coping with change*	*1984-87 Managing change*	*1988-91 Managing diversity*
Control	Management	Participative	Differential
Management	By Objectives	Management	Management.
			Diversification process began in the banking system. It is an era of specialisation and consolidation.

The new business areas explored by Indian banks in the late eighties include:

(a) Merchant banking;

(b) Portfolio management;

(c) Leasing;

(d) Housing;

(e) Consumer banking;

(f) Dealing in stock exchanges as members; and

(g) Mutual funds.

Banks are getting ready to enter hire-purchase business, factoring, venture capital funds, software development and travel-related services. Deregulation has brought in more competition not only amongst banks but also from non-banking institutions.

Erosion in Management of Banks

Despite this commendable progress, serious problems have emerged, reflecting a decline in productivity and efficiency, and erosion of profitability in the banking sector. The major factors responsible for these are: *(a)* directed investments; and *(b)* directed credit programmes. In both these cases, rates of interest that were available to banks were less than the market-related rates or what they could have secured from alternative deployment of funds. There has been a deterioration in the quality of the loan porfolio which in turn has come in the way of banks' income generation and enhancement of their capital funds. Inadequacy of capital has been accompanied by inadequacy of loan loss provisions. The accounting and disclosure practices also do not always reflect the true state of affairs of banks and financial institutions. The erosion of profitability of banks has also emanated from the side of expenditure as a result of fast and massive expansion of branches, many of which are unremunerative, especially in the rural areas a considerable degree of over-manning, and in the urban and metropolitan centres and inadequate progress in updating work technology. Both management weaknesses and trade union pressures have contributed to this. There have also been weaknesses in the internal organisational structure of the banks, lack of sufficient delegation of authority and inadequate internal controls and deterioration in what is termed 'housekeeping' such as balancing of books and reconciliation of inter-branch and interbank entries. This apart, banks have also suffered from excessive administrative and political interference in individual credit decision-making and internal management. The deterioration in the financial health of the system has reached a point where unless remedial measures are taken soon, it could further erode the real value of and return on the savings entrusted to them and even have an adverse impact on depositor and investor confidence. This diagnosis of the problems indicates the lines of solution which the Narasimham Committee proposes with a view as much to improving the health of the system as for making it an integral part of the ongoing process of economic reforms.

HOW THE MONEY KEPT ROLLING OUT

(Rs. crore)

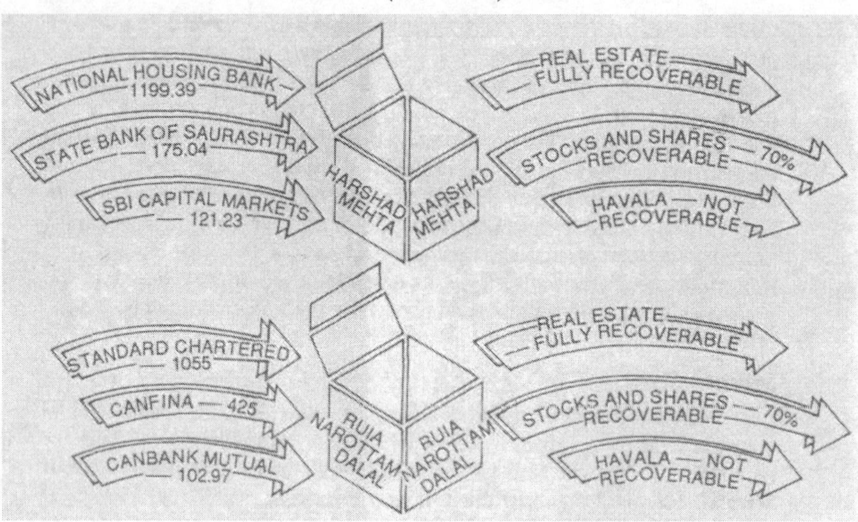

Fig. 10.2 How the Money kept Rolling out.

The Janakiraman Committee which went into the banking securities scam of Rs. 3542.79 crores found serious deficiencies in the functioning of banks, lack of internal controls, fraudulent misappropriation, mass collusion between the concerned officials and brokers, gross violation of rules, utter disregard of instructions, diversion of funds, absence of internal supervision in monitoring, breakdown of essential discipline and failure of the system. In short, it opens up the serious gaps of banking management in India. The principles of management have been wilfully violated or thwarted by the few in a systematic manner.

Highlights of the Interim Report

The highlights of the interim report of the Janakiraman Committee which went into the securities transactions of banks and financial institutions involving a hefty exposure of banks' money to the tune of Rs 3,542.79 crores are:

- The Committee found serious deficiencies in the functioning of the banks and financial institutions involved, lack of necessary internal control in various functions, mass collusion between the concerned officials and brokers involved in dealings in government securities, public sector banks and units.
- *Prima facie* evidence of fraudulent misappropriation through devices adopted for diversion of funds from the banking system to the individual accounts of certain brokers confirmed.
- Fund management operations conducted in gross violation and with utter disregard of instructions and guidelines issued by the RBI from time to time.
- The total amount of exposure of banks/institutions involved in these dubious transactions amount to Rs. 3,542.79 crores.
- The Committe found that an increase in the volume of transactions in securities and capital market instruments since July 1991 in the form of ready-forward deals led to the indiscriminate issue of banker's receipts (BRs) and even securities general ledgers (SGLs) which led to the diversion of funds to selected brokers.
- Funds were diverted to Mr. Harshad Mehta and his associate concerns in a host of transactions put through by the National Housing Bank (NHB), State Bank of Saurashtra, and the State Bank of India and the SBI Cap.
- Several transactions, the counter parties mentioned in the contracts provided by Mr. Harshad Mehta were only in name.
- Irregularities detected by the Committee in regard to SBI's transactions with Harshad Mehta were extremely "disturbing" as investment account in SBI's books and SBI's accounts with public debt office (PDO) were obviously "manipulated" to accommodate the transactions of the latter.
- The Committee noted the serious implications of the flow of proceeds of the account payee cheques drawn on RBI in favour of SBI and ANZ Grindlays Bank in the account of Harshad Mehta, without any authority of the drawers of the cheques.
- Serious damage has also resulted from the issue of banker's receipts by the Bank of Karad and Metropolitan Co-operative Bank, without having the capacity to honour the BRs in the transactions put through by Mr. Hiten Dalai in the cases of Standard Chartered Bank, CANFINA and CANBANK Mutual Fund.
- In providing adjustment to the broker Mrs. J.H. Mehta (wife of Harshad Mehta), UCO Bank has had to purchase certain shares whose value has depreciated markedly.
- NHB's deals reveal an absence of internal supervision in monitoring, non-positioning of prudent procedural safeguards and absence of proper records.
- The public debt office of the RBI requires considerable speeding up and computerisation to effectively handle the large number of transactions of the banks for reconciliation at regular intervals to detect fraudulent/irregular transactions.
- The Committee favours restricting the practice of banks entering into ready-forward and double ready-forward deals with other banks to government securities only and calls for prohibition in other securities, including PSU bonds, units and shares.
- Ready-forward and double ready-forward deals need to be prohibited under portfolio management schemes.

- The RBI's prohibition about banks entering into buy-back deals with non-bank clients to be strictly followed.
- Banks should formulate internal exposure limits for transactions, including limits to brokers.
- Brokers' contract notes should indicate counter party and broker age charged.
- When banks act as custodians of brokers' or other parties' securities, the documentation of all transactions effected for such customers should show the banks' status.
- The existing ban on banks issuing cheques drawn on their own account with the RBI for third-party transactions should be strictly enforced.
- Banks' transactions on behalf of their merchant banking subsidiaries should be transparent, giving full details to the subsidiaries.
- To obviate the need to issue BRs, a separate body like the Stock Holding Corporation should be set up to conduct all bank transactions in PSU bonds, units and similar securities.
- A widening of the scope of RBI inspections with greater emphasis on treasury transactions and supplementing of on-site inspection by RBI by report of banks' compliance certified by the statutory auditors with prudential and other guidelines has been suggested.
- The RBI should review the adequacy of the internal audit departments of banks.
- A separate audit by banks' statutory auditors for the portfolio management operations of the banks and a strengthening of the RBI's organisation responsible for market intelligence has been suggested.
- What is ambiguous is that the Reserve Bank of India (the Central bank of the country) did not act promptly and efficiently.

Fig. 10.3 Courtesy; Times of India, Mumbai.

Basic Functions of Management

"Management is what management does" — points out the functional approach to management and emphasises the importance of distinctive managerial functions which together give us a unified concept of the process of management. Functions of management are also called elements of management.

An analysis of the functions of management points out what management does. It also provides the basis for defining precisely the word 'management.' Broadly speaking, a manager is called upon to perform the following managerial functions: (1) Planning, (2) Organising, (3) Staffing, (4) Directing, (5) Motivating, (6) Controlling, (7) Co-ordinating, and (8) Communicating. Some authors include staffing within organising and consider co-ordinating and communicating as vital parts of direction, motivation and leadership.

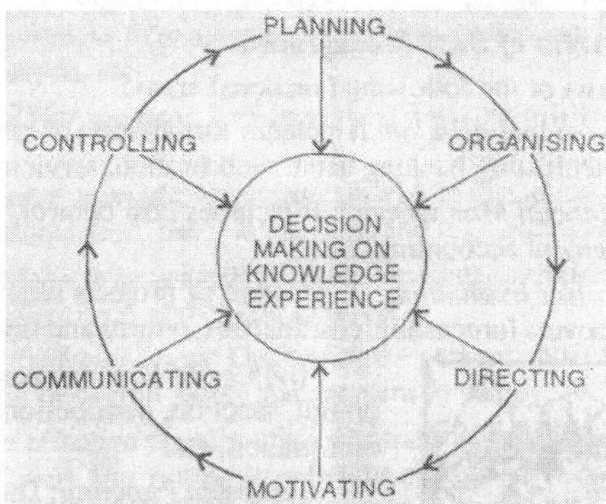

Fig. 10.4 Functions of Management.

Fig. 10.5 (Courtesy: Times of India, Mumbai)

Scope of Management in Banking

Almost all the functions of management are introduced into the banking system. It consists of planning, organising, personnel, directing, controlling, co-ordination, communication, motivation, human resources development and systems.

Functional Areas of Bank Management

It consists of the following functional areas:

(i) *Deposit mobilisation:* It includes formulation of savings schemes, marketing, inculcating banking habit, mobilisation, servicing, etc.

(ii) *Financial Management:* It includes cost control, financial planning, management accounting, etc.

(iii) *Project Evaluation:* Evaluation of projects requires a dynamic approach. It covers forecasting, cost analysis, returns and flow of funds, etc.

(iv) *Credit Management:* It covers appraisal, sanction, distribution, recovery, administration, etc.

(v) *Credit Planning:* The objective is to apportion the available resources among the various types of borrowers in accordance with the government policy and market demand.

Fig.10.6

You are on long leave are you? So am I! You are the head of which bank, may I Know?

(vi) *Liquidity Management:* It relates to cash, statutory liquidity ratio, cash reserve ratio, trading in B.R. etc.

(vii) *Investment Management:* It relates to regulation, underwriting, securities, trading and accounting, etc.

(viii) *Organisation Management:* It covers the structure, functioning, supervision, delegation, etc.

(ix) *Personnel Management:* It includes aspects such as recruitment, training, transfers, promotions, discipline, industrial relations, motivation, social security, etc. In recent years, it is also known as Human Resources Management.

(x) *Marketing Management:* It includes marketing of services, segmentation, mix, planning, customer service, public relations, advertisement, publicity, marketing research, etc.

(xi) *Office Management:* It is concerned with office layout, staffing, equipment of office, etc.

(xii) *Maintenance Management:* It relates to the proper care and maintenance of the building, equipments, etc.

Fig.10.7

All the time you are asking questions — what are forward trading, scrips, bank transfers, SQL, PDO, bears ... when will you ever finish the investigation?

(xiii) *Information Management:* It covers collection of feedback, information, analysis, etc.

(xiv) *Legal Management:* It relates to documentation, titles and related issues.

(xv) *Administration Management:* It relates to discipline, controlling, direction, communication, motivation, rules and regulations, etc.

(xvi) *Portfolio Management:* It encompasses selection, appraisal, evaluation, right decision at the right time, etc.

(xvii) *Assets Management:* Optimising the performance of assets is the most critical part of overall assets management in banks.

Having an effective plan for crisis is usually about 90 per cent of the solution to that crisis. But getting ahead of the change curve does not mean that business people must make advance plans for each and every contingency. You can go broke buying insurance. And you can paralyse an institution with too much planning.

Steps in Business Planning

The basic job of the bank executive is to conceive business visions and turn them into business realities. Vision has two parts. The first is the intuitive discovery of a potential business pattern, involving the so-called "right brain" activities. The second part of building a vision is often the tedious yet crucial work of business planning. In business planning, you convert your intuitive vision into an action plan. The two parts of vision cannot be done sequentially. The task alternates rapidly between the creative — thinking up ways the business could unfold — and the analytical — figuring out the concrete implications of the intuitive vision.

Business planning involves documenting as best as you can everything that is important to the business, such as:

— Your destination.

— The strategies for getting there.

— Where you would like to be at specific times.

— The obstacles you may encounter.

— The approaches you plan to use in overcoming these obstacles.

Use of a Business Plan

Many people think of a business plan as a tool for raising money or getting corporate approvals. Actually, its value as a selling tool is a small part of the value of business planning. The benefits of the planning process include training yourself to become more intrapreneurial, screening your ideas, attracting a venture team, building team consensus, as well as getting the money and permission to proceed.

Banks have adopted national planning, corporate planning, branch planning as well as functional planning to achieve their targets rather than the corporate objectives. A few of the banks have also introduced manpower planning as a process of human resources development.

Business Plan Outline

Cover Sheet
- Name of business
- Names of principals
- Address and telephone number of business

Statement of purpose (executive summary)
- Description of business — product or service
- Business structure

Description of
- Amount of money being requested
- How funds will be used
- How funds will be repaid

Marketing Plan
- The industry
- Competition
- Market size and opportunity
- Market segments served
- Marketing mix
- Key factors to success in market

Financial Plan
- Sources and application of funds
- Capital equipment list
- Balance sheet
- Break-even analysis
- Income statements
- Pro-form a cash flow statements

Organisational Plan
- Location of business
- Organisational structure
- Management
- Non-management personnel

Summary
- Application and expected effect of loan on business *Supporting Documents (as required)*
- Personnel resumes
- Job descriptions
- Credit reports
- Letters of reference
- Copies of contracts
- Copies of leases
- Copies of letters of intent
- Legal documents
- Production requirements

Source: Reprinted by permission of the publisher, Robert D. Hisrich and Candida G. Brush, *The Woman Entrepreneur: Starting, Financing, and Managing a Successful New Business* (Lexington, Mass: Lexington Books, D. C. Heath and Company, Copyright, 1986), 64.

Organising

The form of organisation employed in commercial banks most closely resembles a line-and- staff type. In small banks, the line type of organisation is the predominant form. Larger banks have been organised on a functional basis, each department looking after a specific function. In the case of branch banking, a group of branches are supervised, guided, motivated and directed by a regional office; a group of regions are put under the control and supervision of a local office and all local/zonal offices are supervised by the central office. The authority percolates from the top to the bottom.

Departmentation

Departmentation is the process of dividing the work of an organisation into various units or departments. 'Department' means a section or division or branch of an institution over which a manager has authority and responsibility for performance of specified activities.

Principles of departmentation are:

1. Clear statement of lines of authority and they should run from top to bottom.
2. Existence of unity of command.
3. Clear establishment of responsibility and authority of each manager in writing.
4. Resting the responsibility with the top managers for the acts of their subordinates.
5. Authority and responsibility should be delegated to the lowest possible level in the organisation hierarchy.
6. There should be a minimum number of levels to the possible extent.
7. The principles of specialisation should be adopted wherever possible.
8. The functions and relations of managers and staff should be kept separate.
9. The span of management should be reasonable and optimum.
10. The organisation should be simple and flexible to the BEST test possible extent.

Advantages of sound departmentation are:

1. Conflicts between individuals over jurisdiction can be kept at a minimum level.
2. Minimisation of duplication and overlapping.
3. Establishment of career planning and promotional channels would be easy.
4. Clear-cut communication channel can be established.
5. Effective co-ordination and control is possible.

Bases of departmentation are: (1) functions, (2) product/service, (3) territory, (4) customers, and (5) matrix organisation.

Organisational Planning Vs. Human Resources Planning in Banks

Organisational planning and human resources planning in banks are highly interrelated. Human resources planning in most cases is based on the bank's organisational planning. In fact, human resources planning may become the basis for organisational planning in some cases. Organisational... is an organic process-oriented approach to organisational change... management effectiveness of banks. Further, organisational development in banks, referred to as organisational planning, stresses individual human adaptation and development to bank's organisational changes. Thus, organisational planning and human resources planning in banks are highly interrelated.

The important steps in human resources planning in banks are:

1. Formulation of long-range and short-range objectives, plans, programmes and budgets of banks regarding branch expansion, deposits and other resources mobilisation, loans and advances, various services and the like.

2. Estimation of overall human resources requirements — occupational, category and skill-wise analysis at different levels of the bank's hierarchy.
3. Find out the current inventory of human resources, principal dimensions of manpower inventory being: Forecast the changes in human resources inventory due to employee turnover, transfers, promotions, demotions, training, development and the like based on career plan and development.
4. Find out the difference between the current inventory and future total human resources requirements.
5. Correcting the imbalances between demand and supply.
6. Action programmes for recruiting and selecting for the needed human resources or adjusting the employees through transfers, promotions and adjusting human resources through moulding and developing.
7. Prepare the plans for training, development, promotions, transfers, demotions etc.
8. Evaluating the performance.

Human Resources Development

The development role played by banks in India, particularly after nationalisation, has indeed no parallel in the world. The concept of banking has undergone a dramatic change in the last two decades in the country. There have been many innovations and much adaptation to meet the developmental needs of the economy. No doubt, the national planners and thinkers have provided a direction and given new concepts towards the objective of national growth through banks. The credit for executing these novel ideas, however, goes to the vast human resources developed over the years by the banks. The dedication with which the new tasks have been carried out and the success of these tasks speak volumes about the quality of human resources the banks possess today.

It took long for management experts to realise the importance of human resources in an industry, but having realised their importance, it is now agreed by all that these resources need special care. All the resources required in an industry have to be carefully selected. The next task is to ensure that resources are preserved in the same condition in which they were procured. While raw materials need to be properly stored and checked, from time to time, to see that no deterioration sets in due to storing defects, machines and equipments require lubrication and regular maintenance. In the case of human resources, however, it is not merely preservation or maintenance, but a further process of development that is vital. Human resources do not remain static. Some development is always taking place. What is required is to ensure that the pace of development is accelerated. The process of development has to be given proper direction so that organisational objectives can be achieved. A negative development can prove disastrous for the organistion, and a positive but slow development will also not help in winning the race. So the organisations have to stimulate speed and provide direction to the human resources. The management experts recommend achieving this through various Organisational Development (O.D.) interventions.

What type of O.D. interventions are required by an organisation for its human resources is a complex but fascinating study by itself. Each industry has its own requirements. Each organisation has its own problems. While the fundamentals remain the same, there cannot be tailor-made schemes of O.D. interventions. Seeds for the same plant sown in different soils in different climates will have different needs for watering and fertilisers. The flowers grown will be of the same type but the size and the number will depend on how well the plants are tended. The same is the case with the human resources. The employees recruited initially are good, how useful they ultimately prove will depend on how we shape them.

While the development of human resources is vital for all the industries and all the organisations, for a service industry like banking, its importance is many-fold more. In fact, it is said that all development comes from the human mind. Human resources management is responsible for the transformation of traditional economies into modern and industrial economies. Successful management depends upon the management of human behaviour. If a company is successful, it means it is efficient in the management of its human resources. It is more so in a service-oriented industry like banks. The quantity and quality of service in a bank are entirely dependent upon the human mind, behaviour and physical ability. The man behind the counter counts much more than other resources. It is no exaggeration to say that the life-blood of the economy (credit) is pumped from the human blood of the bank employees. Efficient human resources management and maintenance of congenial industrial relations and harmonious human relations in banks determine not only the performance of the banks but affect the growth and performance of the entire economy. It is said that human resources management is a central sub-system in banks.

Though the management of human resources is a significant and crucial task, a lot of complexities are involved in it because people are essentially self-managing. They decide the nature, time and place of their employment. They react to the changing conditions unlike other resources. The other factors which complicate the task of human resources management in banks are: technological innovation and the consequent increase in the requirement of skilled and experienced people, increase in formal education of the recent entrants which broadens the vision of the employees, increasing the involvement of the government in the management of personnel, changing employee roles and their values, changing the structure of employment, the increasing share of women employees, employees from scheduled castes and other backward communities etc., increasing their strength and thereby regulation of trade unions, increasing and diversified demands of the customer having influence on employer's mind, etc.

Banks and their human resources should develop and progress simultaneously for their survival and attainment of mutual goals. So every management has to mould and develop the human resources in order to develop the organisation. In fact, organisation development is basically the development and adaptation of human resources to meet organisational requirements. Organistional planning when it stresses human adaptations to organisational changes is referred to as organisational development.

Human resources development of a bank may be thought of as moulding and developing of the knowledge, skills, creative abilities, talents, aptitudes, values, attitudes and the like of the employees of a bank so as to match them with the job and bank requirements. Development of human resources is possible through training, development, interaction with superiors through participative management schemes and the like. Performance appraisal is useful to identify the need for an area to be moulded and developed.

Profit Planning: In the latter part of the eighties, a greater awareness was created among banks to improve profitability and housekeeping. It is recognised that emphasis on quality leads to improvement in operational efficiency, resulting in profit. The corporate planning and performance budgeting systems in banks are getting increasingly geared to improve profits and profitability.

Profit as a main area of concern for banks was expressed, perhaps for the first time, in the Annual Report of RBI in 1983-84. Since then both the Government and RBI have been giving considerable attention to viability. It is one of the thrust areas in the two-year action plans introduced since 1985. Greater attention to profit is given in the third round of Action Plan 1990-92. Benchmark estimates of profits and profitability are to be prepared for each bank for judging the performance in the coming years with reference to such benchmark. The significance attached to profitability by the authorities is evident from the fact that at the quarterly meetings of chief executives of each bank with the Reserve Bank, profitability is specially discussed.

While policy support from the authorities will help banks, the main burden for improving profit is with the banks themselves. The banks have to develop profit consciousness and a spirit of cost effective functioning at every level. The spending outlets are many. Hence each and every item of expenditure needs to be preceded by a self-raised question by every functionary: Whether the expenditure is absolutely necessary and whether the same purpose can be achieved at a lower cost. The expenditure control is particularly relevant is respect of all areas of controllable costs.

Income, expenditure and profit budgeting should be a part and parcel of the planning process at the corporate level, zonal/regional offices, and at branches. The monthly expenditure, income and profit budgets have to be monitored by higher authorities closely in each bank.

A constant vigil on funds management is crucial for profit planning in banks. Idle cash needs to be monitored and reduced to the base minimum. Refinance from IDBI, NABARD etc. should be to the full extent of the eligible amounts. The refinanced amount is not subject to statutory preemptions. This will help lending at higher rates and improve the credit deposit ratio.

Increase in ancillary income is yet another area that needs critical attention of planners in banks. The banks on their part should constantly enlarge the volume of ancillary services handled. Several activities such as factoring, leasing, mutual funds, venture capital assistance etc. provide considerable scope for banks to increase their earning avenues. A larger volume of ancillary business gives larger income.

Quality of Work Life

The Indian banking services scenario of the nineties will be dominated by competition between banks and financial institutions. The expectations of customers in the wake of consumerism, equity cult, high technology and marketing strategies adopted by foreign banks will be on the rise necessitating the banks to excel for customer allegiance. Banks should offer various types of services and execute them with speed and quality. To increase the market share, banks should go in for aggressive marketing. Banks should realise that they have to operate in a market-driven environment. To meet the challenges and varied expectations of customers, the total involvement of employees is necessary for the generation of quality products and services as discerned by customers. Motivation of employees is very important to make them committed to organisational goals, viz., increased market share, extending quality services to customers, etc. Promotion of employees to higher positions is one of the motivators in this direction. These opportunities are, however, gradually shrinking. Hence, quality of work life (QWL) and its improvement in the organisation may be the only way to retain the level of employee motivation.

QWL is also concerned with the overall climate of work situation. One recent analysis of QWL described it as (i) a concern about the impact of work on people as organisational effectiveness and *(ii)* the idea of participation in organisational problem-solving and decision-making. The recognised purpose is to change the climate at work, so that human, technological, organisational interface leads to a better QWL.

Peter Drucker observes that, in the context of diminishing opportunities for promotion, to provide satisfaction and achievement to the younger generation of employees, the jobs should be designed providing for more challenge with more autonomy. Lateral transfers to different assignments as a reward for a high degree of performance can also be thought of.

Banking Ombudsman to be made more Customer Friendly

With effect from January 1, 2006, the Reserve Bank of India will ensure that the Ombudsman will be fully staffed and funded by it. The RBI has also revised the existing scheme of Banking Ombudsman to enable the customers to file their complaints in any form including online. The bank customers would also be able to appeal to RBI against the awards given by Banking Ombudsman. All in all, the Banking Ombudsman will be revamped making it more customer-friendly.

It may be recalled that since its introduction in 1995, the Scheme of Banking Ombudsman has been revised just once, in the year 2002, mainly to cover RRBs in its ambit. This time the RBI has enlarged its scope to include customer complaints on new areas such as credit card complaints, deficiencies in providing the promised services, levying service charges without prior intimation and non-adherence to the fair practice code as adopted by individual banks. The new scheme also provides a Forum for Customers to seek the redressal of their most common complaints against their banks.

The new scheme is applicable to all the Commercial banks, Regional Rural Banks and Scheduled Primary Co-operative Banks. The RBI is also in an advanced stage of setting up an independent Banking Codes and Standards Board of India to ensure that comprehensive code of conduct for fair treatment to customers are formulated by banks and adhere to.

Bank Policies and Procedures

This area of training is to be provided with a view to acquainting the new employee with the bank rules, practices, procedures, traditions, management, organisation structure, environment and services that are rendered by the bank.

This acquaintance enables the new employee to adjust himself to the changing situations. Information regarding bank rules and policies creates confidence of the new employee in the bank and its services as well as it develops in him a sense of respect for the existing employees of the bank and the like. The bank also provides first-hand information to the employees about the skills needed by the bank, its development programmes, quality of services and the like. This enables the new employee to know his share of contribution to the bank's growth and development.

Training in Particular Skills

This area of training is to enable the employee to become more effective on the job. The trainer trains the employee regarding the various skills necessary to carry out the actual job. For example, the clerk in a bank should be trained in the skills of making entries correctly in the ledger, skills of arithmetical calculations, quick comparison of figures, entries and the like. Similarly, technical officers are to be trained in the skills of project appraisal, supervision, follow-up and the like.

Human Relations Training

Human relations training assumes greater significance in banks as bank employees have to maintain human relations not only with other employees but also with their customers. Bank employees are to be trained in the areas of self-learning, interpersonal competence and relations, treating people as human beings rather than as machines, treating human beings as social and psychological men rather than as economic men, and the like.

This training enables the employees to achieve better team-work, which leads to improved efficiency and productivity of the bank.

Most of the bank problems are common to the officers/managers engaged in the same activity at different levels of the bank like branch, regional office and central office. Further, some of the problems of different managers may have the same root cause. Hence, bank management may call together all managerial personnel to discuss their common problems so as to arrive at effective solutions across the table. This not only helps solve problems but also serves as a forum for the exchange of ideas and information that could be utilised. The trainer has to organise such meetings, train and encourage the trainees to participate actively in such meetings.

Managerial and Supervisory Training

Even non-managers sometimes perform managerial and supervisory functions like planning, decision-making, organising, maintaining interpersonal relations, directing and controlling. Hence, management has to train the employees in managerial and supervisory skills.

Conclusion

In the post-nationalisation period, the management process in banks has changed from rigid or regulated management to flexible management. Although banks have adopted the management process *in toto,* the skills are yet to be deepened and spread out. It is yet to accomplish participative management at the branch level. There is ample scope for improving the level of management in banks.

Chapter 11

MANAGEMENT BY OBJECTIVES

Introduction

Management by Objectives (MBO) is a successful philosophy of management. It is an improvement in the management process. Since the early 50s, it has acquired momentum.

The term 'management' may be defined as organisation and control of human activity directed towards specific ends. According to John Humble, a leading management expert, "Management by Objectives (MBO) is a dynamic system which seeks to integrate the company's need to clarify and achieve its profit and growth goals with a manager's need to contribute and develop himself.

According to Howell, the concept of MBO has passed through different stages of management development, viz.,

(1) MBO for performance appraisal.

(2) MBO for integrating the individuals with the organisation.

(3) MBO for long-range planning.

Management by objectives has been defined as "a result-centred, non-specialist, operational managerial process for the effective utilisation of material, physical and human resources of the organisation, by integrating the individual with the organisation and organisation with the environment."

In other words, MBO is a process by which managers at different levels and their subordinates work together in identifying goals and establishing objectives consistent with the organisational goals and attaining them. Thus, MBO is not only an aid to planning but also a motivating factor. In short, it is a comprehensive managerial system that integrates many key managerial activities in a systematic and organised manner.

The need to replace subjective values of working behaviour, attitude and co-operation with less subjective quantifiable measures at all levels in the organisation and manage in accordance with the basic objectives was originally advanced by Peter F. Drucker in 1954 in his famous book *The*

Practice of Management. Since then, this approach to management has attracted increasing attention and is now becoming widely adopted. It has turned into a movement in management. The important areas where objectives are to be set according to Drucker are: 1. Market standing, 2. Innovation, 3. Productivity, 4. Efficiency, 5. Physical and financial resources, 6. Profitability, 7. Managerial performance and development, 8. Workers' performance, 9. Attitude, and 10. Public responsibility.

What is Management By Objectives?

Essentially, the term "Management by Objectives", as it is now understood throughout business and industry, means a method of managing that involves:

(i) Critical appraisal and restatement of unit objectives at all levels of the organisation;

(ii) Agreeing with each manager the essential results he must aim to achieve in line with both unit and corporate objectives;

(iii) Agreeing with each manager, a plan for realising these work targets;

(iv) Making systematic reviews of progress towards the attainment of work targets as a basic for appraising managerial performance;

(v) Taking action to deal with the unresolved problems thrown up as a result of these reviews.

Management By Objectives (MBO) is, therefore, simply a system of managing effectively. It is not a new technique. Apart from commercial organisations, non-profit making service or religious bodies also have a great need to identify and clarify their goals.

Management by objectives has been increasingly adopted by various Indian organisations, including commercial banks, as an effective approach to a dynamic system of management. Management by objectives is not a panacea for all management ills. It focuses on vital areas of one's job position with a systematic insistence and tenacious result-orientation. It calls for continuous search for improvement and provides a forum for meaningful dialogue within the various units and departments of a modern organisation. All these contributions of MBO are of singular importance in the context of Indian management.

Characteristics of MBO

The main characteristics of management by objectives are:

(a) Long-Range Plans and Unit Plans: The top management defines the objectives of the organisation together with the outline of the steps required to achieve them. This information is disseminated to the management team.

(b) Key Result Analysis: Each manager analyses his job in order to identify the important areas and he expresses these in terms of the result which he has to achieve. He gets his superior to agree to this analysis and in addition they agree on a plan of action with target dates to achieve the results. The decisions are recorded on paper.

(c) Control Information: The manager runs his job using control information (daily/weekly/monthly) to determine whether he is achieving the pre-determined results.

(d) Performance Review: The manager will have normal contact with his superior at regular intervals (every three or four months). He sets aside time to meet his superior formally to report progress. During this process difficulties are discussed, new targets are agreed upon and training needs identified. The session culminates with a fresh plan of action for the next period.

(e) Manage by Objectives: The process of control and review continues both for the managers and the organisation as a whole. The top management reviews the progress towards objectives and at least once in a year updates the long-range plan. There will be regular review meetings between manager and his superior.

Advantages of MBO

The advantages derived by applying management by objectives are:

(1) It forces management to clarify their aims and overcome the inbred idleness that inclines people to devote all their attention to the day-to-day problems.

(2) It encourages participation of subordinates in the formulation of objectives and work targets and thereby helps to improve people's effectiveness.

(3) It enables the individuals to know what is expected of them.

(4) It helps in drafting plans and helps in achieving them.

(5) It improves communication in the organisation.

(6) It makes the evaluation process more equitable by focusing on specific accomplishment.

(7) It aids the development of subordinates to make them fit for greater responsibility.

(8) It attracts the commitment of staff at all levels to the future growth and prosperity of business.

(9) It aids concentration on essentials.

(10) It brings unresolved problems to the open, and

(11) It helps to disclose opportunities and encourage their exploitation.

Responsibility and Authority

It has been customary in the past to define delegated roles in a somewhat negative manner in terms of 'responsibility' and 'authority.' Under 'responsibility', there used to be given a long list of matters for which subordinates were held responsible and accountable. Similarly, under 'authority', the list of specific actions one is empowered to take used to be given. But, under management by objectives, 'responsibility' has been redefined in terms of positive objectives — the essential goals the subordinate should aim at.

Benefits of MBO

An effective MBO system results in several benefits to the organisation. They are:

(1) As the managers at all levels are involved in setting their objectives, they are more committed to the goals fixed and generally they work hard to achieve them.

(2) Managers at all levels become more aware of the overall objectives and this helps them in understanding their role in the total organisation.

(3) MBO implies that the objectives of each department are consistent with the overall objectives of the organisation. This ensures that people and the department do not work at cross-purposes.

(4) MBO also helps in making a more systematic evaluation of performance. This is made possible, as MBO not only states what one is expected to achieve but also measures the criteria to judge the performance. This also helps the organisation in taking corrective action if required.

(5) We find in the MBO technique clarity of objectives, role clarity, periodic feedback of performance and participation by managers in the management process. Because of these, resources and activities are put to use in such a way that they result in better performance.

(6) MBO provides greater opportunity to managers for personal satisfaction. This is possible, because of the two important features of MBO, viz: (i) participation in objective setting and (ii) rational performance appraisal. Participating in objective setting makes them feel that they are important to the organisation. Further, as their performance is measured in terms of their actual performance without any managerial prejudices or biases, the managers feel that their interests are protected.

(7) MBO is the basis for organisational change. If the MBO is applied, there is a constant process of interaction between superior and subordinates in objective setting and performance review. In this system, the change process becomes easier when compared to arigid system of objective setting and performance evaluation by the superior without associating subordinates.

Limitations of MBO

MBO has certain limitations and weaknesses. They are:

(1) Sometimes, it is difficult to set verifiable goals. For example, it is difficult to set verifiable goals for the staff people and research departments.

(2) Differences in the status of subordinates may not create an open atmosphere which is necessary for appropriate goal-setting.

(3) This may involve much paper work and holding of many meetings. Because of this, managers may not have time to do their normal work.

(4) There is a tendency on the part of managers to emphasise on short-run goals to become more precise in goal-setting and its achievement.

(5) Managers fail to understand and appreciate MBO philosophy. There are number of doubts about MBO like what purpose is served by MBO, how the performance is to be appraised etc. They take MBO as another tool of control. Because of this way of thinking, it is difficult to introduce the MBO successfully.

(6) Environment in which an organisation operates is dynamic and because of this, a particular objective may not be valid for ever. But many members often hesitate to change the objectives during a period of time. This inflexibility may cause harm to the organisation.

The Process of MBO in Banks

Banks can also adopt the MBO philosophy in their planning activity. The steps in the process of MBO in banks are summarised as follows:

(1) Preliminary Setting of Objectives at the Top: The managers at the top level set the overall objectives of the bank by taking planning premises into account. These objectives set by the superiors are preliminary as they must be regarded as tentative and subject to modification as the entire chain of verifiable objectives is worked out by the subordinates. Verifiable objectives are developed in terms of branch expansion, deposits, loan recovery, customer service, profit, etc.

(2) Clarification of Bank Goals: The relationship between the results expected and the responsibility for attaining them should be established as every goal and sub-goal should be someone's clear responsibility and accountability.

(3) Setting of Subordinates' Objectives: The bank's objectives should be accomplished by a number of individuals in the bank, if all the individuals in the bank are to be jointly made responsible for attaining the bank's overall objectives. Therefore, each individual should be assigned a specific task and he must know in advance what he is expected to achieve. In view of this, the subordinates' objectives should also be set in conformity with the preliminary objectives of the bank. In some cases, the preliminary objectives of the bank may be modified or changed in view of abilities, strengths and weaknesses of the subordinates and their objectives.

Recycling of objectives: Goal-setting is not only a joint process but also involves recycling. It means, first, goals are fixed in consultation with the subordinates; in turn, the subordinates set goals for their subordinates and this process goes on and on. Thus, in recycling, subordinates at every level are involved in goal setting and to that extent, they are made to commit. Commitment is necessary for attaining the goals.

Appraisal: In this step, a periodic performance review is made in relation to the goals set and thus the employer is provided with feedback on the actual performance as compared to planned performance.

Steps in MBO Process

Some banks have adopted MBO as the management style with the objective to introduce a concept of management that would increase the bank's efficiency, competitive potential and profitable growth by encouraging managerial improvements in attitude and skill.

Banks and other financial intermediaries can also adopt the MBO philosophy in their planning activities.

The steps in MBO process of banks are as follows:

(1) Organisations need objectives.

(2) Objectives should be dynamic.

(3) Every member of the organisation should work towards these predetermined objectives.

(4) Survival and growth are essential objectives.

(5) Objectives should be in a written form and should be communicated to everyone.

(6) Sub-objectives of Departments/Units should be sacrificed for the broader objectives of the organisation.

The raison d'etre of a commercial organisation is to carry out certain activities to achieve certain goals. The bank has to carry out certain activities; in order to do these effectively, the bank must earn reasonable profits, and also grow. Lower the profits from its activities, lower would be its capacity to optimise the activities for which it is set up. Thus the objective of the bank has to be profit and growth. Without these, the bank would fail to achieve its mission.

Essentials of MBO Programme in Banks

Management by objectives (MBO) seeks to integrate the banks' objectives with individual goals and satisfaction of their managers.

The essentials of MBO programme are:

(1) Periodic critical review and restatement of a development bank's overall tactical and strategic plans.

(2) Clarification with each manager of his key results and performance standards.

(3) Acceptance by each manager of his contribution and commitment to these results and standards.

(4) Establishment of procedures for control and self-control of progress, performance and potential review objectively.

(5) Provision of imaginative MBO development programmes.

(6) Provision of conditions in which these results can be achieved: (i) an effective organisation; (ii) sound managerial control information.

(7) MBO programme should be implemented within the organisation at all levels.

(8) Integrate the MBO programme of individual banks with the overall programmes.

Proper adoption of the MBO programme would increase a bank's efficiency, competitive potential and profitable growth by encouraging managerial improvement in attitude and skill. Thus it will accelerate the process of development.

MBO Programme at Branch Level

The essentials to make an MBO programme effective at branch level are:

1. Pace and Complexity of Programme with particular emphasis given to (a) the skilful use of pilot exercises, (b) the integration of sub-systems, viz., planning and management information to ensure common purpose and cumulative benefits, (c) questioning organisation structures, particularly the role of area and regional managers and (d) ensuring that support is given by head office.

2. Evolution of Documentation: The branch manager should beware of the danger of too much or too little commitment to paper. He should also recognise that planning/review documents will develop over the first two or three years.

3. Briefing and Coaching Managers: Most of the managers do not have a proper idea about MBO programme due to poor communication of objectives of the programme, inadequate knowledge about integrating the individual course and group sessions and absence of major briefing programme, absence of adoption of the scheme throughout the bank, absence of support of the regional managers and manager at the head office. Further, managers have little understanding of the purpose or principles behind the programme and managers' objectives are not linked to overall bank's goals. Consequently, regional managers have the problem of co-ordination and comparison.

4. Motivation: The sustenance of the mind depends upon the extent of satisfaction and happiness they derive from what they perform. They need constant motivation to perform. Unless he is motivated, he cannot find a meaning in what he is expected to do and does not enjoy his work; he becomes a robot, programmed by others, making no contribution of his own. Based on Herzberg's experiments, the following diagram will illustrate an "ACHIEVEMENT MOTIVATION MODEL" for a typical branch manager:

Checking the model with the ingredients of

— happiness

— responsibility

— achievement

— recognition

— meaningfulness

— growth and development

indicates that motivation is a key factor of management by objectives. The model highlights the fact that if the branch manager is motivated, he starts realising the meaning and purposefulness of the bank's policies; he appreciates how his achievements are contributing to the total corporate goals, and he enjoys his work. He is no more a grim individual serving a prison-term or making a martyr of himself. As a leader, he is enabled to induce the personnel placed under him to work for the achievements of the branch goals. He might have received leadership inputs theoretically in training programmes he attended but now he gets an opportunity to apply the precepts in practice because he is himself a happy and involved person.

Skills of Management

To enable a branch manager to function efficiently and effectively, he requires to consciously cultivate skills. These are:

(a) ***Technical Skill:*** Without adequate job knowledge, a manager will neither be able to lead his team nor enjoy the members' respect and confidence.

(b) ***Human Skill:*** "Respect for the individual" is the foundation of human relations. This is the guiding factor in interactions with seniors, juniors and peer-level colleagues, as well as customers and other outside agencies. A branch manager has essentially to deal with other human beings, attending to their human problems; he is not just an accountant compiling balance sheets.

(c) ***Political Skill:*** In order to secure the involvement pf his staff, a manager needs the ability to debate and negotiate logically. The desirability of branch activities cannot be pushed down their throats by a mere issue of fiats. In other words, this skill enables him to communicate convincingly with all relevant individuals/ organisations.

(d) ***Diagnostic Skill:*** Unless the important is shifted from the unimportant, solution to problems can prove infeasible. Every situation can be broken down into its basic elements which would need to be prioritised and tackled.

(e) ***Conceptual Skill:*** The ability to draw lessons from the past experience and project them to the future scenario is essential for a manager to be proactive and innovative. (This is not to be confused with being reactive, applying the past to the future in toto.)

In spite of these limitations, MBO is considered to be one of the important techniques of managing the business and more and more organisations are adopting this technique. Full benefits of the MBO programme can be derived if certain basic requirements arc taken care of. They are:

(1) Top management support the MBO programme.

(2) Defining the purpose of MBO clearly.

(3) Setting individual's objectives jointly by the superior and subordinates.

(4) Evaluating individuals periodically and providing them with feedback concerning their performance.

(5) Rewarding individuals on the basis of the objective evaluation of their attainment.

(6) Implementing MBO at lower levels also, i.e., it must be carried all the way down to the first line of organisation.

Management of Change

Transformation of any system could be triggered either due to environmental pressures or internal needs arising out of dissatisfaction with the status quo. Change, therefore, could be planned. Such a change process would involve deliberate, purposeful and explicit decisions to undertake a programme of transformation. It could also be a multi-dimensional, qualitative, discontinuous and radical change.

The proposed changes in the system could almost be similar to organisational design strategies aimed at fulfilling certain basic criteria. For instance, the systems approach to organisational design suggests some criteria like steady state criterion, operating responsiveness criterion, strategic responsiveness criterion, etc., which are to be met to ensure effective functioning of a designed organisation. The contingency model of organisational design, on the other hand, assumes that there is no one best organisational structure for an enterprise. The model recognises the conditional dependence of the appropriate organisational structure on the dynamic interaction between environmental factors, the characteristics of organisational tasks and the composition of management team.

What is critical to the design exercise would be the objectives or goals of (re) design of the system. Given the overwhelming presence of the Indian banking system in the Indian financial system, the suggested model should not view the systems independent of each other. The solution suggested should, in fact, strengthen the link and congruence between the systems. Thus the objectives of redesign could be viewed at different levels as:

I. At the Banking System Level

- Promotion of domestic savings and efficient mobilisation of such resources so as to facilitate the developmental process.
- Achieve spatial expansion to assume real national character in branch network, but at the same time, avoid overlapping of efforts and concentration of branches (horizontal and vertical disparities).
- As a corollary of the above, work towards removal of regional economic imbalances.
- Minimise resource misallocations and evolve a system design which could foster genuine competition between the constituents and yet accommodate the changing demands of the society at large.
- Bring about closer co-ordination between banks and the central banking authority to facilitate effective transmission of monetary policy.
- Evolve a compatible number and size of institutions within the banking system so as not to defy regulatory framework, while at the same time, foster the competitive element.
- With an increasing deregulatory process, there will be need to ensure lower structural regulation and better prudential regulation.
- Following the market segment approach, the inherent weakness in banking operations in each such market segment need to be overcome by adoption of suitable strategies.
- Reorient the cartel-like institutional arrangement between banks (more specifically the Indian Banks Association — IBA) so as to remove rigidities in individual banks realising their individual strengths.

- Last but not the least, ensure and preserve the soundness of individual banks and the stability of banking and financial system. In other words, the system design should enable the evolution of a robust and efficient banking structure where individual institutions gradually move towards achieving economies of scale and fulfil the stipulated capital adequecy norms.

II. At Individual Bank Level

- Provide efficient service to the banking clientele.
- Through optimal resource management, achieve economies of scale and enhance productivity.
- Move towards attaining even geographical spread as well as vertical spread (rural/ suburban/urban etc.)
- Improve performance in key areas of banking activity so as to enhance profit levels.
- To evolve better monitoring and control on branches so as to reduce strains on managerial control. Evolving a suitable organisational design keeping with growth is thus called for.
- Enhance the capital base gradually so as to fulfil the international norms. At the same time, under a deregulated regime, strict adherence to prudential accounting practices will be required.
- To be responsive to the various changes taking place and flexible enough to manage such changes. The organisational design should enable the natural growth of the organisation in such environment.
- Human resources management has to be given a thrust in keeping with the changes. Towards this end, depending upon its individual strength, the manpower policies of banks could be shaped. This, in turn, would require that the present centralised recruiting system (through the respective banking service recruitment boards) be examined for its continued suitability.

Conclusion

Management by objectives requires planning. Hence, we can minimise crisis management where managers deal with problems as they develop. M.B.O. motivates performance of managers because it involves managers in the planning and overall managerial process at each level of management. Subordinates actively participate in defining their area of responsibility in terms of the results expected. M.B.O. also offers ways and means to integrate individual goals with the goals of the organisation. M.B.O. encourages innovation as it lays more emphasis on results and less on the methods employed in achieving the goals. Not only the subordinate managers participate in goal-setting but they also enjoy a lot of freedom in selecting their own means for achievement of the goals. In short, M.B.O. makes the job of a subordinate manager meaningful and interesting and offers ample job satisfaction.

For management by objectives to be truly effective, there should be a two-way interaction between the goals of the organisation and those of the individual manager. Management by objectives is not only a planning and control system, it is also a means of motivating managers. To put it more precisely, it provides a means for the manager to motivate himself towards the goals he himself has identified with the active help of his superiors.

The manager is required to follow the steps mentioned below in order to build up an effective managerial system:

(1) To determine the pattern of delegated tasks — definition of subordinates' role in terms of principal objectives and constraints.

(2) To select people to perform the tasks.

(3) To give them guidance by formulating general policies and issuing instructions.

(4) To set up control measures.

(5) To instal systems which enable results to be attained:

  (i) An effective organisation;

  (ii) Sound managerial control information.

Thus management by objectives has been a successful philosophy of managers at the grassroot level.

Chapter 12

Credit Management

Introduction

Advances play an important part in the gross earnings and net profits of commercial banks, and promote the economic development of the country. The basic function of credit, whether provided by scheduled commercial banks or by other sources, is to enable individuals and business enterprises to purchase goods and/or services ahead of their ability or desired to pay. Demand for credit by business firms arises because of the time-consuming nature of the productive and distributive processes. Consumers demand credit to acquire goods in advance for which they pay in future. The time gap between production, distribution and consumption gives scope for the wide use of credit; and with the development of the economy and its complexities, a number of financial institutions have come to birth — general and specialised. Credit demand gap is accommodated by savings; but the demand for credit for productive purposes outstrips savings, and hence the need for additional funds from financial institutions. Commercial banks fill the credit demands that are not accommodated by the savings process and other financial institutions. As a result, the commercial banking system is a residual supplier of credit.

Credit Management

Credit management is concerned mainly with using the bank's resource both productively and profitably to achieve a preferable economic growth. At the same time, it also seeks a fair distribution among the various segments of the economy so that the economic fabric grows without any hindrance as stipulated in the national objectives, in general and the banking objectives, in particular. Credit management is concerned with planning, selection, analysis, budgeting, designing and implementation of schemes and plans. It is interwoven into the fabric of the management itself.

Objectives of Credit Management

Credit management evaluates how funds are used. In all cases, it involves a sound judgement of men and projects, combined with a logical approach to decision-making. The core of the credit policy is to channelise the flow of funds into the various sectors in accordance with the socio-economic objectives and also to maximise earnings in the long run and optimise them in the short run. This calls for an evaluation of the conditions of alternative uses of funds and of the allocation of resources after the consideration of production and marketing inter-relationships. Credit management is concerned with the efficient use of records, mainly of capital funds and deposits.

The objectives of credit management are in consonance with the bank's objectives:

(1) Sectoral flow of credit.

(2) Giving support to agriculture, industry and exports.

(3) Ensuring productive utilisation of funds.

(4) Maximisation of profits.

(5) Monitoring the end use of funds at the micro-level.

(6) Minimising risks and ensuring safety.

(7) Recovery and flow of funds productively.

(8) Increasing the earnings of the bank.

(9) Credit planning and control at the macro level.

Importance of Credit Management

Credit management is important because it has an impact on all the activities of the bank. Its primary responsibility is to discharge the credit function successfully. It touches on all other banking functions. Credit management may be considered to be the management of the credit function.

Selective Credit Policies: Policies such as loan rate ceilings and restriction on the portfolios of financial institutions constitute implicit subsidies or taxes. They can be very complex. The implicit taxes could fall on depositors through low deposit interest rates, thus affecting savings. Interest subsidies by the central bank may reduce transfers to the budget, thus affecting the stance of fiscal policy. Banks' lending to non-priority sectors at below-market interest rates affects resource allocation. To the extent that they rely on unconditional refinancing by the central bank of loans to favoured sectors, selective credit policies reduce the flexibility of monetary policy. The accumulation of a whole range of contingent liabilities to the government resulting from its guarantees of the repayments of priority credits makes the government the ultimate guarantor of the financial system's stability. The long-term solution to these problems is to limit the scope of selective credit and guarantee policies as much as possible, and to transfer to the budget the associated implicit subsidies and taxes. This action will limit the monetary impact of these policies and make it possible for the government to compare the costs of credit subsidy programmes with those of other budgetary expenditures.

Credit Analysis: A cardinal principle of the management of bank assets is to conduct it in a profitable and safe manner. Lending is the most profitable as well as the most risky function performed by the banks. Therefore, it must be done efficiently and with a minimum risk factor. To manage the funds effectively, credit management must be operative and credit analysis should be perfect. The objectives of credit analysis are to determine the capacity of the applicant to borrow and his ability and willingness to repay a requested advance in accordance with the terms of the advance contract. Credit analysis must be sufficiently complete to ascertain the risks associated with the advance and the willingness and ability of the borrower to repay. It implies engaging in economic forecasting. Economic forecasting is necessary because we live in a dynamic rather than a static society. Other influencing factors will be the size of credit, the structure of business, the risk factors involved, the purpose of the advance, the length of time the advance will be outstanding, the source of funds for repayment and the principals involved. The amount and type of security also will influence the credit analysis. This apart, location, product, market, infrastructural facility will also influence credit analysis and credit rating. The amount of time devoted to credit analysis by a bank varies considerably with each advance application. And, each will require meticulous investigation and evaluation for better and effective credit management.

Credit Appraisal: The objective of a revised system should be to examine the financial, technical and managerial viability of a firm's operations in order to determine the need and end-use of short-term funds and not an attempt to justify a pre-conceived decision on a credit demand. After all, the best risk to a banker is a well-managed firm rather than the goodwill alone or the quantum of assets the firm commands.

From the banker's point of view, credit appraisal involves a detailed financial analysis of the past and projected viability of a firm's operations, determination of the need, purpose and quantum of short-term credit, and what follow-up and control measures require stipulation to ensure that the firm's operations continue to be viable, and short-term funds are utilised by it for approved purposes.

Installing a Sound Credit Culture

A credit culture is the glue that holds everything related to credit together. It consists of policy — the guardian of the credit ethic; process — the line-driven arm of lending; and audit — the procreator of assets and of the credit mechanism. A glitch in one brings problems in another. For example, an ambiguous or obscure articulation of policy by senior management leads to confusion in market definition at lower levels. A sound credit culture can't be created overnight. It must evolve. When it is first installed, it needs close attention and must be given time to develop and work on an integrated basis. Then it must have continuing close attention. If there is a change of management or a change of focus or emphasis, it may not work at all.

Administering Credit Culture as a Whole

The joint task of policy, process and audit is to be a check and balance and to see that lending tracks a bank's strategy and objectives. It safeguards against surprises and unpleasant complications, whether they be administrative shortcomings, gaps in training or loan officer development, poorly conceived or executed marketing thrusts, or exposures to unnecessary risk.

BOX 12.1

TRANSACTION COSTS AND THE SUPPLY OF CREDIT

The impact of financial intermediation and interest rate ceilings on credit can be demonstrated geometrically. In the diagrams in Box figure 64.1 the horizontal axis measures the quantity of borrowing or lending per unit of time (*X*), and the vertical axis measures the cost of borrowing (*r*) and the return for lending (*i*). The economy's demand for credit is depicted in the first diagram by the downward-sloping curve labeled *D*. Its negative slope reflects, in part, the increasing quantity (per unit of time) of profitable investment as the cost of borrowing declines. The upward-sloping curve labeled S depicts the economy's supply of credit, the amount of saving offered to others either directly or through intermediaries such as banks. Its positive slope reflects, in part, the increasing share of total saving provided for financial assets as their return rises relative to the return on real assets or investment abroad. If there were no transaction costs or interest rate regulations, the market-determined rate of interest would be $r = I$, and the amount of credit per period would be *X*.

It is costly, however, for lenders to locate creditworthy borrowers directly. In the center diagram, the amount lenders must charge borrowers to cover that cost is reflected in the curve S_d. The vertical distance between this curve and the supply of funds curve (S) is the amount of these transaction costs (including the cost of covering the expected default). If lenders had to find borrowers on their own, they would be willing to supply X_d in the expectation of earning (after deducting expected costs) i_d. For that amount of credit borrowers would be paying r_d. Transaction costs introduce a wedge between the cost to borrowers and the return to lenders, which reduces the amount lent.

Banks or other intermediaries exist, in part, because they are able to reduce the transaction costs of borrowing and lending. This is reflected in the curve S_b. The wedge between the cost to borrowers and the return to lenders is now the banks' spread. Assuming that bank spreads are less than the costs of direct lending, the amount lent increases from X_d to X_b the return to lenders increases from I_d to I_b, and the cost to borrowers falls from r_d to r_b. The better banks are at reducing transaction costs, the greater these effects. Reducing taxes on banking (such as unremunerated reserve requirements, which are a part of these costs) has the same effect.

The third diagram shows the effect of an interest rate ceiling (the horizontal orange line at i_c). If the ceiling is applied to deposit rates, it will reduce the amount lent (to X_c) and raise the cost to borrowers (to r_c). If the ceiling applies instead to lending rates, banks will set deposit rates at i'_c deducting transaction costs. The amount deposited (and lent, when abstracting from reserve requirements) will be X'_c. The excess demand for credit ($X_o - X'_c$) cannot be satisfied, and lenders will ration the available supply.

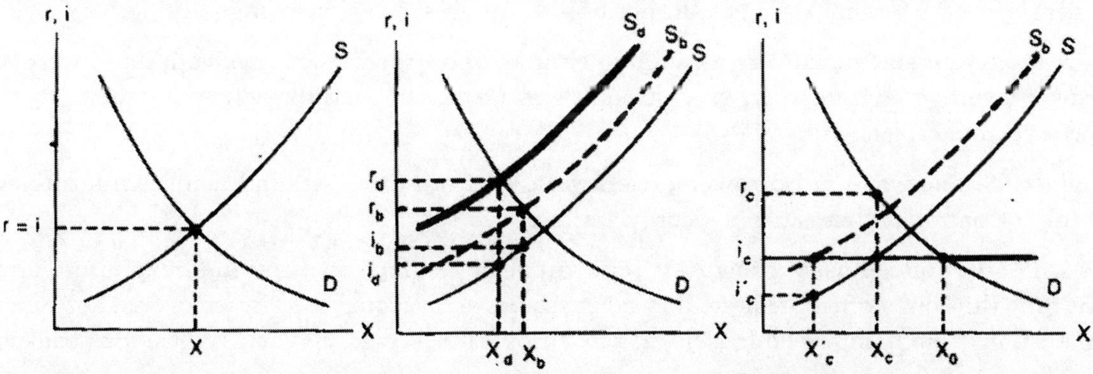

Fig. 12.1 The Supply of and Demand for Credit

This is why a credit culture should be viewed and administered as a whole, not as a series of unrelated parts. Credit policy should be in writing, regarded as a living document, and reviewed regularly. A good credit system will sound bells and whistles when things get off the track, and it should be free of loopholes, able to pass audit.

Well-run banks are always introspective about lending, and senior managements concentrate on credit issues. They understand their bank's proper lending turf, carefully target their markets, ask themselves what they do well and why, and they examine what they don't do well and why. They ask how the credit function can be better organised and supervised. They are careful in selecting and developing lending talent, see to it that their officers stick to lending that they understand thoroughly, follow credits closely, and anticipate rather than just react to problems. They have an effective damage control capacity in the event something should go awry. Credit policy is clear, and each loan officer knows what's expected of him.

Common Credit Problems

Some of the more common credit problems are caused by:

1. Lack of or a deficient credit culture: In such a situation, loans would be made without application of sound basic credit criteria or excessive emphasis on earning in difficult markets, going down-tier or pressing for market share. The devastating impact of the Penn Square illustrates what unsound practice can do at every lending level. Breakdowns occur when early warning systems don't work, when follow-through is inadequate, when documentation doesn't work, when follow-through is inadequate, when documentation isn't carefully done and when the plain nitty-gritty of process is poor.

2. Large borrowers, to which banks have large exposure, that encounter serious difficulties or become marginal for one reason or another: This includes shared credits. Each bank should do its own homework. When trouble is in the offing, the writing is usually on the wall, and alert loan officers should be able to position themselves defensively in good time.

3. Moderate-size borrowers, when hog chunks of borrowing are involved, that increase borrower leverage significantly: When trouble strikes, the bank has only one way out and is, in effect, a venture capital partner.

4. Small one-way-out borrowers, overleveraged from the start, and using bank money as equity: Control and measurable security are essential.

5. Poorly policed asset growth or repayment dependent on continued economic and profit growth: This is often predicated on dream sheets and accompanied by excessive short-term debt, possibly from uninformed lenders, too much overall leverage, and an overgenerous banker.

Knowledge of Borrower

The lender with a close knowledge of his borrower has an offensive and defensive edge, provided his relationship is not so close as to cause him to overemphasize the customer's interests or such that is difficult for him to shift the tone of his relationship when problems arise.

Loan officers often find that they know more about their credit when business turns down or other difficulties develop than they did when they approved them. But their radar dishes are expected to detect, in timely fashion —

(1) Weak financial and management controls

(2) Losses in one part of the business obscured by profits elsewhere

(3) One-man shows, headstrong mismanagement

(4) Fad products (like CB radios)

(5) Marginal products

(6) Brilliant but erratic behaviour

(7) Over-reaching

(8) Poor business strategy

(9) Untested borrowers and management

(10) A lack of appreciation of business fundamentals on the part of the borrower.

Success doesn't necessarily last, and size is no guarantee of good performance or survival. Factors such as technology and changing consumer tastes frequently must be dealt with.

Loan officers in small communities, with a fixed customer base, can best understand their borrowers. The broader the market place and the larger the borrowers, the more fluid and impersonal the customer base. In a setting characterised by deregulation, proliferation of new banking products, heavy transactional volume, and electronic banking, the behavioural factor gets a perpetual stress test.

Senior Management and the Behavioural Factor

Senior management's commitment to sound credit practice must be perceived and believe at every lending level as real, not something that blows hot or cold with marketing or profit centre needs. Nothing related to a good credit practice would be possible to achieve without this. With the focus of public concern on banking, to do otherwise would be anachronistic, and, of course, unwise. In fact, the intensity of this attention, combined with depressed bank share prices, would mandate that managements assess the behavioural factor.

Basically, viability appraisal consists of five major studies:

(a) Analysis of past and projected financial statements to ascertain the spread of shareholdings, range and marketability of products manufactured, the liquidity of the firm's operations and so on.

(b) Trend analysis *(i)* past data based on audited/final financial statements for the previous 3 to 5 years; and *(ii)* projections/ estimates based on projected financial statements and other related data for the ensuing year or two.

(c) Analysis of past and projected funds flow in order to determine the flow patterns of short-term funds, and how these have been planned and controlled as well as how they are proposed to be planned and controlled by the firm.

(d) Assessment of the funds requirement both short-term and long-term of the firm.

(e) The types of reviews and control measures that need to be introduced to determine *(i)* the accuracy of past projections and estimates, and pinpoint reasons for deviations, if any; and *(ii)* whether any improvements could be made in the forecasting or budgeting techniques of the customer to ensure better accuracy in future.

Safety of a loan or advance is directly related to the basis on which the decision to lend to be taken, the type and amount of credit to be provided and the terms and conditions on which the advance will be made available. A banker consequently adopts a two-pronged approach to ensure the safety of each loan or advance:

(a) Pre-sanction appraisal to determine the "bankability" of each loan proposal, and

(b) Post-sanction controls to ensure proper documentation, follow-up and supervision of each loan or advance.

Pre-sanction appraisal is concerned with the measurement of the riskiness of a loan proposal. Over the years, bankers have evolved sound principles of lending. These principles are neither infallible nor are they a part of any legislation. They do, however, lay down parameters with the help of which each advance proposal can be tested. Broadly, these principles can be categorised as follows:

(a) Acceptable Borrower: The banker must have confidence in his customer's integrity and ability to run the business. The customer must have adequate financial stake in the business. He should neither be overtrading nor undertrading; nor should be indulging in speculative activities.

(b) Acceptable Business: What an acceptable business is for the purpose of bank lending depends upon the policies of the Government and the Reserve Bank of India, and the bank's own policies. Owing to the scarcity of their resources, banks are reluctant to finance solely trading activities and other low-priority sectors. An acceptable business must moreover be viable, i.e., it must be making reasonable profits.

(c) Acceptable Purpose: Looking to the nature of bank resources, i.e., deposits repayable on demand or after fixed maturity periods, a banker prefers to lend on short-term. He does not wish to be a partner in the business but is only interested in meeting the gap in the short-term resources of his customer. For specified purposes, a banker can and does extend long-term loans but term lending is not his principal business.

(d) Acceptable Repayment Programme: Since a banker lends on short-term, he expects that his loans will be repaid within short periods. In other words, he desires to keep his loans portfolio as liquid as possible.

(e) Acceptable Security: The best security is a well-managed business owned and run by capable and honest people. But even a good business may face a depression or may fail due to circumstances beyond its control. A banker must, therefore, have an insurance against such events.

Security in the form of goods and collateral serves the function of insurance against untoward happenings.

Post-sanction controls to a large extent depend upon the findings of the pre-sanction appraisal. If a customer is considered to be a first class risk, the banker may be prepared to relax some of his requirements of security. If the business is less than a satisfactory risk, the banker may not lend at all or if he does, he may impose stringent follow-up and control measures.

Successful lending, thus, depends upon the careful selection of the customer, proper appraisal of his credit needs and adequate control to ensure that his dealings with the bank are above board and that he is complying with the terms and conditions on which credit has been sanctioned to him.

Reporting Relationship, i.e., Follow-up Mechanics

The task of banks does not end with the sanction and disbursement of financial assistance. The follow-up of projects is of crucial importance to ensure that the fervour with which a project has been launched or financed by a financial institution results in the desired socio-economic gains and the deviations, if any, therefrom are not such as to vitiate the very concept or thwart the objective of the project. A relationship, therefore, begins between the institutions and the beneficiaries of the assistance, right from the day the first brick is laid, and continues so long as the project continues to be the beneficiary of the assistance granted by the financial institutions. There are basically two prime objectives of the follow-up policies of the financial institutions — one is to have a watch on the progress of the project, i.e., whether the project has been proceeding satisfactorily on the agreed lines and the other is to create a relationship as partners in the projects so that the beneficiaries and the term-lending institutions may realise and continue to have the mutuality of interest throughout the tenure of assistance.

The banks in India maintain a regular reporting relationship with the assisted concerns by *(a)* obtaining monthly production reports which the assisted concerns are required to submit to the concerned statutory/administrative authorities, *(b)* obtaining of monthly/quarterly progress reports, copies of the reports/statements submitted by the assisted concerns to their bankers, etc., *(c)* calling for half-yearly/yearly statements of accounts, working results and financial position, *(d)* carrying out periodical site visits/inspections and verifying the performance of the assisted concerns vis-a-vis their operating plans, *(e)* insisting upon a need-based system of management information and control within the organisation, and *(f)* having reports from nominees on the Board of Directors/ managements of assisted concerns as regards developments from time to time pertaining to their operations and management.

The reporting relationship is supplemented by structured informal discussions with the promoters/senior executives of assisted concerns periodically. Periodical reports are also asked for from internal/concurrent auditors and/or management/technical consultants appointed specially to monitor the progress of the assisted concern(s) in specified cases.

In their follow-up measures and reporting relationship, the endeavour of the financial institutions has been to inculcate among the entrepreneurs and promoters a better awareness of financial disciplines and managerial imperatives for success of an industrial venture. Enlightened promoters and competent managements are now able to appreciate in an increasing measure, the benefits derived by them from the various exercises which the financial institutions require them to carry out during the implementation and operational stages of the project. The follow-up procedures and the reporting relationship of the financial institutions have now been so streamlined that only that much information is called for which any prudent management in-charge of a project would itself like to have and analyse with a view to ensuring successful operations of the project.

Conclusion

The creative and contributive role of banks is neither limited to their decisions to finance a project nor to the supervision of a project's implementation during the currency of the financial assistance granted by them. The relationship between the banks and the assisted concerns is not merely that of a creditor and debtor; they are, in fact, partners in the industrial ventures. It is, therefore, all the more necessary that their relationship with the assisted concerns should be intimate and continuous, drawing upon each other's expertise and experience to create a vibrant industrial ethos and accelerate the process of economic growth.

It is in this light that banks require the management of every assisted concern to develop a proper organisational set-up and suitably broad-based Board of Directors to oversee the operations of the concern, as a whole. The ultimate objective is only to ensure that the assisted concerns do develop within themselves certain self-regulating mechanisms so that they continue to maintain their operational viability and financial credibility. Despite all that, if a concern runs into difficulties, or becomes sick, the institutions, like a good friend, do provide need-based succour to enable it to overcome its difficulties and regain its normal health. Truly, the banks share both prosperity as well as adversity of the industrial units and other enterprises assisted by them, and endeavour to act as their friend, philosopher and guide.

Chapter 13

Marketing of Banking Services

Introduction

The banking sector is passing through a period of rapid changes in response to the changes in the social, economic, political and cultural spheres the world over. Banks are also faced with a major challenge of competition and greater awareness among the customers and their increased demands for special services. At the same time, some of the existing services offered by banks for years have been subjected to closer scrutiny and there is a wider diversification of services to the customers.

What is Marketing?

"Marketing" may be defined as a scientific reconciliation of customer needs with the capabilities of the supplier or producer, so that there is mutual satisfaction. Banks make profit from selling competitive services and this must involve the creation of a marketing strategy which precedes all their other activities.

Deryk Weyer has come out with by far the most comprehensive definition of bank marketing. According to him, it consists of identifying the most profitable markets now and in future, assessing the present and future needs of customers, setting business development goals and making plans to meet them and managing the various services and promoting them to achieve the plans — all in the context of a changing environment. Briefly, this definition lays stress on identification and assessment of customer needs, setting business goals, planning, managing the various services and promoting them to achieve the plans in a changing environment. It means that it is a continuous process of managing the banking affairs in an innovative manner to the full satisfaction of customers — depositors, borrowers, investors etc.

Concept

Marketing implies the following:

- Identifying profitable markets.
- Assessing the existing and future needs of customers.
- Setting business development goals.
- Formulating operational plans to achieve the business goals.
- Implementing and reviewing the operational plans.

The marketing function encompasses both the planning and operation, the existing as well as potential business.

Emergence in India

Marketing has assumed significance in the context of Indian banking owing to the numerous market-related developments that have taken place in recent years. In the Indian context, the concept of marketing the banking services began in the early 80s. In the latter part of 80s, the concept underwent a significant change, mainly due to the introduction of sophisticated technological services in the banks. Thus, the idea of consumer (customer) satisfaction became an integral part of the bank management in the 90s. A wider choice of investment is now open to the savers. With competition from other institutions intensifying, walk-in business for banks in respect of deposits can no longer be expected. This is the challenge.

In this context, growing competition, emergence of a new range of banking services, need for innovative product development to keep pace with the level of economic development, compulsions in the area of profitability of banking business, coverage of far-flung areas make it imperative for ensuring optimum use of the branch banking infrastructure that has already been created. A weakness in the system is the lack of adequate focus on customer satisfaction, professionalisation and a better appreciation of the long-term perspectives. What is called for is a total marketing orientation in banks to overcome these weaknesses. A clear understanding of the marketing concept and the experience of foreign banks can be very useful for Indian banks for evolving and implementing appropriate marketing strategies.

Dynamics of Bank Marketing

Banks are important financial intermediaries which accept deposits from the public for the purpose of lending and investment. Through this function, they get related businesses or ancillary services like remittances, demand draft issue, mail transfers, telegraphic transfers, collection of bills, sale and purchase of foreign exchange, safe custody and safe deposit vault, guarantee facilities, sale of travellers' cheques, trustee and executor services, etc. Apart from these traditional services, others such as merchant banking, portfolio management, leasing, hire-purchase, etc. are services that have been added in recent years. These services are being rendered by the banks mainly with a view to attracting and retaining deposits and advances, customers and thus develop their business further. Some of the services which were earlier the preserve of specialised agencies like investment banks have been taken over by commercial banks. As a result, the wall separating investment banking and commercial banking has been cracking.

But then, for commercial banks whose main resources come from deposits mobilised from the public, there are many competitors. Today deposit mobilisation is not the exclusive preserve of banks. There is intense competition for deposits not only among banks but also from non-banking institutions. Public sector as well as private sector companies are collecting large amounts of deposits directly from the public through various methods. Similarly, the corporate sector has direct access to the saving and capital markets, and has succeeded in raising sizeable resources by way of equity shares and debentures in the capital market. Public sector bodies are allowed to raise funds from the public directly by way of bonds on attractive terms. A number of Government-sponsored savings schemes such as PPF, Indira Vikas Patras, NSCs, etc. have mobilised huge amounts of public savings, thus adversely affecting the banking system in their deposit mobilisation efforts.

Apart from this, the diversification of activities of banks, which were catering mainly to the credit needs of big business, industry and trade until their nationalisation in 1969, to hitherto neglected areas like agriculture, small-scale industries, tertiary sector and weaker sections of the society did affect the profitability of banks. And this forced the banks to go in for new avenues for improving earnings and profit. In the seventies, the major thrust of banks was on social banking and achievement of quantitative targets. During the eighties, the emphasis changed to qualitative aspects of banking. And today, there is a growing awareness among the bankers about the need for increasing profitability as this aspect will be the main criterion for deciding the soundness or otherwise of a commercial bank during the nineties. To meet the challenges and to take advantage of opportunities in a competitive environment, it has become imperative for banks to sharpen their marketing strategies and efforts.

Indian banks, unlike their counterparts in other parts of the world, are yet to adopt effective marketing strategies. More thinking and action in the sphere of marketing are being generated, now that walk-in business can no more be relied upon any more. This is one of the messages that has been conveyed through a recent study on marketing. This book contains the developments that have taken place in Indian banking and is an effort to bridge the gap in the existing literature on marketing in Indian banks. The author has brought home the importance of bank marketing by placing before the readers a fund of information covering the rationale, the principles, the concepts, the practices and the framework relating to marketing of banking and other financial services. The topics covered in the book include relevance of marketing to banking, study and analysis of the financial and marketing information system, bank marketing in rural areas and market planning at the corporate level of banks.

Marketing constitutes an inter-disciplinary approach. The understanding of the subject, therefore, necessitates recourse to several disciplines. The preferences of the customers are determined, for example, by levels of income, saving, price elasticity of products, etc. which constitute the realm of economics. The savings or investment decisions of the customers are very often conditioned by the value system within the society which belong to the discipline of sociology, while the responses and behavioural patterns of the people in the market can be explained in terms of concepts like hierarchy of human needs, transactional analysis, interpersonal relationships, etc. which are in the sphere of psychology. Many of the decisions relating to business planning are based on the available data and therefore, statistics is another discipline that has found useful application in bank marketing.

The Process of Marketing

The process of marketing in banks comprises three stages:

(a) discover what the consumer wants;

(b) create the product or service which satisfies him;

(c) then see that the customer gets it by selling to him or her.

When marketing is a product of any sort, the basic task of marketing is to create the need for it in the consumer's mind. The consumer has then to be convinced that this product is the best one to satisfy his need. Much of the actual selling is carried out through advertising. In the case of services, it is usually the already established needs that the consumer has which have to be met and it is the performance of service which counts — in the sense that satisfactory performance probably leads to a repeat of the order and this encourages "word of mouth" advertising. It is worth mentioning here that it is regarded as unethical for the medical or the legal profession to advertise, and yet this practice grows through the good performance of the services. When we are considering the marketing of services, irrespective of whether we are looking at a youngster who provides a newspaper round service for the local news-agent, or the work of rail, we find that the task is basically the same as for a physical product. The service-provider must make the customer (client) aware of the need which he or she has, to be prepared to cope with the need, and provide the best possible performance. We shall also discover that there are various means by which services may be sold in this way, for example, a car rental firm may direct potential customers' attention to reliability and convenience, whereas a hotel chain may point out how well travellers are looked after to take away the strain of their business or holiday journeys, and so on. In every single instance, remember that: "a need exists ... a need is met ... and a service is carried out well."

Here we may consider products and services and draw a distinction between them. A product is able to be identified through taste, touch, smell, or sight. It may be moved or driven, or lived in perhaps, or it may be used to help produce other products. But a service may very well use a product and convert it into something which can be bought (or rented, or leased and so on) at a price (or for a fee). When, however, does a service change into a product, or a product change into a service? This could matter, from a marketing standpoint. In theory, a building is a product. If a hotel chain buys it, it becomes part of a service. A motor vehicle becomes an instrument used to provide a service if it is used by a car-hire or van-hire firm.

Financial Services

The contribution of the services sector, particularly of the financial services, to the total economic pool has been rising rapidly the world over.

Services are distinct from goods. They are the activities which are not necessarily tied to the sale of a product or another service. They cannot be felt or seen. They can only be realised.

Marketing of services is different from marketing of goods. Its unique features are intangibility, inseparability, heterogeneity and perishability. Lovelock has tried to classify exhaustively the nature of services marketing into four categories:

(a) Those which are tangible to people, like health, transport, restaurant ... etc.

(b) Those which are tangible to goods, like air-freight, equipment-repair, laundry ... etc.

(c) Those which are intangible to people, like education, information service, broadcasting ... etc.

(d) Those which represent intangible actions directed to intangible assets of people like banking, insurance ... etc.

The financial services fall clearly under the category of a service, which is an intangible action directed towards the intangible assets of people.

The communication technology explosion is steadily converting the globe into a planetary village. Consumer aspirations are growing. The markets are being steadily globalised.

The Marketing Mix

In the fast-changing marketing scenario, it is essential to define the target markets and to assess the alternative markets. The marketing mix has to continue to evolve.

"Marketing Mix" is the term used to describe a combination of the seven inputs that constitute the core of the bank's marketing financial services system. They are popularly known as the Seven P's.

(1) Product variety — range as well as branding.

(2) Pricing — customer's perceived value, quality and price differentiations.

(3) Place — location/distribution channels.

(4) Promotion — public relations, advertising, publicity, merchandising, etc.

(5) People — training, incentives, articulation and work culture.

(6) Physical— environment in the various service outposts.

(7) Process — policies, procedures etc.

Adequate and appropriate marketing mix designing has to remain in constant focus, particularly in the light of dramatic developments that are taking place round the world. In fact, the whole world is stunned by the sheer rapidity of the environmental metamorphosis.

Characteristics of Services

Now, let us have a look at the six features of services marketing. These are:

(i) Intangibility: Financial services are intangible and it is, therefore, necessary that, while drafting the strategies, tangible clues are traced so as to reduce intangibility. Brand positioning can be one of the effective attempts in reducing intangibility. The *benefits* of a financial instrument rather than its *features* should be highlighted. The customer must be able to distinguish how the product of a particular kind of financial service is different from others and what unique benefits it will bring to bear. The crucial issue is in managing the atmospherics. Some of the financial institutions in the Indian market have been able to boost up their sales by managing, manoeuvring and manipulating the environmental factors. The word of mouth communication, which can be stimulated by increasing the number of satisfied customers and by developing loyalty clubs can be of great assistance in reducing much of the intangibility in marketing a service product.

(ii) Inseparability: The service cannot be separated from the person who serves. The human element comes foremost. The customer in the case of service products can have access to a facility. Payment is for the use of items. Advantages of non-ownership by the customer, e.g., easier payment through the credit card, have to be stressed.

While on the one hand, reducing the time-lag in rendering services has to be attempted as an on-going process, the capability development and reinforcement in the human resources have to be constant. The higher the customer orientation of the human resources, the greater is likely to be the success of marketing endeavours. The process of selection and training has to be well thought-out.

Automatising the routine in the performance to eliminate the drudgery and boredom of the personnel increases speed and efficiency. A customer satisfaction monitoring system needs to be established to have regular information and data as to the success of the endeavours of the marketing team and help in timely correction.

(iii) Heterogeneity: The uniqueness of the individual will insist on the development of financial products as *personalised* product innovations. The developers of the service instrument will have to remain informed of the environment and of the emerging light on the skyline so as to formulate products in consonance with the aspirations and preferences of customers. The product development exercise has to be constant, continuous and coordinated. It has to be data-based. It has to keep in mind the bottom line of the institution. Eventually, the services must become customised.

(iv) Perishability: This feature poses the problem of the short supply as well as the excess supply syndrome. There are times when the demand is much more and there are times when it is below the production capacity level. The financial organisations have to develop flexibility in the movement of personnel from one service to another, from one kind of job to another. The organisations will also have to consider keeping a back-up of part-time employees to meet a peak time demand situation.

(v) Speciality: Here individual services are quite different in style and content from each other having developed mostly over a long period of time. Note that the services offered by banks must be marketed differently from, say, those offered by a marketing consultancy.

(vi) Partiality: Here there is a special client (as opposed to a simple buyer-seller) relationship so that the provider of the service is very much in control of the situation with the client in his hands. This is clear if we think of a doctor-patient relationship, since the producer of the service is the one with a specialist knowledge.

The responsibilities (or functions) of marketing consist of providing satisfaction to a customer, resource allocation, stimulating and directing demand and providing distributive channels. Marketing activities include the various activities which go to make up the function of marketing. They are: search for marketing strategy which covers fixation of targets for the marketing activity, programme giving a clear idea of the marketing activity, production, i.e., creation of the good or service, transportation, distribution, promotion and prices.

In the growing scenario, the best possibly would be for the organisations marketing financial services to become a financial supermarket — an umbrella organisation. The customers will have the facility of a single window for buying a variety of financial services like banking, mutual funds, housing, securitisation of mortgages, factoring etc. While, on the one hand, this will bring about facilities to the customers, on the other, it will help the organisation to develop the capability to become more competitive. The customer-canvassing as well as customer-retention costs can be substantially reduced.

Technique and Strategy of Marketing

The technique and strategy of marketing in banks and development banks covers a very wide segment. Today, there are over thirty crore depositors and over ten crore borrowers, spread over a vast geographical track both in urban and rural centres. A large segment of these customers are ignorant of many a thing relating to banking and more particularly, development banking. Hence, there is a need for agents, development managers, consultants and other specialised cadre to sell the development services to accelerate the process of economic development.

The technique is a method of providing various need-based services to the customer. The tools of technique should be comprehensive but at the same time, simple, free from jargon, etc.

The strategy deals with matching the techniques with the needs of various market segments so as to foster economic development. In this context, the development of varied skills and providing necessary motivations also form an integral function of marketing strategy. Service innovation and market planning by development banks are significant to meet the needs of the customer. Expansion of the service basket is itself a good strategy. Development banks should, therefore, develop new techniques and adopt new marketing strategies to help the integrated development of human personalities, economic development and banks' productivity.

Market Segmentation

Market segmentation is the process of dividing the total, heterogeneous market for a product or service into several markets or segments, each of which tends to be homogeneous in all significant aspects. Market segmentation is a customer-oriented philosophy.

Markets can be segmented on demographic bases like regional population distribution, urban-suburban, rural population, age, sex, family life-cycle, miscellaneous such as race, religion, nationality, education, occupation, etc.

Market segmentation on the basis of income levels is:

1. High Income Group (Higher-higher, Higher-middle, Higher-lower).
2. Middle Income Group (Higher-middle, Middle-middle, Middle-lower).
3. Lower Income Group (Lower-higher, Lower-middle, Lower-lower).

Market segmentation based on sociological factors such as: (a) cultural group; (b) large social classes; (c) small groups, including the family.

Market segmentation based on psychological factors such as: (a) Personality; (b) Attitudes; (c) Product benefit desired.

Though the above list seems to be comprehensive, it may not suit exactly market segmentation in the banking industry. Bank marketing can be broadly divided into four segments on the basis of the types of customers, i.e., depositors, borrowers, casual customers and other banks.

Borrowers

It is often felt by most bankers and academicians concerned with the banking subject that depositors are the pillars of the bank and the bank is virtually dependent on them. Though it is true in nature to a certain extent, it is always doubtful regarding its validity. Though it is accurate in all senses, only a few bankers realise that the borrower is also as important as a depositor. Rarely do the bankers agree that the borrower is their first-rate customer and the depositor a second-rate customer. That is why bankers give VIP treatment to the depositors and treat the borrowers as parasites on the bank. So this is the most unfortunate situation presently existing in almost all the commercial banks. At this juncture, it may be suggested that banks should realise the importance of the role played by the borrower in making a substantial contribution to the bank's business. The borrower provides employment to the bank's funds. It is no exaggeration to say that bank employees have been getting their livelihood, and enjoying all the privileges at the cost of the bank borrower. Hence, a banker should study the case of each borrower separately in order to give due importance to each type of borrower. The following is the market segmentation based on the types of borrowers.

Bank borrowers are broadly divided into two categories: (i) Conventional borrowers; and (ii) Priority sector borrowers.

Conventional Borrowers: Working capital requirements of large-scale industries producing different types of products or rendering a variety of services. (Example: cotton textile industry, jute industry, sugar industry, chemical industry etc.). Bankers should also categorise these borrowers on the basis of region, type of loan like overdrafts, cash credits, bills purchased, bills discounted, credit against security and mortgage of property, etc.

Medium-Scale Industry: Bankers may classify this category of industries also as in the case of large-scale industry.

Small-Scale Industry: Working capital finance, bridge finance, finance for procurement of raw material, production finance, marketing finance, term loans, etc. Banks should categorise the sick units separately in order to rehabilitate and nurse them. Ancillary industrial units and agro-based industries should be given due importance under this category.

Cottage Industries: Borrowers can be classified on the basis of period of loan. For example, term loans and working capital requirement of industries should be classified on the basis of the nature of the industry: (i) Wholesale Trade; (ii) Retail Trade; and (iii) Small and Petty business.

Agricultural Sector: Banks classify agricultural borrowers on the basis of term loans and crop loans. Agricultural advances include crop loans to all types of crops, term loans for minor irrigation schemes, procurement of fertilisers, land levelling, land development, sinking of wells, installation of pumpsets, farm mechanical equipments like tractors, installation of gobar gas plants, finance to animal husbandry like dairy, piggery, sheep husbandry, poultry, sericulture, fisheries, goat rearing, etc.

Loans to weaker sections of the society like cobblers, barbers etc.: (1) Educated self-employed; (2) Uneducated self-employed; (3) Technocrats; (4) Road transport operators; (5) Water transport operators; (6) Educational loans; and (7) Loans to professionals.

Depositors

Bank deposits play a significant role in running a banking industry. A bank purchases deposits in order to produce and sell loans. Thus, purchase of deposits is an important activity of bank marketing.

Bank deposits can be divided on the basis of two factors: (1) Time factor; and (2) Customer factor.

1. Time Factor: Bank deposits are mainly divided into four categories on the basis of time; (1) Time deposits or Fixed deposits; (2) Savings Accounts; (3) Recurring Deposits; and (4) Current Accounts.

2. Customer Factor: Bank deposits can be divided into 19 categories on the basis of customer segmentation. They are: (i) Public limited companies; (ii) Private limited companies; (iii) Partnership firms; (iv) Joint Hindu family firms; (v) Sole proprietary firms; (vi) Social organisations; (vii) Religious organisations; (viii) Charitable institutions; (ix) Trusts; (x) Educational institutions; (xi) Hospitals; (xii) Liquidators; (xiii) Governments — State, Central, Local; (xiv) Individuals; (xv) Minors; (xvi) Lunatics; (xvii) Drunkards; (xviii) Married women; and (xix) Joint accounts.

Further, bank marketing (in the case of purchasing deposits) can also be divided or segmented on the basis of:

1. Economic status of the potential depositors like higher, middle and lower.
2. On the basis of geographical region like rural, semi-urban, urban and metropolitan.
3. On the basis of age like pre-schooling, schooling, employment, preretirement age. For example, Kiddy bank deposit schemes of the Andhra Bank are designed to encourage thrift among the school children.
4. On the basis of need and convenience of the customers. For example, housing deposit scheme, small savings scheme, cash certificates, gift cheques, cumulative deposit schemes, monthly interest payment schemes, pension plans, deposit schemes to meet the financial requirements of daughter's marriage or children's education, etc.

Marketing Service Structure

Marketing service structure and mix include planning and developing the right services needed by customers at the right time and place to be marketed by the bank. The bank should first know the changing customer tastes, preferences and needs and then innovate and develop the services to satisfy the customer. However, with scarce resources and growing concern for social responsibilities, the priority sector and weaker sections of society as well as for environment, service innovation becomes even more important. The new services marketed by a bank are a prime determinant of the bank's image or goodwill among the public as well as of its growth rate, profits and total marketing programme.

Service innovation by banks is significant as service is a basic factor for satisfying customer needs. Service is a basic profit determinant. New services are essential to growth as customer selectivity has been increasing day by day. Bank management should be careful in developing the new services at each of the six stages, whether or not to move to the next stage, abandon the service or such additional information. The six stages in service development are: (i) generation of new service ideas, (ii) demand-supply analysis, (iii) screening of ideas to determine which ones warrant further study; (iv) service development, (v) test marketing, and (vi) commercialising the service.

Top management of the bank should be deeply involved in service innovation, and support this activity in a creative fashion. For the success of service development, banks may use the service planning committee or new service department, or service-management system or venture team to make the service development programme a success.

A service mix is a full list of all services offered by a bank. The structure of service mix has dimensions of both breadth and depth. Its breadth is measured by the number of service lines carried, viz., acceptance of deposits, granting of loans, public utility services, merchant banking activities including underwriting, etc. Its depth is measured by the assortment of different types of deposits, loans, public utility services for different amounts to different types of people, underwriting for different amounts and companies, etc.

It is imperative that bank management select appropriate strategies for the bank's service mix. One strategy is simply to expand the existing service mix by increasing the number of lines and/ or the depth within a line. An alternative is to prune the service mix by eliminating an entire line or simplifying the assortment within a line. Another strategy is to alter the terms and conditions of service.

Service differentiation and market segmentation are two related service strategies. Annuity plans and mobilisation of deposits through different schemes from older and employed people and deposit schemes meant for children's education, daughter's marriage are examples of service differentiation and market segmentation.

An especially controversial service strategy is that of planned obsolescence built around the concepts of style, fashion and the fashion cycle. Fashion, essentially a sociological and psychological phenomenon, follows a reasonably predictable pattern. Declining demand for the traditional type deposits, increasing demand for newly developed deposits, advances and public utility services like traveller's cheques, gift cheques, credit cards are examples of this concept.

Marketing Plan

The marketing plan is a key document which sets down precisely who is to do what, when, where and how. There must be liaison with production to determine product requirements and scheduling; ample stocks of the product must be available at the time required by the sales organisation. The advertising and promotional programme must be worked out in detail — the amount of money to be spent, the media to be used, the kind of advertising to be run. What is to be the basis of the advertising appeal, to reach what kind of audience with what degree of frequency and impact? Are there to be any introductory consumer efforts, coupons, premiums or competitions? On the sales side distribution and product sales targets must be set by sales territory and by individual sales representatives. Physical distribution facilities have to be organised, delivery schedules worked out and so on. The financial people have to provide costing and profit estimates based on proposed expenditures and forecasted sales volume. Every part of the marketing plan has to be costed out and budgets prepared.

A workable marketing plan, the starting place for the adoption of the marketing concept, can be synthesized in five simple questions. They are: 1. What is the situation now? 2. What do you want it to be in future? 3. What part of the work can reasonably be expected to be accomplished by advertising, public relations, sales promotion, direct selling effort, pricing and other lesser marketing influences? 4. What, specifically, do you want people to do, or how do you want them to think as a result of exposure to the marketing activity? 5. Have they done it? That is, have the people reacted favourably and positively?

The next stage is the implementation of the paper plan through coordination and interaction of the physical field selling and distribution effort and the company's advertising and promotional activities. The functions of the former are to see to it that the company's distribution and sales targets are met, that wholesale, retail and direct customers are efficiently serviced and at all times carry adequate stock to meet their anticipated requirements, and that customer information is fed back regularly to the sales management in the form of daily, weekly or monthly reports. An efficient field intelligence system is of utmost importance in keeping headquarters appraised of the latest situation and expected developments in the market and in checking and controlling the actual field performances against planned performance.

Advertising and sales promotion activities run parallel to the physical selling and distribution operations, and include advertising and display material aimed directly at the consumer; trade and technical press advertising to distributors, trade buyers, professional groups, etc., direct mail, trade receptions, and planned sales presentations to trade buyers, committees or associations; consumer and trade incentive schemes, such as special offers, bonuses, competitions, premiums, etc.

The Nature of Marketing Problems

Any marketing problem involves a situation requiring a decision to act or not to act, in the face of uncertainty. The major sources of uncertainty are the difficulties of trying to anticipate and influence the future course of events, in determining the interactions of cause and effect, in allocating limited resources among competing ends, of choosing between different courses of action, and in obtaining accurate and reliable information. The existence of uncertainty and, therefore, the necessity of taking risks — and a decision not to take action can involve as great a risk, if not a greater degree of risk — is a characteristic of all problems. Decisions to alter the prices of existing products or services, to introduce a new product, to increase the level of advertising for a product or to discontinue advertising for a product, all involve uncertainty and risk as to their probable outcomes in terms of achieving company objectives.

Seen in this light, problem-solving means finding ways of progressively reducing uncertainty and risk in business judgements, assumptions, decisions and actions, at least to more tolerable limits.

The scientific approach to problem-solving involves the basic steps shown in Chart 1.

Chart 1

The Six Basic Steps in Problem-Solving

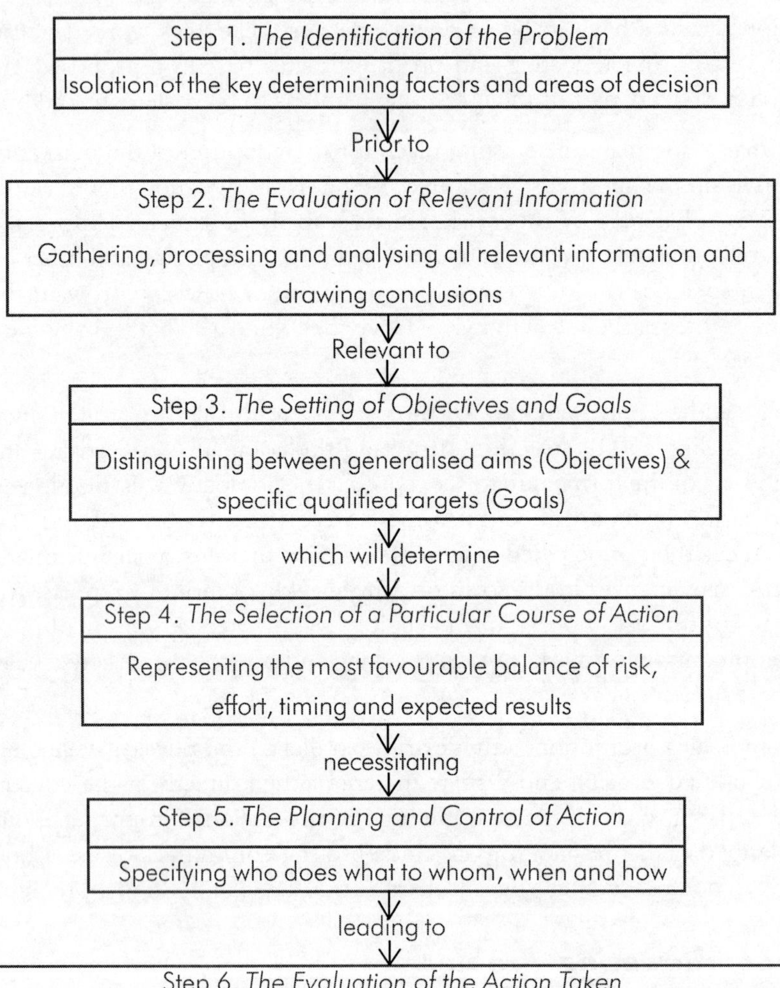

The ability to identify and assess a particular problem is related to the quantity, accuracy, relevancy and timeliness of the information available, and to how well the information is analysed and interpreted.

The setting of objectives and goals and the selection of the particular course of action to follow are related, on the one hand, to management's ability to forecast or anticipate events over which it either can or cannot exercise some degree of control and the probable customer of its own and other's actions; on the other hand, it is also related to management's capacity for perceiving the possibilities and potentialities in a given or expected situation not apparent at first sight, and what can be made to happen by purposeful action.

Planning and control relate to the organisation and allocation of limited resources to a particular course of action, chosen from a number of possible alternatives, and to the evaluation of the results achieved by such action against planned performance. If at the end of this sequence of steps the original problem remains, then the cycle must start again in the hope of coming closer to the final solution through successive approximations and corrections. The original as well as any new information, including the result yielded by the previous plan of action, must be reappraised; assumptions, conclusions, objectives and goals must be critically re-examined and either reaffirmed or changed in the light of newer or more accurate knowledge; a fresh course of action must be embarked upon and its results evaluated.

Linear Programming

It is a mathematical technique for selecting the most favourable or desirable course of action in terms of least cost, highest profit, least effort from among a number of alternative courses of action, using limited resources. Programming means planning activity to achieve a given objective through the optimum use or allocation of available resources. Programming is linear when there is a straight-line relationship between the variables as when a change in the number of calls a salesman brings a proportional change in the number of value of orders he collects. A non-linear relationship would exist where change in the former produces a less than or more than proportionate change in the latter. A very large number of computations usually called for in all but a limited range of linear programming problems makes access to a computer almost essential and this represents a major limitation on the extension of the use of the technique at this time. The cost of marketing problems that linear (and non-linear) programming should help to solve include determining the most profitable combination of products to be made from limited resources, determining the optimum location of warehouses and depots to minimise transport and delivery costs, determining the optimum stock levels to meet the sales requirements.

Communication Theory

As its name implies, this theory originated in the electrical communications field and is concerned with evaluating the effectiveness of the flow of information and communication within a given system. Consequently, many problems in communication theory can be translated into models. One branch of the theory, cybernetics, deals with self-regulating and control mechanisms and has provided greater insight into the workings of human behaviour systems. The study of the mechanism of 'feedback' has been of particular importance to communication and control theory, for control of an operation involves reporting back whenever it goes outside certain specified limits so that corrections can be made. When a human being, sensing that he may fall, corrects his balance, he is making use of a built-in, self-regulating, information feedback control process. Industrial automation is one practical commercial result of the theory of cybernetics.

The two best known applications of the network principle are PERT (Programme Evaluation and Review Technique) and CPM (Critical Path Method). The PERT technique was developed as a method of planning and controlling the co-ordination of the Polaris Fleet Ballistic Missile Programme for the Special Projects Office of the U.S. Navy's Bureau of Ordnance. Several thousands of contractors and agencies involved in the programme had to be integrated and as a result of the use of PERT the completion date is reported to have been reduced by more than two years. Both PERT and CPM have found their widest application to date outside of military uses, that is, in the programming of construction and installation work.

J.S. Pickup and D. A. Thwaites have summarised the main advantages of these network techniques as follows: (i) they record all the activities necessary for the completion of a project; (ii) they display the reasoning behind the forecasting of completion dates; (iii) they enable potential trouble areas to be foreseen; (iv) they pin-point responsibility; (v) they save time and money by simulating changes in cost variables; (vi) they define objectives; (vii) they provide a good communication medium; (viii) they permit management by exception whereby only significant deviations from planned or standard performance, abnormal situations and trouble spots are brought to the attention of management. The authors conclude: "One of the greatest benefits of drawing up networks is improved communication throughout an organisation horizontally and vertically. The necessity to analyse in detail the activities and events of a project not only bring out the relative 'time' importance of interrelated activities, but for people to think and discuss with others the sequence in which operations are done and the associated problems which emerge. Management by exception is a natural outcome of using networks, for by concentrating control on the critical path activities, time is not wasted by progressing other activities which could not shorten the overall length of the project."

The application of network analysis to marketing operations is still in an experimental stage. Its use in planning new product development, test marketing, planning and the co-ordination and scheduling of selling and advertising plans and programmes can be expected to become much more widespread during the next few years. Networks can give the marketing executive a better planning perspective in which the relative importance of time, costs and profits can be taken into account. Operating management is concerned with two basic problems. On the one hand, activities must be organised, scheduled and co-ordinated. On the other hand, limited resources must be assembled and allocated to various tasks at the time and place and in the quantity necessary so as to maximise or minimise some magnitude of importance to management. It is not enough to merely allocate resources to ensure a successful and efficient plan. Although the simultaneous optimisation of all phases of a project may be desirable, in some cases it is usually necessary for the different parts of the programme to be optimised in a particular sequence. But there is always a danger that the whole programme is actually weakened rather than strengthened by making one part more efficient in isolation from or at the expense of others. For example, spending a sum of money on advertising too far in advance of the sales force's capacity to obtain the minimum level of distribution necessary is a common error of marketing policy.

Promotional Programmes and Sale of Services

Role of Promotional Programmes in Accelerating Deposit Mobilisation

Because of the vital role that it plays in the economy of a country, a bank needs to publicise its own activity. So every bank must prepare a well-thought-out programme of advertising, keeping in mind the twin objectives of its own progress and the progress of the country.

It may be true that a good wine needs no bush. But it is not so with a bank. A bank needs advertising since it plays a vital role in the economy of the country. Advertising is one of the four major tools by which a firm directs communication to the prospective buyers and the public. The purpose of advertising is to direct the potential buyers' responses to the organisation and its offerings. It seeks to do this by providing information, by trying to canalise desires, and supplying reasons for preferring a particular organisation's offerings.

Advertising, therefore, plays a key role in the banks by providing useful information to the public. Advertising for the bank is not easy to plan or write. It is much more difficult than most producers' and retailers' advertising which sells, along with the products, its price, colour, flavour, brand names, style and so on. Bank advertising is aimed at breaking the old habits and forming new ones; for example, persuading people who have never had the banking habit to open accounts in a bank and show them the advantages that go with the different types of accounts; convincing those who keep themselves aloof from the banks for one reason or another of the advantages that they get by having accounts in a bank and wean them away from other financial institutions.

There are five major areas in bank advertising which must be given careful consideration. They are: (i) Preparing budget, (ii) Flexibility, (iii) Appeals and strategy, (iv) Media, and (v) Finish.

(i) Preparing budget: The best way to prepare an advertising budget for a bank is to estimate the bank's appropriation on the basis of the job to be done. The banker should first determine which services he wishes to promote and rate them in the order of importance. He also should decide which groups are likely to be interested in these services. This information will help the bank to select the advertising media that will place his messages before the right people with maximum economy and impact.

(ii) Flexibility: Flexibility is the keynote of any good advertising plan. The banker must move with the times instead of repeating the familiar pattern from year to year. So the banker will have to evaluate and adjust his budget annually in the light of its operations, changes in market, time, economic conditions and many other factors.

(iii) Appeals and Strategy: "If the appeal is right, even sub-staff can write the copy", so goes the saying; and it is true of bank advertisements also.

The banker's appeal must, therefore, involve one or more of the basic urges in order to make certain that his advertising will inspire people to act. Effective advertising also involves making proper use of one of the two strategic approaches, viz., (1) the customer approach and (2) the product approach. In the bank's advertising programme, the customer approach generally works better than product approach.

(iv) Media: The banker should give importance to this aspect. There are different types of media of advertising for the banker and he may select anyone of the following: (i) newspapers, (ii) magazines, (iii) outdoor hoardings, (iv) direct mail advertising, (v) transportation advertising, (vi) radio, (vii) television.

Different media of advertising have to be selected for urban and rural centres to achieve maximum response from customers. Newspapers, magazines, outdoor advertising, radio and television may be suitable media of advertising in the urban centres.

(v) Finish: Finish refers to the style, taste and other physical attributes of the bank's advertisement presentations. This will have its impact on the minds of the people. The principal elements of finish are layout, illustrations and colour.

Nowadays, it appears that to use mass media to publicise different schemes of fixed deposits with attractive rates of interest (even compound rate of interest) is a better way of attracting depositors and investors.

Personal Selling

The goal of all marketing efforts is to increase profitable sales by offering want-satisfaction to the market over the long run. Personal selling is by far the major promotional method used to reach this goal. Personal selling is essential when developing close relationships between the buyer and the seller of services. Personal selling is quite suitable to promote the sales of banks' services as it consists of individual, personal communication in contrast with the mass, impersonal communication of advertising, sales promotion, etc.

Bank management should take into consideration while planning for personal selling the following set of predictions relative to the sales process derived by Robertson and Chase: (1) The sale may take place when the physical, social and personality characteristics of customer and salesmen are closely matched. (Example: if the task of mobilising deposits from a rural depositor is assigned to an employee with a rural background and the task of recovery of agricultural loans is assigned to an employee with an agricultural background, the sale is likely to take place). (2) The sale will probably take place if the customer perceives the salesman to be more believable and trustworthy. (3) A sale will result when the customer is known personally to the salesman. (4) A sale will result if the salesman makes more prospective buyers view themselves favourably. (5) The second sales person to call on the prospects will generally have an advantage over the first one.

Publicity for Bank Activities

Bank publicity involves the gathering, preparing and distribution through various means of newsworthy information about banks and the banking industry in general, and individual banks in particular. The basic purpose of publicity is to inform the public about the bank and its activities.

The following are some cardinal rules for the publicist in a bank or any other corporation: (1) Cover your "beat" — that is, your bank — thoroughly; but be discriminating. DO NOT flood editors with trivia. (2) Be fair and impartial with media representatives. Play no favourites. (3) Let your release "stand on its own feet." Never use pressure or leverage in order to sell a story. (4) Be responsible. This means that it is your duty to help the press as diligently on an unfavourable story as when things are going in your favour. (5) If you do not know the answer to a question asked by a newsman, admit it; but if you can reveal the answer, or find an officer who can, do so. Be a good "legman" as well as a reporter. It is part of your job. (6) When a publication makes an error, be philosophical, unless the error is serious, do not insist on a correction. (7) Never try to "kill" a story. This may spur newsmen to dig even harder into what you are trying to conceal. (8) Avoid speaking off the record. Newsmen are not bound to withhold information gained in this fashion — if they can find someone else to reveal the same information. Usually, they can. (9) If you must refuse information, tell the newsmen frankly what your reasons are. Usually, he will respect you for it.

Always remember that the road of the publicist leads between two camps. It is a road of compromise, yet it is a way that can be travelled with dignity and with great usefulness to society as a whole.

You must, on the one hand, keep faith in your employer by doing as effectively as possible the various tasks assigned and on the other, you must fulfil an obligation to the media representatives and to the general public doing a workman-like job in putting out news.

You must perform this task with integrity, honesty, and reliability. If you follow these basic tenets in your performance, whatever your capacity in the field of publicity, you will find your experience richly rewarding and well worth your devoted attention and utmost energies.

The bank management has to devise what combination of advertising, personal selling and other promotional tools will make the most effective promotional programme. Factors influencing the promotional mix are: (1) The amount of money available for promotion; (2) The nature of the market; (3) The nature of the service; and (4) The stage of the life cycle of the service.

Marketing Research and Customer Analysis

Marketing research systematically develops facts about the existing customers and the potential market opportunities. Plans stating realistic short and long-range market and profit objectives as well as blueprints for attaining these objectives efficiently and economically are based on these facts developed by marketing research. This specific activity in some banks is part of the business development or business promotion department.

Some of the large banks in the United States of America have already begun to use marketing research techniques. These banks have found that marketing research provides data on which management can base its decisions. Marketing Research has been called the launching pad for the machinery of successful marketing function for a bank. A writer commented that marketing research makes it possible to prepare confidently for the retention of the existing customers and the attraction of new ones.

Customer Analysis: Customer analysis can help management analyse the present in preparation for the future. The bank management should consider the following questions at the time of customer analysis: (1) Has there been a significant change in the type of business your bank attracts? (2) Are your new customers as profitable as were your close-outs? (3) Are the balances of retainer customers growing, standing still or declining? (4) What are your short and long-range marketing and profit goals? (5) What progress is your bank making against your competitors?

Customer analysis is a beginning area of marketing research. The other areas include research on trading and business areas, residential population, working population, business community, competition analysis, local banking attitudes and habits, deposit potential, business potential etc.

One expression of criticism about bank marketing is that bankers may just be giving lip service only. There will be no fundamental improvement in the marketing of bank services unless there is a will to market where they are needed. There are no pet solutions to the problems. Change means challenge, and the ability to meet challenge is a sign of good management.

Bank marketing activities cannot, obviously, be carried on successfully without the full support, interest and encouragement of top level bank management. In its most basic meaning, bank marketing and bank marketing research are an intelligent communication between the bank customer and the bank.

Obstacles

There are a number of obstacles which hamper the efforts to realign customer service with marketing. At the outset, it must be mentioned that commercial banks find it difficult to take their own decisions independently because of the regulatory controls imposed by the Government and RBI. As a result, they face problems while finalising the pricing strategies to mobilise the savings of the public. Besides, because of the high rates of interest companies are offering on deposits and debentures, it is not possible for commercial banks to raise their rates correspondingly so as to compete with them.

The downward trend in the collection of loans advanced to the priority and weaker sections of people like small and marginal farmers or entrepreneurs has had a cascading impact on the accretion of deposits.

Though the top managements of banks talk about effecting improvements in the customer service, all their plans and programmes tend to remain in cold storage as persons responsible for the distribution of services do not extend their wholehearted co-operation in this regard.

Innovation and imaginative competition has virtually outwitted the commercial banks, specially in respect of mobilisation of resources. It is also felt that synchronisation of banking operations with manpower planning has not been achieved. This has resulted in the quality of customer services deteriorating day-by-day. The RBI Report indicates that the credit squeeze experienced by banks is caused by the stagnation in the mobilisation of deposits and not by the RBI's policies. Experts feel that management practices have been by and large become static. At this juncture, the following measures would prove to be helpful in overcoming some of the banks' deficiencies.

Organising the Marketing Function

The marketing organisation in a developing bank lays stress on promotional and/or development operations and advertising the services both through the media and personal selling or melas for educating the people, marketing information and research and development.

The marketing function is now co-ordinated with development finance and personnel. Marketing management is finally responsible for coordinating and integrating the promotional and development, information and research, advertising and promotion, market and project planning functions of the bank. Marketing management in these circumstances is responsible for the administration and control of the bank's total marketing effort, for initiating marketing research and the preparation of marketing plans, and for presenting to and obtaining the approval of top management for all plans and proposals to achieve the agreed objectives.

Chart 2

Marketing-Centred Bank Organisation

TOP MANAGEMENT

FINANCIAL MANAGEMENT | PERSONNEL MANAGEMENT | MARKETING MANAGEMENT | PROJECT MANAGEMENT

PROMOTIONAL OPERATIONS	ADVERTISING AND PROMOTION	MARKETING INFORMATION & RESEARCH	DEVELOPMENT PROJECT PLANNING
Promotional Office	Advertising	Library	Project Selection (Company product mix)
Field Sales	Promotion of Activities	Information Service	Project Features Packing Pricing
Promotional & Sales Training	Merchandising and Display Services	Market Reseach Services	Project Servicing
Sales Planning	Public Relations	Innovative Schemes	Project Servicing
Promotional Evaluation and Statistics	Personal Selling	Counselling	

Suggestions

1. The banking services make a call in favour of realigning of marketing innovative concept where realignment should be in the background of changing socio-economic scenario.
2. Professionalisation of administrative apparatus is a *sine qua non* for initiating momentum at the operational level. Hence, a massive reform is needed. The introduction of professional

management at all the levels of banking operations would be meaningful. It is found that branches are opened in the rural areas but the branch managers hardly get any special training. The RBI, Union government and the top management need to divert their attention to such a sensitive issue.

3. The topmost priority to the consumer needs and preferences, particularly while tailoring the location and timing of services, is the need of the hour. The development of an effective communication system or formation of a communication mix so as to transmit the right information of the right prospects at the right time, should not be delayed.
4. The mounting inflationary pressure and the various incentives offered by the other financial agents have made it urgent that the commercial banks also revamp their pricing strategies. This means an increase in the rate of interest.
5. It is generally felt that the existing credit squeeze is mostly due to the failure of bankers to entice the customers of different groups. The acceleration of deposits would make possible credit expansion. It is essential that the rate of lending is maximised. Say, 1 per cent increase in the maximum rate of lending and 1 to 2 per cent rise in the yield on SLR/ CRR would neutralise the loss as a result of the hike in the rate of interest.
6. Performance budgeting, introduced in the mid-seventies, is still to get a special treatment. The policy-makers have to assign due weightage to the same.
7. The hallmark of behavioural management, personal touch in service, could be evaporated during the post-nationalisation period but it could not be momentised in tune with socio-economic conditions. This disequilibrium in the bankers' behavioural management is required to be removed.

Conclusion

It is not suggested that all development-minded managements think and act along the lines indicated any more than all marketing-minded managements do. But it is a good deal more likely that managements will view the various banking functions and activities in the ways indicated, depending on their traditional perspective.

To change one's fundamental views or methods of operation is not an easy thing to do at the best of times. It is, however, all too easy to change the organisational structure, without a corresponding real change in the underlying mental attitude or approach. The marketing concept is to be supported and acted upon by top management and the same to be supported and acted upon down the line. Unless this is done, confusion, misunderstanding and disillusionment are likely to follow.

Behind any changes in the organisation charts lie a number of critical personnel and personal relationship problems — problems of explanation, communication, re-education and staff training — which management has to tackle successfully if a different way of doing things is to be made acceptable to all concerned.

Chapter 14

Customer Service in Banks

"Customers' crare to be taken out of their high strung and highly competitive environs to some place where they feel they belong. A setting where they would enjoy learning new ideas, values and benefits of the brand and store experience. The transformation need not be cultural or academic in nature, but go a long way in assisting customers through a lifecycle curve or simply, a mood-altering catalyst of choice."

Introduction

"A customer is the most important
visitor on our premises.
He is not dependent on us.
We are dependent on him.
He is not an interruption in our work.
He is the purpose of it.
He is not an outsider on our business.
He is a part of it.
We are not doing him a favour by serving him.

Gandhiji,
Father of the Nation

He is doing us a favour by giving us an opportunity to do so." Thus spoke Gandhiji, the Father of the Nation.

Customer satisfaction is a dominant factor in the success of an enterprise. In the service industry where intangible products are to be marketed, the importance of customer satisfaction is all the more significant. The customer has, therefore, necessarily and consistently to be the focal point in all decision-making relating to the policies, programmes and practices of an organisation. While there is a growing need to improve customer service, there is no corresponding motivation at all in those who are required to deliver the service. The motivation will spring only when there is recognition of the worth of the individual, recognition of one's duty to the organisation and above all, a sense of pride in the organisation one belongs to.

Service organisations such as financial institutions, banks and insurance companies help in the creation and protection of individual and corporate wealth by making their products and services available to society at large.

The Approach

Banks are community-based organisations. Banks are also business organisations. The two roles are complementary. As business organisations, traditionally, they accept deposits for purposes of lending and investment with a view to making profit. As part of business, they also provide ancillary services, like remittances, collections, custody of valuables, etc. In fulfilling their role as community-based organisations, banks have to be alive to the aspirations and total needs of the community and endeavour to satisfy these needs by themselves and in co-ordination with other community-based organisations. It is also a part of banker's task to anticipate the needs and provide positive responses — this task is rendered more challenging as the society's needs are ever-changing.

It would be unrealistic today to believe that banks are mere financial institutions, working for profit, and serving a social purpose, if any, only incidentally. As we see, banks essentially are social organisations, rendering financial services to sub serve the socio-economic objectives of the society. It is important to recognize that the social purpose of banks is rot peripheral but vital to the banks themselves, and, in a way, the very reason for their existence. We also believe that fulfillment of this social purpose does not militate against surplus generation; indeed, generation of surplus, in the aggregate, is itself a component of this social obligation.

Service to the Society

Service to the society, at the micro level, means service to customers, present and potential. From this point of view, the prime function of banks can be defined as the creation and delivery of customer-needed services in a customer-satisfying manner. To begin with, therefore, a banker's task is to identify his customer and his needs.

Broadly, a customer can be defined as a user or a potential user of bank services. So defined, a customer would obviously include an account holder, or his representative, or a person carrying out casual business transactions with a bank, or a person who, on his own initiative or on banker's initiative, may come within the banking fold. The problem would really arise in locating or identifying a potential customer. This would call for vision, on the one hand, and the right marketing and developmental attitude, on the other : vision for grasping quickly and intelligently (and with futuristic perspective) the 'heart' of policies and priorities, and the right marketing and developmental attitude for creating, in a planned and organically co-ordinated manner, customers, products and delivery systems. Such 'creation and delivery' naturally presuppose bank marketing as an active, creative and outgoing process.

Customer Needs

Identification of a customer should be followed by identification of his needs — articulated and inarticulated. Often, the inarticulated needs are like the submerged part of an iceberg, invisible but real and, in fact, of greater relevance and import. Here, too, the 'active' role of the banker would add to his functions yet another dimension, viz., generation of healthy and socially desirable needs. An 'active' banker may not rest with just responding to a customer's needs. He may, by creating awareness through customer education, himself encourage generation of new needs or surfacing of silent needs.

The process of fulfilling customer needs so identified or generated would necessitate tailoring bank services to what the customer wants, rather than making him helplessly accept whatever banks can conveniently provide. This approach has particular relevance in serving a multitude of small customers.

Designing services to suit the requirements of customer is one part of the story. The other part is good delivery, because bad delivery of a perfectly designed service is as disastrous as perfect delivery of a badly conceived service. Both are indicative of poor marketing. The five elements of good delivery could be said to be speed, timeliness, accuracy, courtesy and concern.

Having ascertained customer needs and designed appropriate services and delivery systems to meet them, it is necessary to continually assess and reassess how customers perceive bank services. Good service and good delivery (as perceived by a banker) do not automatically or necessarily lead to customer satisfaction. Maybe, the spirit does not percolate to the lowest operating levels. Maybe, and this is important, customer's perception does not agree with the banker's perception. And, in a service industry, customer's perception is what matters. Or, should matter. Meaningful appraisal of customer service has, thus, to be an essential activity for all banks. Admittedly, such an appraisal is not an easy job. More so, because customer service is an extremely dynamic concept. What is good customer service today may become indifferent service tomorrow, and bad service the next day.

Unfortunately, there has been so far no integrated, unified and organised effort for a study of customer service in all its aspects by banks in India. Even individually, we are afraid, not much attention — at least not on a regular basis — has so far been devoted to this by banks. The low priority given to such appraisal and study might have been due to inadequacy of bank services compared to large unsatisfied demand all these years; banks have been operating in a seller's market. Banks had, and continue to have, ready customers and large waiting lists. Public opinion was also, till recently, not very articulate or organised nor was the total environment conducive to self-improvement measures within banks.

Despite the absence of any regular or comprehensive appraisal of bank services, there is a general consensus that the service presently rendered by banks needs, and is capable of, vast improvement. Bank users criticize, and bankers themselves concede, that customer service rendered by banks leaves much to be desired, and, in certain respects, has indeed reached very low levels, both absolutely and in comparison with the past. This can be ascribed to many reasons. Maybe, the enormous branch expansion programme undertaken by banks, along with the ever-widening range of their activities and responsibilities, particularly after nationalisation, has weakened the structural fabric of the organisations. Simultaneously, public expectations have been constantly, often justifiably, increasing, and with the growing public awareness, dissatisfaction over the service rendered by banks has assumed growing expression. The near obsolescence of reward and punishment systems, increasing security available to employees, pressures from powerful employee organisations and managerial deficiencies have all had their impact on the quality of service rendered. In a much broader sense, the atmosphere of indifference and casualness prevalent in the society could not but have had repercussions in banks. It is not our intention here to go into the merits or the relative impact of individual causes. It would be enough to say that bank services need considerable improvement on an emergent basis. And, the time has come for banks to look inward to find out what is the nature and quality of the products they sell, what is the product demanded by the customers and how to go about matching the two.

Fortunately, in recent times there has been some improvement in discipline and attitudes amongst bank employees, as a result of the changed climate. The acceptance of the interim report by the Government also seems to have added to the awareness, on an industry-wide basis, for rendering better customer service.

Assessment of customer service of banks should take into account the following four important, interdependent factors which influence customer service:

— demands on, and expectations from, banks;
— quality and job knowledge of bank personnel;
— attitudes and motivation of bank employees; and
— back-up systems and procedures.

Public Expectations

Public expectations from the banking system and consequential demands on banks, especially at operating levels, have been growing since Independence. With national energies concentrated on economic resurgence, it is only natural that the role of banker has come into sharper focus. A new edge and a new direction were given to the public expectations when the major commercial banks were nationalised in 1969. As is well known, expectations vary not only over time, but also from one class of customers to another — the underprivileged, the common man, the agriculturist, the artisan, the professional, the trader, the industrialist, etc.; also, as between rural, semi-urban and urban customers. Understanding and responding to the dynamics of customer expectations, therefore, call for multidisciplinary skills, sensitivity and perspective, supported by perspective research capabilities for assessing customer needs so as to be able to provide appropriate and timely responses. It must, however, be mentioned that not all the public expectations may fall within the banker's role, and it is also true that the banker is sometimes a recipient of ill-informed criticism. This only highlights the fact that customer education is an essential component of customer service. The public can rightfully demand and would be happy to receive information about the various things a banker is doing or is capable of doing and those he is unable to do, and the whys and wherefores.

Customer service is considerably influenced by the quality and job knowledge of bank personnel. Inexperienced and ill-informed staff tend to postpone decision-making, and their decisions, when taken, might turn out to be unsound. Quite often, their anxiety for playing safe leads them to taking decisions which may not be of much help to customers. The indecision often finds weird expression. Some may indulge in paper-pushing. Some others may take refuge behind excessive paper-work — preferring to deal with papers rather than with people. Yet another set may seek prescriptive solutions for every situation and refuse to go beyond the written word. The spirit of progressive measures, thus, gets killed under the weight of paper. There is need for re-orientation here. But, because of the massive branch expansion programmes undertaken by banks, the training systems have come under severe strain with inevitable dilution in the quality of training facilities provided, apart from the sheer inadequacy of such facilities. Even the limited training facilities available generally suffer from lack of direction and integration with comprehensive human resources development plans, if any. The training is still, by and large, procedure-oriented, and that too geared to the procedures of conventional banking business. What is more serious, the branch expansion programmes also led to drafting of inexperienced junior employees for handling important tasks in uncharted fields. The difficulty has been aggravated by the fact that the new challenges have had to be met in a large number of widely-scattered small rural centres. In the last few years, happily, banks have taken steps to meet the situation, and more and more trained and experienced men are becoming available to banks. What, however, needs to be taken care of is that the training facilities not only keep pace with the growing requirements but also are geared to progressively reducing the gap.

Perhaps, the single most significant factor, having a vital bearing on the quality of customer service in banks, is employee motivation, which is influenced by and, in turn, itself influences employee attitudes. It is quite understandable that, in a service industry, motivation acquires crucial importance. If motivation could be said to be that inner force which propels a person and directs his behaviour towards or away from particular goals, bank employees could hardly be said to be so motivated in rendering customer service. In all fairness, it must be stated that banks, with their staff scattered widely in thousands of locations, with a small complement of staff at most of the locations, have genuine problems in employee motivation. Remoteness from the controlling office creates a crisis of identity because it tends to dilute the sense of belonging. In addition, it also creates communication gaps. Over and above such emotional isolation, there is also the problem of lack of integration with society, which has been, at least until recently, a feature of Indian banking. Historically speaking, this lack of integration with society, which is a result of a harrow perception of customer and customer service, is true for almost all levels in banks, and continues without significant change despite the transition from class banking to mass banking. In such a situation, it is only natural that motivation for customer service has not been of a particularly high order.

Apart from the low motivation, the climate of permissiveness further contributed to the lack of attention to customer service which it deserved. Bank managements also had their share of responsibility in the total situation, as it developed, and they were not much supported by the surrounding socio-political climate either. In all the resultant confrontations, the worst sufferer was the customer. For a number of years, the customer suffered in silence but the discontent was seething within. A situation of utter helplessness pervaded the banking scene. The first impor-tant breakthrough came when the Government of India appointed the Working Group on Customer Service in Banks in April 1975 to give unified direction to banks for improving customer service. A development of far greater significance and consequence was the recent change in the national mood which ushered in a new era of discipline, hard work and social orientation. The new climate enabled banks to take many steps for improvement in customer services including implementation of the specific action points suggested in the interim report.

Lastly, systems and procedures. Systems and procedures are vehicles for delivery of customer-satisfying services. Historically, the primary objective, and we suspect quite often the only objective, of systems and procedures, as they evolved in banks, was, essentially, a satisfactory maintenance of books of accounts and records and safeguarding banks' interests. Systems and procedures were not seen as aids for promotion of client satisfaction. The systems and procedures, as such were, probably adequate to meet the demands of the traditional customers. For decades, banks were dealing in class banking which did not call for continuous systemic introspection. Also the tradition-bound, conservative banker was unlikely to encourage innovativeness in banking. The systems and procedures developed in such conditions were, naturally, not geared to the new customers and the new demands. The inadequacies came into sharp focus with the influx of tens of thousands of new customers, crash programmes for marketing of a wide range of unconventional services and opening up of fresh avenues in banking. Since banks had accorded a very low priority to systems development and since they did not possess significant or professional capabilities to grapple with this task, this also had its inevitable impact on customer service. Regretfully, the position has not improved materially, although there are signs of organisational awareness; O & M activities continue to suffer under the low priority that has always been their lot. It needs to be borne in mind, however, that reorientation of systems and procedures should strike a fine balance between advantages of improved customer service and risks of reduced safety for bank funds.

Inadequate attention to any or all of the above-mentioned factors, which, we are afraid, has been the case so far, leads to customer dissatisfaction. The totality of customer dissatisfaction can be attributed to —

(a) delay and inaccuracy in putting through transactions;

(b) delay and inadequacies in correspondence;

(c) delayed, faulty and unhelpful decision-making;

(d) absence of elementary discipline;

(e) undue emphasis of staff on observance of rules and procedures, and generally, lack of organisational support for reasonable and bonafide departures;

(f) in regard to credit applications, particularly —

  (i) scheme-designs lacking the essential adaptability or flexibility to cater to individual customer needs;

  (ii) questions asked and data required, not always relevant and or available, and, perhaps, expensive to obtain;

  (iii) all queries not raised at one time;

  (iv) complicated documents and cumbersome procedures regarding documentation;

  (v) lack of counseling; and

  (vi) malafides of the bank staff;

(g) lack of uniformity in bank charges — some of these are also perceived by customers to be high;

(h) customer being viewed as a 'faceless' unit of business — and the resultant absence of any meaningful banker-customer communication; and

(i) general attitude of unconcern and apathy for clients.

Incidentally, an important factor responsible for the poor quality of service is the soul-destroying monotony and drudgery in the bank clerk's work: as matters stand today, it offers no variety and no scope for self-expression, nor for identification with customer. By and large, the customer is represented by a bit of paper, or a token, or an illiterate messenger, and the clerk develops no involvement in the customer's needs and aspirations.

Admittedly, the list of complaint areas, as outlined above, is formidable. But the dimension of the problem has to be viewed in the light of the fact that not all customers of banks have complaints — in fact, the number of satisfied customers is larger than generally believed — nor do all the dissatisfied customers have complaints under all the above-mentioned heads, nor of the same intensity; as against this, there is the countervailing thought that not every dissatisfied customer cares to lodge a complaint. Sometimes, complaints are not genuine, and, sometimes, some customers adopt unreasonable and annoying postures. Occasionally, complaints arise due to differing perceptions — but, to reiterate, for a service industry, it is the customer's perception that should matter. Additionally, one has to reckon with the fact that there are pockets of poor service, probably owing to environmental influence.

Such customer dissatisfaction over the performance of banks has acquired sharp overtones because of the salary structure of bank employees amidst large unemployment, low wage economy and pervasive poverty. It will be idle to ignore this profile of bank employees in the public mind, while studying the problems in customer service in banks.

Customer Service : A Survey

Customers are almost unanimous in decrying bank's customer service. However, when asked to rate the quality of customer service given by their banks, most bankers rated it as either very good or good. Clearly, bankers and clients have different views of the concept of customer service. Interestingly, some bankers who were personally interviewed, did admit — under their breath though — that the customer service in their banks left much to be desired. But on record, only 12.5 per cent of the total sample acknowledged that customer service in their banks is bad.

The most important reason for the poor quality of customer service, bankers have explained, is work pressure (47.5 per cent). However, a quarter of the sample also admitted that complacency due to job security was the reason behind poor customer service. Some 15 per cent also thought that banks lacked in work ethics. Many earlier surveys on customer service have given customer behaviour as a common reason for poor service. But in this survey, only 5.7 per cent of bankers held this opinion.

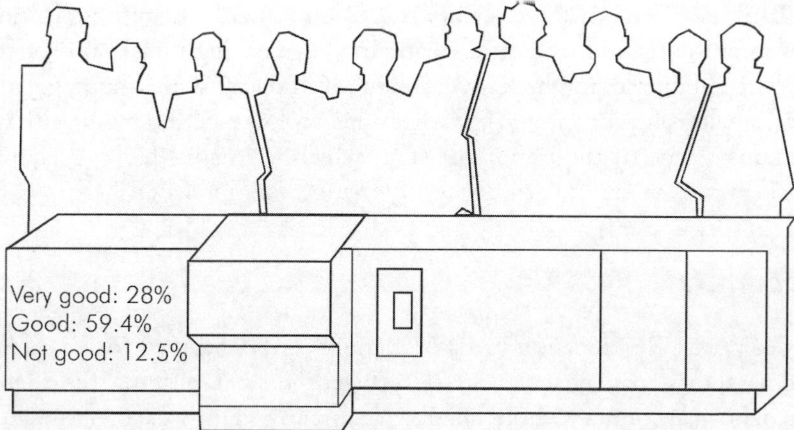

Fig. 14.1 How would you rate the standard of customer service in Indian banks?

Some Popular Banking Beliefs

Issue	*Agree strongly*	*Agree slightly*	*Neither agree nor disagree*	*Disagree slightly*	*Disagree strongly*
Management style in banks is Autocratic	172	399	204	143	117
Banking urgently needs restructuring to improve efficiency	780	170	37	38	43
The profit performance of banks can be improved	705	256	49	41	20
There is a lot of overlap in different commercial banks' roles	504	295	138	69	48
Different types of banks should be set up for rural areas	311	170	114	103	367
Unions in banks affect work and lead to poor customer service	451	344	97	93	86
Corruption in banks is very high	52	215	216	285	303
Bank employees have low motivation and a negative attitude	184	335	164	190	187
Nationalised banks serve development objectives	447	419	114	59	26
Nationalised banks serve the rural and poor	473	413	97	60	24

Note: Totals may not add up to the full sample size as 'Don't know/Can't say' category, being negligible, has been omitted.

Banks and Customer Service

Whether for mobilising deposits or lending money or for providing ancillary services like remittances and collections, commercial banks are primarily service institutions. Speedy, timely and courteous service to customers is the essence of banking business. This aspect has been emphasized by the Reserve Bank in several of the circulars addressed to banks from time to time, as well as in the circulars covering the recommendations made by the Working Group on Customer Service in Banks in its report submitted to the Government of India and the findings of reviews made periodically by the small group constituted by Government to oversee and monitor the implementation of recommendations. Some of the important steps which the banks have to take for maintaining customer-needed services in the most satisfactory manner are indicated here.

Deposit Accounts

Pay books or postal identification cards or identity cards of armed forces/police/government departments or passports may be considered sufficient for establishing the identity of persons desiring to open deposit accounts without cheque facility. In other cases, banks may obtain adequate information about the creditworthiness and reliability of persons. Cheques should be printed in English and Hindi. However, customers may fill in the cheques in regional languages.

It should be clearly mentioned in the savings account passbook that, as far as possible, the depositor has to collect it duly filled up and completed immediately after the transactions on the same day. If a passbook is tendered for posting after a long interval of time or after many transactions, a printed slip requesting the depositor to tender it periodically must be given. And whenever a passbook is given for posting, a paper token indicating the date of its receipt and the date when it is to be collected may be given to the tenderer. Temporary overdrafts for small amounts may be allowed in savings bank accounts for meeting contingencies like non-receipt of salary advice and delay in crediting the proceeds of some instruments already lodged. Statements of accounts may be sent to current account holders in a staggered manner instead of by a target date every month. Obtaining periodic confirmation of balances in accounts from customers may be dispensed with.

It is important that the term deposit holders are advised well in time about the maturity of their deposits. Deposit receipts should be transferable between one branch and another branch of a bank. If any customer so desires, he may be supplied with a plain passbook to enable him to keep his own account of the fixed deposits held by him with the bank.

Banks should introduce incentive schemes for branches and outside agencies for the sale of traveller's cheques. Rupee traveller's cheques issued by one public sector bank may be made encashable at any other public sector bank under reciprocal arrangements.

Loans and Advances

Banks should take decisions on loan applications as speedily as possible. Delay in the disposal of loan applications can be minimized by the banks by helping borrowers to fill in the necessary forms. The field staff attached to branches may be increased if necessary. In cases where there is lack of response from borrowers or where the borrowers are not interested in getting the credit facility, their applications may be treated as withdrawn, with due notice given to the parties concerned. Priority sector advances must be sanctioned mostly by branch offices to which adequate powers need be delegated. For small loans, security should be secondary to viability of proposals. Loan documents may be obtained in duplicate, one copy being given to borrowers for their record. Loans up to Rs. 500 can be disbursed on the basis of demand promissory note or simple loan agreement. While giving loans to small borrowers, banks should take into account their minimum consumption needs also. Training programmes may be organised by banks for small-scale entrepreneurs; participation in the programmes may be made a pre-condition for grant of loans to them. A more liberal approach may be adopted in sanctioning advances against gold and silver ornaments.

Besides schemes for providing credit to artisans, village/cottage industries and tiny sector units, the banks have to evolve specific schemes to meet the credit needs of small vendors and traders (especially in urban and metropolitan centres) such as vegetable vendors, fish vendors, iced-water vendors and small peddlers who require only small amounts of loans. Banks must provide larger assistance to the physically-handicapped persons, particularly under the plans drawn up by various organisations for their welfare and rehabilitation. Besides formulating special bankable schemes for ensuring a larger flow of credit to scheduled castes and tribes for self-employment, the banks must consider the loan proposals of these communities with the utmost sympathy and understanding.

Banks can waive the requirement of insurance cover against fire risk for securities taken from small-scale industrial units for advances up to Rs. 25,000, in respect of composite loans sanctioned to artisans and village/ cottage industries, term loans and working capital advances against non-hazardous goods. In other cases, they may waive such requirement for advances up to Rs. 10,000 except where insurance of vehicles or machinery or other equipment is compulsory under the provisions of any law.

Ancillary Services

Payment of drafts should not be refused because of non-receipt of drawing advice. Just one authorized signature on drafts should suffice. The validity period of demand drafts may be clearly indicated on the draft forms. Every care must be taken to reduce delay in mail transfers. Funds sent through telegraphic transfers (TTs) have to be paid to the parties concerned latest on the third working day from the receipt of instructions from customers. Anticipating their need for funds at another place on future dates, some customers may instruct their banks about such needs well in advance. Banks can meet such requirements by introducing the facility of value date telex/telegraphic transfers of funds on pre-determined dates.

Against outstation cheques lodged for collection, banks can give immediate credit except in cases where they feel that the accounts are unsatisfactory. Special regional collection centres may be set up for outstation cheques/bills. Improvement in cheque/bill collection service can be ensured if work at the realising bank offices is made easier by preparing the forwarding memos in triplicate for cheques and in quadruplicate for bills. The originals of forwarding memos will serve as vouchers at the realising offices, the duplicates being returned to the remitting offices as payment/ non-payment advice. While the triplicates (which can be filed in a bound register) serve as a record at the remitting offices, the additional copies available in respect of bills serve as presentation advice to the drawees. Boxes for depositing cheques for collection and clearing may be provided at the larger bank offices. Whether the outstation cheques over Rs. 5,000 sent for collection have been cleared or not can be ascertained by telegram at the cost of customers. Banks may consider opening special offices for handling inward bill business at metropolitan and large commercial centres. Bills for collection should be sent direct to the banks concerned at the realising centres.

Customers should be provided with booklets giving details of the services and facilities available at banks. Complaints should be studied and corrective action initiated. Pension payments should be promptly credited to the customers' accounts.

Banks should bring out booklets containing basic exchange control rules to be observed by foreign visitors to India and give them free of charge to visitors at all air/sea ports and customs counters. Advisory services will have to be made available to Indians going abroad for various purposes such as business, information tours and study/training. Small exporters deserve special attention. Export advisory cells may be established at major centres to provide a package of services to such exporters.

In their classic book "In Search of Excellence", Thomas J. Peters and Robert H. Waterman Jr. cite a 1980 effort by Dinah Nemeroff of Citibank — as the best outside analysis of the 'close to the customer through Service Concept.' According to Nemeroff, there are three principal themes in an effective service orientation:

(i) Intensive active involvement on the part of senior management; she calls it' Service Statesmanship.' If service is a top goal, sales would increase, revenue would be generated and profits would naturally follow. In short, service is regarded as a revenue builder in the long run.

(ii) A remarkable people orientation — because customer relations simply mirror employee relations.

(iii) A high intensity of measurement and feedback. In fact, how well service-oriented companies manage their people is transparent from the intensity of their measurement and feedback systems. These companies are for ever working out new rewards and incentive programmes for their employees.

The message is thus two-fold in character. For customer service to improve in the banking industry in India, the senior management must be deeply involved and it will be their business to involve the employees in turn. Every time a customer puts through a banking transaction, he interacts with the products and services offered by the bank; this in itself is a reflection on quality, because chances are that if a service is performed shabbily, he may leave the bank.

To become the best bank, very small characteristics count. All banks are selling similar products, at similar prices, at similar locations, with the same opening hours. The attitude, responsiveness and personal skills of staff could be the vital characteristics which mark one bank from the other.

Concern for the customer should, therefore, become an obsession with the banking industry and it should be transparent at all levels. They should be in a position to declare that they have no orphans amongst their customers anywhere in the country. Unless this happens, it would be difficult to bring about an enduring and long-lasting improvement in the quality of service rendered by them. Such a change in their outlook is going to be a key to their survival as a viable industry in the future.

Further, elsewhere in the world, technology has brought about far-reaching changes in the business model of space and time. Automated Teller Machines (ATMs) have moved into bank offices and they are available all the 24 hours in a day; in the process, the traditional approach to customer service and the larger operating rules have changed too. The new buzz words of customer service for the morrow would be:

(i) Consumers need products and services ANY-TIME.

(ii) Producers who deliver their products and services REAL-TIME, relative to their competitors will have a decided advantage.

(iii) Operating in real time means no LONG-TIME between identification and fulfillment of the need.

Surely, the winds of change would sweep over our land sooner or later, and unless the banking industry is ready and prepared by moving close to its customers, it may be swept off its feet.

In order to establish rapport with the customers, many banks have introduced the system of customer calls and customer meets, as well as strict control over the disposal of customer complaints at the branch level. Procedures have been prescribed as to how to keep track that these activities are meaningfully performed; and, whether these are regularly followed or not is periodically verified by the branch auditors and the branch controller. But what should be more important than following the procedures is whether the data that emerge out of these contacts are collated and whether they are then processed and analysed for throwing up specific schemes or plans of action. More often than not, the relative routine is attached more importance than the contents and the outcome of these efforts. If the contacts made in customer calls or customer meets are to be fully utilized, the following issues would need to be tackled. Then and then only can these be strictly deemed to be endeavours towards improving customer service and not merely for improving the bank's own business somehow. Improvement of the bank's business will flow from the improvement of customer service and not the other way round.

An approach of "buy what we have to sell" can make the person contacted irrelevant to the bank and, consequently, the bank itself becomes irrelevant to the customer or another prospective customer. Do customer needs for new services come out of the contacts? And, if so, how is that knowledge utilized?

The efforts may be directed only to identify such customers as have needs which can be met by the bank's existing policies, schemes and systems and procedures. That is only a myopic approach. The concent of customer service which emanates from the larger concept of "Marketing" has to accept the customer as the central element and the satisfaction of his needs the super ordinate goal.

For the satisfaction of customer needs, the bank's systems and procedures or even policies may sometimes have to be bent rather than customers being bent to conform to the bank's rules. No doubt, all that a customer needs cannot always be met or provided. But here comes the ingenuity of the organisation to "re-position" its services while trying to come as near as possible to what the customer desires.

Customer Service: You are the Key Man

We tend to take for granted anything that comes to us easily and regularly.

Take, for instance, our cup of morning tea. While sipping in comfort our cheering cup, we seldom think of the complex machinery that must be set up to ensure that we can enjoy our favourite beverage whenever we feel like it. To this end, tea estates had to be set up, tea bushes grown, leaves gathered and put through all the stages of the manufacturing process. Then the tea had to be tested, packed and shipped across hundreds of kilometers before being warehoused by the wholesalers, delivered to the retailers and finally sold to the customers. Thus, a steaming hot cup of tea placed before you climaxes the co-ordinated effort of thousands of people engaged in scores of different industries.

But this is not all. Behind these thousands of people, who are directly engaged in producing and selling tea, there are thousands of others whose work is equally necessary to bring about the end result. These include the workers who built the machinery for manufacturing tea, those who supplied wood for the packing cases, and the railway staff who transshipped the packed cases. To remember this is to understand the interdependence of industries and to realise how complex is the superstructure that must support a modern industrial society.

All these industries needed money to set up their business and carry on their operations. Plant and machinery had to be paid for, land had to be purchased, and wages and salaries had to be paid to workers and executives.

Without the capital, credit facilities and the mechanism of exchange which banks provide, a modern industrial society is unthinkable. It is easy to see, then, that banks have a hand in producing that morning cup of tea. This is equally true of course, of every other convenience of modern living.

Banks are the backbone of our society!

We have seen how the pooling of the effort of thousands finds fruition when a customer uses the end product. And so it is with all banks.

The resources built up over the years, the expert staff developed through successive training programmes, the far-flung network of branches set up at great cost in money and organisation — the culminating point of all this is reached when a customer deposits his money, or draws a cheque or a loan, or submits a bill for collection. The work of each one of us in banks — no matter how far in the background — is vital to this consummation.

A bank must meet the financial *needs of a customer,* by acting as a custodian of his assets, providing credit facilities and assisting him to speedily put through financial transactions of one type or another.

Banking, when you come to think of it, is people. It is not figures, files or ledgers. We employ all these and much more merely to meet our customers' needs. Naturally, we have to be careful in conducting our business. We hold in trust large sums of money which may be the life-savings of a person, a widow's mite, the property of an orphaned minor. Or, they may well be the funds that enable a huge business to run, providing livelihood to thousands of people. Or a small industrialist, or an entrepreneur or an agriculturist, who is assisted in his productive effort. We dare not take chances. That is why absolutely accurate records, figures, files and ledgers are necessary. But the end in view is, always, *service to our customers.*

What is a customer?

Not an interruption in our work — but the reason for our existence. Without him, we would not exist. His confidence in us is the measure of our security. His dissatisfaction, for whatever reason, is a symptom of a serious disease. If ignored, it will undermine the health of your bank, and darken your future.

Every time a customer comes to you, he casts a vote of confidence in your bank. It is up to you to keep faith with him. He turns to you when he faces a banking problem because, in his eyes, you are the expert who can help him with what, to him, is a complicated problem.

The first step in customer service is courtesy. Extend to your customer the same courtesy that you have a right to expect from the staff of any establishment that *you visit as customer.* Any customer will be unhappy if he feels that he is being ignored. On the other hand, he will not fret and fume if he only knows that his work is being attended to, even while he waits. You can chalk up a *plus* if you can induce a customer to await his turn for you to take up his case without feeling lost or forgotten. Have you, when out shopping, felt the difference between being asked for time and being ordered to wait? You create a friendly atmosphere when you say "Could you please give me a minute?" — instead of "Please wait."

Service delayed is service denied. So do not keep a customer waiting any longer than you have to. The customer will not be slow to realise that this is your approach to work. The chances are that he will be patient, if his case ever takes time to be disposed of.

To serve a customer well, you must listen well. Only then will you find out what his problems are. Your customer service is as good as your understanding of your customer's problems.

You have won half the battle if you begin by putting yourself in his place.

If you do not have the answer to a problem which a customer may bring to you, consult someone who might have. Nobody is expected to know the right answers to all possible problems. You will lose nothing if you check on facts before you answer. But you will lose face, if you give him information which later turns out to be wrong.

Never give the impression that you are serving a customer grudgingly. The old-fashioned slogan, "service with a smile," is as valid today as it was when it was coined. A cheerful greeting will put the customer at ease.

It is more than likely that you have been — and will be — approached by customers for help on matters outside the scope of your own responsibility. When this happens, bear with the customer. He does not know who deals with what in your organisation. He knows only you and he relies on you for help and guidance. Guide him to the right person. Better still, if you have the time, accompany him there.

So many things have gone into building up the image of your bank — many things which seem quite insignificant at first sight. Taken together, they add up to that priceless asset — customer goodwill. *You* are the man on whom it all hangs.

On the one hand, the respect and affection of that host of people who come to your bank, and a satisfying customer relationship; on the other, indifference, or worse, disgust and a chorus of complaints.

You have tremendous advantages in serving a customer. The most important of these is your own job knowledge. This is backed by the assets of your bank, the various facilities that your bank offers to its customers and your bank's goodwill. *But everything ultimately centres on you. Serving a customer is more than job knowledge, more than the backing of an organisation. The decisive factor is yourself.*

Banks have a social purpose. Banks have been entrusted with a worthy cause. Banks belong to the nation. Only through you can your bank discharge the responsibility that rests on it. Your bank's reputation, its future prosperity and the extent of its participation in the country's economic advancement rest ultimately in your hands. The key factor remains — will always remain — *YOU.*

How to Improve Customer Service?

1. Incompetent and demoralised staff cannot render good service. Hence, training becomes important in order to change employees' attitudes and build up their morale and interpersonal skills.

2. Motivating the staff and showing that the organisation cares and respects the employees is equally important.

3. Introduction of computers to support customer service is of great value to the organisation. It improves efficiency, productivity and the quality of services.
4. Delegation of appropriate authority to employees who deal with customers so as to enable them to take on-the-spot decision.
5. The best way to develop a service strategy is to listen to the customers. Conduct regular customer surveys to improve the services. Communicate with the customers constantly through press advertisements.
6. There has to be greater appreciation of the problems between the customer and the organisation.
7. Setting up of customer service cells to handle complaints/grievances, projects a favourable image of the organisation.
8. Keeping an eye on the competitors and how they handle their customers and their problems can help us to shape the strategy.
9. It may be necessary for the customers to organise themselves into forums and associations so that their voice is heard.
10. In large organisations, complaints/grievances are bound to be received from the customers. What matters is the manner in which these customer problems are resolved. The image of the organisation will improve if these complaints are handled with sympathy, consideration and conciliary attitude. They can highlight, through proper literature, their limitations and how complaints/grievances would be met for speedy redressal.

An organisation should be more responsive and pro-active in fulfilling the rising consumer aspirations and the changing consumer preferences. A mere policy decision, a directive, or a circular, though necessary, cannot help to bring about improved customer service. Employee conduct must demonstrate to customers at all times, at all levels, a feeling of concern and earnestness in their efforts and approach. Every customer visiting the banks (i.e., branches etc.) should leave the premises bearing goodwill for the organisation (bank). Nothing worthwhile can ever be achieved without total commitment and comprehensive involvement.

Customer Relationship Management

One of the delicious ironies of customer relationship management (CRM) in the middle of a communications technology revolution is the problem of plenty. So much so that the points of contact with the customer — the telephone, Web-based chat, e-mails, SMS and WEb self-service — almost constitute an embarrassment of riches that become difficult to manage.

To solve the problem of technologies functioning disparately and punching far below their weight, a new-generation approach — CRMv.2 — has been conceived which is characterised by its focus on external interactions rather than internal processes. CRMv.2 aims to put the customer back at the forefront of CRM. The new era of CRM is characterised by self-service and peer support models, knowledge-based applications and on-demand delivery.

Putting the customer first: As Forester Research's John Ragsdale notes, improving customer experience is about "building loyalty, not customer satisfaction." This means that lower cost channels like the Web or chat must not only provide at least the same perceived value as traditional channels like the phone, but also offer unique features and benefits not available elsewhere.

Reading from the same hymn-sheet: A common challenge lies in integrating customer-facing technologies like advanced search, chat, user forums, SMS etc. with existing CRM processes. At the same time, content created for one channel should be leveraged across all others for consistency and economies of scale. For instance, content in a support centre knowledge base should also be available for Web self-service.

Metrics: Going beyond operational metrics like Average Handle Time, measuring the success of service and support initiatives must span multiple channels, user segments and even organisations, if certain functions are out-sourced. These could include user-centric metrics such as site traffic, experience indicators like customer satisfaction and service level agreements and outcome merits like increase in conversion and referrals. The benefits that come out of implementing CRMv.2 are:

1. Greater empowerment for users.
2. Lower cost of service delivery by shifting certain interactions to self-service and chat.
3. Better visibility across service delivery channels.
4. Gains in customer communication, accountability and improved organisational efficiency.

As an illustration, a decision support company which deployed the new-generation solution incorporating e-mail, chat and Web self-service saw that by providing a combination of Web self-service and chat to customers, inbound phone inquiries came down by nearly 50%. Just what are the building blocks of such a strategy?

View self-service as part of an integrated strategy: Selecting the right balance of channels, and how/when to escalate from online self-service to chat, e-mail or even VoIP is essential. At the same time, delivering the value of true customer insight requires having the right reporting and analytical tools in place for thorough cross-challel analysis.

The value of enterprise: As solutions have become more scalable and customisable to specific tasks, organisations are applying enterprise chat more widely, and seeing impressive results. For sales and marketing, the ability to provide live answers online and in-context is often resulting in higher close rates. At the same time chat is a proven technique for making self-service support more interactive, and can keep customers from abandoning a support site in favour of placing a call. And in a growing number of cases, when deployed correctly, some organisations are even seeing higher customer satisfaction rates with their chat-based support compared to the phone or e-mail.

E-mail still has a key role: While spam and security concerns have tempered the growth of e-mail as the ubiquitous business communications channel, many consumers still prefer e-mail to other modes of interaction.

The evolving role of Websites: With more consumers embracing Web applications and information delivery, many organisations are focused on evolving their sites from being primarily transactional (e-commerce, account management, registration) to being more informational and interactive via advanced search, online knowledge delivery and collaboration.

Conclusion

Customer service is to put yourself in the other man's shoes, and being concerned about him. Customer service covers all aspects of the banking interface — from courtesy to efficiency and speed.

Ted Levitt, of Harvard Business School, widely acclaimed as an authority on marketing, observes in *The Marketing Imagination:* "All energies should be directed towards satisfying the customer, no matter what.... The purpose of business is to get and keep a customer, or, to use Peter Drucker's more demanding construction, to create and keep a customer.... To do that, you have to do those things that will make people want to do business with you. All other truths on this subject are merely derivative."

Besides, putting yourself on the other side of the table, good customer service hinges on three critical factors:

- to treat each customer as if he is the only "king" you have. Successful polygamy depends upon pretending to each spouse that she is the only pebble on your beach.
- to encompass the interpersonal influences (in the case of industrial products) in the organisational buying behaviour. The users, the influencers, the deciders, the buyers and even the gate-keeper(!) must all perceive satisfaction.
- Evolving strategies to improve the quality of customer service. Serving as a catalyst and a visionary to make the dreams, aspirations and expectations of the banking industry come true.

Chapter 15

Public Relations in Banks

Introduction

"Public relations" is the art of projecting the image of an institution to its employees, its customers and to the public at large. It is the deliberate planned and sustained effort on the part of the institution to establish and maintain mutual understanding between it and the public. It is a management function which evaluates the public attitudes, identifies the policies and procedures of an organisation with the public interest, and executes a programme of action and communication to earn public understanding and acceptance.

Public relations is being increasingly accepted as a management philosophy pervading all the facets of industrial and business organisations, profit and non-profit-making bodies, public and private undertakings, social and service organisations and even the governments. Not long ago PR in India was confused with mere lobbying for favours from an individual, an authority or a government. Even now, barring a few exceptions, PR is being perceived by most organisations primarily as maintaining effective relations with the media. And there are people who still believe that PR and publicity are synonymous. PR and publicity are two different wings, playing two different roles, yet for an identical objective.

PR is a prime management function aimed at building and maintaining sound, effective and productive relations with the public, thereby creating the best possible image of the organisation concerned. Good PR builds bridges of understanding, helps the organisation to fashion its policies and programmes to the needs, desires and aspirations of the society. The belief that the success of an organisation is made up of "90% good work and 10% PR work", is gaining universal acceptance in the corporate world.

The growth of public relations from when it was just a press relations function has been phenomenal. Today, public relations encompasses a vast area of activities, including corporate public relations, public affairs, employee communication, investor relations and research.

What is Public Relations?

Public Relations (PR) is a distinctive management function which helps to establish and maintain mutual lines of communication, understanding, acceptance and co-operation between an organisation and its policies. It also involves the management of problems or issues; helps the management to keep informed on and responsive to public opinion and defines and emphasises the responsibility of management to serve the public interest. Over and above these functions, PR also helps the management to keep abreast of and effectively utilise the changes, serving as an early warning system to help them anticipate the trends in the industry. It is the systematic promotion of a mutual understanding between an organisation and its target groups.

Many definitions of public relations have been attempted. Some say it is the distribution of good reputation, some others describe it as an art or practice of giving expression to the personality of an organisation and a third group says that public relations stands for "personality and recognition."

Whatever the definition, it is generally agreed that public relations attempts to evaluate public attitudes, expectations and aspirations and helps the organisations concerned to identify their policies, practices and procedures with the public interest and then execute a programme of action to earn public acceptance.

Organisations in India are becoming large in size, and as a result, a vacuum is developing between organisations, their employees, their customers or clients, their shareholders, parliamentarians, bureaucrats and the public in general. This gap can best be filled in by an organised programme of sustained public relations.

Importance of Public Relations

Today public relations has come to be associated with image-building — building the image of the organisation, the products of an industry, the party, the institution or the government. There seems to be a misconception that a good product or a good institution does not require any publicity and it is only the bad and indifferent ones which require image-building.

However, facts do not always speak about themselves. A good case or a good product is nothing but a mere seed. To do any good or to reach it to the masses, it needs to be planted and PR is just the right nutrient to make it blossom.

Public relations, of late, has come of age. It has become a specialised body of knowledge, skills and methods. It is also a management function which deals with the relations between two or more organisations, producing the kind of relations desired by them.

The PR man seeking to serve the public interest is, therefore, well aware of the influence of public opinion on decision-making and decisions because he acts as a two-way conduit between an organisation for which he works and the public whose interest he seeks to take care of.

In theory, the practice and principles of public relations as a management discipline, may it be in the private sector, public sector or in the government, ought to be the same. However, taking a realistic approach towards the end-goals of these organisations, one finds a thin line of demarcation between them, as public and private organisations depend more on public goodwill and support for their survival and growth.

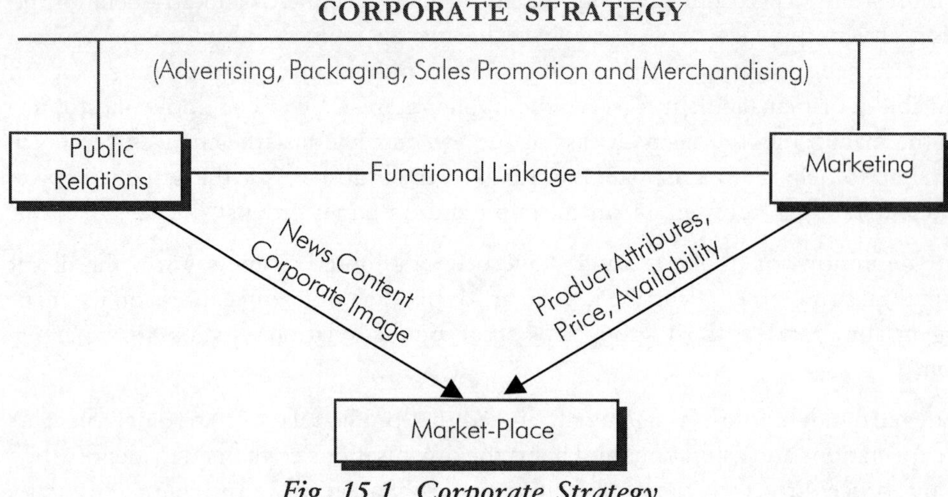

Fig. 15.1 Corporate Strategy

The PR practitioner should sharpen his communication skills and maintain good rapport with the media by both reviewing and transmitting news of interest to the organisation. This, of course, presupposes that, within the organisation, the PR man is kept fully informed of the organisation's goals, achievements, problems and so on.

The unfortunate situation presently prevalent in the country is that while PR today is accepted as a profession everywhere, its services considered essential, the PR men are seldom included in the brain trust that runs the administration. The administration, at times, requires the services of the PR men, but they are still kept away at a respectful distance. PR cannot effectively work when it becomes an appendage of the authority. In order to win the confidence of the public, the organisation too should have confidence in its PR department.

Public Relations in Banks

Public relations in banks should and does, therefore, reflect the objectives and interests of the banks. At the same time, it should be able to create banking awareness amongst the masses. It is the general tendency of the public to decide the public sector banks and snipe at their reported lack of efficiency, lack of experience, mismanagement, prevalence of corruption and so on. However, much of this criticism is motivated. One of the major tasks of the PR man in the public sector banks today is to remove such distortions arising out of one-sided or negative presentation and project the total picture in the overall perspective before the public eye.

Complaints are a universal phenomenon of business life today. Banks, being a service-oriented industry, are in no way an exception to it. A PR man plays a major role in this field too, even though redressal of the grievances is the responsibility of a specialised section of the bank. However, a PR man goes to the root causes of such occurrences and finds out the circumstances which led to such complaints. Thereafter, he is able to persuade the policy-makers to formulate and lay down such procedures which would hardly give anyone a chance to complain any more.

Good PR practice is a two-way process. It is not enough for a PR man to tell the public what the banks can do for them, but it is equally important for him to listen; to listen to what the public feel about the banks. Only through listening with understanding can he assist the management in the policy-making process. He also makes an endeavour to project not only what the bank is, but also what it has been in the past and what it aims to be in the future by interpreting it to the public in terms that people can understand.

However, when one talks about PR in banks, the onus is not on the PR department alone. Under the prevailing social, political and economic structure of the society, the definition and scope of PR activities need to be widened. With the nationwide spread of branches and diversified service-oriented activities, the time has come when each and every employee of the banks is made aware of the public relations functions for image building.

Role in Attracting Talent

Public relations is now becoming an active aspect of HRD. An example is the employment exhibitions where major organisations met aspiring candidates either for immediate or for future recruitment. Such exhibitions go a long way in attracting the best talent in an informal atmosphere where the tensions of the normal interviewing process are absent.

The "catch them young" slogan can effectively be undertaken, with proper public relations exercises, by conducting seminars and plant visits by institutions; to make the youth aware of the organisation, its social role, security, growth plan and career opportunities.

There is a change in the attitude and profile of employees in organisations. Their demands and expectations are much higher than what they were a decade ago. Hence, one has to make use of new practices to have a good PR within the organisation. A new practice followed by some industries to take the families of employees to the factories so that they can get a feel of the work place. They can also know the type of work the employees are doing, their contributions as well as their role in the organisation.

Environment consciousness, concern and participation in eco-restoration are engaging the society's attention as never before. The 1990s are being perceived as the decade of environment greening. To facilitate this eco-restoration process, the PR will have to play the role of a catalyst, by providing the right information to the right target to promote both the interests of the environment and the business.

As all businesses are directly or indirectly involved with environment, discerning consumers now prefer companies with eco-consciousness. An example would be the growing trend of using day-to-day products that are not harmful to the environment by way of raw materials used, packaging materials used and also the manufacturing process itself. This has led to the introduction of the "Green Seal" which classifies the product as "environment friendly."

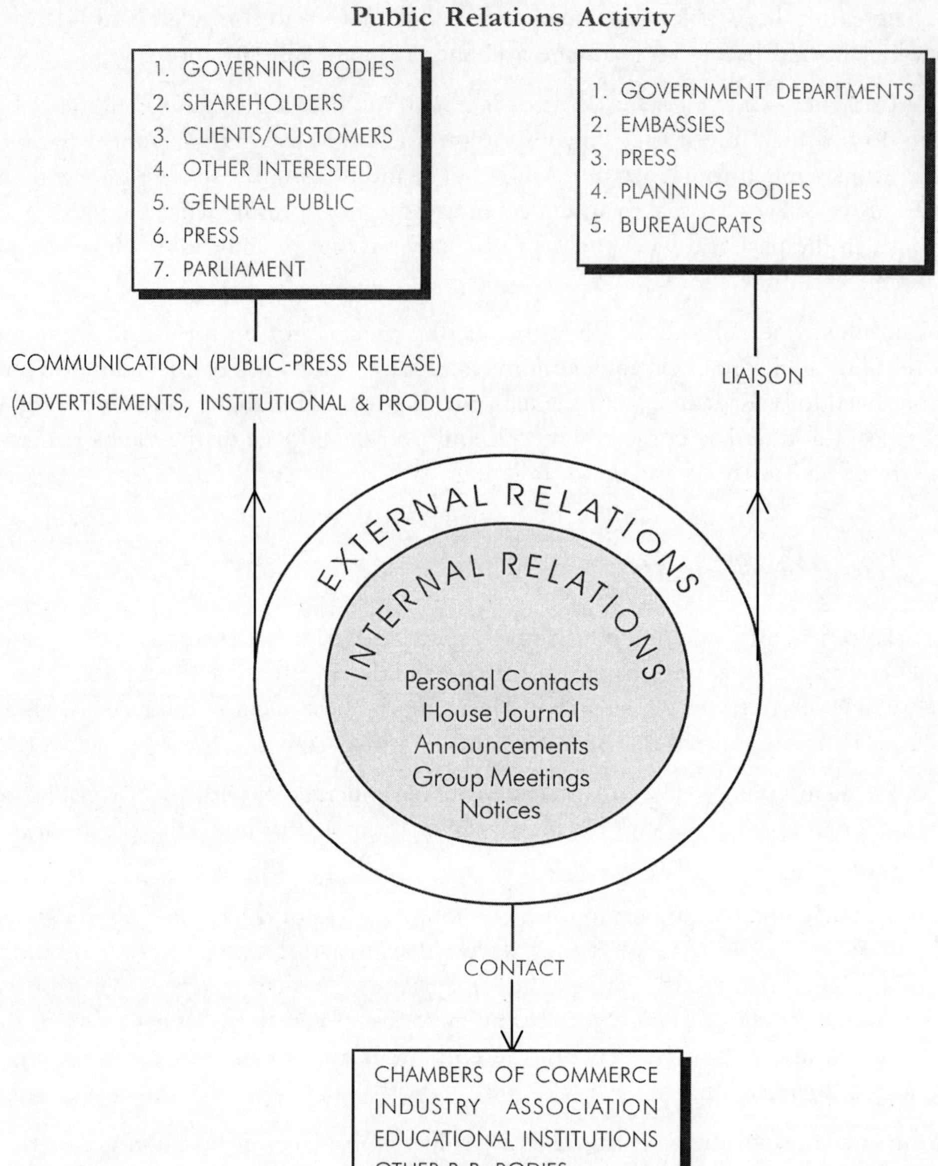

Fig. 15.2 Public Relations Activity

The public relations functions and tools are summarised in the following table:

Functions	*P. R. Tools*
Moulding public opinion	Ascertaining viewpoints systematically and responding to needs.
Internal public relations	Understanding the human need for recognition as an individual and not as a "cog in the wheel"
Consumer awareness	Making customers aware of their rights.
Environmental concern	Public awareness campaigns.

The importance of public relations in banking is all the time being emphasised today. However, this is not something new; may be the same words were not used before but every action of the bank management and its staff was public relations. The reputation that our big banks enjoy today is mainly due to their polite and courteous behaviour towards the public and the image of their institution which they have built up over the years.

Merchants deal in goods while bankers deal in money and the services allied with it. Imagine being in a business in which all the merchants operate in about the same way and have the same goods to sell at almost identical prices. Bankers are in just such a business. All banks look much alike, offer much the same customer services in the same way, lend money at the same rates of interest, and then pay the depositors the same interest on their savings. This being the case, why should customers prefer one bank to another? This is where public relations comes in.

Banking comprises a great deal of advising. The business transacted is often of such an intimate nature that a great deal of its success depends upon the human relationship that exists between the individual bank officers and customers. The personal qualities of a bank's staff probably comprise the largest single source of good relations with the public. The first reaction of an average man, on being asked for his impressions of his bank, is to think of the person or persons whom he usually meets and talks with at the branch where he keeps his account. Staff can create a more favourable impression of the bank in one day by friendly, positive action than can be done in a whole year of advertising effort by the institution.

Every bank official is a Public Relations Officer of his bank. Each time we cash a customer's cheque, discuss stocks and shares, arrange a loan or decline an application, we are adding in quite a substantial way to the public image of the institution we represent. A customer would rather deal with an official who always has a smile and a greeting for him than with an official who has a sour face and gives that "now what do you want?" look.

In addition to the direct face-to-face relations with the public, managers and staff are responsible for a very large part of the public image of their bank through their treatment of correspondence and telephone calls and their social contacts outside the bank. To most customers, the man they see when they call at the bank, the man who signs the letters they get through the mail, the official who is the treasurer of a local club — all these constitute the Bank. What they do, what they say and the way they behave are the acts of the bank itself.

The place of business is more important to the image of a bank than it is to many other institutions. Since banks deal in a service, their location must be convenient for the businessman and the small depositor whose savings aggregate to give banks their working capital.

The public image of banking, and of particular banks, derives much from the impression made by the bank premises. The manifestation of the bank itself is found in the bank building rather than in its balance sheets or in the ability and integrity of its staff. Because the bank building is so much a personification of the bank itself, it frequently appears in advertisements and upon letter-heads.

In the past, the trend was to make the banks look as solid as possible as implied by the heavy bronze plates, granite pillars and marble halls. The forbidding aspects of bank facades and the solemn atmosphere of the banking hall had much to be said for them — the image was one of security. Nowadays, it is more important to create an atmosphere of welcome and friendship rather than an impression of safety. This change in attitude is reflected in the exterior and the interior decoration and design of new branches of banks that are being opened. Some take the view that the vast non-banking public can best be brought into the fold by an increasing use of informality in building design. There seems little doubt that the reluctance of non-customers to enter a bank can often be partly attributed to the "not for the likes of us" image inherited from the policy of past general managements. The accent is now on more intimate, more helpful, less formal relations with the customers.

Whereas public relations in branches is public relations at the "point of sale", that is, between the staff and individual customers, public relations at the central office takes the form of communication between the central office and the general public. Until recently, public relations was not thought of as a conscious function of general management, although it goes without saying that some communication did take place between the banks and the general public, so that there may be a link between the bank as a whole and the public as a whole. Public Relations Officers are appointed by most banks today. The Public Relations Officer must speak with the voice of the bank on those occasions and on those subjects where it is believed that to so speak will inform the public on matters of interest both to them and to the bank. It is a two-way communication; for the Public Relations Officer also receives opinion from the public and transmits it to the management.

To enable the Public Relations Department to do its job effectively, the person selected to head the public relations operation should be a person with sufficient background in communications, advertising and allied fields to speak with authority on the various ways of putting across the image. His official status in the bank should be such that his opinions will command at least some attention at high places. There should be a clear and uninterrupted channel of contact and communication between those at the top and the Public Relations Officer. All public communication should be channeled through the same department so that the "voice" or the "personality" of the institution, that is, its "corporate image", will always remain the same. All departments should consult one another on communications that affect the bank but the public image should always be painted by the Public Relations Department under the direction of those who frame the policy. It is the business of the Public Relations Officer to discover the policy of the bank and interpret it in terms of public relations.

In the execution of his duties, the Public Relations Officer has to do many things. Among the first may be listed answering enquiries from the press. If any important event takes place, such as the bank rate going up, or a robbery having taken place, or there is a case of a forgery, the Public Relations Officer has to be as helpful and informative to the press as possible. He has to maintain good relations with the press as he may himself need them one day.

Many people appeal as individuals to the Public Relations Officer for information. Perhaps they are writing an article for a magazine, composing a talk to be given to a local gathering, or they may be students who are required to prepare a thesis on some subject connected with banking. None of these persons is turned away empty-handed. A simple request may be answered by the dispatch of a booklet. A more complicated one may involve a man's calling on the Public Relations Officer for a discussion which may often prove lengthy. In some cases, a precise or a complete article is specially written in the Public Relations Officer's office.

A part of every Public Relations Officer's day is spent in meeting people. In his own office he sees the ubiquitous seller of advertising space or new publicity gimmicks, printers, editors, lecturers, and, of course, his own colleagues on the staff of the general management. Out of the office there are consultations with the advertising agents, managers, district managers, luncheons (as guests or hosts), press conferences, and quite often, visits to centres throughout the country to give talks.

Much of his work is deliberately created. Here may be included advertising, press releases and publications.

All the banks employ one or more advertising agents. But the planning and control of advertising still represents a substantial part of the Public Relations Officer's job. Although the agents carry out the donkey-work and most of the specialist tasks like layout, art-work, copy-writing and block-making, the responsibility, not only for the campaign but also for its execution, is that of the Public Relations Officer and it has to be designed to further the objects the general management has chosen; these may be, at any given time, to add to its prestige in the long run, to encourage the use of the bank as agent by overseas banks, to attract wage-earning customers, to expand loans, to augment deposits, to extend the use of some special service or any of an unlimited number of objectives.

In addition to the normal advertising campaign, paid space is also taken for publicizing matters such as the chairman's annual speech, any striking innovation such as computer installations, and sometimes, new departures in policy. On the local level, space is taken to advertise the opening or extension of branches, changes in hours of attendance at sub-offices, and also any special matters which might arise in connection with local events, for which a special copy has to be written. All this falls within the aegis of the Public Relations Officer and involves him and his staff in a lot of research.

Letting people know is the backbone of all effective public relations programmes because no matter how virtuous one's actions may be, they can have little effect unless they are widely known as can be seen from the following case.

The Case of the Non-Merging Bank

A rumour which threatened to be embarrassing was turned into a benefit by the alert public relations management at the American National Bank and Trust Company of Chicago in 1960.

The American National was the youngest member of the Chicago La Salle Street financial community, having been founded in 1933, but had grown rapidly and by 1960 ranked fifth in the city. During that year, a merger was made between two other major loop banks, and rumours started circulating that the American National was also going to be part of the merger. In December, The Chicago Tribune carried a story that the American National was considering joining another large bank. Officers of the American National were deeply concerned about these rumours, for one of the principal points of the bank's marketing strategy was its emphasis upon personal and individual attention to each account-holder. Many of the customers made enquiries, for they feared that if the American National were absorbed by a larger bank, they would lose that valued personal touch. It was decided to issue a vigorous denial.

The denial first went to the bank's own staff, assuring them that the rumours were not founded on facts and that none of the 700 staff members need worry about losing their jobs because of rumoured merger with another institution. Later, reports from the four daily newspapers received the same emphatic denial. Despite the bank's efforts to contradict them, rumours continued to circulate.

At this point, the bank's public relations director and counselling firm had an inspiration. For some time, the bank had been considering signing a twenty-year lease for two additional floors of space in the building which it occupied, with an option upon six additional floors. In normal times, this would have made only slight news, but as an answer to the rumours of consolidation, it would definitely be page-one material. Why not expedite the signing of the lease and with it also release the news of the bank's expanded earnings and success in the year just ending?

A press conference was scheduled between the President of the bank and the four financial editors of the daily newspapers, at which the news could be released and all questions could be answered. At the same time, an advertisement was prepared to run in the Chicago dailies and in the New York Times covering the same facts, reprints of which were mailed to 6,000 correspondent bank customers and prospects. And a direct mailing piece of a similar nature was also prepared to go to all checking-account customers along with their statements at the end of the month.

News coverage and response were excellent. Not only were the rumours laid to rest but, in addition, many people not connected with the bank received a new conception of its size, growth, and determination to remain an independent part of Chicago's banking community. The response from many customers expressed their approval. Had this situation been allowed to drift, it could have been injurious; but by the timely seizing of news interest, it became a benefit.

Public relations, like charity, begins at home. It is not confined to dealing with the customers of the bank and the public at large only, but it also deals with people within the bank. The bank has to have effective public relations with its shareholders and its employees. The shareholders who have shown confidence in the bank by investing in it will require to be assured that everything is well with the bank and that they will get a good return on their investment. This is done by the publication of the balance sheet and the Annual Report and by holding meetings. The shareholders themselves should be the Public Relations Officers by commending the bank to their acquaintances and by directing to the bank all business in their control. They should willingly do this since they own the bank and earn profit in direct proportion to the bank's progress.

A bank's greatest resource is its staff. Good public relations cannot exist without good personnel relations and therefore, the bank must have a contented staff whose fundamental wants — salary, security and job satisfaction — are catered to. There must be a continuing two-way communication between management and personnel: (a) a realistic appraisal of employee hopes, desires and ambitions, and (b) a constant flow of information to the staff regarding management purposes, policies and achievements. Good public relations outside the bank grow from good public relations inside the bank.

All phases of a bank's public relations centre round the basic relationship — the relationship between the bank employees and the customers — which is the key to its survival and development. The customer is not only to be treated properly but also to be made aware of the bank's activities, and services on an ongoing basis. In short, it is an image-building exercise, as well as laying a sound edifice for growth. Essential requisites of a PR programme are awareness of the importance of the participation in local activities of the bank's community and plan for such participation. Bank's participation in community activities should be on the basis of team work to promote the welfare and prosperity of the community. It is through such growth that the bank prospers. Careful selection of projects should be made by laying emphasis on economic feasibility and social viability in which the bank can be most helpful.

Bank Personnel and Public Relations

The most important means of interpretation and communication of public relations of a bank is through its personnel. Since public relations is concerned with all the functions and services of the bank, it cannot be set up as a separate department. It cuts through all department lines, concerning itself with all phases of human relationships.

Wider participation by each employee in the bank should be secured to create, maintain and develop sound public relations. To get wider participation by each employee in the bank, the levels in the organisational hierarchy should be avoided, without indicating any distinction among officers, clerks, cashiers and sub-staff. It is obvious that the success of public relations programmes hinges on all members of the bank, with each individual employee enthusiastically participating in planning and sharing equally as a member of the bank staff.

Public relations is concerned with a two-way communication within the bank so that all personnel may be fully advised of the bank's policies and services; then informed and inspired to properly interpret and project them before the public. Public relations must be interested in the quality and training of the bank's personnel.

Advertising

Advertising is an important means of communication which is vital to a good public relations programme. It plays a key role in banks by providing useful information to the public. The purpose of advertising is to elicit the potential buyers' responses to the organisation and its offerings and it seeks to do this by providing information, by trying to channelize desires, and supplying reasons for preferring the particular bank's offerings.

Relationship with Print Media

A number of publications that have come up on the Indian scene discuss various aspects of the economy in general and industry in particular. With increasing readership concern for the health of the economy, it is necessary that there should be an ongoing relationship and communication between organisations and these publications, as otherwise the organisations may suffer because of half-baked facts and distorted reports. As Abraham Lincoln remarked in one of his speeches, "Public sentiment is everything: with public sentiment nothing can fail, without it nothing can succeed. He who moulds opinions is greater than he who moulds laws."

Public relations activities by and large cover communication, liaison and contact. These three activities are practiced both internally and externally. In fact, "internal" public relations is far more important than the "external" one. A handful of satisfied employees can give their organisation, in terms of image and reputation, greater mileage than what a large external public relations campaign can. Internally, apart from personal contact and liaison with different departments PR keeps channels of communication open through house journals, announcements, group meetings and sports meets.

External public relations keeps communication open with the press and the public. And in respect of marketing it plays a vital role in providing uniformity to institutional advertisements and the company's image, products and services.

It is quite common to find a single "communication format" developed and sent to different segments of the society having varied expectations from a given organisation. For example, a women's college wanting to raise funds for building a hostel or class rooms sent the same appeal letters for funds to the controlling university, government, parents, students and the general public, without realising that the information needed by each of these could be different. The controlling university may like to know the academic performance, admission graph, utilization of funds etc. and the parents may want to know about discipline in the college, relations between teachers and students, teaching innovations and comparative examination performance.

Similarly, public relations functionaries need to disseminate different sets of communications to their governing bodies, shareholders, customers or clients, press, Parliament, bureaucrats and the general public.

The activity of "liaison" is more or less confined to government departments, embassies, press and planning bodies. Unfortunately, however, the emphasis of liaison work is more on dinners and cocktails than on dissemination of worthwhile information.

"Contact" is by and large with chambers of commerce, industry associations, educational institutions and other public relations bodies.

A large volume of advertisements are today intended to promote sales and increase the scope of marketing activities. A wide variety of means (the advertising media) are used to communicate these advertisements to consumers, the most important of which are the press, television, radio, illuminated signs, billboards, and direct mail.

Fig. 15.3 broadly classifies advertisements according to the advertising medium used. Advertisements prepared for exposure through the mass media, as well as those for display on public transport vehicles and on telephone poles are communicated via media companies such as newspapers and commercial broadcasting stations. On the other hand, means such as billboards, illuminated signs, direct mail, and shop-window advertisements are media in their own right, and communicate directly to the consumer.

Public relations have always been one of the most significant aspects of banks in determining its level of success. At the micro-level, i.e., bank branch, the bank employee comes face to face with the consumer as well as the general public, who are the potential customers. The branch can spread the message of banking, inculcate thrift, banking habits through public relations. Public relations in banks is a continuous process and will go a long way in improving the economic and social standards of the people.

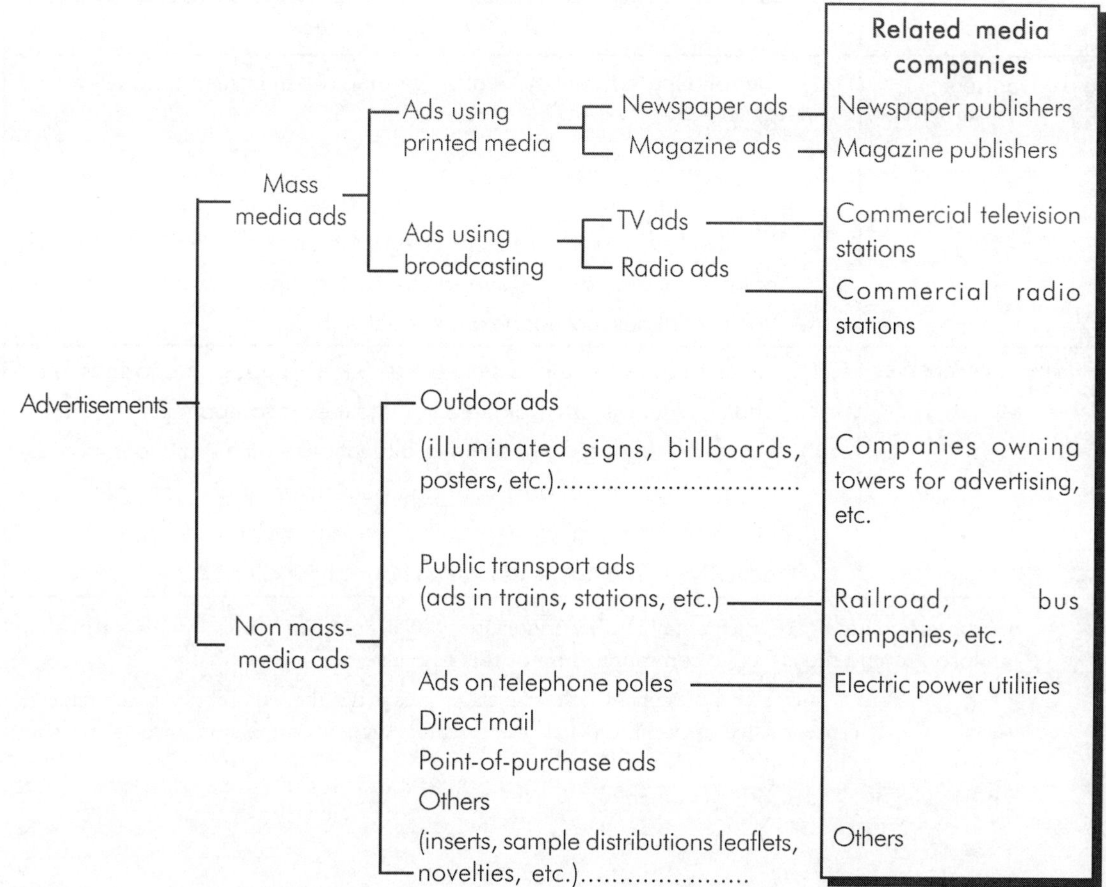

Fig. 15.3 Types of advertisement and media used.

Note: Unbroken lines — denote cases in which all advertisements are communicated through media companies.
Dotted lines ...... denote cases in which some advertisements are communicated through media companies.

Sources: Based on Nihon Keizai Shimbun and other data.

	Outline of Services
A. To advertisers	(1) Negotiating complex matters with media companies on advertiser's behalf. (2) Meeting advertiser's needs in respect of planning and preparation of advertising, selection and obtaining of advertising media. (3) Feedback of advertising effectiveness based on market research, collation of information, etc., and support for advertiser's marketing activities. (4) Public relations, corporate identity activities, etc.
B. To media companies	(1) Locating advertisers and selling space (newspapers, magazines, etc.) and time (television, radio, etc.) for the media companies. (2) Upon receipt of space and time, allocations from media companies, payment to them of advances and guarantee monies, or payment to them of advertising fees, irrespective of whether these are collected from advertisers. The agencies take a financial risk.

Note: 1. Corporate identity activities entail the harmonization of a company's image with its business philosophy, and the effective communication of this to consumers.

2. Only the large agencies and certain middle-sized agencies have the capabilities to provide the services to advertisers listed in A (1) to (4) above. Smaller Agencies often specialise as space and time brokers as listed in B (1) above. The services to media companies listed in B (1) and (2) are undertaken by all advertising companies.

Conclusion

The public judge a bank both by what it does and what it says. If a bank's policies are sound, its operations technically competent, its services good, and if the bank acts fairly and justly towards its customers, employees, shareholders and the community, then it is only good business to publicise these virtues. No business can continuously attract the public unless it projects its services constantly before the public. This combination of sound policies and good practices, projected to the public by effective publicity, produces good public relations.

Finally, public relations can help humanize a company through feature write-ups on its executives which advertising cannot do as successfully and convincingly.

Even though public relations is a powerful function, it is not adequately used to help and assist marketing efforts. Unless these two functions are linked and synchronized, a company will waste its resources. When a high cost function like marketing is linked to a low cost function like public relations with a much better impact and response at the marketplace, the "cost benefit" factor becomes much clearer.

Chapter 16

Organisation of Banks

Introduction

Behind every bank — successful or otherwise — lies the most intricate instrument the world has ever evolved, an organisation. It is this instrument which transcends its immediate use and reveals qualities and forms that lie hidden in the inert matters around it. Organisation is the basic input for any activity, enterprise, venture or business. Organisation makes management easier, effective and result-oriented. An organisation designed and structured on planned lines promotes collaboration and negotiation among individuals in a group and thus improves the effectiveness and efficiency of communication within the organisation. This function creates clear-cut lines of authority and responsibility in the organisation. Banking organisation is a process of combining and interrelating in a sequence the various organs of a bank like individuals, customers, working and social groups, borrowers, tasks, responsibilities, jobs, services, guidance, etc.

An banker who has a high level of administrative capability, flair and ability for decision-making, computational skill, delegation skill, organisational skill, good at communication and has a sound technical knowledge stands a much better chance of success than his counterpart who possesses none or a low level of these basic qualities. It is the possession of these scarce qualities that confers an advantage over others. Organisation is a basic tool of management on which depends the success of banking. In recent times, organisational structure should be presentable to the customers, employees and managers alike.

The Concept

The word "organisation" has two meanings. Firstly, it means an institution or structure, viz. a bank is an institution with its organisational structure of head office, local office, district offices and branches. Secondly, it means a process of an ongoing activity, i.e., the process of organising, allocating and bringing about relationships among men, money and services. In fact, organisation establishes relationship among the people so that they collectively contribute to the attainment of organisational goals effectively. Thus organisation is a means to an end. It is also an important part of management.

The Process

Ernest Dale has described organising as a multi-step process, viz.,

(i) Detailing all the work that must be done in order to attain the organisation goals;

(ii) Dividing the total work load into activities that can logically and conveniently be performed by one person or by a group of individuals;

(iii) Combining the work of a company's members in a logical and efficient manner;

(iv) Setting up of a mechanism to co-ordinate the work of organisation members into a unified, harmonious whole; and

(v) Monitoring the effectiveness of the organisation and making adjustments to maintain or increase effectiveness.

Need for an Organisation

A proper organisation would assist in the most effective use of the physical assets and the human resources so that the unit may be perpetuated and the objectives, including that of profit, may be achieved. The need for organisations grows with the increase in the size of the unit. An organisation involves division of work among people whose efforts must be co-ordinated to achieve specific objectives and implement pre-determined strategies. An organisation is thus the foundation upon which the whole management structure is built.

The concept of organisation has five basic elements, namely:

(i) The assembly of men, materials, machines and money to produce a product in the unit in accordance with the plan;

(ii) The identification and grouping of the work, i.e., work division and work allotment;

(iii) Definition of responsibility for every function;

(iv) Delegation of appropriate authority; and

(v) The establishment of structural relationships.

These five basic elements enable an organisation to co-ordinate its varied activities to achieve its objectives. Moreover, they ensure the smooth performance of the operations of various organisational activities.

Definition of Organisation

An organisation provides the mechanism for purposive, integrated development. It has been variously defined by different authors. Dimmock in his book, *Public Administration*, has rightly observed: "An organisation is the systematic bringing together of interdependent parts to form a united whole through which authority, co-ordination, and control may be exercised to achieve a given purpose. (Because the interdependent parts of this are made up of people who must be directed and motivated and whose work must be co-ordinated in order to achieve the objectives of the enterprise, an organisation is both structure and human beings.) To try to deal with the organisation as merely a framework without considering the people who make it up and those for whom its services are intended would be wholly unrealistic."

According to Herbert Simon, the term "organisation" suggests "the complex pattern of communication and other relations in a group of human beings. This pattern provides to each member of the group much of the information, assumptions, goals and attitudes that enter into his decisions, provides him also with a set of stable comprehensible expectations as to what the other members of the group are doing, and how they will react to what he says and does."

Louis A. Allen defines organisation as "the process of identifying and grouping the work to be performed, defining and delegating responsibility and authority, and establishing relationship for the purpose of enabling people to work most effectively together in accomplishing objectives."

Organisation is defined as a system in which individuals and groups operating at different levels perform the tasks assigned to them within the framework of delegated authority and responsibility which are rationally coordinated to achieve the desired organisational goals. It is an effective mechanism with which an entrepreneur directs, coordinates and controls the activities of man, machine, money and materials. The success or failure of an enterprise depends upon the organisation.

An organisation thus involves:

(i) A determination and an enumeration of the activities necessary for the achievement of the goals of an enterprise;

(ii) A grouping of these activities and assigning authority and responsibility to a particular position;

(iii) A co-ordination of authority relationships so that the efforts of individuals are directed towards achieving the corporate goals.

Other Definitions

1. "An organisation is the formation of an effective executive and the administration of an effective direction. Administration determines the goals; the management strives towards it. Administration determines the organisation; the management uses it. An organisation is a machine of management in its achievement of the ends determined by its administration. An organisation tries to establish an effective behavioural relationship among selected employees and in selected work places in order that a group may work together effectively." — Sheldon

2. "Organisation involves the grouping of activities necessary to accomplish goals and plans, the assignment of these activities to appropriate departments and the provision for authority and delegation and co-ordination." — Koontz and O'Donnell.

3. "An organisation consists of people who carry out differentiated tasks which are co-ordinated to contribute to the organisation's goals." — G. Dessler.

4. " Organisation is the form of every human association for the attainment of a common purpose." — Mooney and Reiley. They visualise it as a process of "relating specific duties or functions in a co-ordinated whole."

5. "An organisation is the rational co-ordination of the activities or roles of a number of people for the achievement of some common explicit purpose or goal, through division of labour and function, and through a hierarchy of authority and responsibility." — E. H. Schein.

6. "Organisation is a structured process in which individuals interact for achieving the stated objectives." — Ernest Dale.

Approaches to Organisation

The organisational approaches assumes importance because of the constant interface between the organisation and the environment, which is changing fast and unpredictably. The experts have identified —

(i) Systems approach,

(ii) Process approach, and

(iii) Organisational change approach.

Under the systems approach, an organisation is treated like an open system requiring different structures in different environments. The basic conceptual elements in the systems approach are:

(a) Key organisational process — communication, decision-making, control and planning.

(b) External environment.

(c) Employees and other tangible assets.

(d) Formal organisational arrangements.

(e) Social system.

(f) Technology.

(g) Small group coalition — the internal relationship of the minimum group (e.g., unions) which control its basic policy-making.

A major finding of the systems approach is the inter-relationahip between the prime components of the organisation. When change is to be made in one of these components, there will be an impact on all other elements.

The key concept under the process approach is the 'crisis' aspect of organisational change. One of the main features of the approach is its ability to accommodate superficial changes without changing its structure. Large organisations are far more committed to routinisation of change and adjustment than they are to allowing organisations to continuously adjust and change.

It deals with the nature of change process. The evolutionary association reflected the view that change was a part of one major adjustment after another fuelled by time and subtle environmental forces largely outside the direct control of the organisation.

Systems Approach to Organisation

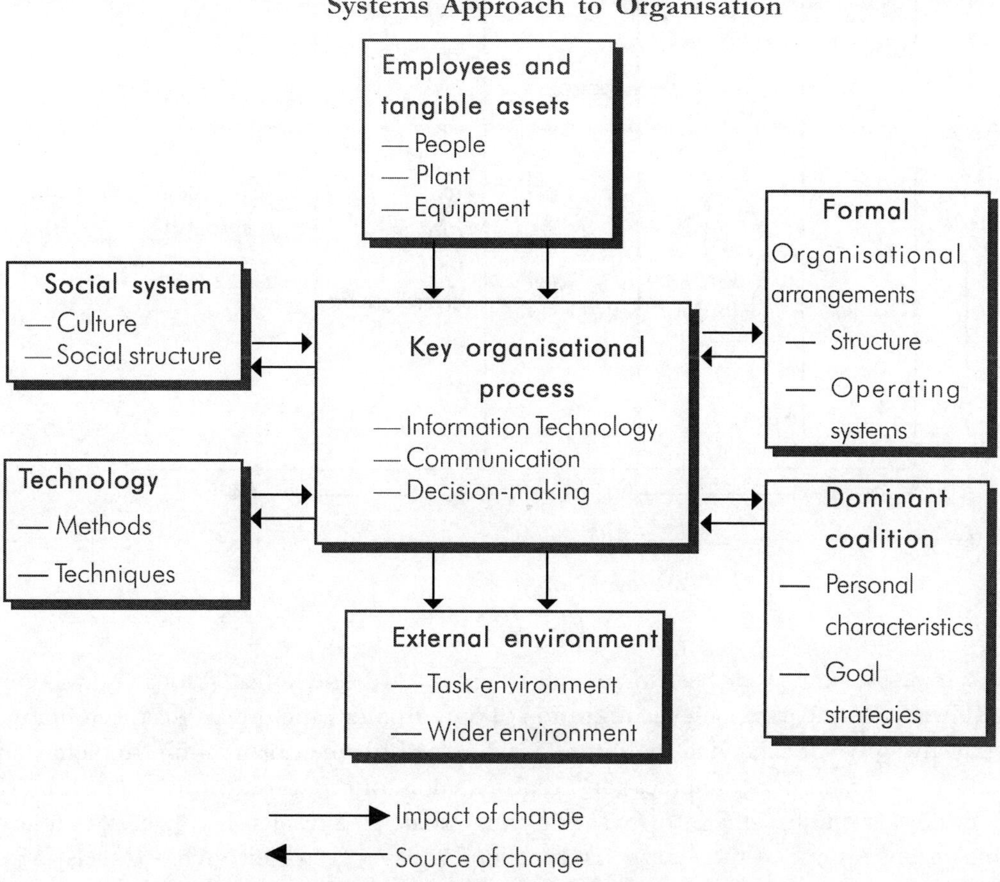

Fig. 16.1 Systems Approach to Organisation

Organisation is defined as a living being. It has a life cycle and it grows. There are five phases of organisational growth as depicted in next page.

According to M. Tushman, "The most innovative organisations are highly learning systems. Organisations that can be self-critical and can learn to keep improving on today's work while aggressively preparing for tomorrow will be more successful than those organisations that evolve towards greater stability and complexity."

The concept of organisational change is not new to the banking industry. The constitution of Sarayya Committee (1972), James Raj Committee (1977) and Luther Committee are a testimony to the awareness of the change concept.

The aspects of behavioural change which received attention in banks include managing change through training, organisation development approaches, job description to alter the control system, performance appraisal system, value clarification of employees to improve organisational climate

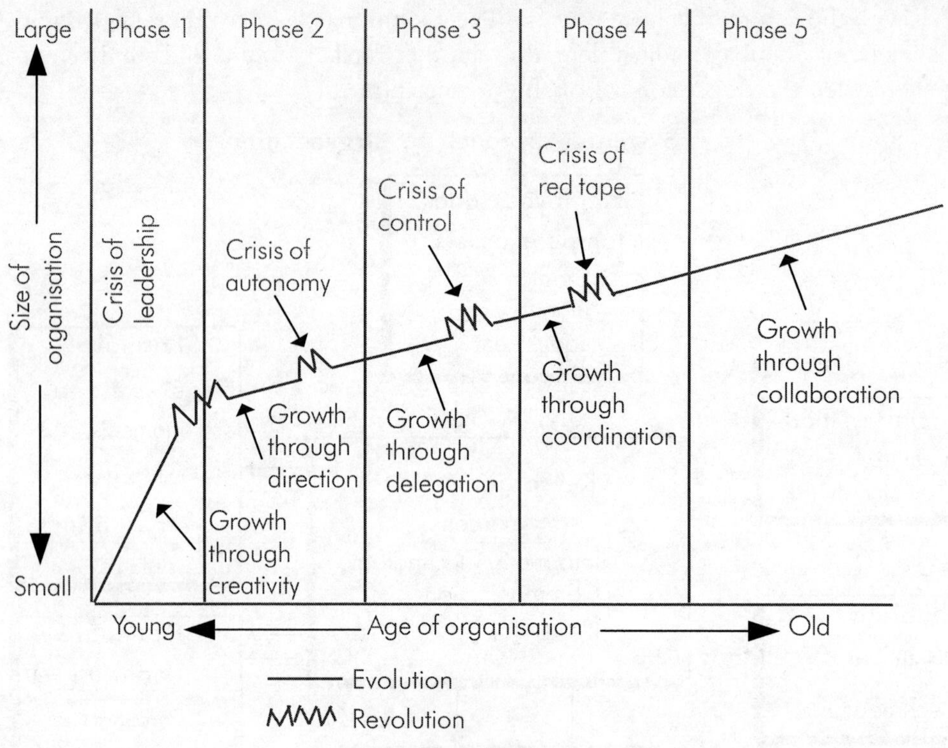

Fig. 16.2

and the most important areas have been long-range planning (LRP) and human resources development (HRD). LRP was aimed at systematic identification of opportunities and threats that lie in future and to frame effective ways of achieving the future goals framed for the organisation. Implementation of HRD efforts suffers from communication, feedback, monitoring, consultation and measurement problems. Besides, such one time effort will not bring the desired results. It is necessary to accept that planning change is one of the managerial functions, irrespective of hierarchical levels and only limited planning is carried out in the banks while designing any major change. Further, organisational health basically relies upon the manner in which changes are planned and institutionalised. Therefore, what is important is to understand the levers of change. There are seven inter-related levers of change called 'Seven S' framework — these include structure, strategy, staff, style, skills, system and superordinate goals as shown in the diagram.

Executive Structure

Organisation is the executive structure of an enterprise — a basic framework within which the executive's decision-making behaviour occurs. Organisation, as an element of management, is concerned with the following aspects: (1) Identifying and grouping of activities to attain corporate objectives and goals. (2) Assignment of these activities to appropriate divisions, departments and sections and individuals. (3) Provision of authority, delegation, co-ordination, and communication. (4) Provision of facilities and equipment, i.e., physical factors of good work environment. These are the four basic elements of all forms of living organisations. The process of organisation centres

A New View of Organisation

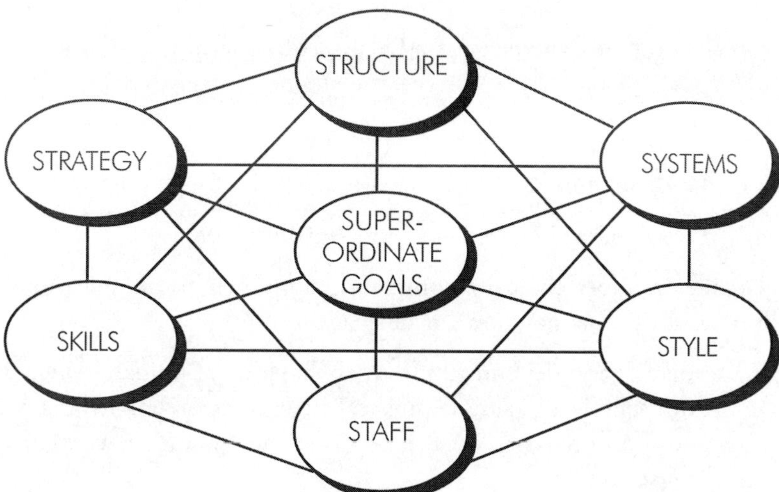

Fig. 16.3 A New View of Organisation

round: (1) The Work, (2) The People, (3) The Authority-Responsibility Relationships. A clear-cut division of work defines and prescribes each part of the work to be handled by each person, allocating of duties and responsibilities, and defining authority or power at each position in the organisation chart. Co-ordination and integration will ensure elimination of duplication of work and unity of action.

An Ideal Organisation

A good organisation has to fulfil four special functions:

(1) It must enable management to maximise the outputs or resources through provision of an efficient man-machine system.

(2) It must ensure smooth and effective network of communication and information.

(3) It must offer interesting and meaningful jobs to all individuals working in the organisation. This alone will ensure job satisfaction. Organisation is developed for people. It must be also humanistic and not merely mechanistic. Both approaches can be reconciled.

(4) It must create, maintain and develop its own image or individuality. This ensures customer goodwill; investors will have confidence in the enterprise. Employees can develop a sense of belonging to the organisation.

The managerial function of organising is the process of establishing relationships among available organisation resources so that their structure enables the achievement of objectives of the enterprise. Resources are personnel functions and physical factors. Relationships centre around status, role, responsibility, authority and accountability. Structure may be functionalised — line, line and staff, committee and project.

Characteristics of a Good Organisation Structure

(i) It focuses on the achievement of a balance of short-run and long-run objectives.

(ii) It recognises the importance of the interface between the customer and the bank.

(iii) It groups activities of a similar nature together, recognising, however, that at different stages in the development of a bank, the pattern of groupings will change.

(iv) It clearly differentiates between line and staff positions.

(v) It establishes a short chain of command, simplifies communications and speed of decisions and discourages upward delegation.

The success of an organisation depends upon the behaviour of human beings. It is, therefore, very important to view it not merely as a simple physical structure of relationships but as a complex structure influenced by social and psychological behaviour and by informal groups governing the interactions of human beings.

An organisational structure is a framework which holds the various functions together according to the pattern, order, topical and legal arrangements and in-built relationships. According to some authors, an organisation is a system with such inputs as men, materials, machines, goods and services, profits, etc.

Importance of Organisation

Organisation is the foundation of management. It is a process in which individuals interact to accomplish definitive objectives. Organisation has the following advantages:

(i) It encourages specialisation and ensures higher productivity.

(ii) It streamlines the process of activities and ensures their smooth functioning. Duplication of, and consequent confusion as well as wasted efforts are likely to be removed if there is an adequate organisation and a fixing of responsibility.

(iii) It fosters co-ordination of various activities in an integrated manner towards the attainment of specific objectives.

(iv) It facilitates precise and effective delegation of authority.

(v) It ensures proper direction, motivation, co-ordination and control.

(vi) It aids in the expansion and growth of an enterprise. A sound organisation plan avoids all the pitfalls that occur during rapid growth.

(vii) It provides for the optimum use of technological improvements and manpower for higher growth.

(viii) An effective organisation promotes growth and diversification through decentralisation and divisionalisation on geographical or product basis.

Formal and Informal Organisation

An organisation is broadly classified into formal and informal organisations.

A formal organisation is one resulting from planning where its pattern or structure is pre-determined to carry out specific jobs or to achieve goals. The structure, procedural rules, membership and work process of a formal group/organisation are explicitly stated in clear terms. It is based on the delegation of authority with official leadership.

An informal organisation develops when people work together towards a specific objective or goal. In this type of organisation, people with common interest generally get together and work. It represents a pattern of interpersonal and inter-group relations which develop within a formal organisation without any prescribed position, duties, responsibilities, authority, etc. By and large, the informal group develops its own leaders. It has a natural existence and performs unique functions.

Principles of Organisation

While choosing a viable organisational structure, every person, whether a small entrepreneur or a large one, must first determine the scientific principles on which it has to be based. The fifteen basic principles laid down by Urwick will serve as guidelines in determining the organisation pattern best suited to a unit. These fifteen principles are:

(i) Objective;

(ii) Specialisation;

(iii) Co-ordination;

(iv) Clear unbroken line of authority;

(v) Responsibility;

(vi) Efficiency;

(vii) Span of control;

(ix) Balance;

(x) Communication;

(xi) Personal ability;

(xii) Flexibility;

(xiii) Grouping;

(xiv) Definiteness; and

(xv) Continuity.

Table 1

Distinctions between Formal and Informal Organisations

Formal Organisation	Informal Organisation
1. It is a prescribed structure of roles and relationships consciously co-ordinated towards a common objective.	1. It is a natural and spontaneous structure arising out of the social tendency of people to associate and interact.
2. Its goals and tasks are oriented towards productivity, profitability, growth and so on.	2. Its goals and tasks predominantly centre round individual and group satisfaction, affiliation, friendship, etc.
3. It is hierarchical, pyramid-shaped and bureaucratic in structure.	3. It is shapeless and unchartable.
4. Emphasis is on status differentials and based on superior-subordinate relationships.	4. It is based on friendship, common values, and interests.
5. There is a prescribed system of behaviour. People are rewarded for their "desired behaviour" and punished for their "undesirable behaviour." Rewards can be both monetary and non-monetary.	5. There are unwritten norms of behaviour enforced by common consent by all the members. Rewards for obeying the norms can take the form of continuous membership, social esteem, group leadership, etc. Punishments are isolation, censure etc.

Steps in Organising

The process of organisation follows the formulation of objectives. The work is then divided into component activities, which are then grouped into practical units of similar activities. George R. Terry states: "Organising is the establishing of effective behavioural relationships among selected workers and work places in order that the group may work together efficiently."

Briefly, the following are the logical steps involved in organising:

(i) Identifying the activities in order to attain the objectives of the unit;

(ii) Determining the activities which are needed to execute plans and policies with a view to attaining objectives;

(iii) Classifying and grouping these activities on the principles of functions, products:

- (a) grouping activities into individual jobs;
- (b) grouping jobs and people into sections;
- (c) grouping sections into departments;
- (d) grouping departments into administrative units;

(iv) Defining responsibility and accountability, so that each person knows what is expected of him in terms of the attainment of the unit's objectives;

(v) Delegating the requisite authority and adequate facilities to enable each one to carry out his responsibility; and

(vi) Establishing clear structural relationships among individuals and groups.

The organisational structure of a small-scale industry differs from that of other business organisations. Its outstanding feature is the personal character of the organisation and management.

In analysing the organisational structure of a small-scale industry, we may broadly discuss the pattern of ownership (social organisation) and input organisation, i.e., the physical aspect of an organisation covering production, marketing, planning and control.

Functions of an Organisation

There are three kinds of work which must be performed whenever an organisation comes into being, viz., division of labour, combination of labour and co-ordination, i.e., the work, the people, and the relationship among them. These are fundamental in every successful organisation.

(i) Division of Labour: Since an organisation is a structure of human association for the achievement of common goals, it involves individuals and groups of individuals. When two or more individuals join together to perform certain tasks, it follows that some division of work is done. Properly or improperly, fairly or unfairly, work is divided among those who participate in a productive organisation. With effective planning and organisation in an enterprise, the division of labour leads to a fixing of responsibility, the delegation of authority, specialisation, and other conceptual schemes which are frequently called the principles of an organisation.

(ii) Combination of Labour: With work divided and assigned to the members of an organisation, their activities are grouped together, forming operations; and operations are arranged to establish systems and procedures. From a structural point of view, this grouping of activities results in units, departments and divisions in an organisation. The basis for this grouping of activities may be the skills of the workers, the tools and machinery used, the nature of the product, the materials employed, or some other element. Whether it is logical or not, there is always some reason for the arrangement of tasks in a work place.

(iii) Co-ordination: This all-inclusive principle emerges because of the need in every organisation for the integration of activities and the coordination of individuals and groups of individuals performing their tasks. Co-ordination is achieved through leadership; in the structural sense, it involves the fixing of responsibility and the delegation of authority. It establishes controls which provide for an efficient scheduling and performance of activities.

Functional Organisation

Departmentation on the basis of enterprise function (functional organisation) is the most logical and widely accepted practice. The important functions of any commercial organisation are:

(i) Production/Service Management rendering service, (ii) Marketing Management, (iii) Financial Management, (iv) Personnel Management, and (v) Research and Development. Though it seems that the acceptance of deposits and granting of loans and advances are two important functions of a commercial bank, they are, in technical sense, not the functions of a bank but two important processes of a production. In other words, banks produce loans (output) with the help of deposits (input). Hence the above classification of functions is also applicable to banks. The process of functional analysis, classification and diversification may continue through several successive levels in the hierarchy.

Chart 16.1

Departmentation, i.e., Logical Grouping of Activities (Creation of Manageable Units)

Functions	*Product*	*Geography*	*Customer*
Functions are the main entities around which a manager builds the organisation structure. *Typical functions:* (1) Servicing, (2) Marketing, (3) Finanace & Accounting, (4) Personnel, (5) Purchasing, (6) Engineering, (7) R. & D. *Advantages:* (1) Easy coordination within the function, (2) Simplified training, (3) Economy and efficiency of operations, (4) Simple, logical to decide, effective in practice, proven over time. (5) Helps in tight control by chief executive, (6) Follows the principle of specialisation.	For each product or allied products, we have one autonomous unit having its own functional departments, self-sufficient product-wise units. *Common example:* Department store. One department for one kind of merchandise. *Advantages:* (1) Steady growth. Product expansion, diversification. (2) Effective control of work. (3) Best for management development. (4) Satisfies product characteristics of manufacturing, engineering and marketing.	Each region has its own set up. Complete self-sufficient unit of administration with its own marketing, finance and manufacturing departments. Entire service area of enterprise broken up into territories and positions grouped by the territory served. *Advantages:* (1) Marketing advantage — serves local markets. (2) Management development. (3) Economy in transport cost. (4) Economy in purchases. (5) Lower cost of production.	More attention to depositors and borrowers may lead to departmentation by customers. The service area is decentralised into divisions. These are supported by mass media campaigns. *Departmentalisation:* Banks have special sections for exporters, small industries, agriculture, large industries, etc. *Advantages:* Service advantage. Technical service easily made available. Quick decision. Efficient service at low cost.

Disadvantages: (1) Too much specialisation, narrow outlook, (2) Delay in decisions, (3) Excessive centralisation, poor co-ordination between departments, (4) Over burdening chief executive, (5) Poor training ground for managers. *When to use Functional Departmentation?* (1) Stable and predictable environment. (2) Efficiency more important than flexibility. (3) Products, markets, customers not diverse. (4) Personal centralised leadership is required.	*Disadvantages:* (1) Increasing service cost. (2) Duplicate service functions at the top and at operating levels. (3) High cost of management. (4) Small companies cannot adopt it.	*Disadvantages:* (1) Difficulty of co-ordination and control of all divisions. (2) Divisionalisation requires adequate planning and longer time of 5 to 10 years. (3) Costlier to initiate and maintain than functional organisation. (4) Divisionalisation is a major surgery. It must be thoroughly planned and phased in two or three stages — first marketing, then manufacturing and then financing.	*Disadvantages:* Difficulty of co-ordination and control. Preferential services. Personalised and decentralised leadership is required. Bank staff should be motivated to provide quick and excellent service by delegating more responsibilities.

Note: As an organisation grows the organisation structure expands vertically as well as horizontally. Addition of activities or functions create new departments. It leads to horizontal growth. Addition of levels to an organisation structure is due to the operations of scalar process brought about by the delegation of authority and assignment of responsibility to the subordinate managers. Levels are added to the organisation structure as a result of vertical growth. Scalar process creates vertical growth. Functional process creates horizontal growth. Span of control or management is responsible for the shape of the structure — flat or tall. Flat structure has few levels of management. Tall or pyramidal structure has many levels of management.

Functional organisation can be effective and can continue only as long as it is used to the fullest extent.

Advantages

(i) Efficient utilisation of human resources in view of specialisation;

(ii) All functions are oriented towards the attainment of objectives;

(iii) Easy control and coordination;

(iv) Suited to a stable environment;

(v) Fosters development of expertise;

(vi) Requires fewer interpersonal skills.

Disadvantages

(i) Managers may try to build their functional empire;
(ii) Functions cannot always be clearly delineated and they are interdependent;
(iii) May create conflicts over product priorities;
(iv) Less innovative and has narrow perspective.

Departmentalisation of Bank Activities

Commercial banks are organised on the basis of geographical divisionalised structure, i.e., rural, semi-urban, urban and metropolitan. Management organisation is on the basis of hierarchy of organisation structure, viz., head of office, local offices, divisional offices, and branches. Bank activities are grouped on the basis of functional type or departmental type of organisational structure within the geographical, hierarchical structures. The amount and degree of departmentalisation vary with the size and the work load of the bank/branch. Some of the key departments in banks are enumerated here. At the branch level, many of these functions are handled by officers themselves.

Operations: The operations function of a commercial bank includes a wide variety of functions, the most important of which are the handling of deposits and withdrawals, book-keeping, record-keeping and analysis. The handling of deposits and withdrawals is sometimes referred to as commercial functions. The paying and receiving tellers are responsible for the acceptance and paying out of demand deposits. Fixed deposit division accepts term deposits, issues receipts, calculates interest, etc. The savings division is concerned with receiving savings deposits, computing the interest on the various accounts, and paying out funds that are withdrawn from the savings accounts. At the branch level, the operations functions are under the supervision of the accountant — second in command.

The operations function in most banks, especially in larger ones, also includes those responsible for maintaining the building and for planning the necessary future space requirements and equipment needs. In large and growing banks, these functions are extremely important and necessary for efficient operations.

Accounting: The accounting and analysis department is concerned with the bank's accounting and cost analysis. Since a bank makes charges for various services performed for customers, it is necessary that it knows the cost of performing these services, just as it is necessary that it knows what departments are being operated at a profit or a loss. This is a responsibility of the accounting and analysis department. Since most small banks do not have such a department, many of them do not know much about the costs of their various services. Banks are increasingly realising the importance of an accounting and analysis department, and more of them are establishing such departments or are at least employing capable persons to perform such work. At the branch level, it rests with the manager.

Advances: The lending function is one of the most important functions of a bank. The size of the department handling advances will vary with the size of the bank and with the types of loans granted. Sometimes, the advance department is composed of officers and employees who make all types of loans. The officers of the department may be specialists in certain types of loans such as real estate or commercial loans. In larger bank branches, there may be sub-divisions within the credit department, handling, for example, real estate, personal, and commercial or business loans. Such banks often have a number of separate loan departments such as commercial, agricultural, small-scale industry, large industry, real estate, instalment loans, loan recovery and credit analysis.

The analysis of credit requests is a very important phase of commercial bank lending. In large banks, a separate department is sometimes maintained under the supervision of the loan department, to collect information regarding borrowers, to prepare and analyse information in order to determine the creditworthiness of the person or business under investigation, and to keep credit information for future use. This department formulates policies relating to loans and advances to different sectors and borrowers on the basis of directives from the Reserve Bank of India and Central Government. It also formulates schemes of advances, margins, subsidy, refinance, rediscounting, etc. In branches this function rests with the manager.

Investment: This department is responsible for utilising idle funds and invest them under the Statutory Liquidity Requirements in Government and approved securities. This department takes into account the liquidity and profitability requirements while planning investments.

Foreign Exchange: The important functions of this department are:

(i) Providing information to branches about trade control and exchange control regulations;

(ii) Making arrangements with other banks in foreign countries as correspondents;

(iii) Purchasing and selling of foreign currencies;

(iv) Formulating policies regarding pre-shipment and post-shipment loans, issue of letters of credit, guarantees, refinance, rediscounting, etc.

Auditing: Auditing in commercial banks is concerned with the review of transactions for accuracy and in determining whether or not such transactions have been recorded in conformity with the acceptable accounting theory and banking regulations. Supervisory authorities strongly encourage the performance of the auditing function and nearly all require an annual or semi-annual general audit. Many large banks have an auditing department that performs a continuous audit. Many small banks that lack sufficiently competent auditing personnel conduct an occasional "spot" audit and sometimes employ a certified public accountant to perform an audit once or twice a year.

Personnel: The basic objectives of this department is to generate, develop and maintain human resources in order to contribute to the attainment of organisational goals. This department performs various functions of personnel management like manpower planning, job analysis, recruitment, selection, training, development, wage and salary administration, providing fringe benefits, negotiating with trade unions, redressing grievances, disposing of disciplinary cases, maintenance of sound industrial relations, etc. The chief personnel manager thus asserts, counsels and advises various departmental heads and managers on personnel matters by assuming the role of a staff manager. To a great extent, the personnel department of a bank determines the efficiency of the organisation. Due to the increase in the cost of labour in recent years, banks have shown greater interest in personnel than ever before. The department has also HRD division under its wing. At the branch level, it is delegated to an officer.

Inspection: This department inspects the functioning of the various branches relating to deposits, loans and advances, issue of drafts, cheques, maintenance of books, issue of travellers' cheques, clearing or accounts, staff matters etc. This department follows up the irregularities pointed out by it and submits its report to the higher authority.

Legal: Some of the large banks have a legal department organised for the purpose of keeping the management of the bank informed on legal questions relative to the bank's business. Its function is not to render legal advice to customers, but to prepare certain legal documents and forms and to represent the bank in legal proceedings. Small banks do not have legal departments but usually retain outside attorneys to pass upon legal questions, handle all suits, and give advice on loan collection procedures. Legal work is delegated to an officer in local, divisional and large branches.

Economic and Planning: This department collects and analyses the data and submits Memos, Circulars, Statutory Returns, Control Returns on Advances, Monthly Flash Reports, etc., to the top management and the Reserve Bank of India. It also conducts surveys regarding lead districts, location of new branches as well as market and economic surveys. It also appraises the performance of the branches. It conducts cost studies, publishes economic journals and manages the information system in banks.

Safe Custody: Many depositors of a bank have certain documents, deeds, abstracts, stocks and bonds, insurance policies, and other papers upon which they place great value. Since home or business is not the safest place in the world to keep such valuables, the bank vault has become a depository for their safekeeping. Most banks provide safe-deposit vaults which they rent to customers. These vaults are owned by the bank. All the large and medium-sized banks have this facility.

Trust: Many persons and corporations turn to banks, because of their permanence and stability, to perform trust services for them. Trust services performed by banks consist of settling estates, administering trusts and guardianships, and performing agencies. This department is quite large in old and established banks and often requires the services of several officers and employees. In smaller banks, the trust powers, if exercised at all, are delegated to an officer of the bank.

Organisation and Methods: This department is in charge of review of bank's procedures and rules, forms and registers. It also suggests simplification, effectiveness and standardisation of forms, procedures, etc. By and large, these functions are performed at the head office. At local offices, an officer acts as a link officer.

Public Relations: The public relations department, sometimes called the new business department, is found in all large banks and is becoming more common in smaller banks. This department is concerned with all activities that place the bank in a favourable light, including advertising and promotional programmes and calling upon new residents and potential customers of the bank. This department is essential for the growth of a bank, especially in those communities where competition is great. In large banks, the public relations department may include a relatively large force. In a smaller bank only one officer may devote his full time to this work, but he will be aided by other officers and employees as the need arises. This is especially true of a programme involving the visiting of present and potential customers of the bank. Some banks publish and distribute monthly letters, house journals and bulletins. Such activities would probably be the responsibility of the public relations department, providing space for meetings of various industrial, agricultural, and civic groups. At the branch level, the manager discharges some of these functions.

Organisation Structure in a Bank: The organisation structure of banks differs from that of other enterprises. The form of organisation employed in banks resembles a line-and-staff type. And, at times, authority flows through one executive to the subordinates, although overall authority rests with the Board of Directors and its numerous committees.

Further, the organisation structure facilitates administration, growth and diversification, provides for the optimum use of technological improvements, encourages the human resources, use of human beings, and stimulates activity.

The banking business is becoming more and more complex. The accelerated pace of expansion and the influx of unfamiliar business in new sectors have made the entire operation much more difficult. Though there have been rapid and complex changes in the business, the structure to deal with these changes remain more or less the same as in the past. In most cases, the structure is too centralised to deal effectively with the new challenges of business, far flung along the length and breadth of the country. The policies of the banks (lending, personnel, etc.) are largely informal and legalistically circumscribed. Their information, inspection and control system are not adequately conceived and organised. Their procedures (recruitment, documentation, etc.) are not scientifically designed and often these are cumbersome, costly and anachronistic.

No doubt, there are differences between banks based on their size, history, and nature of business etc. which should be reflected in their organisation. However, considering the commonality of their objectives and basic roles, there are many generic elements which should be common features in the organisation of all the banks. To deal effectively and expeditiously with the problems at the branch level, it is essential to evolve a more decentralised structure with an adequate system of control and coordination. This would need:

(a) A decentralised decision-making structure based on geographical units of varying sizes, ranging from branches through areas/ divisions/regions which operate as complete units of banking, disposing of a major part of the banking business at the lowest possible level within the overall framework of corporate policy and performance.

(b) A control system based on an agreed budgeting, performance review, and systematic communication and consultation. There should be an alignment between responsibility and authority with accountability for performance.

(c) Reduction in hierarchy and status-based structures with greater emphasis on team-building, committee system and consultative processes.

(d) A central office mainly devoted to policy formulation, planning, co-ordination and maintaining overall-control. This would require that the central office is free of routine transactional decision-making, these being effectively delegated to lower levels of the structure.

(e) Properly designed systems aimed at integrating the operations of the various functional and geographic units.

(f) Streamlined operating procedures geared to the needs of mass banking and quick and efficient customer service.

(g) Built-in arrangements in the organisation to ensure adequate development of managerial talent.

Keeping in tune with the changes in the scope and scale of the functional activities of the unit bank, the Head Office has to be oriented to meet its developmental and socio-economic obligations. Management is the most important problem in the banking industry, which deals in an intangible product called service; and the entire range of services marketed by banks, multifarious in nature as these are, is, by and large, the product of clerical activity.

The Board of Directors: Each bank, whether it is wholly-owned by the Government, a subsidiary of a bank or has been promoted by shareholders, is governed by a Board of Directors. The bank's statute determines the number of directors for each bank. These directors shoulder a high degree of responsibility. Shareholders, depositors, creditors, and regulatory authorities look to directors for policy decisions and management ability which will result in the safety of funds and profitable operations. Although the Board of Directors is not directly concerned with the day-to-day operations of the bank, for it delegates authority to various officers who, in turn, delegate authority to other employees, it is ultimately responsible for the success of the bank's operations.

Responsibilities of Bank Directors: Bank directors' responsibility is multifarious and multi-directional. The first responsibility is to the depositors of the bank. That is why they have to adopt a course of action that will be sound from the standpoint of the safety and liquidity of funds. They are also responsible to the shareholders, who are interested in a sound investment and a fair return. Finally, they are responsible to the various supervisory and regulatory agencies (the Government of India, the Reserve Bank of India) which are interested in the bank management that will result in the safety of the funds of the depositors and adequate banking service to the public.

Functions of the Board of Directors: In meeting their responsibilities to depositors, shareholders, the Government, the Reserve Bank of India and the public, the members of the Board of Directors of a bank have many functions, the performance of which varies considerably from bank to bank. The progress of a bank solely depends upon the quality and calibre of the Board of Directors.

Bank Objectives and Formulation of Bank Policies: The most important functions of a Board of Directors of a bank are the determination of bank objectives and the formulation of its policies. Objectives reflect the personality and image of a bank. It is mandatory to employ a sound policy to achieve the objectives. The term "Policy" refers to a planned course of action. With definite policies, the goal becomes concrete and comprehensible. Policies also give meaning to the objectives.

Supervision of Credit and Investments: The bank's Board of Directors is charged with the responsibility of seeing to it that the acts of lending and investing are carried out in accordance with the sound principles and in conformity with the regulatory banking laws. This involves a periodic review of the lending and investments portfolio.

Counselling: A very important function of the bank's Board of Directors is to give direction to the management (officers) of the bank which assists them in making decisions, and to bring new clients to the banking fold, i.e., depositors as well as borrowers.

The internal organisation varies from one bank to another, depending upon its size and its area of operations. Organisational charts are helpful in explaining the organisational structure of a bank.

Tasks Before the Central Office: The principal areas of the tasks of the central office are planning, policy-making, and control of circle performance, besides guiding local head offices and sanctioning very large advances. It has also to look after audit, investment, and research activities.

The executive director of the bank is the co-ordinating head for all operational functions. He relieves the chairman of ongoing operational responsibilities and enables him to concentrate on policy. The three general managers have complete functional control of banking operations, staff and services, and planning and research respectively. The general managers have under them a number of chief managers who look after the different areas of the bank's activities, such as individual market segments, personnel, premises, public relations, management science, economic research, etc. Here, too, as in the local head offices, the line and staff wings will have to constantly engage in mutual consultation if realistic policies are to be evolved and implemented.

Management Control System: In order that the bank management may be able to ensure that organisational objectives are achieved, it is necessary to institute a proper system of control. Consultants have recommended the introduction of a budgetary control system, so that a definite programme of action may be drawn up and implemented, and the bank's performance evaluated at regular intervals. The budget is the most widely used control device, for it incorporates, in numerical terms, the objectives, goals, and operational programmes of an enterprise. The performance budgeting system in the form of an annual plan for each branch, covers deposits, loans and advances, expenditure and profits in the different customer segments. A tentative budget is prepared by the branch manager, which is based on certain guidelines furnished by the circle management, after which it is finalised and accepted by the regional manager on the basis of personnel discussions. The final branch budgets together form the circle budget. The bank's annual plan is an aggregate of seven circle budgets.

In actual practice, planning starts at the central office, where the business expectations of the bank as a whole in the forthcoming year are carefully projected on the basis of various economic trends and other factors. These planned growth levels are then communicated to the local head offices which relate them to the local conditions obtaining in each circle. The overall circle expectations in each market segment are then determined (if necessary, after further consultation with the central office) and communicated to branches to serve as authoritative guidelines for the preparation of tentative budgets.

In a meeting of the top management of the bank just prior to the commencement of the budget period, the allocation of performance targets among the seven circles under the various heads of business are finally decided and accepted by the central office. It is against this final budget that the performance of each circle is evaluated at monthly intervals, and such remedial action is taken as is necessary to keep in line with predetermined standards. The performance of branches is, of course, similarly checked and appraised at regular monthly intervals, and deviations from the set goals are corrected by taking suitable measures.

Budget forms have been so designed as to ensure that the data on the past performance of a branch and critical environmental information (such as extent of industrialisation, population characteristics, etc.) are readily available in the forms themselves. These particulars are collected and

Chart 16.2

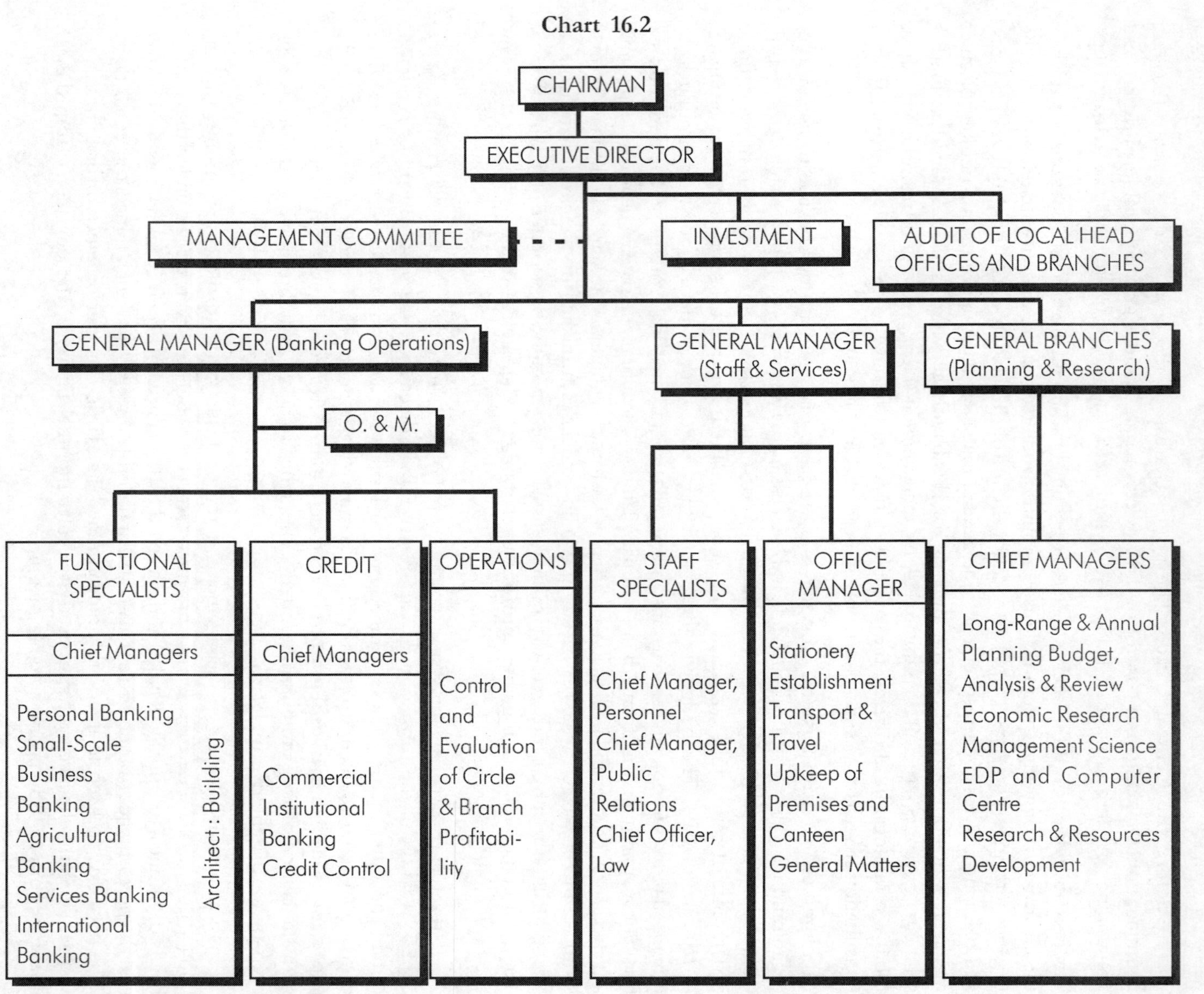
CHAIRMAN
EXECUTIVE DIRECTOR
MANAGEMENT COMMITTEE
INVESTMENT
AUDIT OF LOCAL HEAD OFFICES AND BRANCHES
GENERAL MANAGER (Banking Operations)
GENERAL MANAGER (Staff & Services)
GENERAL BRANCHES (Planning & Research)
O. & M.
FUNCTIONAL SPECIALISTS
Chief Managers
Personal Banking
Small-Scale Business Banking
Agricultural Banking
Services Banking
International Banking
Architect : Building
CREDIT
Chief Managers
Commercial
Institutional Banking
Credit Control
OPERATIONS
Control and Evaluation of Circle & Branch Profitability
STAFF SPECIALISTS
Chief Manager, Personnel
Chief Manager, Public Relations
Chief Officer, Law
OFFICE MANAGER
Stationery
Establishment
Transport & Travel
Upkeep of Premises and Canteen
General Matters
CHIEF MANAGERS
Long-Range & Annual Planning Budget, Analysis & Review
Economic Research
Management Science
EDP and Computer Centre
Research & Resources Development

incorporated in the forms by the branch manager before determining his business expectations. There is also a detailed form for reporting the performance of the branch at monthly intervals. The budgetary system thus provides various officials at the local head office as well as the branch manager and other operating personnel with an easy mechanism which facilitates a continuous watch on the progress of the actual performance in relation to pre-established operating plans. Moreover, the proposed budgetary system gives the operating personnel a sense of direction and confidence in developing business, a certain degree of freedom in running branches, and an assurance that results would necessarily be evaluated in the context of the availability of adequate resources.

Activities of the Local Head Offices

The local head office constitutes the second tier in the organisational structure of the bank. It is primarily established to strengthen the developmental functions of, and to co-ordinate and control, a group of branches within a compact area. The local head office is entrusted with the following activities:

(a) ***Planning:*** Formulating the strategy of business growth over specified periods in the context of such external factors as economic trends, Government policy, etc., and the optimal utilisation of internal resources of personnel, premises, etc.;

(b) ***Promotional Work:*** Determining policies, schemes, procedures, etc., for each customer-group with a view to exploiting the business potential;

(c) ***Specialist Services:*** Making available expert advice to managers at all levels on personnel, premises, law, and public relations; and

(d) ***Operations Control:*** Implementing and reviewing performance plans (through budgeting) allocating manpower and other resources, and generally administering branches.

Every regional manager should, apart from his own departmental setup, have area managers whose principal job will be to maintain a liaison with about 25 branch managers by frequent visits, and to guide them in discharging their responsibilities. The area managers are particularly effective in helping junior branch managers, who are placed in charge of the smaller branches, in improving their own managerial performance. By discussing with the branch manager some of the past decisions taken by him at the branch and generally reviewing these and other matters, the area superintendents offer a valuable counselling service to him in developing his decision-making capabilities. The area managers are, moreover, capable of eliciting useful information, based on an on-the-spot study and observation, for a realistic policy formulation at the local head office level.

Nature of Tasks at the Branch

It is evident that the nature of the tasks at the branch level is quite different from that in the controlling offices. The aim of the branch manager is, therefore, to achieve the following objectives:

(a) Sustained profits for the bank and to maintain its position of leadership in the banking industry;

(b) A deeper penetration and coverage of its markets by looking "outwards";

(c) A better control system for performance and co-ordination;

(d) A better delegation of work so that senior management is released from routine work for more futuristic tasks;

(e) A clearer perspective of objectives and tasks shared by all the employees of the bank;

(f) An adequate flexibility of the organisation to accommodate growth and rapid change; and

(g) The development of managers by the bank's administrative practices so that they may be able to cope with plans for rapid growth.

In keeping with the foregoing goals, the organisational set-up in branches is determined by the types of customers served, instead of the traditional grouping of work according to the nature of activities and services, such as deposits, loans and advances, remittance of funds, collection of cheques and other instruments. In other words, the bank's efforts should be geared to meeting the total range of banking needs of each of the various categories of customers. Customers are, therefore, classified into five major groups, viz.,

(a) Commercial and institutional customers, comprising the larger units engaged in trade and industry, and including institutions such as universities, clubs, societies, etc.;

(b) Individual customers;

(c) Small-scale industries and small business customers;

(d) Agriculturists; and

(e) Governments, State and Central.

How to make an Organisational Diagnosis

Organisational diagnosis technique involves asking questions like "where are we" in the life cycle of the organisation and "where we want to be?" Answers to these questions are not complete unless we give a prescription suggesting the steps involved in the process of organisational change, i.e., "how do we go about there?" The major steps involved in this change process, according to W.A.G. Branddick Butterworth (Management for Bankers), are given in Chart 16.5.

Conclusion

Managing a business is not just planning. It includes putting life into the plan by bringing together the executive personnel, workers, capital, machinery, materials, physical facilities and other things or services to execute the plans. When these resources are assembled, the enterprise comes to life. Organising involves determining and noting activities needed to fulfil the objectives, grouping these activities into manageable units or departments, and assigning such groups of activities to

Chart 16.3

ORGANISATION OF LOCAL HEAD OFFICES

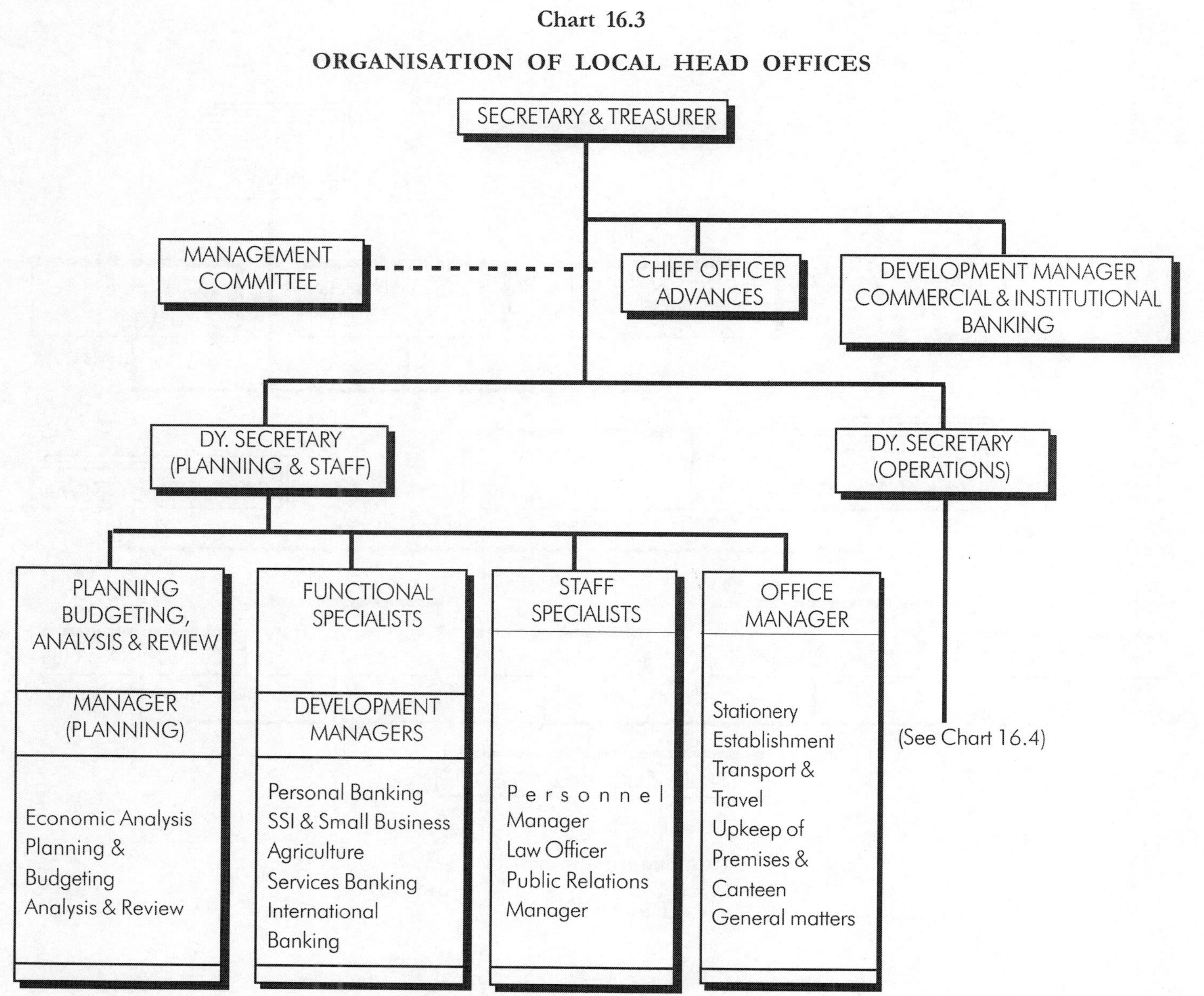

Chart 16.4

Operating Management

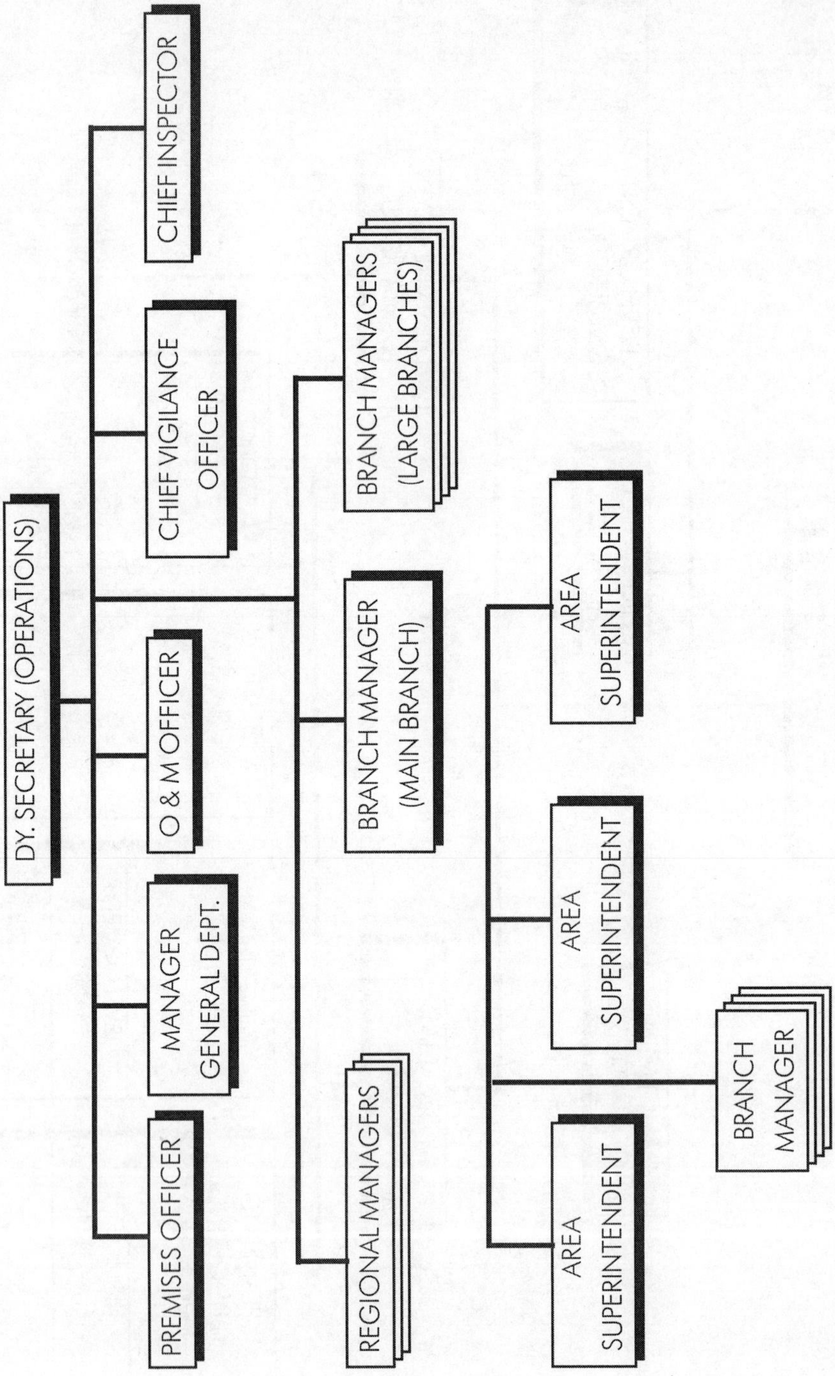

Chart 16.5

Organisational Change Process

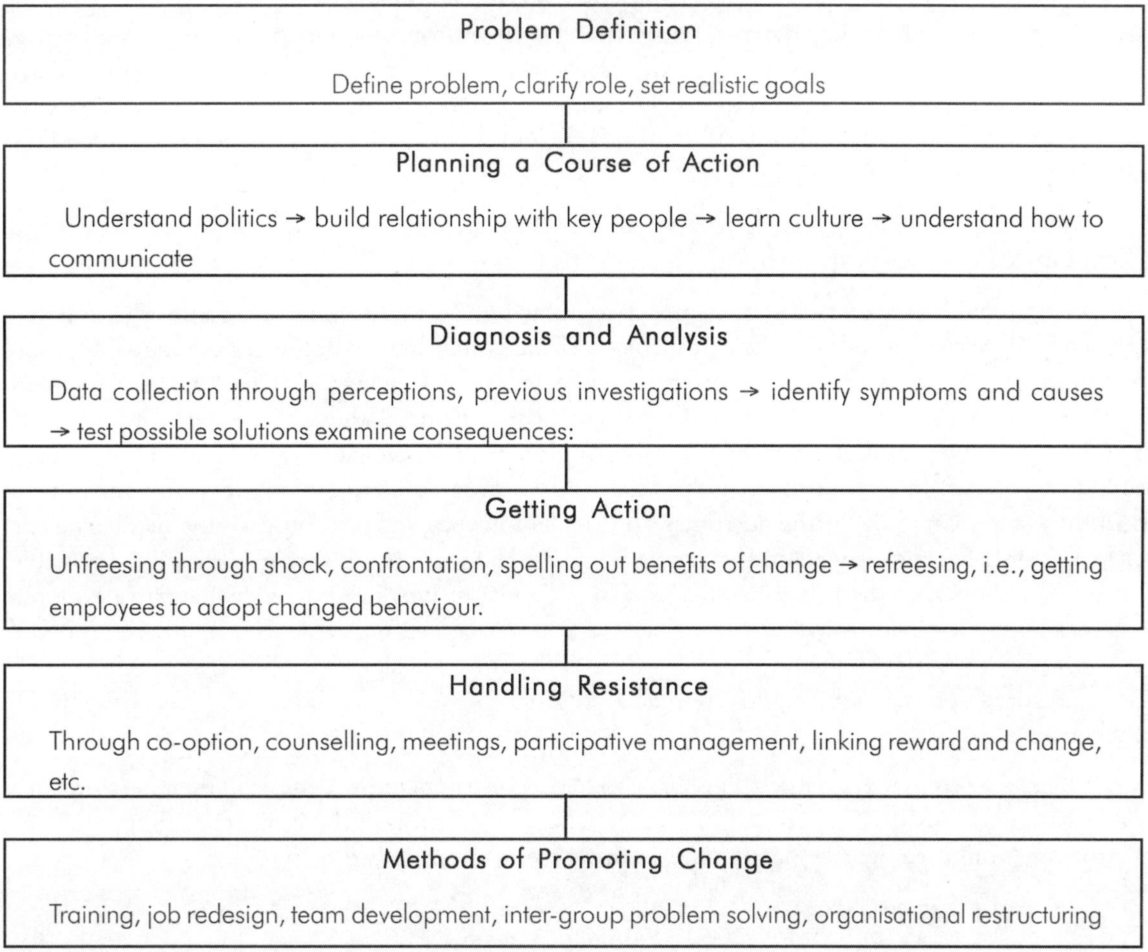

Problem Definition

Define problem, clarify role, set realistic goals

Planning a Course of Action

Understand politics → build relationship with key people → learn culture → understand how to communicate

Diagnosis and Analysis

Data collection through perceptions, previous investigations → identify symptoms and causes → test possible solutions examine consequences:

Getting Action

Unfreesing through shock, confrontation, spelling out benefits of change → refreesing, i.e., getting employees to adopt changed behaviour.

Handling Resistance

Through co-option, counselling, meetings, participative management, linking reward and change, etc.

Methods of Promoting Change

Training, job redesign, team development, inter-group problem solving, organisational restructuring

managers. Delegation of authority creates an organisation. It determines authority-responsibility relationship. These relationships must be properly co-ordinated to secure unity of organisation.

Organising provides a framework of management or a mechanism for purposive, integrated and co-operative action by many people in a joint effort to implement any plan. Planning decides what management wants to do, while organising provides an effective machine for achieving the plan or objectives. Under organising, we have mechanical as well as human aspects. Mechanical aspect provides an organisation structure or chart, describing the authority-responsibility relationship. Side by side with the formal organisation structure, we have also an informal or social organisation having unwritten conventions and code of conduct, and the manager has to integrate both these types in order to execute the plans and policies.

The form of organisation employed in banks is a line-and-staff type. The immediate management of a bank is entrusted to the senior officers of the bank under the chairman. However, the organisation of banks for management purposes varies considerably because of the differences in size, location, personalities and capabilities of officers and employees; the importance of different functions performed and services offered; and the work load of the bank. The number of employees also varies from one branch to another. The functional activities are departmentalised. It results in improved and expanded services rendered to customers, and specialisation on the part of the officers and employees leads to greater efficiency. The ultimate objective is to improve bank services and to reduce costs of operations. The amount and degree of departmentalisation vary with the size and work load of the bank. All banks, large and small, perform the same types of lending, investing, accounting and banking operations.

All in all, banks are organised, departmentalised and meet the demands of their customers and community in an efficient manner.

In any banking organisation, the impact of an activity, a philosophy or a value system is felt only if it is all-pervading and only the culture of excellence can bring about the desired transformation in achieving the enormous goals and objectives expected of us. Reluctance or apathy in any segment of the organisational associates can take the wind out sails. The need, therefore, is to involve the total strength at all levels and at every centre of operation to the "philosophy" of the origins of the banking organisation, its objectives, its policies and its programmes. The organisation's march to meet the rising aspirations of the customers, agents, employees, the government, the media and the citizens at large has to be constant, sustained and unrelenting. Then and then alone can it be possible for excellence to reach the horizons of perfection. To institutionalise, the banks have to develop a dynamic culture of their own. This culture should lead to openness, receptivity, sensitivity, and urge for excellence so as to keep the banking organisation dynamic and alert to the changing environment. Thus, the march on the path of perfection and excellence should be the avowed goal for the banks in the nineties.

Organisations as they go into future have to make consistent improvement in their performance for survival and growth. The catalyst of change would move around three pillars — improvement in processes, improvement in people and improvement in corporate culture.

The lean principles involve:

(a) Specifying **value** from the standpoint of the customer

(b) Identification of **value stream** for each product

(c) Removal of **non-value** added activities

(d) Making **value** flow towards the customer as quickly as possible

(e) At the **pull** of customer

(f) Striving for **perfection** in products and processes

And finally corporate culture is the ultimate in the overall change of organisations. Culture influences the behaviour of people that impacts performance and business results. Culture refers to behaviour pattern that people express during decision making process and implementation of decisions. The behaviour, i.e., supported, expected, reinforced and valued by a group of people over a long period of time. Corporate culture is thus an amalgam of shared values, beliefs, attitudes, behaviour patterns, the customary way of thinking and conducting the business. It also differentiates one organisation from the other. Thus, it creates a unique identity, generates commitment to a common objective, develops a sense of pride, acts as a social binder to keep people together and serves as a control mechanism to guide attitude and behaviour of an employee.

The desired corporate culture can thus be seen as an *intrapreneurship* which is a combination of *Entrepreneurship* and *Employeeship* which represents a unique type of commitment by every employee and company. Some pre-requisites for Intrapreneurship Culture in any organization are openness, honesty, trust, mutual respect, commitment and a genuine interest in helping each other. *Intrapreneurship* involves believing in breakthrough for improvement, development and innovation. Empowering employees with a strong sense of ownership with well defined roles, responsibilities and goals. It is strongly customer focused, flexible organisation, promoting growth of employees. Employees are not just seen as responsible for their results or work but also for development of their own competence and overall performance of organizations.

As the needs and expectations of customer change, quality of products and services of competitors improve, market forces get realigned and mood of people change, excellent companies wanting to retain their market leadership will renovate, reform, revamp... and in short change their corporate culture. The biggest challenge and success of banks will be in their ability to achieve successful integration of their processes, people and culture.

Chapter 17

Human Capital Management

Introduction

The Indian banking sector has been witnessing tremendous changes which have been driven by heightened competition, ever rising customer expectations and increasing use of technology. This transformation has brought to the fore the need for grooming the staff to face such volatile times. It requires much greater and relevant HR interventions to create a facilitating environment, nurture talent and retain the staff. Thus banks need to adopt a new way of looking at the HR function.

In fact, the stage is appropriate that HR function leverages the human strength and creates a best fit between organisational growth and human growth. In service industry like banks, the intangible assets, especially the human resources, contribute significantly to the building of shareholder value. The critical success factor for any knowledge based company is its highly skilled and intellectual workforce since no organisation can achieve anything without its people. Human resource management implies a strategic and coherent approach to the management of an organisation's people who individually and collectively contribute to the achievement of organisational goals. Thus maximization of shareholder value is paramount and this is best achieved by treating employees as valuable assets rather than as variable costs. Competitive advantage of the organization can be achieved only through harnessing the potential available in the employees by creating a positive work culture and ensuring a voluntary support of all the employees to the organisational goals. This in turn implies that there has to be a "strategic fit", i.e., human capital development strategies have to match with business strategy.

The transformed banking sector would expect the banks to be more creative, innovative and proactive if they are to sustain themselves and their success. They and their staff will need to manage rapid and complex changes. With the growing importance of knowledge economy around the globe, the importance of learning for both the organisation and the individual has become crucial for survival. The challenge before the managers is to be able to harness employees' initiative and commitment through appropriate support and direction. Further, retaining key employees is likely to be a major challenge in future for the banking sector. Banks wishing to retain their knowledge workers will need to address the issues of balance, flexibility, learning, careers as well as management development. They will also need to find ways of turning knowledge gained to competitive advantage through the development of human capital.

The liberalisation and deregulation in the financial services sector along with the rapid advancements in computing and communication technologies coupled with the foreign competition has brought in sea-change in the banks.

The new economic paradigm characterized by speed, innovation, short cycle times, and quality and customer satisfaction is highlighting the importance of information-centred assets, such as technologies, brands, workforce skills, and strategic relationships. New workforce practices like team based work, cross functional integration and supplier partnerships are slowly evolving. There has been an all round change in employer-employee relationship. The evolving style of functioning indeed differs from that of even the recent past in many ways. For instance, the growth of technology has had two significant effects on the workforce of banks.

- One, technology has reduced the sphere of activity for semi-skilled labour; and
- Two, with the diversification of banks beyond their core area under a highly competitive environment, existing workforce is under pressure to deliver multiple tasks.

Consequently, there is increasing pressure on banks to impart multifarious training to employees. But on the other hand there is also quick obsolescence of imparted training due to rapidly changing nature of banking technology. In such an atmosphere it is imperative that human resources are valued and their utility assessed at every point of time. The current emphasis is on developing human resources which can contribute to sustained competitive advantage by facilitating the development of competencies that are firm specific.

Human Capital

The term human capital refers to the recognition that people in an organisation is an important asset who contribute to the development and growth of the business, in the same way as other physical assets do. Thus the collective skills, abilities and expertise of the people in the organisation contribute to the performance and productivity.

Human Resources (HR), at one time, used to be a drab, secondary function, typically manned by people whose main job was to keep track of employees' payroll, leave and sundry mundane activities. Now, though, HR is as critical to a company as any other function. That's because HR is now actively involved in fashioning career paths for employees, improving their skill sets, and honing in on and developing leaders for the future who can take the company forward. After all, it takes more than just good strategy to make a company a success.

All this has been made possible due to the evolution of technology tools, particularly Human Capital Management (HCM) solutions, that have automated the mundane activities almost totally, and allowed the HR department to play a more strategic, thinking role.

It is now well-recognised that people are the key to success in any service industry. Banking is a large organisation having a massive work force. The work force in the banks has the competence and capability to innovate not only in the area of product development and service sophistication,

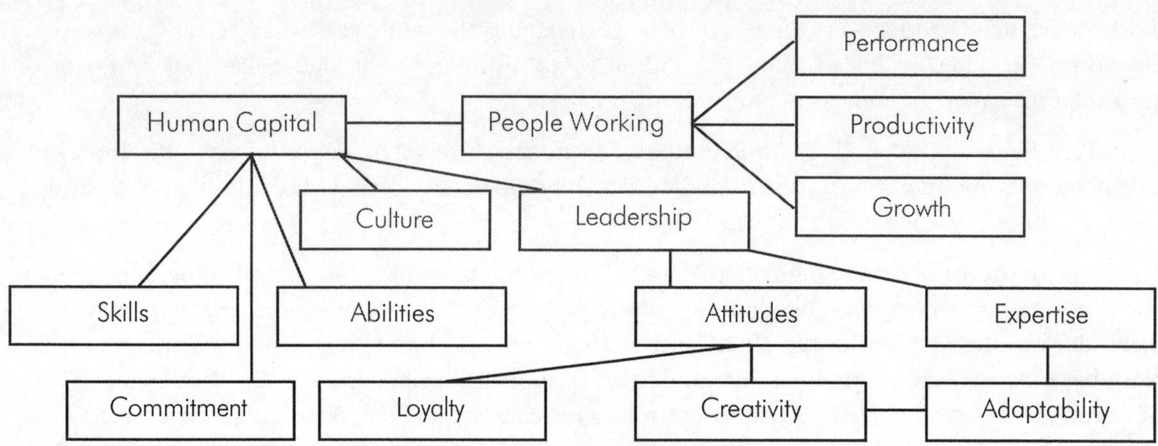

but also in the area of enhancing the image of the organisation. The markets are growing global; consumers' expectations have also heightened. With easy exchange of technology, homogenisation of products and services is bound to surface. It is only the human element that would possibly make a difference and help the organisation to succeed. The focus should be on human resources development and channelising it for productive purposes.

Why HRD?

HRD (Human Resource Development) as a process helps employees of an organisation in a continuous and planned way to:

- acquire or sharpen capabilities;
- develop their general capabilities as individuals and discover and exploit their potential for their own and/or organisational development purposes;
- develop an organisational culture in which team-work, relations and collaborations are strong;
- make both the individual and the organisation more effective and strong.

HRD as a system, seeks to develop individuals working in an organisation as "organisational men." HRD as process helps an organisation on an ongoing basis to:

- build managerial resources of quality and leadership;
- inculcate an effective team work culture;
- create value systems that are conducive to growth;
- motivate people to bring innovation in their work culture and extent prompt service;
- creating a sense of belonging.

Redefining HR

The world over, HCM solutions are mostly built into a larger ERP (enterprise resource planning) framework. A recent survey conducted by Aberdeen Group and the Human Capital Institute brings out some interesting numbers:

- 22 per cent of HR executives will purchase employee and managerial self-service applications within the next months.
- 96 per cent outsource some portion of their HR solutions today (38 per cent use ADP; 21 per cent Ceridian).
- 40 per cent manage HR with ERP solutions (Oracle, SAP, People Soft, or JD Edwards).

The numbers, though, are not a major surprise, given the business benefits that IT tools bring to the table. Some examples:

- **Improved corporate performance:** Align your workforce with business objectives, and ensure that every employee understands and acts upon those objectives.
- **Optimised development and use of talent:** Find the best people and leverage their talent in the right place and right time. Identify and track high-potential employees to ensure future leaders are identified for key positions.
- **Cost-effective compliance and administration:** Reduce the cost and effort of complying with local regulations through features and functions, support structures and expertise.
- **Global and local coverage:** Enable flexible processes that balance global demands with local needs.
- **Improved employee satisfaction:** Build better relationships with employees through personalised self-services, e-learning and e-recruiting applications, and more flexible compensation and reward models.
- **Improved decision-making:** Integrate HCM information and processes into the core of your business to provide line managers and executives with the means to make better decisions.
- **Scalability and support that lower risk:** Adapt your processes quickly to changing business needs with a flexible, scalable solution.
- **Proven return on investment:** Transform your HR function, lower costs and improve service.
- **Opportunities for value-added activities:** Streamline all HCM processes and free employees to concentrate on value-generating activities rather than on routine tasks.

A Valuable Asset

People are not a liability. They are a potential asset. Dr. Mahbub Haq observes that, "the end of development is to expand human capabilities and to provide opportunities for the full use of human potential, to enlarge the range of choices at the disposal of the people. Besides income and employment, these choices include better health, more education, cleaner physical environment, greater community participation and a democratic framework of personal and political freedom." It is essential today that banks should prepare their own human development strategies and reflect them in their plan and budget framework. Sustainable human development must move to the top of the bank's priority agenda for the year 2,000 A.D.

Top Challenges Designated by HR Executives

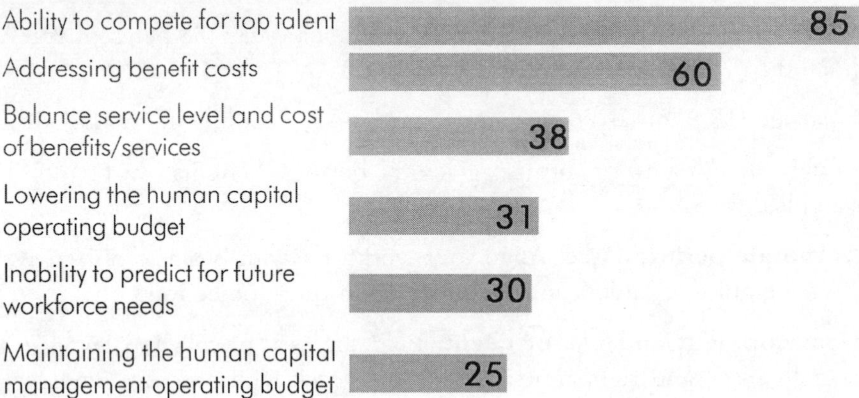

Figures are per cent of respondents in a Human Capital Institute/Aberdeen Group survey of 98 HR executives.

Source: Aberdeen Group, September 2005.

Current Use & Procurement Plans for HCM Applications

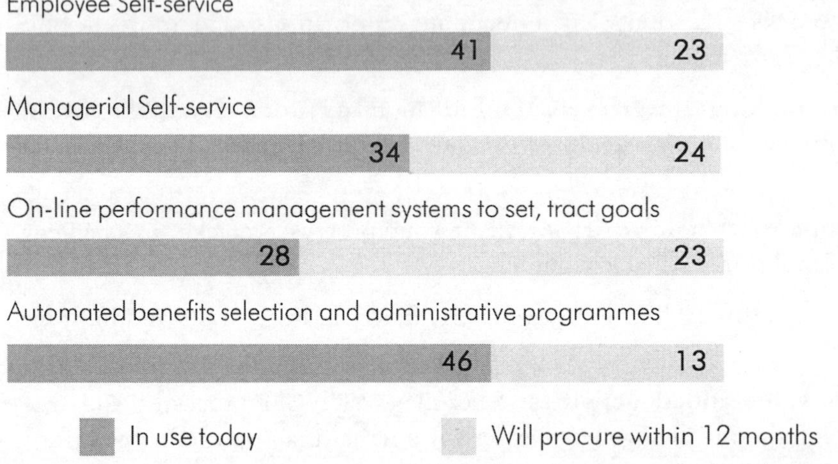

Figures are per cent of respondents in a Human Capital Institute/Aberdeen Group survey of 98 HR executives.

Source: Aberdeen Group, September 2005.

Constituents of Human Resources

Human resources constitute the principal asset of an organisation. They consist of the total knowledge, skills, creative abilities, talents and aptitudes of an organisation's work force as well as the values, attitudes and beliefs of the individuals involved in them. They are the sum total of the inherent abilities, acquired knowledge, skills represented by the talents and aptitudes of the employees.

The quantity and quality of human resources of an organisation thus become their edifice. An organisation such as a bank, industry or government can only be as strong as the people manning it are at various levels. It is, therefore, obvious that any organisation interested in real and rapid progress should exercise particular care about the personnel manning the posts at the various levels. One of the important and dynamic activities is the management of people, of the human resources. Management of human resources is the heart and soul of a manager. It is a challenging task because of the dynamic and unpredictable nature of the people. The employees should be equipped to handle their jobs effectively. They should also be given opportunities to expand their knowledge and thus extend its utility to other jobs so that they may develop themselves and get equipped to handle higher responsibilities efficiently.

Measurable Benefits

The benefits are not abstract, intangible ones; they are measurable, and show how HCM solutions can result in significant savings for companies across the globe. Some examples:

- US-based IT major Dow Coming's HR work-force has been reduced by approximately 60 per cent, savings attributable to the organisational management business process was $2.3 million, and the cost-savings attributable to the personnel administration business process was $2.7 million. Then, transaction times for personnel administration business processes were brought down from 10 business days per transaction to a remarkable three days.
- The world's #2 brewer, South Africa's SAB Limited, streamlined its HCM business processes and systems, and projected a 10-year savings of 8.24 million euros.
- Canada-based TransAlta, a leading North American utilities company, realised significant cost and time savings with HCM, projecting an ROI of 102 per cent, with a 10-year annual savings of CAD$31 million.

With numbers like that to show, it is no wonder that according to AMR Research, over the next five years, the HCM solutions market will grow the second fastest (8.3 per cent), second only to strategic sourcing (12 per cent), and ahead of customer relationship management (CRM, at 7.6 per cent). Keeping the employee, it appears, is now as critical as keeping the customer.

Quality and Utilisation of Human Resources

The success of any organisation depends on the quality of its human resources. Studies in the growth pattern of advanced countries have shown that improvements in the quality and utilisation of personnel have been a major factor in accelerating the pace of economic growth. It is the effectiveness of the human system, therefore, that differentiates successful, dynamic and progressive organisations from the others. As noted by Thomas J. Peters and Robert H. Waterman in their management classic, *In Search of Excellence:*

"Treat people as adults. Treat them as partners; treat them with dignity; treat them with respect. Treat them — not capital spending and automation — as the primary source of productivity gains. These are the fundamental lessons from the excellent companies' research. In other words, if you want productivity and the financial reward that goes with it, you must treat your workers as your most important asset."

"There was hardly a more pervasive theme in the excellent companies than respect for the individual. That basic belief and assumption were omnipresent. But like so much else we have talked about, it is not any one thing — one assumption, belief, statement, goal, value, system, or program — that makes the theme come to life. What makes it live at these companies is a plethora of structural devices, systems, styles and values, all reinforcing one another so that the companies are truly unusual in their ability to achieve extraordinary results through ordinary people."

BOX 17.1

WHAT SMART EXECUTIVES DO

- Use time efficiently. Jot down a day plan in your diary and stick to it.
- De-clutter. Clear each day's e-mail then and there and handle today's tasks now before they become too big.
- Delegate. What's the point of having a team if you have to do everything yourself?
- If your company provides flexi-time and work at home options, make full use of them.
- Family time is sacrosanct. Go for your kid's Sportsday before he grows out of his childhood and you find you have missed it all.
- Don't let peer pressure get to you. Just because a colleague has a nicer car or a bigger house, it doesn't mean that you should also plunge into a 17-hour work day.
- If you can afford to, switch off the phone and the Blackberry after work.
- Spend time with yourself. Find a hobby, plug in the iPod, hit the gym and take annual vacations religiously.

Changing People

Change of people has always been a more tempting proposition than bringing about change in people. This is where HRD has a vital task to perform. Much has been said and written about bringing about a change of attitude in people. The ironical aspect of it is that at each level of the organisation, they feel that all others need to change except themselves. The task of HRD is to help focus the analysis on one's own self and the factors impeding the change rather than worrying about how to change others!

Even Indian scriptures have precisely emphasised this point. Emphasis on values will go a long way in this regard. According to Prof. S. K. Chakraborty, who has researched extensively into the Indian methods, some of the most widespread and perverse human response syndromes in Indian organisations today are a restless quest for self-centred need satisfaction, without giving back much to the organisation; the common tendency to lament over the alleged absence of any zone of discretion in one's own work environment for making self-motivated changes; the disquieting lack of sanctity about promises made in the course of work; and the pathetic toll of regionalism, linguistic parochialism and the like in all types and sizes of organisations.

External and Internal Pressures for Change

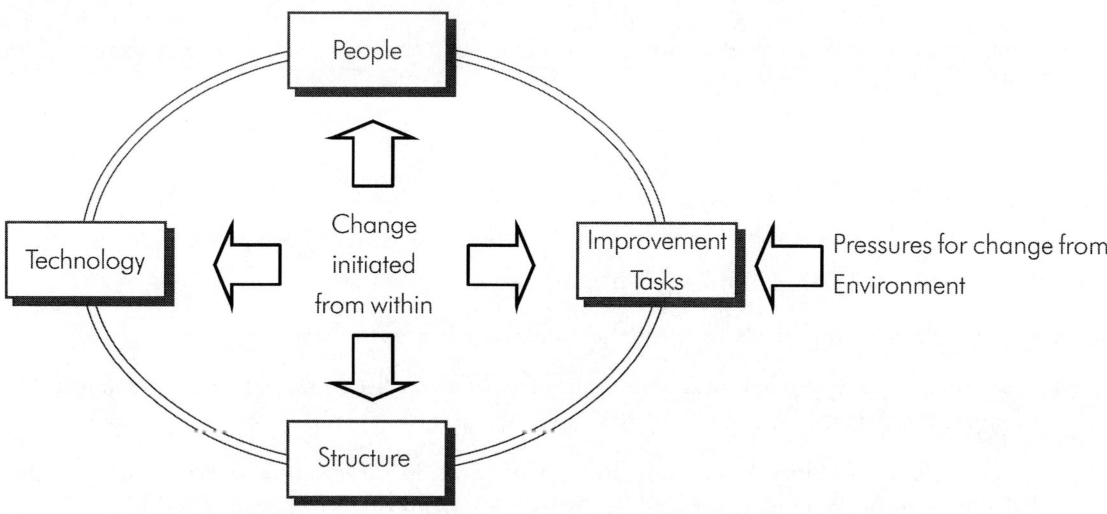

Fig 17.1 Aspects of Change

Talking about human response, he adds that Indian culture and value-systems are like a three-layered cake. The visible top layer of social infirmities and normlessness is not the place to seek for remedies. It is in the out-of-view but deeper layers of psycho-philosophical theories and principles that the answers have to be sought. The Japanese success in managing its economy and enterprises is entirely rooted in those very social and psychological values. Many of these value systems also form an important part of the core of Indian culture too; for example, respect for the head of the family, hierarchical relationships, relevance of seniority, paternalism as a cohesive social bond and the, like. Therefore, there is an urgent need for greater inquiry by HRD specialists into the Indian psycho-philosophical system based on which the HRD strategies can be properly formulated. This alone will give an answer to the nagging question of motivation of people for change.

BOX 17.2

WHAT SMART EXECUTIVES DO

You will have a realistic and enjoyable learning experience, where you actually manage a multimillion company and benefit with:

- Understanding the cross-functional relationships among various management functions.
- Exposure of running a company in a simulated environment without causing damage to a live company.
- Honing operative and strategic decision-making skills under constraints of time, finances and information.
- Understanding the financial implications of the decisions taken.
- Helping in finding and employing the available information for the data analysis of their own and competitor's business.
- Understanding the importance of team work under trying business situations and above all.
- Getting a synoptic view of a company's operations and experience the thrill of running a company in a competitive environment.

Advantages of HRD

The advantages of managing the human resources are many. In fact, a careful examination would reveal the following advantages:

(a) It will help the banks to reach the set goals.

(b) It will help to effectively utilise the skills and abilities of the work force.

(c) It will help to provide the banks with motivated and developed employee potential.

(d) It will help to develop employee job satisfaction.

(e) It will help the employees to meet their self-actualisation needs.

(f) It will help to develop and maintain the quality of work life, rendering employment in the organisation a highly merited and desirable occupation.

(g) It will help to develop desirable behaviour patterns in the employees which will in turn help them to become better social beings thus enabling them to develop and maintain the quality of life itself.

(h) It will help to effect and manage change to the advantage of the individuals, groups, the organisation and the society.

It can thus be seen that effective management of the human resources will not only provide motivated and efficient work force which will help achieve the organisational goals but will also enable them to become more functional citizens, thus improving the social set-up itself.

What is Human Resources Development?

HRD is defined as "activities and processes undertaken by an organisation to promote the intellectual, moral, psychological, cultural, social and economic development of the individuals in an organisation, in order to help them to achieve the highest human potential as a resource for the community." It means to bring about a 'total all-round development' of the people so that they can contribute their best to the organisation, community, society and the nation. HRD does not cover only a set of mechanisms or techniques but it is a process by which employees in an organisation are helped in a planned way to:

(a) acquire or sharpen capabilities required to perform the various functions associated with their present or expected future roles;

(b) develop their general capabilities as individuals and discover and exploit their own inner potentials for their own and/or organisational development purposes; and

(c) develop an organisation culture in which superior-subordinate relationships, team work and collaboration among sub-units are strong and contribute to the professional well-being, motivation and pride of employees.

The human resources development (HRD) concept is much wider and embraces almost all areas of an organisation. In the context of banking, HRD would mean not only the acquisition of knowledge and skills but also acquiring capabilities to anticipate and manage both internal and external environment and attaining self-confidence and motivation for public service. Further, HRD is not a piecemeal or a one-time exercise; it is a continuous process requiring to keep pace with the changes and developments taking place.

Environmental Role of HRD

HRD environment essentially means such actions, tendencies and commitments which support the following:

Openness and Risk-Taking: Employees feel free to express their ideas and the organisation is willing to take risks.

Collaboration: Employees collaborate with each other and have a feeling of belonging to the same family.

Trust and Authenticity: Employees, departments and groups (union/ associations and management) trust each other and can be relied upon.

Proactivity: Employees are action-oriented, willing to take initiative.

Autonomy: Employees have some freedom to act independently within the boundaries of their role/job.

Confrontation: Employees face problems and issues without hiding or avoiding them for fear of meeting each other.

HRD Process

The HRD process, under a systems approach, constitutes as subsystems, which together form a network of organisational action, leading to the desired goals. Some of these sub-systems are Manpower Planning, Recruitment Placement, Training, Performance Appraisal, Career planning, Organisational Development, Feedback, Counselling, Job-rotation or Role Analysis.

With the aid of these sub-systems and the overall climate-creating endeavour, the organisation would fulfil its role and responsibility in the process of helping employees acquire skills and competencies.

Evolution of HRD in Banks

In the early sixties, the new concepts of personnel management were being experimented in India by some of the enlightened managements, based on the successful experiments carried out by companies in Europe and the U.S.A. after the Second World War to overcome the problem of surpluses and stagnation arising out of a fall in demand and therefore, profits. Multinational companies having their network in India also introduced personnel management techniques they had adopted successfully in their home countries. Naturally, the banks could not have remained unaffected for long by such environmental changes taking place all round.

The first signs of these changes were seen in the mid-and late sixties. The banks started setting up Personnel Departments. Some of them engaged professionals with personnel background to work in these departments. With the expansion of branches gaining momentum, lack of experienced personnel became a serious handicap. To equip the existing as well as the new staff for manning the new branches, it became necessary to arrange for their training, both in class room as well as at the desk. So projects for opening training schools and training colleges were taken up. The banks also streamlined on-the-job training by formulating structured programmes for rotation of desks for trainees.

The two awards, viz., Sastry Award and Desai Award and the First Bipartite Settlement at the industry level, had brought about considerable improvement in the service conditions of bank employees. As a result, bank jobs became quite attractive. In the forties and fifties, people were reluctant to take up bank jobs due to long working hours, lack of security and low remuneration. At present, however, bank employees' pay and perquisites are one of the best in India. Besides, their working hours are fixed and there is security of service.

Due to rapid expansion, a lot of additional staff was required. The number of candidates applying for new jobs was very large. It was not possible to handle such a large number of recruits in the traditional way. So, gradually, the concept of zonal recruitment, all-India recruitment, objective tests etc. developed.

As the employees' unions got more organised and it became necessary to have continuous dialogue with them to sort out various staff problems, the need for separating the industrial relations function was felt. Many banks employed specialists to man these departments. In the early seventies, the management institutes in the country had started producing a good number of specialists in the area of personnel management and industrial relations. Many of these young graduates found their way to banks.

After the personnel administration and industrial relations were professionalised in banks, the concept of HRD got attention of the bank managements. It was felt that it was not enough to recruit good employees, have effective personnel administration and maintain satisfactory industrial relations. It was also necessary to ensure that employees were treated as the most important resource in the organisation and received all the care and attention throughout their stay in the organisation. As the machines require continuous lubrication and other maintenance, as it has to be ensured that material is stored properly and is rotated regularly so that it does not deteriorate, it was felt necessary that human resources are also looked after well. It gradually dawned upon the bank managements that human resources was not only the most important resource but was also the most expensive and most delicate resource which required very gentle handling. Human resources is the only resource which has feelings and a behaviour pattern which is not easy to predict. Hence the need for special care.

With these developments, the banks started setting up HRD Departments and some have even taken encouraging initiatives in this area.

This is more especially true of banking as it is essentially a 'people's business' and improvements in service and quality of work as also the commitment towards social and developmental policies of government, will largely depend on the attitudes and calibre of its employees at different levels. It is for this reason that all organisations including the banking institutions have started laying much greater emphasis on the development of the most important resource, i.e., 'Human Resources', and the Human Resource Development (HRD) has become an important corporate philosophy over the past few years. In fact 'HRD' has emerged as a profession in itself with tremendous relevance to the service sector like banking. The emphasis of HRD is not only on production and productivity, but also on the overall quality of work life.

In so far as HRD is concerned, it is a multi-faceted process involving areas like selection, placement, induction, training, objective performance appraisal, career planning and potential development. It also includes areas like motivation and development of the entire work force within an organisation. It not only aims to provide knowledge and skills to employees but also brings about changes in the attitudes of people with a view to developing them. HRD policies and exercises within an organisation help the individual employees in sharpening their existing capabilities and acquiring new capabilities. In fact, an effective HRD policy enables an individual to improve his overall personality and career prospects and helps him to perform existing and future roles effectively. It also develops a sense of belonging of the employees towards the organisation and society and a commitment to work. In the Indian context, commercial banks have given their major thrust on training.

BOX 17.3

MARCHINEG WITH A SMILE

H.G.Wells once said, "The crisis of today is the joke of tomorrow." Indeed today's daunting problems often seem trivial when viewed in retrospect. So why not take the trials and tribulations at the workplace with a pinch of salt and match on with a smile?

Here are a few tips to get you off the starting blocks:

- Encourage staff to laugh with each other and not at each other by sharing jokes or humorous anecdotes during a coffee break or amidst a stressful situation.
- Diffuse the tension or animosity with a 'difficult' or 'hostile' employee by going for the 'jocular' instead of the 'jugular.' A light-hearted comment rather than a heated argument can make the sternest of men crumble at times.
- Make the office a fun place rather than a dull, humourless space devoid of colour and comedy. Put up a notice board for jokes or funny stories in the recreation room and greet the sound of laughter from employees with applause rather than disapproval.
- Join in the fun! Being on top can be a lonely place with awesome responsibility and tensions. There's nothing like 'letting your hair down' with employees so that they feel the boss is a guy with emotions and not just a dictatorial figure.

HRD For Women Employees

Women are making their presence felt on the banking scene. The percentage of women to total employees is on the increase. But while there appears to be a confident and gradual march of the first generation of competent female executives, there are also a large number of women clerks who forgo promotional opportunities because promotion entails transfer and uprooting of their family lives. Women officers' enthusiasm is also dampened due to male attitudes. Banks as employers also feel that although women employees are bright and hard-working, they pose special problems due to high absenteeism and by rejecting promotions and transfers.

Against this backdrop, the real HRD of women employees means an understanding of the unique problems faced by women as a category and a search for bold innovative alternatives which can result in assimilation and growth of this resource. It is necessary to explore the concern for women employees at clerical and officer levels and to identify organisational mechanisms which can respond appropriately.

The problems of women relating to their 'dual role demands', transfer and promotion problems, social isolation at work, stereotyped and attitudinal barriers, sex labelling and lack of proper guidance are some of the problems faced by women employees in banks. Banks appear to have ignored the unique problems faced by women and women employees have been left to their own limited individual resources to grapple often unsuccessfully with these problems. HRD for women employees in its true sense entails a concern for these problems faced by women employees and a proactive organisational stance to help female employees overcome obstacles to their growth.

Developing proper data on women in banks, different and suitable career paths, creating awareness on women-related problems and skills training to all employees, mentorship for women and childcare are some of the areas which need early attention. And unless banks cultivate a developmental concern for their women employees and act now, problems will worsen as more women enter banks. Banks need to undertake some radical measures to enable their women employees to grow within the bank as its valued members.

Prerequisites to HRD

Before introducing HRD in a bank, it is therefore necessary to study the culture and tradition of its own, and create an HRD climate, which is done by stressing the importance of developing people, creating effective teams, solving problems by bringing these in the open and working together to find solutions to the problems. HRD climate can also be created by exposing most employees in the bank to the general approach of HRD and helping them understand the concept of HRD. And once the climate is created, it is advisable to create HRD spirit by laying emphasis on the development of individuals through the help of their supervisors. Reorganising the training systems, introducing appraisal system in phases are the next stages in the process of HRD introduction. It is useful to prepare a systematic plan like a PERT Chart for the entire HRD system to be introduced.

Role of Top Management in HRD

HRD is an integral part of every manager's responsibility and need not be looked upon merely as the responsibility of the corporate office or the personnel department. The top management, the HRD personnel and the branch managers have their respective roles in promoting HRD in banks. The role of top management in HRD is described in the following ten points:

(1) Developing HRD corporate policy.

(2) Developing congruent top management leadership style.

(3) Action planning for HRD.

(4) Appointment of competent persons for HRD functions.

(5) Examining appraisal systems.

(6) Starting Organisation Development (OD) exercises.

(7) Developing training policy.

(8) Developing HRD climate.

(9) Developing HRD personnel.

(10) Exercising patience with HRD.

A management innovation like HRD can be initiated and institutionalised only with a deep commitment and involvement of the topmost managers. But between the acceptance of the idea and its institutionalisation lies the process of giving shape, flesh, blood and life to it. This part is generally left to the HRD managers within an organisation whose main roles are:

(1) *Supportive role play* which calls for the preservation of existing strengths of an organisation as building strength is a major way to develop individuals and organisations.

(2) *Systems development and research,* which means to continuously undertake research to understand the needs of the people and the organisation and make the necessary review and modifications of existing systems and also to develop new ones.

(3) *Developing competencies* not only in the two traditional areas of technical and managerial competence but also behavioural competence in terms of conflicts, problems of commitment, co-operation and related matters.

(4) *Process role,* which means to develop capability in the organisation to cope with several important dimensions like growth and expansion of organisation, impact of outside forces, etc. It is within this role that falls the task of creating a desirable culture and values within the organisation, diagnosing problems in various parts and designing and facilitating interventions to make the organisation more capable of handling its problems with greater confidence and innovativeness.

Developing HRD awareness in the organisation is the primary role of HRD managers. Their secondary role is to shape, delineate and develop a role for themselves. This is followed by diagnosing organisational problems from the HRD viewpoint. And lastly, to educate people in the organisation about the potential of HRD. The roles of HRD managers will obviously vary at corporate, zonal/regional and at the branch levels.

The most important agent in developing human resources in any bank is the branch manager. Just as the effectiveness of any bank depends on the collective effectiveness of its branches, the effectiveness of HRD function also depends on the collective effectiveness of its branch manager as agent for developing the branch staff. Most of the banks today have excellent training facilities provided by their training institutions. But while training institutions do well in imparting the necessary job knowledge and technical skills, they are not able to develop the right kind of attitudes, motivation and work culture in the bank employees. This is mainly because attitudes, motivation and work culture get influenced and developed much more in the work place than in a training institution. Given this limitation of the training institution, it becomes the responsibility of the leadership at the work place to take care of these more complex areas.

A branch is the first place where every employee of a bank begins his work life and gets socialised. A branch is the main and most important agent of socialising a bank employee and inducting him into its culture. Therefore, the branch becomes an important place for developing employee motivation, attitude and work culture and the branch leadership plays a crucial role in HRD.

Managing Complexity

Managing Human Resources in a Dynamic and customer driven environment has its own set of challenges. What becomes critical in such an environment is the easy availability of information, which helps HR make intelligent decisions based on their resources over the long term. The challenge for such a system is to be robust enough to cover various facets of the employees. Apart from that it should provide single-window, role-based access to various users of the system. The system over and above this should be able to support analysis of the information for planning and identifying development needs.

SAP HCM (Human Capital Management) is a solution built keeping in mind the specific challenges of your industry and therefore adapts to the requirements based on the needs of your organisation. It helps you manage the service perspective by better aligning employees to business strategy. It gives your employees easy access to their information, thereby reducing the administrative burden of the HR department, and finally it addresses the organisation's requirements by providing metrics and analysis to meet customer expectations and also align them to employee SLAS.

Managing Talent

Acquiring quality talent and developing it is critical in today's business. SAP HCM identifies and develops a talent pool and provides means and ways to maintain communication with this pool of candidates. And internally, talent management can be used to manage the internal employees.

Using talent management as the fundamental building block, SAP HCM helps organisations plan for training, individual development plans and appraisals that are aimed at improving efficiency, while ensuring progressive development happens for employees.

BOX 17.4

WHAT COMPANIES CAN DO

In a survey conducted by the Association of Executive Search Consultants, 87% of respondents felt that work-life balance considerations were critical in their decision to join, or remain with an employer. And 53% said that they hadn't achieved satisfactory work-life balance. Some respondents were even willing to "down-size both their salaries and their prospects within large organisations in favour of quality of life." These findings pertain to the US but they increasingly hold true for India as well. Is there anything that companies can do to make things easier for employees? Perhaps yes, and a handful of companies have already started taking steps in this direction.

Enabling environment: IBM has a flexi-time policy and allows employees work-from-home options. That means providing broadband access at home, laptops, phones, the works. Others like Texas Instruments has a counselling helpline for employees.

Connect with families: For 15 years, A.G. Krishnamurthy, former chairman and MD, Mudra Communications, and now chairman of AGK Brand Consulting, would send the families of Mudra employees a Diwali gift with a personal note recognising the employee's contribution and thanking the family for enabling it. The idea being that the family will be more supportive of the employee's work.

HR Initiatives: There are other simple things that HR departments can implement. For example, at UBS India, leave is non-encashable, forcing people to utilise it. Says the company's executive director (HR), P.N.S.V. Narasimham, "We are trying to send the message that we value your personal life. We also force employees to take at least 10 days off at a stretch." The idea is simple: if they have to take 10 days off in a bunch, they will be forced to take a vocation — and will be able to unwind. Once in five years, employees can take a sabbatical for one-two months.

The system would also help in deployment of resources based on various parameters like skills, requirements and workload, and suggest the optimum fit for a particular task. The system also helps in setting up compensation structures and guidelines, which can be effectively used to manage employee compensation.

Developing motivation means getting every employee filled with a desire to perform well the tasks assigned to him and getting them to work hard and work with the right kind of attitudes towards the branch, the bank, towards objectives of the bank, towards its clients and similar other matters.

With this understanding of HRD at the branch level, the role of branch manager in this exercise becomes very crucial. Some of the important roles of a branch manager in this direction are:

(i) development of styled leadership role,

(ii) creating HRD climate in the branch,

(iii) developing a family culture in the branch,

(iv) inducting new employees, socialising them and creating a good work culture,

(v) managing the boundary role — ability to contain shocks received from the top so as to maintain a high level of morale in his subordinates,

(vi) performance appraisal, development and counselling,

(vii) grievance handling and maintaining good relations with employees.

Review of Performance

For human resources development in banks, the following aspects would need active consideration:

The *first step* in the implementation of the HRD concept is to review the performance of employees at fixed intervals, say, once or twice in a year and pick up a percentage of promising persons with the definite purpose of grooming them for holding higher management posts in the coming years.

Depending upon the aptitude of each employee, the *next step* would be to plan the nature of the exposure to be given to each employee. It is needless to stress that an individualised approach is a must, and stereotyped training is not what is called for. Some people may have to be deputed to external specialised organisations for adequate training whereas a few others could be groomed with in-house training programmes. In either case, job exposure is a must, so that the selected employees can have a feel of the higher responsibilities they may have to shoulder in due course. This could well be achieved by special workshops organised in simulated working conditions.

By integrating performance appraisal with future promotions, a major breakthrough has been achieved, especially with regard to the attitude of the appraisees towards it. Still it requires a great attitudinal change in the employees who have to accept and seek merit-based promotions and extricate themselves from the web and security of the programmed patterns of seniority-based promotions and the accompanying work culture and standards.

Need for Training Systems Training in Banks

The banking scenario is undergoing a metamorphosis and the industry is facing many a challenge. The new challenges call for appropriate changes in the perceptions and attitudes of the staff at all levels. Therefore, if the banking system is to effectively cope with these, it will have to adopt a proactive approach through initiation of steps to ensure that the HRD/ training system is adequately reinforced through appropriate streamlining of the training strategies and training techniques. The policy makers and senior level managerial personnel should be made aware that 'continuous training/ retraining is perhaps the only available means to effectively cope with the fast approaching obsolescence in the areas of attitude dimensions, knowledge diemnsions and skill dimensions.

This naturally will require the thrust of 'HRD' to be on the specific areas of training and perhaps continuous retraining. In this context, inasmuch as training methodologies do play a vital role, in the matter of transfer of 'training inputs' to the job situation, research into 'designing of appropriate training methodologies is an acutely felt need.

Banks being a technical field, persons directly handling banking Affairs, especially at the branch level, must necessarily know their job in all its technicalities. Proper and timely training of the concerned personnel both in theory and practice becomes imperative, particularly when new spheres are being constantly added to the present-day banking and demands and expectations from the community are growing.

With a view to making training useful and bringing it in consonance with costs involved, it has to be meaningful, need-based, effective, broad-based and purpose-oriented. Generally speaking, need for training can be best judged by the employee himself or his immediate superior who knows the gaps of knowledge and skills required or to be acquired. But in the case of specialised types of skills, it should be left at the administrative control points to judge the training gaps and the required manpower to fill up such gaps depending upon the overall corporate policy.

Training, are Integral Part of HRD

Training is an integral part of the HRD activity of a bank. It is a potent instrument for preparing its personnel to meet the challenges of change. In India, training in banks has assumed greater importance in the eighties and more so towards the end of the decade. Explosive and excruciating changes are taking place in the banking environment. Increased disintermediation and deregulation are introducing keener competition and hitherto untrodden areas are opened up by newer financial services such as the mutual funds, venture capital, factoring, etc. Rural development and in particular, the Service Area Approach is another field which calls for the development of skills in collection, analysis and interpretation of environmental data as also towards its suitable linkage with the development process.

While national and social compulsions have already trimmed the profitability of banks during the present decade, competition, increasing wage bills and mounting frauds and losses are posing serious challenges. To face these challenges, a banker is required to be an allrounder. He must be able to understand the changes taking place in the environment and accordingly come out with new products, new schemes, systems and services and thus meet the changing requirements of customers. It has rightly been said that in the emerging environment, a banker is expected to be a creative innovator and a critical evaluator. Training and education system in banks, therefore, assumes paramount importance in developing the requisite professional competence.

Training is an integral input of managerial development. The lack of adequate and skilled personnel is one of the bottlenecks in a developing economy. Staff training is essential for entrepreneurs and workers employed in small enterprises.

What is Training?

Training is the systematic instruction of staff at all levels in new attitudes or new skills; random bits of continuing education or mere learning on-the-job cannot be called training. The term implies a scheme of instruction which is more or less formal and ongoing, which is planned, systematic, consistent, pervasive, and monitored to measure its effectiveness. Although it may usually be re-active, a response to a perceived demand or pressure, it should be developed to become proactive — an advance response, instigating new services, skills and methods, identifying unsuspected problems, and leading the way towards an improved standard of service. As a term, it implies a trainer and a trainee; it suggests an institutional context, but it is in fact open to anybody to be a trainee and we should not mislead ourselves into assuming that an institution is essential.

Why Should We Train Staff?

Very few individuals indeed do their jobs in an 'ideal' way; many jobs are done for the wrong reasons, or in the wrong place, or by the wrong staff, and many jobs that should be done are overlooked. Currently, the pressures on the public sector make any of these 'mistakes' insupportable. The costs of staff are so great and their role in a service profession so crucial that their work must be demonstrably effective. Effective staff do not happen; they must be created through training.

A service profession must enjoy a careful relationship with its public; attitudes of staff towards their clientele is the most vital area of training. Banks are becoming more market-oriented; there is a change in emphasis, and to cope with this, staff need training to understand the need to change, and to become familiar with the needs of their clientele.

All individuals have a need for training; new recruits need induction into the rationale and objectives of their jobs, and need to be trained in specific skills and routines. New professional staff may need additionally a programme of training to enable them to obtain their professional qualification. Certain individuals may need training for a specific purpose, the development of a new service, taking on a new role in the organisation or preparing for retirement.

But, in a world where development and promotion occur rarely, everyone still needs training, or rather needs it even more; if a job at any level becomes drudgery, then it cannot be effectively performed. The role of training is to develop a critical awareness of staff and prevent in-growth. An employee who can make some appraisal of her or his role can compare the situation of colleagues elsewhere, can feel that management promotes this process and is likely to feel a satisfaction in the job, however great the constraints on achievement. And job satisfaction is a clear way towards effectiveness if individuals at all levels can contribute towards the formulation of goals, then those goals are more likely to be the most appropriate in the context.

The Benefits

Training is pervasive; if there is a climate of training, then individuals become more efficient, their motivation is increased, standard of work improves. Groups of employees will develop their own group training needs, and from this type of training comes greater flexibility, co-operation, continuity and interchangeability of staff. The needs of the organisation, the management needs, are obviously also achieved through training; apart from the simple mechanism of conveying new information and attitudes to employees, a learning climate aids management to pin-point areas of service needs, and helps give a better response to pressure.

The various benefits of a training programme are as follows:

1. Training programme helps in increasing the quantity and quality of output.
2. It helps each individual member to utilise and develop her/his full potential.
3. Employees feel that they are being taken care of by the management and this results in raising their morale.
4. By training, the worker is enabled to make the most economical and best use of the materials and equipment. This results in reduced cost of production.

5. Trained employee needs less supervision. Because of this, the supervisor can increase his span of management costs of supervision.
6. As training helps in building a second line of competent officers, there will be competent replacement for more responsible positions.
7. The availability of trained personnel ensures long-term stability and flexibility in the organisation.
8. As managers are exposed to the latest concepts, information and techniques, they become better qualified. By this, they increase their market value and earning power.

Objectives of Training

The training programme is designed to subserve the following objectives:

(i) To impart basic knowledge about the organisation services methods;

(ii) To build the necessary skills of new executives and workers;

(iii) To assist the executives/workers to function more effectively in their present position by exposing them to the latest concepts, techniques and information;

(iv) To build up a second line of workers and prepare them to shoulder additional responsibility and/or switch on to the production of a new product, if there is any diversification;

(v) To expose executives/supervisors to the latest developments which directly or indirectly affect them;

(vi) To broaden the vision of officers and workers by providing them suitable opportunities for an interchange of experiences within and outside the industry;

(vii) To impart customer education;

(viii) To impart knowledge of the marketing of services; and

(ix) To instil confidence and imbibe leadership and entrepreneurial qualities.

Training and Development Methods

There is a large number of training and development programmes meant for different types of employees at different levels. Broadly speaking, the various training and development methods can be classified into the following two categories:

A. On-the-job Methods:

1. On specific job:

   (a) Experience, (b) Coaching, and (c) Understudy programme.
2. Job rotation.
3. Special projects and task forces.
4. Vestibule training.
5. Committees and junior boards (Multiple Management).

B. Off-the-job Methods:

1. Special courses and lectures.
2. Conferences.
3. Case studies.
4. Simulation — role playing.
5. Sensitivity training.
6. Incident method.

A periodic review would be an essential element. Further, in order to prevent the training system from becoming simply a number game, proper balance has to be evolved between intensive and extensive training for better results. In addition, the exercise of training has to be continuous, keeping in mind future promotions and placements so that neither the person concerned nor the organisation is taken by surprise due to maladjustment which may be caused due to insufficient preparation for higher or new roles to be performed. Lastly, training and placements must find a direct and close relationship as far as possible for the optimum utilisation of both human and material resources. As a bank becomes larger, it may become more difficult to match the 'Available' personnel with the 'Needed' personnel but this task can be made easier if HRD sections are created at RO/ZO levels for this and related purposes and development of 'human resources' becomes a total concern at all levels of administration.

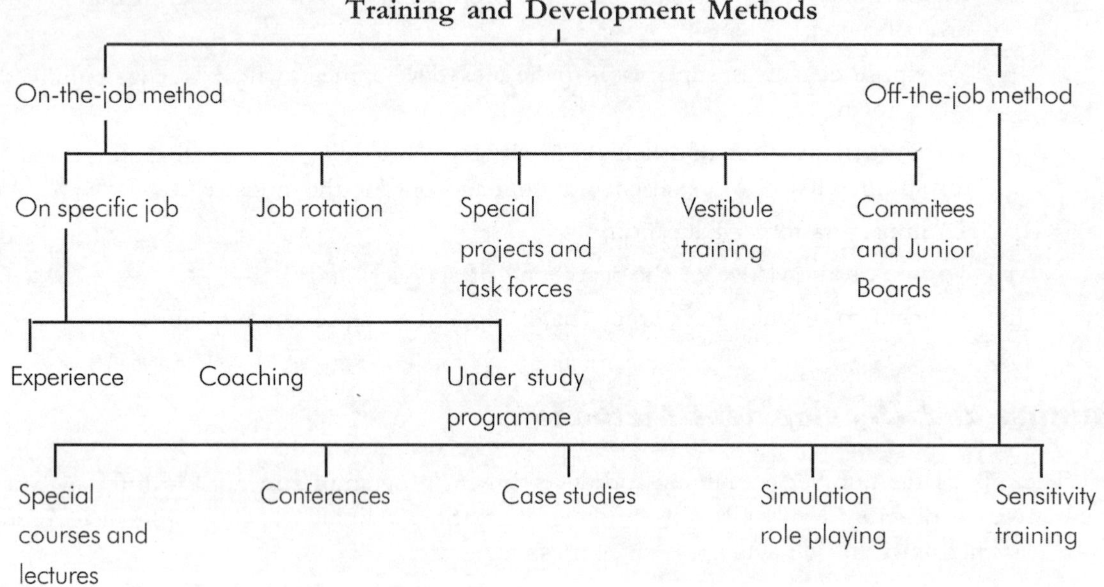

Fig. 17.2 Training and Development Methods

Appropriate Strategy — The Need of the Hour

- There must be sincerity on the part of management, the trainers and the trainees, so that the entire system has credibility.

- Training programmes must be specific and tailor-made.
- Trainee must feel the relevance of training for himself and the institution.
- Focus should be more on skill, attitude and techniques.
- Environment should be conducive to learn, both in terms of 'psychological preparedness' and 'physical conditions.'
- Methodology must be appropriate so as to create and sustain interest.
- Training must be need-based and be given on the spot.
- Opportunities must be made available and systems established to use the skills immediately after training.
- Training programmes for clerical/sub-staff cadres need to be participant-oriented with more practical methodologies and the programmes should, as far as possible, be in the regional language in the case of sub-staff. In the case of officers, experience sharing could be the main plank with more active participant-oriented inputs like in — basket exercises, management games, experiential learning, meaningful structured and unstructured role playing and case studies forming a regular feature of programme modules.
- Appropriate audio-visuals enhance the intrinsic worth/quality of the programmes and make the learning process easier and appealing to the participants. Audio-visuals remove the boredom and monotony and hence should be a regular feature of programme schedules for all categories of staff.
- It would be desirable to offer all the employees broadly four types of training exposures, in the areas of HRD, attitudinal change, functional and self-development on an ongoing basis.

Simple Model of the Training Process

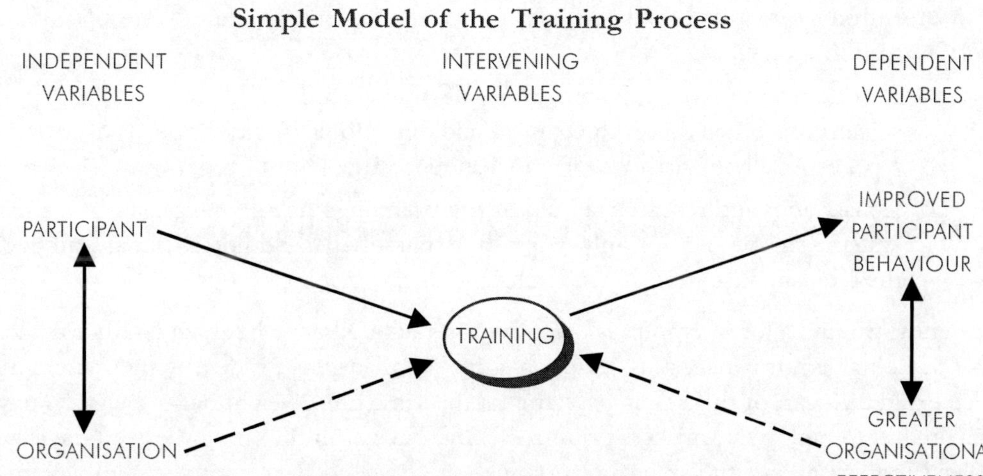

Fig. 17.3 Simple Model of the Training Process

The Ten Commandments

For enhancing the overall effectiveness of the training system, banks may follow the ten commandments enumerated below:

(i) Focus on on-the-spot training programmes, organised on a vertical integration basis.

Elaborated Model of the Training Process

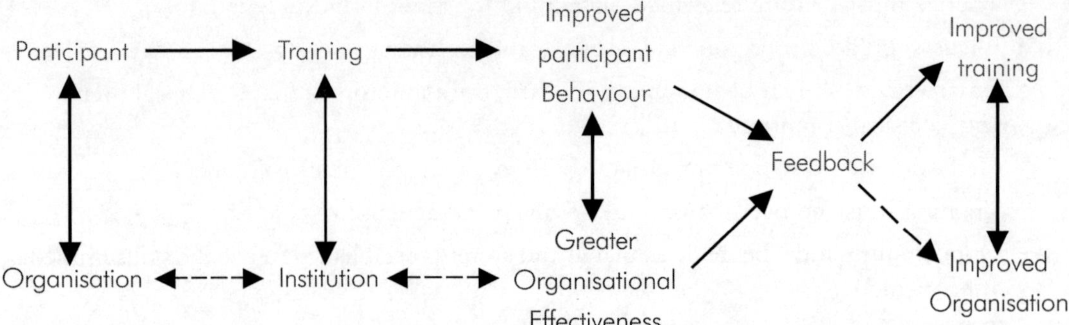

Fig. 17.4 Elaborated Model of The Training Process

(ii) To the extent feasible, use appropriate computer-aided gadgets.

(iii) Introduce distance learning with a view to encouraging 'self-learning.'

(iv) Introduce 'interactive sessions' with the operational personnel concerned as well as zonal/corporate office executives.

(v) Incorporate experiential learning as a teaching methodology invariably in the programme structure.

(vi) Task assignments/paper presentation to individuals/groups of participants should be a regular feature.

(vii) Provide for experience-sharing among the participants to facilitate meaningful interaction.

(viii) Introduce to the extent feasible, structured and unstructured role plays in training sessions.

(ix) Introduce, exclusive programmes on self-introspection/self-sensitivity/hypnosis/auto-suggestion, etc. The teaching methodology should basically be of a demonstrative type, especially in sessions of transcendental meditation/yoga.

(x) Consultancy and research should be made an ongoing and integral part of the training system. This would not only help refine training methodologies but also in developing the requisite insights/ conceptual skills of the training faculty.

Presently, we find a lot of emphasis being laid on the number to be trained rather than the type of people to be trained. It is necessary to involve the line managers to identify the training needs of their people and be a part of the training system. At the same time, weight has to be given to the area of training that the employee identifies for himself. And once both the employees and the supervisors are involved in this process, the system of nomination as well as the training system will improve.

When all is said and done, training in banks is growing in importance as it contributes greatly towards developing better and brighter bankers for today and tomorrow. It is time to further strengthen the training infrastructure already set up and ensure a more streamlined nomination system. This coupled with a closer monitoring of post-training utilisation will go a long way in improving the efficacy of training system in banks. At the same time, banks need to draw up a suitable training policy at the corporate level and follow it up meticulously for implementation from year to year. Separate HRD and training departments at the corporate level may have to be set up to look at the training matters more objectively and give them the degree of attention and importance that they rightly deserve.

Table 17.1
Comparison of Six Training Strategies

Strategy	Emphasis	Characteristic Methods	Assumptions	Action Steps
1. Academic	Transmitting content and increasing conceptual understanding	Lecture Seminar Individual reading	1. Content and understanding can be passed on from those who know to those who are ignorant. 2. Such knowledge and understanding can be translated into practice.	Devising a syllabus to be covered in the programme Examination to test retained knowledge and understanding
2. Laboratory	Process of function and change Process of learning	Isolation Free exploration and discussion Experimentation	1. It is useful and possible to pay attention to psychological factors for separate attention. 2. Understanding of own and others' behaviour helps in the performance of the jobs.	Unfreezing participants from their usual expectations and norms Helping participants see and help others see their own behaviour and develop new habits
3. Activity	Practice of specific skill	Work on the job under supervision Detailed job analysis and practice with aids	1. Improvement in particular skill leads to better performance on the job. 2. Production and training can be combined rather simply.	Analysing skill and dividing it into parts Preparing practice tasks, standards, and aids.

Strategy	Emphasis	Characteristic Methods	Assumptions	Action Steps
4. Action	Sufficient skills to get organisational action	Field work, setting and achieving targets	1. Working in the field develops people 2. Individual skills and organisational needs will fit together	Preparation of field programmes Participation according to schedule
5. Person-development	Improved individual competence in a wide variety of tasks and situations	Field training, simulation methods, incident and case sessions, and syndicate discussion	1. Training in job requirements with emphasis on process will help a participant develop general skills and understanding 2. Organisation will support the individual in using understanding and skills acquired	Identifying training needs Preparing simulated data
6. Organisation development	Organisational improvement	Study of organisational needs Work with small groups from the organisation	1. Attention to organisational needs as process develops understanding 2. Organisational change will result in individual's change	Survey of organisational needs Determining strategic grouping for training Working on organisational requirements

The selection of an appropriate strategy depends on a number of factors. One is the training goals. Once the training institution is clear about the goals, it can choose a strategy that leads to them.

For example, the goal of developing individuals with sufficient skills to be able to perform more effectively on their jobs cannot be accomplished by the academic strategy of training. For that goal an activity or person-development strategy is more appropriate. The activity strategy will be appropriate if the job calls for limited skill and is not likely to change much in the near future. The person-development strategy is more appropriate if the job is complex and developing. If the main emphasis is on changes in the total organisation, it is necessary to use the organisation-development strategy.

The second consideration when choosing a strategy is the resources available for training. The resources include the faculty of the training institution in the first place, the extent to which it can draw on additional professional resources and community contacts, and the availability of various other facilities necessary for successfully using a particular strategy. Above all, so long as available trainers are not competent to operate a particular strategy, attempting it would only create a frustrating situation likely to lead to failure.

Placement

The concept of the right person for the right jobs is the crux of a sound placement policy. It is true that such a concept cannot be applied with mathematical precision due to the largeness of the number of persons as well as the various varieties of jobs involved in a large bank. All the same, the importance of a conscious and sound placement policy cannot be under-emphasised. For this, a data bank at different administrative levels can provide a good solution. In addition, a factoral analysis of crucial jobs and personality characteristics of eligible personnel for matching purposes and its timely utilisation can be extremely useful. A majority of right placements would not only create a majority of satisfied employees; it would also help the organisation from both control and developmental points of view. More suitable and satisfied manpower would be less vulnerable to commit errors and create a more conducive work climate in furtherance of achievements of long-term objectives which an organisation may envisage for its excellence. Like any other organisation, a bank would also have to successfully handle the problem of succession which if not handled properly and in time may lead to uncertainties, break in continuity and retardation. The policy of succession has to be pursued in a continuous and planned manner in such a way that persons who have to be succeeded and their successors are involved in the process of succession well in time.

Development of Healthy Attitudes

Attitudes of an employee towards work, towards his colleagues, towards seniors, towards juniors, towards the organisation and its declared objectives can determine whether his behaviour in different situations would be positive or not. Before we proceed further, it may be expressed that an attitude of a person towards something is his predisposition towards that thing which gets reflected in his behaviour. Such predispositions become stronger and stronger as the age of an individual progresses. However, there is always scope for varying improvements in the attitudes of individual employees. Such an improvement can be made through clearer communications flowing from higher levels of management, reflecting its sincerity by way of words as well as deeds. These can also be improved through well-designed training programmes. In addition, employees' general satisfaction can also act as a catalyst towards improvement in positive attitudes towards work as well as towards involvement with the organisation. Although transformation of attitudes in a favourable direction is a slow process, but once it takes place it may lead to a chain reaction with broader advantages for the organisation and in turn for the individuals.

Employee Satisfaction

An employee joins the bank for the satisfaction of his basic needs through the remuneration he gets. Gradually, his needs develop in the direction of higher needs like belongingness and recognition. Any unavoidable obstacle in the satisfaction of these needs is perceived as a distraction and results in frustration which may retard his efforts. But the satisfaction of such needs creates a feeling in him that he is doing something worthwhile for himself and for the bank, a feeling that he is not merely a cog in the wheel, a feeling that by his contribution he along with all his colleagues would benefit. These feelings can act as a motivational force and this can be facilitated by the conscious devotion of time and efforts by the organisation, mainly through job enrichment, training at different levels and projecting a perception that an employee as an individual is a welcome person. Here HRD can help. There would be, of course, a small number of employees who on their own would travel along the path of self-actualisation with very strong internal motivation within their own selves. But even in such cases, HRD can facilitate increase in the number of such persons.

Appraisal System

Appraisal of an employee is a critical analysis of his abilities, performance, conduct, strengths/ weaknesses and utility relevant to the organisation over a period of time. Appraisal is useful for promotion, placement and development of the employees. It is, therefore, essential that the performance of each employee is appraised and that the appraisal system is reasonably objective both in procedure and practice. Normally, in banks, there is no system whereby an employee is communicated the appraisal off him except in cases where his performance has been assessed as unsatisfactory. But if the objective of appraisal system is, *inter alia,* to develop the employee, there may not be any harm if he is informed about his appraisal, irrespective of the rating he gets from the appraising or reviewing authority. As a consequence of this, he would get a chance to introspect himself vis-a-vis the organisation, and this would provide him an opportunity and impetus to improve.

Leadership and Morale

Leadership is the ability to persuade others to seek and achieve predetermined objectives wholeheartedly. In an organisation like a bank, there is a structured behaviour legitimatised by virtue of role behaviour as superiors and subordinates. Leaders essentially provide both task and psychological support to the followers and sometimes, serve as role models using a combination of technological and conceptual human skills. Leaders tend to apply different styles like authoritative, participation, etc.

In banks, by and large, almost every employee is well educated and enlightened. There are written rules, regulations and instructions. The tasks involved need a good degree of team work. Keeping these factors in mind, there should be a stress on development of democratic leadership quality amongst members of management cadre. In addition, if they are trained in human behaviour, they would be in a better position to understand their colleagues. Such a situation can create a more conducive and motivated work climate within the organisation, leading to high morale amongst the growing number of men and women.

Motivation: the Functional Employee

One of the greatest challenges facing the banking industry today is the requirement of motivating the work force. The traditional patterns of motivation which were largely founded on the economic rewards and authority have failed to deliver the goods on a long-term basis. Further, the highly structurised and traditional compensation systems operating in the industry coupled with the need to avoid leap-frogging tendencies tend to eliminate the possibility of individualised monetary rewards. The complex milieu of labour welfare approach, growth of unions, rising standards of living, better educational backgrounds and awareness have raised the expectation levels of the employee. However, when the employee joins a bank and becomes a part of the multitude of the employed, the inevitable organisational anomie takes over, devoid of recognition; and individuality; alienation and frustration set in.

The achievement motivation depends on varied styles. The principal ones are: routine, avoidance of trouble and the attainment of pleasure.

The characteristics of true achievement motivation are:

- The desire to excel, to achieve greatness.
- No fear of trying even though failure may be a possibility.
- A route is followed by which, if success is achieved, it is recognised and acclaimed. Success achieved through gambling, chance and unfair means is eschewed.
- The goals are attainable — the possibility of success having been indicated by preliminary successes, for example, a businessman who succeeds with an idea in a small way may try to expand and apply the idea in a wider area.
- The attitude that obstacles can be overcome. In fact problems are welcome and there is a feeling of excitement in tackling problems and unusual situations. There is a fondness for winning.
- Unlike those who seek pleasure as a goal, achievement motivation does not let personal likes come in the way or influence one's decisions.
- Unfinished tasks weigh heavily on the mind.
- Money and reward are measures of achievement — not ends in themselves. Growth, opportunities for action and advancement are as important as the immediate reward.
- There is boldness in the face of the unknown but prudence in the face of risks.
- Ancestors, relations and contacts do not play a significant role to blame for one's failures, to be ashamed of or to be depended on for success. Independence and self-reliance are valued more than connections.

Success gives encouragement for further ventures. It generates courage to overcome difficulties and failures. Success breeds success. Nothing succeeds like success.

There are, however, many possibilities in the management of motivation. For example, an appropriate job evaluation system which will provide equity by internal analysis of job values is a prerequisite to organisational effectiveness. The modern appraisal philosophy which concretises specific goals after mutual goal setting is one which would be worth emulating. Coming to the issue of rewards, there are possibilities which could be monetary or non-monetary. Recognition of employee efforts, quality circles, proper care and attention to the employee in his work setting, etc., will further help the situation.

Discipline — Positive and Negative

For the efficient and smooth functioning of any organisation, it is necessary that specific norms of behaviour are laid down, understood and followed by those who form a part of such organisations. Viewed in this vein, discipline is the mode of life in accordance with the rules of conduct. The term 'discipline' itself could be categorised into positive which presupposes a situation where the employee willingly follows the prescribed norms and negative which stresses the need for correction.

Discipline could be viewed from an individual point of view as also in a collective fashion. On an individual plane, discipline has the single employee as its focus with the positive and negative forces converging. Discipline, on the other hand, on a collective plane is a much broader issue and has the group as its focus.

It has to be noted here that the need for improving discipline and maintaining it has been recognised by both the management as also the All-India Trade Unions of Bank Employees which have signed the Fourth Bipartite Settlement. In fact, both the Indian Banks' Association (DBA) on behalf of the managements of the banks and the All-India Trade Unions of Bank Employees which signed the Fourth Bipartite Settlement have specifically agreed *inter alia* under Clause XVIII pertaining to the improvement in working in banks' branches/offices as under:

> "Having regard to the vital role of the banking industry in the national economy and the various social and economic responsibilities they have been entrusted with from time to time, parties agree that there is need to improve the housekeeping in the offices/branches of the banks throughout the country to ensure efficient, cordial and speedy customer service at all times in the banking industry, and to promote harmonious industrial relations and better discipline at all levels."

Discipline, particularly at senior levels, must arise largely as a self-imposed exercise — not having to be administered externally. Such self-discipline will come in greater measure if we were to hold ourselves accountable in the manner that we should. Accountability has come to be a major area of concern in the way we function.

Customer Responsiveness

"In the new marketing environment, companies must prove that the ways they operate guarantee their ability to keep promises. Perhaps that is why a new kind of advertising is emerging, one that describes the company's internal management processes", says Rosabeth Moss Kanter.

An organisation can be customer-and-market-friendly only if everyone right from the leader of the organisation to the last man in the service output force is responsive to the customers' needs and necessities. The philosophy which can help the organisation to survive, sustain, and see through the turbulent waves of environmental tides will be the 'Superiority of the Customer.' The eighties have seen considerable change in consumer profiles. The consumer today is more sophisticated, more sensitive, more selective and more sceptical than ever before.

Communication

There is no gainsaying the fact that effective communication is a basic imperative for the success of an organisation and this has been testified by the results of research analysis. We talk a lot, we write reams of paper and circulate bundles of messages. Do we really communicate? Are we able to bring the internal audience on the same wavelength? Are we able to make the internal audience appreciate our decisions and decision-making processes? Are we able to know and understand the aspirations of both the internal and external audience and use them for product development, service sophistication or other decision-making areas? Let us examine our systems of communication, enhance their capability and reinforce their viability.

The Future Needs

The 21st century, unlike any other era in our history, will offer major challenges to our human resource capacities as we enter a period of rapid social, technological, and economic fluctuations. To meet these challenges, our people must be knowledgeable, trained, competent and inventive. All of our people, not just a few, must be able to think for a living, adapt to changing environments and to understand the world around them. They must continually learn and develop new skills throughout their lives. We must recognise that education is a life long pursuit, not just an endeavour for our children. Towards this end, the accent of training programmes in banks needs to be changed from one of concentrating only on job knowledge to that of developing motivating aspects and behavioural traits of its human resources (employees). The need of the hour is to have innovative training programmes which will mould employees in the organisation.

Thus, proper and purpose-oriented training, logical and rational placement, development of healthier attitudes, objective appraisal systems, realistic level of employee satisfaction, better leadership and higher individual/group morale are the most important ingredients which would form the core of human resources development. But once the HRD systems have been developed and imbibed by an organisation to a fairly good degree, employees would develop greater involvement in the working of the organisation. They would also tend to be more objective in their behaviour. Development of any cracks in such systems may endanger the resultant frustrations and other consequences which may adversely affect the health and excellence of the organisation. Therefore, while establishing HRD system in banks is important, it is equally important to keep them continuously strengthened at all levels.

Organisational Development

As human resources is inducted on a mass scale by an independent agency, there is not much scope for the individual banks to pick up persons in regular cadres on the basis of personal scrutiny and specific requirements. As such, there is greater need to mould and develop the human resources, keeping in view the organisational development (O.D.) requirements.

Edwin B. Flippo in his book *Personnel Management* has beautifully analysed this requirement in the following introductory paragraph of the Chapter 'Individual and Organisational Development':

"After the employee has been recruited, selected and inducted, he or she must next be developed to better fit the job and organisation. No one is a perfect fit at the time of hiring, and some training and education must take place. No organisation has a choice of whether to develop employees or not; the only choice is that of method. If no organised programme exists, then development will largely be self-development while learning on the job. Development would include both training to increase skill in performing a specific job and education to increase general knowledge and understanding of our total environment."

The HRD function which was in its infancy in the mid-seventies has now reached the puberty stage. Banks have a wide network of training establishments for their employees. Employees are also deputed to outside training programmes. Thus, employees have adequate opportunities to develop themselves.

Knowledge Management

In the world of banking, the banks are presently operating in the buyers' market in which the customer loyalty and customer delight continue to hold key to the business growth and profitability. Value addition to the customer satisfaction can be effectively achieved through application of right knowledge at right time and place. Banking is steadily shifting from 'labour-intensive enterprise' to 'knowledge-driven economy' and as such in the futuristic outlook, the effectiveness and success of the banks largely depends on the level of intellectual capital build and utilise it effectively.

The knowledge management is a process encompassing various steps, viz., gathering, organising, sharing and analysing to generate a new set of value system in the banking organisation. Knowledge management is a systematic and holistic approach to capture the collective experience, wisdom including the tacit knowledge which is the intellectual property of the individuals and make it available and useful to every one in the organisation.

The characteristics and attributes of knowledge management are:

- It is a process through which organisation generates value and their intellectual and knowledge-based assets;
- It is not a one-time activity but a continuous and on-going process;
- It envisages getting the right information, in the right context, to the right person, at the right time and also for the right business purpose;
- It is the transformation process and a process of creating, capturing, storing, sharing and applying such knowledge for achieving business goals;
- It is an effort towards bringing up new work culture and intellectual capital from within by evoking the best in the workforce;
- It removes mental inertia among the workforce and creates inner urge for excellence;
- It is also an effort to inculcate a desire among the workforce for acquiring knowledge, efficiency and productivity by creating a learning environment;

- It addresses problems particular to the business — whether relating to creation and delivery of innovating products or services or to manage and enhance relationships with all stakeholders.

It may therefore, be observed that Knowledge Management is not only a process of creating and transferring knowledge right across the organization but also adds value to the existing treasure of knowledge. It is an asset which can be leveraged for customer delight, operational excellence, product innovation and for enhancing profits and organizational effectiveness.

The objectives of the Knowledge Management systems in any organization may encompass — to optimize the use of knowledge besides other assets, to leverage internal and external expertise and intellectual abilities to the competitive business advantage, to provide right knowledge at right time to the right person, to inculcate a habit of continuous learning among the workforce to drive the organisation towards a 'Learning Organization.'

Management Development

Management development is a systematic process of training and growth by which individuals gain knowledge, skills, insights and attitudes and apply them to manage work in banks/organisations effectively. Objectives of management development in banks are:

(1) To increase the effectiveness of the bank by —
   (a) better utilisation of managing abilities;
   (b) assisting managers to function more effectively in the present jobs;
   (c) developing managers who think broadly from the overall bank viewpoint rather than the specialists;
   (d) increasing team work in the management group.
(2) To build a reserve of qualified personnel to back up key positions;
(3) To devise methods of testing executive competence of the managers before they are promoted;
(4) To improve the morale of the members of the management group; and
(5) To attract desirable personnel to the bank.

Subject matter and course content for the management development programme include:

(1) The bank organisation (objectives, philosophies, policies, services, organisation structure and dynamics, etc.)
(2) Management principles and techniques.
(3) Human Relations.
(4) Technical knowledge and skills.
(5) Economic, social and political environment.
(6) Skills for self-development.

Manager Development Programme

In the 90s, banks have introduced a high-priority training and development initiative, called the Manager Development Programme (MDP), to enhance the managerial skills of the current and potential future managers.

The need for MDP arises from the fact that the banks have moved forward into the 1990s with expanding and more diversified operations, including new modalities of development assistance. Banks are faced with complex, though exciting challenges. To keep pace with the rapidly changing external environment and to effectively respond to the challenges which the banks now face, they have to rely on the responsiveness, skills and productivity of their staff. The quality of leadership provided by the banks' senior staff and their overall performance and managerial capabilities are, therefore, of vital importance.

A major focus of the MDP is on the behavioural aspects of management, i.e., increasing the self-awareness of one's strengths and weaknesses, developing communication skills, and improving leadership qualities.

The full programme consists of five modules:

1. Leadership and performance management;
2. Communications and negotiations;
3. Strategic planning and organisation;
4. Resource Management; and
5. Management Information Systems.

The overall programme consists of case studies, including some focussing on the banks' specific problems and issues, lectures, self-assessment tests, role playing, group exercises, real-time problem solving, and audio-visual presentations. Thus MDP aims at not only equipping the leaders with information and knowledge in the various facets of banking, but also instilling confidence in handling various competitive situations. This apart, imbibing them with leadership and entrepreneurial qualities can also lead others on to the right path.

Training System for Modern Banking

Modern Banking has changed the concept of "brick banking" to "click banking." To adapt to these changes, it has become important to correctly identify the branch units, which are contributing and those that are unviable and are proving to be a drag on profitability, depending on the mix of customers. For the purpose of identifying such branches, a thorough knowledge of the factors effecting performance like reduction of earlier potential, economies of scale and extent of business flowing in/out of the area and level of technology and competition, is crucial, with excellent communication facilities. Knowledge and experience with loyalty account for 90% of resource of a Bank. We need to churn it with care to get the best yield in terms of profitable business. The Training System need to focus on strengthening on strengths of each individual, branch and cluster of branches in line with the goal oriented needs of individuals along with their team leaders.

Modern Training in Banking Need to Focus on:

— Building mindset at different levels to facilitate mergers, acquisitions and collaborations as these will be order of the day with growing focus on strengths of organizations and where the size matters.

— Building the belief in the strength of technology to facilitate the fast growing size of the cake resulting in a bigger and a larger piece for each.

— Inculcating the culture to pass on the solutions thought for problems faced and better performance of assignments to be analyzed and improved upon by the experts for continuous innovative incorporation to improve the system and strengthen it.

— Building the appetite for soft skills among the employees and providing opportunities for its satiation.

Once these areas can be focused in the training system of Banks there seems no reason why unforeseen growth cannot be achieved.

Conclusion

Human resources development is an organised and deliberate process not only for the advancement of deserving employees in their career but also to help the management in its long-range planning to plant the right person in the right post in the days ahead. The concept embraces almost all areas of an organisation and places emphasis on the all-round development of individuals. It requires a "developmental climate" — an HRD climate in the organisation which is characterised by the presence of values and openness.

"Objectives of HRD are laudable. But they cannot be achieved overnight. It is important that HRD is relatively a new concept in the Indian context and needs to be nurtured with care."

"Each of the HRD areas can make organisations better places of work and make them healthier institutions for pursuing a better future for the human race. The direction of HRD efforts in banks has to be competence development, competence utilisation, motivation for public service, integrity and character-building, building of self-discipline and team work."

Changes in human resource policies should be based on the projected market potential of the organisations. Probably, organisations should have to reallocate funds towards HRD functions to prepare manpower for the future. There will be more sharing of powers with employees than what has been conventionally in practice so long. Identification of appropriate knowledge and talent is a must. Innovations should be encouraged not only in technology but also in human resources management. Employees will have to be trained in understanding the present and future environment and the demands that are expected to be fulfilled.

Creating an atmosphere of spontaneous will to cooperate is not all that easy. Resistance to change can be resolved by involving people in the process.

The problem lies in fostering an entrepreneurial spirit among employees. Rotation of jobs can help in preparing leaders for general management. Decisions by consensus have to be encouraged.

Specialised training programmes must be conducted to influence the thinking and perceptual processes of the employees.

Peter F. Drucker observes as under:

"The secret may lie in what the Japanese call continuous training. This means, first that every employee, very often up to and including the top managements, keep on training as a regular part of his job until he retires."

The organisational challenge cannot simply be met by technological innovations or by financial resources but it can be met only through the management's ability to organise human beings in such a way as to generate opportunity. Opportunities have to be created to make him feel more participative in the decisions which affect him. Thus a more result-oriented work force will emerge.

The HRD experiments in some of the banks have stressed on the following salient points:

(i) Top management commitment to HRD has to be continuous;

(ii) HRD should focus on improving HRD climate;

(iii) Innovations and experimentation should be encouraged;

(iv) HRD should be decentralised;

(v) There is need for a strong line orientation;

(vi) There is need for development-oriented Human Resources Management policy; and

(vii) The specialists should be integrated in the HRD system.

The rapid changes in the business environment and the resultant reorientation in business strategy call for similar shifts in people management in banks. The Government of India has recently provided full autonomy to the banks in respect of their HR policies including, recruitment, placement, promotion, pay structure etc. While some banks have moved forward, many banks are yet to utilise such new found freedom and link their HR policies to business strategies. The apparent disconnect between HR practices and business strategy needs to be bridged quickly. Banks run the risk of strategic failure if this situation does not change. For the best of strategies will fail if the people to implement them are ill-equipped in terms of skill sets and attitude.

The writing on the wall is quite clear. Banks need to look beyond their current HR practices and achieve a fundamental shift in their people management policies. HR strategies should be imaginative, innovative while at the same time, flexible to adjust rapidly to change. This would be possible only if employees are explicitly recognized as assets and the investments on development of human capital are viewed as critical.

Training and development of human resource to man the multiplicit points of critical importance in the third millennium Banking Industry is a challenge with which staff Colleges and training centres of the Banking system have to deal. The continuous introduction of new control mechanisms, as well as, reporting systems in modern Banking, smoothening business cycles, changing public expectations, new trends in demographic distribution and fast moving Banking technology have made the captains of the industry sit up and take notice of quality training inputs and specialization of personnel.

In the ultimate analysis, the success of banks in managing the human resources will be commensurate with the effort that is put into this vital area. In fact, the banking industry has a vital role to play in this area of developing an effective management style in relation to human resources. Thus, human resources development is a continuous process to ensure the development of competence, dynamism, motivation and effectiveness among employees in a systematic and planned manner. The focus of attention has been on improving the quality and strength of employees who alone can take the banks towards their avowed goal of growth with profit.

Chapter 18

Manpower Planning in Banks

"A good Bank is not only the financial heart of the community, but one with an obligation of helping in every manner possible to improve the economic conditions of the common people."

— *Shri A. Subba Rao Pai*

Introduction

Of all the "M's" in management, i.e., the management of money, methods, manpower, materials and machines, the most important is manpower or human resources. It is the most valuable asset of an organisation, and, more particularly, in the service organisations like banks. Manpower is utilised to the maximum possible extent to achieve individual and organisational goals. Manpower planning is, therefore, an important segment of the business plan. In a service-oriented industry like banking, manpower planning is quite significant. It is a means to human resources development.

What is Manpower Planning?

Manpower planning is a useful guide. It gives both balance and direction, i.e., manpower input and its multi-faceted uses. It is the identification of various action steps committing human resources towards achieving results beneficial to the organisation. It involves clarity of objectives. In the words of Peter F. Drucker, "Objectives must be derived from *our need both in quantitative as well as qualitative* (italics author's) terms. They are the fundamental strategy of a business." Manpower planning is the process of examination and re-examination, of continual consideration of the future, of constant searching for more effective methods of accomplishment and improved results.

Definitions of Manpower Planning

Coleman has defined "manpower planning" as "the process of determining human resources requirements and the means for meeting those requirements in order to carry out the integrated plan of the organisation."

Edwin B. Flippo states: "An executive manpower planning programme can be defined as an appraisal of an organisation's ability to perpetuate itself with respect to its management as a determination of measures necessary to provide the essential executive talent."

Edwin Geisler defines it thus: "Manpower planning is the process (including forecasting, implementing and controlling) by which a firm ensures that it has the right number of people and the right kind of people at the right place, at the right time, doing things for which they are economically most useful."

Welter has defined manpower planning as "the process by which a management determines how an organisation should move from its current manpower position to its desired manpower position. Through planning, a management strives to have the right number and the right kinds of people at the right place, at the right time, to do things which result in both the organisation and the individual receiving the maximum long-range benefits."

According to Wickstrom, manpower planning consists of a series of activities, viz.,

(a) Forecasting future manpower requirements, either in terms of mathematical projections of trends in the economic environment and developments in industry, or in terms of judgemental estimates based upon the specific future plans of a company;

(b) Making an inventory of present manpower resources and assessing the extent to which these resources are employed optimally;

(c) Anticipating manpower problems by projecting present resources into the future and comparing them with the forecast of requirements to determine their adequacy, both quantitatively and qualitatively; and

(d) Planning the necessary programmes of recruitment, selection, training, development, utilisation, transfer, promotion, motivation and compensation to ensure that future manpower requirements are properly met.

Thus, it will be noted that manpower planning consists in projecting future manpower requirements and developing manpower plans for the implementation of the projections. This planning cannot be rigid or static; it is amenable to modification, review and adjustments in accordance with the needs of an organisation or the changing circumstances.

Human resources planning is a double-edged weapon. If used properly, it leads to the maximum utilisation of human resources, reduces excessive labour turnover and high absenteeism; improves productivity and aids in achieving the objectives of an organisation. Faultily used, it leads to disruption in the flow of work, lower production, lower job satisfaction, high cost of production and constant headaches for the management. Therefore, for the success of an enterprise, human resources planning is a very important function, which can be neglected only at its own peril. It is as necessary as planning for production, marketing, or capital investment.

For an individual, it is important because it helps him to improve his skills and utilise his capabilities and potential to the utmost. For an organisation, it is important because it improves its efficiency and productivity. It is only through initial human manpower planning that capable hands are available for promotion in the future.

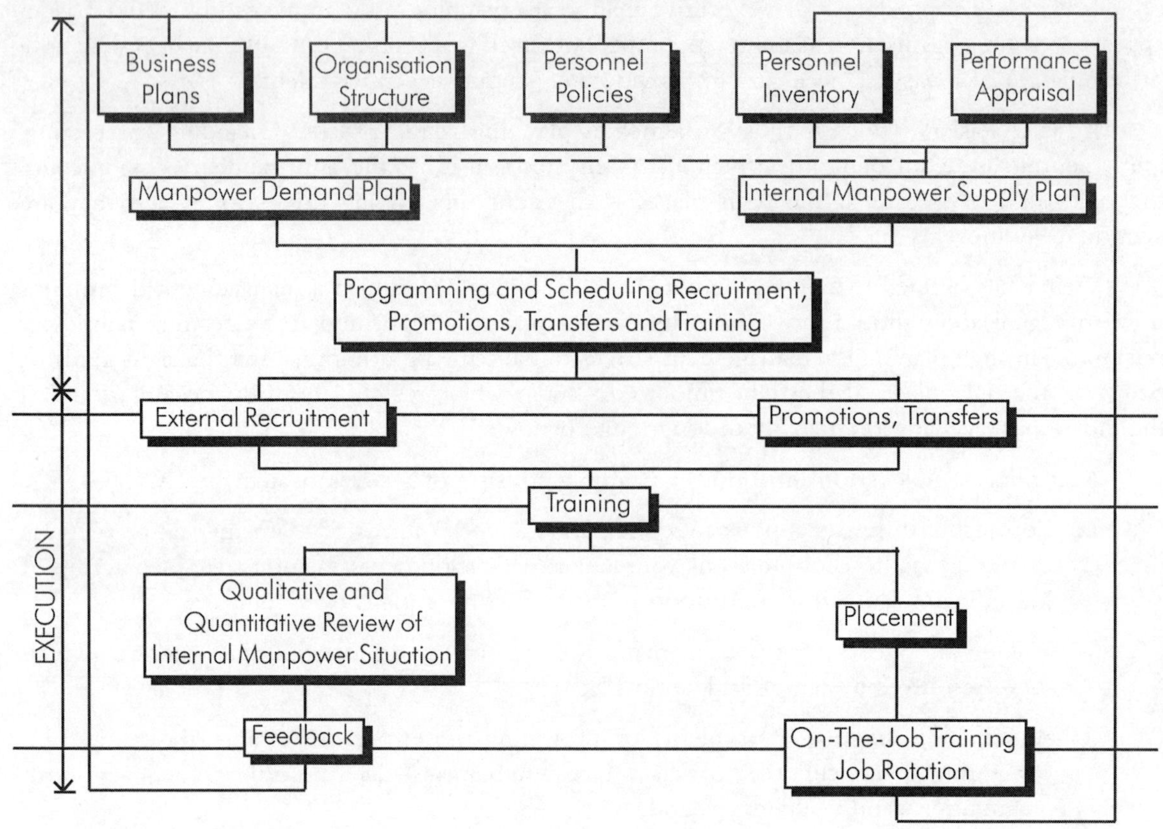

Fig. 18.1 Diagrammatic Representation of Manpower Functions in a Bank.

Source: The Chartered Accountant, Vol. XXII — Part II

Salient Features

The definitions of manpower planning stated above possess the following features:

(1) It includes all activities in regard to human resources.

(2) It is concerned with finding out the manpower requirements of the organisation in the right number and at the right time.

(3) It determines in advance the manpower requirements so that there will be enough time for training and development of manpower.

(4) It includes inventory of present manpower of the organisation. An analysis of the existing inventory helps in determining the status of available personnel and to discover the untapped talent presently within the organisation.

(5) With the knowledge of total needs of manpower and the present supply of available personnel, it takes decisions to meet the difference between demand and supply of manpower. If future needs are more than the available talent, it initiates programmes for

recruitment and development of manpower. On the other hand, if future needs are less than the available talent, it takes measures such as retiring personnel, etc.

(6) To be effective, manpower planning must include not only recruitment, development of workers, etc., but also their working conditions.

Objectives of Manpower Planning

Manpower planning fulfils individual organisational and national goals. The principal objective of manpower planning is to match the power or integrate it with the organisational plan to achieve the goals or objectives.

The objectives of manpower planning are:

(1) To relate future human resources to future organisational needs so as to maximise the future return on investment in human resources.

(2) To match employee abilities to organisational requirements, with an emphasis on future instead of present arrangement.

(3) To plan for the required human resources in terms of skills, knowledge, aptitude, attitude of the existing and newly-recruited human resources.

(4) To ensure optimum use of human resources currently employed.

(5) To assess or forecast future skills requirements if the organisation's overall objectives are to be achieved; and

(6) To provide control measures to ensure that the necessary resources are available as and when required.

A few more specific reasons for attaching importance to manpower planning and forecasting exercises are:

(1) To determine recruitment level;

(2) To anticipate redundancies and avoid unnecessary dismissals;

(3) To determine optimum training levels;

(4) To provide a basis for management development programmes;

(5) To cast the manpower in new projects;

(6) To assist productivity bargaining; and

(7) To assess future accommodation requirements.

Need for Human Resources Planning in Banks

Human resources planning is deemed necessary for all banks for the following reasons:

(1) To carry on its work, each organisation needs personnel with the necessary qualifications, skills, knowledge, work experience and aptitudes. These are provided through effective planning.

(2) Since a large number of persons have to be replaced who have grown old, or who retire, die or become incapacitated because of physical or mental ailments, there is a constant need for replacing such personnel.

(3) Human resources planning is essential because of frequent labour turnover which is unavoidable and even beneficial because it arises from factors which are socially and economically sound such as voluntary quits, discharges, marriage, promotions; or factors such as seasonal and cyclical fluctuations in business which cause a constant ebb and flow in the work force in many organisations.

(4) In order to meet the needs of expansion programmes which become necessary because of increase in the demand for goods and services by a growing population, a rising standard of living, which calls for larger quantities of the same goods and services as also for new goods; the competitive position of a firm which brings it more business arising from improvements effected in the slump period; and the rate of growth of the organisation, human resources planning is unavoidable.

(5) The nature of the present work force in relation to its changing needs also necessitates the recruitment of new labour. To meet the challenge of a new and changing technology and new techniques of production, existing employees need to be trained or new blood injected into an organisation.

(6) Manpower planning is also needed in order to identify areas of surplus personnel or areas in which there is a shortage of personnel. If there is a surplus, it can be redeployed; and if there is a shortage, it may be made good.

Organisational Planning vs. Human Resources Planning in Banks

Organisational planning and human resources planning of banks are highly interrelated. Human resources planning in most cases is based on the bank's organisational planning. In fact human resources planning may become the basis for organisational planning in some cases. Organisational planning is an organic process-oriented approach to organisational change and management effectiveness of banks. Further, organisational development in banks, referred to as organisational planning, stresses individual human adaptation and development to bank's organisational changes. Thus, organisational planning and human resources planning in banks are highly interrelated.

Steps in Manpower Planning in Banks

Manpower planning is a process. The important steps in manpower planning in banks are:

(1) Formulation of long-range, short-range objectives, plans, programmes, and budgets of banks regarding their key activities like branch expansion, deposits and other sources of mobilisation, loans and advances, organisation and other key services.

Commercial banks take into consideration the long-run objectives and plans while planning for human resources relating to: (i) branch expansion in different areas like backward, unbanked, underbanked, rural, urban etc.; (ii) deposit mobilisation from different sections of the economy; (iii) deployment of credit to priority and conventional sectors (in detail); (iv) improvements or changes in the quality as well as quantity of customer service; (v) end-use of credit; (vi) improving the recovery performance; (vii) educating the borrowers; (viii) conditions/regulations to be imposed by the Reserve Bank of India or Government; (ix) changes in the economy, society and other environmental factors; (x) technological changes like computerisation in banks.

(2) Estimation of overall manpower requirements — occupational, category and skill-wise analyses at different levels of the bank's hierarchy.

(3) Find out the current inventory or manpower, principal dimensions of manpower inventory being:

(a) Head counts — total, department, sex, designation, skill-wise.

(b) Job family inventory — clerks, typists, officers — General, Technical, and at different levels like grade A, B, C and D.

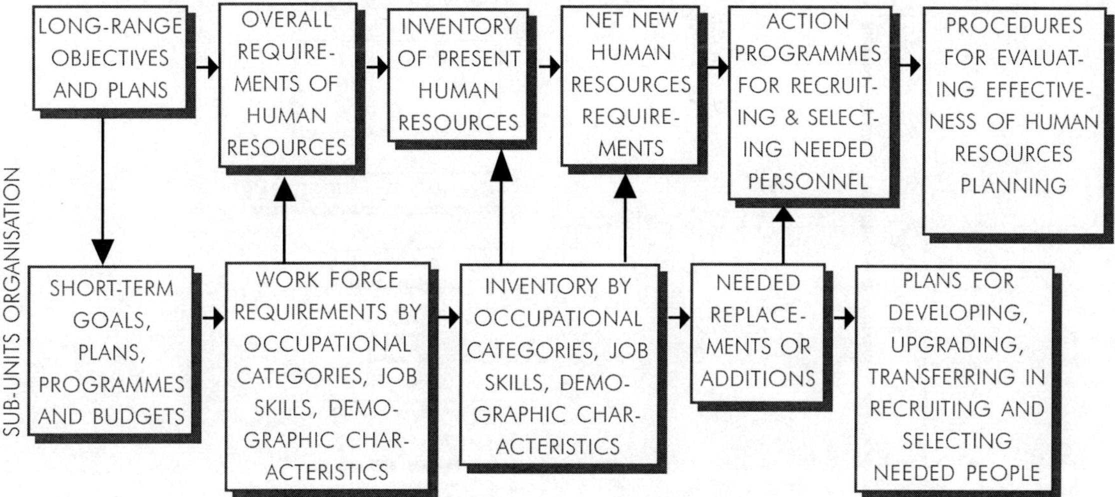

Fig. 18.2 Human Resources Planning System.

(c) Age Inventory.

(d) Inventory of experience, skill, talent, ability, aptitude, knowledge and the like.

(e) Inventory of qualifications, training and executive development.

(f) Inventory of salary grades.

(g) Inventory of performance.

(h) Inventory of potential.

(4) Forecast the changes in human resources inventory due to employee turnover, transfers, promotions, demotions, training and career plan and development.

The plan factors and forecasts will help the banker to determine the quantity and quality of work to be turned out and thereby to estimate the total number and kind of personnel (branch-wise, department-wise, category-wise, job-wise etc.) required to meet the future demand in terms of knowledge, skill, creative abilities, talents, aptitudes, attitudes, and the like, in this connection, the banker also takes into consideration short-term goals, plans, programmes and budgets, etc.

(5) Find out the difference between the current inventory and future total human resources requirements.

(6) Correcting the imbalances between demand and supply.

(7) Action programmes for recruiting and selecting for the needed human resources or adjusting the employees through transfers, promotions or adjusting human resources through moulding and developing.

(8) Prepare the plans for training, development, promotions, transfers, demotions, etc.

(9) Evaluating the performance.

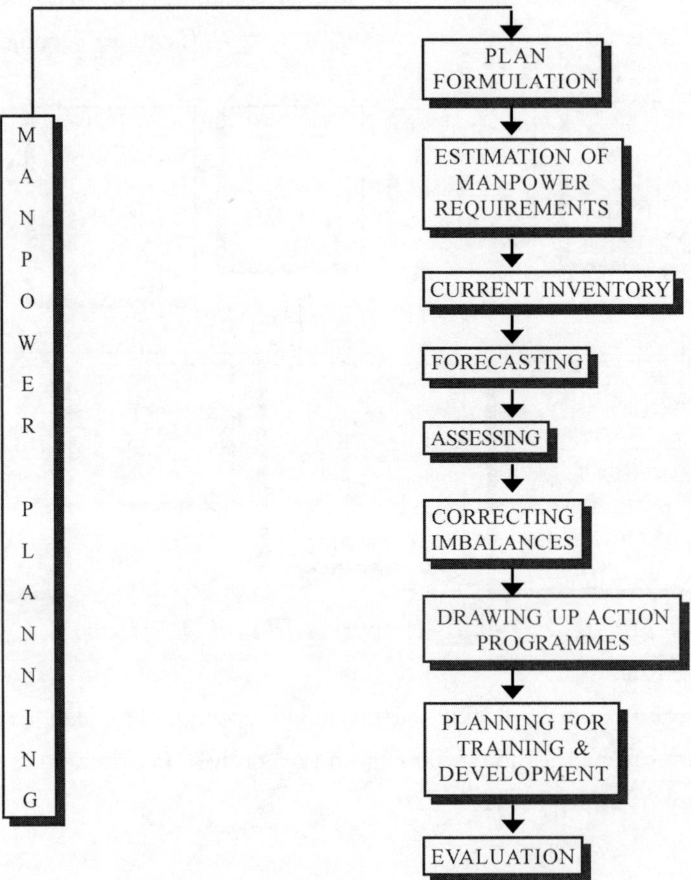

Fig. 18.3 Steps in Manpower Planning.

Factors affecting human resources supply are:

1. **Internal Factors:** (a) Present inventory; (b) Possible changes in the present inventory.
2. **External Factors:** (a) Local population density in the area, local unemployment level, availability of employees on part-time/temporary basis, current competition for similar categories, outcome from local educational institutions, pattern of immigration, residential facilities available, local transport and communication facilities.

(b) National: Trends in the growth of the working population, training institutes, schemes, technical, professional, vocational and general educational institutes, social security measures, unemployment benefits, lay-off, retrenchment, cultural factors, customs, social values and the like.

Time Period for Manpower Planning

Manpower planning can be classified on the basis of time span. On this basis, manpower planning can be made short-term, medium-term or long-term. Generally, short-term planning is made for a period of up to two years, medium-term planning up to 5 years and long-term planning for more than 5 years. While short-term manpower planning is essentially concerned with matching the existing jobs with the existing individuals and filling current vacancies with the available talent, medium and long-term manpower planning is concerned mainly with future vacancies.

Manpower Planning Process

Manpower planning process consists of three phases:

Phase One. This phase is mainly concerned with job analysis and skills inventory. It tries to find out its current position and match the existing jobs with the existing individuals and filling current vacancies with the available manpower, because the time is too short to make any changes in personnel or to recruit or to develop personnel or to create or eliminate jobs.

Job analysis is the process by which pertinent information relating to the nature of a specific job in the organisation is obtained. Job analysis involves job description and job specification. While job description describes the job and specifies the requirements of a job, job specification states the qualities needed for an individual to perform the job successfully. Skill inventory as we have already observed helps the organisation in getting information about the quantity and quality of its current human resources. Thus, through job analysis, an organisation can know its current resources needs and through skill inventory, it can know the quantity and quality of its current human resources.

Phase Two. This phase is concerned with personnel forecasting. Personnel forecasting is a process by which the future personnel requirements of the organisation to achieve the organisational objectives is determined. For making personnel forecasting, many variables such as composition of present work force, skill required in the potential new business venture, future sales projections, technological changes etc., are considered. Because of the important role human resources play in attaining enterprise objectives, all levels of management should be involved in the personnel forecasting process.

Phase Three. This phase is concerned with the taking of measures to obtain the quantity and quality of human resources to achieve the enterprise objectives. In the second phase, human resources requirements have been estimated to achieve enterprise objectives. These human resources needs indicate gross personnel requirements. The skills inventory which has been done in the first phase of the manpower planning process indicates the current quantity and quality of human resources with the enterprise. The difference between the gross personnel requirements and the organisation's current level of human resources is referred to as the net 'personnel requirements.' It may be positive or negative.

The organisation takes measures to bring the current level of quantity and quality of its human resources in tune with the requirements as forecast. To achieve this, the methods adopted are recruitment, selection, training promotion, transfer, layoffs and retirement of employees.

Career Planning

Career planning is choosing an occupation keeping in view one's resources and environmental conditions. Career planning is not an event or an end but a process which requires continuous examination of the goal, the strategies to be chosen, the resources and limitations on the part of the individual, the organisation and the environment. Career planning is of less importance in a stable society but has greater importance in an adaptive society. Career planning requires that individual employees, particularly those in the supervisory and managerial role, develop early in their careers insights into their suitability for creative vs. ordinary or routine work. Those who do not possess or cannot develop the ability required for top level managerial positions might look towards routine jobs in large organisations.

From the above, it clearly follows that career planning is an essential aspect of managing people to obtain the maximum performance. It is aimed at:

(a) improving the performance of subordinates on their present job in terms of results to be accomplished;

(b) to prepare employees to accept increasing responsibility in their present jobs; and

(c) to help subordinates grow and develop for higher level jobs.

Career planning is thus an important and an integral part of the manpower planning and development system.

The overall aim of career planning is to give individuals the guidance and encouragement they need to bring out their potential and have a successful career in the organisation matching their talents and aspirations.

Myths of Career Planning

There are many myths related to career planning which have surfaced over the years. These myths are often misleading and can inhibit career growth. One such myth is that there is always room for one more person at the top. The major lesson to be learned is to choose career paths that are realistic and attainable. The second myth is that career planning is the sole responsibility of the organisation. But career planning and development is a two-way process and both the organisation and the individual must play their part. The ultimate responsibility for career planning, however, rests with the individual. Successful career planning results from the joint efforts of the individual and the organisation. The individual does the planning and the organisation provides the necessary guidance and resources.

A person is more likely to experience satisfaction as progress is made along the career path. A good career plan identifies certain milestones and when these are consciously recognised and reached, the person is likely to experience a sense of achievement. The feeling of accomplishment increases the individual's personal satisfaction and motivation.

Responsibility for Career Planning

A fundamental question regarding career planning arises as to who is responsible for career planning: is it the employee or the management? Career planning is basically an individual's responsibility. However, in the organisational context, it is the organisation's responsibility to guide and direct the employees to develop and utilise their knowledge, abilities and resources toward organisational development and effectiveness. Employee goals have to be integrated with organisational goals. The organisation must provide career counselling services. Such a programme has the following objectives:

(a) Provide a normal, mature person with guidelines to help him understand himself more clearly and develop his thinking and outlook.

(b) Enable the individual to study the immediate and personal world in which he lives, a world different from all others and possibly more exciting.

(c) To bring about a closer relationship between people as well as increase one's awareness of human needs.

(d) To understand the forces and dynamics operating in a system.

(e) To achieve and enjoy greater personal satisfaction, pleasure and happiness.

The individual and the organisation will have to operate in close coordination in the 'career exercise' and the organisation has to provide timely intervention at various stages of the career programmes to make it a fruitful and satisfying experience, both for the employee and the institution. Any ' attitudinal slackness' on the part of the organisation can result in demoralisation leading to frustration and ultimate collapse of the Career Planning System. The phase-wise close monitoring remains the prime responsibility of the organisation.

At the start of the career, new skills are acquired, knowledge increases rapidly, and aspirations and inclinations are clarified. Job rotation programme opens up 'career paths' that were previously blocked to a person because he lacked the necessary experience.

The first step towards attaining the skills for a higher position in the hierarchy is identifying and defining those skills. This can be done either by the organisation or by the individual aspiring for promotion. The relative importance of the various skills at different levels can be highlighted diagrammatically. As one moves higher, the importance of technical skills is reduced, and that of conceptual skill gains prominence. Broadly speaking, the skills at different levels are as shown in Fig. 18.4. The organisation plays a prominent role at this stage in providing opportunity for all-round experience and enables the employee to identify skills and qualities needed for the current and future jobs.

The all-round multifarious experience gained in the initial years brings the employee to a critical point, where he has to choose his career path. The skill and knowledge gained in the formative years is applied, tested, identified and consolidated, and aspirations are confirmed and amended accordingly. The organisation's role in the career development of the employee at this juncture is to help him align and integrate personal aspirations with organisational objectives. The organisation also, keeping in view the future needs, should make available career paths not just for upward mobility but lateral too.

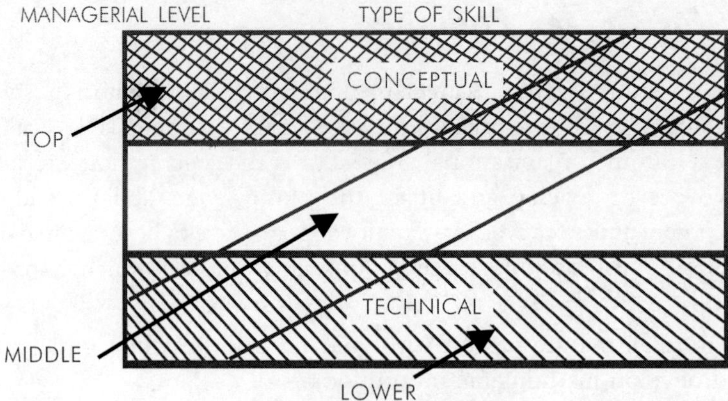

Fig. 18.4 Types of Skills.

Persistent people know they can succeed where cleverer and more talented people fail. It involves making choices, which is risky. Successful people understand that no one makes it to the top in a single bound. What truly sets them apart is their willingness to keep putting one step in front of the other — no matter how rough the terrain.

Career Planning Process

On the basis of manpower planning, the organisation will have the following information:

(a) An inventory of manpower resources.

(b) Manpower needs, in terms of numbers, types, skills, levels and time dimensions.

(c) Changes in functions and activities expected in the next two or five or ten years hence, if not for a longer period.

(d) Nature and extent of behavioural changes required to meet the manpower needs.

(e) Availability of human resources within and without the organisation, training opportunities, training resources, and training time, etc.

On the basis of the above information, an effective organisational career planning process should include the following:

A. Assessment of occupational and career choice.

B. Personnel assessment.

C. Annual appraisal and development programme.

Career Growth of Employees

Employees can feel the organisational interest in their growth, if they are provided with constant information on banking, its schemes, ways of improving business, etc., as this would give them confidence and motivation to achieve better and give them a taste of success. A news letter providing this relevant information which also encourages their participation and suggestion would facilitate "information explosion." Open communication should be encouraged through various ways and employees should talk about bank schemes. Without proper dissemination of work-aiding information, the employees are conspicuously oblivious of the progress of their own bank and its services and do not get a visible feel of the organisation. By professionalising in this fashion, they would feel that the organisation means business. For instance, if newly inducted employees are straightaway put in the field to collect deposits, it would help in developing them as field people and also help the organisation by adding to its deposits.

BOX 18.1

HOW TO BE OPTIMISTIC

- **You can only have one thought at a time**

This is the key to feeling optimistic, enjoying your life, and fulfilling your vision for a delightful life. You only can keep one thought in your head at a time. So, what should your one thought be? Dwell on what you want to accomplish. Do not dwell on what you do not want.

- **Expect the best**

What are you thinking about? Do you have a goal or an exciting vision for living your life? Ralph Waldo Emerson once said, "A man is what he thinks about all day long." Generally, as you begin your day or a project, your frame-of-mind proves extremely important.

- **Strong ambition**

Wishy-washy people do not go very far. They get swayed by whatever crosses their paths. In contrast, the people who move mountains, people who get things done, are people who feel a profound sense of mission. They dive into their projects with gusto. Every highly successful person is a maniac on a mission.

- **Gumption to change how you think**

The way you handle situations has served you to some degree. Now, you have a tremendous opportunity to feel more confident and optimistic than you ever may have dreamed possible. You can unleash your energy and hone your focus on what you most want.

- **Persistence**

Persistence is a key to feeling happy. Fascinating research done at Stanford University proves that persistent people achieve more than their less persistent colleagues.

Successful Career Planning Programme

(1) An organisation must have clear corporate goals for the next five, ten and fifteen years.

(2) On the basis of corporate plans, an organisational analysis should be conducted periodically to determine the types of changes, its functions, activities, procedures, technology, materials.

(3) Unless the above two are completed, an organisation cannot develop the manpower planning system, thus reducing the need for career planning.

(4) Career planning requires selecting the right man for the right job. Job design systems require understanding employee resources and clarity of organisational, divisional and unit goals. In an employment-oriented organisation, there is hardly any place for career planning except at the top level. In most government organisations in India, employees stagnate at the very level they join. In most cases, getting a job and holding on to it is a blessing and an achievement.

(5) Career planning is a top management philosophy and commitment. The success of career planning programme will depend upon the sincerity of the top management and the interest it takes in the development and utilisation of the employee to achieve organisational effectiveness, development, innovation, health and vitality.

(6) Career planning is a continuous process. This process may be followed yearly, two-yearly or five-yearly. In organisations such as space research, electronics and other adaptive organisations, the process should be carried out more frequently and consistently.

(7) An effective career planning programme requires interested, goal-directed, motivated and hard working employees. An organisation can create an environment and show genuine concern for the development of the employee but the employee must be willing to make use of the resources and opportunities available.

Career planning is an integral part of manpower planning. It contributes towards individual development and utilisation as well as organisational development.

Career Counselling

Career Counselling or Vocational Guidance is the process of facilitating a person to make a suitable career decision based on his individual abilities and expectations in keeping with the job context. Vocational guidance includes proper psychometric testing and further one-to-one counselling session with the parents and the child along with the report/profile of the child/individual.

Banks should have a professional career counsellor to play the role of catalyst to bring about the desired outcome and groom the employees to cater to the changing needs in banking.

A career counsellor is by qualification and not by position or designation. One needs a Master's Degree (Psychology/Counselling Psychology/Educational Psychology or other related) or a Post Graduate Diploma in Guidance and Counselling, and undergo a proper vocational guidance training by relevant authorities.

Things to keep in Mind

- There has to be a report/profile handed over by the counsellor to the counselee.
- Psychometric test includes Aptitude, Interest, Intelligence, Personality and Adjustment Tests. These tests are normed and validated. Very few computerised tests have been designed in this regard.
- Most of the scientific instruments are paper pencil tests (3-5 hours), and they are the most preferred tests by counsellors.
- Psychometric tests are not based on any academic syllabus/curriculum. There is no prior preparation required for taking up these tests. One should be relaxed, focused, alert and honest in answering the tests.
- The tests unveil the individual's potentials and options.
- Professional counselling is usually a paid service.

- The counsellor does not take a decision for you, but provides guidelines and facilitates the decision-making process. The objective of a counselling session is to narrow down the choices.
- Ensure that the counsellor is not being biased or non-judgemental.
- Counselling is done on a one-to-one basis with the student and his/her parent/s. Ideally, there should be no group counselling.
- Check if the counsellor is updated with information as regards to various universities, courses, entrance exams, etc.
- In case a person wants to take a second opinion, there has to be sufficient time gap between two assessments.
- The benefits of counselling sessions are intangible and the results may show only after 5-7 years (if you take career decisions in line with counsellor's suggestions).

Responsibility for Human Resources Planning

Human resources planning is the responsibility of the personnel department. In this task, it is aided by the industrial engineering department, the top management and the team of directors of different departments. It is mostly a staffing or personnel function. The overall responsibility lies with the Board of Directors because, as the manpower planning scheme of Hindustan Lever indicates, "these members are in a position to direct the future course of business, set appropriate goals for the management concerned in the formulation of personnel policies." The personnel department's responsibility is "to recommend relevant personnel policies in respect of manpower planning, devise methods of procedure, and determine the quantitative aspects of manpower planning."

The responsibilities of the personnel department in regard to manpower planning have been stated by Geisler in the following words:

(i) To assist, counsel and pressurise the operating management to plan and establish objectives;

(ii) To collect and summarise data in total organisational terms and to ensure consistency with long-range objectives and other elements of the total business plan;

(iii) To monitor and measure performance against the plan and keep the top management informed about it; and

(iv) To provide the research necessary for effective manpower and organisational planning.

The Future of Work

- In the knowledge economy, employees will own the tools of production-ideas-and hence the work itself.
- The work of tomorrow will demand formal education and more cutting-edge knowledge accumulation.

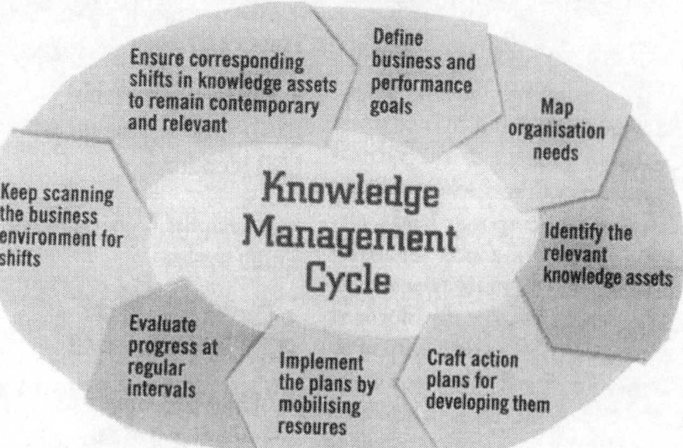

- The focus is on work that adds higl the organisation, work that is spec and not easily duplicable competitors.
- In future corporations, employees will be expected to 'own' their functional responsibilities.
- To achieve the specified goal within the budgeted time and money, t worker would need to accept and est control over all related processes.
- Working smarter would mean not just doing a given job well, but also stretching it into a mini-profit-making project.
- Work is characterised by multiplicity of roles and connectivity between functions.
- The onus of work has moved from the top to the organisation.
- It is possible for people from different locations to combine skills and working together on projects.
- Work will increasingly come to people, rather than people going out for work.
- Work synthesis would also involve matching long-term personal goals with choice of work.
- The future will see smart work, smart roles, and smart teams.
- New economic organisations and start-ups will ask for comfort with ambiguity. And all this without deviating from performance focus.
- The leadership paradigms will have to change drastically. Trust have to replace paranoia.
- **The Autocratic Leader:** Leads through a chain of commands, and demands compliance.
- **The Hierarchical Leader:** Leads through sanctioned power associated with position.
- **The Participatory Leader:** Leads through facilitation and empowerment, enthusing rather than dictating.
- **Leader as Team Player:** The new leader will work and play with his team, and as a hands-on participant in tomorrow's organisation.
- **Leader as Coach:** In future, the onus will firmly be on empowerment and facilitation and not on the top-down chain-of-command.
- **Leader as Rule-Breaker:** The leader will need to steer his team through business and market ambiguity.
- **Leader as Performance-Driver:** The leader will ensure a comprehensive talent assessment, with focus on performance.

- **Leader as Profit-Maximiser:** Profit maximisation, rather than span of control, will decide the leader's course of action and accordingly, the organisation design. Organisations will be amalgamations of profit-making entities with leaders emerging at business levels.

The new leader will combine roles: The new work will straddle functions, industries, and boundaries. And both will combine to create new workers, new work styles, new organisational structures, new career and performance paradigms, and new ways of balancing work and life.

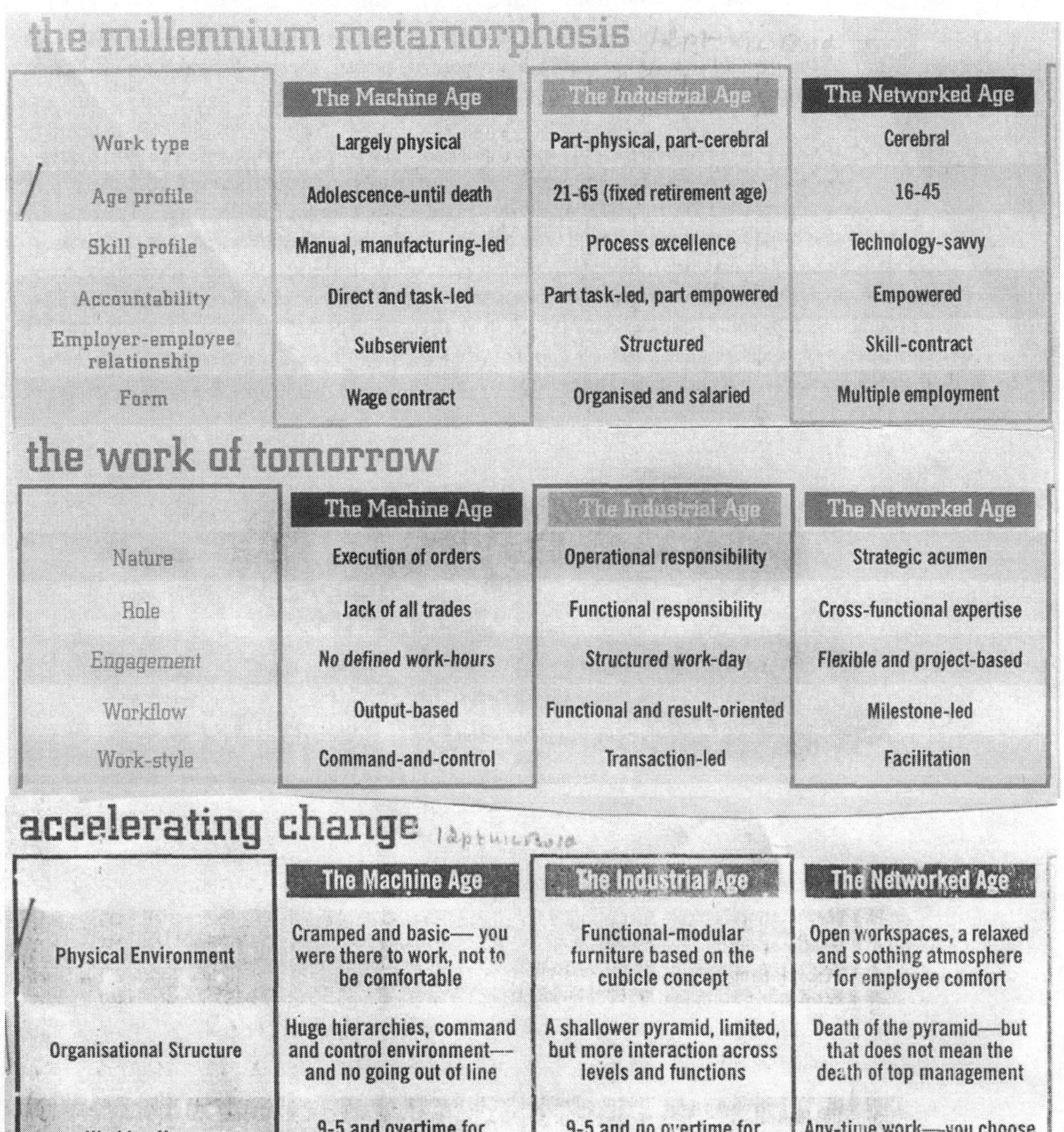

the millennium metamorphosis

	The Machine Age	The Industrial Age	The Networked Age
Work type	Largely physical	Part-physical, part-cerebral	Cerebral
Age profile	Adolescence-until death	21-65 (fixed retirement age)	16-45
Skill profile	Manual, manufacturing-led	Process excellence	Technology-savvy
Accountability	Direct and task-led	Part task-led, part empowered	Empowered
Employer-employee relationship	Subservient	Structured	Skill-contract
Form	Wage contract	Organised and salaried	Multiple employment

the work of tomorrow

	The Machine Age	The Industrial Age	The Networked Age
Nature	Execution of orders	Operational responsibility	Strategic acumen
Role	Jack of all trades	Functional responsibility	Cross-functional expertise
Engagement	No defined work-hours	Structured work-day	Flexible and project-based
Workflow	Output-based	Functional and result-oriented	Milestone-led
Work-style	Command-and-control	Transaction-led	Facilitation

accelerating change

	The Machine Age	The Industrial Age	The Networked Age
Physical Environment	Cramped and basic— you were there to work, not to be comfortable	Functional-modular furniture based on the cubicle concept	Open workspaces, a relaxed and soothing atmosphere for employee comfort
Organisational Structure	Huge hierarchies, command and control environment—and no going out of line	A shallower pyramid, limited, but more interaction across levels and functions	Death of the pyramid—but that does not mean the death of top management
Working Hours	9-5 and overtime for working late	9-5 and no overtime for working late	Any-time work—you choose the hours you want to work

Conclusion

Manpower planning is a key factor in achieving the banking goals and objectives. In particular, banks that are expanding and dynamic in character and have a high labour turnover must systematically plan their short-term, medium-term and long-term manpower needs meticulously. Over and above, it is a continuous process and needs periodic reviews and adjustments to meet the changing conditions. Manpower planning helps banks in effecting and adjusting to new changes without much difficulty. The process of manpower planning is one of the most crucial complex and continuing managerial functions which "embrace organisational development, management development, career planning and succession planning." Career management is essentially managing change. Tomorrow's people have no problem in developing their skills, by being responsive to change. Career plans normally require that the individual acquires skills and training as he proceeds on the chosen career path. The process has gained importance in banks with the increase in the size of business, diversified services, improved information technology, upgradation of technology in working (such as the introduction of computers and electronic instruments) necessitating changes in the skills of employees, as well as a change in the number of employees needed and leadership styles. Banks will benefit much more by manpower planning in the optimum utilisation of its manpower effectively and productively for better performance and excellent customer services. Manpower planning is essential to managing change. Those who fail to do so become yesterday's people and decline and fall.

Chapter 19

Quality Circles in Banks

The Cost of Success

I'm a catalyst for change.... You can't be an outsider and be successful over 30 years without leaving a certain amount of scar tissue around the place.

— *Rupert Murdoch, Chairman, News Corporation*

Introduction

The basic philosophy of participative management is that once the people are committed to the goals of the organisation, they will exercise self-direction and self-control in the service of the objectives to which they are committed. Their commitment to objectives is a function of the rewards associated with their achievement and therefore, external control and the threat of punishment are not the only means to bring about efforts towards achieving organisational objectives. In order to create proper conditions for people to seek and accept responsibility, conscious efforts are required to be made to involve them at all levels — intellectual, emotional and physical — in decision-making process. Employees' participation in the management process at all levels is expected to bring about improved employee morale and increased productivity. With this end in view, the various techniques of participative management have been tried — employee suggestion scheme, work/floor committees, house journals, representation on the board, etc. with varied results. Quality Circle is one such technique which has played a significant role in creating awareness for sustained quality improvement. In this chapter, we analyse Quality Circles' relevance to the banking system.

Complete Quality Process

Over the last fifty or so years, three distinct ways have evolved as to how to phrase the question. "Who will be involved in this organisation's Quality Process?" As the demands of the customer become more and more strident, the changing questions have reflected the fact that companies have had to stray further and further from their traditional (and comfortable) paradigm, wherein all information and all directives flowed from top to bottom.

Is such a process truly feasible? Yes — and an overview of the components of such an effort, called a Complete Quality Process (CQP), will be the subject of the next three articles in this series.

Understanding the CQP approach to defining, implementing and maintaining a 100 per cent employee-involved quality effort begins with two pairs of words:

- Simple vs Complex
- Easy vs Difficult

A quality process is simple but difficult. The concept of quality is not complex, it is that the right thing should be done the right way the first time and every time. That is far short of nuclear physics — or even the dynamics in a moderately interesting family — in complexity. It is, however, very difficult to do — in large part because you have to do it every day, all day. And you have to keep getting better as the definitions of the 'right thing' and 'things right' keep being elevated by either your own employees, your customers or the competition.

There are seven components to a Complete Quality Process:

- Top Management Commitment
- Leadership
- 100 per cent employee commitment — with a structure
- Communications
- Training
- Measurement
- Recognition, Gratitude and Celebration.

Most 'quality consultants' make their money by convincing potential clients that achieving quality is a very complex thing that they (the consultants) will make easy for the top management of the company. That's why a CQP process is designed to have the executives actively involved — with outsiders used as short-term sources of specific technical detail.

This quality stuff can be done. But it is best done if it is recognised that quality is everybody's business, not just the part-time focus of a limited number of people.

What is a Quality Circle?

The term "Quality Circle" is used in a dynamic sense. It refers to the function of participative management which is necessary for bringing people together so as to improve the overall working of an organisation. It may be called the process of management. It is also a means to achieve the ends of the organisation. "Quality Circle" is defined as a "circle of quality-conscious people (workers) organised for quality improvement and also improve their work environment through a systematic approach, i.e., 'bottom up' approach."

A working definition of quality circle which has now become an accepted one in Japan and in all other countries where quality circle is practised is as follows:

"Quality circle is a small voluntary group of people from the same work area who meet together on a regular basis for the purpose of identifying, selecting, analysing and solving quality, productivity, cost reduction, safety, customer service and other work-related problems in their work area, leading to the improvement in their work effectiveness and enrichment of their work life."

The basic idea behind Quality Circle is to fully develop the human capabilities of all employees and thereby lead to the improvement of the organisation. Here also, the basic principle centres around the advantage of worker participation in management — improved personal capability of individual employees, increased self-esteem of individual employees, developing workers' potential to become supervisors of the future, reduced conflicts stemming from work environment and increased involvement of workers in their jobs.

It is a voluntary group of people, say, between 5-8, from the same work area, who meet at regular intervals to identify problems and bottlenecks relating to the work environment, analyse them, work out solutions therefor and implement these solutions, wherever within their jurisdiction, or recommend them to the appropriate authority. The most important feature of a Quality Circle is its voluntary character — nobody is forced to join and nobody is penalised for not taking part in it. Experience has shown that unless the urge for this type of association comes from within, motivation being provided by a desire to seek better job satisfaction and a sense of achievement, worthwhile results cannot be achieved. The Circle, once formed, sets its own terms of reference, selects for itself the problems it wishes to tackle; and in due course, presents its recommendations for implementation to the appropriate authority. In other words, it functions organically — according to its own perceived needs — rather than compulsively in response to externally determined criteria.

Once a Circle has been formed, group meetings take place at fortnightly or monthly intervals. The initial meeting(s) is (are) devoted mainly to the election of a leader whose main function is to enable the people concerned to function as a group rather than as a bunch of individuals. Every group has a facilitator who assists the members in understanding the concept, guides and coordinates the activities of the Circle and generally ensures that the Circle members follow established guidelines. It has to be clearly understood that the facilitator is only an impartial observer during the meetings and does not actively participate in the discussions unlike the leader who is responsible for the effective performance of the Circle. For establishing the policy and guidelines for Circle activities and for effectively monitoring and guiding its programmes, a Steering Committee can be constituted which would be in the nature of a "support group."

Quality Circle in Banks

Though the Quality Circle movement was initially started in the manufacturing industries, it was soon realised that it had much to commend to the service industries like banking which employ a large work force and handles multi-dimensional functional areas. Notwithstanding the fact that the men and women in the banking sector today are amongst the highest qualified and best paid and served, the level of their involvement and motivation towards achievement of organisational and national goals has often been the subject of adverse criticism. It was, therefore, rightly perceived that QC philosophy may perhaps take care of some of the problems leading to better task identity, job

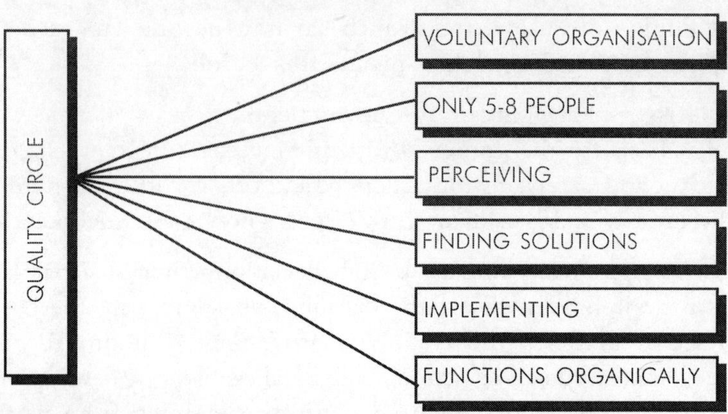

Fig. 19.1 Characteristics of a Quality Circle

enrichment and consequently, customer orientation. The Bhopal Circle of the State Bank of India was the first to appreciate the underlying philosophy of QC and its potential for tapping the innate creativity of the employees not only for tackling the various problems relating to their work environment but also for improving their commitment towards organisational goals. To start with, a number of seminars were organised in which selected senior functionaries were exposed to the manifold facets of the philosophy as the acceptance of the ideas by the senior managers and controllers was considered pivotal to the success of the experiment. This was followed by identification of a few branches, to start with, the entire staff of which was introduced to the concept and all encouragement was provided to them to form QCs. The next step was organising appropriate training programmes for leaders and facilitators of the QC teams of certain quality control techniques, necessary for a scientific approach to the solution. Thence onwards the QC philosophy caught the imagination of the bankers and a number of QCs in the banking industry has been steadily rising covering both the public and private sector banks. The international convention on Quality Circles organised by the Quality Circle Forum of India (QCFI) in December 1989 in Delhi amply proved the growing faith and interest in this particular movement in India and gave the much-desired fillip to it resulting in the philosophy being internalised by a large number of organisations both in public and private sectors and Government agencies. An important fall-out was the formation of similar group activities among management personnel though the scheme was initially conceived for grass-root level workers only.

In a broader perspective, Quality Circle in banks means working together in a group so as to bring about improvement in services as well as in improving the quality of work life. Thus, Quality Circles in banks will benefit customers, employees and management.

Procedure for Meetings

The meetings of Quality Circles are held at weekly intervals. The meetings, which are held during the working hours, normally last for one hour. The day and time for the meetings are decided by members of the QC in consultation with the Branch Manager and other staff members. Normally, the meetings are held at the same time every week and the members gradually develop the habit of assembling for the meetings at the specified time. Usually, the QC meets towards the end of the day to avoid disruption in the daily routine.

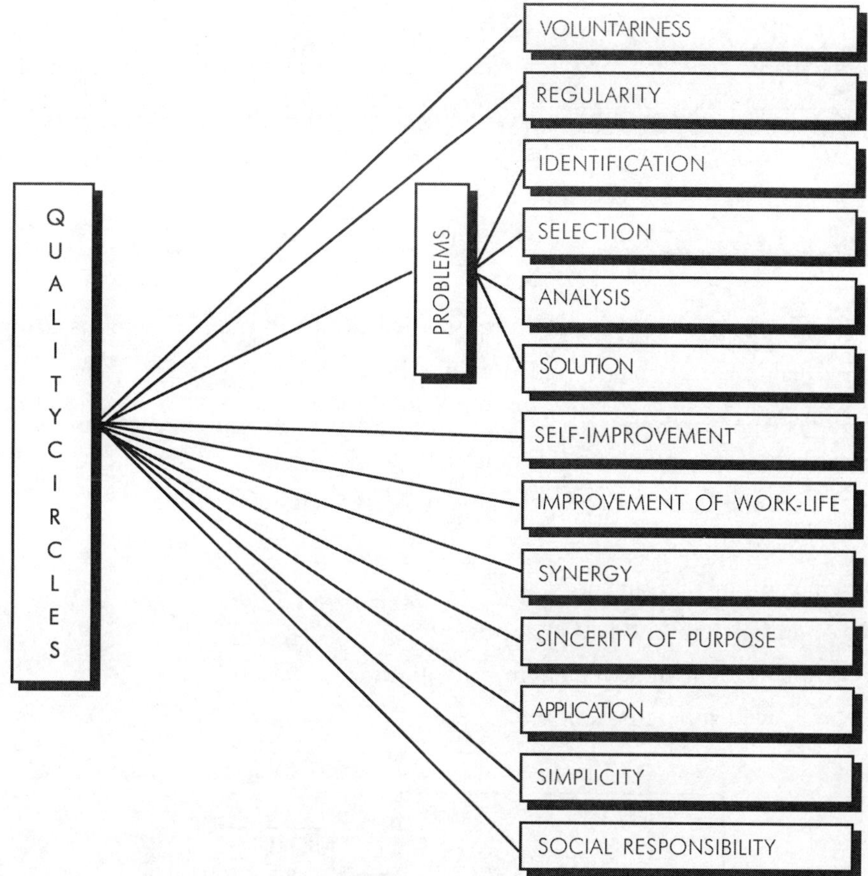

Fig. 19.2 Ten Principles of Quality Circles.

It is interesting to note that in several QCs, the meetings tend to extend up to two or even three hours beyond the office hours. This indicates that the members derive a good deal of inner satisfaction during the meetings.

Objectives of Quality Circles

As Quality Circles in banks are mainly related with human beings such as customers and employees in a predominantly service organisation, they should aim at providing service efficiently and effectively at the minimum cost.

The main objectives of the Quality Circles are:

(i) to improve their work environment;

(ii) to solve their problems in a novel way;

(iii) to cultivate responsive behavioural patterns among workers;

(iv) to improve job satisfaction;

(v) to create healthier industrial relations;

(vi) to improve customer services;

(vii) to improve the quality of services;

(viii) to sharpen and encourage workers' creativity and innovative application of mind and will;

(ix) to bring about improvement in the quality of work life; and

(x) to encourage the establishment of a coherent management philosophy in the organisations and banks in particular.

Areas Touched Upon

Quality Circles in banks have shown impressive results in many directions. Empirical studies show that the Quality Circles have yielded results in the following areas:

(i) customer service;

(ii) streamlining branch functioning;

(iii) increasing business and profitability by reducing overheads;

(iv) recovery of bad debts;

(v) prevention of frauds;

(vi) optimum utilisation of manpower;

(vii) improvement in work environment; and

(viii) improved job satisfaction.

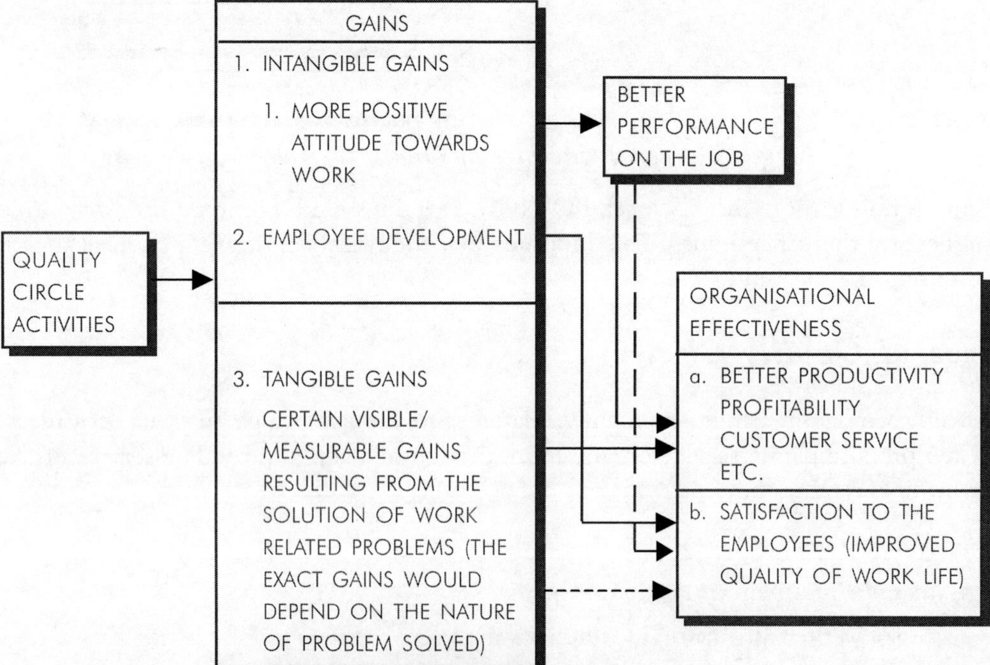

Fig. 19.3 Benefits from Quality Circle

Source: P. Amsa, "Benefits from Quality Circles", Vinimaya, July-Dec. 1987, National Institute of Bank Management, Pune.

The impact of Quality Circles on the banking activities are summarised in Table 19.1.

Steps Involved in Quality Circles

(1) Identification of the problem: Problems for possible solution can be identified by any one of the members. These may arise, for example, from customer complaints, management information or feedback received from other departments.

(2) Description of the problem: The identified problem is looked at from the various points of view and then taken up for discussion. The various aspects of the problem are considered in detail with the help of the cause-effect diagram, which assists in an organised approach to the solution.

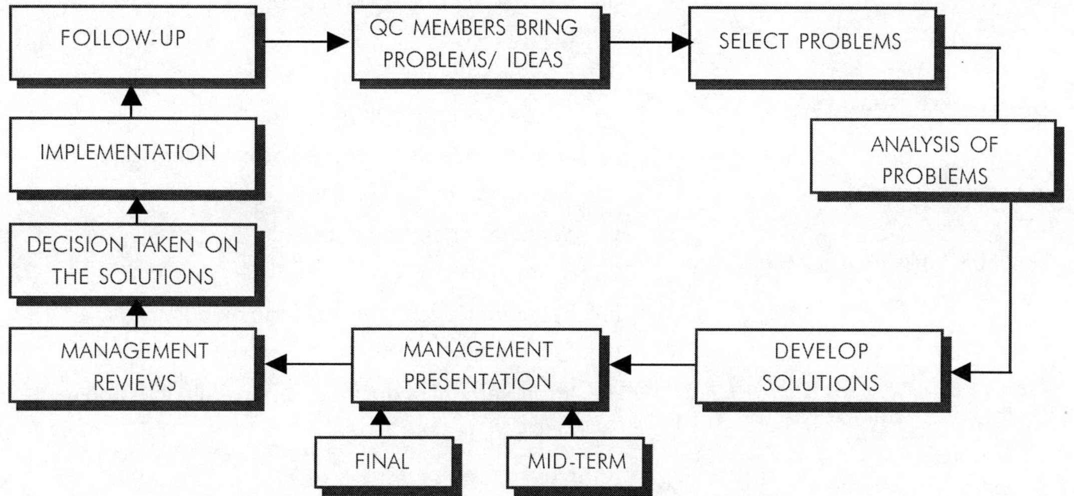

Fig. 19.4 Quality Circles Operation Cycle.

Table 19.1
Areas Covered by Quality Circles in Banks

Areas Covered	Project Completed
I. Customer Service	(i) Reduction in transaction time
	(ii) Timely payment of pensions
	(iii) Timely payment of salaries
	(iv) Prompt issue/payment of drafts
	(v) Statement of accounts
	(vi) Updating of pass books
	(vii) Timely despatch of letters/advices to customers
	(viii) Guidance to customers
	(ix) Improving staff-customer relations
	(i) Smooth and quick flow of vouchers

II. Streamlining Branch Functioning	(ii) Reconciliation of drafts issued
	(iii) Timely balancing of cash book
	(iv) Coping with heavy work on salary days, etc.
	(v) Easing the problem of handling SIB ledgers
	(vi) Smooth financial year closing
	(vii) Effective functioning of electronic accounting machine
	(viii) Miscellaneous subjects related to branch functioning
	(i) Reduction in overheads and augmentation of incomes
III. Increasing Profitability	(i) Growth in resident deposits
IV. Business	(ii) Growth in non-resident deposits through prompt services to NRIs
	(i) Recovery in PB/RD accounts
V. Recovery of Bad Debts	(ii) Recovery of agricultural advances
	(i) Safety of transit vouchers book, tokens & ledgers
VI. Prevention of Frauds	(ii) Prevention of frauds in instruments sent for collection
	(i) Systematic deputation of staff
VII. Optimum Utilisation of Manpower	(ii) Saving man hours
	(iii) Systematic deployment of staff on busy days
	(iv) Overcoming shortage of messengers
	(i) Improvement in arrangements within the branch
VIII. Optimum Utilisation of Space	(ii) Utilising unused space
IX. Amenities to Customers/Staff	(i) Drinking water
	(ii) Seating arrangements
	(iii) Easy availability of voucher forms, pens, etc., to customer/staff
	(iv) Canteen for staff
X. Personal Growth of Staff Members	(i) Improvement in job knowledge
	(ii) Increasing general awareness of staff members
XI. Improvement in Work Environment	(i) Reduction in noise level
	(ii) Cleanliness of premises
	(iii) Beautification of the branch/office
XII. Other Areas	(i) Problems related to demand loans, guidance to illiterate customers, enhancing the image of the Bank and other miscellaneous subjects.

(3) Solution and Implementation: Each aspect or cause of the problem is brainstormed to throw up possible solutions. The Circle leader should encourage all members to contribute freely, ensuring in particular that the ideas thus thrown up, rather than the people who suggested them, become the target of comments or criticism. During the process of detailed execution of possible solution, the Circle may require uninhibited interaction and consultations with the specialist departments and staff members who are not necessarily members of the Circle. This should be encouraged as this will enhance acceptability of the final solution. After a workable solution has been evolved, it is evaluated at the unit level if possible and implemented by the Circle members, themselves, if found feasible. In case a solution has to be submitted for the consideration of higher authorities, management presentation is organised which is the culmination of the entire process. A representative flow chart for such a presentation could comprise:

— Identification of problems — selection of problem

— Description of problem — objective of the study

— Analysis of the study — evolution of solution — implementation of solution — benefits.

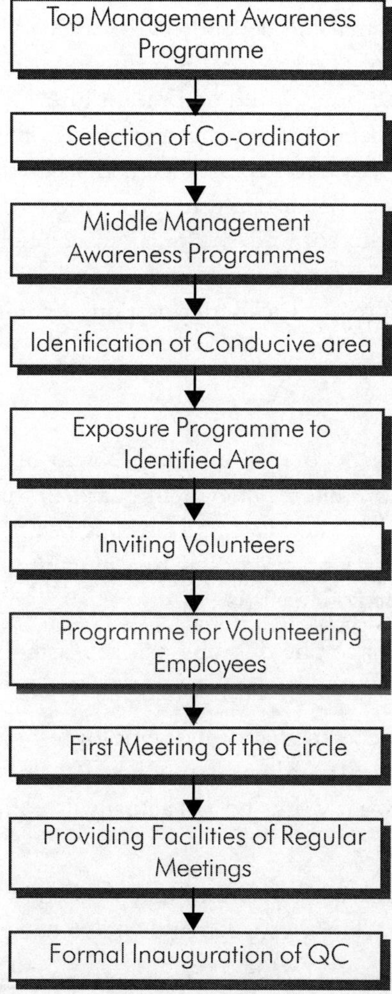

Fig. 19.5 Sequence of Events in Implementing Quality Circle.

Mutual Independence

For improving the industrial relations climate in the banks, it is imperative that there is a mutual understanding and appreciation of the roles of management and unions. The managers must realise that a dynamic and vibrant organisation is one which is in touch with the people and is alive to their aspirations and that it is difficult to maintain consistently high levels of productivity without commitment and high morale of people. It is, therefore, imperative that a manager learns to work more like a leader of the team (rather than a BOSS) and develops skills and capabilities of carrying his entire team with him. At the same time, trade unions should also appreciate that in the context of fast-moving changes taking place in the banks and increasing social complexity, greater demands and higher expectations by people, there is a need for change in their attitudes too and that they cannot survive for long by only feeding on the frustration of their people and concentrating on their bargaining role. They must take positive steps for bringing about perceptible improvement in the quality of life of their members and enthuse the employees for a better performance. This is possible only by improving the quality of their work life. In other words, there has to be a growing awareness, both on the part of managements and trade unions, of mutual interdependence between the employees and the management for the continued growth of an organisation. With this realisation, it is possible for both the parties to work together as collaborators in the pursuit of a common cause. When this happens, the employee will experience no cognitive dissonance or grudge against the management. A QC programme recognises the need and validity of this interdependence and seeks to sort out the various problems relating to improvement in the work environment through a process of identification of problems and bottlenecks, a meaningful analysis thereof and working out solutions therefor. QCs give working people an opportunity to control their own work and make it more enjoyable without any fear, concern or conflict and can, therefore, lead to better working conditions.

Managing Your Aces

What is the best way to manage the gifted people who are increasingly important in the knowledge economy? By acting more like a benevolent guardian than a traditional boss, argue two business school professors. Writing in the *Harvard Business Review,* Rob Goffee, a London Business School professor, and Gareth Jones, who teaches at Insead in France, say the first thing you need to do is acknowledge how difficult your task is.

They write: "If clever people have one defining characteristic it is that they do not want to be led."

The authors define such people as the handful of employees whose ideas, knowledge and skills give them the potential to produce extraordinary amounts of value at work. After studying these people, the authors conclude that what works best is actually listening to how these talented people say they should be managed.

"Clever people want a high degree of organisational protection and recognition that their ideas are important," the authors write. "They also demand the freedom to explore and fail."

You already know what does not work, but the authors remind you just in case: Gifted employees hate bureaucracy, tend not to respect the corporate hierarchy and have little respect for leaders who are not accomplished.

One more thing. If you do manage these people well, do not expect to hear many 'thank-yous.' "Even when you are leading them well, clever people will be unwilling to recognise your leadership. Remember these creative individuals feel that they don't need to be led."

Organisational Support Systems

The culture of QCs, in their applicability to the bank, are fundamentally people-building instruments that facilitate flowering of people in an organisational context. They cannot be looked upon as instruments explicitly for the purpose of productivity increase. It has been a carefully nurtured attempt to ensure that QCs are seen at all levels as being totally voluntary and free from organisational diktats. All support rendered to foster the growth of QCs is only by way of structural assistance rather than through organisational control.

A parallel structure symbiotically linked to the organisational structure has been devised by the Bhopal Circle to support the growth of the QC movement. This support system is depicted as a flow chart to bring out the congruence it bears to the organisational structure at the Circle (see Chart 19.1).

At the branch level, the Branch Manager acts as a co-ordinator. However, most of the guidance regarding the functioning of the Quality Circle is provided by the 'Facilitator', who is nominated by the Branch Manager. The Facilitator, normally a middle-level officer, is a vital link between the members of the QC and the management. Though the Facilitator does not involve himself directly in the meetings, he has to exercise leadership qualities in a tactful manner. It was noticed in the Bhopal Circle that the chances of success of a Quality Circle increased, if the right person is chosen as the Facilitator.

The leadership patterns of Quality Circle in banks reveal that:

(i) In some cases, the members chose to elect new Leaders and Deputy Leaders for every project. This system worked quite well as all the members got a chance to develop leadership qualities.

Chart 19.1

Chart of Organisational Structure Compared to QC Support System (Functionaries Shown in Brackets)

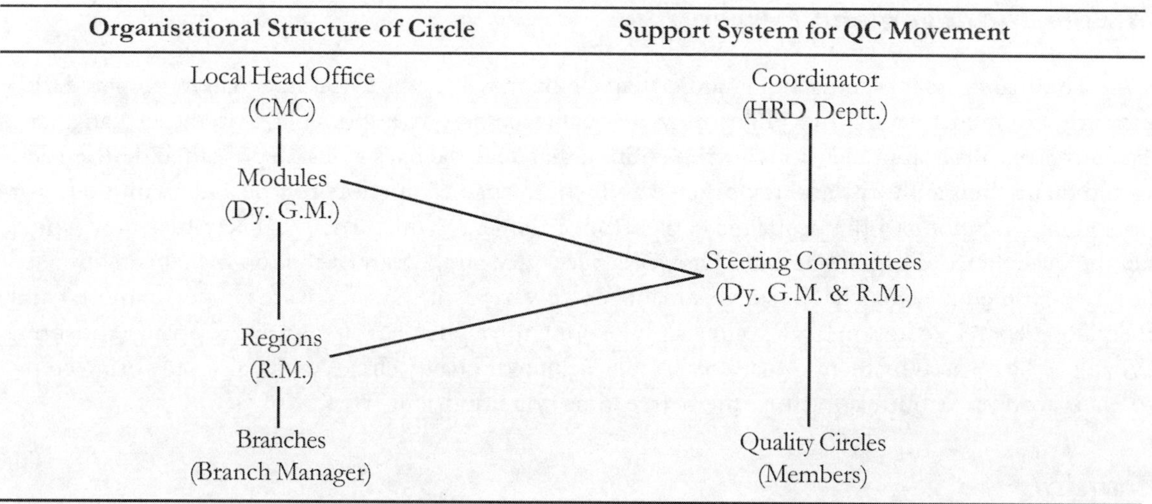

(ii) The leadership of the employees' unions rarely coincided with QC leadership. A number of union leaders joined Quality Circle as ordinary members. The number of members in Quality Circles normally varies from 5 to 8. The membership is open to all categories of staff, viz., the officers, clerical staff and the messengers. Due care is taken to ensure that all members, irrespective of their status, are treated as equals during the course of QC meetings.

As QCs are work-area specific, members of a QC are normally drawn from the same work area. Large branches having divisions have separate QCs for different divisions. In smaller branches, any one can become a member of the Quality Circle that is formed. This is possible as in such branches there are frequent job rotations and all the staff members are familiar with the different functions and job areas of the branch.

Management Support

Although Quality Circles are voluntary, they represent a management philosophy characterised by the belief in people and their development, open communication, management by objectives, promotion of self-esteem and a sense of achievement among people. The implications of this management philosophy are that the top management should be genuinely concerned about human resources development and the quality of work life; it should be willing to listen and follow through employees' suggestions; decision-making should be decentralised and a corresponding authority/ power should be shared; it should be willing to invest time and money on employee development and training; it should encourage people to try and experiment new ideas/methods/procedures etc., and it should set standards of excellence for organisational performance and the performance of employees. Developing a trusting climate between employees and the management is a very essential pre-requisite for the success of quality circles. A diagnostic study into the prevailing management philosophy will have to be made and whatever changes are necessary in the organisational structure and style will have to be brought about to strengthen the above qualities.

Middle Management Perception

The managers/executives at middle management will have to be adequately prepared and properly oriented towards the philosophy of quality circles. It is possible that these managers/ executives may have apprehension or wrong notion that quality circles would expose their deficiencies, would dilute their authority and importance and would enable superiors to find fault with them for not finding solutions to the problems earlier. Once they have this fear, it is likely that they would kill the quality circles in a subtle way. Thus, it is necessary on the part of the top management to see that the middle management executives/managers in various departments are properly advised and mentally prepared to accept quality circles philosophy through adequate and appropriate exposures. What is to be realised by them is that successful working of quality circles would not only bring credit to their work area but also afford them free time for important work.

Training

One of the major principles of quality circles as has been pointed out earlier is that they are to be formed entirely voluntarily. There should be no force or compulsion, direct or indirect, for the employees to form the circles. In order to enable the employees to consider whether it is worthwhile for them to form circles, a general awareness among them about the basic philosophy of quality circles, the likely benefits that accrue to them and to the organisation and the mechanism of working through quality circles will have to be brought about.

During this phase of training itself, the emphasis will have to be given to bring about an awareness in them that the quality circle is not a technique/ method for redressal of their grievances regarding service conditions, transfers, promotion, wage revision, etc. The appropriate forum for this purpose is the union and it would continue to take care of these issues. Quality circle is essentially for bringing about a better work culture/ environment and it promotes the use of brain power of the people and brings about a closer rapport between the worker and the work, and that too through his own efforts.

It may also be necessary to impress upon them that initially it is better for them to take up small problems of immediate relevance to them, the solutions and implementation of which would be easier. After all, it is not the magnitude of the problem that is always important. However small the problem is, it is their efforts in identifying and solving it that get recognition.

Quality Audit

The goal of quality circles as far as the banks are concerned is to bring about improvement in the quality of work life and overall productivity through a better way of working together. In order to see whether there is improvement in this direction, there is need for evolving a system of quality audit in terms of

- quality objectives/goals of the bank;
- the key areas concerning quality from the clients' point of view;
- the key areas of quality from the point of view of having a competitive edge;
- ways to make better use of human resources in the bank;
- threats coming over the horizon; and
- cost-benefit analysis.

Managing Time

Time is something none of us have control over. So managing your time is clearly impossible. However, if we try and read between the lines, we will realise that it is not time, that we need to manage, but ourselves. Wise usage of time is what we need to do. Whether you are a student, employee, employer or even a housewife, one cannot deny the importance of managing time.

Issues in managing our time

- Shifting priorities and crisis management
- The Telephone
- Unplanned schedules
- Attempting too much
- Drop in visitors

- Ineffective delegation
- The cluttered desk
- Procrastination
- The inability to say "No"
- Meetings

There are many ways we can manage our time. Here are some methods that you may find helpful.

Analyze your use of time

Are you spending enough time on the projects which may not be urgent now, but are the things you need to do to develop your career. If you constantly ask yourself "What is the most important thing to do, right now?" It will help you focus on important tasks.

Have a plan

Your yearly plan should be reviewed daily and reset as your achievements are met. Successful people make lists constantly and prioritize their tasks. This should be done for both personal and business goals.

Action plan analysis

Problems will always occur, the value of a good plan is to identify them early and seek solutions. Good time management enables you to measure the progress towards your goals because what you can measure is what you can control. Always try to be proactive.

By setting goals and not wasting time, we can find extra time in the week to spend on those people and activities, which are most important to you.

Conclusion

The Quality Circle concept has played a significant role increasing the necessary awareness of sustained quality improvement. It is basically a bottom-up management technique, derives its strength from the vast pool of knowledge, experience and skills of the work force of the organisation. It canalises the potential, energy and a craving for job satisfaction on the part of the employees, directing their efforts for improving the quality of service and work life. Briefly, Quality Circles enable the employees to look to their worth and the organisation positively. The team culture is itself a motivator of achievement.

The endeavours of Quality Circles in banks have yielded results that are truly novel in their simplicity. Problems that the staff had learnt to live with or had ignored hitherto were solved. Introduction of Quality Circle is facilitated in service organisations like banks by the fact that the service industries normally employ people with higher educational qualifications. Quality Circles are an appropriate medium for utilising their talents and creative abilities for the growth of the organisation. There has been an attitudinal metamorphosis among the members of the Quality Circles. This radical transformation in the work ethic has manifested itself in more responsive behavioural patterns, improved customer service and healthier industrial relations climate.

Quality Circles in banks viewed at one time as a strange mutation from the industrial sector have proved to be perfectly compatible with the requirements of this demanding service industry. Empirical experience has established that Quality Circles have come to stay in the banking industry. Quality Circles will continue to tackle the problems and concerns of the various work areas that foster them and in the process, offer to their members a medium for creative and innovative application of mind and will. This calls for a significant shift in the attitude of the management.

(i) Quality Circle activities involving small groups at grass-roots level for identifying and solving work-related problems prevailing at their work area through team culture will enable the employees to contribute their ideas.

(ii) The employees' recognition is considered as a powerful achievement motivator through the enhancement of self-worth of the employees, since it is a positive public acknowledgement of employees' abilities and efforts.

Human resources is the greatest asset of banks. No matter how sophisticated we become on the technological front, the future of banking depends on the full participation of its employees. At the branch level, this alignment can be established through Quality Circles. Only through people can banks have a better performance and build a better society. People through Quality Circles can effectively contribute to the success of banks through their work organisations. The key to this is Quality Circles.

Chapter 20

Management Information System

When you focus on something, no matter what it happens to be, you are really calling that into existence.

— The Secret

Introduction

Banking industry plays a vital role in rejuvenating and revamping the economic growth of a country. Indian commercial banks woke up from their splendid isolation during 1970s, especially after nationalization in June 1969. The banking sector is the major purveyor of money in an economy; hence the banker is the best 'cash flow' manager of a country. During industrialization, 'finance' was considered the major input for achieving industrial growth. But in the latter half of this century, 'marketing' evolved as an important variable for achieving sustained growth of industries. During 1990s, the world witnessed a tremendous advancement in the field of Information Technology (IT), which has become an inevitable essence for the steady growth of the industries. In the 21st Century, Finance-Marketing-Information Technology combination should be the corner-stone for the success and development of an organization.

Information is power; it is a resource and a key input in decision management. Harnessing and managing that resource power will make all the difference between success and failure of an organisation. Information is the critical ingredient of human interaction and organisation; it only naturally follows then that the technology of information will fundamentally revise the way of organisations.

The overall performance of an organisation, with no exception of banks, can be improved remarkably through an integrated system of information technology. Every organisation has to strive to achieve a high level of systems integration and information-sharing across functions. This requires a cultural change in the organisation as well as an efficient flow of information from 'top-down' and 'bottom-up' directions on an ongoing basis. This is most required in an organisation like banks.

Information Synchronism

Information is the basic power without which no enterprise can plan and implement its strategies. This power, from whatever channel it flows, is to be used judiciously and effectively and has to be necessarily shared amongst people involved in a venture. Sharing information not only brings about a greater degree of authenticity, involvement and total commitment, but also helps in putting into action collective wisdom for working out policies, plans, practices and programmes. Information sharing can be defined as an exchange of intelligence and/or knowledge between two individuals, between an individual and a group of individuals, and/or between groups and/or between offices of a corporate unit.

An individual quite often is possessive of the information he has acquired, particularly if it is of a vital and critical nature for his own advancement and hesitates to share it. However, in a corporate unit, the information acquired by an individual, a group or a unit office is meant for the benefit of the entire organisation. It should be shared without any reservation and diffidence, because without pertinent information/data, the marketing strategies of our organisation could face rough weather.

In an organisation, if information-sharing is to become a cult, efficacious systems have to be developed and sustained. For a constant and continuous flow of information, both upwards and downwards, sharing of information cannot be accomplished only by the medium of written communications. This has to be executed by all the three methods, viz., written, verbal and non-verbal.

It is just not enough if the information is shared at the top, senior or middle management levels. Information-sharing systems should encompass the entire organisation and its people, including the customer base. However, a word of caution. The element of discretion will have to be built within the systems to ensure that only relevant and desirable information is shared and that too at the appropriate time. Indiscriminate sharing of information could cause more harm than good. Hence, no uniform structured system for information-sharing can be good enough for all organisations or for any particular organisation at all times. The systems have to be constantly evolved and need to be modified and adjusted depending upon the situational requirements and the nature of information to be shared. Information-sharing has to be a deliberate exercise and done with full consciousness and utmost discretion. What should, however, always remain in focus is the need to share the information in essence — to give as well as to receive.

The information received is to be analysed, stored and retrieved at appropriate times to make full use of its value.

One of the important elements in the sustained growth of the organisation has been the initiation of the information-sharing process. Yet that practice has not reached the desirable level. Hence the system has to be reinforced by monitoring constantly their efficacy at all levels. No information, on the face of it, can be judged as useless and inconsequential unless the same is properly analysed. Availability of the right information at the right time to meet the changing environs of our times will go a long way in evolving and in re-evolving our marketing strategies so as to derive the best out of even the worst situation.

This chapter evaluates and discusses the management information system in banks as an effective tool of management process. Banks especially are to benefit much more by information technology than other organisations. The rewards of information are enormous when it is both functional and geographical, covering all services. Activities get transformed into a well-oiled machine with respect to banking operations and management.

Management requires complete information relating to a problem or issue in the right time in order to make effective decisions. The proper collection, handling and providing the right information to the right manager at the right time not only reduces the risk of wrong decisions being taken but also works as an effective controlling technique. Complexities involved in business and economic activities and voluminous government regulations create the need for supply of right information to the right manager at the right time.

What is Management Information System?

Management Information System (MIS) is a system to provide selected decision-oriented information needed by management to function effectively. It is an organised process of providing information for decision and action. James A. F. Stoner has defined management information system as "a formal method of making available to management accurate and timely information necessary to facilitate the decision-making process and enable the organisation's planning, control and operational functions to be carried out effectively." The system provides information on the past, present and projected future and on relevant events inside and outside the organisation.

Generally, an organisation's MIS consists of a series of information systems of varying degrees of complexity, competence and scope. They are:

(a) Transaction processing and inquiry response;

(b) Management information for operational planning, decision-making and control;

(c) Management information for tactical planning, marketing, and decision-making; and

(d) Management information system for strategic planning and policy planning and decision-making.

New Developments

Information providers these days are watching a number of developing trends:

- The business environment is undergoing sweeping changes in everything from technology to deregulation, to the restructuring of companies and industries.
- Technology, and increasingly the technology of the personal computer, is making it easier to get that information and at the same time, is creating more customers for information delivered electronically.
- The demand for real-time information, information delivered electronically, is growing and will grow even faster as the technlogy improves and as business people realise the advantages that real-time information offers.
- The information and communication technologies at our disposal — computers, telecommunications and video — are becoming increasingly intertwined.

Present Environment and Information System

The function of management involves planning, staffing, organising, directing and controlling. These sets of activities are intertwined systematically. All these activities have to be designed and implemented rationally for completing the management process. Planning is a very complex function. For planning, analysis of internal and external information and drawing up of inferences

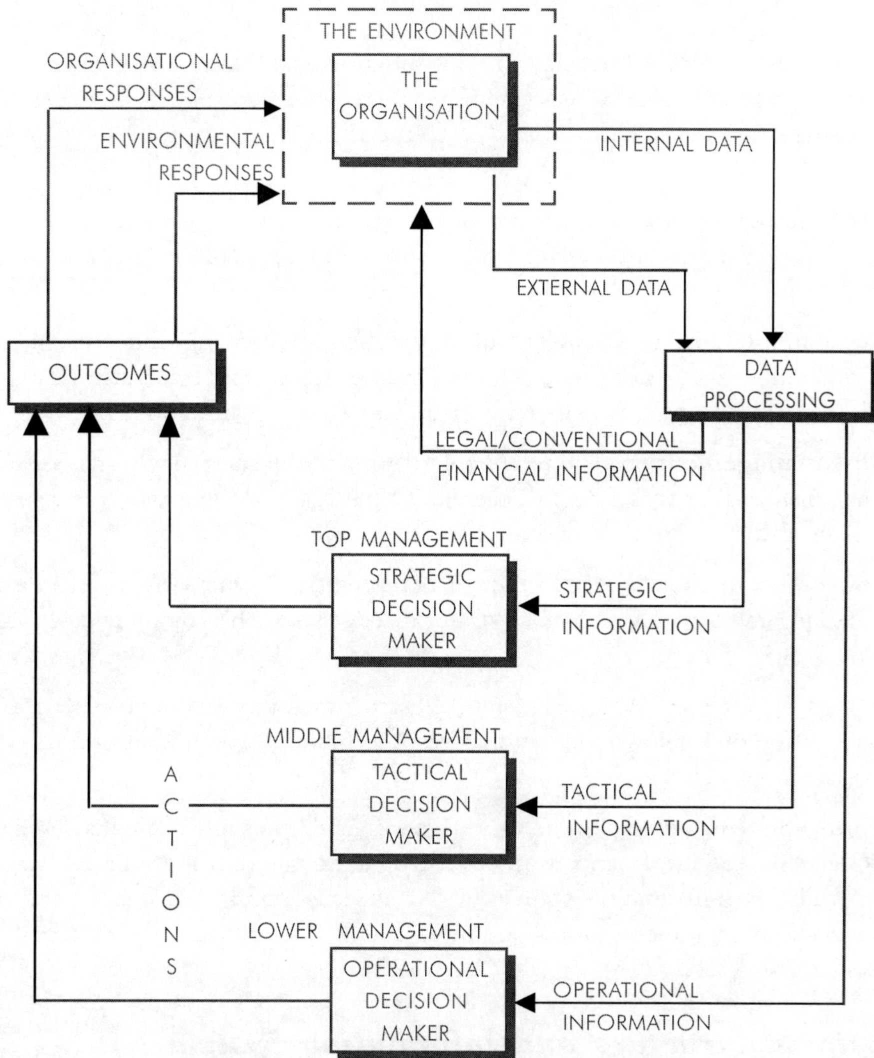

Fig. 20.1 Information System Model.

are absolutely necessary. A detailed SWOT analysis is also a highly desirable activity for carrying out the planning function. A thorough market analysis is also an indispensable factor, particularly in a competitive field.

Market research and analysis involves collection of data and analysis of an interpretation thereon for using them in the plan preparation. Planning requires forecasting of internal variables and extrapolation and analysis of external data for drawing up of suitable inferences. On the whole, analysis of data and designing of necessary information are the basic requirements of the planning process.

Similarly, staffing and organising functions need the help of an information system. For planned implementation, organising of various resources is essential. One of the important resources is manpower. Development of manpower by providing the necessary training, proper deployment of manpower, etc. are necessary for the success of any plan. Other resources have also to be organised and channelised into the process of implementation of any plan. Control function is as important as the process of plan formulation. This function enables the management to have proper control over the process of plan implementation. Reviewing the progress of implementation and applying correctives, whenever necessary, is very crucial for the success of any plan. Control and review depends heavily on the information system.

Top management needs information for prediction, strategic planning, and overall control. Information is mostly external, predictive, qualitative and of reasonable accuracy. It is of a long-term nature, i.e., futuristic.

Middle management needs information for tactical planning and control. It is current information with a time frame not exceeding one year. Mostly it is internal, historical. It is primarily financial and relatively accurate. It is mainly for decision-making and control.

First line management needs operational information, instant, day-to-day or real time. It is mostly internal, historical or real time, i.e., current. Often it is non-financial. It is very precise. This information is used for action and routine operations.

The flow of information is a key input of management, particularly in relation to planning, organising, directing and controlling. In fact, strategic decisions are based on the quality and adequacy of information.

An organisation's information system must provide the various levels of organisational hierarchy with different levels of operational responsibilities, operational control, management control and strategic planning.

Information requirements of the various managerial levels must be considered in the design of an MIS. Generally, the information sources for operational control are based largely within an organisation, while the information sources for strategic planning are outside the organisation, whereas sources for management control are more evenly distributed among internal and external origins as shown in Fig. 20.2.

Organisational Structure and Information System

Commercial banks normally have a multi-layered organisational structure. They have two or three layers in between the head office (macro level) and the branches (micro level). Head office is vested with policy formulation and other macro level functions. The middle levels have more of control functions, apart from taking up the responsibility of designing, formulation and implementation of policies on local issues. The internal information/data are generated at the grassroot levels, viz., the regular reporting system. Depending upon the specific needs, information system is designed for compilation and analysis of data and for generating information at various levels. In addition to the internal information, different levels of banks require data/information on different environmental factors which influence the growth of business of the bank. These are also collected from time to time for interpretation and use.

Structurally, organisational pattern and information system are related to each other. Information system needs to be designed in such a way that the organisational structure facilitates smooth functioning of such a system. One of the basic infirmities in the information system relates to this particular aspect. Due to the short-term demands for data and information, sub-systems of the

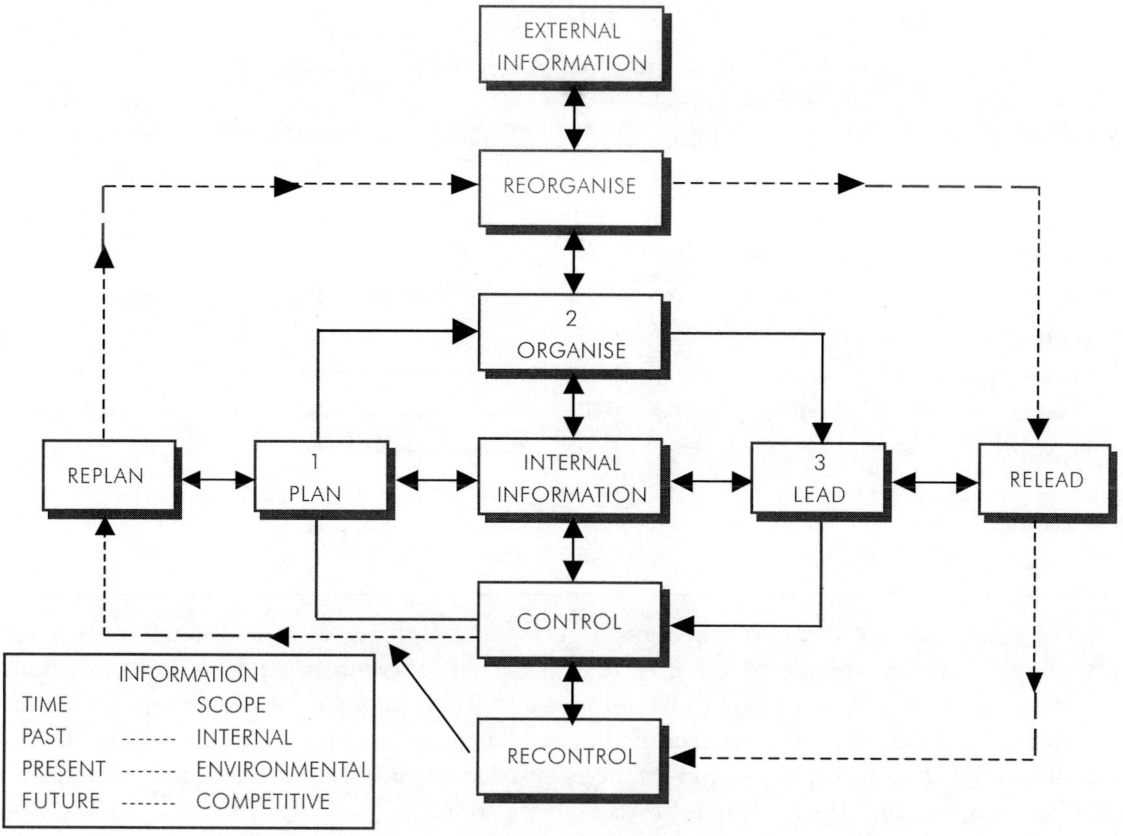

Fig. 20.2 Role of Information in the Management Process.

information system are created many times, with a shorter perspective. Such sub-systems, however, have been able to serve short-term purposes only. But many times, such demands have been continuous in nature and the sub-systems of the information system so designed, have failed to deliver the goods in the long run. These shortcoming require corrective measures on an ongoing basis. Banking being highly challenging and being subject to the impact of new environmental factors from time to time, newer demands for data here arise very often. To meet these requirements, smaller information systems are also designed at a very short notice.

Basic Resource

Information is now regarded as a basic resource of the organisation along with other resources such as personnel, money, materials, machines, and facilities. Information is a critical or crucial resource to the success of the enterprise. It can be used at a cost. It must be at the right place and at the right time. There are three major areas of information system: (1) financial information; (2) personnel information; (3) logistics information — physical flow of goods through an organisation, etc. Logistics function covers such activities as purchasing, receiving, inventory and distribution. An organisation with a well-designed MIS will generally have a competitive advantage over firms with poorer systems.

Table 20.1

Information Requirements by Decision Category

Characteristics of Information	*Operational Planning and Control*	*Management Planning and Control*	*Strategic Planning and Control*
Source	Largely internal	⟶	External
Scope	Well-defined, narrow	⟶	Very wide
Level of Aggregation	Detailed	⟶	Aggregate
Time Horizon	Historical	⟶	Future
Currency	Highly Current	⟶	Quite old
Required Accuracy	High	⟶	Low
Frequency of use	Very Frequent	⟶	Infrequent

The primary purpose of MIS is to assist managers in making *timely, informed decisions* in their areas of responsibility. Information is received by the MIS from all sources. MIS identifies relevant information and offers it to managers to be used for decision-making/problem-solving. Effects of decisions both on the external environment and internally are then compared against given standards. If necessary, corrective action is taken at the decision-making stage or at the information-sources stage. MIS is an ongoing process. It has also a systems approach.

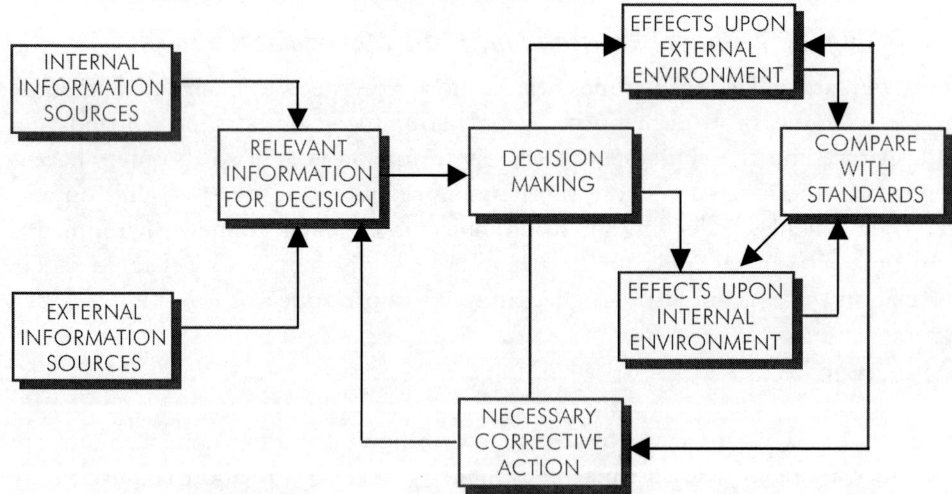

Fig. 20.3 Basic Components of a Management Information System.

Notes: 1. Management Information System (MIS) is a combination of sub-systems based on functions performed in an organisation: (1) Marketing Information, (2) Production, (3) Logistics, i.e., buying, receiving inventory and distribution, (4) Personnel, (5) Finance and Accounting, (6) Top Management Information, and (7) Information processing.

2. A manager plus the decision procedures for directing an activity is called decision centre. It is also a control centre.
3. Decision centre plus activity is called a functional unit.
4. A number of functional units connected with a network of information flows is called an organisation in designing an information system.

Management Information System in Banks

Accurate information necessary to facilitate decision-making is made available at the right time to the management at different levels, viz., Branch Office, Divisional Office, Circle Office, and Head Office by way of (a) Memos; (b) Circulars; (c) Statutory returns; (d) Control returns on advances; and (e) Other control returns. Control returns provide the information such as recovery performance, out-of-order advances, half-yearly credit programme, calculation of salary/overtime payments, staff requirements, performance of employees, expenses incurred, cash holdings, interbranch/ bank drawings, furniture/fixtures, profitability, pending and unadjusted items, and performance and progress made by the branch. Monthly flash reports from branches contain important banking indicators such as deposits, credit, credit-deposit ratio, deposit and borrowal accounts, priority sector credit, credit to weaker sections, important items of expenditure, and staff position.

Now, we discuss the characteristics of information required by the management at different levels, viz., (i) Operating; *(ii)* Management control; and *(iii)* Strategic planning, separately.

(i) Operating Management: (Branch Management and Regional Management Level): Though the branch manager is at the operating level, he requires both planning and controlling information. The information requirements of the branch manager can be broadly divided into: *(i)* planning decision areas and (ii) control decision areas. Planning decision areas include: obtaining deposits, lending policy and level of discretion, investment policy, management levels and budgeting, human resources and marketing of services, forecasting business mix with volumes, etc. Control decision areas include: providing statutory returns, accepting new business, recovery position and bad debts, performance of credit sanctions, controlling costs, complaints, training, programme, actual staff levels, utilisation and productivity of staff, budget staff levels in relation to the level of business etc.

Though the top management is mostly concerned with the planning areas, it allows the regional manager/branch managers to participate in decision-making and allows certain scope for discretion to the operating management level. Hence management has to identify the decision areas and people and clearly delegate the authority of decision-making to individuals specifically.

Thus, the management has to (i) think through the key decision areas for the whole functional areas; *(ii)* decide which people are responsible for which decision areas; and *(iii)* identify the information needed to make the key decisions.

(ii) Management Control: Information required at this level is somewhat widen scope, both historical and future in the time horizon, both current and old in currency, moderate in accuracy, not of much detail at the level of external. Herein information flows in both directions. At this level, executives or organisations use information for control and for planning as well as decision-making. More so, they are also a source of information, too.

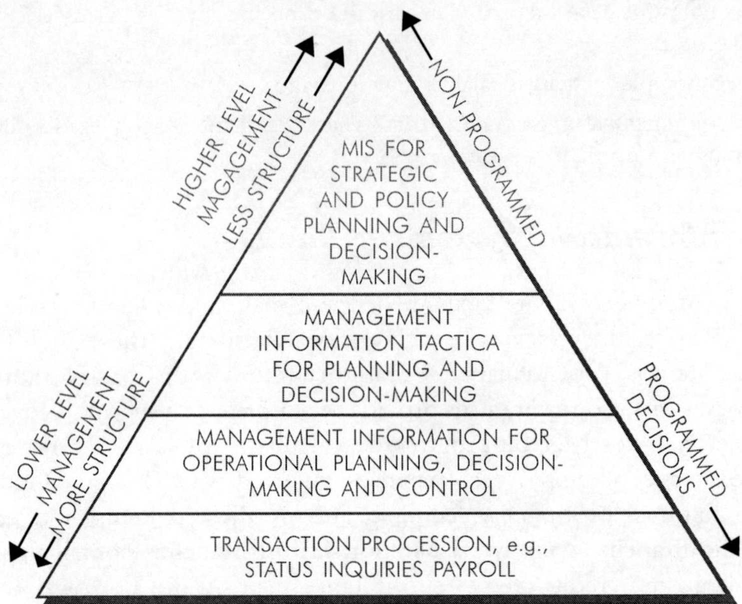

Fig. 20.4 MIS and Planning/Decision-making/Control

A good bank agent has a clear knowledge of the relation between his several customers and also of the transactions which each bill originates; the permanent officials at the Head Office may acquire much of the same knowledge from the returns, and by the intelligent use of the progressive ledgers may see very clearly how the relations of the customers change.

What is needed today is reorientation of our approach from —

(i) data collection and transaction analysis to information gathering and processing; and

(ii) mere control and monitoring of operations to issues of strategy, not only of marketing and development of new services, but also of pricing and profits.

All Indian banks have time-tested accounting procedures, scheme of delegation of powers and control mechanisms and it is only recently that branch level accounting machines have been introduced. These are expected to bring about greater efficiency in book-keeping, operations and information gathering. But as Shri D. N. Ghosh, Chairman, State Bank of India, observed, while speaking at Hyderabad on 9th January 1987,

"Mechanical aids are an obvious necessity to assist in controlling the day-to-day operations. But mechanical aids are not ends in themselves. These are like aids available to an organisation to develop a type of information systems."

The banks should therefore seize the present moment to design and create a comprehensive, but appropriate information system, best suited to their requirements.

In actual practice, this would mean the creation of an "information systems pyramid" by each bank — consisting of three layers and resting on a solid data base foundation.

(iii) Top Management Level: Decision-making at this level is not confined to control and technical planning. It is concerned with strategic planning which plays a pivotal role in the entire planning, information and control system. Strategic planning decision areas relate to future products and services, growth, merger and acquisition strategy, organisation structure, organisation change and development, corporate image, etc. Information required at this level is of a very wide scope, mostly external in source, aggregate in level, future in time horizon, quite old in currency, low in accuracy, and infrequent in frequency of use. The internal source of information generated and presented forms the basis of policy framework, planning and introducing corrective measures for the dynamic growth of the bank.

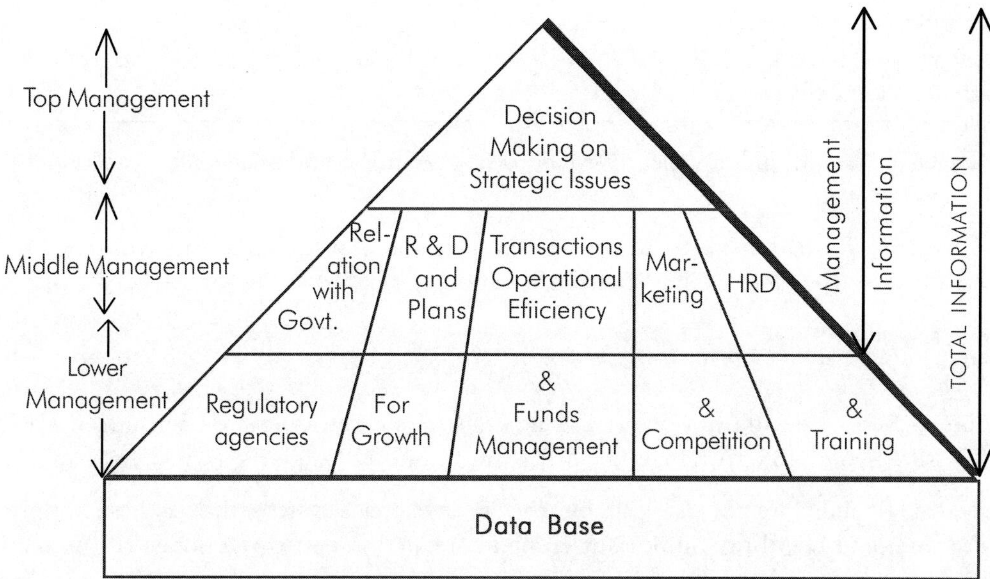

Fig. 20.5 Information System Pyramid in Indian Banks.

Generation of Information

Management information can be broadly classified into external and internal. While external information is all about the economy, banking, international markets at the macro-level, internal information is operative in nature and originates at the micro-level or grass-root level. It flows bottom-up for control and planning.

Economic planning and research departments and management advisory and services division of various banks play a significant role in collecting, collating and analysing external information for the benefit of the top management on an ongoing basis.

Internal information flows in the form of performance reports, various control reports, audit reports and guidelines received from the Reserve Bank of India and the Government of India.

After the above-said information has been collected, the management at different levels have to check it so as to make sure that it is adequate for the purpose:

1. Identify and check the objectives of the department/organisation concerned.
2. Identify the key decision areas of planning and controlling.

Planning	Controlling
The use of resources	Resource
Standards of performance	Costs
To delegate	Waste
New Projects/loans	Quality
Priority sector advances	Projects
Profit	
Customer service	
Improve weaknesses	
Staff Development	

3. Delegate responsibilities clearly to persons identified and make them accountable for performance.
4. Identify information needs to the minute levels and at the frequency you need it. Also identify sources and methods of presentation.

HR Audit

A Human Resource audit not only tells one volume is about the state of health of HRD in a bank, it also shows one how to remain agile for the future. HR audit is a must for banks.

Periodical HR audits are not just desirable; they're an exercise in strength-weakness-opportunity-threat assessment and help bring important company-related issues to the notice of the directors. Audits also suggest ways for companies to fine-tune personnel management practices, and keep up with the latest laws and directives. More importantly, audits help organisations shape a vision for the future, channel their resources into their people more effectively, and help the company sail smoothly through testing times of change.

Some of the generic conclusions that an audit report seeks to establish are:

1. Is everyone who is responsible for doing something, doing everything they have to do — i.e., are they doing their job?
2. Are managers handling non-HR functions extending help and taking initiative to work with the HRD?
3. Are all employee needs being met? If not completely, what is the solution?
4. Does the company meet all personnel standards and compare favourably against the rest of the industry?

Using the Information

The information that is gathered is corroborated against past audit reports and a final HR audit report is drawn. The report essentially highlights good and bad performances, classifies items as 'high', 'medium' and 'low' priority, and puts the organisation back on track as far as long-term plans are concerned. Ideally the report should address a wide range of concerns and even if no immediate solutions are possible, it must explore the source of the problem and serve as a reference point to compare progress in the future. "Of course the measure of success will depend on how seriously and effectively the recommendations are implemented. It is in this area that success rates/success stories may vary from organisation to organisation," appends Dutt. Audits are like yearly visits to your dentist — they might seem like a bore, but they are necessary if you want to avoid nagging problems down the line. And in the final analysis, what counts is that your HRD will be the better for it.

What exactly is organisation looking for during an HR audit? Information that falls under the following heads:

- Efficacy of existing systems and procedures such as communication, staffing and training, employee benefit programmes and an organised and systematic approach to the future. Most importantly, audits determine if HR is 'visible' at every step.
- Whether there is adherence to labour, safety, employment, payroll and other related acts or regulation.
- Is the company's spending on HR optimal and adequate? Problematic areas need to be identified. Are there undesirable practices or behaviours such as absenteeism or negligence that contribute to spiraling HR costs?
- A strategic design to help the company improve upon existing plans and fill lacunae. An audit revisits the HRD's goals and suggests priority changes if needed. The important thing to remember here is that inefficiency or wastefulness caused by a stagnant HR policy will eventually cascade down and affect the company's bottomline. Audits can stop this decline cold in its tracks and turn things around for you.

Audit and Management Information

An incidental but very important fall-out of a comprehensive audit exercise is in the area of management information and management control. This requires computerisation of the findings of the branch audit in a synoptic manner. Thus, a branch can be measured on any number of parameters and sub-parameters, from audit to audit, and its overall performance as well as performance in specific fields can be watched at any given periodicity. Trend analysis can be prepared for information of the branch itself and its controller. The trend analysis will show whether the branch is improving in housekeeping or not and even within housekeeping, whether its performance in inter-branch reconciliation is going up or down, and how it compares with other branches. The trend analysis can become a vital tool of management information and control. The total picture of any branch in key areas (branch profiles) as on a given date can also be prepared from the computerised audit reports. Such profiles are very valuable from the point of view of a controller.

If such computerised audit reports are aggregated, they would present a good and reliable picture of a region or a zone or even the bank as a whole, which should have great utility for corporate management and also for the Reserve Bank and Government of India. Such a report will reflect the health of a bank as a whole on predetermined parameters, brokern up into the health of a zone or of a region. Weightages can also be given to the parameters and sub-parameters. It is true, the picture will not be as on a given date, since it will represent the aggregation of audit reports of all branches *up to* a particular date; still, it will be a good indicator of the overall health of a bank or specific health of its zones/regions as also the health trends. Such information would obviously be of help in initiating timely remedial action.

Source of Information

Management at this level mostly requires the information available within the branch/regional office. The branch manager would mostly require highly current information as he would be concerned with the current operating performance. The branch manager/regional manager requires information through daily/weekly/monthly reports regarding: *(a)* quantum and structure of deposits like current, savings, term, recurring, from rural branches, urban branches etc.; *(b)* volume of mix of advances like advances to agriculture (crop and term loans), advances to small-scale industry, small business, weaker sections, craftsmen, artisans, transport operators, business and trade and other priority sectors, large and medium industry, loans to export and import business etc.; *(c)* cost of deposits, establishment, stationery, premises, furniture, lighting etc.; *(d)* revenue earned on loans and advances, investments, commission on issue on drafts, collection of bills, transfer of funds etc.; and *(e)* maintenance of CRR, SLR requirements.

Use of Information

All this information is useful and should be sent very frequently to the branch manager/regional manager to compare his actual performance with the budgets, to find out the deviations and take corrective action immediately. Thus, information at this level is of great importance for operational control and for attainment of predetermined operational goals.

Scope of Information

Scope of information required at this level is narrow as it deals with only the day-to-day and routine operations of the bank as discussed earlier. The requirements of information are defined clearly.

The System

The all encompassing framework that describes how these units interact is the system. A system is a set of interrelated components. A system is a set of arrangement of things so related or connected to form a unity or organization. For a banking organization, a system is an array of components designed to accomplish a particular objective according to plan.

Systems modules

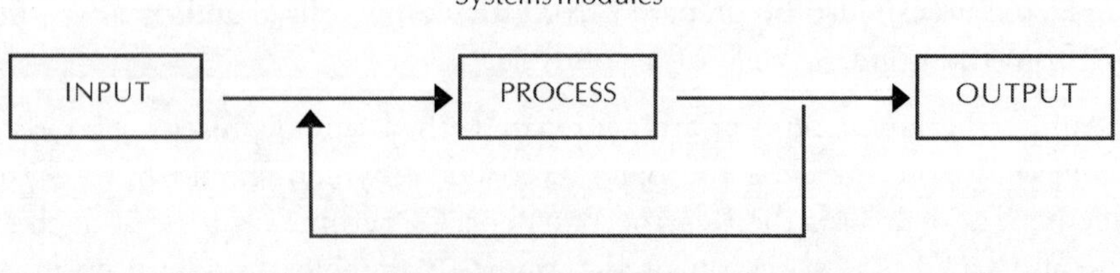

Feedback/Control

There are four basic elements of systems, viz., input, processing, output and feedback/control. A banking industry receives operational information from the branches and economic information from the Government, etc. This will form the input into the system. The information so gathered is processed at the management control and at the strategic management level. Some times the sub-systems may operate at the input and output levels but not at the processing level. Such sub-systems are called black boxes.

The MIS in a banking industry receives input and produces information from data according to the instructions. The bank has to capture and store the data as and when they occur. The stored data becomes input to the system and the processed data is also stored awaiting future use. Thus, the bank has to add storage function to the basic system model of input, process and output.

The management control information systems mainly center on providing managers with information to control operations and make decisions that optimize the delivery of banking products and services to customers. These systems often help the managerial personnel in the banking industry to take decision rules and algorithms that help manage the process. This information system is used to project the operations of the banks at the branch level. The management control system work directly with the operational control systems, but at a higher level, in that the goal is not to focus on individual transactions, but to manage the resources and facilities that control the total process.

Conclusion

To sum up, in these days of information-based management, the best way to motivate the employees is to share inside information with them, share information about the external environment with them and encourage them to take interest in such information sharing. This also means that field people would likewise share their grass-root data with their superiors. With the mutuality and respect so developed, the organisation would achieve better results through better motivation of the employees and better evolution of strategies on the basis of shared information.

Management activities in an organisation comprise planning, organisation, leading and controlling operations. Framework of decision-making needs problem recognition, formulation, data collection and solution by operations research techniques. The optimum solution is then validated and the decisions are made for implementation. The decision-maker must monitor and control the progress of the implemented decisions.

MIS facilitates the job of data collection, estimation and forecasting of parameters. Once the decision is made to implement the solution, the MIS further aids in tracking key parameters and monitoring the progress towards the goal. The MIS development has been instrumental in widespread use of O. R. tools in decision-making situations.

In an organisation like banks, issues have to be considered both horizontally and vertically. Issues like streamlining data sources, standardisation of branch procedures, security and control are to be examined horizontally across the offices of banks. Issues like providing timely information at ZO/CO levels for prompt decision-making or ensuring availability of vital information for top management would be vertical issues involving the study of information flow and control among offices, converging at the top. This contributes towards an overall effective management of the bank as a whole. The development of a Management Information System requires breaking away from some traditional methods which includes changing management styles and ways of thinking. Unfortunately, many of the benefits that can be envisaged at the start of a project are not easily expressed in tangible terms.

Now is the time for the leaders of the banking industry to make certain that the banking system will become competitive in the year 2000 A.D. First, develop a long-term information plan. Second, make sure that the integrated software application packages are a part of the information plan, freeing your staff to develop unique and competitive systems which cannot be packaged. Third, move long-term decisions on information technology to the Board level. Fourth, restructure your management for the next decade, utilising the Chief Information Officer concept. Future banking growth will further depend upon the innovative software and information system that the bank will have at its disposal. The future of any bank depends on the timely information on which to base decisions. Begin now the planning process to ensure that the banking system will be competitive in the twenty-first century.

Chapter 21

Management Audit in Banking

Management in action is always through systems. Systems may be defined as any scheme or arrangement of things which work in a predictable manner.

Introduction

Management audit is a new concept in the sphere of auditing. However, Indian banks have adopted it as an integral part of bank management. Management audit in simple terms means the audit of management functions. It is distinctively different from audit of specific functions or systems. The need for such an audit has been increasingly felt with the growing complexity and spread of functions and expectations of the organisations, where efficiency is more dependent on the performance of the management. It is, in fact, a comprehensive audit of management and throws much light on the following areas:

(1) The ability of the organisation to respond to the changes in the environment.

(2) The effectiveness of the various management processes like decision-making, communications, public relations, management information, leadership management styles, collaborative processes, human resources development, motivational climate, building process, etc. so as to have cohesive work groups at various levels, geared to tap opportunities for the achievement of the organisational objectives and goals.

(3) The adequacy of the system in a changing and competitive environment for achieving the mission, goals and objectives of the organisation.

Origin

Management audit owes its origin to the United States of America where the professional accountants have a management services wing which conducts management audit. Often, the concept of management audit is used to cover operational auditing. In reality, it is a step ahead of internal audit.

Concept

We can define the objectives and scope of auditing as:

— Reviewing and appraising the soundness, adequacy and application of accounting, financial and other operating controls and promoting effective control at reasonable cost;

— Ascertaining the extent to which company assets are accounted for and safeguarded from losses of all kinds;

— Ascertaining the reliability of management data developed within the organisation;

— Appraising the quality of performance in carrying out the assigned responsibilities; and

— Recommending operational improvements.

Management audit is an audit of the management for the management by the management. It is an evaluation of the performance of the management. It is a qualitative assessment of the management efficiency and effectiveness. It is described as an independent, critical and systematic analysis of the adequacy of the organisational structure to accomplish the objectives, suitability of the systems introduced, ability to implement the systems properly and of the overall performance of the organisation in all areas of management such as planning, organising, staffing, co-ordinating and controlling. It evaluates the processes and functions of the management, the quality of decisions, standards of MIS, systems and management effectiveness and adequacy of delegated powers.

Definitions

Several authorities on audit have defined "management audit" covering different aspects of management.

The concept of "management audit" was first focused by T. G. Rose in 1932 and since then it has been refined by many authors, adding to its qualitative dimensions and branching out in its various ramifications. A few important definitions are:

"Management audit is a comprehensive and constructive examination of the organisational structure of an organisation or a component thereof, its plans and objectives, methods of control, means of operations and its human and physical facilities." — Leonard

According to Norbeck, "Management audit is a control technique which provides management with a method for evaluating the effectiveness of operating procedures and internal controls. It is a constructive method of assisting management to improve operations of its busines: by alerting it to any breakdown of operational controls, by pinpointing areas of cost reduction, by suggesting potential operating improvements and by pointing out where breakdowns in the implementation of functional responsibilities in various areas have significantly affected these areas."

The most comprehensive definition is given in a Research Report titled "An Evaluation of Selected Current Internal Auditing Terms" and published by the Institute of Internal Auditors Inc., USA, which states: "A management audit is a future-oriented, independent and systematic evaluation of the activities of all levels of management performed by the internal auditor for the purposes of improving organisational profitability and increasing the attainment of the other organisational objectives through improvement in the performance of the management function, achievement of programme, purpose, social objectives and employee development. Financial data are some of the sources of evidence. The primary sources of evidence are the operational policies and management decisions as related to the organisational objectives. Included are an evaluation of the management control system in terms of existence, compliance and adequacy; the management decision-making process in terms of existence, compliance and relevance to the attainment of organisational objectives; the management decision itself in relation to the organisational objectives; and the quality of management. The resultant audit report both identifies problems and recommends solutions."

Another clear and precise definition of the term 'management audit' is, "management auditing is a method to evaluate the efficiency of management at all levels throughout the organisation, or more specifically, it comprises the investigation of a business by an independent body from the highest executive level downwards, in order to ascertain whether sound management prevails throughout and to report as to its efficency or otherwise, with recommendations to ensure its effectiveness where such is not the case."

According to Leslie R. Howard, "Management audit is an investigation of a business from the highest level downward in order to ascertain whether sound management prevails throughout, thus facilitating the most effective relationship with the outside world and most efficient organisation and smooth running of internal organisation."

An analysis of the above definitions would indicate that management audit presupposes the existence of:

- a clear perception at all levels of the expectations of the corporate management from the unit/division being audited,
- formulation of policies/strategies by the unit in line with the corporate goals for meeting the expectations,
- existence of an adequate supporting organisation at the division in terms of structure, systems, procedure, personnel, rules, regulations, etc., for the above purpose, and
- a set of expected standards in these areas of management functions (e.g., the Regional Manager will raise demands on the Planning Officer for making specific studies, their relationship will be informal, etc.) However, these standards differ from the standards set for, say filling up a form, and would focus on the roles and role linkages in relation to the key functions rather than the functions themselves.

The following points emerge from the above definitions:

(1) Management audit is an 'audit of management' while internal audit and operational audits are audits for management.

(2) Management audit is futuristic in nature as distinguished from other audits which are historical.

(3) It is an audit of performances of management in the field of plans, policies and designing of organisational structure.

(4) The approach of management audit is primarily constructive, while the other audits are primarily protective.

(5) Management audit depends on and covers 'management practices', while other audits such as financial and statutory audits cover 'accounting practices.'

(6) Like other forms of audits, it is not structured. It is objective.

(7) Management audit is a novel concept which includes other recently developed concepts such as 'propriety audit', 'efficiency audit', 'systems audit', 'performance audit' and 'social audit'.

(8) Management audit lays emphasis on 'organisational objectives.' It is highly result-oriented.

(9) Management audit not only identifies the problem areas but also recommends possible solutions to the problems.

(10) Management audit is a constructive exercise. It is not a fault finding exercise. The aim of this audit is not to comment on or rectify individuals but to suggest improvements to the systems and policies which will contribute to the effectiveness of the management.

(11) Management audit has to cover basically three areas — the prescribed structure, i.e., the organisational structure, the 'level' entity, i.e., the management and the results achieved, i.e., the performance.

Objectives of Management Audit

The basic objectives as contained in the above definitions are:

(1) To identify the overall objectives of the organisation.

(2) To ensure that management objectives are being met.

(3) To help the management to manage its affairs better, i.e., to achieve the most efficient administration of the operations.

(4) To assist all members of the management in the effective discharge of their responsibilities.

(5) To improve organisational profitabilitiy.

Scope of Management Audit

The scope of Management Audit is much wider than any other audit, and it includes all the decisions taken by the management in achieving the objectives the oganisation strives for. It covers the diverse area of management functions, such as Planning, Organising, Staffing, Directing and Conferring. The following definitions of management audit are useful in assessing its scope and areas of activities.

Management Audit is an examination of the conditions and a diagnosis of deficiences with recommendations for correcting them. It is basically constructive in its conception and objective in its approach. It has but one purpose that of helping the management to improve the position of the organisation. The net result is the diagnosis of the present state of health of the business with attention focussed on what needs improvement and with clearcut recommendations.

Management Audit is a systematic fact finding approach that examines, appraises and reports on the understanding and effectiveness of an organisation's objectives, policies, standards, structure, procedures and controls, to spotlight friction, waste and red tape etc. and to identify areas for improvement. The purpose is to spotlight problem areas so that corrrective action may be taken.

The management auditors act strictly as diagnosticians with treatment being outside their purview.

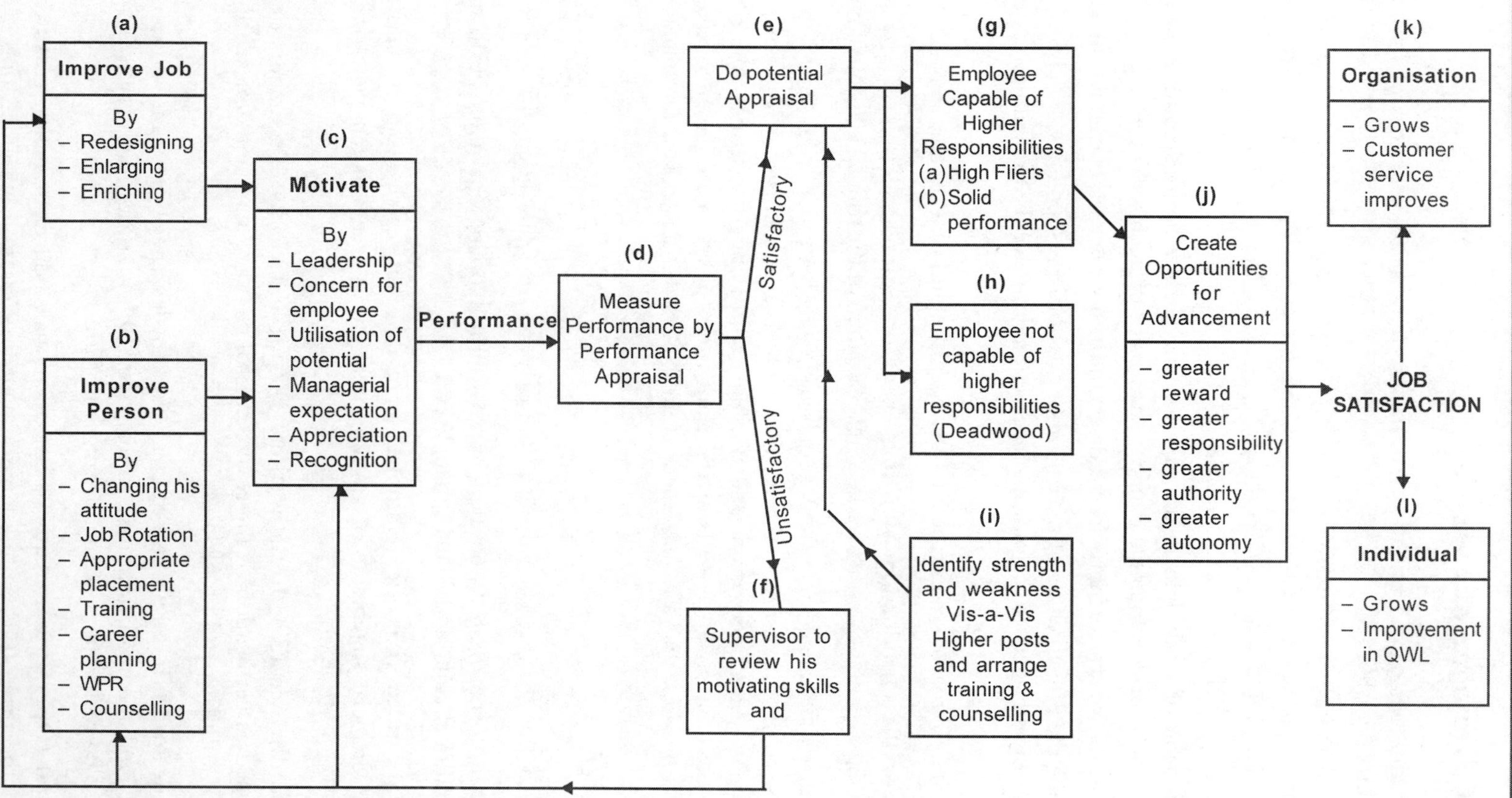

Fig. 21.1 HRD System — Flow Chart

Activities of Management Audit

From the definitions considered above we may summarise the activities of the management audit to consist broadly of:

- Analytical and objective examination of the organization, the plans, the policies, controls in the different functional areas of the business to ensure optimum utilisation of resources and facilities available.
- An objective evaluation of the performance of the business.
- Identification of weak links in the organisation and the internal controls with a view to giving signals on the potential dangers arising out of such weakness.
- Identification of waste, inefficiency, delay and other area which require improvement.
- Reporting the effectiveness of the organisation, objectives, policies, standards, procedures and control with a view to helping management to improve the organisation's performance.
- Make recommendations for improvement.
- The entire approach is constructive in conception and objective in analysis.

The time for the introduction of management/operational audit is ripe when the top management develops a genuine desire to have a full evaluation of the total management performance.

It is so because the Management Audit requires change in attitude. Although the functions of the financial as a watch dog, attesting the financial statements as forming a true and fair view satisfies the legal requirements, the modern management in the present day complexities to find the systems and to diagnose the company's ailments at the right time for the managemet to take corrective action. It is in this position that a management audit can render services to the management.

Types of Audit

The various audits that are carried out in the organisations can be classified as under:

Financial audit, cost audit, revenue audit, internal auditor, operational audit, performance audit, social audit, operational audit and Management Audit.

I. Financial Audit: It is the traditional form of audit, carried out by certified Public Accountants that financial statements of an enterprise give a true and fair view of its business positiion.

II. Cost Audit: According to the Institute of Cost and Works Accountants of India, cost audit can be defined as verification of the correctness of cost accounts and adherence to the cost accounting principles, plans and procedures.

III. Revenue Audit: It is a process of identifying the leakages of revenue and causes thereof. Systematic, procedural or human; it should also suggest suitable modifications in systems, procedures, civil controls, to plug recurrences of such leakages in future.

IV. Internal (Operational) Audit: The operational audit examination covers a review of the objectives of the firm, its operating environment, organisation structure, operating plans &

policies, its personnel and physical facilities. Operational audit is oriented towards the efficiency of operational activities rather than thrust of managerial activities.

V. Performance Audit: This is an audit which mainly covers only the outside directors in the organisations (Board members not connected with day-to-day management). Besides making a more constructive use of the expertise and experience of the outside directors, performance audit is also designed to get greater involvement of the full board of directors in the corporate affairs.

VI. Social Audit: Social audit is an approach for measuring and appraising the social performance of an organisation. The audit, to be carried out by a high level independent group of outsiders, is expected to be recommending in nature and is only for internal usage of the organisation.

VII. Management Audit: It has been described in a variety of ways. In its general form, management audit is an examination of the administrative operations and organisational arrangement of a company using commonly accepted standards of good management for evaluation.

According to Washbrook, Management and Administrative audit is an independent assessment of the soundness of the business unit and its ability to face the business problems of the future. In conclusion management audit may be described as a forward look concerned with way and means to assist management in improving its business position.

Issues of Management Audit

The concept of management audit covers a very wide spectrum of issues such as objectives, policies, strategies, effectiveness of the structure, work systems, work culture and the organisational processes. Broadly, however, these can be classified as the issues relating to:

— organisation

— management

— performance.

In his diagnosis, the management auditor has to examine the problems/ deficiencies in the organisation that he has been examining and relate the causes to any one of the following sets which follow from the above broad heads:

Organisation

— the structure, the linkages and the role relationships;

— the various systems in vogue, like the control system, information system, the performance appraisal system, etc.;

— the role designs, their effectiveness, conflicts and the clarity of the occupants and the quality and adequacy of their perceptions to play these roles;

— the organisational processes;

— the informal organisation, etc.

Management

— delegation of power and authority;
— administration of reward and punishment;
— leadership patterns, styles, effectiveness, etc.;
— levels of motivation and management efforts to have motivated work groups; the management practices in relationship to their ability to generate a disciplined, innovative and responsible work force with optimum productivity;
— managerial skills like conceptual skills, behavioural skills, etc., at different levels of management;
— authority, responsibility and accountability, etc. (in terms of perceptions and actions).

Performance

Some of the more important dimensions are:

— achievement of goals/objectives;
— tapping of business opportunities;
— profit optimisation;
— discharge of social responsibilities;
— exercise of effective and pro-active control over branches/work units;
— optimisation of deployment of resources;
— utilisation of the various integration mechanisms; and
— discharge of various functions vis-a-vis the roles.

In this task, unlike the usual audit, the management auditor has to visualise clearly what was expected to happen, and under what circumstances. He has also to perceive the internal and the external force fields (releasing the facilitating and restraining factors) operating in the situation and having a direct effect on such performance, and to identify which of these are uncontrollable and, as such, demand changes in our original expectations. Once this is done, and he is in a position to identify the strengths and the weaknesses of the unit being studied, he is in a position to give constructive feedback to the management with data-based, carefully analysed observations. Though impressionistic feedback may not always be ruled out, it will be often required to the user to make further probe/evaluation before initiating actions on the basis of such feedback.

A clear-cut compartmentalisation of the functions of a management auditor as above, for the basic purpose of having a clarity and perception of the areas being examined may, however, not always be possible. For instance, employment of financial resources for earning profits is an important management function. However, linked with this function are also such management issues as marketing activity, ability to appraise risks and the like. It may not be functional if the management auditor mechnically divides his areas of investigation under these heads since this may open up possibilities for omission of significant information on areas of enquiry. The process of audit has, therefore, to be integrated and the diagnostic or the prescriptive part of the report can be drawn up separately only after the entire audit has been completed.

Before a management auditor can decide the strategies and methodology for undertaking a specific audit, he has to undertake the basic preparatory work. This relates to:

— understanding the environment of the particular unit, the local culture, the social sub-systems, and the past history;

— acquiring adequate skills in interviewing and understanding human behaviour;

— getting full brief from the corporate office about the structure of the organisation being studied, the description of the roles to the extent specified, the various structured integration mechanisms in force and the work systems in vogue. The brief will also include the expectations of the management from the work unit as a whole and the senior managers in particular. Such expectations will be linked to the current management concerns in areas like profitability, business growth, market development, etc.

With the expectations of the top management clearly known and the areas of audit perceived, the management auditor would set out to translate his activities in the form of finding answers to specific questions and issues and analysing the causes for the variances. Such questions and issues may be framed with reference to each area of performance, in sufficient detail, so as to throw light on the areas of organisation and management as well. To give an example, if the relevant questions (illustratively) to which he may try to find answer may be:

— What are the systems introduced to collect information about the environment?

— How useful is the available information in shaping the management strategies?

— Are the systems adequate? Are they too cumbersome? Do they enable the sources to provide valid information promptly and efficiently?

— How scientific is the process of budget formulation?

— How much use of the information so generated is made for formulation of the targets and the strategies for their achievement?

— What is the process of integration of the operators and the planning staff?

Scope in India

A progressive management may conduct management audit periodically to assess the performance of various managers and link a system of incentives with such an assessment. The aim may be to improve internal efficiency of the management and make it effective to cope with the demands of stake-holders and the society.

The government may order a management audit with a view to examining the efficiency of the management before taking over a sick unit. In case the government finds the management of the sick unit inefficient, it may decide to take over the unit. However, if it is found that sickness is due to some other reason beyond the control of the management, government may try to remove such basic constraints rather than taking over the unit.

Similarly, a bank or a financial institution may like to get a management audit conducted before advancing loans or before agreeing to participate in the equity capital of a company. Foreign collaborators may also like to get management audit conducted before agreeing to participate in joint ventures in India or abroad. This would help them in assessing the managerial strengths and weaknesses of their prospective associates.

The concept of management audit in reality offers an entirely new dimension to the audit function and has a great potential from the viewpoint of realising efficiency in the functioning of an organisation.

The need for conducting management audit in banks became imperative after the reorganisation of the most of the major commercial banks which gave rise to a three-tier structure with the formation of controlling offices at Zonal and Regional levels. As a result, during the past few years, many of the commercial banks in India have either opened a separate department for conducting management audit or have assigned the task on an experimental basis to the management services department operating at their central offices.

Benefits of Banks

Bank's central office and other controlling offices such as Zonal Ofices and Regional Offices work as the brain and nervous systems of the banks respectively. They control the functions of the branches by issuing various policy guidelines, deciding systems and procedures of functioning and designing plans and programmes for operation etc. besides evaluating, monitoring, guiding, co-ordinating the work of the branches. If these controlling offices do not function properly and effectively, then the operational units, viz., the branches, cannot function effectively. The effective management of these controlling offices can give strength to the branches.

In the normal course of statutory audit and internal inspection, these controlling points are not subjected to rigorous audit. Further, the scope of these audits and inspection is limited only to the financial transactions and procedural systems. The style of management, the quality of decision-making, appropriateness of the organisational structure, functional effectiveness for the attainment of goals etc. are not questioned or subjected to any form of tests.

Hence management audit is vital for the banking sector to prevent it from any form of breakdown. No other form of audit will be able to highlight this aspect. In the post-nationalisation period, the concept of banking has changed from class banking to mass banking and service has taken the need-orientation in place of safety/security-orientation. Management audit can also be a useful tool for the government/RBI to assess the extent to which a bank is able to discharge its social responsibility. It can, again, work as a warning system for detecting incipient sickness in the organisation and suggest appropriate corrective measures for the timely removal of the causes of sickness.

Application in Banks

The scope of management audit can be as broad as the management process itself which involves planning, organising, directing, staffing and controlling etc. The objective of management audit is to identify the various problem areas relating to the functioning of the management and to recommend suitable solutions to the problems with an aim to make the management both efficient and effective in achieving the desired objectives. The process of enquiry would involve examination of three major areas, viz., the prescribed organisation, i.e., the organisation structure, the live entity, i.e., the management and the results achieved, i.e., the performance. Management audit may be conducted in the central office, other controlling offices at Zonal and Regional levels and in major branches.

The following sequential steps may be followed for management audit as suggested by Mr. A. B. Roy Chowdhary in his book titled *Modern Internal Auditing — A Workbook on Operational & Management Audit:*

(a) Study management plans, policies, objectives, organisational structure and chart, nature of activities, volume of business and broad spectrum of organisational workings.

(b) Collect documents like operational manual, various management and operational data including periodical reports, operational process chart, flow process charts.

(c) Discuss with the operating personnel and management to find out the relevant information. For the discussion, a bottom-up approach may be found useful. Initial discussions may be held with lower level officials followed by middle level officials and finally with top level officials. The authors found this approach useful for both collecting independent views of officials at different levels and in resolving controversies, if any, in the thinking process at different levels. The discussions may be held in a free and frank atmosphere where the auditors may preferably work as facilitators, helping the officials at various levels in the auditors office to identify the problem areas and seek various possible solutions to the problems themselves. Though it may be found useful to take the help of a pre-designed structured questionnaire to give a definite direction to the discussion, the discussion should be made as far as possible non-structured and objective to accommodate the views and genuine feelings of the respondents.

(d) Record the facts for appraisal, review and evaluation. It may not be possible for the management auditors to remember all the facts and figures. Hence it is necessary to record vital and relevant facts systematically in an audit notebook. These facts may be used at a later date for drawing flow charts and for writing reports.

(e) Examine the facts critically through analysis, verification and evaluation. It may be useful for the team members to examine the day's proceedings at the end of every day.

(f) Verify the various relevant documents, reports, returns, statements etc. which may help in evaluating the overall performance.

(g) Observe through insights into the organisational process, the bottlenecks, ineffectiveness, conflict of interest and unforeseen constraints which have thwarted the achievement of organisational objectives and goals.

(h) Develop the methods to be instituted after assessing the requirements and taking into account the prevailing circumstances and the pros and cons of the alternative methods.

(i) Discuss the findings and observations with the operating personnel (auditee) and with the management to elicit their views.

(j) Recommend the best method for effective and efficient management towards higher productivity and profitability.

(k) Implement the accepted recommendations in close collaboration with management and the concerned operating personnel in the auditee office.

(l) Follow up review at regular intervals to ascertain that the accepted recommendations are in operation.

Management Audit Team

Management audit requires an interdisciplinary approach since it involves a review of all aspects of the mangement function. Thus it should be conducted by a team of experts. The team may consist of persons with a background in accountancy, operations research, industrial engineering, social sciences, O & M etc. Each member of the team should have an analytical mind and an ability to look at a management function from the point of view of the organisation as a whole. In banks, the team members should be mainly chosen from the senior management who should have a clear understanding of the management process. The team leader should be of the rank of a DGM/ AGM. If necessary, the team may consist of one or two specialists at middle management level to provide technical assistance and secretarial support. A balanced team would ideally have one DGM/ AGM, two senior officers in Scale IV level and one junior officer in Scale H level.

The frequency of management audit for banks may be fixed once in three years for each auditee office/unit.

Reporting and Follow-Up

The team should submit its report to either the Executive Director or the Managing Director of the bank. This is necessary for giving the necessary importance to the report and for its subsequent implementation and follow-up.

The report should be balanced, giving credit to achievements while highlighting shortcomings and weaknesses.

The report may highlight the strengths and weaknesses of the various functional heads of management such as planning, organising, directing, staffing, controlling etc. while pinpointing the typical areas of management study such as structure, strategy, style, staffing etc. to which the strength or problem is related.

The suggested recommendations may highlight the action plans to be taken both at the auditee unit and other relevant units and offices, to make the desired system/structure/style effective. Though the report may touch upon the style of functioning of the top-management of the auditee office, it should not be interpreted as the efficiency or inefficiency of the individual incumbents as its aim is to make the structure, system etc. appropriate in order to make it possible for the individual incumbents to function most effectively and efficiently. Management audit is a constructive exercise and in no way is it a fault-finding mechanism. The reporting style should be such that it facilitates follow-up.

Management audit has a great future in banks. In view of the increasing social responsibilities and growing demands of other stake-holders such as Government, RBI, Bank employees, customers etc., it has become all the more necessary at present that the banks should not only function efficiently but also function effectively. Management audit can help in putting the banks on the fast development track. Banks may in future even conduct management audit for their major clients before committing themselves to financing them or in participating in any form of financial ventures.

After the Audit

On completion of the audit, the auditor has to specially ensure in his report that:

— the diagnosis flows from sufficient data are duly analysed and sorted out;

— their opinions and views on the basis of impressionistic data are separately spelt out:

— at all stages, no effort is made to focus on a mere evaluation of individuals or groups of persons;

— instead of giving specific prescriptions, an attempt is made to develop the maximum number of alternatives, with the likely pros and cons of each of them being clearly indicated.

If the above practices at each stage are followed, the effectiveness of the audit would improve over a period of time and the system of audit will get established and accepted. As a result, the management auditor would be looked upon and received as a management consultant and a guide and help.

The pre-audit work through preparation of questionnaires for self-use and direction may not always be possible while examining the structural and process areas. In the area of structure, where the role linkages and the functions are mostly prescribed, the discretionary element of the management auditor does not lie in evaluating the structure so much as in evaluating the implementation of the working, adequacy or otherwise of the structure in relation to the corporate goals. This would require a management auditor to comment on appropriate remedial steps. His gamut of information needs will, therefore, be wider than simply trying to ascertain if the prescribed structure is properly functioning. In the area of processes as well, the information need in areas like the ones given below, would be wider than what can be gathered by finding answers to structured questions such as:

— issues relating to informal delegation,

— atmosphere in which decisions are made,

— unstructured decision-making,

— fear and anxiety levels of officials, etc., and

— climate on the work scene and motivational levels of the staff.

Such areas should be carefully identified and data relating to them collected and analysed qualitatively for a diagnosis. A management auditor' s task in this area will always remain a little ambiguous and it would be up to his skill and capability to handle such issues and come out with authentic data and meaningful diagnosis.

It is common knowledge that no organisation can be more effective than what the chief executive wants it to be. If the chief executive realised the need for improving efficiency at all levels, the management audit becomes relevant and useful. It is, therefore, of paramount importance that for stabilisation of management audit, an environment prevails where:

— at all levels in the organisation, people carry a zeal to excel;

— the chief executive entertains and encourages efforts and supports actions for introducing changes for the improvement in the functioning of the work group;

— the top management, as a corporate policy, does all such things which reinforce such attitude at the lower levels. If the environment is different, management audit will have only a limited success to the extent of providing the right diagnosis but the treatment of the illness following the prescription may often not begin at all.

The areas of enquiry for the management audit being what they are, the natural question that would arise is whether any management would like such an exercise to be undertaken and if so, whether officials inside the organisation are well-equipped to undertake the task. This is where the top management has to take a conscious decision. Having regard to the fact that an insider is likely to have a better insight into the organisational processes, set-up, climate and its needs, he should be in a better position to make an objective appraisal of the efficiency/efficacy of the management than an outsider, provided all the support is made available to him. It is, therefore, necessary that sufficiently senior people are drawn for the purpose, who have the experience or understanding of working in the environment of the unit being audited, and have a reasonable knowledge and skills in the areas of:

— Management sciences.

— Behavioural sciences and also insights into the working of organisational processes.

It would, therefore, be beneficial if the members of the team are given sufficient training to develop knowledge and skills for sharpening their —

— process skills,

— diagnostic abilities, and

— abilities to understand organisational behaviour.

The selection and training of the members may affect significantly the success of management audit.

In dealing with management audit reports, the following factors must be kept in mind and practised: Unlike other forms of audit, it is not the disposal of the report which is important. What is necessary is to take a deep look into the various observations, suggestions of the management auditors and see in which areas and in what form interventions are necessary for trying out actions for the desired improvement. Thereafter, a detailed plan for changes/interventions should be drawn up and so also the plan for managing the changes, carefully perceived and introduced. The purpose of management audit is met, as soon as the top executives start initiating actions on these lines. On the other hand, if they resort to a routine approach centred around disposal of the report, management audit fails to generate the expected results.

Despite the best efforts made by the management auditor, very often he cannot go beyond identifying the symptoms. It is possible that he may end up in prescribing that certain symptoms are dysfunctional and should be tackled without being able to identify the real causes. For example, he may suggest that for having a collaborative and participative management, communications through interdepartmental memos should be discouraged. A deeper scrutiny may, however, reveal that such memos arise out of feelings of 'insecurity', 'passing the buck', etc., prevailing in the organisation and as such it is a must to tackle these process areas first for getting the desired results.

The Success

For the success of management audit, both the auditor and the user have to seek deeper analysis if they intend to get the expected insights/ solutions.

A common experience with most of the organisations has been that the intitial enthusiasm and the impact created on receipt of the report decays with the passage of time. This happens, as the resistance against change mounts up and the top executives find out a compromise by taking up initially the periphera and the minor issues. As such, if management audit and its effectiveness have to be what are desired of them, a proper machinery headed by a top executive should take it up from the beginning in right earnest to sustain the process of change and stabilise the structure, systems and procedures. It is, therefore, desirable that an inhouse team constantly monitors the process of change till such time it is internalised.

The management audit department is not the only dapartment which provides feedback to the top management and suggests improvements. It is also not desirable that the top management will respond only on receipt of the management audit report and not on the basis of needs felt by regular operating/functional departments. As such, if the process of change has to be supported by all and accelerated, it is necessary that a relook is given by all other departments and steps initiated first in such areas where a consensus exists. In other areas also, conflicts have to be resolved and willing cooperation of the other departments has to be offered to create the desired harmony in action and synergy in results.

Conclusion

Management audit in banks has come to stay. In a dynamic organisation, management audit serves as an effective tool of management in sharpening the management skills and at the same time, strengthening the weak points. The banking system is undergoing a sea change and the management audit is a key to success. The success of management audit depends upon the sincerity, flexibility, innovativeness and vision of the management. Management audit will not only improve bank management but also improve the management system in banks.

Chapter 22

Efficiency Audit in Banks

Introduction

The Indian banking system at present is over-regulated and over-administered. Supervision should be based on evolving prudential norms and regulations which should be adhered to rather than excessive control over administrative and other aspects of bank organisation and functioning.

In the context of the extensive branch banking that is in existence in India now and also the anticipated further enlargement of the branch network in the near future, management of branches has, indeed, assumed great importance and also places greater emphasis on internal audit and internal inspection systems of banks. The inspection by the supervisory authorities should be based essentially on the internal audit and inspection reports. Their main concern should be to ensure that audit and the inspection machinery (which will cover the credit appraisal system and its observance) is adequate and conforms to the well-laid down norms. Of the various techniques adopted to make branch management effective, numerous administrative as well as structural steps have been taken by all banks from time to time. Of these, a very significant step has been to decentralise operational decision-making to the maximum extent possible and desirable, as also to move the controlling offices as close to the areas of operation as possible, in order to ensure locational relevance to the decisions made. Nevertheless, a controlling office will have to be at least at an urban centre (a well-developed semi-urban centre would also come under this category), so that adequate infrastructural support is available and this results in some branches still being somewhat remote from their controlling office. Many of such branches would have branch-specific problems which are generally tackled by periodical visits of the controller to the branch locations. Apart from these factors, some branches do continue to be delinquent and somehow or the other their performance continues to be far from desirable. Even if the controller has 25 or 30 branches under him, there is a tendency to stereotype the branches and deal with their problems through widely practiced remedial measures like augmentation of personnel, enforcement of discipline or even formal training. But a positive response is often not perceived, at least not immediately.

We have so far talked of branches far removed from the controlling offices. But there are also branches — large branches — which may not be far away from the controlling centre, but, historically, have been performing at a lower than the expected level. Problems of such branches are also branch-specific. It will be our endeavour in this chapter to describe a system for handling branches of this nature in a simple manner which is not time-consuming. The approach would be from the human relations angle so that involvement of all the relevant functionaries is ensured and their contribution to designing ameliorative action plans and implementing them would be visible.

The performance of a branch is assessed in three broad dimensions, viz., business development, customer service and housekeeping. The resources that are available to a branch manager are personnel, premises, planning, system and procedures, organisational structure and general administration. The efficiency of a branch would be determined by the extent to which a desirable balance is struck among these three facets of performance. Past experience indicates that often only one of these dimensions of performance (that might have been found to be deficient) is emphasised with the result that the others go out of focus. For instance, in the seventies, business development, especially in the priority sector, was emphasised; after nearly a decade, it was observed that customer service had left considerable room for toning up and housekeeping had gone into heavy arrears. Resultantly, the need for up-to-date housekeeping was stressed and, later on, quality of customer service was sharply focused in response to a general impression that banking services were not adequately customer-oriented. Even the regulatory authorities commenced monitoring these aspects. As a result, banks' commercial (conventional) business took a back seat and the problem of deployment of surplus funds assumed serious proportions. This is some kind of a "switch-on-switch-off" situation and there is no gainsaying that it is not helpful for optimising branch performance. In fact, it leads to the branch managers getting confused and perplexed, and eventually overwhelmed.

Diagrammatically, the anatomy of branch performance may be represented in Chart 22.1.

There are 18 boxes (numbered 1 to 18) in the diagram and if any lag in the performance in any of the three dimensions is observed, inefficiency or inadequacy of one or more of the resources can be identified and a specified box or boxes will need to be attended to. In other words, the break-down of the performance into its basic elements would help quickly spot the deficiencies and a holistic approach would be ensured due to the total picture being visible all the time. Such an exercise would really represent a "systems approach" to the problem(s), in as much as it first analyses the areas of deficiency and then synthesises these against the backdrop of the totality of branch operations. This is, however, easier said than done; for, although conceptually, a diagrammatic representation would lead to the identification of issues and suggestion of remedial measures, the task cannot be performed unless there is an appropriate procedure laid down for the purpose. We will now examine some of the existing methods available for achieving the objective of streamlining branch performance, especially those answering the generic name of "audit."

Audit

The dictionary meaning of "audit" is "official examination of accounts." The scope of audit is extending because of the changes in the economy. Holmes observes, "Long-range objectives of an audit should be to serve as a guide to management's future decisions in all financial matters, such as controlling, forecasting, analysing and reporting. These objectives have their purpose — the improvement of performance." According to Schlosser, audit now covers cost audit, management audit, internal audit, statutory audit etc. The objectives of an audit are:

Chart 22.1

	Business Development	*Customer Service*	*House-keeping*
Personnel	1	2	3
Premises	4	5	6
Planning	7	8	9
System &	10	11	12
Procedures Organisational	13	14	15
General Administration	16	17	18

(i) to establish the correctness of the accounts;

(ii) detection and prevention of errors;

(iii) location of errors; and

(iv) detection and prevention of frauds.

However, in practice, especially in the context of banks, this concept has been widened to cover various other examinations of qualitative as well as quantitative aspects of operations. Resultantly, the proliferation of audits in banks has assumed a prohibitive magnitude. Apart from statutory audits and RBI audits, there are concurrent audits, internal (or operational) audits, spot audits, expenditure audits, tax audits, stock audits, management audits, functional audits and so on and so forth. The word "audit" itself has acquired an unsavory taste because they often adversely affect the daily routine of a branch. The normal activities are disrupted so often that an auditor is looked upon as a disturbance whose only business is perceived to be to find fault. While management audit and functional audit are generally at the corporate or administrative level, for all other audits it is the branch which is the target and the common objectives of all branch audits are to physically verify the assets against which the branch has lent funds, to ensure the safety of such funds, to certify that the bank's standard systems and procedures have been followed and to ensure that transactions take place with the maximum economy in the matter of the utilization of inputs. It will be observed that, given an appropriate system, these audits should be able to tackle the problems of banks and help the management to streamline the system by taking a corrective step in time.

Management audit takes care of the various managerial processes by scrutinizing the relationships, communication systems, information systems, extent of decentralisation of decision-making, etc. In other words, it is like a monitoring arm for checking the efficacy of the organisational structure and for assessing the adequacy of the systems and procedures, as well as personality and behavioural traits which go to make the organisation a success. Functional audit, when it is taken up as a regular exercise, would concentrate on the identification of deficiencies and suggestion of remedial measures for a specific function or functions severally. As a bank performs numerous functions, functional audit has to be several in number, by the definition itself.

In this chapter, we would concentrate on a strategy for an integrated development of the performance of such branches as give an impression of not operating at the desired level of efficiency. For, after all, a branch is the field-level operational unit and the efficiency of all the branches would ultimately determine the performance and profitability of the whole bank. We have already discussed how the three dimensions of performance have to be attended to in a balanced and equitable manner. This is not to say that there cannot be some *inter se* priority among these three dimensions depending on the local conditions in which a branch is functioning. What is important, however, is to decide upon this prioritisation, in consultation not only with the branch manager and the controller but also with such other functionaries at the branch as are performing tasks of a significant nature. None of the present systems of audit provides a tool for doing this in an adequate manner.

If we agree to define 'efficiency' as a balanced improvement of the three dimensions of performance as well as optimum use of the resources, then an analytical method for diagnosing the state of the art and suggesting remedies with the active and visible participation of the relevant functionaries can be called "efficiency audit." It is, in effect, an examination of the existing situation at the branch and identification of specific action points, taking a 'helicopter' view of the total branch performance. We will proceed now with the narration of the various aspects of efficiency audit.

Methodology of Efficiency Audit

The basic concept in efficiency audit is to examine all the significant activities at a branch against the backdrop of the matrix of 18 boxes. The effort is on the conceptual lines of zero-base budgeting, where each managerial position(in our case, it would be any significant position — managerial or otherwise) is required to describe the activities performed, examine the relevance or otherwise of each of them to other activities and, in the context of the accepted preferences and priorities, identify the road-blocks as related to deficiencies in resources, and finally, suggest remedial measures. By its very nature, the methodology is direct and simple. It is essentially a commonsense approach to the problems tackled in a systematic manner.

At the start of the exercise, the controller prepares a list (by himself) of the branches which he would like to audit in view of his own perception of the deficiency of their performance. His own perception is to be underscored, because, after all, he is responsible for the results of the branches placed under his control, and if any one of them is deficient, it will reflect on his overall achievement. It is quite on the cards that some of his impressions would be based on the feedback he receives from others, including his superiors.

For the efficiency audit of a branch, the services of three to four officers would be required for a short-term of, say, eight to ten days, depending on the size of the branch. At the discretion of the management, one of them may be identified as the team-leader. In the initial few exercises in a bank, it may be useful to induct the services of an experienced outside specialist to lead the team. A senior member may eventually take up leadership in the subsequent efficiency audits. The seniority of the officers should not be a criterion for selection. However, these officers should possess traits for analytical and diagnostic approach to problems and should not be too much burdened or overwhelmed either with traditions or with the *status quo*. Innovativeness and lateral thinking should come to them naturally. The team-leader should, of course, have some branch experience with a good track record, so that the credibility of the exercise may not be challenged.

The team-leader first sits down with the controller and sketches with the latter a thumb-nail picture of the branch to be audited, taking good care of noting down the controller's impressions and his diagnosis of the causative factors. These causative factors will, however, be validated (or invalidated) after the exercise is completed. The team then visits the branch and discusses with the branch manager along with the significant officials at the branch the problems at the branch as perceived by them and their own views on the sub-optimal functioning of some of the desks at the branch. It would be a good idea to involve in the discussion some representatives of the staff union and the officers' association, so that the entire exercise becomes an open and collaborative effort. At the conclusion of this preliminary discussion, the audit team members convene a meeting of their own where they list out the significant desks to be diagnostically studied and other functions or activities at the branch to be examined and then draw up an action plan on the basis of a time-frame. They should guard against the temptation of commenting on individual accounts, although they should be free to examine whatever books or records they think would be useful for a study of the situation.

It is interesting to record here that, at a branch of a public sector bank where an efficiency audit was undertaken under the guidance of the author, the general impression was that there was large absenteeism among the clerical staff at the branch. But a close scrutiny of the leave record showed that, except for a couple of delinquent clerks who were often absent from work in an unauthorized manner, everybody else was utilising leave within the permissible quota. There were, however, a number of female employees who were going on maternity leave as permitted. The impression apparently was not validated by the observation and the deficiency was in the matter of redistribution of the tasks to be performed among the employees available on a particular day. The branch manager had till now adopted the practice of closing down a counter (or desk) if the concerned clerk was absent.

The preliminary study and generation of relevant data should usually be completed within a week, then, the team members meet and collectively analyse the data and arrive at alternative suggestions for remedies. It would be observed that the whole exercise has been, *ab initio,* an open study (with understanding of the realities, as well as of the efforts being made) and all the concerned members of the staff (officer or otherwise) have been talked to, so that no suspicions are generated at any stage. Another aspect to be emphasised is the generation of alternative suggestions rather than unique suggestions. This is where the faculty of lateral thinking of the members of the team would be of great help.

Armed with the information based on factual data, compiled from the observations made and scrutiny of the branch books, as well as analysis and remedial suggestions, a meeting is organised with the branch manager and his assistants (if the branch manager so desires) in which the controller is also present. At this meeting, the issues that have emerged in the areas of personnel, premises, planning, systems and procedures, organisational structure and general administration and the suggested action points are discussed one by one. One of the most desirable aspects of the exercise is that the auditors are not identified as "outsiders." They are not being deputed by the corporate office (as in internal audit) or by the concerned zonal office. In fact, the members of the team may be drafted from the complement of staff in the controller's office itself. This way, the usual "we-they" situation is avoided and all the participants at the joint meeting have a commonality of purpose. There is also no possibility of the controller and the branch manager "ganging up" against the auditor, as may sometimes happen in other audits. The consensus that emerges from this meeting comprises the final conclusions of the exercise. These conclusions are then recorded by the team-leader in the form of action points only. There is neither formal report-writing involved nor is it necessary to comment and counter-comment on each of the issues identified (as is the case with normal audit reports); for, each item has been discussed and a general agreement has been arrived at. This also reduces the relevant paper-work to a minimum and obviates such administrative activities as 'closing of files', etc.

Another aspect of the list of action points is that each one of them is put on a time-frame. Some of the action points would be implementable by the branch manager himself, some by the controller, while there may be a few which will have to go to the higher authorities for approval. In the last-named group of action points, the controller gets committed to submit appropriate recommendations (again on the basis of a time-frame). It has been the author's experience that compilation of the list of action points in its final shape does not take more than two to three days. This list is prepared in three copies, one of which is handed over to the branch manager, the second one to the controller and the third to the controller's superior who will go through it and monitor the implementation of the action points on the basis of the time-frame already agreed upon. Except in a rare case, there will be no necessity of the controller's superior to express his views on any of the action points, although he can certainly give his opinion on the desirability or otherwise of any of the action points even if they may have been agreed to by all. Generally speaking, most of the action points lead to straightforward remedies which are likely to produce immediate results. Suggestions for long-term remedies naturally need to travel to higher levels of authority; for, they would involve matters of policy.

Special Advantages of Efficiency Audit

As already indicated earlier, the most significant advantage built in efficiency audit is the collaborative nature of the exercise. Also, an efficiency audit is quite brief in its time-span and absolutely down-to-earth. It has been observed that sometimes as the branch business grows, stop gap strategies are adopted to provide merely short-term relief without paying as much attention as is deserved to all aspects of the branch performance. For instance, in a very large branch of a public sector bank, an efficiency audit revealed that a member of the public coming to purchase a draft was required to walk quite a few hundred metres within the branch premises from the point of his filling in draft application form to the point of his receiving the draft. This had taken place because of the fact that a steep rise in business had led the branch to grow in a cellular form without taking into account the convenience of the customer. Wherever some place was available or wherever extension to the branch premises was possible with a minimum cost, it was done and a cell was located there to operate. These cells had turned out to be 'cancerous' in the long run and the branch did require a diagnostic analysis by the efficiency audit team to identify the necessity of redesigning the branch layout. At the meeting with the controller and the branch manager, when a map of the branch premises, showing in it the path followed by the purchaser of a draft, was displayed, everybody seemed to be totally taken unawares.

Another facilitating aspect of efficiency audit is that the controller of branches selects those which need to be subjected to efficiency audit. This selection, as well as the periodicity of efficiency audit, would depend entirely on the controller's own judgement. While, therefore, the performance of the branches under his command is monitored on the basis of the standard systems of performance reporting, auditing, etc., those branches which prove a drag on the performance of the total group can be specially identified and will be under the sharp focus as a result of the efficiency audit.

In the course of efficiency audit, it has also been found useful to speak informally with some of the customers visiting the branch. Care should be taken to see that this is not done by way of a market survey or as an effort to identify defects. It is more by way of a discussion in an attempt to impress upon the valuable customers of the branch that they are also a part of the total system.

Suggestions made by some of these customers have been found to be not only feasible but also very useful. Besides, this is also an effective marketing strategy, in as much as these customers also talk to their friends, relations and acquaintances who start feeling that the branch cares for the customers.

In a branch in a posh commercial area of a metropolitan city, it was observed that it is provided with huge glass windows in front, which would have normally proved ideal for publicity material of an attractive nature. However, only seats for customers were placed against those large windows and the publicity material (of which there was no dearth) was displayed inside the banking hall where they would not be visible to anybody unless he enters the branch premises. These glass windows could have also been beautified with potted plants. These visual attractions are not to be denigrated because they do attract passers-by. This effort is particularly significant when there are a number of banking offices in close proximity to one another, because a prospective customer would first feel attracted to the one which is visually attractive, other services being equal.

At another branch, it was observed that its housekeeping was in serious arrears, because a majority of the returns were not going to the controlling office in time, while, even in the branch manager's opinion, there was no staff shortage. The causative factor which was identified as the lack of friendliness among the officials of the branch, some of whom were not on speaking terms with one another. As a result, various officers were issuing conflicting instructions to the same group of branch staff who did not know which one to comply with when, and there was general chaos. As a remedial measure agreed to both by the branch manager and the controller, the former started meeting all the officers in a group and encouraged them to come forward with their problems and difficulties and discuss them in that forum in order to develop a sense of cohesion at the branch.

In another important city, it was observed that the growth of deposits every year has been at a steady pace and both the branch manager and the controller did not have any complaints about this aspect of performance. Interestingly, however, it was observed that a large shopping complex with a number of departmental stores had in the recent past come up just behind the branch premises and barely 10% of these shops had accounts with this branch. This indicates the danger of determining the growth potential by the method of extrapolation rather than through managerial scrutiny and scanning of locational environment.

Again, at a branch, discussions with customers revealed that there was a general satisfaction about the services rendered by the clerical staff at the branch. In the opinion of some of the old customers, the clerks at the counters were helpful and courteous but they could not say this about the officers. In fact, a comment that was made was that work completed by the clerks reached the officers' tables quite promptly, but it had to await disposal by the officers for, what the customers thought, an unduly long time. Again, while the customers were satisfied with the work and behaviour of the counter clerks, they were unhappy that the cashiers did not come in time in the morning, that the opening of the strong room was, therefore, delayed and that the customers visiting the branch for transacting business in the morning had to wait unnecessarily. Both these were valuable inputs for the branch manager and the controller.

In more than one branch, it was observed that valuable rented space was cluttered with broken furniture and unstacked records, whereas the rest of the branch was acutely congested. It has also been a common occurrence that administrative circulars received at a branch are not perused by all members of the staff, even not by all the officers. Often the availability of circulars is rendered difficult by their haphazard filing and an officer is satisfied by merely reading such circulars as pertain to his own current work and as he can somehow lay his hands on. A proper system of circulation and filing of circulars could go a long way in facilitating their being studied by the staff members.

In sum, the principal beneficial fall-out of efficiency audit is an intensive study of those areas of branch activity or performance which have not received due attention. In the process, some streamlining of the other activities which have been generally satisfactory also takes place. For instance, at a branch, a member of the public has to travel to the fourth floor to reach the Foreign Exchange Department for encashing a foreign currency travellers cheque. However, the cash counter is on the ground floor and he has to make two trips by the common elevator for encashing one cheque; and during office hours, the elevator is very crowded. While attempting to rectify this situation, the exercise naturally has to be enlarged to the relocation of many of the departments of the branch which is functioning on a number of floors in the same building.

Conclusion

The several illustrations which have been cited as immediate results of efficiency audit have been drawn from the author's own experience in more than one bank. The branches referred to belong to more than one bank. It has also been the author's experience that there has never been any reluctance in the extension of co-operation by the members of the staff including the representatives of the staff union and the officers' association. Undoubtedly, some of the suggestions offered could not be recorded as action points, for they were in conflict with the policies and procedures of the bank. But, at least, the exercise provided an opportunity to apprise the members of the staff of certain policy priorities of the bank of which they had not been aware so far. The controllers of branches have found the exercise very gratifying; for, they felt, this gave them an opportunity to have a deep insight into many locational situations which they could not detect during their short visits to the branches. Organisationally, the justification of efficiency audit arises from the fact that no branch should operate from a level of efficiency lower than the desired one. And, the philosophy of efficiency audit is that optimisation of performance in a branch is the joint responsibility of the branch manager, the controller and the controller's superior, as well as all members of the branch.

The prevailing environment offers a constant challenge to the banks. As a natural corollary to the liberalisation and deregulation of the financial sector, its nature and structure is undergoing a morphological change. While, on the one hand, the distinction between banks and non-banks is getting blurred, on the other, new products and services are being introduced by non-banking units for gaining a competitive advantage. Banks, more than ever before, have to be quick in their responses to these changes in the operating environment in order not only to maintain their position but also consolidate it further by making their products more competitive and by offering improved services to their ever-expanding customer-network.

Increased competition — both from within the industry as well as outside — necessitates the adoption of innovative measures to meet the changing and more demanding market requirements. Apart from planning and implementing sound business strategies, we must look beyond the narrow confines of current opportunities to market segments hitherto unexplored or under-utilised, so that banks can expand their base and thereby accelerate the pace of accretion of business, particularly deposits. The deposits provide the basic inputs to the banks for their operations which affect practically all sectors of the society. A slow-down in the rate of growth of deposits, therefore, is bound to adversely affect banks' services to their customers, lead to declining profits and ultimately their viability itself.

Each one of us should, therefore, make some introspection and ascertain whether we are putting in our best efforts for the betterment of our institution which belongs to us all and in whose continued prosperity lies our hope for a better future.

Chapter 23

DECISION-MAKING IN BANKS

The guidelines that I like to follow (in decision-making) include identification of all pertinent information and then a fast decision. And, I would emphasise the word "pertinent" and not the word "all." If you waited until you had every scrap of information, the world would pass you by while you were sorting out all the nitty-gritty.

— *Hicks Waldron, Chairman, Avon Products*

Introduction

What is the most important concern of the managerial set-up? Although all other aspects of management are equally important, organisational dynamics is, however, best sustained and nourished through effective decision-making. "Making effective decisions", therefore, ranks the highest amongst the most important concerns of the management. Decision-making is a process and the decision is the product of such a process. Decision-making is a continuous process. A systematic decision-making culture acts as a strong back-up to the strategies and objectives of the organisation to achieve its committed goals.

Banks are dynamic financial organisations always aiming at excellence and decision-making plays a key role. Decision-making is a process of choosing the best out of the many alternatives available. And this choice determines the level of success of banks. Bankers —managers and employees — keep making decisions of one kind or another day in and day out. In this chapter, the decision-making process in banks is examined and discussed.

Definition

Decision-making is the act of determining in one own's mind upon an opinion or a course of action. Decision-making may be defined as the selection of one course of behaviour chosen from a number of positive alternatives. It is a choice-making activity and the choice determines our action or inaction.

According to Peter F. Drucker, "Whatever a manager does, he does through making decisions." Decision-making is connected with formulating plans, establishing objectives, laying down policies and so on. According to Rustom S. Davar, "Decision-making can be defined as the selection based on some criteria of one's behaviour alternative from two or more possible alternatives. To decide means to cut off or in practical content to come to a conclusion."

According to Manley H. Jones, "the decision is a solution selected after examining several alternatives chosen because the decider foresees that the course of action he selects will do more than the other to further his goals and will be accompanied by the fewest possible objections and consequences." Thus, a decision essentially involves choosing a particular course of action, after considering the possible alternatives. It may be expressed in words or it may be implied from behaviour.

According to Melvin T. Copeland, "Administration essentially is a decision-making process and authority is responsible for making decisions and for ascertaining that the decisions made are carried out." In business, whether the enterprise is large or small, changes in condition occur, shifts in personnel take place and unforeseen contingencies arise. Moreover, just to get the wheels started and to keep them turning, decisions must be made. "The business executive", observed John McDonald, "is by profession a decision-maker. Uncertainty is his opponent, overcoming it is his mission. Whether the outcome is a consequence of luck or of wisdom, the moment of decision is without doubt the most creative event in the life of the executive manager."

Importance

Decision-making permeates through all managerial functions, and management and decision-making are inseparable. Managers use the tool of decision-making for discharging their duties. Whatever a manager does, he does it by taking some decision — the selection of a suitable course of action from a number of alternatives.

All management functions such as planning, organisation, direction and control are settled by managers with the tool of decision-making. Decision-making is important in planning, for in planning, the manager has to decide many things such as what services to give and do it effectively, how to do it, how to develop business and keep the customer satisfied, how to keep his accounts uptodate, where, when, how and so on. In an organisation, decision-making relates to the structure, nature of organisation, division of work and so on.

Decision-making is also an important tool in the management functions of direction and control. In direction, decisions relate to determining the course of action, deciding the type of motivation, deciding the orders and instructions to be given etc., whereas in control, the decisions relate to deciding of quality, control points, procedures, development, etc.

Managerial functions are exercised through decision-making. Decision-making is the key aspect in banks because they deal with money, men, and materials. For example, banks have to mobilise deposits, to give loans for productive purposes, to invest prudently, market the services, organise work, satisfy customers, deal with problems, etc. Thus, decision-making is vital to all bank management activities.

Purpose

Decision-making serves three important purposes. Firstly, it serves as a means to find a solution to a problem. Problems or difficulties are viewed as opportunities to test managerial talents and to make improvements and progress. Secondly, decision-making serves as a tool to direct human behaviour and effort towards translating policies, objectives and dreams into concrete actions and realities. Thirdly, it brings in personal satisfaction and advancement — a sense of accomplishment which is the best reward to satisfy egoistic demands.

Chart 23.1

Decision Criteria Chart

Knowledge of Outcomes	*Explanation*
1. Certainty	Complete and accurate knowledge of the outcome from each choice. Certainty is present if an action is known to lead invariably to a specific outcome. There is only one outcome for each choice.
2. Risk	The possible outcomes can be identified, and a probability of occurrence can be attached to each. Risk exists when an action leads to one of a set of alternatives or possible outcomes, and each outcome occurring with a known probability.
3. Uncertainty	Several outcomes are possible, these can be identified, but there is no knowledge of the probability to be attached to each outcome. Probabilities of occurrence are unknown or not even meaningful.

Steps

The process of decision-making has distinct steps. They are:

1. Defining the problem: The first step in decision-making is finding out what really is the problem. If the problem is not correctly diagnosed, efforts made to solve it will be of no use. To find a creative solution to a problem, it is to be clearly identified and stated. For example, deposit mobilisation.

2. Analysing the problem: After ascertaining the correct problem, it should be thoroughly analysed and information and data relating to it should be collected. This will help the management to get a clear idea of the problem. Various economic indicators like savings, economy and saving habit are analysed.

3. Developing alternative solutions or courses of action: The next step is to develop alternative solutions or courses of action. The management after evaluating the various alternatives can make the decision and the evaluation of alternatives help the management in making the best decision. Alternative strategies are thought of.

1	2	3	4	5	6
Defining Real Problem	Analysing the Problem	Develop-ing Alterna-tive Solutions	Selecting the best Decision	Converting the decision into effec-tive action	Follow-up into the Decision
Careful Identification of objective or gcal	Collection classification analysis of facts and figures	Analysis of alternatives and the probable conscquences from the use of each	Selection of the most promising and desirable course of action (choice-making)	Execution or imple-mentation of the decision (conversion of decision into action)	Measure-ment of result against objective evaluation of results if selected decision and action
		Feedback		Feedback	

Fig. 23.1 Steps in Decision-making.

4. Selecting the best solution: The next step is to select the best solution out of the several alternatives developed. For this purpose, the management has to consider the merits and demerits of each alternative solution and costs and sacrifices involved in each. Select the best-suited strategy for deposit mobilisation.

5. Converting the decision into effective action: After selecting the best solution or decision, the management takes steps to translate the decision into action with the co-operation of the employees. In order to avoid opposition from the employees in implementing the decision, it is desirable that the employees should be associated with the decision-making process.

6. Follow-up the decision: Sometimes, it is possible that a decision taken by a manager may not be a correct one. Hence, the manager, while translating the decision into action, should introduce a system of follow-up. This helps in safeguarding against an incorrect decision and also in modifying or altering the decision without loss of time. Evaluate the deposit mobilisation decision.

Decision-Making Methods

1. Kepner-Tregoe Model: Kepner and Tregoe propose the following seven types as a logical extension and conclusion to their problem-saving format:

(a) The objectives of a decision must be established first.

(b) The objectives are classified in the order of importance.

(c) Alternative actions are developed.

(d) Alternatives are evaluated against the established objectives.

(e) The choice of the alternative best able to achieve all the objectives represents the tentative decision.

(f) The tentative decision is explored for future possible adverse consequences.

(g) The effects of the final decision are controlled by taking other actions to prevent possible adverse consequences from becoming problems, and by making necessary rule or rules, the actions decided on are carried out.

2. Management by Decisions: Charles Ford criticises the step-by-step decision-making process and proposes a provocative concept in conjunction with Kepner-Tregoe's model.

3. Operations Research: This involves gathering and bringing together of required data on a particular problem, processing these data, resolving quantitative reports from these data on the relative merits of a potential course of action.

4. Decision Tree: Decision tree is a graphic method by which a decision-maker can rapidly visualise the various courses of action open to him together with the risks of possible outcomes and information needed in a problem. Decision-making involves several stages and at each stage, each of the choices open will result in a different outcome and pay off. A decision tree is a depiction showing the time sequence of decisions to be made and the possible events that may occur. The simple concept of decision tree is illustrated in Table 23.1

Normally, an organisation consists of hierarchies and information flows upwards through different hierarchies. Most organisations have three common hierarchical levels, viz., Top Management, Middle Management, Lower Management. The concerns and types of decisions made at the three levels as well as the information needed by each vary as can be seen from Table 23.1.

Approaches

There are five approaches to solving the problems of management, viz.: (a) Routine; (b) Scientific; (c) Decisional; (d) Creative; and (e) Quantitative. The routine approach involves solving the problems through traditional measures and by using standard operating procedures, but the problem in scientific approach involves the following steps: (a) Identifying the proposition; (b) Acquiring the preliminary observations about the proposition; (c) Stating tentative solutions to the proposition; (d) Investigating the proposition thoroughly using both current knowledge and controlled experiments; (e) Classifying the data obtained; (f) Stating a tentative answer to the proposition; and (g) Adjusting and stating an answer to the proposition.

Decisional approach involves the stages in problem-solving like: (a) Stating the desired result; (b) Stating the problem; (c) Listing the alternatives; (d) Evaluating the probable outcome of each alternative in terms of critical alternative; and (e) Implementing selected decisions.

Quantitative approach involves the following phases in finding solutions to various problems. They are: (a) Formulating the problem; (b) Building a mathematical model to represent the system under study; (c) Deriving the answer from the model; (d) Testing the model and answer derived to ensure its practicability; (e) Placing the needed constraints over the use of model and answer and implementing the solution.

Effective: Effectiveness of a decision cannot flow from organisational constituents, submission or acquiescence. The merit of a decision lies in its succeeding to acquire the widest sense of ownership by those who have to work on it, those who constitute the organisation. Teams of 'super star' managers, each outstanding in his own way, seldom take effective decisions, largely because

Table 23.1

Decision-Making Tree of Management

Characteristics	*Lower Management*	*Middle Management*	*Top Management*
1. Skill Level	Technological Human Relations		Conceptual
2. Types of Managerial Activities Performed	Direct Supervision Detailed Review of Operations Operations Control Personnel Problems		Strategic & Long Range Planning Analysis of Alternatives & Resource Allocation Policy Formulations Overall Reviews and Evaluation Critical Problems Tackled/Leadership Role/Ceremonial Activities Performed
3. Time Orientation of Managerial Activities	Present or Past		Future
4. Kinds of Decisions Made	Repetitive Structured Information Readily Available		Non-Recurring Unstructured Need for Decision Unpredictable Reqd. Information Not Readily Available
5. Types of Information Needed	Details of Factual Information Exception Reports		Routine, Highly Summarised Versions of Transactions, Costs, Revenue, Profits Cross-Functional Summary Reports Forecasts/Ad-hoc Reports Non-Factual Information
6. Source of Information %			
Computer Bases	55-75 %	30-40 %	
Non-EDP	25-45 %	15-20 %	15-20 %
External	05-10 %	10-15 %	10-15 % 35-45 %

(See *Principles of Management: Information Systems* by George M. Scott, pp. 41 -51)

their ability to analyse and criticise and their vanity and intelligence together make them bad listeners and impervious to new ideas. 'Making it happen means involving the hearts and minds of those who have to execute and deliver.' Participation in direction and decision-making ensures involvement of 'minds and hearts.' And once that be so, the decisions are bound to be effective.

Participative: Participative decision-making process need not be equated with the Westminster style apparatus or the Swiss style referendum systems. It is not an arithmetical democracy. The process takes deep roots only when openness pervades the functional culture and truthfulness is the work ethics. Revealing is encouraged, concealing is looked down upon and fear is extinct. Interaction, vertical and horizontal, is a habit, and respect for the 'individual' is the group culture.

No single decision-making process could be ideally suited for all situations, at all the times. Decision-making process continuously undergoes change in tune with the changing attitudes, perceptions, values and beliefs.

Chart 23.2

Quantitative Techniques (Decision-making)

Statistical Techniques

1. Methods of data collection
2. Methods of classification and tabulation of collected data
3. Probability theory and sampling analysis
4. Correlation/Regression
5. Index numbers
6. Time series analysis
7. Interpolation and extrapolation
8. Survey techniques
9. Ratio analysis
10. Statistical quality control
11. Variance analysis
12. Theory of attributes
13. Statistical interpretation

Programming Techniques (Operations Research)

1. Linear
2. Decision theory
3. Games theory
4. Simulation
5. Queuing (Waiting line) theory
6. Inventory planning
7. Network analysis PERT/CPM
8. Others:
   (a) Nonlinear Programming
   (b) Dynamic Programming
   (c) Search theory
   (d) Data processing
9. Break-even Analysis
10. Input-output Analysis
11. Cost-benefit Analysis

Notes:

1. Linear programming gives profit maximisation or cost minimisation under certain constraints. It solves resources allocation and distribution problems.
2. Queuing theory aims at minimising the cost of both servicing and waiting — balancing these two costs.
3. Inventory planning and control aim at optimising inventory levels — how much/ when to buy.
4. Games theory determines the optimum strategy in a competitive situation.
5. Decision theory involves decisions under certainty, risk and uncertainty.
6. Network analysis controls project scheduling or time table as well as cost rise.
7. Simulation device tries to test a model which resembles real life situation and it is useful before actual performances.

On general analysis, it is felt that there are various ways to ensure synergism in the decision-making process. Level of involvement of those who execute very largely depends on how broad-based they feel the decision-making process is. For that the decision-making process could be:

Informative: By this, the top functionary provides through various channels, information about the matters usually considered important. Information regarding the financial health of the organisation, structural changes, if any, being contemplated, variation in market receptivity to the product and statistical data regarding cash and capital state. This is an enabling methodology. It is left to the constituents to react or not to react. The strength of this system is the existence of a strong belief ingrained in the psyche of the rank and file that their reactions are bound to be respected and valued. Showmanship is not the motive of the top echelons.

Basic and Routine	*Tactical and Strategic*	*Programmed and Un-programmed*	*Organisational and Personal*
Basic Decisions: Unique, one-time decisions, involving long-term commitments, large investments, costly mistakes. **Examples:** Plant locations, product to be made, basic policy decisions, capital investment project. **Routine Decisions:** Repetitive, involving little thought, tending to have only a minor effect on the organisation. These decisions are made with the help of standing plans, e.g., procedures and policies. **Examples:** Salesman's call on customers on a day. A clerk sorting parts into bins.	**Tactical:** Routine, unimportant, containing few alternatives. Situation is given, requirements are evident. The only problem is to find the most economical adaptation of known resources. Decision shall achieve the desired end with minimum effort and disturbance. **Strategic:** Decisions upon basic objectives and basic policies. They involve either finding out what the situation is, or changing it, either finding out what the resources are or should be. **Examples:** Major capital expenditures, productivity, automation, reorganisation, plant layout, location, size, etc.	**Programmed:** Those which are routine, repetitive, have set up procedures, deal with low risk, more easily delegated, subject to quantitative assessment. Programmed into a computer. **Unprogrammed:** New, unique, non-repetitive, high risk, many courses of action possible, no easy quantitative assessment, involve greater expenditure of resources, cannot be programmed into a computer.	**Organisational:** Those made in the role of company executives, reflect company policy, can be delegated. We have policy decisions relating to basic ideas, e.g., financial structure, distribution policy. Then we have administrative decisions involving means of implementing policies, e.g., advertising media, themes, etc. Lastly, there are executive decisions at the points where the work is to be carried out, e.g., grant of merit raise as per top management policy. **Personal:** Decisions made by a manager as an individual cannot be delegated.

Note: 1. Basic, strategic, and unprogrammed decisions are identical or similar.
2. Routine, tactical, and programmed decisions have similar concepts.

Consultative: Here the work force nearly becomes part of the decision-making apparatus. Macro-micro interaction precedes all important decisions. Middle levels also are taken into the interaction system. Such interactions may be for bringing about better working environment. It could cover administration of standing orders and production methods. Here also the work force must see and perceive that these consultations are contributing towards the content and quality of ultimate decisions. Failure here will reduce these actions into an exercise in sound and fury sans significance. Set up as a whole they will stand to lose rather than gain.

Administrative: This is generally experimented in areas where the work force alone has direct interest. These are not the areas where decisions will have far-reaching ramifications. Here the employees representatives are entrusted with the administrative responsibility of carrying out welfare measures. Suggestion scheme could also be taken as an area where such a participation could be practised.

Associative: This is duly formalised sharing of responsibility to take decisions in certain select areas. These are structural fora duly recognised where deliberations are undertaken to arrive at representative decisions. These are generally the areas where the decisions have a direct bearing on the work force. An atmosphere of complete trust is very essential for such a system to succeed, while mistrust will lead to organisational anarchy.

Management Information System (MIS) and decision-making are inter-linked and inseparable in practice. The MIS improves organisational decisions by upgrading the existing systems. MIS provides the basic data to the management to take appropriate decisions in a scientific manner. Fig. 23.2 depicts the relationship of MIS to decision-making in programmed or unprogrammed decisions.

Programmability Vs. Adaptability in Decision-making

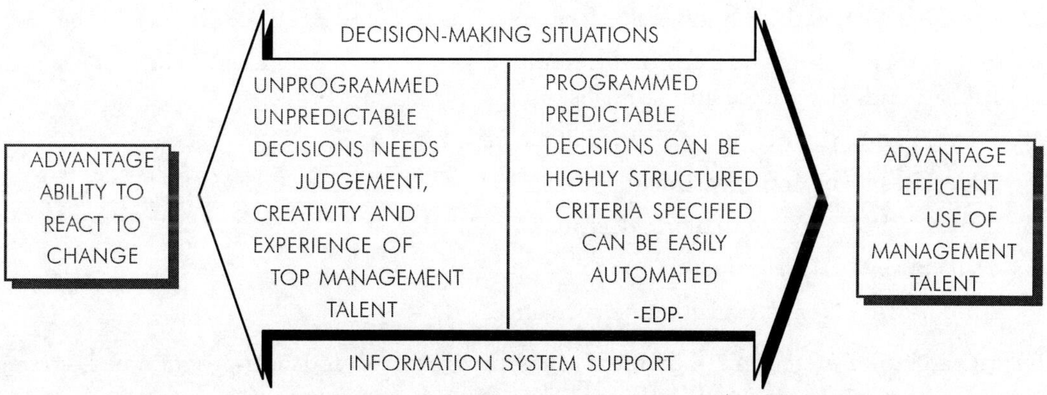

Fig. 23.2 MIS and Programmed/Unprogrammed Decisions.

Decision-making in Banks

Let us now turn our attention to banking.

Almost all the commercial banks are organised on the basis of the geographical divisionalised structure. Bank activities are grouped on the basis of functional type of organisational structure within the geographic divisionalised structure.

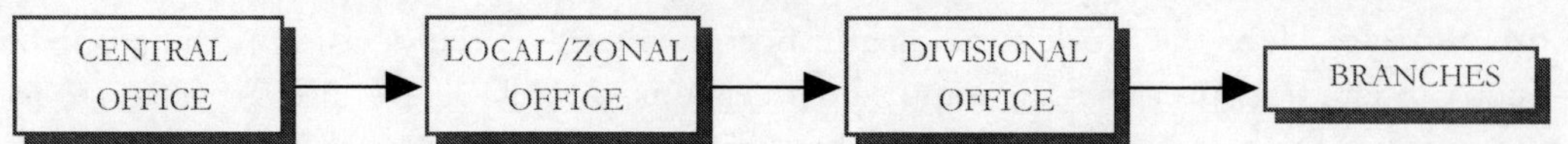

Present-day commercial banks are performing numerous functions compared to those of the traditional ones. Modern commercial banks are working as a developmental agency and not merely as a credit supplying agency. Hence the right structure of the organisation assumes greater significance in the efficient management of modern banks.

The various functions that are frequently departmentalised in commercial banks are auditing, correspondent banking, credit evaluation, foreign operations, investment, lending, legal work, operations, personnel, public relations, safe-deposit vaults, and trust services. Some of these departments would be large in some banks and small in others. At the branch level, the principal departments are deposit-taking (current, saving and term deposits), remittance of money, lending of money, handling of foreign exchange transactions, reconciliation, personnel, estate, despatch etc. The number or size of departments vary with the size of business operations.

The highest level in the hierarchy of the organisation structure of banks consists of a Board of Directors. The Managing Director is the Chief Executive of the bank. The Chairman presides over the meetings of the Board. One person can hold both these offices of Managing Director and Chairman. He is assisted by the Managing Committees, Advisory Committees and Regional Committees etc.

The Board of Directors is responsible for the overall supervision and development of the bank. It performs the following functions:

(1) Setting of bank goals regarding income, liquidity, customer service, etc.

(2) Formulates bank policies like personnel policies, credit policies, financial policies etc., strategies like marketing, diversification, etc.

(3) Selects bank executives from different walks of life taking into consideration their background, experience and specialisation.

(4) Determines authority and responsibility of each manager.

(5) Supervises loans and investments.

(6) Counsels executives in making decisions.

(7) Plans business development.

(8) Appraises bank and executive performance.

In discharging its functions, the Board takes programmed and non-programmed, strategic, policy, organisational and personnel decisions. Though decisions appear to be democratic in form, yet, in reality, they are by and large, autocratic and personal in nature. Decision-making process seems to be a matter of only choice.

The banking management cadre (officers) are broadly grouped into three categories: top management, middle management and junior management. Banks have delegated authority in detail and decisions are taken accordingly. All administrative decisions are taken in terms of detailed rules and regulations formulated by the bank.

At the branch level, the branch manager is the boss and the real decision-maker as far as administrative decisions are concerned. By and large, decision-making is concentrated in the hands of the branch manager. Although authority is delegated in medium and large branches, the will of the manager runs through all decisions. Thus, decision-making in banks is concentrated and autocratic in nature. And many a time, ineffective decisions are taken or decisions are postponed or referred to higher authorities for approval. The post of branch manager should be upgraded with the increase in the business to cut down levels in decision-making. This also calls for a complete decentralised set-up, with several centres. This will improve decision-making in banking in general and at branches in particular.

Search for a change for the better is what keeps the set-up alive. Search for a change involves continuous decision-making and the essence of quality decision-making is to make sure that each decision made is firmly anchored in position before it becomes operational. Instant and "not worked at" decisions may yield results for a while but sooner than later, the results are internal dissensions and bickerings.

Decision-making is neither difficult nor easy. If a decision has to be taken on a scientific basis and time permitting, there are certain ground rules to be followed. These are:

1. State the problem clearly;
2. Collect relevant information;
3. Develop feasible options;
4. Evaluate these options;
5. Choose the best option and decide; and
6. Implement the decision.

Even with all these exercises, decision-making may not result in getting a correct solution. For decisions can be taken only with the available information and according to the prevailing circumstances.

Decision-making is a democratic-cum-autocratic process. You must be a democrat in following the decision-making process — collecting information, consulting men concerned, be adaptive, open, free, frank, candid and discreet in discussing and flexible to explore alternatives before a decision is finally taken. But once the decision is taken, you have to be an autocrat in its implementation. But in many instances the reverse method is followed. Managers are autocratic in decision-making but very democratic in implementation of the decision by leaving the odium to their subordinates!

But many managers do not take decisions on scientific basis outlined above. Sometimes, they take decisions on ideological bases such as:

1. Application of emotions;
2. Power politics;
3. Influence of other people;
4. Decision-making on personal values; and
5. Depending on hunches and instincts.

But still, that leads the managers somewhere — towards the flickering light at the end of the tunnel. After all, a decision has been taken. Is it not better than vacillation and indecisiveness? 'As long as a dog barks which is his job,' says a Chinese proverb, 'it does not matter whether the dog is black or white in colour or whether the barking is pleasant or hoarse to the ears!' What is needed is action. And that's what decision-making is!

Conclusion

A business organisation such as banks is essentially governed by an information and decision-making system. Decision is a solution to a problem. In an organisation, problems may keep on cropping up. Identification of the right problem is not only significant but also crucial in banks. It is evident from the saying of Charles F. Kettering that, "It isn't that they can't see the solution. It is that they can't see the problem." A problem is a deviation from some standard or a desired level of performance to which a person is committed to find a solution. In fact, problems are the diet upon which an achieving manager survives.

Decision-making is defined as "an act of choice, wherein an executive forms a conclusion about what must be done in a given situation. A decision represents a course of behaviour chosen from a number of positive alternatives."

This discerning exercise can be scientific only if appropriate and adequate data are available to back up. The data need not necessarily be in the form of numerical figures alone; it can be in terms of the experience of the past, in terms of the environment and other relevant factors. Decisions taken without sufficient data base are likely to suffer from deficiencies which can lead to a lesser degree of success. It, therefore, becomes not only relevant, but also essential that the data on various facets are collected by an organisation with the utmost exactitude and are made available to the decision-makers on demand. Data-based decision-making can also be termed as scientific decision-making.

The banking scene is undergoing a sea change in conformity with the changes in the social, economic and political environment. In such a dynamic environment, information-based scientific decisions would be of real strategic advantage. Banks will do well in taking the right decisions at the right time and accelerate the process of development.

Banks have been, over a period of time, realising the necessity of data back-up for decision-making. Banks have been gathering data, volumes of them, concerning their operational environs. Systems have been devised for collecting, sifting and storing data. Important and ultra-modern communication technology tools like computers are increasingly being utilised for storing, analysing and retrieval of data. However, there is a need to streamline meticulously the systems and procedures, for collecting, sifting, storing, analysing and retrieving the data. This is essential, particularly in the light of the fact that sometimes we possess the data which are inaccurate and present an analysis which is faulty, thereby leading to a fragile situation in the decision-making process. The time, money and energy invested in developing the data bank does not bear the fruits of labour. This malaise — major or minor — needs to be remedied diligently forthwith.

The first and the foremost need will be to bring about greater consciousness, about the exigency of data-based decision-making to be followed by every individual concerned asking some pertinent questions like what kind of data are needed today and will be relevant tomorrow. Secondly, we must explore what kind of systems are necessary to be developed to store, analyse and retrieve the data; what kind of infrastructural capacity is needed; and what methods are to be devised to ensure their availability on demand with ease and without loss of time. Meeting these questions will possibly help us to identify the issues, chart out the planning path, formulate an action programme and usher in a culture of conscious endeavour to build up an efficient data bank and above all, an era of data-based decision-making — nay, scientific decision-making.

Systematisation of measures and procedures will bring about economy in expenses of management and enhance the effectiveness of the decisions by elimination of irrelevant data. This process of initiation must begin at the top and flow down the lower rungs of the ladder. It must ingrain the ability of the steam surging upwards from the very grassroots to the top. Decisions taken without data support at times are just akin to groping in the dark. Perennial reinforcements will be imperative to sustain the data-based decision-making culture, as a strong back-up to the strategies and objectives of the organisation to achieve its committed goals.

Chapter 24

The Future of Indian Banking

The rise of India's public sector banks is but a pointer to the dramatic changes sweeping through the industry for some years now. A growing economy, greater consumer confidence and appetite for credit, and greater thrust on technology have helped the more aggressive PSU banks not just grow their business, but drum their balance sheets into shape.

India is poised to become a major player in the global economic arena in the near future. At this critical juncture, a vibrant banking system is of crucial importance to the economy as it gives the necessary momentum by providing capital, generating employment, and safeguarding investments. A sound banking system is also imperative in preventing future financial crises.

Introduction

The financial system in India is undergoing structural transformation under the influence of globalization, deregulation, technological advances and institutional and legal reforms. While the liberalized environment has opened new avenues of business for financial institutions, it has led to intensified competition. To survive in a competitive environment, financial institutions have been diversifying into non-traditional activities, altering their pricing strategies and looking for non-fund based sources of income. As a result, operations of financial institutions are becoming increasingly complex and, correspondingly, exposed to greater risks. In order to ensure that financial institutions grow along sound lines, a robust prudential regulatory framework has been put in place.

Globalisation, financial deregulation and improvement in technology have had a profound effect on the financial landscape in recent years. These developments have intensified competition and resulted in financial engineering through product innovation and business strategies. While market participants have now greater scope to diversify risk and manage it efficiently, this has also posed new risks and challenges to the financial system. Growth of financial firms across different business lines and across national boundaries has made the task of designing appropriate policies more challenging. Regulatory and supervisory policies are, therefore, constantly assessed regarding their capabilities to meet the challenges of containing systemic risk in the financial system. The main challenge for the supervisory authorities has been to maintain financial stability without curtailing the incentive to innovate.

Financial regulation and supervision has been progressively aligned with international best practices with suitable adaptations. The corporate governance framework in banks has also been strengthened. At the same time, the Reserve Bank has been making consistent efforts to strengthen credit delivery, improve customer service and encourage banks to provide banking services to all segments of the population.

The Main Challenge

In view of accelerating economic growth, the main challenge for the banking sector in the coming years would be to expand while maintaining sound financial health. With large credit expansion during the last two years, while banking penetration has increased on the asset side, it continues to be relatively low on the liability side. Banks, therefore, would need to focus on reaching the hitherto untapped clients and regions. With increasing competition on the asset side, banks would also need to look for new creditworthy borrowers. While there is an enormous scope, the need is to find innovative methods to reach them. With the expected expansion of banking operations in line with the overall macroeconomic growth and the introduction of Basle II requirements, there is clear recognition of the need for banks to also extend their capacity. Consequently, the Reserve Bank allowed banks to raise capital from the market by way of certain innovative instruments during the year 2006.

Greater Thrust On Credit Portfolio

One of the critical issues facing the banking sector is the flow of credit to all the productive sectors of the economy. Retail financial services, particularly housing and personal loans, continued to traverse a high growth trajectory, fuelled mainly by demographic shifts and rising household incomes.

Credit demand by the corporate sector has also turned robust on the back of strong industrial performance. Furthermore, banks are expected to have greater financing opportunities in the area of project finance, especially in the infrastructure sector, given the conversion of two major Financial Institutions (FIs) into banks. Banks have been focusing mainly on syndication of debt to ensure wider participation in project finance and wholesale lending segment. Banks were permitted to raise long-term bonds to finance infrastructure investments as also to reduce asset liability mismatches. The ongoing effort to develop the private corporate debt market would help banks meet the long-term funding requirements of the industrial and infrastructure sectors on a sustainable basis.

Rural credit has emerged as an important growth opportunity. Several new areas such as agri-clinics, contract framing and rural housing are fast becoming viable revenue propositions for banks. In order to enhance the flow of credit to these emerging areas, the Reserve Bank has been undertaking measures to remove the impediments on timely availability of credit through various means.

- The coverage of rural credit has been extended to include facilities such as storage as well as credit through NBFCs.

- Procedural and transactional bottlenecks are sought to be removed by reducing margins, redefining overdues to coincide with crop-cycles, new debt restructuring policies, one-time settlement and relief measures for farmers indebted to non-institutional lenders.
- Public and private sector banks are being encouraged to enhance credit-delivery in rural areas.
- Banks are urged to price the credit to farmers based on actual assessment of individual risk rather than on a flat rate, depending on the category of borrower or end-use while ensuring that interest rates charged are justifiable as well as reasonable. Banks will also need to devise appropriate risk assessment and management strategies and develop technical capabilities to serve the emerging needs.

While credit to agriculture has tended to move upwards, lending to SMEs has stagnated. This could possibly be due to the perception of higher levels or risk in the sector. Financing the growth of a healthy SME sector is essential for the future sustained growth of the economy. Several measures, therefore, have been initiated by the Reserve Bank to streamline credit flow and address structural bottlenecks in credit delivery to the SME sector.

All scheduled commercial banks, including RRBs and Local Area Banks (LABs), have been advised to undertake pro-active measures to increase the credit flow to the SME sector. Salient among these include fixing of self-set targets for financing, rationalization of cost of loans, expanding the outreach of formal credit, formulation of comprehensive and more liberal policies for granting of loans, adoption of cluster based approach for SME financing and displaying instructions/guidelines formulated by banks as well as the Reserve Bank on their respective websites.

The Reserve Bank has also advised public sector banks to institute specialized SME branches in identified clusters/centers with preponderance of medium enterprises. Further, a simplified, non-discretionary and non-discriminatory mechanism has been formulated for one-time settlement of chronic NPAs below Rs.10 crore in the SME sector. A debt restructuring mechanism for units in the SME sector has also been formulated for implementation by all scheduled commercial banks.

In order to increase the flow of credit to the SME sector, appropriate risk management is essential. With the operationalisation of Credit Information Bureau of India Ltd. (CIBIL), the quality of credit analysis is expected to improve. This should help in reducing the transaction cost and improving the credit flow to the SME sector.

Micro-finance Institutions (MFIs) now provide several non-credit services such as capacity building, training, and marketing of the products of the SHGs and micro insurance. The policy environment has been fine-tuned such that the micro credit extended by banks is presently reckoned as part of their priority sector lending. Banks have been provided the freedom to devise appropriate loan and savings products in this regard.

The benchmark prime-lending rate BPLR system was introduced to increase the transparency in pricing of credit by banks in the recent past. However, with the introduction of sub-PLR lending, spreads between minimum and maximum lending rates have increased significantly. Furthermore, the sub-BPLR lending of the banking system (excluding exports, the bulk of which is at sub-BPLR) has also increased substantially — to the extent of over 60 per cent of total outstanding advances above Rs. 2 lakh. Though sub-PLR lending has enabled corporates to raise funds at competitive rates from banks without incurring any additional cost towards stamp duty, dematerialization costs or fees for issuing and paying agents (IPAs), it is distorting the role of BPLR itself. Many banks have their average lending rate below their BPLR, which is also putting pressure on their spreads. Furthermore, there is a growing perception that there is under-pricing of credit risk for large private sector corporates, whereas there could be over-pricing of risk in lending to agriculture as well as small and medium enterprises. There is, therefore, merit in reviewing the current procedures and processes of pricing of credit.

Customer Service and Financial Inclusion

Liberalisation of financial services and competition has improved customer service. However, experience shows that consumer's interests at times are not necessarily accorded full protection and their grievances are not properly attended to. There have been complaints relating to charges for balance enquiry, cheque status verification, signature verification, address confirmation, photograph verification, punitive service charges for non-maintenance of minimum balance in saving accounts, transaction charges for reorder of cheque book and for cash transaction at the branch beyond a stipulated number.

The Reserve Bank has been issuing guidelines from time to time to facilitate banks' focus on service to the common man. With the Reserve Bank's initiative, the Indian Banks' Association (IBA) has prepared a model 'Fair Practices Code' which is a public document enlisting things that a customer can expect from the concerned bank. The scope of the Banking Ombudsman is also being expanded to cover all individual cases/ grievances relating to non-adherence to the 'Fair Practices Code' evolved by the IBA and adopted by individual banks.

The expansion of banking services and diversification of ownership has led to both enhanced efficiency and systemic resilience in the banking sector. However, there are legitimate concerns with regard to the banking practices that tend to exclude rather than attract vast sections of population, in particular pensioners, self-employed and those employed in the unorganized sector. Banks have been bestowed with several privileges, especially of seeking public deposits on a highly leveraged basis. It is, therefore, imperative that they provide banking services to all segments of the population on an equitable basis.

Customer Relationship Management

In the quest to implement a successful CRM initiative, executives can learn a lesson from this cradle-to-grave philosophy. But it requires a change in thinking and a willingness to take a lifecycle view of CRM.

The key to implementing a successful CRM initiative is to first understand exactly what CRM is. Often businesses begin with an initial understanding — right or wrong — that motivates them to pursue a CRM initiative. Several misconceptions emerge once they attempt to apply CRM to their business. The most common is believing that CRM is the new cure-all for customer management evils that, if implemented, will result in almost immediate benefit. Unfortunately, CRM by itself is no guarantee of customer retention.

Companies at the forefront of CRM think of it as an integrated business strategy that places the customer at the centre of a business's consciousness. CRM provides a holistic view of the customer across all of an organisation's products and channels. At its best, CRM should address the following business goals:

- Increased customer acquisition and retention, as well as greater loyalty
- Expansion of profitable, long-lasting customer relationships
- Delivery of a consistent, relevant, high quality customer experience
- Continuous learning about customers (both business and consumer) and communication of that knowledge across the organisation
- Delivery of the right products and services tailored to meet customers' needs
- Increased customer equity
- Improved cost management

To properly implement CRM, executives must first uncover the root cause of the business problem (or problems) hampering success, and then determine how customer management or integrated treatment of customers can help solve the problem.

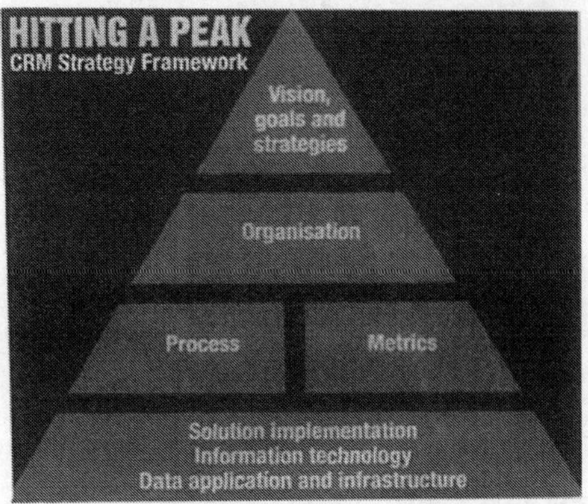

Source: A.T. Keamey

Once the organisation is well-versed in what CRM is, the next stage of the life-cycle is to develop a strategy for implementing CRM. Traditionally, software suppliers have been a major source of information about CRM, and most CRM initiatives have been born in IT departments. So it's little wonder that executives think that all good CRM initiatives begin with the installation of a tool. As the adage goes, if you have a hammer, everything looks like a nail. Yet tools do not create lasting customer relationships — at least not by themselves.

Companies must begin with a clear understanding of the requirements for winning customers, and then determine the best strategies to help them reach their goals.

The scope of a CRM strategy must be broad, consider a wide range of variables and have a business impact that affects a company's revenue performance. For example, the strategy must take a lifecycle view of the customer, complement the business and its brand strategies, and extend across marketing, sales, fulfillment and customer service. In short, successful CRM efforts are integrated enterprisewide and span all business units.

What is Inclusive Growth and Financial Inclusion?

The term "Inclusive Growth" means that the poor and the disadvantaged population should come within the ambit of mainstream growth process. "Financial Inclusion" means the outreach of formal financial system to the vast sections of the rural and urban population who are in the grip of the unorganised forces and trapped in acute perpetual poverty. It is a process of ensuring access to timely and adequate credit and financial services to vulnerable groups at an affordable cost. Major components of inclusive Growth and Financial Inclusion are as below:

- "Inclusive Growth" should include all the poor, deprived and disadvantaged sections of the population both in rural and urban areas in economic development. However, actions should begin in the rural areas, which are relatively more deprived. In later stages, it is essential to extend benefits to pensioners, self-employed and labourers in the unorganised sectors as well.
- Formal Financial System, viz., commercial banks, co-operatives, Regional Rural Banks and insurance companies should participate in the inclusive growth process. Because, the aim is not only to provide loan but also to offer a whole bunch of services to the poor, viz., banking, insurance, advisory services and other hybrid products and services.
- There must be effective coordination among the agencies that participate in the inclusive growth process, viz., Banks, NGOs, Micro Finance Institutions and the Government. The Government should provide the basic infrastructure, banks should provide the financial inputs and the NGOs should lend their leadership and executive skills. In the entire process of implementing such a programme, Reserve Bank of India may play a catalyst role in coordinating with the players and guide orderly execution of the Scheme.

Financial Inclusion: RBI's Initiatives

- RBI has advised banks that they should provide basic banking to the poor with 'No Frills' accounts either with 'nil' or very minimum balances. The inclusive growth by banks should begin with by establishing relationship with the poor, from the deposit front.
- The KYC norms for opening savings accounts for low-income groups in urban and rural areas are simplified.
- Overdraft facilities in 'no frills' accounts without any collateral or linkage to any purpose are allowed.
- 'One-time settlement scheme' (OTS) for all borrowers are allowed where principal loan amount is less than Rs.25,000.
- Borrowers with loans settled under OTS scheme may be eligible to re-access the formal financial system for fresh credit.

- Banks to provide General Purpose Credit Card (GCC) facility at their rural and semi-urban branches. It is in the nature of revolving credit facility with a specified sanctioned limit. A revolving credit limit up to Rs.25,000 without the collateral will enable the rural households to have hassle-free credit.
- Financial inclusion may be achieved by extension of banking services through business facilitators and correspondents such as NGOs/SHGs, Micro Finance institutions etc. Those banks that do not have the requisite branch networking, can outreach the rural poor through the already established institutional infrastructure thereby minimizing expenditure on physical infrastructure.
- RBI has set up a Committee on Financial Inclusion to prepare a strategy for implementation (Chairman: Dr. C. Rangarajan). The recommendations are expected to be implemented by banks in a systematic and phased manner.
- The recommendations of the Committee on Financial Sector Plan for north-Eastern Region (Chairperson: Smt. Usha Thorat, Dy. Governor, RBI) set up by RBI are going to be of great significance for future course of actions and replication in other areas as well.

Imbalance Sheet

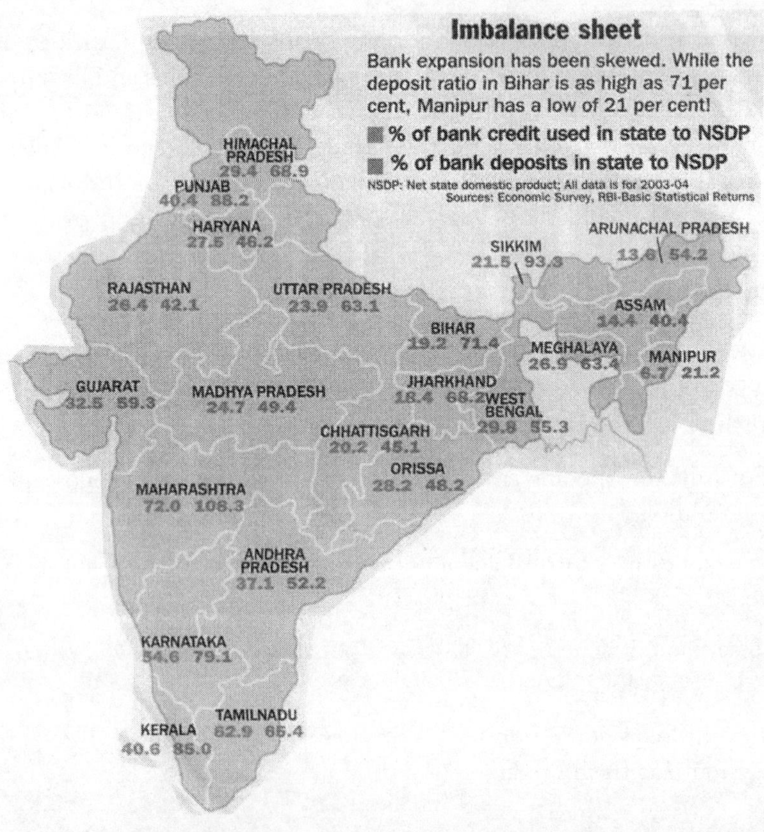

Banks' Role in Inclusive Growth

Commercial Banks have major responsibility in the process of inclusive growth and can proactively participate in Financial Inclusion through various measures as follows:

- ***Technology Applications at Branch Level***

The primary activity at the rural branches pertains to depositing money, disbursing loan and managing small remittances. Appropriate technology at rural branches may focus on networking rural branches using the radio frequency and low cost ATMs. By using PIN or biometric based technology, the validation of customer and the transfer of money to the rightful customer can be authenticated at dispersed locations (i.e., not at the branch premises but where the customer is located) at lower cost. This facilitates rural branches to reach out to rural poor who are hesitant to go to branches for these transactions. Further, by this method it is possible to bring down cost of transactions.

At rural branches low cost ATMs can be installed to transact cash deposit, cash withdrawal and bill payment. Introduction of multi-application Smart Card system can serve as a bank account, and also can function as a store of electronic cash, as a data repository for essential information relating to card-holder, with in-built security features. Banks can also consider the feasibility of using the Smart Cards for the no frill accounts to expand the coverage of the banking services and garnering the low cost deposits.

- ***Appropriate Business Strategy***

Banks should understand that the best way to initiate financial inclusion in rural areas is to start with a deposit account. It helps to build relations with depositors, proves the credentials of the deposit-customer, helps to gauge his income flow and income pattern and capacity to save, helps to assess his loan requirement and finally analyse the expectations of customer. It is feasible to insist on deposit-linked loans or loan-linked deposits. Merely lending to the rural poor under the targetted schemes is not fruitful. Thus a single gateway to banking account may open up a host of opportunities to establish better linkages with customers.

- ***Rural Computer Kiosks***

Government's initiative to set up one lakh Information Kiosks in villages is a welcome step and the same needs to be implemented soon. These rural Common Service Centres (CSC) will be set up with public-private partnership and it is a major step in bringing the rural poor closer to the Government. By getting host of information like birth/death certificates, electricity bills, agricultural prices, weather reports etc., the rural poor can upgrade themselves in health care, employment and modern agriculture as well. Banks can make use of this facility to directly interface with the village customers.

- ***Issues in Human Resources***

Banks may have to re-look at HRD policies and infuse career prospects and provision of incentives for the rural staff. A dedicated cadre of officers may be identified and posted in Priority Sector Departments and the rural offices. Specialized officers such as Rural Development Officers may be recruited afresh to plan, execute and monitor the Financial Inclusion strategies.

- ***Addressing Apprehensions of Rural Customers***

Many rural poor customers have unfounded apprehensions about banks. The attitude of bank staff, documentation process and formal procedures, fear of availing more loan than required, risk of loan default and possibility of diversion of funds are the major mind-blocks of rural population about banks. For greater inclusion, banks should erase these unfounded apprehensions from their minds by continuous interaction with the rural customers. Hence, rural branches should establish healthy links with prospective customers and encourage them to bank with them.

- ***Credit Information***

There is a need to create credit information data to assess the credit-worthy borrowers in rural areas. As such, there is hardly any data on this aspect and the same needs to be strengthened. The RBI, NABARD and the NGOs can coordinate to create such information, which could be shared by all banks. The SLBC data may also be suitably structured to build a reliable credit information.

- ***Suitable Credit Schemes***

As the income flow of the farmers is seasonal in nature, loan disbursement and loan recovery by banks should go in tandem with the sowing and harvesting of crops. Even within that, the credit schemes should be different for Food crops and Commercial crops. With regard to lending to activities such as poultry, floriculture, Sericulture etc. banks have to adopt innovative lending methods. Lending to the poor for construction and up-gradation of houses need be partly in cash, partly in kind and insist on beneficiaries participating in the construction of the houses.

- ***Credit Risk Hedging and Insurance against Loss***

Agricultural activity depends on monsoon and there is a need to hedge the credit risk through insurance coverage. General insurance can be conceived for commercial crops and food crops in the event of failure on account of failure of rain/scanty rain. This will benefit not only the farmers but the lending banks as well. Presently, in respect of crop failures, claims assessments are made on area basis rather than individual basis and this has not benefited the aggrieved farmers. Hence, some leniency can be made in claim assessment on individual basis as well.

- ***Strengthening Linkage with NGOs and Self-Help Groups***

There is an impressive growth in the SHG-Bank Linkage Programme. The number of SHGs linked with banks as of March 31, 2006 stood at 22.39 lakh. The number of participating banks was 501. Of these, 47 were commercial banks, 124 RRBs and 330 cooperatives. The total number of bank branches participating in the programme stood over 41,000. The total bank loan and the refinance availed under the programme amounted to Rs.113.97 billion and Rs.41.56 billion, respectively. The average loan sanctioned per SHGs was Rs.50,913 and the average loan per family was Rs.3,637. The total number of poor households assisted under the programme stood at 32.98 million.

Based on the various experiences, the SHG-Bank linkage programme has shown many benefits: One, the poor have not only the potential to save but also are bankable; Two, through the SHG route, the rural poor are ready to be part of the institutional financial structure and particularly banks and three, banks also find it safe to finance the poor, if they could approach through SHGs route. Hence, the SHG-Bank linkage may be strengthened.

- ***Greater inclusion through Micro Finance***

Banks have greater role to play in micro credit in the coming years so as to achieve greater financial inclusion. Each bank may formulate its own models or choose any conduit/intermediary for extending micro credit. They may choose suitable branches/pockets/areas where micro credit programme can be implemented. Micro credit should be included in the branch credit plan, block credit plan and state credit plan of each bank. Greater dedication and increased involvement of banks in the SHG linkage plan has proved to be successful and hence the same needs to be encouraged.

BASLE-II & Integrated Risk Management

In India, the capital adequacy norms were adopted in 1992 following the Basle Accord, 1988. With the increasing sophistication in banking operations and the growing cross-border activities of banks, the earlier Accord, which focused exclusively on credit risk, did not adequately address the emerging realities of banking. After due consultative process which began in 1999, the New Capital Accord, popularly known as Basle II, was enunciated in 2004 for adoption by banks. The revised Accord takes into account both market and operational risks, reinforced by a three-pillar strategy. Basle II, under which banks' capital requirements will be more closely aligned with the underlying risks in their balance sheets, is expected to promote stronger risk management practices in banks.

In India, commercial banks will start implementing Basle II with effect from March 31, 2007. In particular, they will adopt the Standardized Approach for credit risk and the Basic Indicator approach for operational risk. After adequate skills are developed both at the bank and the supervisory levels, some banks may be allowed to migrate to the Internal Ratings Based Approach.

The Reserve Bank had advised banks in May 2004 to examine in depth the options available under Basle II and draw a road map by end-December 2004 for migration to Basle II and review the progress made at quarterly intervals. Subsequently, all banks were advised to undertake a self-assessment of the various risk management systems in place, with specific reference to the major risks covered under Basle II and initiate necessary remedial measures to update the systems to match up to the prescribed minimum standards.

Banks were also advised to formulate and operationalize the Internal Capital adequacy Assessment Process (ICAAP) as required under Pillar II of the new Accord. The adoption of Risk Based Supervision (RBS) would facilitate in factoring the Pillar II requirements under Basle II. In the interim, banks were also advised to create an Investment Fluctuation Reserve of 5 per cent of the investment portfolio, both in the Available for Sale (AFS) and Held for Trading (HFT) categories plus a 2.5 per cent risk weight on the entire investment portfolio to address the market risk.

In the course of implementation of Basle II, banks are expected to face several challenges. These are as follows:

- Basle II provides scope for the supervisor to prescribe higher than the minimum capital levels for banks for interest rate risk in the banking book and concentration of risks/risk exposures, among others.

BOX 24.1

THE NEW BASLE CAPITAL PROPOSAL FOR BANKS

Jan van der Vossen

Historically, banks incurred credit risk mainly through direct loans and relationship financing. Setting capital requirements for these types of credit risk was relatively straightforward. Since 1988, the Capital Accord issued by the Basle Committee on Banking Supervision has set guidelines for banks' financial buffers against unforeseen credit risk. The accord is intended to promote equal competitive conditions across countries for internationally active banks and to enhance banks' financial resilience. To date, more than a hundred countries have adopted the Basle approach. Major changes in the financial landscape since 1988 have necessitated a new approach. On January 16, 2001, the Basle Committee issued for public comment revised proposals on capital requirements for banks, upon which the IMF has also been asked to comment. The proposals are to be finalized around the end of 2001.

The development of secondary and derivatives markets, in which banks sell credit risk instead of retaining it as loans on their balance sheets, was largely unanticipated when the original Basle Accord was designed. Furthermore, experiences during recent years have highlighted the shortcomings of excessive supervisory focus on capital rules. The development of derivatives, global financial markets, and increased intragroup connections has made it much more difficult to supervise banks mainly on the basis of capital criteria. Since 1988, the prudential value of the capital-adequacy ratio has eroded in countries with advanced financial markets. Banks in the crisis countries of the late 1990s showed vastly overstated capital figures, mainly because they made insufficient loan-loss provisions.

The current proposals, made up of three sections, or "pillars," are a major advance over the 1988 accord. Pillar I links banks' capital requirements more closely to actual risk. Pillar II strengthens the supervisory process, and Pillar III seeks to enhance disclosure and market discipline. Pillars II and III thus go beyond bank capital regulations and underline that these are only one part of effective banking supervision.

Pillar I encourages better risk management by banks. It links capital-adequacy requirements more closely to risk. Banks may choose between what is termed the "standardized" approach, largely prescribed by the supervisor, or an "internal ratings based" approach, which, after supervisory agreement, allows banks to use elements of their own risk-management systems. However, the science of credit-risk measurement is still young and unproven over a full credit cycle, and much attention will need to be given to the quality of banks' internal systems. Pillar I also changes capital requirements for corporate credits and allows differentiation for risk quality. The new proposals can require that up to 12 per cent capital be held against poor risks but can also allow capital held against good risks to drop from 8 per cent to 1.6 per cent. Within the internal ratings based approach, banks can choose a "foundation" or an "advanced" approach, depending on their risk-management sophistication. Importantly, the new proposal abandons the distinction between Organization for Economic Cooperation and Development (OECD) and non-OECD sovereign borrowers and banks by linking risk weightings to quality, rather than to OECD membership. The proposal also recognizes credit-risk-mitigation techniques.

Pillar II gives supervisors more responsibility for reviewing banks' risk-management and capital-adequacy systems. Supervisors will need to become fully conversant with modern risk-management techniques.

Pillar III reinforces market discipline and specifies what information must be disclosed by banks. Banks would, for instance, need to disclose detailed information on credit exposures, including impaired loans.

These changes can facilitate the IMFs work by strengthening financial sector stability. In the meantime, many countries will need to invest heavily in staff, training, and information technology. However, there is no way back. As markets become more sophisticated, so must bank managers and bank supervisors.

- The existence of large and complex financial conglomerates could potentially pose a systemic risk. It would, therefore, be essential to institute appropriate supervisory policies in order to address the challenges posed by the presence of such conglomerates. Capacity building, both in banks and the regulatory bodies, is a serious challenge for implementation of Basle II, especially with regard to adaptation of advanced approaches.

As implementation of Basle II gathers force and banks capture operational risk appropriately and provide for capital charge for market risk, several banks may need additional capital. With the expected high growth of the economy, banks' lending operations are also expected to expand requiring more capital. In the past, banks have tended to rely mainly on retained earnings to strengthen their capital position. However, with the buoyant capital market, it should not be difficult for banks to raise capital from the market, especially when the banking sector is performing well.

Modern day banking is all about management of risks. Banks with proper risk management systems would tend to have a competitive advantage by way of lower regulatory capital charge. Such banks would also be able to properly price their services and make adequate provisioning. Risk Management has assumed added significance in the context of Basle II. In the changed environment various risks are not independent. Banks, therefore, need to adopt Integrated Risk Management Systems, whereby they effectively address all relevant risks in an ongoing and comprehensive manner.

BOX 24.2

ENHANCEMENT OF BANKS' CAPITAL RAISING OPTIONS FOR CAPITAL ADEQUACY PURPOSES

I. Innovative Perpetual Debt Instruments

The innovative perpetual debt instrument (IPDI), which is perpetual in nature, is allowed to be issued up to 15 per cent of total Tier I capital. While IPDI is not allowed to be issued with a '*put option*'. it could be issued with '*call option*' and '*step up option.*' However, call option can be exercised after the instrument has run for at least ten years and with the prior approval of the Reserve Bank. Step-up option could be exercised only once during the whole life of the instrument, in conjunction with the call option, after the lapse of ten years from the date of issue. Further, the step-up should not be more than 100 basis points. As this instrument is eligible to be included as Tier I capital, it would have '*loss absorption*' feature. Interest due on IPDI is not payable and is also non-cumulative in case the CRAR of the issuing bank is less than regulatory minimum prescribed or the impact of such payment results in bank's CRAR falling below or remaining below the minimum regulatory requirement prescribed. However, banks would be allowed to pay interest due with the prior approval of the Reserve Bank even when the payment of interest results in net loss increase, provided CRAR remains above the regulatory norm. As regards *seniority of claim*, the claims of investors in innovative instruments will be superior to the claims of investors in equity shares and subordinated to the claims of all other creditors. Investment in these instruments by FIIs and NRIs are allowed within an overall limit of 49 per cent and 24 per cent, of the issue, respectively, subject to the investment by each FII not exceeding 10 per cent of the issue and investment by each NRI not exceeding 5 per cent of the issue.

Investment in IPDI raised in Indian rupee by FIIs is outside the ECB limit for rupee denominated corporate debt (currently US $1.5 billion) fixed for investment by FIIs in corporate debt instruments. Banks could also augment their capital fund to issue IPDI in foreign currency, without approval of the Reserve Bank, subject to terms and conditions. Not more than 49 per cent of the eligible amount can be issued in foreign currency.

II. Upper Tier II Instruments

The amount of Upper Tier II instruments issued by a bank along with other components of Tier II capital cannot exceed 100 per cent of Tier I capital and these instruments shall have a minimum maturity of 15 years. Similar to IPDI, Upper Tier II instruments cannot be issued with a '*put option*'; they could be issued with '*call option*' and '*step up option.*' As in the case of IPDI, call option can be exercised only after the instrument has run for at least ten years and with the prior approval of the Reserve Bank and step-up option can be exercised only once during the whole life of the instrument, in conjunction with the call option, after the lapse of ten years from the date of issue. Further, the step-up should not be more than 100 pbs. Unlike IPDI, loss absorption capacity of Upper Tier II instruments is limited. Interest due on this instrument and principal on redemption can be deferred, but would be cumulative. Interest due and principal on redemption can be deferred, only if, CRAR of the issuing bank is less than regulatory minimum prescribed or the impact of such payment results in bank's CRAR falling below or remaining below the minimum regulatory requirement prescribed. However, banks are allowed to pay with the prior approval of the Reserve Bank, when the payment of interest results in net loss/increase in net loss, provided CRAR remains above the regulatory norm. While paying such unpaid interest and principal, banks are also allowed to pay compound interest at a rate not exceeding the coupon rate of the relative Upper Tier II bonds on the outstanding principal and interest. The Upper Tier II instrument is not repaid at maturity without prior approval of the Reserve Bank. The claims of the investors in Upper Tier II instruments are deemed superior to the claims of investors in instruments eligible for inclusion in Tier I capital, but subordinate to the claims of all other creditors. As in the case of short-term subordinated debt. Upper Tier II instruments are also subjected to a progressive discount for capital adequacy purposes during the last five years of their tenor. These instruments are open for FIIs/NRI investment, subject to certain restrictions. While investments by FIIs are allowed within the limits as laid down in the ECB Policy for investment in debt instruments. NRIs' investments are subject to the existing policy in force.

Investments by FIIs in Upper Tier II instruments raised in Indian rupee is outside the limit for investment in corporate debt instruments, i.e., US $1.5 billion. However, investment by FIIs in these instruments is subject to a separate ceiling of US $500 million. The total amount of Upper Tier II instruments issued in foreign currency cannot exceed 25 per cent of the unimpaired Tier I capital. This eligible amount is commuted with reference to the amount of Tier I capital as on March 31 of the previous financial year, after deduction of goodwill and other intangible assets but before the deduction of investments. This is in addition to the existing facility for foreign currency borrowings by Authorised Dealers.

Management of Non-performing Assets

The most important facet of risk in India remains credit risk. Banks have been successful in containing their Non-performing Assets (NPAs), despite adoption of 90-day delinquency norm and the overhang problem. Net NPAs have now fallen to about just two per cent of net advances. Banks have been able to achieve this by using treasury profits during the last few years. Various measures initiated by the Government, the Reserve Bank and the banks themselves have also facilitated the recovery and management of NPAs. The Securitisation and Reconstruction of Financial Assets and Enforcement of Security Interest (SARFAESI) Act, 2002 has significantly strengthened the lender's ability to enforce its right to collateral. The Corporate Debt Restructuring (CDR) system has also emerged as a time-bound and transparent mechanism for arriving at a consensual financial arrangement between the creditor and the borrower. The enactment of the Credit Information Companies Act, 2005 will also enable sharing of credit information and progressive formation of credit information bureaus, which should help in reducing transaction costs of banks in extending credit to small and medium borrowers.

BOX 24.3

GUIDELINES ON SALE/PURCHASE OF NPAS — SALIENT FEATURES

The salient features of the guidelines are as follows:

- The guidelines are applicable to banks, FIs and NBFCs purchasing/selling non-performing financial assets (NPFA) from/to other banks/FIs/NBFCs (excluding securitisation companies/reconstruction companies).
- A financial asset, including assets under multiple/consortium banking arrangements, would be eligible for purchase/sale in terms of these guidelines if it is a non-performing asset/non-performing investment in the books of the selling bank.
- A bank which is purchasing/selling NPFA should ensure that the purchase/sale is conducted in accordance with a policy approved by the board.
- While laying down the policy, the board is required to satisfy itself, that the bank has adequate skills to purchase NPFA and deal with them in an efficient manner which will result in value addition to the bank. The board should

also ensure that appropriate systems and procedures are in place to effectively address the risks that a purchasing bank would assume while engaging in this activity.

- The estimated cash flows are normally expected to be realised within a period of three years and not less than 5 per cent of the estimated cash flows should be realised in each half year.
- A bank may purchase/sell NPFA from/to other banks only on a 'without recourse' basis, i.e., the entire credit risk associated with the NPFA should be transferred to the purchasing bank. Selling bank shall ensure that the effect of the sale of the financial assets should be such that the asset is taken off the books of the bank and after the sale there should not be any known liability devolving on the selling bank.
- Banks should ensure that subsequent to sale of the NPFA to other banks, they do not have any involvement with reference to assets sold and do not assume operational, legal or any other type of risks relating to the financial assets sold. Consequently, the specific financial asset should not enjoy the support of credit enhancements/liquidity facilities in any form or manner.
- A NPFA in the books of a bank shall be eligible for sale to other banks only if it has remained a non-performing asset for at least two years in the books of the selling bank.
- Banks shall sell NPFA to other banks only on a cash basis. The entire sale consideration should be received upfront and the asset can be taken out of the books of the selling bank only on receipt of the entire sale consideration.
- A NPFA should be held by the purchasing bank in its books at least for a period of 15 months before it is sold to other banks. Banks should not sell such assets back to the bank, which had sold the NPFA.
- Banks are also permitted to sell/buy homogeneous pool within retail NPFA, on a portfolio basis, provided each of the NPFA of the pool has remained as NPFA for at least 2 years in the books of the selling bank. The pool of assets would be treated as a single asset in the books of the purchasing bank.
- The NPFA purchased may be classified as 'standard' in the books of the purchasing bank for a period of 90 days from the date of purchase. Thereafter, the asset classification status of the financial asset purchased is required to be determined by the record of recovery in the books of the purchasing bank with reference to cash flows estimated while purchasing the asset.
- The asset classification status of an existing exposure (other than purchased financial asset) to the same obliger in the books of the purchasing bank will continue to be governed by the record of recovery of that exposure and hence may be different.
- Any restructuring/rescheduling of the repayment schedule or the estimated cash flow of the NPFA by the purchasing bank shall render the account as a NPA.
- When a bank sells its NPFA to other banks, the same will be removed from its books on transfer. If the sale is at a price below the net book value (NBV)(i.e., book value less provisions held), the shortfall should be debited to the profit and loss account of that year. If the sale is for a value higher than the NBV, the excess provision shall not be revised but will be utilised to meet the shortfall/loss on account of sale of other NPFA.
- Any recovery in respect of NPA purchased from other banks should first be adjusted against its acquisition cost. Recoveries in excess of the acquisition cost can be recognised as profit.
- For the purpose of capital adequacy, banks should assign 100 per cent risk weights to the NPFA purchased from other banks. In case the NPFA purchased is an investment, then it would attract capital charge for market risk also. For NBFCs, the relevant instructions on capital adequacy would be applicable.
- The purchasing bank will reckon exposure on the obliger of the specific financial asset. Hence, these banks should ensure compliance with the prudential credit exposure ceilings (both single and group) after reckoning the exposures to the obligers arising on account of the purchase. For NBFCs, the relevant instructions on exposure norms would be applicable.
- Banks which purchase/sell NPFA from other banks are required to make disclosures in the 'notes on accounts' to their balance sheets relating to details of NPFA purchased/sold.

Corporate Governance in Banks

Corporate governance lies at the heart of building sound financial institutions. Corporate governance has assumed added significance in the current liberalized environment when the banking sector is expected to function on commercial lines. The governance structure specifies the rights and responsibilities of the Board, the management, the shareholders and the other stakeholders. It is only through a proper interaction among these constituents that governance of banks can improve. Since institutions have different business philosophies, each institution would need to develop its own governance system based on the guiding principles as it evolves and develops over time. The quality of corporate governance in banks becomes critical as competition intensifies and banks strive to retain their client base.

Transparency and disclosure standards, which are important constituents of a sound corporate governance mechanism, have been enhanced to align with international best practices. Banks are currently required to make several disclosures about their operations in their balance sheets. However, there are some gaps in the disclosures in India vis-a-vis the international standards, particularly in the area of risk management strategies and risk parameters, risk concentrations, performance measures, components of capital structure. Hence, the standards need to be further broad-based in consonance with improvements in the capabilities of market players to analyze the information objectively.

Consolidation of the Banking System

One of the major objectives of banking sector reforms has been to enhance efficiency and productivity through competition. This involved three elements. First, private shareholding in public sector banks has been injected by permitting reduction in the Government shareholding in public sector banks up to 51 per cent. Second, entry of new private sector banks has been allowed. Third, foreign banks have been permitted additional branches. The roadmap for banking sector reforms, which put forth guidelines on ownership and governance in private sector banks and a two-phase roadmap for presence of foreign banks in India, has also been announced by the Reserve Bank in February 2005.

Various indicators suggest that competition in the banking industry has intensified. New private sector banks and foreign banks with comparative advantage in technology have ushered in highly competitive banking. This has encouraged other banks to devise imaginative ways to maintain their market share.

Although the financial system in India has developed considerably over the years, the ratio of bank assets to GDP in India is still low in comparison with that prevailing in several other emerging market economies. This, combined with the fact that India's economy is growing at a robust rate, would suggest that there is enormous potential for future growth of banking, especially in rural and semi-urban areas.

It is expected that consolidation of the domestic banking system in both public and private sectors would be combined with gradual and calibrated enhancement of the presence of foreign banks. The move towards consolidation also encompassed the financial institutions (FIs), which have been providers of long-term finance. Two large term-lending institutions have already converted into banks. The Government of India has notified on September 12, 2005, under Section 23A of the RRB Act, 1976, the State level amalgamation of 28 RRBs into 9 new RRBs in six states, viz., Bihar, Gujarat, Karnataka, Maharashtra, Punjab and Uttar Pradesh. The amalgamations have become effective from September 12, 2005.

The growing complexity of the financial sector with banks, insurance companies and NBFCs making foray into non-traditional activities, has led to the emergence of financial conglomerates which pose a significant risk to the financial sector. Accordingly, it was felt desirable to move away from the segmented approach to supervision to a comprehensive process involving inter-regulatory exchange of information. Based on a consultative approach, a mechanism has been evolved, which seeks to capture intra-group transactions/exposures of identified financial conglomerates and exchange of relevant information among the principal regulatory authorities, on a quarterly basis. Since different financial conglomerates have different lead area of operations, the oversight framework envisages that the principal regulators obtain data/information in the prescribed format in respect of their conglomerates and address the issues of concerns arising out of the analysis of the data.

Organisational Change

Every one acknowledges the need to radically change organisational structures and systems to survive in the New Millennium. Jerry Yoram Wind and Jeremy Main suggest that the best way to view organisations in the next century is to use a concept they call Integrated Architecture. This describes companies as bundles of capabilities (Intellectual Capital) and assets (Physical Capital) which are connected to each other — a mix-and-match of IC and PC generates a variety of products or services — and to the stakeholders of the organisation. And the relative importance of one set of them over another depends on the company, the industry in which it operates, and the macro-economic variables of the country in which it operates.

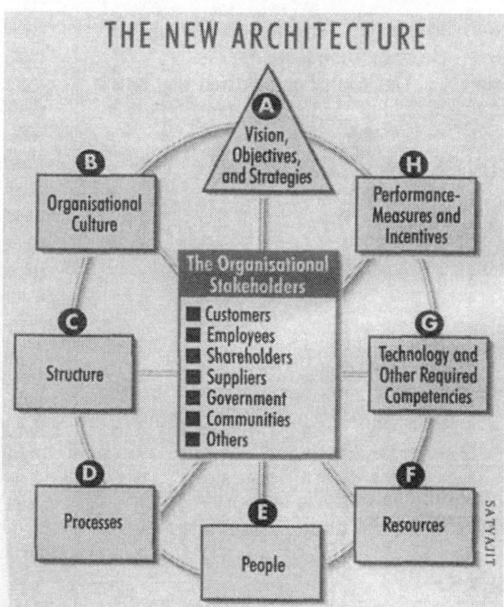

BOX 24.4

AMALGAMATION OF RRBS

The Advisory Committee on Flow of Credit to Agriculture and Related Activities (Chairman: Shri V.S. Vyas) in June 2004 recommended restructuring of RRBs. Following this, an Internal Working Group on RRBs was set up in the Reserve Bank to examine various alternatives available within the existing legal framework for strengthening RRBs. The Group, in its Report submitted in June 2005, observed large variations in the number of districts covered and the branch network of RRBs. While 47 RRBs covered only one district each. 111 RRBs covered 2-3 districts, 29 RRBs 4-5 districts and 9 operated in 6-9 districts. Similarly, 72 RRBs had up to 50 branches, 87 RRBs 51-100 branches, 21 RRBs 101-150 branches and 16 had more than 150 branches. As many as 6 sponsor banks had only one RRB sponsored by them. While 11 sponsor banks had 2-4 sponsored RRBs, 3 sponsor banks had up to 10 RRBs and 8 sponsor banks had more than 10 RRBs sponsored by them in various States. Of these, only 2 sponsor banks had more than 20 RRBs.

In order to improve the operational viability of RRBs and take advantage of the economies of scale (by reducing transaction cost), the route of merger/amalgamation of RRBs was suggested taking into account the views of various stakeholders. The merger process would help in strengthening some of the weak RRBs. A two-phase restructuring was suggested: (i) merger between RRBs of the same sponsor bank in the same State; and (ii) merger of RRBs sponsored by different banks in the same State. Merger of RRBs with the sponsor bank is not provided for in the RRBs Act 1976. Further, such mergers would go against the spirit of setting up of RRBs as local entities and for providing credit primarily to weaker sections.

The Government of India has initiated the first phase of amalgamation of RRBs sponsor bank-wise at State level to overcome the deficiencies prevailing in RRBs and making them viable and profitable units. The process of amalgamation of RRBs sponsor bank-wise at the State level started on September 12, 2005 with the issue of notification in respect of formation of 9 amalgamated entities. As on March 31, 2005, 196 RRBs were operating in 26 States across 523 districts (525 in 2005-06) with a network of 14,484 branches (14,489 in 2005-06). RRBs had a large branch network in the rural areas, which constituted nearly 45 per cent of rural branch network of all commercial banks. Till October 31, 2006, 137 RRBs were amalgamated to form 43 new RRBs, sponsored by 18 commercial banks in 15 States, bringing down the total number of RRBs in the country to 96 from 196. The amalgamation process of phase I is in process of being completed.

RRB Count

State Bank group	22
Central Bank	11
Punjab National Bank	9
Bank of India	7
Syndicate Bank	7
Bank of Baroda	6
UCO Bank	5
United Bank	4
Canara Bank	3
Ind Overseas Bank	3
Allahabad Bank	3
Bank of Mah	3
Union Bank	2
J&K Bank	2
Vijaya Bank	1
Bank of Rajasthan	1

Revised guidelines regarding organisational set-up, appointment of Chairmen and fixation of seniority of staff were issued by NABARD to sponsor banks for implementation in their respective RRBs in the post-amalgamation period. NABARD is providing full guidance and support to smoothen the process of amalgamation.

After amalgamation, RRBs would become bigger in size with a larger area of operation, which would enable them to function in a competitive environment more effectively by taking advantage of the economies of scale and reduction in transaction cost. The process of bringing down the number of RRBs would also make it more convenient for the sponsor banks to manage the affairs of RRBs.

Among the capabilities that must, therefore, be part of the architecture of the New Organisations:

- An organisational culture that facilitates innovation.
- A team- and customer-oriented organisational structure.
- Best-in-class processes at every point of the value chain.
- HR systems that make employees feel satisfied and loyal.
- A vision, strategy, and objective for the company's technologies.
- Non-traditional measures of corporate performance and individual appraisal.

Clearly, the foundations of tomorrow's organisation are already being laid at today's best companies. In that sense, the future is already here.

Banking on Design

The new generation banks have lobbies that provide a view to the street and induce the new client to check the visual ambience. The extensive use of glass walls in the interiors conveys vastness of space and brings down the barriers between the customer and the banker to the minimum. Designs seem to be evolving in a manner, that is reflective of the institution's personality, brand and its proper execution ensures that one cannot just walk across it without lifting an eye towards it. The conservationist bankers may scoff that this new ambience tends to compromise on security, but they are a minority.

The change in the layout has meant that the movement of a customer can now be directed to key products, induced by positive ambience created by warmness of the lush interiors, and it translates the passivity which a consumer may have about the new product of a bank, owing to display into a salability proposition by a banker.

The change, however, has not only been in the interiors but the exterior facade is also being reconstructed to convey a "come hither" look. After all it is the exterior that draws the attention of the customers, so lots of input also is put into creating an externally comfortable ambience for the customer. Facades of modern banks are a clear pointer to this fact.

The success of design and layout of a branch can be attained when the customer who walks inside the facade feels empowered to exercise his option about enquiring from the products on display, rather than helplessly lost in the maze of products on display inside. One of the ways through which the customer is empowered is by using electronic signboards and plasma screens. Its progressive use is dictated by the fact that it facilitates in maintaining promotional information.

Corporate Governance

A strong financial system is premised on principles of sound corporate governance. Corporate governance lays down the fundamental rules by which companies are governed in their management. Each institution needs to evolve its own governance principles based on its changing business philosophy over period of time. These principles would have to be adapted in line with the changing circumstances. The quality of corporate governance has become particularly important in the banking system in view of growing competition and consolidation of the banking system.

The banking sector in India is quite large and widespread across the country. There are several banks of varying sizes and the shareholding pattern also varies significantly. The issues of size and governance are extremely important from the point of view of financial stability. The two major concerns that arise in the context of corporate governance in banks are concentration of ownership and the quality of management that controls the bank. The recent irregularities involving accounting firms in the US have amply demonstrated the importance of good corporate governance practices. The quality of corporate governance in banks assumes critical importance as competition intensifies and banks strive to retain their client base.

Conclusion

It is crucial for the banking industry to meet the increasingly complex savings and financing needs of the economy by offering a wider and flexible range of financial products tailored for all types of customers. With the increasing levels of globalisation of the Indian banking industry, evolution of universal banks and bundling of financial services, competition in the banking industry will intensify further. The banking industry has the potential and the ability to rise to the occasion as demonstrated by the rapid pace of automation which has already had a profound impact on raising the standard of banking services. The financial strength of individual banks, which are major participants in the financial system, is the first line of defence against financial risks. Strong capital positions and balance sheets place banks in a better position to deal with and absorb the economic shocks. Banks need to supplement this with sophisticated and robust risk management practices and the resolve to face competition without diluting the operating standards.

Banking Technology

In an environment of large-scale use of technology, an effective security policy covering physical and other aspects has assumed high importance: Banks need to institute an appropriate security policy to ensure adequate and effective safety. Regular IT-related functions also need to be undertaken to ensure that there are no lapses or deviation from the approved information security policy. Information systems and information technology have an impact on the reputation risk of a bank. While outsourcing of IT related and other services does have certain advantages, it also has its own challenges. This calls for putting in place appropriate and adequate safeguards in place. The future computerization in banks should aim at strengthening the payment system, bring out new products and services and facilitate move towards fool-proof risk hedging techniques.

IT has provided for better asset-liability management, which was a relatively difficult task in a manual based system spanning a large number of branches of banks, geographically spread across the country. This has helped banks in better funds management, thereby improving profitability for banks. IT has also improved information availability as also their timeliness. Concepts such as core banking systems, internet banking, anytime banking and anywhere banking have all been made possible with the help of IT. All these have made banking transactions to be performed in a manner, which is beneficial not only for the customer and his banker but for the economy as a whole.

The Financial Sector Technology Vision document provides a broad overview of the thrust areas of the direction provided by the Reserve Bank in respect of IT for the financial sector for more than two decades and sets out a roadmap for 2005-08. The Vision document focuses on four major areas, viz., IT for regulation and supervision, IT and Institute for Development and Research in Banking Technology (IDRBT), IT for the Financial Sector and IT for Government related functions. The Vision document envisages: (i) emerging challenges in achieving standardisation across a variety of hybrid systems at different financial entities; (ii) need for decision support systems; and (iii) the requisite technology to facilitate risk based off-site supervision. The Vision document visualises the IDRBT to be a premier research institute, concentrating on research and development for the banking and financial sector, providing educational/training facilities. The Vision document proposes that specific attention would be devoted to percolation of technology efforts to all types of banks and all sections of customers in the banks with specific reference to the rural areas. It also emphasises the use of affordable technology products which can be easily used by the target clientele with intershareable resources. The document also details the use of IT in the Government sector transactions (which has the largest potential to grow significantly in the years to come) with specific attention on the need for business process re-engineering and changes in rules and procedures for aligning them with e-governance in a manner so as to achieve implementable objectives.

Concluding Observations

Calibrated deregulation, prudential regulation and supervision and a responsive policy environment have resulted in significant improvement in the efficiency, stability and resilience of financial institutions. This is reflected in their profitability, improved asset quality and higher capital levels. As the economy grows and becomes more sophisticated, the banking sector has to develop in a manner that supports and stimulates such growth. There are, however, several challenges in future which may require new technologies, better processes of credit and risk appraisal, product diversification, robust internal controls and corporate governance and efficient human resource management. Banks are also facing increased market risk uncertainties on account of rising interest rates as a result of growing global financial imbalances. The banking sector, therefore, needs to equip itself to meet these challenges as well as those arising out of introduction of Basle II norms and international accounting standards. Competition, consolidation and convergence are emerging as the key drivers of the banking sector in the years to come.

BOX 24.5

BANKING CODES AND STANDARDS BOARD OF INDIA

The Reserve Bank of India together with 11 other banks in India set up the Banking Codes and Standards Board of India (BCSBI) in February 2006 to monitor and ensure that banking codes and standards voluntarily adopted by banks are adhered to, in letter and spirit, while providing services to individual customers. These industry wide norms have been codified in the form of a Code of Bank's Commitment to Customers (Code), which has been evolved in consultation with the banking industry and released by the Reserve Bank on July 1, 2006.

The Code is a landmark in the development of banking in India as, for the first time, the individual customer has been provided with a Charter of Rights which he can enforce against his bank. The Code sets out minimum standards of banking practices for banks to follow and emphasises transparency in banks' dealings with its customers. To achieve the avowed transparency, it provides for documentation of banks' fees and service charges in the form of a Tariff Schedule and requires banks to set out a cheque collection policy, compensation policy and a security repossession policy. The Code lays great emphasis on providing full information to the customer before a product or service is sold to him. For post sale conduct, the Code insists on banks giving one month's notice to customer before making any change in their tariff schedule or any change in terms and conditions, governing the product, which may adversely affect the customer.

The cardinal principle that runs across all the provisions of Code is that banks should not rely on implicit consent from customers and all product and services should be sold to the customer only after obtaining his explicit consent in writing. As a logical corollary of this principle, the Code prohibits banks from providing unsolicited credit in any form, including credit cards. The Code addresses the issue of Right to Privacy of customers and also provides for automatic compensation to be paid, in accordance with the bank's compensation policy, for any financial loss incurred by an individual customer due to undue delays, failure in executing mandates or erroneous debits.

The provisions of the Code are applicable to third party products sold through bank branches and the banks are under obligation to ensure that their direct sales agents also comply with the provisions of the Code. BCSBI's purview is restricted to scheduled commercial banks and 69 banks have intimated their willingness to become members. BCSBI is in the process of entering into a covenant with 55 of these major banks.

BCSBI combines the best of statutory regulation and self-regulation. It is a collaborative effort between banks and the Reserve Bank not only in its origin but also in purpose. While banks becoming member of the BCSBI agree to observe the Code, the Reserve Bank derives supervisory comfort from banks being members of the BCSBI as it would look into systemic issues that impinge on customer service and financial inclusion. The spirit of collaboration is further reinforced by the general consultative approach adopted by the BCSBI in formulating the Code and in its implementation.

Chapter 25

Indian Banking in 2010: Three Scenarios

The possibility of the opening up of the Indian banking in 2009 should act as a catalyst for action, ushering in a transformational phase of organic and inorganic growth.

Introduction

Financial sector reforms have been introduced in a calibrated and well-sequenced manner since the early 1990s. The sustained efforts by the Government, the Reserve Bank and by banks themselves have resulted in a competitive, healthy and resilient financial system. The asset quality and soundness parameters of the Indian banking sector, on the whole, are now comparable with global levels. This has been achieved in the backdrop of gradual alignment of prudential norms with international best standards and in an environment of growing competitive pressures. There is also an evidence of some financial deepening in recent years. Having achieved substantial success in improving the financial health of commercial banks over this period, there is now need to focus on the further expansion and deepening of financial services so as to serve the needs of those who are underprivileged. This would include particular attention being given to the underdeveloped regions of the country. The reform process is also being extended to the improvement of financial health and prudential regulation of urban co-operative banks, regional rural banks, the rural co-operative banking sector and non-banking financial institutions. In view of the dual regulatory control of urban co-operative banks, the strategy of reform is being conducted through a consultative mechanism involving State Governments.

The Indian banking sector has undergone a major re-rating over the past few years and has been a steady outperformer on the bourses. The re-rating was led by structural reforms in the banking sector, growth in core business operations, improving profitability ratios and improvement in asset quality, among others. Going forward, we expect continued buoyancy in the economy and core banking operations to maintain the growth momentum of banks. Consolidation is also expected to trigger some re-rating in the stock valuation of certain banks.

BOX 25.1

FINANCIAL SECTOR REFORM AND FINANCIAL STABILITY

Central banks have tailored the design of financial sector reforms to country-specific situations, taking cognisance of the threats to financial stability. The relevant considerations are: (i) the recognition that there exist strong complementarities between financial stability and macroeconomic stability; (ii) the pace of reforms to be adopted, i.e., whether a shock therapy approach or a more cautious and gradualist strategy; (iii) deciding the optimal sequencing of reforms in case the gradualist approach is adopted; and (iv) the credibility of reforms. In this regard, the issue of credibility is inter-related with the choice of the pace of reform. A graduated pace wins credibility since it avoids disruptions and roll-backs in the short-run, while building a consensus in favour of continuing reforms in the medium to long-run.

In the pursuit of financial stability, effective regulatory and supervisory initiatives along with a calibrated approach to financial sector liberalisation are critical. Surveillance of the institutions in the financial sector and their interactions, both amongst themselves and with lenders and borrowers outside the financial sector, strengthening of the financial infrastructure and crisis management are also crucial. Financial crises, however, do not necessarily involve just banks and other deposit-taking financial institutions. There is an increasing overlap and interaction between banks and other segments of the economy. Some segments may not have the same rigorous risk management systems or regulatory oversight as banks. There are also market segments, particularly over the counter, which are not tightly supervised but could be of systemic importance such as hedge funds. In this scenario, the financial risks have a tendency to be shifted from well regulated to weakly or less regulated segments.

In emerging market economies, financial sector reforms have greatly helped in strengthening and reinforcing financial stability. It needs to be emphasised, however, that the existing international financial architecture is not adequate to prevent or mitigate the domestic and external effects of a financial crisis in large economies. The impact of instability in times of crisis appears largely to be borne by the domestic public sector rather than the global private sector. The issue of setting the pace of financial liberalisation is important in order to minimise the risks of instability. International experience shows that a faster pace of financial liberalisation was often followed by financial instability and crises. Therefore, in framing public policies, the approach to managing the financial sector, the choice of instruments and the timing and sequencing of policies are issues of crucial importance.

The financial sector reforms in India were initiated early in the reform cycle. In this regard, while prudential regulation of banks was introduced in the early phase of reforms, independent regulatory framework for other entities has been a recent phenomenon where new regulatory bodies for securities markets and insurance sector have been set up.

References

Reddy,Y.V. (2006): 'Financial Sector Reforms and Financial Stability', Reserve Bank of India Bulletin, April.

Mohan,R. (2006): 'Financial Sector Reforms and Monetary Policy:The Indian Experience', Reserve Bank of India Bulletin, July.

Mohan,R. (2005): 'Financial Sector Reforms in India: Policies and Performance Analysis', in Economic and Political Weekly, March 19.

In a white paper produced earlier this month, international consultant Mckinsey lists three different scenarios for the Indian banking sector depending upon reforms the government is able to push through and the vision of individual banks. "Our firm belief is that the shape of the banking sector in 2010 will be the result of a strong interplay between the decisions taken by policymakers and actions of bank managements."

Open Markets

The Reserve Bank of India's (RBI) Roadmap for the presence of foreign banks in India could, if actually implemented, herald a significant change in the competitive dynamics of Indian banking. The impact that this possible opening up could have on the entire banking landscape is significant. Should the regulator permit and should industry participants, particularly public and private sector banks, choose to make the best of the time they have, 2009 could turn out to be an inflection point for the industry — creating a more vibrant financial services industry that in turn has a down-stream effect on the Indian economy. Open markets 2009 impacts the industry on two fronts:

- **External-Consolidation:** Changes in the landscape due to mergers and acquisitions being undertaken across the industry; and
- **Internal-Markets and Efficiencies:** Shaping up of banks, internally with respect to target markets and customers, business models and operations.

Indian Banking in 2010: Three Scenarios

The discontinuities facing Indian banking will force a major change in the industry in next 4-5 years, the onus of which would depend upon the interplay of policy maker's and bank management's actions. The **Policy makers** must address six key issues to create a banking sector which supports faster economic growth along with ensuring social objectives of employment, access to quality products for all and fair competition for different categories. The issues that need to be addressed include areas like consolidation and industry ownership, capital deployment to agriculture and weaker section, coordination across the different regulators, corporate governance (ensuring board accountability and effectiveness), supporting infrastructure (credit bureaus, ARCs and outsourced processing) and implementing labour reforms along with human capital enrichment (introduction of productivity based compensation for PSB employees, creating a training infrastructure, etc.).

While the shape of the regulatory framework will be determined by these policy changes, the action of the **Bank management** will enhance the performance of an individual bank. Three key challenges that the bank managements should address are improving critical skills in people, process and system dimensions, leading consolidation in the sector and leveraging technology to further innovate and develop newer business models. Success will also be dependent on management's ability to drive changes and execute bold moves.

Based on the likely interaction between these two key players we can outline three distinct scenarios for the Indian banking industry in future. Through these scenarios we can have an idea of the outcomes that will be the consequence of the actions of policy makers and bank managements.

Scenario 1 : High Performance: In this scenario, policy makers intervene only to the extent required to ensure system stability and protection of consumer interests, leaving bank managements free to drive far reaching changes. ***Banking becomes an even greater driver of GDP growth***

and employment. These changes reduce intermediation costs which in turn lead to increased growth, productivity and innovation. Higher returns to shareholders increase the capital flow enabling increased investments and a focus on developing people, processes and systems. Industry consolidation takes place within public sector banks, thus resulting in creation of a few large and efficient banks.

Scenario 2 : Evolution: In this scenario, ***though the banking sector emerges as an important driver of the economy and wealth in 2010, it has still not come of age in comparison to developed markets.*** Here some constraints still exist as policy makers are cautious in liberalizing the industry while adopting a pro-market stance. Significant changes in policy and regulation and in capacity building measures are still required by PSBs and old private sector banks.

In this scenario, M&A activity is driven primarily by new private banks as a result of which their growth increases to 35%. Growth in foreign banks is about 30%. The share of private sector banks and foreign banks to total sector assets are to the tune of 30% and 12% respectively. Similarly, the share of banking sector value add to GDP also increases to over 4.7%.

Scenario 3: Stagnation: In this scenario, ***banking sector is unable to support a fast growing economy as restrictive conditions are set by policy makers and management that is unable to execute the necessary changes.*** As a result, there is a low return to shareholders and a low provision of quality product and services to customers leading to low growth and productivity levels. ***There is limited consolidation and most banks remain sub-scale.*** There is a slowdown in growth of PSB and old private sector bank. There is significant risk to the system due to instability caused by weaker banks.

Agenda of Action

Banking sector today suffers from many structural weaknesses which unless addressed could jeopardize chances of faster economic growth. Hence policy and regulatory interventions are essential for strengthening the banking sector.

Agenda for Policy Makers: The policy makers need to act on six fronts, in a phased manner:

1. **Help shape a superior industry structure**
   - 3-4 global banks accounting for 35-45% of total assets by 2010 (Rs. 3-4 trillion assets); this would place most of them in the global 100 by 2010 with one or two among global 50.
   - 6-8 large national banks with assets more than Rs. 1.5 trillion, accounting for 20-25% of total assets.
   - 4-6 India focused foreign banks with assets more than Rs. 1.5 trillion, accounting for 15-20% of total assets.
   - Specialist players accounting for remaining 15-20% of total assets.

This structure will enable them to create scale at a regional or global level and build efficiencies in operations, products and pricing. It will also lead to emergence of 'specialist' players providing superior services to specific product and customer segments. This structure can be achieved through

Implication of Three Scenarios by 2010

	Scenario 1	Scenario 2	Scenario 3
Mergers & Acquisition	Consolidation within PSBs and within private sector banks	M & A activity is driven primarily by new private banks	Limited consolidation
Capital requirement (banks reaised Rs. 30 billioin in capital from different sources on cumulative basis, between 2001 and 2004)	Rs 600 billion to fund growth in advances, NPL write-offs and human capital up gradation	Rs. 400 billion	Rs. 125 billion due to large NPL write-offs
Growth rates: Foreign banks New Private banks Public sector banks	 50% (share: 20%) 50% (share: 35%) 15% (share: 45%) (share in total banking sector assets)	 30% (share: > 12%) 35% (share: 30%)	 25% slowdown
Market capitalization	Rs. 1700 billion to Rs. 7500 billion	Rs. 1700 billion to Rs. 4400 billion	Rs. 1700 billion to Rs. 2400 billion
Share of value added of the banking sector (as a % to GDP)	Over 7.7% from current level of 2.5% 30% of GDP to more	4.7%	3.3%
Banking intermediation	than 100% of GDP 0.9 million to over 1.5 million	30% of GDP to 65% of GDP	30% of GDP to < 45% of GDP
Employment levels		0.9 million to 1.35 million	0.9 million to 1.2 million

three distinct approaches, "Controlled, forcing consolidation, A Free Market Approach, A Managed Transition."

However, India should follow the "Managed Transition" Approach to restructure banking industry. This would enable the policy makers to build strong domestic institutions by maximization of scale advantages through selective consolidation of banks with highly overlapping customer focus, branches and IT systems.

The policy makers have to take ***four critical steps*** to ensure that the banks which may not appear 'weak' today do not become vulnerable in the longer term with increased competition after 2009:

(a) Ensure regulatory mechanism to differentiate between strong and solvent institutions so as to remove regulatory arbitrages which currently favour the smaller and weak entities in the sector.

(b) Lay out clear processes to gutde bank consolidation for which 'anchor banks' need to be identified on the basis of the value and scope of the bank. Then the target banks should be selected which could be merged with 'anchor banks.' Three principles should guide this selection: target banks with complementary areas in customer focus, branches and IT; adequate coverage/ competition and transfer of management skills so as to strengthen critical areas like risk management, marketing and operational efficiency.

(c) Unshackle public sector banks and give them more operational freedom by providing flexibility in recruiting, performance management and compensation.

(d) Increase foreign presence in a 'controlled manner' over time so that the share of foreign controlled banks in India increases from the current level of 7% to 20% by 2010.

2. Ensure adequate focus on social development through explicit market-driven incentives

Explicit directed lending and bank supervision introduces non-commercial elements into decision making causing banks to deviate from core business processes. Current requirement of 40% loans and advances in the priority sector and 25% of branches in the rural and semi urban areas, should be replaced by more 'market based' mechanisms for serving these segments.

Regulation can be reformed in ***four ways*** by setting up credit-guarantee schemes, introducing market-based subsidies, promoting Microfinance institutions and creating a strong consumer protection infrastructure (information transparency, dispute resolution, anti-trust regulation and deposit insurance).

3. Create a unified regulator, distinct from a central bank

Moving to a single regulatory agency will lead to improved supervision and an increased ability to assess the risk of a financial conglomerate; reduction of compliance costs; ensure a level playing field with harmonized regulations across intermediaries and single point accountability for consumers and industry participants.

A transition to a structure with a unified regulator, separate from the central bank can be done in ***three phases:***

(a) Integrate regulations across different entities like NBFCs, RRBs, Cooperative Banks, etc. so as to remove regulatory arbitrage.

(b) All regulatory activities could be taken over by RBI which will internally separate the regulatory and central functions.

(c) The internal regulatory function could be spun off to a separate regulator with legislative sanction.

4. Improve corporate governance

The RBI will need to guide Indian banks towards adopting international standards in corporate governance. The various aspects of good corporate governance are:

(a) ***Board independence*** (majority of non-executive directors, separation of Chairman and CEO roles, independent committees for core processes).

(b) ***Broader role for Board*** and performance orientation (Boards to actively engage in CEO appointment and succession planning, developing and approving corporate strategy/ corporate goals, evaluating corporate performance, conducting senior management appraisals).

(c) ***Board accountability*** (formal and independent process for evaluation of directors).

(d) ***Nomination by committee*** (all directors should be appointed on the recommendation of a nomination committee).

(e) ***Increased board effectiveness*** (through comprehensive training programmes, management comments on performance, committee reports, agenda driven board meetings, etc.).

(f) ***Suitable board size*** (optimal board size varies from 5-11 depending on the size, ownership and business of the bank).

5. Accelerate the creation of a world-class supporting Infrastructure

The need is to take specific actions to ensure robust and world class infrastructure in four areas:

(a) ***Credit bureaus:*** CIBIL is a good initiative. PSBs need to complement their IT and operations initiatives so that their information can be transferred to CIBIL.

(b) ***ARCs:*** ARCIL has already acquired assets worth Rs 165 billion from 25 banks forming around 23% of their book value. However there are still structural and operational hurdles to successful functioning of ARCs. Further need is to strengthen DRTs for speedy case disposals.

(c) ***Payments:*** RBI should focus on building scale in the electronic fund settlement and cheque settlement system. RTGS system is covering 5000 bank branches in over 400 centres, transacting around Rs. 440 billion/day which further needs penetration. On retail payments front, the work needs to be done on increasing the penetration of alternative payment mechanisms like credit and debit cards in tier 3 and tier 4 towns which are feeling the constraint of not having terminalisation of POS systems in these towns.

(d) ***Promoting the outsourcing of back-office functions by banks:*** This lowers costs, improves productivity and enhances quality.The areas which can be covered are credit card processing, data entry, call centres, reconciliations, cheque processing and securities settlement.

6. Accelerate human capital development

Restrictive labour laws have decelerated reforms in Indian banking and inhibited productivity enhancements. Restrictions on recruitment, compensation and deployment of staff will continue to significantly limit PSBs. There is need to:

(a) ***Reskill employees*** by creation of large training infrastructure so as to give the training in areas like leadership, business orientation and other core management skills.

(b) ***Flexibility in compensation*** is necessary to retain leadership talent.

(c) ***Specialization*** is needed in specific skills like treasury, credit, cash management, retail banking, etc.

Agenda for Management: Public Sector Banks

In a radically changed environment bank managements need to complement policy makers by strengthening skill, scale and scope while addressing deficiencies. In case of PSBs, there are some fundamental gaps in skills which need to be closed to remain competitive. Initiatives in four fronts are needed to ensure this:

(1) ***Rapidly implement IT and operations initiatives:*** Currently most Indian banks are spending Rs 1.5 billion on average on software, hardware, centralized operations and core banking operations. PSBs have to close the technology gap with the new private sector banks by reducing the time taken for successful implementation. ***Three themes*** will be very important. First, they need to restructure the platform by centralizing and outsourcing parts of operations. Second, they have to reinvent and streamline operating processes across the platform. Third, they have to re-design within an operating unit.

(2) ***Build sales and marketing capabilities:*** PSBs have to leverage their strength of branch network and staff by refocusing efforts on sales as Indian banking is going to be changed into a sales and marketing led sector.

(3) ***Strengthen risk management skill:*** Rapid growth in consumer finance and Basel II requirements have brought into focus the need to build risk management systems. Banks will need sophisticated models; a risk management organisation with a clearly codified and pervasive credit culture; credit processes with high frequency review mechanisms, early warning systems and streamlined collection and default management; and superior IT systems.

(4) ***Build leadership capacity and equip organizations to adapt to the changing environment needs:*** PSBs will need to strengthen their organisations by expanding leadership capacity so as to change the organisational mindset and behaviour. This includes fostering understanding and conviction, among employees, realignment of performance management systems, development of talents and skills, and role modeling the behaviour of superiors.

Strategies for a Changing World

The question then is, how should banks prepare for change? The strategy each player should adopt would depend on the unique positioning that the player finds itself in. What is needed is for each player to adopt a structured approach towards assessing the implications of changes in the landscape and preparing for what may lie ahead.

The first step would be for each participant in the industry to assess its position along specific dimensions. There are five key dimensions that banks should carefully assess themselves on.

These dimensions include:

Markets

STRATEGISING FOR FUTURE
CUSTOMER
Products
Customers
Geographies
Brand & positioning
CAPABILITY
• Processes
• Technology
• Operations
• Knowledge management
External drivers
STRATEGIC
Present strategy
Growth
aspirations
Internal drivers
COMPETITION
• Competitive actions
• Change in landscape
FISCAL
Investments
Capital adequacy
Profitability

- Positioning with respect to the products and services within its portfolio; its target segments; penetration and reach in terms of geography.
- For example, with a strong retail presence and significant reach through branches in smaller towns and cities, large public sector banks are likely to be concerned with protecting their competitive advantage and cementing relationships with the customer segment in this geography. These markets may prove to be the next frontier of growth as each acquires importance and penetration in tier 2 and 3 towns increases. On the other hand, with restrictions on their ability to expand, foreign banks may focus on strategies to increase their penetration in areas they are already present — other parts of the portfolio can be grown through acquisitions in 2009.

Capability

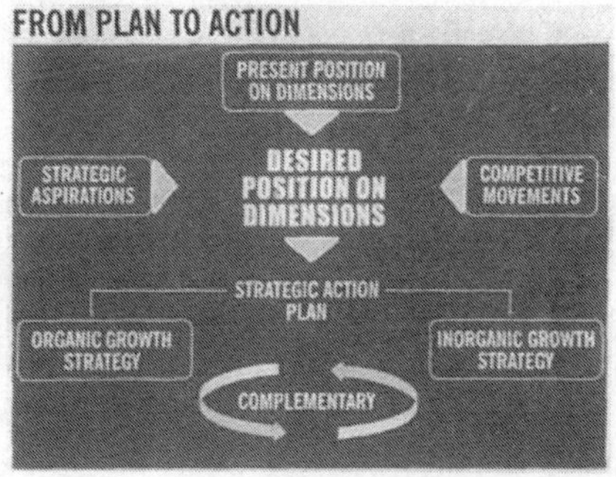

- To be effectively executed, strategy must be supported by internal capabilities that include technology, efficient processes, enabling structure and capable human resources. Banks would need to assess their positioning on these internal capabilities as they drive operational efficiencies that determine their competitiveness in the marketplace.
- For example, public sector banks and old private sector banks are likely to be focussed on ensuring that appropriate processes are in place — supporting innovation in product structuring and efficiency in delivery. Foreign banks would need to ensure that they are well integrated with their global operations — best practices and processes need to be in place and imbibed internally before they expand their operations through acquisitions.

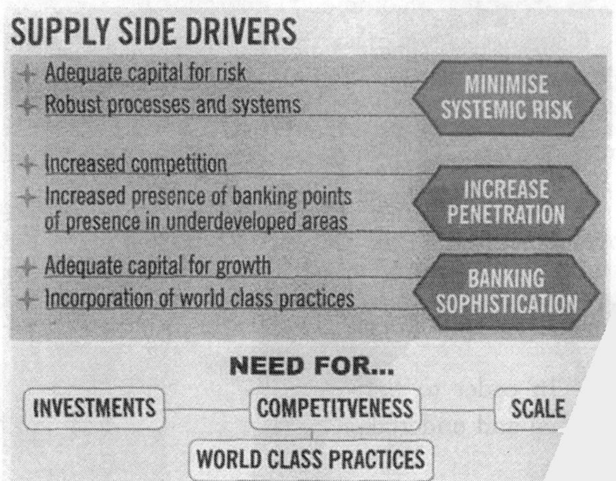

Fiscal

- It would be important to assess the fiscal health the bank is currently in — Is there adequate capital from a regulatory perspective? Are there profitability concerns? Is there adequate capital for growth?
- While weak public and private sector banks would need to assess the

availability of adequate capital from risk and regulatory requirements, the strong private sector banks would be concerned about infusion of capital to support aggressive growth plans.

Strategic

- Strategic aspirations of the bank are also an important dimension — ultimately growth has to be linked to risk appetite of the bank. For instance, some foreign banks may not have the risk appetite to look at expanding inorganically into less penetrated geographies.

Competition

- The above four dimensions are internal to a bank. However, in a situation where consolidation rules, competitive dynamics can change, quite literally, with a signature on the dotted line. Competitive movements can set back all the planning done, if strategies by key competitors are not factored in.

Assessing one's position on these dimensions will enable a bank to understand its relative competitiveness. The choice then some banks would need to make is — do they aggressively grow the business through organic means and inorganic acquisitions or do they merge with larger players for survival —y predator or prey?

In Mckinsey's best-case scenario, Indian banking will contribute 7.7% of the GDP in 2010 and account for a market capitalisation of Rs.7.5 lakh crore. If the worst were to happen to the sector with no reforms and stagnant policies, banks would collectively have a market cap of Rs.2.4 lakh crore and a share of 3.3% in GDP.

To reach the high-performing scenario, banks would need a capital of Rs.60,000 crore to fund credit growth, write off bad loans, and invest in technology and human resources. Policy makers then will intervene only to ensure systemic stability and protect consumer interests, leaving managements to drive change. Consolidation would happen among state-owned banks as well as among old and new private sector banks. Foreign banks would also become active, buying out some private banks. Foreign and private banks would grow at a rate of 50% and state-owned banks would grow at 15%. Private banks would have a market share of 35% and foreign banks would have a share of 20%.

Mckinsey recommends that the government should strengthen the industry structure by allowing managed consolidation and enabling capital availability. It should create three-four global-sized banks that would control 35-45% of the Indian market. About six to eight national banks would control 20-25% of the market and four to six foreign banks would have about 15-20% rket share. The rest would be niche players.

he consultant has also suggested creating a unified regulator, distinct from the RBI, to supervisory difficulties and reduce compliance costs.

nsform Indian banking to world class banking, required changes must be at this stage when Indian banking is at a watershed in its development.